Group Communication
Process and Analysis

JOANN KEYTON

University of Memphis

Mayfield Publishing Company
Mountain View, California
London • Toronto

Copyright © 1999 by Mayfield Publishing Company

All rights reserved. No portion of this book may be reproduced in any form or by any means without written permission of the publisher.

Library of Congress Cataloging-in-Publication Data

Keyton, Joann.
    Group communication : process and analysis / Joann Keyton.
        p.   cm.
    Includes bibliographical references and index.
    ISBN 1-55934-772-4
    1. Communication in small groups.   I. Title.
HM133.K446   1998
302.3'4—dc21   98-44460
                                     CIP

Manufactured in the United States of America
10 9 8 7 6 5 4 3 2 1

Mayfield Publishing Company
1280 Villa Street
Mountain View, CA 94041

Sponsoring editor, Holly Allen; production editor, Melissa Kreischer; manuscript editor, Jennifer Gordon; design manager, Susan Breitbard; text and cover designer, Joan Greenfield; art manager, Robin Mouat; illustrator, Larry Daste; photo researcher, Brian Pecko; cover photo, © Rhoda Sidney / PhotoEdit; manufacturing manager, Randy Hurst. The text was set in 10.5/12.5 Janson Text by Thompson Type and printed on acid-free 45# Chromatone Matte by Banta Book Group.

Text, illustration, and photo credits appear following the References on page C-1, which constitutes an extension of the copyright page.

 This book is printed on recycled paper.

Preface

Group Communication: Process and Analysis is a primary text for undergraduate group communication courses. In writing this book, I was motivated by several goals. I wanted to help students

- move toward a better understanding of their own communication in groups and how it either facilitates or hinders group outcomes;
- develop critical thinking skills and apply them to their group interactions;
- develop an analytical framework from which to approach group work;
- learn how to move beyond analysis of group dynamics to fruitful intervention or change;
- learn basic observation and assessment methodologies so they can become active learners rather than passive observers; and
- gain exposure to the literature of group communication as well as the broader interdisciplinary literature on groups.

The text, then, blends skills, theory, and research in an interdisciplinary context. The group communication classroom is particularly well suited to this integrated approach for two reasons. First, a systematic approach to understanding and improving group interactions, strongly supported by theory and research offers students a way to enhance their daily and lifelong experiences in groups. The practical applications of the study of groups are extensive and highly relevant to students. Second, the group communication class is widely sought both by communication majors and by students from other disciplines, who recognize the value of studying groups for their own academic and professional pursuits. This book is specifically designed to address the needs of all students, both in communication and in other disciplines.

Approach

The title of the book, ***Group Communication: Process and Analysis***, speaks to the dynamic quality of group interaction. The text explores group interaction dynamics, the relationship of the individual to the group, and the situation of groups within their larger contexts. The dynamic capacity of groups also means that one group cannot be treated like another. Students must learn to analyze each particular group experience in order to become effective group members.

To provide a foundation for this analysis, Part One uses a systemic perspective, encouraging students to seek out the unique characteristics of a specific group and to identify and analyze the individual-group-organization relationships. Part Two is based on structuration theory, which encourages students to see how systems and structures within groups are developed and then reproduced by group members. Both perspectives are useful for blending theory and practice.

Features and Learning Aids

To encourage students to apply principles to their own experiences, each chapter reinforces the balance between informative and analytical approaches by giving new information about groups and then providing cases or examples to explore. The text also speaks to students' experience by providing information about a wide variety of groups—family and social groups, work teams and high-performance work groups, civic and community groups, discussion and decision-making groups. The challenge for instructors in covering such a variety of groups is to find common ground for class discussions, exercises, and evaluation. Again, the text helps by providing a broad range of in-text cases for reflective analysis. Once students learn an analytic technique in the context of one group experience, they can write their own case studies or analyze their own group experiences.

To provide additional help for students learning to analyze group experiences, this text offers four different pedagogical techniques. Each technique asks students to be reflective, pose questions, and seek understanding, but in different ways. "Putting the Pieces Together" boxes call for students to use the five core concepts that comprise the definition of a group as a basis for analyzing and evaluating a particular group. "Think About It" boxes ask students to take a moment to apply information to one of their group experiences. "Group Assessment Technique" boxes provide students with the opportunity to use an assessment technique to study a group case or one of their own experiences. And "Building Analytical Skills" boxes teach students what to analyze, how to analyze, and how to interpret group interactions. In addition to these boxes, transcripts from group interactions are placed throughout the text as examples for analysis to further the student's understanding of what constitutes effective group communication. All of these techniques are aimed at providing students with skills for assessing what is happening in their groups, making sense of their observations in a systematic way, and using that information to make their groups more effective.

Learning aids further reinforce these aims. Each chapter concludes with a summary and a checklist review of the knowledge, skills, and assessment/analytical techniques presented in the chapter. Following these items are discussion questions and exercises, designed to help students extend their understanding of chapter material. Key terms are printed in the text in boldface type and included in a glossary at the end of the book.

With its pedagogical features and learning aids, the text offers instructors flexibility in making classroom assignments. Instructors have opportunities to test students' knowledge, their understanding and application of analytical principles, or their performance of group skills.

Organization

Chapters 1–7 comprise Part 1, "The Group as a System." These chapters encourage students to identify, discuss, and analyze groups—what they are, how individual abilities and communication styles influence their dynamics, what could happen if they were approached in alternative ways. Part 1 exposes students to analysis of groups and tasks at both the micro and macro levels.

Chapters 8–11 comprise Part 2 "Meeting Group Challenges." These chapters identify the specific knowledge and group skills that students need in order to become masterful group members and leaders. Part 2 exposes students to the topics traditionally found in group communication texts, including decision making, problem solving, leadership, and conflict management. Several different approaches to these topics are discussed and compared.

Part 3, "Developing the Group," distinguishes this text from others. Chapters 12–15 cover analytical group frameworks that will help move students from information-based work to application-based work. Chapters on meeting management, group facilitation and intervention, observing interaction and giving feedback, and group development and evolution will encourage students to become more proactive in taking responsibility for their groups and the outcomes of their groups.

Supplements

To assist in teaching with *Group Communication*, I have written a detailed instructor's resource manual. This manual includes the teaching philosophy that was a foundation for this book, syllabus examples for a group communication course, methods of obtaining feedback from students about the course and their learning experiences and expectations, chapter-by-chapter teaching resources and exercises, a chapter-by-chapter test bank with both objective and essay questions, as well as suggestions for term-long group projects.

Acknowledgments

Perhaps you find it odd that a book about group communication be written by a single author. I can simply tell you that's not the case. Four groups supported me and helped me see this book through to completion. My first "group" of supporters never came together face-to-face . . . they existed only as a group in my head. But nonetheless, this "group" provided the foundation for how I think about and feel about group communication. Paying off a debt is difficult. But, I would like to think that I've done so partially by completing this book. Many ideas presented in this book originated in my classroom experiences with Steven C. Rhodes, Western Michigan University, and Victor D. Wall, then of The Ohio State University. I owe my love of groups to these two men. But before Steve and Vic, I was generously mentored by two others. My high school journalism teacher, Ron Clemons, initiated the spark of learning and writing. My boss at the Federal Reserve Bank of

Kansas City, Nick Santoro, recognized my analytical ability and provided me opportunities well beyond my level of education and experience. Thank you. Although these men have never had a face-to-face conversation, they have met many times as a virtual group in my head providing me guidance through some difficult writing days.

My second group of supporters are my friends who have never seemed to mind hearing about the book or the long hours . . . and certainly, they've kept calling to check on me when I turned down invitations for socializing. Many thanks especially to Wanda and Tom, and Joanne and Tom. Special thanks to Wanda—who humored me, read the chapters, and provided the soul of many of the experiences used as examples in this book. Thanks to fs; our continuous email discussions provided strength and encouragement. Heartfelt thanks are extended to Jeff Solomon for surviving both an undergraduate and graduate education with me . . . and still being my friend. Now guidance counselor and confidante, his friendship has endured me through many odd, awkward, difficult, and testing times. My love to him always.

Third, I was fortunate enough to have a group of excellent reviewers who pointed out problems, identified difficulties with examples, and so on. I applaud the following scholars for helping me with this text: Carolyn M. Anderson, University of Akron; Dale E. Brashers, University of Illinois; John O. Burtis, Kansas State University; Elizabeth M. Goering, Indiana University - Purdue University Indianapolis; Michael E. Holmes, University of Utah; Michele H. Jackson, Florida State University; Bohn D. Lattin, University of Portland; Michael E. Mayer, Arizona State University; Mary B. McPherson, Boise State University; Renée A. Meyers, University of Wisconsin, Milwaukee; Marshall Scott Poole, Texas A&M University; Barbara Eakins Reed, Wright State University; and Matthew W. Seeger, Wayne State University.

Finally, thanks to the Mayfield book team led by Holly Allen, my sponsoring editor. Thanks also to Kate Engelberg, managing developmental editor; Melissa Kreischer, production editor; Susan Breitbard, design manager; Robin Mouat, art manager; and Brian Pecko, photo researcher.

And, throughout the process of organizing, contemplating, writing, fussing over, and revising this book were my girls, Maggie and Sally. Thank you will never be enough.

Contents

Preface iii

PART 1

The Group as a System 1

1 Introduction to Group Communication 3
Introduction 3
What Is a Group? 7
 Characteristics for Defining a Group 7
  Group Size 7 • Interdependence of Members 8 • Group Identity 11 • Group Goal 11 • Group Structure 12 • Group Size Revisited 13
How Do Groups Communicate? 14
 A Basic Communication Model 14
BUILDING ANALYTICAL SKILLS: Laying out the Pieces of the Puzzle 16
 Communication Opportunities 19
 Other Issues Affecting Group Communication 20
What Do Groups Do? 21
THINK ABOUT IT: Reflecting and Projecting 24
Summary 24
Checklist 25
Discussion Questions and Exercises 25

2 Communicating Within Groups 27
A Micro-System Perspective 28
Verbal Communication 29
PUTTING THE PIECES TOGETHER: Interdependence and Group Identity 30
 Words and Meanings 30
 Patterns of Language 30
 Impact of Verbal Activity 32
Nonverbal Communication 33
 Functions of Nonverbal Communication 34
 Multiple Meanings of Nonverbal Communication 36
 Verbal and Nonverbal Communication as a System 37
THINK ABOUT IT: Cracking the Nonverbal Code 38

The Listening Process 38
   Listening Styles 39
   GROUP ASSESSMENT TECHNIQUE: Rating Verbal and Nonverbal Interaction 40
      People-Oriented 41 • Action-Oriented 42 • Content-Oriented 42 • Time-Oriented 42
   Adapting Your Listening Style 43
   Listening Pitfalls 44
   GROUP ASSESSMENT TECHNIQUE: How Well Do You Listen? 45
   Improving Listening 45
Group Communication Climate 48
   Evaluation Versus Description 50
   Control Versus Problem Orientation 50
   Strategy Versus Spontaneity 51
   Neutrality Versus Empathy 51
   Superiority Versus Equality 52
   Certainty Versus Provisionalism 52
   Altering Group Climate 53
   BUILDING ANALYTICAL SKILLS: Working Through Climate Challenges 54
Summary 56
Checklist 57
Discussion Questions and Exercises 57

3 Structuring the Group System 59

Group Member Roles 59
   Formal Roles 60
   THINK ABOUT IT: Formal Role Performance 63
   Informal Interaction Roles 64
Group Norms 68
   GROUP ASSESSMENT TECHNIQUE: Identifying Informal Role Behaviors 69
   PUTTING THE PIECES TOGETHER: Group Structure, Interdependence, and Group Size 72
   Norm Development 72
      Initiating a Norm 74
   THINK ABOUT IT: How Could You Initiate a Norm? 75
      Why Talk About Norms? 75 • Group Norms Are Unique 77
   Influence of Norms on Groups 77
   GROUP ASSESSMENT TECHNIQUE: Identifying Your Group Expectations 78
   Norms Are Resistant to Change 79
Communication Networks 80
   THINK ABOUT IT: Comparing Networks 81
   Decentralized Networks 81
   Centralized Networks 82
   Identifying Your Group's Network 84
   Determining Which Network to Use 85

The Group's Structure and Its Impact on the Individual 86
PUTTING THE PIECES TOGETHER: Group Structure, Interdependence, Group Goal, and Group Identity 87
Summary 87
Checklist 88
Discussion Questions and Exercises 89

4 The Environmental Context of Groups 90

A Macro-System Perspective 90
  Boundary Spanning 91
    Group Impact on the Larger System 92 • Strategies for Communicating Across Boundaries 93
  Systemic Connections 94
    Connectivity and Embeddedness 96 • Impact of the Group on the Individual Member 98
Expectations and Dependencies 100
PUTTING THE PIECES TOGETHER: Group Structure, Group Goal, and Group Identity 102
The Group's Environment 103
  Physical Environment and Material Resources 103
  Psychological Environment 105
Reacting to the Group's Environment 107
THINK ABOUT IT: External Influences on the Group 108
  Denial of External Threats 109
  Groupthink 109
The Group's Charge 110
  Questions of Fact 111
  Questions of Value 112
  Questions of Policy 112
  Where Do Opinions Fit In? 113
  Identifying Criteria 114
  Goal Setting for Social and Support Groups 114
Final Output 115
BUILDING ANALYTICAL SKILLS: Developing Criteria to Understand the Group's Charge 116
System Theory as a Foundation 118
Summary 121
Checklist 122
Discussion Questions and Exercises 123

5 Types of Groups and Group Activities 124

Types of Groups 125
GROUP ASSESSMENT TECHNIQUE: Identifying Groups and Their Characteristics 127

Types of Group Tasks and Activities 128
   Steiner's Typology of Group Tasks 129
      Disjunctive Tasks 130 • Conjunctive Tasks 131 • Additive Tasks 132 • Discretionary Tasks 132
   BUILDING ANALYTICAL SKILLS: Redesigning Tasks to Take Advantage of the Group 134
   McGrath's Group Task Circumplex 136
      Task Type 1—Planning Tasks 137 • Task Type 2—Creativity Tasks 137 • Task Type 3—Intellective Tasks 137 • Task Type 4—Decision-Making Tasks 138 • Task Type 5—Cognitive Conflict Tasks 138 • Task Type 6—Mixed-Motive Tasks 138 • Task Type 7—Contests/Battles/Competitive Tasks 139 • Task Type 8—Performance/Psycho-Motor Tasks 139
   GROUP ASSESSMENT TECHNIQUE: Breaking Big Goals into Small Tasks 140

Task Characteristics 140
   Task Difficulty 141
   Solution Multiplicity 141
   Intrinsic Interest 142
   Population Familiarity 142
   Acceptance Level 143
   Area of Freedom 143
   Social Complexity 143
   PUTTING THE PIECES TOGETHER: Interdependence and Group Goal 144

Task and Activity Constraints 144

Task and Activity Outcomes 146
   THINK ABOUT IT: Confronting Task Constraints 147

Summary 148

Checklist 149

Discussion Questions and Exercises 150

6 The Individual in the Group 151

GROUP ASSESSMENT TECHNIQUE: How Important Are Communication Skills? 152

Your Group Interaction Style 152
   Interpersonal Needs 154
   Achieving Need Compatibility 157
   Communication Apprehension 158
   BUILDING ANALYTICAL SKILLS: Finding Needs Embedded in Conversation 159
   Communicator Style 160
   THINK ABOUT IT: What Is Your Level of Communication Apprehension? 161
   GROUP ASSESSMENT TECHNIQUE: Determining Your Communicator Style 162
   Group Communication Competence 165
   Informal Interaction 167
   GROUP ASSESSMENT TECHNIQUE: How Competent Are You? 168
   PUTTING THE PIECES TOGETHER: Interdependence and Group Goal 169

Maintaining Identity and Independence 170

Summary 170
Checklist 172
Discussion Questions and Exercises 173

7 Communicating to Build Relationships in Your Group 174

Your Relationship to Others: Dependence 174
Your Relationship with Others: Interdependence 175
  Group Cohesiveness 177
  Group Satisfaction 180
  Camaraderie 181
Power Relationships 182
  Bases of Power 183
GROUP ASSESSMENT TECHNIQUE: What Is Your Level of Camaraderie? 184
PUTTING THE PIECES TOGETHER: Group Structure and Group Size 186
  Analyzing Power Issues 187
  Control of Resources 188
  Situationally Enhanced Power 189
    Primary Provokers 190 • Scapegoats 193
  Equity 194
  Trust 195
Gender Influences in Groups 196
THINK ABOUT IT: How Fragile Is Trust? 197
Cultural Diversity in Groups 200
  Beyond Cultural Diversity 204
  Dysfunctional Reactions to Cultural Differences 205
BUILDING ANALYTICAL SKILLS: What Is Your Diversity Filter? 206
  Overcoming Diversity Problems 208
THINK ABOUT IT: Are You Ignoring Diversity? 210
Summary 210
Checklist 212
Discussion Questions and Exercises 213

PART 2

Meeting Group Challenges 215

8 Using Groups to Make Decisions and Solve Problems 217

Using the Group's Strength to Solve Problems 217
Using Decision Procedures 219
PUTTING THE PIECES TOGETHER: Group Goal and Interdependence 220
  Standard Agenda 220
  Critical Advisor 222

THINK ABOUT IT: Could You Be A Critical Advisor? 224
    Consensus 224
GROUP ASSESSMENT TECHNIQUE: Can Consensus Work? 228
    Voting 228
    Ranking 230
    Brainstorming 231
    Nominal Group Technique 232

Comparing Procedures 234
    Preference for Procedural Order in Groups 236
THINK ABOUT IT: Which Procedure Would Help Your Group? 238
    The Paradox of Using Procedures 238
GROUP ASSESSMENT TECHNIQUE: Identifying Your Preference for Procedural Order 240
BUILDING ANALYTICAL SKILLS: Was Your Decision Effective? 242

Decision-Making Effectiveness 242

Summary 244

Checklist 245

Discussion Questions and Exercises 245

9 Theoretical Lessons for Group Decision Making 247

Group Decision Principles 247

Advice from Functional Theory 249
BUILDING ANALYTICAL SKILLS: Identifying Decision-Making Functions 252

Influences on Decision Making 253
    Prediscussion Influence 253
    Social Comparison Theory 254
    Persuasive Arguments Theory 255
GROUP ASSESSMENT TECHNIQUE: What Arguments Do You Bring to the Group? 256
    Social Identity Theory 256
    Social-Interactional Perspective 257
    Social and Contextual Influence 257
THINK ABOUT IT: Where Does Influence Come From? 258

Reasons for Faulty Decisions 261
    Constraints on Decision Making 263
        Recognizing Constraints 265 • Responding to Constraints 266
    Process Loss 267
    Groupthink 267

Implementing Decisions 269
    Criteria for Successful Implementation 270
    Designing the Implementation with PERT 271
    Dealing with the Pressures of Time 273
    Additional Implementation Considerations 275

Monitoring and Evaluating Decision Outcomes 276

PUTTING THE PIECES TOGETHER: Group Goal, Group Structure, and Group Identity 277
Summary 277
Checklist 279
Discussion Questions and Exercises 279

10 Leadership in Groups 281
Defining Leadership 281
Becoming a Leader 283
  Appointed Leaders Versus Elected Leaders 283
  Emergent Leaders 284
  BUILDING ANALYTICAL SKILLS: What Is Your Leadership Potential? 284
Universal Approaches to Leadership 288
  Leadership Traits 288
  THINK ABOUT IT: What Do You Want a Leader to Be? 289
  Autocratic and Democratic Leadership 289
  Functional Leadership 292
  Leadership Styles 292
Contingency Approaches to Leadership 294
  Contingency Model of Leadership 294
  Situational Leadership Model 295
  Leader-Member Exchange Model 299
Criticisms of Early Leadership Approaches 300
Transformational Leadership 301
A Communication Competency Approach to Leadership 302
  BUILDING ANALYTICAL SKILLS: Evaluating a Transformational Leader 304
  Task Competencies 305
  Relational Competencies 306
  Technical Competencies 306
  Leading Through Communication 306
  Your Leadership Evaluation 307
  PUTTING THE PIECES TOGETHER: Group Goal, Group Structure, and Interdependence 308
Multiple Leaders 308
A Group's Need for a Leader 309
Summary 310
Checklist 311
Discussion Questions and Exercises 312

11 Managing Conflict in Groups 314
Defining Conflict 314
  Ways of Thinking About Conflict 315
    Is Conflict Always Disruptive? 316 • Is Conflict Inherent? 317

THINK ABOUT IT: Did I Do That? 318
   The Importance of Communication 319
Types and Sources of Conflict 320
PUTTING THE PIECES TOGETHER: Group Goal, Group Structure, Group Identity, and Interdependence 322
   The Origin of Conflict 322
   Conflict Between Groups 325
Conflict Management Strategies 326
   Conflict Management Alternatives 327
GROUP ASSESSMENT TECHNIQUE: What Conflict Strategy Do You Prefer? 328
      Which Strategy Do You Pick? 331 • Symmetry in Conflict Management Strategies 333
Balancing Conflict and Problem Solving 333
BUILDING ANALYTICAL SKILLS: Identifying Conflict Strategies 334
BUILDING ANALYTICAL SKILLS: A Case Study in Conflict Management 336
Conflict and Cultural Differences 336
Minimizing Ineffective Conflict in Your Group 339
   Communication Strategies 339
   Mediation 341
      Message Feedback 342 • Working on Problem Solving 344
Summary 344
Checklist 346
Discussion Questions and Exercises 347

PART 3

Developing and Facilitating Your Group 349

12 Group Development and Evolution 351

The Origins of This Group 351
   Group Member Selection 352
   Group Startup 354
   Group Member Assimilation 355
PUTTING THE PIECES TOGETHER: Group Structure, Group Identity, and Interdependence 356
Group Development 356
   Stages of Group Development 357
      Forming 357 • Storming 359 • Norming 361 • Performing 362 • Termination 362 • Progressing Through the Stages 364
   Multiple-Sequence Views of Group Development 365
      The Contingency Model 365
GROUP ASSESSMENT TECHNIQUE: How Far Has Your Group Developed? 366
      The Punctuated Equilibrium Model 366

THINK ABOUT IT: Identifying Group Breakpoints and Transitions 368
Membership Changes in Groups 369
BUILDING ANALYTICAL SKILLS: Reflecting and Remembering 371
Summary 371
Checklist 373
Discussion Questions and Exercises 373

13 Meeting Management and Group Facilitation 375

Formal Meeting Planning 376
Premeeting Planning and Preparation 376
Leader Premeeting Planning 376 • Group Member Premeeting Preparation 379
PUTTING THE PIECES TOGETHER: Group Identity and Group Goal 379
THINK ABOUT IT: Making Plans Count 380
Conducting the Meeting 380
Managing Relational Issues 382 • Using Space 383 • Using Visuals 383 • Making Assignments 386
GROUP ASSESSMENT TECHNIQUE: How Would You Plan and Conduct These Meetings? 387
Ending the Meeting 388 • Taking Minutes 388
Postmeeting Follow-Up 388
Overcoming Obstacles 389
Long Meetings 389
Unequal Member Involvement and Commitment 390
Formation of Cliques 390
Different Levels of Communication Skill 390
Different Communicator Styles 392
Personal Conflicts 392
Building a Team 392
BUILDING ANALYTICAL SKILLS: What Would You Do? 394
Identifying the Effectiveness of Your Team 396
THINK ABOUT IT: The Power of Emotions in Groups 397
Understanding the Problem of Your Team 398
Developing a Group Charter and a Code of Conduct 398
GROUP ASSESSMENT TECHNIQUE: Diagnosing Team Problems 399
Ethical Group Membership 401
Defining Ethical Behavior 402
THINK ABOUT IT: Who Is Responsible? 403
Group Impact on Individual Ethics 404
Summary 405
Checklist 406
Discussion Questions and Exercises 407

14 Making Observations and Giving Feedback 408

Why Groups Need Feedback 409

Message Feedback to Group Members 412
- *Closed-Loop Communication as Feedback 416*
- *Feedback Style 419*

PUTTING THE PIECES TOGETHER: Group Goal, Interdependence, and Group Identity 420

Types of Feedback 420
- *Descriptive Feedback 420*
- *Evaluative Feedback 420*
- *Prescriptive Feedback 421*

Levels of Feedback 421
- *Task and Procedural Feedback 421*

THINK ABOUT IT: How Do You Respond to Feedback? 422
- *Relational Feedback 422*
- *Individual Feedback 422*
- *Group Feedback 423*

BUILDING ANALYTICAL SKILLS: Topics for Group Feedback 424
- *Organizational Feedback 424*

Questionnaires and Surveys as Feedback 425

Other Feedback Techniques 425
- *Interaction Diagrams 425*

BUILDING ANALYTICAL SKILLS: Specifying Feedback 426
- *Taping the Group 428*

Principles for Designing a Group Feedback System 430
- *Getting Started 430*
- *Feedback Advice 432*

Summary 434

Checklist 435

Discussion Questions and Exercises 436

Glossary G-1

References R-1

Author Index I-1

Subject Index I-4

PART 1

The Group as a System

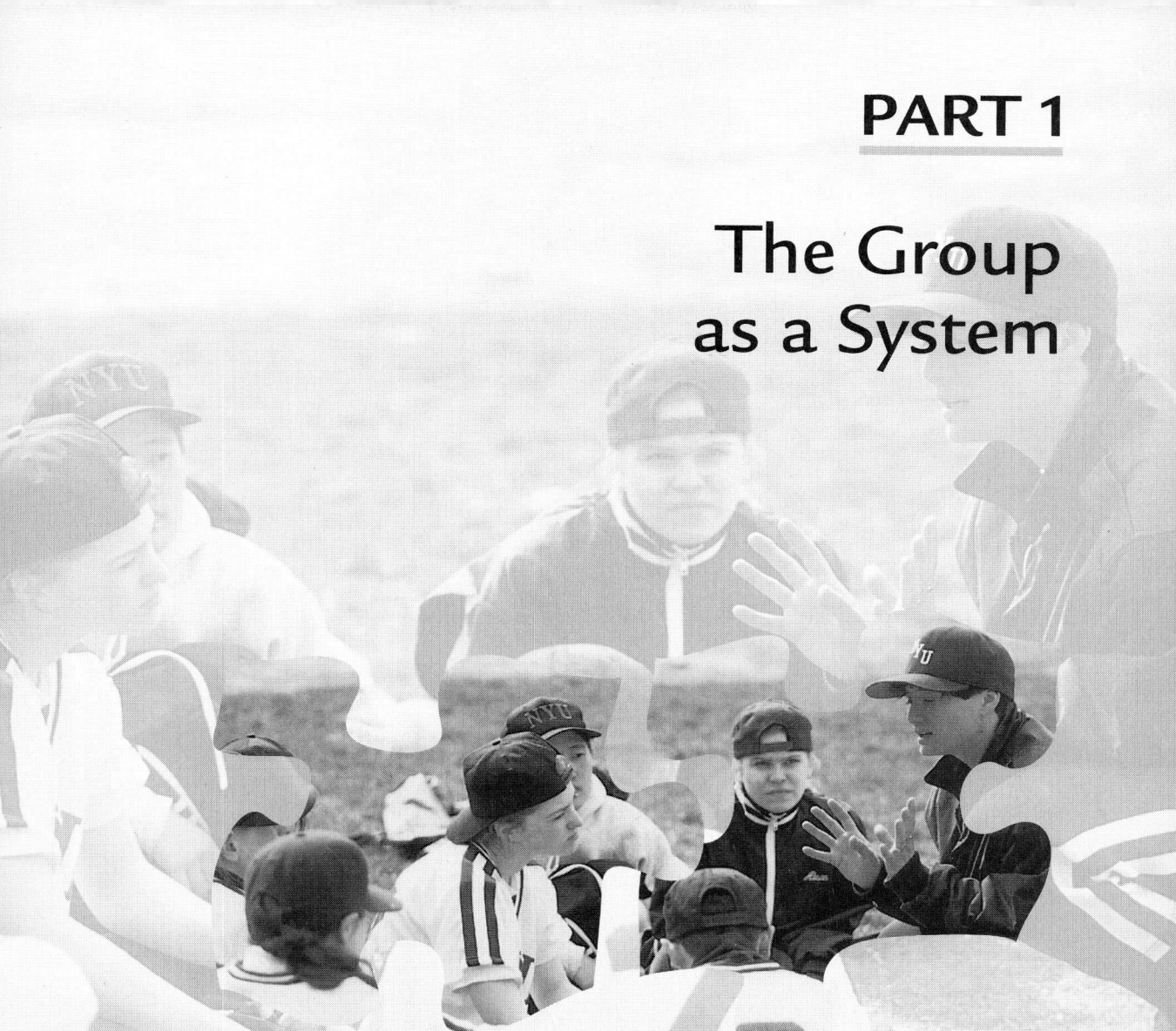

Introduction to Group Communication

What exactly is a group?

Why is it that I am successful in one group and not in another?

How does communication work in groups?

Do all groups have tasks?

As you embark on the study of group communication by reading this book and taking this course, you are entering both familiar and uncharted territory. The focus of your study will be familiar because you have been a member of many groups—groups of people with whom you live and play, with whom you work, manage, or supervise, and with whom you celebrate life. Yet, each group is a puzzle waiting to be solved.

Introduction

You have always belonged to groups. You have lived and played in groups—your family, your class in school, sports teams, clubs. You have worked in groups, and you have socialized in groups. Some of your groups have focused on making decisions and solving problems; others have focused on social activities or entertainment. Although some of the groups were fun, supportive, successful, or effective, others were boring, hostile, unproductive, or ineffective. At some point, the groups to which you have belonged experienced disagreement or conflict that contrasted with the groups that were full of laughter.

What's your attitude toward groups? You have had many group experiences and are familiar with how groups operate. What ideas and attitudes do you have about groups based on your experiences? Some of your memories may be negative: the family events that ended with everyone frustrated and angry, the civics classroom group that couldn't present its project because Jenna didn't do her part. Other groups have been more positive: the committee that had so much fun decorating for the dance, the ecology club that earned recognition for cleaning up trails in the park. Often, however, negative memories outweigh positive ones. If this is the case for you, you may have a pessimistic attitude toward groups or try to avoid groups whenever possible.

People in groups complete activities together and create relationships with one another. This book examines groups in the broadest terms, looking at both the processes of problem solving and decision making as well as the development of relationships. It will help you understand your previous group experiences and reconsider some of your attitudes and ideas. It will also clarify group interactions and show you how they can be improved.

One group is never exactly like another. You can't predict other group members' behavior, nor can you control how other members will react to you. Thus, as a member of a group you are always entering uncharted territory. Regardless of factors that may be the same from one group to the next, even one significant difference creates a new and unique group experience. For example, consider a group of co-workers who effectively solve problems on the job and decide to get together for a relaxed dinner at one member's home. When everyone arrives, the team's leader takes over, organizing and directing the group's social activities. She may think she's just doing her part, but the other group members are both offended and astonished that she needs to manage the group in this social setting. Back at work, the harmony of the group is now disrupted as previously effective task and social roles are confused. Or consider some neighbors who walk their dogs together every morning and who then form a book club. They now have to decide when and where they will meet and how to select a book every month. Their previously harmonious interactions are disrupted by conflicting expectations, desires, tastes, and management styles. An obvious solution may seem to be to not mix task and social groups. But in our complex society, we often find that relationships developed in one context extend to other settings; thus people in one part of our lives may show up as group members somewhere else.

You cannot avoid groups. Regardless of your experiences and feelings about groups, it is unlikely that you will be able to avoid participating in them. In fact, our society is becoming increasingly reliant on groups. Although individuality is emphasized in U.S. culture, we are expected to interact in groups as part of the social fabric of families and other living arrangements. The effective interaction of groups is the foundation of our government at local, state, and federal levels. Group structures are often the basis of the organizations on which we depend for economic survival, as well as for our goods and services. As you progress through organizational hierarchies, you'll be a member of groups and manage groups. In fact, the more professional responsibility you have, the less you will work on your own and the more you will interact with or manage groups or teams.

The objective of this book is to help you "read" the groups or teams of which you are a member or for which you are responsible. By being able to analyze group activities, group interaction, and the environment in which a group operates, you will discover what's unique about a particular group and the most effective way to participate and help the group accomplish its activities. As Figure 1.1 illustrates, you may be good at certain kinds of group interaction but not so good at others. To help you become more sensitive to the many factors that inhibit and facilitate group interaction, each chapter contains exercises—*Building Analytical Skills* and *Group Assessment Techniques*. These exercises will focus your attention on a specific

Figure 1.1 We may be good at some aspects of group communication but poor at others.

group issue and allow you to analyze a group experience or apply analytical skills to a group case. Also interspersed throughout the book are brief stopping points called *Think About It*. These are meant to stimulate your analytical thinking by helping you immediately apply what you have read to your previous group situations. Finally, *Putting the Pieces Together*, which appear in each chapter, will help you quickly identify group problems that are caused by violating basic group principles. (In this chapter, these group principles are introduced in "Laying out the Pieces of the Puzzle.") As you encounter new material, you will see how it relates to basic group issues. At the end of each chapter is Checklist for the group skills, information, and assessment techniques introduced. Use this Checklist to chart your course through group communication.

Groups are like individuals—no two are alike. The better equipped you are to analyze what is happening in and around the group, the more successful and satisfying your group experiences will be. To guide you through your investigation of group communication, this book is organized into three parts. The first part describes basic communication concepts as they apply to groups or teams. This part also defines core group concepts and skills. By increasing your ability to analyze group interaction, you will have accomplished the first step to achieving more effective group participation. Part 1 will also explore the types of task groups you are likely to encounter. Although it may seem obvious that group members must know what their task is to accomplish it, group members frequently assume they know what the group is supposed to do without getting verbal consensus or commitment from other group members. Learning to assess the group's task or activity will help you in deciding which interactive processes will be most productive for your group.

The foundation for our exploration of groups is the systemic perspective. This perspective acknowledges that a group is complex, comprised of many elements. Using this perspective, we can examine each of the many layers of a group's system. Each layer is worthy of exploration by itself, but, by focusing first on one layer and then another, we might miss the extent to which a group's multiple systems interact with and affect one another. One layer—the interpersonal level—contains the interpersonal interactions within the group. This most micro layer allows us to examine the group by looking at the communication among individual group members. At this level, we would examine the skills of individual members as well as issues of power and roles. Another layer of the system—the group level—is the entirety of the group's activity. At this level, we would examine how the group makes decisions and resolves conflict, as well as leadership issues. The third level—the environmental level—is the broadest level, and it is any interaction between the group and its larger context. Groups do not exist in isolation, rather, they are composed of members who are also members of other groups with competing claims on their time and resources. You've probably felt the pressure of rushing from one group activity to another. In the same way, groups feel pressure when they have to meet deadlines set by others or when they are constrained in some way by those outside the group.

The second part of the book focuses on group interaction opportunities and problems that surface regularly. Bringing individuals together creates a natural opportunity for differences to occur. These differences can benefit or harm the group. Increasing your skills in decision making, problem solving, leadership, and conflict management will help you maximize your group interaction efforts.

Part 3 brings together the information presented in the first two parts. With all that has been researched about group interaction, there is no blueprint for group success. What works in one group situation fails in another. Moreover, what works at one point in time may not work later as relationships among group members mature or the group takes on different tasks or activities. This part of the book covers group facilitation and intervention skills. Whether or not you are the leader of a group, if you can recognize group interaction patterns and know how to help a group stay or get back on track, you will be a valuable group member. Thus it is important that you learn to analyze the group task, environment, members, and interaction. Armed with more than just a gut feeling will make you a productive group member and allow you to positively affect your group.

There are no magic formulas for group interaction or set procedures that work in each group setting. Each group is different, therefore, your approach to each group must be different. This book is a guide for your exploration of groups. It is based on theory and research studies. Theories from a range of disciplines including communication, counseling, management, and psychology provide frameworks that both describe and explain group interaction. Research studies provide information about application and procedures. By basing your assessment of the group and its task on theory and research, you will be able to develop viable solutions to the group interaction problems you encounter.

What Is a Group?

Through your experiences, you probably already have your own definition of a group. However, you may have overlooked a few of the critical elements that differentiate group communication from other communication contexts. So, although you may have great familiarity with groups, you may not know the defining characteristics of a group. Are two people having dinner together a group? What about five people waiting for a bus on the street corner? Or 50,000 fans in a football stadium? And how about your favorite "X-Files" chat room on the Internet? How exactly is a group differentiated from other forms or contexts of interaction?

Characteristics for Defining a Group

We'll examine five characteristics central to the definition of groups: group size (number of members), interdependence of members, group identity, group goal, and group structure. In addition to defining what a group is, these characteristics are also a good place to start in understanding how members of a group interact effectively. These characteristics can help us isolate and understand why group interaction problems develop. As you read in more detail about each of the characteristics, you will understand why a **group*** is defined as three or more members who identify themselves as a group and who can identify the activity of the group. Together, members use the structure, roles, and norms generated from their own interaction to work together interdependently on an agreed-upon goal or objective.

Group Size One of the primary characteristics of a group is **group size.** The minimum number of members in a group is three. The maximum number of members depends on the other factors discussed shortly. Early in the study of group interaction, many researchers examined **dyadic interaction,** or interaction between two people (a dyad). In the communication discipline, this form of interaction is now regarded as interpersonal interaction.

The interaction of three people is significantly different from the interaction of two. The introduction of the third person sets up the opportunity to form coalitions. As an example, **coalition formation** occurs when one member takes sides with another against yet another member of the group. When the third person identifies with or takes sides with one of the other members, this creates an imbalance of power. This type of imbalance can only occur when at least three group members are present. A coalition creates interaction dynamics that cannot occur with two people.

Introduction of a third group member also allows hidden communication to take place. These hidden interactions are often attempts to build alliances, which underscores the role of relationship building as groups work on tasks. For example, let's say that Nancy and Michelle meet on their way to the group meeting; Jeff is waiting for them in the conference room. Nancy takes this opportunity to brief Michelle on the background of the project as well as her evaluation of her previous

Some families interact as groups—making decisions about vacation travel, planning holiday activities, and celebrating significant achievements of family members.

interactions with Jeff. Jeff does not have access to this hidden interaction, but Nancy's musings to Michelle will certainly affect the interaction among these group members. In this case there was no strategic attempt to manipulate Jeff, but Nancy and Michelle's interaction still affected the group. Naturally, the larger the group, the more these hidden interactions are likely to occur.

The size of a group has an impact not only on how members interact with one another but also on how roles are taken (or assigned) within the group and how interactions are regulated during group meetings. It may be more difficult for members of larger groups to decide who takes what role as many members may have the skills necessary for any one role. Also, larger groups typically have more difficulty in scheduling time to interact together. On the other hand, members of smaller groups may find that no one in the group possesses a critical skill or knowledge essential to the group's activity. You may be thinking that smaller groups are better because fewer interaction problems arise, but artificially limiting the size of the group forces more responsibility on each of the members. Thus, group size is more appropriately fixed by the group's task. Let's return to the topic of group size after we consider the other characteristics of a group.

Interdependence of Members A second important characteristic of a group is the interdependence of group members. **Interdependence** means that both group and individual outcomes are influenced by what other individuals do in the group (Brewer, 1995). Group members must rely on and cooperate with one another to

Normally, when we think of groups, we think of formal work teams like those in organizations that make decisions and solve problems (top). Likewise, sports teams are groups that play together usually under the direction of a group leader—the coach (bottom).

complete the group activity, as group members are attempting to accomplish something that would be difficult or impossible for one individual (DeLamater, 1974). For example, members of a softball team are a group. It's impossible to play effectively without a catcher, pitcher, *and* shortstop. Each member of the softball team fulfills a specific role that functions interdependently with other team players. Even if your team has one outstanding hitter, the team will not win very often without members who specialize in defense. Not only do these team members have to fulfill their specialized roles and depend on one another, they have to communicate with one another, both verbally and nonverbally. It is not enough for the necessary roles to be identified and members assigned to them; the individuals in these roles have to be actively engaged and in interaction with one another.

For example, consider a project team at a computer company that has been given the task of developing a new software program. This task can be seen as a **superordinate goal**—that is, it cannot be completed by one person because it would be too difficult, time-consuming, and burdensome. The team, however, brings together several people with different strengths and skills. Team members can share ideas and experiences in the early stages of the project; later, they can test various ideas with one another before engaging expensive resources. Such interdependence is likely to save time, energy, effort, and money; it is also likely to create a better software program.

The communication among group members also illustrates the interdependence of group members. Let's look at a student group concerned about course and faculty evaluation. Jennetta asks the group to think of ways to improve the evaluation process. Her question prompts group members to respond with ideas that she writes on the board. When they finish, Jerome comments about one trend he sees in the list. Sara asks him to explain it further. As Jerome and Sara continue their conversation, Jennetta circles the ideas they are talking about and links them together while she gives them affirming nods to indicate they should continue. Pamela, who said very little during the idea generation process, says, "But the ideas you are circling are ones we as students can do little about. What about working through student government to develop an independent evaluation process that could be published in the student newspaper? Student government set up their own book co-op in spite of opposition from the administration." Jennetta, Jerome, and Sara turn to Pamela. Their silence encourages Pamela to continue talking. "What I'm saying is that the ideas on the board are attempts to fix a system that is not under our control. So, why not develop an independent system that students control?" Jerome replies enthusiastically, "Great idea, Pam. . . . Do you mind if I call you Pam?"

Notice how the verbal and nonverbal messages in this group depend on one another to make sense. Jennetta first invites their participation, and all members generate ideas. The list they have generated motivates Jerome to make an analytical comment, which is further encouraged by Sara's question. Although Pamela is quiet, this action has an impact on other group members' communication by giving Jerome and Sara more opportunities to talk. Jennetta's nonverbal messages further contribute to Pamela being quiet as she acknowledges Jerome and Sara and not Pamela. Pamela's interjection into the conversation startles the others, and their conversation stops. Her acute observation reminds them that Pamela has not been ignoring what's going on; rather, her assessment helps them see that they may be wasting their time.

In this example, the communication itself was interdependent. One statement can only make sense when it is placed before and after other strings of the conversation. Each individual in the group is influenced by what others say (and don't say). The group's success depends on the extent to which the verbal and nonverbal messages make sense together.

Group Identity A third defining characteristic for a group is group identity. Group members must know and act as if they are members of this particular group. They must be able to identify the other group members and the group's task or activity. Without this type of identification, group focus and interdependence will weaken. Unfortunately, many times people are identified as a group when they have little or no expectation that group interaction will occur. Such gatherings or collections of people are more appropriately called **groupings**.

Throughout our lives, we are constantly identified by the groupings people assign to us. For example, I live in Memphis, Tennessee, I am female, I own Dalmatians, and I drive a Sebring. But being identified according to these categories does not necessarily place me in interaction with others as a group member or cause me to be interdependent with anyone else. These categories make it easier to identify who I am, but they do not in any way make me part of an interacting group. On the other hand, individuals may join particular groups because they want to be identified as members of a group (for example, fraternity, sorority, community chorus). But doing so will not result in group interaction opportunities unless the individuals are motivated to talk to others. **Group identity** means that people identify themselves with other group members and the group goal.

Remember that just because individuals have some reason to be together or there appears to be a surface connection among individuals, true group interaction may not occur (Zander, 1982). Simply being identified with others who share similar characteristics doesn't create "groupness" as we are interested in the concept. Rather, group members who identify with one another and the group's goal must communicate about and work toward that goal for identity to be meaningful in the group environment.

Group Goal Identity, then, is a necessary but not sufficient characteristic for a group. We also need a fourth characteristic: group goal. A **group goal** is an agreed upon task or activity that the group is to complete or accomplish. This goal may be long term and process-oriented (such as a family functioning as a social and economic unit), or it may be short term with specific boundaries and parameters (for example, your church group is having a car wash to raise money). Regardless of the duration or type of goal, group members must agree on the group's goal to be effective (Larson & LaFasto, 1989). That does not mean that all group members have to like the goal, but it does mean that there is clarity on what the goal is and that it is perceived by members as being worthwhile.

Having a group goal gives a group direction and provides members with motivation for completing their tasks. A group's goal should be cooperative. This means that as one member moves toward goal attainment, so do other group members. A group goal is cooperative when it integrates the self-interests of all group members (Deutsch, 1973). Groups that are having trouble have often lost sight of their goals, sometimes because of distraction or sometimes because of external forces (other people, changing deadlines or objectives, and so on). Groups that cannot identify why they exist and what they are trying to achieve are doomed to failure.

For example, as a student in the class for which you are reading this textbook, your goal is probably to get a good grade. But getting a good grade is your individual goal—not a group goal. Each student in the class may have the same goal, but it is not a shared, consensual goal that motivates interaction and activity. If it were, everything you did in preparation for class would be designed to help you, as well as others, achieve the "good grade" goal. Thus, agreement on a common goal among individuals, not similarity in individual goals, defines individuals as members of the same group. Group goals create cooperation whereas individual goals often create competition.

Group Structure The final defining characteristic of a group is its structure. Whether informal (a group of friends) or formal (a parent-teacher organization), some type of structure must develop. **Group structure** tends to develop along with, or emerge from, group rules and norms—patterns of behavior that others come to rely on. Pat, Emily, Donna, and Greg regularly meet for social activities on Friday night. If the group does not set plans for the next week, Pat takes it upon himself to call everyone to get suggestions for next Friday night. No one has appointed him to this role; he does it naturally in reaction to the other group members' lack of initiative. Pat has taken on the role of being the group's social organizer, and the group has come to depend on him to play that role. His role playing has created a certain structure in the group, and that structure has become a norm—a behavior that is expected by the other group members.

In more formal settings, a group may elect someone to record what happens in the meetings as a way of tracking the group's progress and keeping an account of details. Again, the person taking on the recorder or secretary role is providing structure for the group as well as behaving in a normative pattern—a pattern of behavior that others come to rely on. Thus both the recorder's actions and the recording of the meeting provide structure for the group. Anytime a group member takes on a formal or informal role, group structure is created. Likewise, any discussion or outcome that provides direction for the group is considered group structure. Your family decides to visit Disneyland on vacation. That decision creates structure for your future family discussions because now your interactions will center around the logistics of traveling to California and planning your vacation.

Whatever structure is initiated in a group, it is also likely to change as a group matures and develops or as its activities change. To be viable, groups must have some form of structure, but the structure does not have to remain constant throughout the life of the group. **Group roles,** which are the micro components of a group's structure, must also be visible to the group's members. But like group structure, roles are not necessarily fixed. Formal roles—those filled through appointment, assignment, or election—are likely to be more permanent. Informal roles—functions that emerge from the group's interaction (such as the group member who eases tension in the group)—will change as the talents of group members become apparent or are needed by others.

To summarize, we have defined a group as three or more people who work together interdependently on an agreed-upon activity or goal. They identify themselves as members of the group, and they develop structure and roles, based on norms and rules, as they interact and work toward their goal. Your family may have been your first group according to the characteristics we've established. If your family had a family council in which all members participated to help establish family norms or rules or decided how to spend family time (vacations and weekends), then your family was a group. Unfortunately, today many families are simply groupings. These individuals may have group moments when family members come together and take on the characteristics identified earlier (for example, at the dinner table when everyone sits down to discuss a common topic and the conversation results in a consensual decision), but for the most part they remain groupings—failing to achieve the reality and potential of true group interaction.

Group Size Revisited You can probably see that although we identify the minimum number of members of a group, the maximum number depends on the other four characteristics. Rather than limiting group membership to some arbitrary number, we need to consider issues such as task complexity or interaction opportunity to identify the maximum number of group members.

However, research has demonstrated that size is often a factor of diminishing returns, affecting both the group's tasks and the relationships within the group (Bettenhausen, 1991; Hare, 1982; Wheelan & McKeage, 1993). Although more group members help expand the pool of skills and talent from which to choose, when group size increases certain disadvantages develop. There is a point at which groups become too large and members become dissatisfied. Smaller groups generally are more cohesive as well. When a group becomes too large, members are less satisfied and have less identification with the group. The larger the group, the fewer opportunities each member has to talk, and as group size increases, what the group can achieve decreases because of the logistical efforts in coordinating many people. Thus increased group size affects group productivity because members have less opportunity to participate, which affects the relationships among group members. Large groups require more attention to group norms and group roles, and they can create the illusion that someone else is responsible so individuals fail to do their part. There are also greater demands on group leadership in large groups.

But large groups can be effective—if the goal is clearly identified for all group members, if groups members are in consensus about the goal, and if members are aware of, and fulfilling, their roles. Clearly, groups need to be the appropriate size to effectively complete the task or activity before them. Three members may be too few for a complex task or goal. When there are too few members and too much work to do, group members are likely to become frustrated, even angry, about the task and toward the group. Relationships, as well, are affected by group size.

Twenty members are probably too many to deliberate on a problem and make recommendations in one written report. When group members feel as if they are not needed to produce the group's outcome, or if their individual efforts are not recognized by others, they become apathetic and feel distant from the group. This form of detachment is known as **social loafing**, which means that individual efforts decrease as the size of the group increases. Conversely, five members are too few to make up a baseball team.

Although some groups and teams (juries, sports teams) have specific size limits or standards, other groups (for example, work groups) can be designed with size in mind. Generally, research has demonstrated that the optimum group size is five (Hare, 1976). Members of five-person groups are generally more satisfied and believe that they have adequate opportunities to talk in the group. Too few members may make members feel pressured into talking; too many members decreases the opportunity to participate. An odd number of members is also preferred for decision-making groups to avoid a deadlock.

Due to the defining characteristics of groups, each group takes on a life of its own. Each is unique, not replicating others and seldom replicating itself. What we as individuals bring to group interactions is a compilation of all our past group experiences, good and bad (McCanne, 1977). This set of expectations is like no one else's set of expectations, and the expectations we take from the group differs from other group members. As a result, we live in a world of constant ebb and flow of group interactions from our personal, social, and professional lives that overlap and affect one another. It is to our benefit to understand these interactions and our ability and skills to influence them. Not only are our groups charged with completing tasks and activities, they provide us with the opportunities to develop and maintain relationships, to learn about ourselves, and to enhance our personal and professional skills. And, all of this is accomplished through communication. "Laying out the Pieces of the Puzzle" illustrates how these five elements that define groups can help you determine if a group is effective or not.

How Do Groups Communicate?

This is a simple question, but the answer is quite complicated because at any one time there is not just one communication system within a group. First, let's examine a simple communication model. Then we will apply it to a group.

A Basic Communication Model

Communication models identify the sender, the receiver, and the message as the most fundamental elements. The **sender** is the source of a **message,** or information, which is sent through verbal, nonverbal, written, or electronic channels to the **receiver.** The message, however, is not always transmitted or received with the meaning intended by the sender. **Physical noise** (for example, a construction crew working just outside the building) or **psychological noise** (a son trying to remember what his mother asked him to bring home from the store) can distort the message for either the sender or the receiver—sometimes both. For example, Jason is trying to tell Becky about his ideas for the picnic they are planning. But, just as he launches into his description his beeper goes off, and Jason looks down to find out who is calling. Becky, who dislikes the interruptions of beepers, starts to wonder how reliable Jason will be in planning the picnic. She thinks, "If he is rude enough to let a beeper interrupt our conversation, will he listen when the deli manager gives him quotes for food?" In this very simple transaction, there is both physical noise (the beeper) and psychological noise (Becky's attitude about the intrusion and Jason's attention to the outside caller). When Jason and Becky have the opportunity to restart their conversation, the interaction environment has been changed by their previous attempt to talk about the picnic and the interruption. Noise causes distortion in most sender-receiver interactions and is a primary cause of ineffective communication. Although the noise described in this example is rather severe, most interactions are affected by some level of noise. It is rare that a sender and receiver give each other 100 percent of their attention.

When we consider the interaction of the group, we need to notice several interaction tendencies that can further distort the communication process and ultimately affect the message that the receiver hears or sees. One tendency in groups is for people to talk over one another. This may happen because a member wants to make sure she's heard. It can also happen when members have great enthusiasm for their group activity. Another tendency is for several conversations to occur at once. These are called "side conversations" and can occur when friends sit side by side and use the group meeting as an opportunity to catch up with one another. They can also occur when group members are disinterested in the conversation or unmotivated to participate. Feeling like the conversation has little to do with them, several group members start discussing another topic. Now the group is split into two separate discussions. When this occurs, members do not have access to both conversations. Thus time is wasted, and information intended for everyone is received by only part of the group's membership. Both types of side conversations create additional physical noise that may prevent a receiver from hearing a sender. Moreover, both tendencies are likely to create psychological noise (for instance, negative attitudes) for at least some of the group members, further distorting the interaction.

Thus groups need to take special precaution against distortion in messages. To be interdependent and to share understanding of the group's goal, all group members need to hear what is being said and need the opportunity to discuss ideas. Too frequently, group leaders use meetings to provide information (send messages), leaving little time for other group members to respond or ask questions. This introduces another component of the group communication model—**feedback.** Without this opportunity to ask questions, to restate the message in the receiver's own words, or to overtly agree or disagree with the message sent, the sender cannot be certain that other group members received the message he intended. Feedback is critical in group settings because of the many interaction opportunities that exist.

The communication model in Figure 1.2 consists of the sender as the source transmitting a message through one or more channels (verbal, nonverbal, written,

> ### BUILDING ANALYTICAL SKILLS
>
> *Laying out the Pieces of the Puzzle*
>
> The five characteristics that define groups—group size, interdependence, group identity, group goal, and group structure—can provide a foundation for analyzing the effectiveness of a group. The following exercise will lead you through this analysis.
>
> **The Group and Its Interaction**
>
> Like most students assigned a group project, Gayle, Rebecca, Sean, Jim, and Sonya waited too long to begin work on their assignment. Now, pressed for time, each member has other obligations and, quite frankly, more pressing interests and motivations. Still, the group has to produce what the professor expected in order to receive 20 percent of their course grade. Meeting once to get organized, Rebecca, Sean, Jim, and Sonya each took responsibility for one area of the project while Gayle agreed to take responsibility for later integrating these parts. The group gave itself two weeks before getting back together to turn in their finished materials to Gayle, who would pull it all together before their oral presentation to the class. Due to their late start, there would be only a few days between the group's second meeting and the oral presentation, putting extreme pressure on Gayle to integrate the project's parts and get it back to the other members so they could perform effectively during the presentation. These members are juniors and seniors, and they had done this type of group project many times in the past. They know they could pull it off.
>
> Group Size
>
>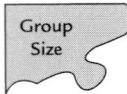
> This group had five members. Deciding to separate responsibilities into four distinct parts and one integration role makes sense if there are four major parts of the topic or project to be researched. Or does it? What other factors could come into play? Does it make sense to have one person be responsible for integrating the results of others' work?
>
> Interdependence of Members
>
>
> The group decided to break up the task into distinct parts. This seems reasonable given their tight deadline. Or does it? As Sean completes his research, his findings could impact the research of others. What other interdependence issues could arise? Think about the lack of interdependence in coordinating the research and then forcing interdependence in the oral presentation. Does the class project described represent a superordinate group goal? What supports your argument?

or electronic) to the receiver. The sender acknowledges the feedback of the receiver, and is aware that both physical and psychological noise are present in the interaction. This model illustrates that thinking of communication as sending and receiving messages is an oversimplification.

To better represent the process, we need to think of each person in the communication opportunity as being *both* sender and receiver:

JARROD: I think we should consider his past performance.

ANGEL: Performance at school or performance on the job?

Group Identity

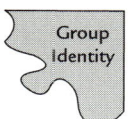

How do these group members identify with one another? What steps could they take to enhance their group identity? As the leader of the group, what could Jim do to enhance the group's identity? Or, do they need a group identity, given their limited time for interaction?

Group Goal

What are the boundaries or parameters of the group's goal? The goal was given to the group by someone external to the group. How will this affect group members' perceptions of the goal? The goal is primarily task-oriented. What relationship elements does the group need to consider to successfully complete the assignment?

Group Structure

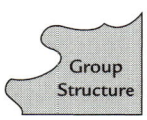

This group appears to have developed some type of structure and identified functional roles (four researchers and one integrator of the material). Are these the only work roles the group needs to consider? Is the structure developed useful for the project? Could individual group members bring differing group norms from past experiences into this interaction that could inhibit the group's effectiveness?

Which part of this group's puzzle is strongest? Weakest? Most critical to the group? If you were in charge of this group, which element would you work on first?

Putting the Pieces Together

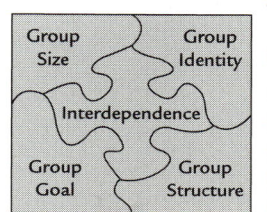

Using the five defining characteristics of a group can help you understand what factors may be inhibiting your group. Knowing, for example, that identity is weak in your group, you might want to suggest that your group spend some time getting to know one another better before working on the task. Or, if the group goal is not clear and agreed upon by everyone, it would be helpful to spend a few minutes talking specifically about what the group is trying to accomplish. When one or several of the defining characteristics is weak or missing, the sense of "groupness" may be too fragile for the individuals to function effectively as a group.

JARROD: Probably only his job skills.

ANGEL: Why? His ability to do well at school would tell us if he can learn quickly and make adjustments to conflicting demands on his time.

MALCOLM: Let's just interview him, and get this over with!

In this short exchange, Jarrod and Angel identified different issues they wanted to bring before the group. Jarrod initiated their interaction, but because feedback occurred, Angel also became a sender when she initially disagreed with Jarrod's proposal. As Angel explained why she disagreed, she became the sender and Jarrod

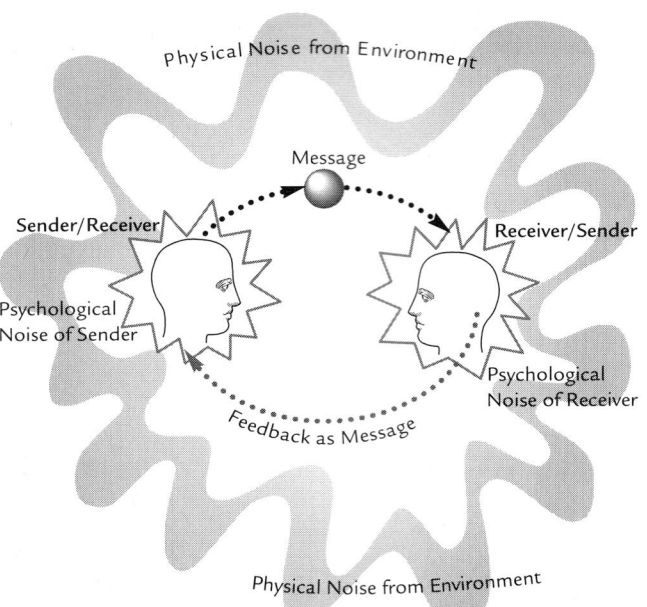

Figure 1.2 Interactional Model of Communication

became a receiver while Malcolm was another receiver for both of them. This fluidity between sender and receiver roles is further heightened when you consider that as Angel explained why she disagreed, Malcolm was sending nonverbal cues to which both Angel and Jarrod reacted. So, now for every interaction relationship (Angel and Jarrod, Angel and Malcolm, Jarrod and Malcolm), the model would look like Figure 1.3; it emphasizes that messages are being simultaneously sent and received.

This brief example demonstrates that group conversations are **multichannel** because group members make use of both verbal and nonverbal messages. Sometimes a written or electronic channel, like writing on the board or e-mail, is used in addition to the verbal and nonverbal channels. Also, notice that both the verbal and nonverbal channels are used simultaneously. We interpret much of what others say by paying attention to their facial expressions, tone of voice, and use of hands and arms. For example, Angel can tell that Jarrod is serious—his words indicate this, but his tone reinforces it.

The model also shows communication to be a **transactional** process—one in which participants together create mutual meaning and understanding. In the previous example, notice how group members question the word *performance*. Groups must work to create mutual understanding because each group member may have a different interpretation of a word or phrase and because each member may create a different understanding of what has been said. In the example, do you believe that the three group members have a common understanding of the phrase "past performance"? If the group stopped right now

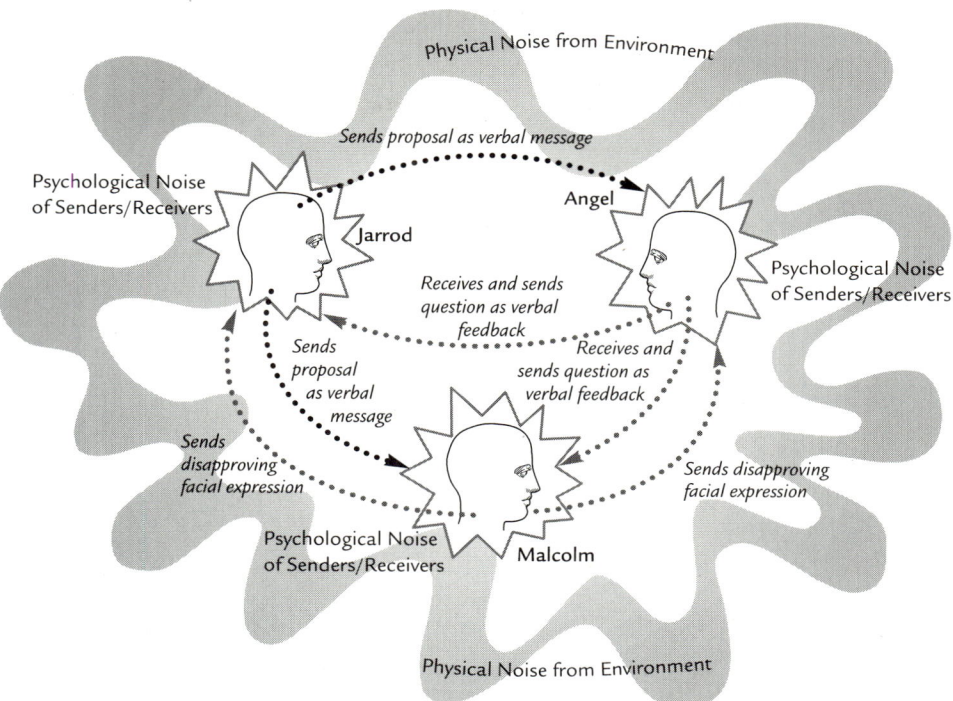

Figure 1.3 Transactional Model of Communication

and reviewed the applicant's performance, would they be evaluating the same thing?

Also note that modeling communication in this way demonstrates that communication is a **process**. As a process, it is difficult to know where the communication event starts and stops. Did Jarrod, Angel, and Malcolm start communicating when Jarrod spoke, or was it when the three group members became aware of the others' nonverbal messages? Because communication is a process, it is also difficult to determine when the disagreement started. Did it start with Angel's first question, Jarrod's response, or Angel's second question? As a process, communication is ongoing and continuous, dynamic and ever changing. As a process, this specific communication event can also affect other communication events. In this example, the disagreement expressed in this meeting will likely influence the group's future conversations.

Communication Opportunities

Another way of thinking of communication in a group is to consider the many interaction opportunities that exist. Look at Figure 1.4; it identifies the ten dyadic relationships in a five-person group. Each possible dyadic relationship is

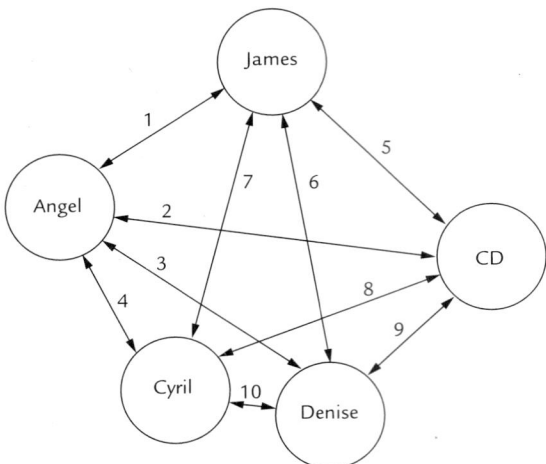

Figure 1.4 Ten Dyadic Relationships in a Five-Person Group

numbered. So not only must each group member maintain a relationship with the group as a whole, he or she must maintain a relationship with each other group member because all of those interaction opportunities exist. It is naive to think that James will receive undivided attention from all of the other group members when he is communicating.

You can see, then, that there are many opportunities for interaction within a group, and this complicates the communication process. Further, it is likely that multiple messages are being sent and received at the same time within the group setting. Even when James is the only person talking, other group members are sending nonverbal messages, which act as feedback. This feedback can be directed to James, in which case it will affect what James continues to say or how he delivers the next part of his message. Nonverbal feedback among other group members while James is talking will also affect how other group members hear and receive messages from James.

Other Issues Affecting Group Communication

Intentionality, impact, and shared meaning are three additional elements that need to be considered in the model of group communication. First, **intentionality:** Does the sender purposely intend to communicate with the receiver? Or, is the sender unaware that she has sent a message? Most of the time verbal messages are intentional. Group members are generally conscious that they are speaking. On the other hand, nonverbal messages can be intentional but generally are not. Nonverbal messages are those that accompany or substitute for verbal messages. For example, you've had a busy day, and you're really not paying much attention to the discussion. To occupy yourself, you start to draw pictures on your notes. Although you may not intend for other group members to interpret this as a message, they probably are. Just as you make decisions to communicate, others are making assessments about your intentions.

Impact is the effect or the result of your message on other group members. In choosing our words and verbal strategies, we attempt to regulate the impact we have on others. For example, you know that Susanna is sensitive to being the only female in the group. As a male member of the group, you try to avoid any negative impact by selecting gender-neutral descriptors. You also ask Susanna questions when others are leaving her out of the conversation. These are attempts at regulating your impact. However, it is the receiver who determines the impact. Depending upon Susanna and other interaction dynamics established in the group, Susanna could have two completely different interpretations of the impact of your communication: She might think you are including her in the conversation, or, alternately, she might think you are bullying her. In the first interpretation, your communication is perceived as being helpful and supportive. She might trust you as a valued colleague because your attempts to include her seem sincere. But a completely different interpretation can also occur. Susanna might think you're trying to highlight the fact that she's not talking but calling her by name in front of others. This more negative interpretation is likely based on Susanna's past group experiences, either with members of this group or with a similar one. The point here is that the impact you have as a sender is largely determined by the receiver. Although senders should always carefully choose their words and monitor their verbal strategies, be aware that receivers determine the ultimate impact. This is why the feedback process is so critical in interaction.

It is through the feedback process and the fluidity between sender and receiver roles that shared meaning is created. **Shared meaning** is the degree to which group members agree on the interpretation of the message. Do not assume that everyone agrees with what you have said, or even understood your primary point. By watching for nonverbal feedback (such as, a puzzled look) and by taking turns at the sender and receiver roles, group members can greatly increase shared meaning in the group.

What Do Groups Do?

Groups have many interaction opportunities. This is the primary reason why a group can do a variety of things. Some groups are focused on a task—winning a basketball game, registering first-time voters, or making recommendations to increase business results. Other groups are more socially or entertainment focused. Support groups that help members with their weight loss and exercise plans or groups of friends that meet regularly to play cards are examples of these types of groups. When we consider the **task dimension** of the group, we are talking about what the group does, whether it is called a task, an activity, or a goal.

Yet, even when groups focus on tasks, the relationships that develop among group members are vital. This **relational dimension** of groups provides social and emotional support as well as a mechanism for developing and maintaining role identities. And, even when groups are primarily social or relational groups, groups still have some task. Perhaps that task is simply to be there for others, or the task may be more specific, such as to provide a place for members to explore their feelings. Regardless of groups' primary focus, both task and social dimensions are present, and they are inseparably interdependent (Fisher, 1971).

Beyond task and social, there is one other important dimension of groups that is frequently overlooked: This is the **learning dimension**—two types of learning occur. First, group members learn or acquire information through their group experiences. This is content knowledge. The learning may be direct (such as learning about children's needs by participating with your group in an after-school child care program), or it may be indirect and vicarious. In a group setting, you have the opportunity to listen and learn from each of the other group members. For example, you can indirectly learn more about your campus by joining a group and listening to others with more experience on your campus.

Learning is often one of the greatest benefits of group interaction (Hackman, 1990; Senge, 1990). Although it is most common to speak of the decisions groups make (for example, which movie to see) or the problems they solve (how to cut the budget by 10 percent), group members can use their interactions to become skilled at managing the group process or group relationships. This second type of learning is relational or process knowledge. For example, learning to solve the inevitable conflicts that arise as members work out solutions among themselves is one type of process learning. Thus, as a group member you have the opportunity to learn how to manage group interaction. An example of relational learning would be using the group setting to ask others questions so they can feel comfortable being part of the group. As they become comfortable and now freely reveal information about themselves, you develop a relationship with one member that lasts beyond the time span of the group.

This multidimensional aspect of groups—task, relational, learning— is important because a group that concentrates solely on work without attending to its members' social or relational needs becomes boring and ineffective. Likewise, a group that focuses solely on having a good time can become tiresome if that social interaction does not lead to new information or provide opportunities to complete meaningful activities. The learning dimension is vital because we tend to carry forward new information or new process or relational skills to our next group setting. Those who are responsible for group management must recognize this group multidimensionality and keep each of these dimensions in balance relative to the activity at hand. With an appropriate balance of group functions, groups effectively accomplish their goal.

Given the amount and variety of resources that are available in a group, it makes sense that groups should work on tasks, or engage in social activities, that are different from the tasks and social activities of individuals. People often believe that groups can do anything. It might be more accurate to say that groups can try anything. But actually, there are some tasks that are better for groups and some that are better for individuals. A few very simple examples explain these concepts.

For the most part, groups do not need to be engaged when the answer is known. For example, why waste the resources and time of several people to solve a crossword puzzle? Steve may enjoy the process of working the puzzle, but the answers to the puzzle are provided. Steve can check the answer to see if he is correct; interacting with others won't change the answer. If a group were charged with the task of completing the puzzle, it is likely that the member most accomplished at completing crossword puzzles would be given the task on behalf of the group. As a result, the other members would be likely to become disinterested and unmotivated as they realize their help is not needed. Moreover, these types of tasks (balancing a checkbook, completing a crossword puzzle) are difficult for a group of individuals to accomplish. For the most efficient use of resources, individuals should be assigned to these types of activities.

On the other hand, when the outcome cannot be predicted, or when many different outcomes could be acceptable, groups rather than individuals should be used. The synergistic effects or the collaborative efforts that accrue from group interaction can be especially fruitful. **Synergy** exists when the performance of a group goes beyond the capabilities of group members as individuals (Schweiger & Sandberg, 1989). When synergy occurs, individual group members feed off one another's energy and interest. The communication among group members promotes positive synergy (Salazar, 1995).

You are probably familiar with synergy, but may know it by another name—team spirit or teamwork. Whatever you have called it, you probably know the effects of synergy. For example, marketing employees in an organization were charged with the responsibility of recruiting new business. Individually, each made cold calls and followed leads on potential business. As individuals, they were fairly effective collectively—claiming at least ten new customers each week. But when all of the marketing employees started to work interdependently as a team, they increased their goal to fifteen new customers a week. To meet this goal, they exchanged information and expertise with one another. If Melody experienced problems with a potential customer, she had Jeff and Dave join her on a conference call to be more persuasive and contribute their specialized knowledge. The marketing team met regularly before work, before lunch, and in the middle of the afternoon to see where they were at in meeting their goal, to pass on information, and to encourage one another. After a few successful weeks, they were able to increase their goal to twenty new customers—something that would not have been possible without the synergistic effects of working together as a team. Clearly, the marketing employees could have worked together and maintained their performance of ten new customers a week. But their willingness to communicate as a group integrated their efforts, which allowed them to capitalize on one another's strengths and create group synergy.

Groups are also appropriate when a decision or solution outcome will affect many people. When the people affected by the decision or solution are involved in the process, they are more likely to be committed to finding and supporting the most effective and efficient answer. "Reflecting and Projection" poses some questions for you to ponder about your past group experiences.

> **? THINK ABOUT IT**
>
> *Reflecting and Projecting*
>
> Think about the last group you were in. Identify the group's goal. What were the tasks or activities? How would you characterize the relationships among members? How did those relationships help the group accomplish its task? Did relationships among members impede task accomplishment? Did the group achieve synergy? If you could change one thing about the group, what would it be? If you encountered this type of group in the future, what would you do differently?

Summary

This chapter has introduced group communication—something that is familiar to you and at the same type a bit confusing. You have always belonged to groups so you have already developed attitudes and habits about working in groups. Although you may have lumped all of your group experiences together, each group is an unique experience. One group is never exactly like another. Because you cannot avoid groups, this book is designed to help you "read" your groups and teams. By analyzing group activities, engaging in reflection after group interaction, and assessing the environment in which groups operate, you will gain a better understanding of group interaction and optimize your group interactions.

The first part of the book will review basic group concepts and basic group skills. The second part focuses on typical types of interaction that require special knowledge or skills—decision making, leadership, conflict management, meeting management, and so on. The final part of the book will integrate information presented previously into analytical techniques that can be used whether you are a group member or a group leader.

A group is defined as three or more members who identify themselves as a group and who can identify the activity of the group. Thus five characteristics will guide our exploration of groups—group size, interdependence, group identity, group goal, and group structure. Using these defining characteristics as avenues of analysis can help us understand the uniqueness of each group. They will appear in exercises throughout the book to help you understand the complexity of group interaction.

Because groups are complex, our model of communication focuses on the fluidity of roles between senders and receivers. Because group members can be both sender and receiver simultaneously, monitoring group interaction and selecting appropriate and effective interaction strategies can be difficult. If we emphasize the role of feedback, however, we can help groups become more effective because feedback increases the opportunity for shared meaning to develop among group members.

We also examined the three dimensions of groups—task, relational, and learning. Although many of our groups are established to make decisions or solve problems, we should not forget the importance of groups in learning or acquiring information, in providing emotional or social support, in managing conflicts, and in socializing or entertaining. Although all groups represent each of these dimensions to some extent, groups must balance these dimensions to support the primary task, goal, or activity group members seek to accomplish.

✓ Checklist

Group Knowledge

You should be able to:
- name characteristics for defining a group.
- describe the communication process in groups.
- describe the task and relational dimensions of group activities.

Group Skills

You should be able to:
- recognize and use the unique communication opportunities of being in a group.
- recognize and eliminate physical and psychological noise from group conversations.
- help your group by facilitating its learning about group process.

Analytical and Assessment Techniques

You should be able to:
- use criteria for defining groups to identify problems.
- assess which of the five characteristics—group size, interdependence, group identity, group goal, and group structure—may need adjustment when group members are having trouble communicating.

Discussion Questions and Exercises

1. Think of a group to which you belonged in the past. Analyze it according to the five characteristics for defining groups.

2. Reflect on one of your childhood groups. Compare that experience to one of your adult group experiences. What has changed? What is similar? What do you believe accounts for the differences and similarities?

3. Think of your past classroom group projects. What characteristics made them interesting? What characteristics made them unbearable?

4. Social loafing is more likely to occur when groups are large. When circumstances dictate many individuals work together as a group, what strategies could group members use to control social loafing?

5. Thinking back on the different groups in which you have been a member, develop two lists—one for groups you consider successful and another for

groups you consider unsuccessful. Review each list and identify three elements that contributed to group success or kept the group from being successful. How many of these elements were under your control as an individual group member? For which elements did you need to depend on other group members?

6. Review the table of contents for this book. Thinking about your current level of group skills, develop three lists: (a) group skills and knowledge that you have now; (b) group skills and knowledge that you'd like to learn; and (c) group skills and knowledge that you've mastered and could share with others.

2

Communicating Within Groups

How can my communication skills make a difference in a group?

Does how I behave in a group communicate more than what I say?

Is listening really a group process?

How can I create a better climate for my group?

Many disciplines study group process (for example, anthropology, counseling, management, psychology, sociology), but communication researchers and consultants have a unique perspective on groups. Group process relies on interaction—both the verbal and nonverbal communication among members within the group. In some contexts, communication may also include written and electronic channels (such as with brainstorming or computer technology). Most group researchers believe that communication is the medium through which individuals constitute a group. Communication creates and sustains interdependency among group members. Groups cease to exist when interdependency and group identity are threatened by lack of communication.

The study of groups originated in the field of social psychology, as a result many of the early studies examined individual behavior in groups. Later, social psychologists (for example, Bales & Cohen, 1979) focused on the entirety of the group process, but they examined the perceptions of group members rather than actual behavior. Researchers in counseling and management also study groups, but they are restricted in the types and contexts of groups they study. Anthropologists study groups in relationship to their role in society or their impact on culture. These foundations provided a natural bridge for communication scholarship on groups.

Communication scholars interested in groups have traditionally focused on task groups or decision-making groups (Bormann, 1994; Poole, 1994), and much of those studies were conducted on groups of students. More recently, group researchers have expanded their interests to groups in natural settings (Frey, 1994; 1995) and groups in organizations (Hirokawa & Keyton, 1995; Seibold, 1995). Now, group scholars focus on children's groups (Keyton, 1994b; Socha & Socha, 1994), community/civic groups (Barge & Keyton, 1994), health care teams (Berteotti & Seibold, 1994; Keyton, 1995), and social support groups (Adelman & Frey, 1994).

Any type of group can be studied from the communication perspective, although communication may function differently from context to context. A counseling group that provides support for those grieving the loss of a loved one is quite different from a committee planning a golf outing for a community fundraiser. Some groups focus on relationships; others focus on tasks. But for each group to exist, communication must occur. What results from or what is achieved in a group is a function of what is communicated (or not communicated) in that particular group environment and situation. Thus communication is central to what it means to be a member of a group.

A Micro-System Perspective

Using a **system perspective,** a group's communication can be described as a set and series of interrelated communications—first as relationships within the group, second as group interaction as a whole, and third as interaction between the group and its environment. A **system** is defined as an organized set of interrelated and interacting parts that attempts to maintain its own balance with the influences from the surrounding environment (von Bertalanffy, 1968). A group as defined in Chapter 1 can be thought of as a system (Fisher & Hawes, 1971).

As a system, the group consists of inputs, throughputs, outputs, and feedback. Through interaction, the group maintains its system by adding information as **input** and using communication to process that information. The result of the processing is **output,** or outcome of the interaction. This output, in turn, can become **feedback** that generates new input for the group's system. Thus the group system is cyclical and ongoing but never repeatable, as the interaction process within the group actively directs or reflects any input brought to the group. Communication is central to this process. It is the medium by which new information is brought into the system. Communication among group members is also the process by which input is processed as **throughput.** Communication is the process by which output is determined and presented. Finally, communication is the process by which output becomes feedback for the group.

Because of these systemic effects, one group member does not represent his or her group because we cannot understand one member of a group in isolation. In other words, one group member is not a true replication of any aspect of the group—its knowledge, its motivation, its desire. Thus, knowing one group member does not allow us to know the group. To understand the group, we must have access to group members' interactions with one another. This **micro-system** level is only one of the systemic levels of a group. Within the group's micro system (among group members) even more micro systems exist in the subgroups or dyads of the group. Moving to a broader systemic view, we can examine the interaction of the group with its environment. This macro-level system—or the relationship between the group and its environment—will be explored in Chapter 3.

A group of friends provides a good example of micro-system interactions that occur within groups. First, each group member constitutes his or her own system. Each person—Rachel, Monette, Penny, LeVar, Russ, and Derrick—has a series of experiences that is independent of the other group members. For example, Rachel works with individuals not well known to the others, has a unique family experience, and has other friends with whom she interacts. This uniquely constitutes the experience of Rachel; no other group member is exactly like Rachel. Second, Rachel brings an unique set of experiences, knowledge, and skills to the larger group. Third, Rachel has a unique relationship with each of the other five friends. Her relationship with Monette is not like Penny's relationship with Monette. Thus, Rachel's relationships with the other group members and her personal experiences together affect how Rachel interacts with this group. Thus, both Rachel's individual system and her interpersonal system with each of the group members affect how the group as a system operates.

In one group outing, Rachel, Penny, and Derrick are commiserating about their lack of finances (input), especially when it is time to celebrate the triumphs and successes of the other group members. Wanting both not to complain but also to be included in celebrating Monette's new job, they join Monette, Russ, and LeVar for dinner at an expensive restaurant (throughput). Instead of a full-course meal, Rachel, Penny, and Derrick order appetizers and soup (ouput) because they have very little money to spend on this type of extravagance. Their unusual behavior (feedback which acts as input) starts a conversation (throughput) among the six-member group about wanting to belong and to be a member of the group but not having the resources to do so. Together, they decide that helping one another through difficult times is what friends do (output).

This example illustrates that group members do not come innocently or naively into group experiences. Rather, they bring with them the totality of their previous group experiences as well as their individual perceptions of what works and doesn't work in group interactions. Coupled with the roles enacted within their group, these individuals create a system in which the verbal and nonverbal communication of one member affects or changes the subsequent interaction of others.

Verbal Communication

Words are the lifeblood of group interaction. Even when we communicate nonverbally, those behaviors are interpreted into words as we construct meaning for the behaviors. **Verbal communication,** or what we say, can hold a group together or erect a wedge among members, hindering the effective accomplishment of goals. Because the definitions of words can be found in dictionaries, many people falsely believe that words have specific meanings for everyone. However, because words are abstract and can act as symbols for different referents, meanings are not centrally located within words themselves. Rather, meaning is derived by the communicators (both sender and receiver) based on the communication context, previous experiences with the words, previous experiences with this person, and even previous experiences with the task. Meaning is perceptually based; thus, meaning is not predictable. For example, think of the word *group*. Before you read this book, it was likely that you had a different definition of group than the one presented here. Check out "Interdependence and Group Identity" to see how words can affect a group.

> **PUTTING THE PIECES TOGETHER**
>
> *Interdependence and Group Identity*
>
> Identify a recent group activity of your friends. Recall a statement that someone said that had impact on the group (for example, "You know, we should do this again; I had fun" or "This is the last time I bail you guys out"). How did the statement affect the interdependence of group members? Was interdependence highlighted, or did the statement strain the interdependence among members? Did the comment strengthen members' willingness to identify with the group, or did the comment cause group members to wish they were not a member of the group?

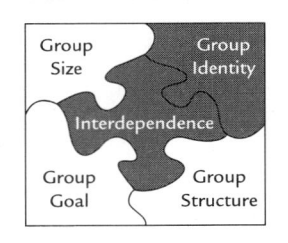

Words and Meanings

Because verbal communication relies on language and because we have more receivers (and more potential errors) in group settings, we must choose our words carefully to communicate clearly. To be effective communicators, we should choose words that are specific and concrete in meaning rather than abstract. **Abstract** words paint broad generalizations whereas **concrete** words help the sender and receiver agree upon what was said. In a group setting, "be on time," may mean come when you think the meeting starts and could even encourage someone who is habitually late to arrive well after the perceived starting time of other group members. "The meeting starts at 2 P.M." is more precise and will generate questions about the starting time if group members have different ideas about when the meeting starts.

Moreover, some words used in groups will not appear in any dictionary. Words or phrases can be specific and unique to the group because the group develops meaning for its own use. For example, "the report" to one specific group means no less than a twenty-page detailed recommendation with an executive summary for Mr. Santoro on his desk by 8 A.M. Monday. Group members will come to use the shorthand "the report" to refer to this detail. Unless all group members mutually understand these details, the verbal message using "the report" is meaningless.

Patterns of Language

We should also consider verbal communication as patterns of language that exist within the group. Verbal messages can direct ("Let's have a moment of silence, please"), structure ("Harriet, you give your report first, then Rashad will talk about the budget"), or dominate ("Shut up!") the communication system within the group. As these messages accomplish these functions, they create positive or negative relationships among group members.

Naturally, the patterns of verbal messages that emerge and the relationships that follow differ among types of groups (Ellis, 1979). For example, decision-making groups can develop messages that indicate symmetry, or equality, among members. When group members perceive themselves as equal to other group members, the discussion is more likely to create a spirit of inquiry and participation. On the other hand, decision-making groups will also experience competitive messages as members compete for leadership and other group management roles. Members of support groups display different types of verbal messages. In this context, messages are almost exclusively symmetrical. Such messages provide a foundation for members to share their feelings. Examine the following two conversations:

Golf Fundraising Committee

TYLER: Okay, let's get rolling.

NAOMI: I'd like to hear about what corporate sponsors we've got lined up.

TYLER: I think it would move us along quicker to see which golf courses are willing to donate green fees.

NAOMI: But, I have to leave the meeting early, and I want to let everyone know about the sponsors.

Grief Support Group

DEBBIE: It's been a really hard week. I'm glad you're all here tonight.

KARL: Me too. At least here, I can let all of the emotion just be, without having to explain myself.

AVERI: Do you want to begin, Debbie?

Notice how the communication functions differently in these two conversations. In the first, communication directs and structures the activities of the group as Tyler and Noami compete with each other about what should be first on the agenda. If this pattern of competitive messages continues, their relationship in the group will likely suffer. Certainly, their messages to each other will have to demonstrate more equality if they are to communicate effectively. In the second conversation, communication is less directive and more focused on building relationships. No one member is trying to dominate the group or its activity. Averi's comment to Debbie suggests structure for the group, but the request has a completely different tone than Naomi's.

Another way to think of the patterns of language is to consider the feedback concept introduced earlier in this chapter. At an interpersonal or dyadic level, how one group member responds to another is feedback. By examining the quality of the feedback within the group, we can assess the overall quality of the group's verbal messages. Let's return to the two conversations. Tyler's feedback to Naomi ("I think it would move us along quicker to see which golf courses are willing to donate green fees") is confrontive. Although his feedback is direct and clear, it is not positive nor does it demonstrate that Naomi's suggestion is welcome. But Karl's feedback to Debbie in the second conversation ("Me too. At least here, I can let all of the emotion just be, without having to explain myself") confirms Debbie's emotional message by agreeing with her and then extending what he thinks she means. In both cases, these patterns of language are sustained by feedback. Feedback can also change a group's language pattern. How would you characterize the pattern of language if Tyler said to Naomi, "Great! Then we'll hear the report about the golf courses"?

Research studies support the conclusion that problem-solving groups using high quality communication—or high quality feedback—produce higher quality solutions (Leathers, 1972). High quality messages are deliberate, relevant, specific, clear, relaxed, and concise. Such high quality feedback unifies meanings and create ideas, as well as demonstrating the sender's flexibility and involvement. Thus the language patterns we create in group settings are a powerful influence on a group's micro system.

Impact of Verbal Activity

Some group members talk more; some talk less. But because it is difficult to hear more than one person talking at a time, it is important to note the person who does the most talking in a group. Differing amounts of **vocal activity,** or the amount of time a member talks in a group, can create different perceptions of group members (Daly, McCroskey, & Richmond, 1977). In general, group members are perceived as being credible—competent, sociable, and composed—as they increase their level of vocal activity. However, if a group member talks too much or consumes all of the talking time in a group, perceptions of credibility decline. Likewise, a group member who contributes regularly to the group's interaction will be seen as a positive influence on the group. But if the group member consumes too much talking time, that influence turns from positive to negative. It appears, then, that participating in group interaction will increase positive perceptions about you as a group member. However, if you talk too much—not giving other group members an opportunity to participate—those positive perceptions can deteriorate.

Vocal activity in a group is also noticed when there is silence—no group member is talking. In a conversation between two people, we expect one person to talk until finished, when the other person takes over. In a group, it is a bit more complicated. Often, there is no obvious way to decide who has the next talking turn (Dabbs, Ruback, & Evans, 1987). When silence occurs, two members may compete to talk next. This is not to say that the competition to talk is negative—members may be enthusiastic about joining the conversation.

Even though you may be unaware of your own nonverbal communication in a group, you are interpreting other members' nonverbal behaviors.

Nonverbal Communicaiton

Group conversations are a mixture of sound and silence (Dabbs, Ruback, & Evans, 1987). Some group members use their speaking turn to perform a monologue, only to be followed by a monologue by another group member. Other groups may present more complex patterns by interrupting one another—several group members may even be speaking at once. Because a group conversation contains silence or multiple verbal channels, meaning is also derived from how words are said or how behaviors are used to replace or substitute for verbal messages. This is known as **nonverbal communication.** Nonverbal communication occurs in many forms: through the tone and sound of your voice (vocalics), your facial expressions and other body gestures (kinesics), and your use of space (proxemics), touch (haptics), time (chronemics), and objects (artifacts). Even when you are not talking in a group, you are communicating nonverbally. Sometimes you do something purposely—for example, you look at your watch and tap at it to draw attention to the few minutes the group has left. At other times you are unaware of the nonverbal signals you are sending—for example, you continuously lace and unlace your fingers or you close your eyes when your least favorite person is mentioned. Even when you do not mean to, you are creating powerful signals that others will interpret.

One type of nonverbal communication, **vocalics,** accompanies everything we say. Meaning can be derived from how we use our voice in saying words. Vocalics include inflection (upward as in asking a question, downward as in making a statement), tone (monotone, excited), accent (Southern, Eastern seaboard), rate (fast, slow), pitch (deep, nasal), volume (fast, slow), number of vocal interrupters (aaaahhh, well-uh) and quality of voice indicators (clear, scared). This type of nonverbal communication is particularly important in group settings because although we can usually hear what others are saying, sometimes it is difficult to see everyone in the group. Subtle (and not so subtle) cues—like irony and sarcasm—about intensity and emotion are given through nonverbal voice qualities. Group members display dominance in teams and groups through rapid speech and a loud and sure tone of voice whereas more submissive members use a passive tone and a slow rate of speech. Friendliness toward other group members can be demonstrated by warm voice qualities whereas unfriendliness comes through with irritability and cynicism.

Other elements of nonverbal communication include **kinesics** (facial expressions, eye contact, hand gestures, body posture), **proxemics** (use of space), physical appearance, **haptics** (use of touch), **chronemics** (use of time), and **artifacts** (use of objects) (Burgoon, 1985). Eye contact, a form of kinesics, is particularly important in group settings because it regulates who will talk next. When a group member is willing to talk, she is more likely to look at the current speaker or at the leader/facilitator, signaling her intention to communicate. On the other hand, someone who wants to avoid conversation will look away or down at their lap. A shy member may even push his chair away from others in the group (proxemics). When it is difficult to get into the conversation, a group member can lean forward with the upward torso (kinesic behavior) or lightly touch the speaker's shoulder (haptic behavior) to signal she wants to say something. Raising his voice and talking a little faster (vocalics) is usually effective when a group member wants to be recognized. If those cues fail, a group member may raise his hand (kinesic behavior). This nonverbal cue is nearly universally recognized as an indication that the group member wants to be called on to talk. A group member who wants to demonstrate her affiliation with a sorority might wear a sweatshirt monogrammed with the sorority's initials. Using artifacts can provide cues for other members about appropriate ways to start conversations, especially when group members are unfamiliar with one another. A leader who starts the meeting on time (chronemics) is indicating that time is valuable and that the group will start to consider its business even if some group members are absent. Each of these examples describes how nonverbal communication can regulate group interaction.

Functions of Nonverbal Communication

Even when they are not aware of it, group members use nonverbal messages for some communication functions that are important in group settings (Andersen, 1992; Infante, Rancer, & Womack, 1997). Nonverbal communication indicates intensity and emotion, regulates who will talk (turn taking, initiating and terminating conversations), reveals comfort level, symbolizes community, helps to develop or clarify relationships (dominance, power, intimacy), and influences others. Nonverbal communication can also provide cues about other group members' culture, race, gender, and personality. When you think about it, you realize that nonverbal communication is the primary form by which we develop and manage impressions. The group member that others believe you are is primarily guided by your self-presentation of nonverbal cues (Burgoon, 1980, 1985).

In group settings, some nonverbal behaviors like physical distance, posture, and touch will change relatively little once the group has settled into its interaction setting and created norms for the use of such behavior. Other nonverbal behaviors, however, like facial expressions, body movements, and the use of silence, are powerful indicators about the dynamic process occurring within the group (Argyle & Kendon, 1967). Nonverbal cues are particularly good for detecting deception, especially when there are mixed messages. What you say is controllable; the nonverbal cues you provide are often more spontaneous. When these two channels of communication do not match or reinforce each other, group members will suspect that you are deceiving them (Burgoon, 1980, 1985).

Nonverbal cues are powerful indicators about the quality of a group's conversation and the status of group members. Once a week, Gloria, Marcia, Linda, and Anika meet over breakfast to discuss common issues they face as nontraditional students returning to undergraduate life. Although their conversations generally stay on school topics, the primary outcome from the group is the support each feels from the other group members. It is easy to tell when it has been a bad week for one of the women. The conversation starts slowly, but then it builds to such an intensity that others in the restaurant turn to look at what is going on. Their voices get louder as they all complain about Wednesday's midterm and then softer when Anika reveals she will return to Czechoslovakia after the semester is over. The pace of their interactions quickens, emphasizing their interest in the current topic. Those who overhear and can see their conversation can tell that even with all of the complaining, these women are best friends: Hugs are routinely given, bodies are hunched over the table in toward one another, one woman leans across the table to playfully poke at another. Even if you could not hear exactly what the women were saying, you could make interpretations about their conversation based on the displayed nonverbal dynamics. Thus, their nonverbal communication serves specific functions within their group as it also provides information to outside observers.

Nonverbal messages can be used to signal that one is uncomfortable. Individuals often find it easier (but not necessarily more effective) to send nonverbal messages indicating that they are uncomfortable. Perhaps the group is talking about an issue that Merv finds too personal. It is unlikely that he will state his objection overtly. More typically, Merv will withdraw from the group and become silent. This will be accompanied by decreasing eye contact with other group members and physically drawing his body in toward his center. His face may even redden. These nonverbal messages will let other group members know that he is uncomfortable in the group.

Nonverbal messages can also be used to establish or clarify relationships between group members. For example, Hillary shifts her eyes from the speaker to Sam. As she does this, she widens her eyes, arches her eyebrows, and smiles slightly. This seemingly innocuous behavior may be the first signal that a coalition is forming between Hillary and Sam. If Sam returns her glance with a smile or a wink, these nonverbal signals will probably alter their relationship from merely colleagues in a group to a relationship that is unique and separate from other group members.

When group members use more direct eye contact and more face-to-face body orientation, it indicates that greater intimacy is developing within the group. These nonverbal behaviors suggest two things: first, that members are developing greater positive regard for one another and, second, that members have a greater desire to affiliate with one another (Mabry, 1989a). Generally, as group members interact over time and through multiple sessions, their nonverbal behaviors give cues to the relationships that are developing among group members.

Finally, physical appearance, vocalics, and the use of time are especially important in influencing others in groups. The image you present of yourself often influences how others receive what you say. If you come to group meetings dressed comfortably but neatly and you speak confidently, group members will likely pay attention and remember what you say. They will see you as a credible source of information. On the other hand, if you disregard standards of dress or cleanliness, you may unknowingly create an impression that what you say cannot be taken seriously. Finally, group members often pay specific attention to how other group members use time. Group members who habitually arrive late may create the impression that they cannot be trusted with important group business or activities. Lateness may suggest the unimportance of the group, its members, or its activity.

Proxemics, or the use of space, is also important in group settings. How group members are seated affects the flow of interaction within the group (Burgoon, 1996). Members who are most centrally located and members who have visual access to others are likely to participate more in the group's interaction. Frequently in decision-making meetings, members sit around a rectangular table. If someone takes the end chair, members typically look to that person to start the conversation and to identify who talks next. Because it is difficult to see others on the same side of the table, members are more likely to talk to those sitting across from them or to those sitting next to them. Generally, it is better to hold meetings at a round table so all members can see one another and communicate directly.

Group members who have developed relationships outside the group structure usually sit next to one another. Individuals in a group who do not know one another are more likely to first develop a relationship with the person sitting next to them. In either case, when relational acquaintances sit beside each other in a group, detrimental side conversations are more likely to occur.

Multiple Meanings of Nonverbal Communication

Like verbal communication, nonverbal communication is highly symbolic; thus, precise meanings are sometimes difficult to determine. You may like wearing black—your favorite color—but another group member may think you are sad. If you always have a smile on your face, others may perceive you as happy-go-lucky. You, on the other hand, were taught as a child to be pleasant to everyone, to smile and nod your head while listening to others. In such cases, these behaviors are automatic and are performed unwittingly. However, others in the group may attribute a specific meaning to your nonverbal actions.

Reading nonverbal cues from others is both a conscious and unconscious activity. It is conscious when we are looking to attribute meaning to words and then develop attitudes toward others based upon those meanings. But many other attributions are made unconsciously. Our perceptual abilities to select and pick up nonverbal cues affect what we hear and how we perceive others. Alternately, we are often unaware of the nonverbal cues that we display. Because many nonverbal cues are physiologically based (for example, your face reddens when you are nervous; you shuffle your feet while sitting because your knee hurts), many receivers believe that nonverbal messages are more credible or believable than verbal messages. Thus knowing what nonverbal cues you display and how they are read by others is important to your success as a group member.

To a large extent, our use of nonverbal communication and the interpretations we make of others' nonverbal behavior is culture-bound. As children, we learn many nonverbal practices by watching others and gauging how others respond to our use of nonverbal messages. As you take this class, you already have participated in hundreds of groups. These culturally bound experiences have formed your expectations for the use of nonverbal behavior. You have learned how to use nonverbal communication to indicate your willingness to join groups and talk with others, to leave groups or avoid interaction with others, and to protect your individuality in groups (Cathcart & Cathcart, 1996). Thus groups with culturally diverse members may have some difficulty making sense of nonverbal communication. If someone says something we do not understand, we are likely to ask for clarification. If someone gestures or makes a facial expression we do not understand, we are more likely to develop an interpretation without checking with the other person. See "Cracking the Nonverbal Code" for some practice in recognizing nonverbal communication.

Verbal and Nonverbal Communication as a System

Obviously, you cannot communicate verbally without some nonverbal elements. Others interpret your verbal messages as they develop meaning for your actions. Simply, verbal and nonverbal are intertwined. However, the two message systems are not always in agreement. You can probably recall when someone said something to you, but you responded more to how the person said the message (nonverbal communication) than to what the person said (verbal communication).

Research has demonstrated that when receiving inconsistent messages—messages in which the verbal and nonverbal messages do not agree—receivers are more likely to believe the nonverbal message. When inconsistent messages are sent, receivers respond with one of three reactions (Leathers, 1979). First, receivers acknowledge that they cannot determine the meaning of the inconsistent message. So they tell you they do not understand. You are lucky—you have a second chance to get your message across. Second, receivers become more diligent and pay more

> **? THINK ABOUT IT**
>
> *Cracking the Nonverbal Code*
>
> Think of one of your recent group experiences. Concentrate on remembering the nonverbal messages that other group members used or displayed. Were you particularly drawn to one member? If so, how would you describe his or her use of nonverbal communication? Were you particularly repulsed by another member? How did his or her nonverbal communication differ from the communication of the member to whom you were drawn?

attention to you, thinking that they have missed something. Finally, receivers withdraw from the interaction when they cannot clarify the inconsistency. You probably do not want to send messages in which the verbal and nonverbal components do not match. However, this happens frequently in groups, for example, when a group member feels pressure to commit to something he knows he cannot deliver. Inconsistent messages also occur when group members do not think they can be honest with criticism or feedback in talking with other group members. To the extent that you can deliver clear verbal and nonverbal messages in your group's interaction, your participation in the group will be more favorably received. Use "Rating Verbal and Nonverbal Interaction" to see if your perceptions about the power of verbal and nonverbal communication match the perceptions of others in your group.

The Listening Process

When we think about how we communicate in groups, we often forget that besides the verbal and nonverbal aspects of communication there is one other major communication process involved. Particularly in group settings, we spend far more time listening than talking, yet we often fail to assess our listening ability in groups. Unfortunately, most listening research focuses on listening to one other person in instructional, public, or relational (dyadic) contexts. Although these findings can tell us something about listening, they do not address the complexities the group context imposes on the listening process. In group situations, there are frequently competing side conversations or multiple speakers striving to gain other group members' attention. But the basic principles of listening identified from these other contexts can help us become better listeners in groups.

Why is listening in groups so complex? One reason is that you often do not realize when others are not listening. When one group member is speaking, there are multiple group members as listeners. Some members may fake listening, believing that the presence of other group members covers for their lack of attention. There is less social pressure to listen in groups, and, as a result, ineffective listening goes unnoticed (Watson, 1996). Second, group settings can lend themselves to

Contrary to what most people believe, you spend much more time listening than talking in groups.

extraneous interaction, which gives some group members the license to take a holiday from listening. Finally, sometimes it is difficult to listen to many points of view being presented; some of us simply concentrate better on one person speaking or on one idea at a time.

What can be done to increase listening effectiveness in groups? First, group members should try to consciously focus on improving their listening. Second, recognizing that listening is a multistep process helps group members acknowledge and deal with the many types of listening errors that occur. Too frequently listening is associated with hearing. And excellent hearing does not ensure good listening. Listening is both a physical and perceptual process. After you actually hear the sound of others talking (the physical process), you must make sense of it (the perceptual process). What was said? What does it mean to me? How will I reply? These stages occur rapidly, making it difficult to distinguish one stage from another. Listening errors can occur in any of these stages. Listening can be improved when group members pay attention to the process and make conscious attempts to practice effective listening.

Listening Styles

Differences in listening styles must also be acknowledged. Effective presenters of ideas know that other group members have different listening styles, and they accommodate those differences in the organization and presentation of ideas

GROUP ASSESSMENT TECHNIQUE

Rating Verbal and Nonverbal Interaction

Pick a discussion topic from current national or local events. Identify the major positions, and ask class members to identify the position they most strongly support. Assemble class members into groups of three to five with as many different positions represented in each group as possible. The goal of the group is to address the different positions represented so that group members have a better understanding of the various points of view. It is not necessary to come to an agreement about which point of view is best, correct, or most preferred. After 30 minutes of discussion, stop and rate yourself and each of the other group members using the adjectives below.

To what extent did you or the other group members communicate in this fashion?

0 = never/seldom   1 = sometimes   2 = frequently/always

Adjective phrase	You				
1. active, dominant, talks a lot					
2. extroverted, outgoing, positive					
3. domineering, tough-minded, powerful					
4. friendly, egalitarian					
5. unfriendly, negativistic					
6. looks up to others, appreciative, trusting					
7. depressed, sad, resentful, rejecting					
8. passive, introverted, says little					

There are several analyses to perform. First, add up the numerical scores for your ratings and your ratings of the other group members.

Add the scores for items 1, 2, and 3. This is the *dominance* score.

and opinions. There are four distinct listening styles—people-oriented, action-oriented, content-oriented, and time-oriented (Watson, 1996). Because listening styles develop over a lifetime, individuals bring a predisposed listening profile to group settings. Each listening style is distinct with its own advantages and disadvantages. Although there is no single best listening style, more people prefer people- and action-oriented styles to content- and time-oriented ones. In the descriptions that follow, which style seems most like you?

Add the scores for items 6, 7, and 8. This is the *passive* score.
Add the scores for items 2, 4, and 6. This is the *friendly* score.
Add the scores for items 3, 5, and 7. This is the *unfriendly* score.
For each characteristic, the score will range from 0 to 6.

Characteristic	You				
dominance					
passive					
friendly					
unfriendly					

Are your scores balanced between dominance and passivity? Why would you want to display some passive behavior in a group setting? Examine the balance between the friendly and unfriendly scores. Which characteristic should be stronger in group settings? Why? What would cause you to rate a group member as unfriendly?

Second, examine your ratings of yourself in comparison to your ratings of other group members. Do these ratings reflect effective verbal and nonverbal communication for a discussion group like this one? How did others' nonverbal behavior influence your consideration of their verbal behavior?

Third, if all group members are comfortable in sharing their ratings, compare your ratings of yourself to the ratings others made of you. Are the ratings similar? If other group members saw you differently than you saw yourself, ask how they saw you displaying these characteristics. What verbal or nonverbal messages did you send to be rated that way by other group members?

Four, what would you consider to be ideal scores for group members in a situation similar to the one you just experienced? Why? Are there verbal or nonverbal messages you can use or introduce to the group to move the group in that direction?

Source: Adapted from Bales's (Bales & Cohen, 1979) dominant-submissive and friendly-unfriendly SYMLOG dimensions.

People-Oriented Group members with a **people-oriented listening style** are attuned to the emotional aspects of the conversation and to relationships with other group members. A people-oriented listener is the person you would likely seek out in a group when things are not going your way. A group member with this listening style demonstrates care and concern about others, is nonjudgmental, and provides clear verbal and nonverbal feedback. A people-oriented listener has the ability to quickly identify emotional states and is interested in building relationships. Those with a people-oriented style, however, can become overly involved in the feelings of others or can be blind to others' faults. A person with this type of listening style may internalize the emotional states of others and may be seen as intrusive. People-oriented listeners also tend to be overly expressive in giving feedback (Watson, 1996). In a group of close friends, a people-oriented listening style might be preferable. But in a fast-paced work group where there is pressure to produce something, too many group members with this style might slow the process unnecessarily and introduce emotion when other behaviors might be more effective.

Action-Oriented Those with an **action-oriented listening style** are almost the opposite of people-oriented listeners. Action-oriented listeners concentrate on the task and help others stay on task as well. Action-oriented listeners get to the issue at hand quickly and give clear feedback about expectations. This type of listener helps the group by concentrating energy on understanding the task or activity, helping others focus on what is important to the group, and encouraging others to be organized and concise. Individuals with this listening style, however, can be impatient with speakers who ramble, jump ahead, and move quickly to conclusions. Action-oriented listeners can become distracted by unorganized speakers and ask blunt questions. When this happens, this type of listener can appear overly critical (Watson, 1996). When we examine the advantages of this listening style, it may seem that a group would want all its members to be action-oriented. But there are drawbacks, including fostering a defensive or negative climate in the group. In general, groups are more effective when group members represent both people-oriented and action-oriented listening styles.

Content-Oriented Individuals with a **content-oriented listening style** take on the role of critical evaluators when they carefully examine everything they hear. These group members can see all sides of an issue and enjoy the complexity that group discussions offer. Group members demonstrating a content-oriented listening style appreciate technical information as they test for clarity and understanding. When a group member is presenting an idea, they give encouragement to support others' ideas. Content-oriented listeners welcome complex and challenging information because they have the ability to look at all sides of an issue. On the other hand, content-oriented listeners can be overly detail-oriented, which may intimidate others. This type of listener may also minimize or overlook the value of nontechnical information or may discount information from unknown sources. Because content-oriented listeners like lots of detail, they can take a long time to make a decision (Watson, 1996). There is a great deal of congruence between the attributes of a content-oriented listener and a devil's advocate or critical evaluator (Watson, 1996). However, a content-oriented group member should not always take on this role. To help others improve these skills, groups should rotate this role whenever possible.

Time-Oriented Finally, there is the **time-oriented listening style.** As you might guess, this type of person values time and encourages other group members to do the same. Although it sounds as if having a time-oriented group member would keep the group from wasting time and other resources, too much of a time orientation can arbitrarily cut off discussion before the group has had a chance to examine solutions or think through the ramifications of its decision. Time-oriented listeners can manage and save group time by setting guidelines about time for meetings and conversations, discouraging speakers from wasting time, and giving cues to others when time is being wasted. These are all important functions in a group. Alternately, group members with this listening style can be impatient with those who they perceive are time wasters. They may interrupt others in discussions or rush other speakers by looking at their watch or the clock. Each behavior limits others' contributions by heightening time pressures (Watson, 1996). No doubt we all have been in meetings where time was wasted, and it sounds as if having a time-oriented listener in the group would be a benefit. But we must also recognize that too much time pressure on a group from internal sources could be disastrous. Most decision-making groups already work under external time constraints, adding additional time constraints from inside may cause a group to shut down, allowing or forcing the leader to decide without the input of group members.

Adapting Your Listening Style

Each listening style has its own advantages and disadvantages. Although some people are predisposed to a specific listening style, others can move fluidly among the styles. Thus you need to recognize that different group situations require different listening skills. Your primary goal as a listener is to analyze the group situation, decide what is required of you as an individual member, and then work to develop and apply the most effective listening orientation. It is helpful to not only do this analysis for yourself but to also analyze the listening style preference of other group members. If you want your interactions with others to be effective, you must adapt your messages to them.

When encountering people-oriented listeners, use "we" instead of "I" statements to emphasize the relationship between you and the listener. Stories can also be used to draw the attention of people-oriented listeners. It is not necessary to neglect facts and information; simply embed them within the story. Action-oriented listeners will appreciate it if you keep your points to three or fewer. Number them for clarity as you talk. Content-oriented listeners respond best to data and facts. When multiple viewpoints are available, present each side and then give your recommendation. When encountering a time-oriented listener, it is best to assess and acknowledge time limitations up front and then get to the point quickly.

Acknowledging others' listening styles is fairly easy when the conversation is one on one. But what happens when several listening styles are involved? First, be adaptable; good communicators can demonstrate flexibility. Second, use group members' names when you are adapting your response specifically for them. For example, you have noticed that Fuller seems particularly responsive to stories—evidence that he is a people-oriented listener—whereas Chavon appears responsive to data and facts, indicating that she is a content-oriented listener. How can you satisfy both of these listening styles? You could say, "Fuller, that reminds me. Have I told you how we solved that problem before? We had a difficult time because we failed to identify three important issues: (1) how our salespeople would respond to an incentive program, (2) what types of incentives they might prefer, and (3) on what basis we would give the incentives. Basically, we just assumed that everyone would be motivated by time off. In the end, we really blew it! Chavon, the three issues we didn't pursue before—are these similar to the issues you wanted to discuss?"

Listening Pitfalls

Not only are there different listening styles that affect listening effectiveness, there are pitfalls or barriers to consider. These can occur in any context but may be especially hazardous in group settings because many people have committed their time, energy, and resources to being part of the group. Poor listening has been identified as a major obstacle to group participation (Gastil, 1993). One of the most frequently occurring listening pitfalls is to prejudge the speaker or the content of what is being said. What evidence of prejudging can you find in this example?

MELESSA: (to Ken) I can't find Ricky. (Ricky comes in late to the meeting.) Ricky, where were you?

RICKY: Just went to do some business for the group.

KEN: Right, Ricky . . . You? Business?

RICKY: You know, I had to cash some checks at the bank.

KEN: Please don't tell me you're in charge of our finances!

MELESSA: I asked Ricky to open an account for us.

KEN: Yeah, what kind of account is that?

The more heterogeneous the group, the more likely it is that group members will express ideas or opinions different from your own. Although these differences can add positively to group outcomes, we can only negotiate these differences if we allow ourselves to hear what others say. If we prejudge others because their views are different, ignore views that are different from our own, or reinterpret what was said to fit our own ideas, we have generated our own listening barriers. Not only have we failed to hear what was said, we have arbitrarily created a barrier to establishing positive relationships with those members.

Another type of listening pitfall is to rehearse a response. This happens in two ways. First, it occurs when we have convinced ourselves that we know exactly what the other person will introduce into the group. Being so convinced that we know what another group member will say, we rehearse our response before we get to the group meeting. Thus we are armed with a response to something we have not even heard! The second way the pitfall occurs is when we rehearse a response while another group member is speaking. In doing so, we may miss important

> **GROUP ASSESSMENT TECHNIQUE**
>
> *How Well Do You Listen?*
>
> Organize yourselves into small groups of no more than five members. For this exercise, it is best if you are grouped with people whom you do not know well. The goal of your group's 20- to 30-minute discussion is to get to know one another better. Throughout your conversation, try to identify at least five common elements. Examples could be favorite vacation spots, how you came to select this school, what you expect your salary to be when you finish college, favorite television shows, how you picked your major, what you consider to be unique or unusual about yourself.
>
> When you are finished, talk about the listening process that occurred in this discussion. These questions can help guide your evaluation: What listening styles were evident? How did group members demonstrate that they were listening? Did anyone make an attempt to respond specifically to another group member's listening style? What made it easier to listen? What made it more difficult? Did any listening pitfalls occur? What could have been done to overcome these pitfalls? Overall, how would you assess your listening effectiveness in this exercise?

aspects of the speaker's comments that come later in his or her speaking turn. This type of silent arguing usually revolves around our overly selective attention to flaws in the argument or to irrelevant factors. We hear something that catches our attention—often because we are looking for something negative—and then focus our attention internally on creating a response rather than completely hearing the other group member. Try "How Well Do You Listen?" to see if you can identify listening styles and listening barriers.

Improving Listening

What is the result of poor listening in groups? Poor working relationships, ineffective group outcomes, or time lost to faulty group processes. When a group finds that it is rehashing the same material or that individual tasks are not carried out to the group's instructions, faulty listening may be to blame. Replace these ineffective listening habits with **active listening**—paraphrasing what the speaker has said, asking questions to confirm what was said, taking notes, and so on. In active listening, the receiver tries to paraphrase what the previous speaker meant. But the receiver does not stop there. To make sure that group members are in sync, the receiver must also ask for confirmation or correction of what the receiver heard. See how Matt uses this active listening technique during a meeting with Rea and Clinton.

> REA: If we want to pursue this science and public issue grant, I think we need to find out which problem is more serious.
>
> CLINTON: Yeah, but isn't it obvious that the ozone problem is worse than the respiratory disease project?

MATT: Guys, I'm not sure what we're proposing. Clinton, it seems that you favor the ozone project and Rea hasn't made up her mind yet. (This statement clarifies for others what Matt has heard.)

REA: Well, yeah. But the ozone project is okay with me.

CLINTON: Okay, let's talk about the ozone problem first. See, to me, if there's this huge hole in our atmosphere caused by CFCs in some places and a concentration of ozone in other places, that causes this build up, or the greenhouse effect. Scientists think that this is what is causing the increase in respiratory disease. So, it seems a moot point to worry about respiratory problems when that issue itself is probably determined by ozone. Right, Rea?

REA: Well . . . ?

MATT: Let me see if I got this right. You believe that environmental issues are connected and that some problems are more primary than others. And, more importantly, you believe that the ozone problem may actually be that primary problem. Is that right? (This response is Matt's paraphrase of what Clinton said.)

CLINTON: Right. I agree totally. (This statement is Clinton's confirmation that Matt understood him correctly.) But now that I think more about it, I am wondering if an ozone project may be too big of an issue for this group to tackle before the grant due date.

This may seem cumbersome in a fast-moving group conversation, but it is well worth it in the long run as the group avoids recurring discussions and miscommunication. You have probably been a member of a group in which each member left the meeting thinking he or she understood the instructions. Later, when the group reconvened and members compared their results, it became obvious that there were great differences in their understanding of the instructions.

Most group members have to consciously practice the art of active listening. In addition to the critical advisor role described in Chapter 3, groups may want to appoint a **process advisor,** or facilitator, to monitor the group's listening. It is particularly important for the process advisor to be wary of signs of **pseudolistening** in which group members respond with cliché phrases such as "right," "yeah," and "I know what you mean." Some people are extremely good at using these phrases to indicate that they are listening when, in reality, they are not paying close attention to the content. They simply use these phrases to move the conversation along.

Taking notes is another good way to improve your own listening skill. This is not to suggest that you write down exactly what is said, never looking up at the group members who are speaking. Rather, you listen and then write down a paraphrase of someone's comment. This gives you a good record of the group's interaction, a chance to reflect on important points, and an opportunity to assess how your opinions and ideas can move the group toward its goal. Another way to increase your listening effectiveness is to ask questions. If you have a question, other group members are likely to have similar ones. If no one asks a question, then the group has lost an important step in the critical evaluation process, and a poor idea may proceed unchecked. You can also increase listening effectiveness by looking at the speaker. If you do not, you will miss nuances and nonverbal cues that get you involved in the conversation. You sabotage listening effectiveness if you use group time to take notes on another meeting or to plan your next day's schedule.

Is it worth your time to be a good listener in a group? One study demonstrated that group members who were rated "most like a leader" were also rated "good listeners" (Bechler & Johnson, 1995). The development of effective listening skills seems to enhance others' perceptions of your leadership ability. Moreover, those group members who were perceived to be poor listeners were more likely to be eliminated from consideration as leader of the group.

Now, what about the group? Is there a way to improve the overall listening effectiveness in the group? Whoever plans for the group meeting should make every effort to secure a meeting space that is quiet—preferably behind a closed door. Groups need an opportunity to concentrate, and quiet meeting areas help them do that. Groups also make noise; closed doors prevent group interaction from spilling out into areas where others are trying to work or communicate. Another technique for heightening the importance of listening in group settings is to audiotape a group session. In listening to just a few minutes of interaction, group members often find they missed much of what transpired. This simple technique reinforces the need for good listening skills.

In groups where members are brought together because of their specialized knowledge or because they represent different interests, effective listening becomes even more important. Group members representing different departments, factions, or interests bring with them a unique perspective or frame for listening. Such a frame may make it difficult for them to hear or understand what other groups members are trying to say. In other words, they are using **selective listening.**

Let's examine how easily selective listening operates in the following group. Several individuals have been appointed to an advisory group. Their goal is to recommend a solution to improve the city's park and playground facilities. The mayor insists that all interested parties be involved. Thus the group is composed of a member of the city's planning department, a member of the city's park commission, several residents from the proposed park site (several elderly residents without children or grandchildren, and several residents with elementary schoolchildren), and a social worker with knowledge about gang violence. Because each individual is a part of this group due to his or her special interests or knowledge about the group's task, it is going to be difficult for each of them to avoid selective listening. When selective listening occurs, group members do not hear other points of view; it also encourages group members to change what was said to fit their personal expectations:

PARK COMMISSION REPRESENTATIVE: It looks like we all agree that this park needs to be kept in better physical shape than we have been doing. Now, let's talk about what type of activities we want this park to support.

RESIDENT WITH YOUNG CHILD: I think we should have plenty of playground equipment . . . slides, swings, that kind of thing.

RESIDENT WITH OLDER CHILD: Tim really likes to play softball with his friends. And, I like him to be close to home. So, I suggest we have a ball diamond.

RESIDENT WITH YOUNG CHILD: Okay, but I don't want the bigger kids hitting balls into the area where the smaller kids are playing.

ELDERLY RESIDENT WITH NO GRANDCHILDREN: Parks are for us too. Just because we're senior citizens you want to leave us out!

PARK COMMISSION REPRESENTATIVE: No one's trying to leave you out—we don't want to leave anyone out. Have you been to the Elmway Park? Plenty of senior citizen activities there. If you'd like, I could introduce you to the activities coordinator.

ELDERLY RESIDENT: Thank you, I'd like that.

SOCIAL WORKER: I thought we were discussing park activities.

PARK COMMISSION REPRESENTATIVE: We are; what are your ideas?

SOCIAL WORKER: Well, I'm most concerned about gangs and gang violence. I certainly don't want to see the neighborhoods around the park deteriorate because we create a space for illegal drug activity.

Can you identify the filters and biases created by selective listening? When the park commission representative asked about park activities, each member of the advisory board heard something a little different. One resident was concerned that her child have a play area close to home. Another was more concerned about how the activities of different age groups would fit together. The elderly resident became defensive, feeling that others on the board were leaving her out. The social worker certainly let her bias about preventing gang activity be known. From the same stimulus question, advisory board members recreated the message to fit their own interests and then responded to further strengthen those positions.

Listening effectively in this situation is certainly more difficult than when a group of individuals is brought together to share ideas from similar points of view. Thus to listen effectively in a diverse group, you must first analyze your own feelings and attitudes and attempt to not prejudge others and their positions before you hear them.

Group Communication Climate

A group's **communication climate** results from group members' use of verbal and nonverbal communication and their listening skills. Assessing your group's climate is much like checking the weather when planning a trip: If you know what to expect

Six different types of behavior contribute to a defensive communication climate; each is based on some type of threat or other negative interaction. Another six behaviors contribute to a supportive communication climate; each is based on supportive or friendly interactions. Although most groups generally prefer a supportive climate, groups differ in the amount of support they need to be effective.

when you get there, you are more likely to pack the appropriate clothes. Similarly, when you interact in group situations, you should assess the climate of the group. Doing so will help you present your ideas and opinions in ways that are more likely to be accepted. By paying attention to your presentation strategies, you are also likely to strengthen your relationships with others in the group and avoid unnecessary confrontation. Thus a group's communication climate is the tone, mood, or character of the group that develops from the way in which group members interact and listen to one another.

Early research on groups (Gibb, 1961) demonstrated that climates in groups could be described on a continuum between defensive and supportive. Of course, you would not want to be a member of a group that has a **defensive climate**—a climate based on negative or threatening group interaction. Initially you may believe that all groups should have a **supportive climate,** or a positive environment. But, to be most effective, we must be able to assess and then create the level of supportiveness we desire in our groups. A counseling group would need a more supportive climate than a task force making decisions about personnel policies. And the task force would need a more supportive climate than a group deciding on discipline for inmates. Some level of a supportive climate is needed by all groups, but groups vary in their position on the supportive-defensive continuum.

Gibb observed that climate is built on the following six aspects of how people communicate: evaluation versus description, control versus problem orientation, strategy versus spontaneity, neutrality versus empathy, superiority versus equality, and certainty versus provisionalism. Bringing together a group of people to establish and fulfill a group goal always creates an unique interaction context and presents some challenging interaction moments—moments you will recognize as you read the descriptions of the following six categories.

Evaluation Versus Description

To arrive at a good idea, group members toss many ideas into the interaction for consideration. Not every idea is great, and when a group member suggests an idea that is considered less than ideal by other members, there is a tendency to evaluate the person rather than the idea. This is the basic notion behind evaluation and description. **Evaluation** occurs when a group member uses evaluative language or content that criticizes the other person. A good example is when a group member uses "you" language to assess the person who introduced the idea. For example, John appears critical of Betsy when he says, "You know, your idea isn't very good; in fact, they never are!" As a result, Betsy, who introduced the idea, is likely to withdraw to some extent—maybe even to the point of not participating. It is also likely that other group members will withdraw as they become afraid that they will also be evaluated harshly when they introduce ideas.

As an alternative to evaluation, **description** occurs when a group member describes the idea—its weakness and strengths. A better way for John to give Betsy feedback about her idea would be to say, "I appreciate your idea, Betsy, but do you think that we can fit that within our budget?" Asking for more information and analyzing an idea and not the person provides a more constructive framework for the entire group. Describing what is wrong with an idea gives the group member who introduced it the opportunity to clarify its presentation or amend the idea for consideration by the group. Describing the idea may also stimulate other group members to join in and help transform the poor idea into a better one. Description is almost always preferable to evaluation. It is better for a group to know why an idea is rejected; this provides a learning experience for all. Evaluation simply humiliates the other person and is likely to result in a defensive relationship and a defensive group climate.

Control Versus Problem Orientation

Controlling behavior causes a defensive reaction because implicit in controlling is the assumption that controllers know what is best for those whom they are attempting to control. Controlling language or nonverbal behavior makes others feel ignorant, uninformed, or immature. "You meant to say that the budget is $250,000. Isn't that what you meant?" said with a belligerent voice and wide-eyed stare belittles a group member in front of others and asserts the dominance of one member over the other. To make the most of group situations, members need to exhibit the spirit of group participation and democracy, and control does not fit well with those concepts. When controllers assert their superiority, it decreases the likelihood that everyone will participate.

An alternate to controlling behavior is problem orientation. A group member practicing **problem orientation** strives for answers and solutions that will benefit all group members and satisfy the group's objective. A member with a problem orientation would not assume that there is a predetermined solution to be found. Thus the sender is seeking collaboration on solving the problem. When group members take on this attitude and it is reflected in their interactions, it is easier for members to receive cooperation from one another and achieve group cohesiveness and effective outcomes.

Strategy Versus Spontaneity

At the outset, strategy sounds like a good thing. In this case, however, **strategy** denotes manipulation of others. Strategy is apparent when a group member places him- or herself above the group or its task. In other words, the member is perceived as having a hidden agenda and wants group members to unknowingly help him or her achieve it. For example, to achieve your own goals, you might withhold necessary information or ask others to perform tasks for you that might otherwise put you at risk. When a group member fakes sincerity or tries to hide motivations, the member is likely to be accused of being strategic.

At the opposite end of this dimension is **spontaneity.** A group member who acts spontaneously is open and honest with other group members. This group member is known for his or her immediacy in the group and willingness to deal with issues as they come up. If a member is straightforward with others, the other group members are likely to reciprocate that honesty and openness, which creates a more supportive communicate climate for completing the group's task or activity.

Neutrality Versus Empathy

We have all had bad days and not performed at our best in group situations. In a supportive group climate, other group members express empathy for our situation because we have expressed empathy for them. **Empathy** does not mean that another group member is excused from doing his or her assigned tasks but that group members express genuine concern and are helpful if their help is requested. Empathic communication conveys members' respect for and reassurance of the receiver. Nonverbal behaviors are especially good at conveying empathy. **Neutrality,** on the other hand, is expressed when group members react in a detached or unemotional way. When group members react with a lack of warmth or caring, other members often feel as if they are not important.

As an example, Detria comes to the group hesitant to ask for more time to complete her assignment. A series of unfortunate events—her mother's illness, a poor performance on a biology test, and a roommate who just announced she was leaving at the end of the month—kept Detria from completing her responsibilities to the group. A group member responding with empathy would say something like, "Sure, Detria, we understand you need until Monday. Is there anything we can do to help you out?" Said quietly and respectfully, this response demonstrates concern for Detria's situation but doesn't let her disregard her responsibility to the group. Detria would have been met with neutrality if a group member had responded with an offhand "okay, whatever" to her request for more time.

Superiority Versus Equality

Each of us has our strengths and weaknesses, but it usually leads to a more defensive communicate climate when a group member continually reinforces his or her **superiority** over others. Name dropping is a good instance of superiority. Another example of superiority is when a group member continually assumes leadership functions in the group without regard for other roles. Often other group members will regard these attempts at superiority as a lack of substance and style and begin to polarize themselves from that group member. Attempts at superiority also discourage others from entering into collaborative problem solving.

Groups are more likely to create supportive communicate climates when **equality** is stressed. This does not mean that everyone does the same thing. Think of this more in terms of equity. Equitable assignments for group members are one aspect of equality just as are trust and respect. Remember that trust and respect are earned and given incrementally. It is every group member's responsibility to work for trust and respect, and to give trust and respect when these are due. And because each group member must establish his or her own trust relationship with each other group member, creating a sense of trust within the group is a long-term and complex process.

Certainty Versus Provisionalism

No one likes a know-it-all, especially in a group. Group members who believe they have all the answers or who "know" what another group member is going to say or do create a defensive environment. Often when one group member acts with **certainty,** it creates a chain reaction, causing other group members to respond with certainty in hopes of proving the other group member wrong. Now the group is moving away from its goal as it is stuck on the issue of who is right! A more effective alternative is to act with **provisionalism.** This state is one of flexibility and commitment to solving the group's problems. Rather than taking sides, provisional group members want to hear all of the ideas so they can make better, more informed choices. Provisionalism encourages the experimentation and exploration of ideas in the group. To encourage provisionalism in your group, use descriptive and nonevaluative language to summarize the different positions before the group, and then ask group members if you have correctly summarized the major issues. This type of action creates an opportunity for group members to ask more questions, and it can diffuse the dominance of one or two group members.

Defensive communicators also become defensive in their reception of others' messages. As you might guess, the more group members exhibit the behaviors that lead to defensive communication climates, the more likely the group will become focused on relational problems. In turn, this deters the group from working on its task, completing its goal, or providing support for one another. Each of us is probably guilty of some defensive behaviors. We may even fall into a rut of behaving defensively because of our personality attributes, our negative feelings from past group experiences, our negative feelings about a group member from other interactions, or our negative feelings about groups in general. When negativity and defensiveness become routine, it is difficult to recognize what is contributing to the ineffective communication climate of the group.

Altering Group Climate

If any of the defensive conditions describe you in group situations, try to monitor your behavior and adopt more positive behaviors. The behaviors that create a supportive communication climate require you to assess the group situation, think about what you want to say, and evaluate your statements for their potential impact. Finally, you must follow through. Good intentions will not create a supportive communication climate. Use description rather than evaluation to assess the input of others. Create opportunities for all group members to participate. Be open and honest, but tactful. Express empathy for others in the group. Create a sense of equality through equitable assignments and responsibilities. Finally, be flexible and open. It is impossible for one group member to have all of the answers to all of the group's questions and needs. If you can adopt some of these supportive interaction strategies, you will strengthen your relationships in groups and help your groups achieve more effective outcomes.

You can also assess others' behavior in your group and address your interaction with them in a more productive fashion. For example, you may find it easier to react to superiority with superiority—but a more effective way to neutralize superiority is to respond with equality. It is every group member's responsibility to break destructive cycles in group interaction, and the development and maintenance of defensive group climate is one such destructive cycle. Effective group interactions are more likely to occur in supportive group climates where members feel at ease with one another.

It is useful to think adaptively about climate. If you perceive the climate of your group as being static, you may unknowingly reinforce characteristics you find unproductive. Climate is changeable, but first you must recognize what needs to be changed and what your role has been in sustaining the defensive climate. Even if you have not directly used defensive strategies, you subtly reinforce their use by others when you just let it go. Try "Working Through Climate Challenges" to practice improving communication climate.

BUILDING ANALYTICAL SKILLS

Working Through Climate Challenges

The case that follows is taken from a group problem-solving discussion. On the left is the transcript of the group's interaction. The right contains Arden's notes and evaluation of the group's climate after reading the transcript. Review both the transcript and Arden's comments. Do you agree with his assessment? What other conclusions could you draw? What could you do as a group member to improve the climate of this group? Try editing or rewriting the transcript of the meeting to turn this group's climate around.

Transcript of Meeting	Arden's Comments
Arden: I mean, a professional secretary types 70 words a minute. Boom, it's done. Ten-page paper done in 20 minutes. Jane's a professional secretary.	Climate is pretty neutral here. Although, group members are letting me talk about Jane. That made me feel good.
Marissa: Really?	I can see now how this side conversation kept the group from building a positive climate and from working toward our task.
Arden: Yes, my girlfriend—Jane. It's the most amazing thing you've ever seen.	
Marissa: I type 70 words a minute, but 35 of them are mistakes, so . . .	
Colin: Would she type things for me?	
Elinor: Can we get back to the issue? (calmly, but firmly)	I think most of us took Elinor's comment as negative because we all felt she was evaluating us for getting off task.
Arden: This is the timetable. Like I said, the budget's not . . . well . . . it's not complete.	
Tracy: I don't see that part. (putting Arden down)	Tracy was definitely into control here!
Arden: Of course you don't. It's not done! (loudly)	And, then I got defensive.
Tracy: Oh.	
Colin: Shouldn't the budget take into account labor costs? (nastily) You'll have to excuse me. (now apologetic, submissive) I woke up this morning with my sinuses in extreme rage, and while the pain is gone, the fuzziness is still there.	In Colin's first statement, he was acting superior to the rest of us like he's never made mistakes or taken a group's conversation off track. I loved it how he backtracked and made an excuse we could all empathize with.

Transcript of Meeting

Marissa: At least *you* have an excuse. (sarcastically)

Tracy: Do we know how many managers and employees, or do we have to find that out? (confused)

Arden: We need to find that out. (dominantly)

Tracy: So we know who to pass them out to. Okay. Do we know how much copies are? (regaining control of her emotions, pleasantly)

Marissa: We knew what it was for one side. Did we find out for two?

Arden: Well, I had . . . I did have the price (as he searches through his papers for the note about prices), but I turned it in. I think. (defeatedly)

Marissa: Wasn't it 3 cents for copying on one side? (exasperatedly)

Arden: We're talking about two different things.

Marissa: What are *we* talking about? (angrily)

Arden: I was talking about the number of copies for the managers and staff.

Marissa: Oh, I thought we were talking about the price.

Arden's Comments

Marissa must have taken the same nasty pill that Colin did. The comment was said in reference to Colin, but her intention was to put down others in the group.

Tracy tried to bring us back to task by asking what she perceived to be an easy question for us to answer.

Instead, it brought up another topic that confused us. We sure didn't use a problem orientation here.

Tracy's trying to be supportive, being spontaneous, and putting the question to the group as a whole.

But, looks like I blew it again. Someone tries to get the group into a supportive climate, and then I don't follow through with the content.

Marissa was giving factual information, but, boy, she sure was being evaluative.

Why can't I get ahold of what I'm doing and help the group here?

Our sense of confusion really contributed to a defensive climate.

Summary

The study of groups is wide and diverse, but the communication discipline has its own unique perspective. Group process relies on verbal and nonverbal interaction. Without it, a group ceases to exist. The system perspective allows us to view group communication as a set and series of interrelated communications: specific communication relationships within the group, group interaction as a whole, and interaction between the group and its environment. This chapter focuses on a group's micro system—a system of messages as inputs, throughputs, and outputs. Because of the systemic properties, communication also creates a cyclical process that provides feedback or new input for the group.

Therefore, verbal communication or verbal messages are central to group communication. To be most effective, group members need to use concrete rather than abstract words and to recognize that definitions are not simply found in dictionaries: Groups are capable of creating unique meanings for words and phrases. Verbal communication also creates structure for the group. Feedback creates patterns of symmetrical or competitive messages contributing to each group's uniqueness. Remember that although it is good to actively participate in a group, consuming too much of a group's time will damage others' perception of you. Likewise, how you communicate is as important as what you communicate.

Nonverbal communication is also important in group settings. Members can effectively communicate nonverbally at the same time, but that is not true for verbal communication. Your use of vocalics, kinesics, proxemics, haptics, chronemics, and artifacts creates messages and meanings for other group members. Nonverbal communication fulfills functions within groups that are sometimes difficult to communicate verbally. But interpreting nonverbal messages requires a great deal of skill because multiple meanings abound in these messages.

Remember that verbal and nonverbal communication are intertwined. How you interpret messages from others relies on both the verbal and nonverbal components. But when verbal and nonverbal messages are inconsistent, receivers tend to rely on the nonverbal message.

Listening is another type of critical communication in group settings. In groups there are always more receivers or listeners than senders. There are four different listening styles—people-oriented, action-oriented, content-oriented, and time-oriented. To be an effective group member, you should be knowledgeable about each style and know how to adapt your messages to each. Listening pitfalls are prevalent in groups, and all group members are occasionally guilty of poor listening. Improve your listening in groups by practicing active listening or by taking notes when others talk.

Your verbal and nonverbal communication styles, and your listening styles, help create the communication climate within your group. Knowing how you contribute to the micro-system structure of the group through your communication patterns and strategies will help you analyze the complexity of group interaction. Effective group members practice description, problem orientation, spontaneity, empathy, equality, and provisionalism. When these are evident, a supportive group climate develops.

✓ Checklist

Group Knowledge

You should be able to:
- explain how words can express multiple meanings.
- describe how nonverbal symbols communicate.
- explain how verbal and nonverbal symbols work together to make a complete message system.
- identify the characteristics of different listening styles.
- differentiate between a supportive and a defensive group climate.

Group Skills

You should be able to:
- use verbal symbols to clearly express yourself about group tasks.
- use nonverbal symbols to build positive group relationships.
- develop and deliver positive messages to build a supportive group climate.
- use different speaking strategies to adapt to listeners with different styles.

Analytical and Assessment Techniques

You should be able to:
- assess your verbal and nonverbal communication style and the style of other group members.
- identify your primary listening style(s).
- adapt your messages to the listening styles of other group members.
- identify the climate of your group's interaction.
- help a group climate move from defensive to supportive.

Discussion Questions and Exercises

1. Attend a public discussion group. This might be a group on your campus (for example, student government or student organization meeting) or in your community (an advisory hearing, a support group). Pay particular attention to the words group members use. How specific and clear are members about describing concepts? How can you tell if group members share meanings for the words that are used? How do members display attentiveness or lack of attentiveness through nonverbal communication? Does any member display a particularly annoying nonverbal behavior? How well do other group members

listen when someone is speaking? Can you identify any listening pitfalls? Write a short evaluation of your experience. Identify three things you learned from watching this group.
2. In groups, develop a list of arguments that support the statement "Group members need to be good listeners." Rank-order your list of arguments and provide a rationale for your rankings.
3. Thinking of a specific and recent group experience, write a short essay analyzing the communication climate within the group. Give specific examples to support your conclusions. Provide three recommendations for maintaining or increasing a supportive climate.
4. How would you explain to someone with no knowledge of communication the importance of communication in group settings?

3

Structuring the Group System

What roles or functions does a group need?

Can more than one group member perform the same role?

Why should I be concerned about group norms?

How do groups structure their interactions?

Group structure develops from the relationships between and among group members. As members talk to one another, patterns start to emerge. Once formed, structure also predicts how group members will interact in the future. In fact, a group's structure can be so prominent that it is difficult to change. Group structure creates a foundation for the group. When structure is present, members can more easily identify with the group. In turn, this enhances members' interdependence and commitment to group goals. In this chapter, we focus on the structure provided by adopting formal and informal roles, developing group norms of behavior, and creating networks of communication.

Group Member Roles

It is the communication process that transforms a collection of people (a grouping) into a group. In that process, formal roles emerge, are assumed, or are assigned. Formal roles are those we can easily label: leader or chair, vice-chair, secretary or recorder, program planner, and so on. Each of those roles has rights and duties toward the group, and the roles are consciously performed (Hare, 1994). Accepting or taking on the responsibility of such a role, however, does not ensure that the task and interaction responsibilities of the role are enacted effectively. Arliss may agree to be the group's leader after much prodding from other group members. But if Arliss places more importance on other activities and misses group meetings, Arliss is not engaging the leadership role. It is at times like these when informal roles emerge to substitute for missing or ineffective formal group roles.

While formal roles are developing (or not being fulfilled), informal roles emerge through group member interaction. For example, any group member can perform leadership duties for his or her group without being the formal leader. When Arliss misses a meeting and does not notify other group members, Concha emerges as the group's informal leader. Other group members respond favorably when she calms them down and gets them refocused on the group's task. Informal

Usually group members communicate in both formal and informal roles. In the top drawing, Saundra is the work teams formal leader. When she represents the team, she dresses more professionally to indicate her formal role status. Interacting with members of the work team (bottom drawing) her leadership role is more informal as she coordinates the team's activities. Making the transition from a formal to an informal role is not always easy. In this case, by relinquishing some of her formal leadership responsibilities, Saundra is encouraging other team members to take on task responsibilities for the team.

roles do not always emulate the formal roles of a group. Someone who is good at keeping the group on track by asking questions has developed an informal role for which there is no formal equivalent. After all, we do not elect back-on-trackers. As formal and informal interaction roles develop, a group further develops and defines its micro system, or the structure of the group.

Formal Roles

There are several ways a group can acquire its formal role structure. Sometimes roles are appointed. The mayor appoints a task force to explore opportunities for developing summer jobs for low-income high school students. When she appoints members to the task force, she may appoint a chairperson or leader of the group. Groups can also elect members to formal roles. Most of the clubs and organizations on your campus use this procedure for fulfilling formal group roles.

Sometimes group members allow members to emerge from the group's interaction. The member who is most dominant and attempts to direct the group's activity becomes the leader; the member who takes notes without being asked becomes the group's secretary. Groups are often happy that members want these responsibilities. When someone adopts a role and then accepts implicit confirmation for that role from group members, it saves the group from holding an election. However, without discussion about role responsibilities or elections that encourage the identification of all interested parties, the group may be **satisficing,** or settling for less than what can be maximally produced by the group (Janis & Mann, 1977). When all group members do not contribute to role decisions, jealousy, conflict, and confusion can occur. Several group members may compete for the same role while another role goes unfulfilled. Moreover, it may not be obvious to all group members exactly who the leader is. Rayleen appears to be the leader from Victor's point of view, but Raymond is more comfortable with Meg's communication style. When Victor and Raymond talk after one group meeting, they discover they have different ideas about who is leading the group. As you might guess, role emergence is not an effective way for groups to identify their formal role structure.

Often the connections one group member has with other groups help determine the formal roles group members play. It is not unusual for a group member who is well connected throughout an organizational system to be asked (or expected) to take on a leadership role in another group. Other group members may feel that the connections this member has already established within the system will be useful as they complete their work. Relying on who has the most connections to identify a leader does not guarantee that this group member will be the most effective leader. Asking Nicolas to take on the leadership role of the student entertainment committee because he is also a vice-president of your university's student government may overburden Nicolas, contributing to his ineffectiveness in both roles. In fact, Nicolas may be more effective in helping the entertainment committee if other group members use Nicolas's knowledge as a springboard rather than expecting Nicolas to take charge of the group.

These issues describe some of the difficulty in naming, electing, and placing group members in **formal roles.** How structure is formed for the group can be as important as the structure that develops. Formal groups of all types, and especially decision-making or problem-solving groups, can benefit from carefully considering at least three formal roles. Although the role profile and what the roles are called may be unique for each group, the roles of leader, secretary/recorder, and critical advisor are three central roles that can help groups stay focused on their goal or task.

First, many groups need a **leader**—someone to plan for and facilitate meetings, encourage and motivate group members, and be the group's link to its external environment. Unfortunately, taking on the leadership role is often synonymous with doing all of the work, and that is why many group members hesitate in taking on this responsibility. The leadership role, however, is crucial to the successful completion of the task and to the relationships that form among group members. Many leaders believe that simply showing up and directing the meeting is the extent of their responsibility. Unfortunately, such an attitude leaves many elements to chance and reflects poor planning. Take a look at the following suggested typical responsibilities for leaders.

Leader Responsibilities

- preparing an agenda
- making sure minutes are kept
- identifying and locating meeting space
- getting to meetings early to secure space and welcome group members
- calling the meetings to order
- bringing up most of the issues to be discussed by the group
- identifying when decisions need to be made
- managing conflict when other strategies fail
- appointing members to subcommittees
- motivating or encouraging other members to participate
- finding resources for the group
- representing the group to others
- focusing the group's task or activity
- notifying members or distributing notices between meetings

Frequently, students placed in small groups with their peers simply wait for a leader to emerge. That way, motivated, enthusiastic members can make a claim for leadership by demonstrating their worth to the group. Group members who allow this to happen may want to avoid the humiliation of an election defeat or the high profile or responsibilities of leadership. Unfortunately, sometimes a leader does not emerge until it is too late. Now the group is behind in its task and is in crisis because an effective leader has not laid the foundation for the group's work. In executive or management groups, the highest ranking person often takes on the leadership role. Although this may seem natural, this norm does not guarantee that this group member will be the most effective leader. Moreover, such a norm does not develop the leadership skills of the other group members.

Sometimes group members assume that several people can share the leadership role. "But shared responsibility may mean that no one has the responsibility for focusing the group's attention" (Wood, 1989, p. 445). If one member of the group does not perform the minimal leadership duties of setting time deadlines, encouraging a sense of responsibility and accountability among members, and setting group agendas, there is greater likelihood that the group will fall apart. When group leadership is shared, it is recommended that co-leaders take on distinct role responsibilities and that other group members know who is responsible for what. Because the leadership role is so important, we will explore it in more detail in Chapter 10.

A second formal role that should be considered for each group is **secretary/recorder.** Groups that meet over time (particularly decision-making or problem-solving groups) need someone who is formally charged with capturing what happens in the group's interaction. The secretary/recorder can also make a list of who

> **THINK ABOUT IT**
>
> *Formal Role Performance*
>
> Think about the last formal role you were assigned or assumed in a small group. What was the role? How effectively did you perform that role? What advantages were there to performing that role for that group? How could you have improved your role performance? How did your role integrate with the other formal roles of the group?

is responsible for what assignments and make an agenda for the next group meeting. If this role is left to chance, then no one may take notes. It is also a good idea for the secretary/recorder to review his or her notes with the group at the end of the meeting. That way, differences in perception can be checked, and all group members can reach agreement. Having a history of the group's action can help a group avoid repeating mistakes or wasting time.

A third formal role is the role of **critical advisor.** You may know this role as the devil's advocate. "Critical advisor" as a label is preferred over "devil's advocate" because of the negative connotations the latter can imply. The task of the critical advisor is to constructively criticize ideas brought before the group. Evaluating ideas before the group in a tactful manner creates an environment that encourages others to join in the constructive evaluation. Individuals with particular personalities often emerge to take on this role. But this is rarely effective because those individuals then may be viewed as troublesome or negative for the group. When this role emerges, it relieves other group members from critically examining the process or actions of the group.

When the devil's advocate or critical advisor role is formally assigned, it should rotate among members on a regular basis. Then when someone constructively criticizes an idea before the group, other group members are more likely to attribute the criticism to the formal role the person is enacting rather than attributing any negativity to that individual. The critical advisor can also help the group by reminding members to stay on course with the problem-solving or decision-making procedure they chose to use. Groups that use the critical advisor role make better quality decisions because they are less likely to use poor information processing, make faulty assumptions, or allow one group members to dominate the group's discussion (Schultz, Ketrow, & Urban, 1995). "Formal Role Performance" helps you recall the roles you have fulfilled in the past.

Together, these three roles—leader, secretary/recorder, and critical advisor—provide a basic functional structure for your group. Your group might require other formal roles as well. Although the group might wait to see who emerges to fulfill these roles, it may waste time and leave some roles unfilled. Group members should directly take responsibility for these roles or assign them. Imagine playing softball without knowing your assignment. The batter hits the ball, and everyone runs to center field to get the ball. The problem is that no one is covering first base to get the throw-in and tag the runner out!

Informal Interaction Roles

In addition to formal roles, group interaction generates **informal roles** as conversation becomes patterned and group members repeatedly perform interaction functions (Benne & Sheats, 1948; Mudrack & Farrell, 1995). Members are not elected to or assigned informal roles. Rather, these types of roles are sanctioned by other group members through interaction. You might think that informal roles develop from the task or activity the group is working on, but that is not necessarily so (Guetzkow, 1968).

Informal roles can develop in response to formal role assignments when the formal role structure does not satisfy all the activities necessary for the group to be effective. They can also develop in opposition to the formal roles of the group (Homans, 1950). If the formal leader is too dominant or too strict, a group member may develop an informal role that balances social behavior with the leader's strict adherence to the rules. In other situations, roles develop and are accepted as group members gain a better understanding of the roles to be played. For example, Shanita tries to coordinate the activities of the members and provides information when it is requested. This behavior helps the group accomplish its task, and she may become the group's informal leader. She could enhance her position in this role if she also talks about the characteristics of a good leader and includes the characteristics she is displaying. Thus, she designates herself in the informal leader role by behaving in a way that reinforces the role information available to the group (Guetzkow, 1968).

Many informal roles emerge from how group members interact within the group. **Task roles** are those that function to move the group forward with its task or goal. **Group maintenance roles** help define the group's relationships and develop the group's climate. Whereas task and group maintenance roles help the group become more productive and cohesive, **individual roles** are typically counterproductive for the group; individual roles focus attention away from the group and its goal. Sometimes group members perform these behaviors consciously; other times group members are oblivious to the impact of their behavior on the group. This type of group role framework is different from the formal roles just discussed in that any group member can assist or inhibit the group's interaction by stepping into these roles. They also differ from formal roles in that informal roles tend to develop over time as the group interacts. Informal roles become established through repetition when other group members accept or encourage a group member's behavior (Bormann & Bormann, 1988).

Because these are informal interaction roles, they are contextually bound in terms of appropriateness and definition (Biddle, 1979). This means that a role that is appropriate in one group setting can be inappropriate in another group setting. For example, a task role in your work group probably would not be appreciated when your family is celebrating a holiday. You also should remember that roles are not always enacted similarly in different groups. For example, a group maintenance role in your group of friends is likely to be enacted differently than a group maintenance role in your community action group. With your friends, maintenance roles are likely to be more personal because you know the other members so intimately. In your community group, maintenance roles focus more on the professional relationships that exist among group members. Finally, you should recognize that not all roles will be evident or needed in all groups. The type of group task or activity and the relationship histories among group members will have a great deal to do with which roles develop. The specific roles (Benne & Sheats, 1948) in each category are described below.

Task Roles

Coordinator	Pulls together related ideas or suggestions; clarifies the relationships between various ideas or suggestions; tries to coordinate the activities of various members or subgroups.
Elaborator	Expands on suggestions; offers a rationale for suggestions previously made; tries to figure out how an idea or suggestion would work out if adopted by the group.
Energizer	Tries to prod the group to action or decision; attempts to stimulate or arouse the group to greater or higher quality activity.
Evaluator/Critic	Gives a critical analysis of a suggestion or idea; evaluates or questions the practicality, logic, or facts of a suggestion; holds the group to a standard of accomplishment.
Information giver	Offers facts or opinions; relates one's own experience directly to the group task or problem.
Information seeker	Asks for facts, opinions, or interpretations; seeks clarification of suggestions made.
Initiator/Contributor	Proposes tasks, goals, or actions; suggests solutions, procedures, or ways of handling difficulties; helps to organize the group.
Opinion giver	States beliefs or opinions pertinent to a suggestion made or to alternative suggestions; emphasizes what should become the group's view of pertinent values, not primarily relevant factors or information.

Opinion seeker	Asks for a clarification of the values pertinent to what the group is undertaking, rather than primarily the facts of the case; considers values involved in a suggestion or in alternative suggestions.
Orienter/Clarifier	Defines the position of a group with respect to its goals by summarizing what has occurred; points to departures from agreed-on directions or goals; raises questions about the direction that the group discussion is taking.
Procedural technician	Does things for the group; performs routine tasks such as distributing materials, taking notes, typing, photocopying.
Recorder	Writes down suggestions, records group decisions, or notes the product of discussion; provides group memory.

Maintenance Roles

Compromiser	When an idea or position is involved in a conflict, tries to offer a compromise (for example, by yielding status, admitting error, maintaining harmony, or meeting the group halfway).
Encourager	Praises, agrees with, and accepts the contributions of others; friendly, warm, and responsive to others; offers praise and acceptance of other points of view, ideas, and suggestions.
Follower	Passively goes along with the ideas of others; serves as an audience in group discussion and decision.
Gatekeeper/Expediter	Attempts to keep communication channels open; encourages the participation of others; tries to make sure that all group members have the chance to participate.
Harmonizer	Attempts to reconcile disagreements among group members; reduces tension; gets people to explore differences.
Observer/Commentator	Comments on and interprets the group's internal process.
Standard-setter/ Ego-ideal	Expresses standards for the group to achieve or applies standards in evaluating the quality of group processes.

Individual Roles

Aggressor	Expresses disapproval of the acts, values, or feelings of others; attacks the group or the group's problem; shows

	envy toward another's contribution or tries to take credit for it; jokes aggressively.
Blocker	Tends to be negative; resists the direction in which the group is headed; tends to disagree and oppose beyond reason; attempts to bring back an issue the group has bypassed or rejected.
Dominator	Tries to assert authority or superiority and to manipulate the group or certain group members (for example, through flattery, giving directions authoritatively, or interrupting the contributions of others).
Evader/Self-confessor	Uses the audience that the group setting provides to express personal interests, feelings, or opinions that are unrelated to the group's purposes; stays off the subject to avoid commitment.
Help seeker	Attempts to call forth sympathetic responses from other group members by expressing insecurity, personal confusion, or self-deprecation.
Player	Makes a display of lack of involvement in the group's processes (for example, through cynicism, nonchalance, horseplay).
Recognition seeker	Works to call attention to self (for example, through boasting, referring to personal achievements, or acting in unusual or inappropriate ways).
Special-interest pleader	Speaks for those with low status in the group, usually cloaking any prejudices or biases in the stereotype that best fit individual needs.

Another type of role is procedural roles. These are different from task roles. Procedural role players help the group decide how to work through problems or perform functions vital to group cooperation (for example, someone who records the group's decisions or someone who helps facilitate the flow of group interaction). Task role players help group members decide what the task is or what information is needed. Both of these types of role players are different from group members who, through their interactions, build, maintain, or repair relationships by taking on group maintenance or social-emotional roles. Finally, group members who take on individual roles are actually working against the group and its objective. By emphasizing their individual agendas, these group members destroy group cohesiveness and keep the group from achieving its task or goal objectives.

As you read through the list, you likely recognized that you have enacted several of these roles. You may have assumed one set of roles in one group and a different set in another. When a group meets over a long period of time, say several months, you may have favored one type of role in the beginning of the group and another role near the end. "Identifying Informal Role Behavior" helps you examine the extent to which task, procedural, social-emotional, and individual roles are present in group interaction and which roles you are most likely to play.

Although promoting teamwork and cooperation will help the group, it is not enough to establish you in a procedural role. Group effectiveness also depends on how complementary members' roles are to one another. Too many members in task roles or too many members in social-emotional roles will create an imbalance in the group. Although research has demonstrated that task role behavior is seen as most valuable by other group members (Mudrack & Farrell, 1995), the inability to demonstrate social-emotional or group maintenance roles is likely to diminish effective work relationships within teams. Not only do formal roles need to be balanced, but there must be a balance between formal and informal roles.

Roles are fluid, and any role affects both the task and social-emotional dimensions of the group (Salazar, 1996). The group's activity and context help members enact the role at the same time as they constrain or define what the role is. This is how a group member knows what is acceptable and appropriate role behavior. If Jackee deviates from her expected group maintenance role, other members may let her know it by suggesting that she work with Kirk before the next meeting so she can include him in the next group discussion. This behavior suggestion creates both an expectation for Jackee's role behavior as well as a sanction (working with Kirk between meetings) for not actively pursuing her role.

There are several issues that are important to remember about group roles. First, group members perform roles in both the group's formal *and* informal group role structures. When you assess your role effectiveness in a group, do not forget to examine which roles you play in both structures. You might also want to assess how congruent your formal role is with your informal role. For example, if you have been assigned the formal role of the group's recorder, and you have also assumed an informal role as the group's joker, other group members may not trust your abilities to help keep the group focused and on track. Make sure that your informal role is not sabotaging your formal group role. Second, there will likely be competition for roles. Frequently members compete for the formal role of leader. When this happens, a member may perform task and procedural functions as an informal leader for the group until the formal leadership role is settled. Or the role may go unfilled, resulting in an unproductive group. When there is too much competition for group roles, the group can be sidetracked and ignore its goal. Try *Putting the Pieces Together* for some practice in analyzing group roles.

Once established, formal and informal roles often become fixed or accepted by other group members. When group members come to expect that certain people will continue to effectively (or ineffectively) play certain roles, norms have been created.

Group Norms

We all bring a set of norms to our group experiences. A **norm** is an expectation about behavior, an informal rule adopted by a group to regulate group members' behavior (Feldman, 1984). It can be developed from past experiences, from what

GROUP ASSESSMENT TECHNIQUE

Identifying Informal Role Behaviors

Use your most recent group experience to reflect on your own behavior. Complete your assessment first. Then complete the assessment a second time for a group member you consider to be most unlike yourself.

First circle the number for each question that reflects how often you used these particular behaviors in the group interaction you identified. Then circle the number for each question that reflects how often a group member who is most unlike you used these particular behaviors in the group interaction you identified.

1 = never   2 = seldom   3 = sometimes   4 = often   5 = always

	Assessment of Self	Assessment of Person Most Unlike You
1. Do you offer lots of ideas and suggestions by proposing solutions and new directions?	1 2 3 4 5	1 2 3 4 5
2. Do you ask for clarification or evidence, or ask for suggestions and ideas from others?	1 2 3 4 5	1 2 3 4 5
3. Do you ask how others view the issues or look for agreement and disagreement among others' comments?	1 2 3 4 5	1 2 3 4 5
4. Do you act as a resource person for the group by providing relevant and significant information based on expertise or personal experience?	1 2 3 4 5	1 2 3 4 5
5. Do you explain, expand, and extend the ideas of others by providing examples and alternatives?	1 2 3 4 5	1 2 3 4 5
6. Do you draw together the ideas of others by showing the relationships between facts and ideas?	1 2 3 4 5	1 2 3 4 5
7. Do you keep the group on track by guiding discussions or reminding the group of its goal?	1 2 3 4 5	1 2 3 4 5
8. Do you regulate the group's activities?	1 2 3 4 5	1 2 3 4 5
9. Do you bolster the spirits and goodwill of group members by providing praise and acceptance of others?	1 2 3 4 5	1 2 3 4 5
10. Do you include less talkative members in the discussion?	1 2 3 4 5	1 2 3 4 5
11. Do you maintain peace in the group by reducing tensions through humor?	1 2 3 4 5	1 2 3 4 5
12. Do you help smooth over differences between members?	1 2 3 4 5	1 2 3 4 5
13. Do you control the flow of information by encouraging evenness of participation?	1 2 3 4 5	1 2 3 4 5

(continued)

Identifying Informal Role Behaviors continued

		Assessment of Self	Assessment of Person Most Unlike You
14.	Do you promote open discussion of issues?	1 2 3 4 5	1 2 3 4 5
15.	Do you monitor feelings and moods of the group by suggesting discussion breaks when the mood turns ugly or energy levels drop off?	1 2 3 4 5	1 2 3 4 5
16.	Do you seek recognition and attention by monopolizing conversations?	1 2 3 4 5	1 2 3 4 5
17.	Do you prevent others from expressing their opinions fully?	1 2 3 4 5	1 2 3 4 5
18.	Do you withdraw from participating in the group?	1 2 3 4 5	1 2 3 4 5
19.	Do you exhibit indifference or uninvolvement in group meetings?	1 2 3 4 5	1 2 3 4 5
20.	Do you resist efforts by others to be included in the team discussion?	1 2 3 4 5	1 2 3 4 5
21.	Do you engage in horseplay or thrive on practical jokes?	1 2 3 4 5	1 2 3 4 5
22.	Do you divert other team members' attention away from serious discussion of ideas and issues?	1 2 3 4 5	1 2 3 4 5
23.	Do you thwart the progress of the team by being uncooperative?	1 2 3 4 5	1 2 3 4 5
24.	Do you oppose much of what the group is attempting to do?	1 2 3 4 5	1 2 3 4 5
25.	Do you reintroduce dead issues?	1 2 3 4 5	1 2 3 4 5
26.	Do you make negative remarks to team members?	1 2 3 4 5	1 2 3 4 5
27.	Do you try to dominate the team by being competitive?	1 2 3 4 5	1 2 3 4 5
28.	Do you pick fights with members?	1 2 3 4 5	1 2 3 4 5
29.	Do you interrupt others to have your opinion the focus of the discussion?	1 2 3 4 5	1 2 3 4 5
30.	Do you display a sour outlook or engage in faultfinding?	1 2 3 4 5	1 2 3 4 5
31.	Do you focus on the negatives and try to predict the failure of the team?	1 2 3 4 5	1 2 3 4 5
32.	Do you promote teamwork and cooperation?	1 2 3 4 5	1 2 3 4 5
33.	Do you perform critical thinking?	1 2 3 4 5	1 2 3 4 5
34.	Do you galvanize the group with energy, provide enthusiasm, or prod action from other participants?	1 2 3 4 5	1 2 3 4 5

	Assessment of Self	Assessment of Person Most Unlike You
35. Do you serve as the group's memory function by taking minutes and keeping track of the group's records and history?	1 2 3 4 5	1 2 3 4 5

A. Count the number of 4 or 5 responses to questions 1 through 8. _____

B. Count the number of 4 or 5 responses to questions 32 through 35. _____
   Add these totals together.   A + B _____

C. Count the number of 4 or 5 responses to questions 9 through 15.   C   _____

D. Count the number of 4 or 5 responses to questions 16 through 31. D   _____

Team members playing the task and procedural roles identified in A and B help the group maximize their productivity. Strong task and procedural group members would have combined A and B scores of 6 or higher.

   A + B score _____ / out of 12

Team members playing roles identified in C see their objective as gaining and maintaining the cohesiveness of the group. Strong social-emotional group members would have a C score of 4 or higher.

   C score _____ / out of 7

Team members playing individual roles identified in D focus attention on themselves and away from the group's tasks. In doing so, they diminish the team's productivity and cohesiveness. A group member with a D score of more than 3 is probably seen by others as having a negative impact on his or her group.

   D score _____ / out of 16

This assessment illustrates that it takes more than one type of interaction to perform and occupy a particular role. Items 1 through 8 represent the behaviors associated with task roles whereas items 32 through 35 represent behaviors associated with procedural roles. For example, scoring high on item 8 ("Do you regulate the group's activities?") would not be enough task interaction to establish yourself as the group's informal task leader. Likewise, promoting teamwork and cooperation by itself is not enough procedural behavior to make the group effective. Group effectiveness is only achieved through multifaceted group interaction.

Source: Adapted from Benne & Sheats (1948).

> **PUTTING THE PIECES TOGETHER**
>
> *Group Structure, Interdependence, and Group Size*
>
> Identify a recent group activity where there was a specific task or goal. Think about how the roles played by group members provided structure for the group. How did you know that all necessary roles were fulfilled? Did the formal and informal roles fit together comfortably and effectively? How did role behavior affect the interdependence among group members? How did the size of the group affect role development? Were enough formal roles needed by the group so that each member could contribute to the group's formal role structure? If not, what informal roles did these members develop? If there were not enough members to fill all the formal roles, what happened?

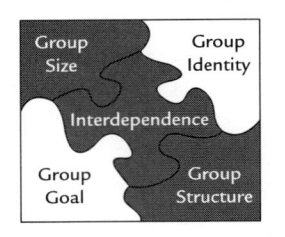

others have told you to expect, or from interaction with others in unique settings. Norms shape your beliefs and attitudes about what will happen and even how you might respond in certain interaction situations. But, most importantly, norms provide clues about the appropriateness of your behavior in group settings (Jackson, 1965). You probably have developed norms about how groups should complete their tasks and activities (for example, you prefer that your group use voting as a technique to give everyone in the group a voice). You also have developed social norms (you expect group members to talk about themselves and what is going on in their lives before getting down to the group's business).

It is unlikely that you have said to other group members, "You know, we have a norm about that." But you have probably identified or talked about customs, traditions, standards, rules, or values that are practiced in your groups. These are synonyms for norms, and when they exist, they guide your behavior by telling you what is appropriate and acceptable in group settings. Whatever norms you believe in, they are the least visible yet most powerful form of social control that can be exerted in a group (Bettenhausen & Murnighan, 1985). How powerful are norms? Very. The greater the degree of psychological closeness and the greater the number of communication linkages among group members, the more powerful the norm is in influencing group member behavior (Festinger, Schachter, & Back, 1968).

Norm Development

Early in the interactions of any group, norms develop from one of two sources. First, a norm can be brought into a group from other experiences of group members. Think of this as a script—or a sequence of activity to follow—that a group member used in a previous group experience. For example, in her rehearsal group, Jasmine suggested that someone should be responsible for calling each performer before the next group rehearsal to remind them of meeting date and time and what music they would be practicing. This was done regularly in Jasmine's rehearsal group at her previous college, and she thought it was really helpful. If other group members accept or do not question this procedure or practice, it is likely to be adopted in this group as well. If Jasmine offers to be the group member to call and remind others, the norm has a chance to develop and take hold in this group. If the norm helps the group rehearse more effectively, then other group members may offer to take on this responsibility. However, if group members find the reminder call annoying or Jasmine calls them too late for the call to be beneficial, the group may fail to adopt this norm. When someone attempts to introduce a norm into a group, he or she either has to take responsibility for the normative practice or be its champion. Either way, if group members do not adopt the norm, it will soon be forgotten. Unless the initial interaction of a group is so unique that group members have nothing to compare it to, group members will import norms that worked in other groups to be tested in this group.

Norms can also develop in reaction to some unique event in a group. In this case, group members implicitly compare their reactions to the event. If their reactions or interpretations are dissimilar, the group as a whole must develop a group-based understanding of the novel situation (Bettenhausen & Murnighan, 1985). This group-based understanding becomes the group norm. Zeb, Caitlin, and Dorothy belong to an honors fraternity on campus. To help the organization reach its goal of collecting 1,000 children's books, Zeb, Caitlin, and Dorothy meet to discuss strategies for getting merchants to donate or purchase books. During their meeting in the lobby of a campus building, Professor Darwin approaches the group and says "If you'll let me know where to drop them off, I'll give you ten books." The threesome's immediate reaction is "Great!" As they continue to talk, however, they realize that no one knows Professor Darwin or why he offered to donate the books. Caitlin says that he must have overheard them talking. Zeb thinks that some other honors student told Professor Darwin about the book drive. Dorothy's not sure what to think, but she offers, "If Professor Darwin is willing to donate ten books, wouldn't other professors do the same thing?"

The group immediately shifts its conversation to strategies of approaching professors for book donations. Zeb, Caitlin, and Dorothy go to the building's directory. There are twenty-one professors listed so they divide up the list and start knocking on professors' office doors. When they meet back in the lobby, they find that together they have secured pledges from thirteen professors for ten books each. The group is excited about their success. Zeb suggests that the group meet the next afternoon in the neighboring building to try the same approach. The group is developing a norm about how to complete its task. Something happened (Professor Darwin's offer to donate books) that was unexpected. When group members discussed this unique turn of events, their interpretations for why he offered to donate books were dissimilar. But now that the group has tried and achieved some success towards their goal, Zeb, Caitlin, and Dorothy have explicitly agreed to try the approach again. Thus a pattern emerges in their behavior, and they accept it because they believe it is effective.

A group norm can also develop when members share a common experience. Matt's health and nutrition study group has been meeting since the beginning of the semester. Now it is time for the first big exam. After studying together, group members go home to take a break before the exam that evening. When the exam is over, they gather to talk about their answers. Amazingly, each one has the same answers on about 80 percent of the questions. Noticing the similarity, they ask one another what they did during the break. Although there are some minor variations, each study group member went home, had dinner, and reviewed the note cards made during the last group study session. These group members feel successful. They agree. They will use the same study technique for the next exam—study together and develop note cards, break for dinner and a quick review of the notes, and then take the test! Similar experiences by each group member reinforced their previous behavior encouraging them to accept it as a norm.

Norms also develop when one member's behavior deviates from the behavior of others. Even when members have not explicitly talked about what they expect from one another, a group member's behavior can still be at odds with how other members believe they would behave. When this happens, members feel like a norm has been broken. Let's return to Zeb, Caitlin, and Dorothy. Approaching professors for book donations has turned out to be so successful that the group has dropped its idea about approaching local merchants. For the last six days, the threesome has met after classes to work on the book drive. But today, when Dorothy met Zeb and Caitlin, she was dressed in her exercise clothes. Her skin was damp with perspiration, her face was flushed, and her hair was in a messy ponytail. Sensing Zeb and Caitlin's disappointment, Dorothy explained that her afternoon class had been canceled and she took the opportunity to get in a workout at the gym. The group had never talked about being dressed a certain way when they were approaching professors. Dorothy simply thought it would not make a difference. But Zeb and Caitlin were pretty distressed. Without having to address the issue directly, Dorothy conceded, "Okay guys. I won't do it again." Without knowing it, the group had developed and accepted a dress norm when approaching professors to donate books.

In this case, Dorothy challenged the norm. But the group could have had one of three reactions. First, other group members could have ignored how Dorothy was dressed. This could have dismissed the norm, encouraging members to dress however they want, or it could have deepened the conflict between Dorothy and other group members. Second, Dorothy's attire could have prompted the group to talk about how to dress. After some discussion, they could have agreed that it did not really matter; professors were accustomed to seeing students in a variety of attire. Third, the group could have perceived Dorothy's challenge as a real threat to the norm, reinforcing their belief in the norm. This third scenario is what happened with the group.

Initiating a Norm Although norms usually develop over time and informally, the process can be shortened (Feldman, 1984). If you see that a norm is needed in your group, what can you do? You can use several methods to initiate a norm. First, the

> **THINK ABOUT IT**
>
> *How Could You Initiate a Norm?*
>
> Think about a social group experience. What norms exist in the group? What norm would you like to introduce (for example, giving each other presents on birthdays and at holidays; getting the group to make faster decisions in planning movie outings). How would you go about initiating that norm? How do you believe other members would react? What could you do if you met resistance to the norm?

leader or another high-status member can talk explicitly about the desired behavior. This strategy is particularly good for procedural norms such as setting standards for how and when the group meets. Second, norms can be set when there is a critical event in the group's history. After a group has had a particularly good or bad experience, group members can comment on the effect of their behavior and agree to continue or to cease that behavior. For example, instead of birthday gifts, Keiji asks his friends to bring a toy for the local Toys for Tots campaign to his party. Together, these friends recognize the good they have done and agree that they will celebrate future birthdays of group members in this way.

A third way to establish a norm is to control the initial interactions of the group. If you use yourself as a model, you establish expectations for other group members' behavior. As a member, Gwen wants to make sure the Citizens Police Review Board, to which she has been appointed, develops a professional, nonpartisan voice. To help ensure this, before the meeting she writes down a list of issues and then examines each one from the viewpoint of a variety of community groups. When one of these issues is raised at the first meeting, Gwen is able to interject comments from viewpoints other than her own. Seeing her level of preparedness and her ability to be inclusive, other board members are less politicized in their contributions. Practice creating a norm with "How Could You Initiate a Norm?"

Why Talk About Norms? A norm of many groups is tardiness for scheduled meetings. If the group does not confront the tardiness of a particular group member, then it becomes implied to all group members that it is acceptable to arrive late. Soon, everyone expects the others to be late, which makes it an acceptable standard. It is important to discuss group norms to avoid destructive behavior and ambiguity. Although most are hesitant to do so, groups should spend some of their first meeting time talking about how the group will operate. Explicitly stating rules of conduct for group interactions can help groups avoid two problems: (1) the difficulty of confronting a member whose behavior is detrimental to the group, and (2) the development of destructive group cycles.

Moving from implied or informal norms to explicit or formal norms is more difficult than people realize. To do so requires conscious group attention to rules and procedures that group members are willing to adopt. The more such rules and procedures are discussed, the more likely that all group members will feel they have had a part in their development, and thus the more likely they are to adhere to them. Behavior, positive or negative, that becomes routine in groups, is often ignored, which actually serves to reinforce the behavior pattern (Gersick & Hackman, 1990). Thus the behavior becomes automatic for group members without raising attention or discussion from the group. When the behavior becomes part of the accepted routine, the norm is implied and usually left unexamined until the inappropriateness of the violation becomes so severe that the group must stop what it is doing and talk about it. Being unprepared, like tardiness, is another common behavior that group members tolerate and allow to become a norm. Take a look at transcripts from meetings of one student group preparing a class project. To what degree is the pattern that develops in the example familiar to you?

First Meeting

BOB: Sorry, I didn't have time to work on this last night.

KERRY: Okay, man. I understand.

PENNY: Yeah, we understand.

BOB: Next time, I promise, I'll get it done before I work on anything else.

Second Meeting

KERRY: You know, guys, I was supposed to do the budget. I'm sorry, I didn't get it done.

PENNY: Oh, okay.

BOB: It's okay, man, I messed up last time.

Third Meeting

PENNY: I'm sorry, guys. I didn't get your things until late, and I just ran out of time. Sorry.

BOB: Yeah, we're sorry, too. Next meeting, though, we'll get it all together.

KERRY: Don't worry Penny. We'll get it done.

Fourth Meeting

BOB: Who's got their part done? Sorry, but I don't.

PENNY: Not me. I had to work late last night. Kerry?

KERRY: Not me either. Sorry about that.

PENNY: Now what do we do?

Group Norms Are Unique No two groups will develop the same set of norms. What becomes accepted as group norms will differ as each group member brings his or her own expectations into the group setting and as the group develops norms based upon its purpose and goal. Group members' familiarity with one another will also affect the extent to which norms from other experiences are initially accepted. If members have high familiarity, they will move more quickly in developing norms for their group. Members with less familiarity are more likely to rely on their past experiences. In either case, however, the importing of norms does create the interaction expectations of the group. These expectations can be modified as group members create new or additional norms as they react to threats, opportunities, and key dilemmas associated with their task (Bettenhausen, 1991). As interpretations of these events are shared among group members, new norms are created and assimilated as part of the social reality of the group.

Regardless of how norms develop, they will not take hold in a group unless members hold similar beliefs about them. Norms help group members know what to expect from one another and what is expected from themselves. Norms create routines that allow group members to predict the responses of other members, which is necessary for coordinated actions (Gersick & Hackman, 1990).

Influence of Norms on Groups

Norms can have both positive and negative consequences for the group as they allow us to identify what is acceptable or appropriate behavior for group members. For example, many will import the expectation that people in groups waste time and accomplish little. This normative belief is based on our past group experiences. Unfortunately, negative group norms can affect our current group experience by becoming self-fulfilling prophecies. If we expect the group to be unproductive, we may unconsciously let that happen. If we expect the group to accomplish little, we might enter the group interaction unprepared, thereby contributing to the group's ineffectiveness. As the group concludes its interaction, we have helped to prove our norm true—that the group spent time but accomplished little. However, we often fail to see our own role in that destructive cycle. Attribution theory suggests that we are more likely to blame the group's other members or external influences for our own ineffectiveness. Such rationalization allows us to forgive our own transgressions while overemphasizing other negative elements.

On the other hand, many of us are energized by group experiences and bring that expectation or norm to new group settings. With such a normative belief, we become the group's cheerleaders, facilitators, and leaders. Just as a destructive cycle can be developed, so can positive cycles. Coming into group settings with a positive attitude and bringing positive group norms—such as arriving on time, being prepared, and encouraging every member to contribute—will help the group be more effective. So, once again, we have validated our past group experiences. Group

GROUP ASSESSMENT TECHNIQUE

Identifying Your Group Expectations

Identify below the next group interaction you expect to have. This can be any type of group—a school group, work group, community group, and so on.

Group: _____

How likely is it that the group you have identified will have this attribute?

1 = not likely at all   2 = unsure   3 = very likely

1. Some group members will do too much whereas others will do too little. _____
2. There will be greater input because we will work as a group. _____
3. There will be scheduling conflicts. _____
4. I will get to know more about other people. _____
5. There will be difficult group members to deal with. _____
6. There will be greater objectivity about the problems or issues the group is considering. _____
7. Different people in the group will use different methods to solve problems or make decisions. _____
8. I will be able to learn "people" skills. _____
9. It will be hard to get all group members to agree. _____
10. We can specialize; each group member will get to use his or her own talents. _____
11. Not all group members will have the same sense of purpose. _____
12. Group members will brainstorm with one another. _____
13. Some group members will move at a different pace than I do. _____
14. I will get to meet other people. _____
15. I will have to rely on others in the group. _____
16. There will be more resources because many people are involved. _____
17. The group will get the credit instead of the individual who did the most or the best work. _____
18. I will get feedback on my ideas. _____

settings can be places for positive or effective interaction, largely based on the norms brought to the group's interaction. In "Identifying Your Group Expectations" is a list of group interaction attributes. Check the ones that you believe will be characteristic of your next group interaction.

19. Some people will be shy around others. _____
20. The group's interaction will break the monotony. _____
21. Some of the group members will not be in the mood to work in a group. _____
22. I will be able to understand different points of view. _____
23. This group will be compared to other groups. _____
24. Others' strengths will complement my weaknesses. _____
25. Some of the members will not show up. _____
26. I will learn how to work as a team member. _____
27. I will have to play catch-up when a group member does not show up or does not do his or her part. _____
28. There will be the chance to network with others. _____

Number of even items marked "very likely" _____

Number of odd items marked "very likely" _____

Let's review your expectations by examining how you responded to the questionnaire. For any characteristic or attribute you indicated would very likely occur, you are importing a norm into the group through your interaction expectations. The even-numbered items are positive group attributes; the odd-numbered items are negative group attributes. For example, if you said that it was very likely that you would get feedback on your ideas (item 18), you will look forward to such feedback and accept it when given. You will probably also give feedback to others. Giving and receiving feedback is critical to group success. By bringing that particular norm to the group, you can facilitate the group's acceptance of positive group interaction processes. If, on the other hand, you marked "very likely" more often on negative than positive group attributes, you may be bringing a poor attitude into the group. Not only will you have to overcome this negativity, but others in the group will have to as well. Your group may have to spend more time on building and developing relationships and identifying and maintaining positive interaction techniques, rather than working on the task or issue at hand.

Source: Adapted from Keyton, Harmon, and Frey (1996).

Norms Are Resistant to Change

Once a group norm has been established, it is remarkably resistant to change—even if the norm creates negative consequences for the group. When new members join the group, a group norm that has been developed and practiced by others persists (Cartwright & Zander, 1968b). This norm persistence is why newcomers have difficulty figuring out the rules the group is using. A norm that has developed without group awareness makes it difficult for members to effectively explain to a newcomer why or how a particular group procedure works the way it does: "That's just how we do it!"

One way to change a norm is to bring it up for group discussion. When all the group members decide to change a norm or standard, the agreed-upon change is more likely to replace the old norm. The discussion and vote create a public pledge or commitment by all group members to change the expectation that group members have of other members' behavior.

Communication Networks

The norms established in a group and the roles that members take on often create another type of structure for the group—a structure of who talks to whom. A **communication network** is the interaction pattern or flow of messages between and among group members. A network creates structure for the group because patterns emerge of who can (or will) talk to whom. A network also reinforces social norms in the group. Each group develops its own unique communication network, but two general types—decentralized and centralized—can be identified. These two types are shown in Figures 3.1 and 3.2.

Communication networks can be developed based on interpersonal relationships among group members or on the type of group task or activity. For example, you are more likely to talk frequently with your next-door neighbor in your neighborhood watch group than your neighbor down the street. You and your next-door neighbor might share similar concerns about the broken corner street lamp, which reinforces the need for you to communicate with each other. At neighborhood meetings, you will probably sit next to your neighbor so when adequate lighting is discussed, the two of you can jointly describe the problem and raise concerns. On the other hand, group activities can dictate who talks to whom in a group. If you

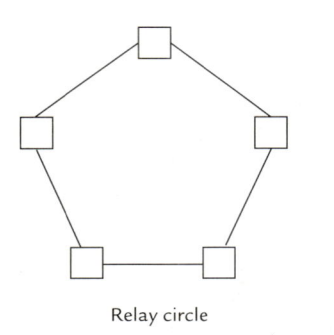

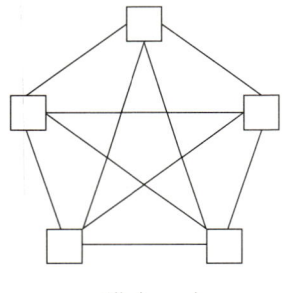

Relay circle   All channel

Figure 3.1 *Decentralized Networks*

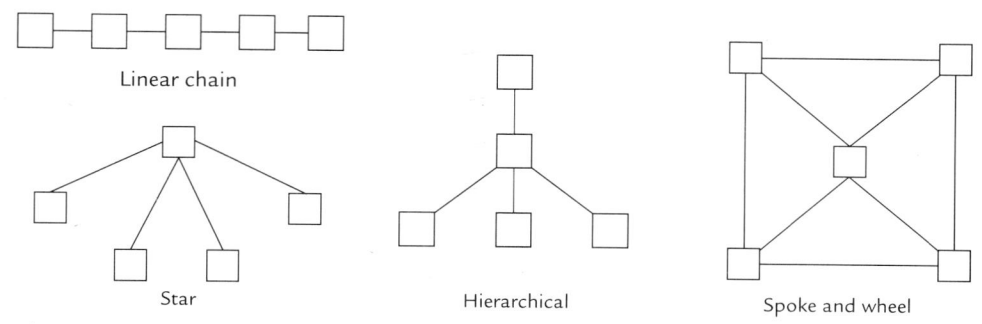

Figure 3.2 *Centralized Networks*

are the catcher for your softball team, you will talk to the pitcher and the member playing first base more frequently than you will talk to the outfielders. By virtue of your position on the team, you must talk to infielders to coordinate your team's defense strategy. See "Comparing Networks" to reflect on your communication networks.

Decentralized Networks

Most groups use an all channel or open network that allows each group member to talk to every other group member. This decentralized pattern operates without restrictions and is typical of most group interactions. Although this is the best communication network to use for group discussions, problem solving, and decision making, it may slow down other types of group activities. Imagine having to talk to everyone in the group to get approval before completing a simple task that has been assigned to you. An open network provides the most input, but it can also produce **communication overload**—too much or too complex communication from too many sources. When overload occurs, messages may compete or conflict, causing stress and confusion. Even in discussions, groups using an open network need a facilitator or coordinator to monitor turn taking so everyone has a chance to be heard. When open networks are not monitored, it is easy for subgroups to develop. This severely limits the advantages of using an open network in the first place.

Another type of decentralized communication network is the relay circle. In this pattern, one group member communicates to only one other member, who then communicates the same message to yet another member. Relaying of messages continues until all group members have received the message. This pattern is decentralized because any group member can be in charge of or control the message that is sent, and the initial sender chooses to whom to send the message. Relays seldom occur as the primary conversation of a group, but they do develop as side conversations.

During their discussion of health precautions, members of the child care cooperative use an open network. Everyone is involved in the conversation, and

> ### ❓ THINK ABOUT IT
>
> #### Comparing Networks
>
> Think about your current or most recent work experience. What kind of communication network did you establish to complete tasks with your co-workers? How did this network differ from the network you established with co-workers with whom you ate lunch and took breaks? Did the information flow in one network cause problems in the other? What was your position in each network? How would you have changed the task network to be more effective?

messages flow easily throughout the group's micro system. About halfway through the meeting, Ori pulls out pictures of his daughter and shows them to Rosemary sitting next to him. Although the other conversation is still going on, Ori takes time—and Rosemary listens—to describe the ordeal in getting his child to smile for the camera. Rosemary laughs, takes the pictures, and turns to Ralph sitting next to her. Ralph is listening to the other conversation, yet Rosemary pokes him with her elbow to get his attention. Ralph sees the pictures and smiles, encouraging Rosemary to launch into the story that Ori told her. And so the relaying of Ori's difficulty in taking his daughter's picture continues around the circle while another conversation is going on.

There are two situations in which a relay can be used effectively. Many counseling or support groups use a relay to start the meeting. This way, each member, in turn, can talk about what is important to him or her. Having this opportunity to hold the floor encourages all members to talk. A relay can also be effective when sensitive or emotional issues are being discussed by a group. In an open network session of the student government executive council, it becomes apparent that there are radically different viewpoints about continuing the homecoming queen tradition. In such a situation, it can be difficult for members to completely present his or her ideas. A relay can be effective because it gives each member the opportunity to present his or her ideas without others interrupting.

Centralized Networks

Any type of centralized network imposes restrictions on who can talk to whom—and one or two group members control those restrictions. As a result, some members may experience communication underload. **Communication underload** occurs when messages are infrequent and simple. Group members in an underload situation often feel disconnected from the group. Look at the star network in Figure 3.2. In this pattern, one group member acts as the controller of messages, passing out information to other group members. From the controlling position, Darrin can pass along similar or different messages to each group member. Group members do not talk with one another, but communicate only with Darrin. This type of pattern often develops when there is a strong, domineering leader. If this is the only communication pattern within the group, group members are not likely to be satisfied with the group experience. This pattern also restricts the development of a group identity. The star pattern can be used effectively after decisions are made and individuals are assigned particular tasks to complete. But as a general pattern of communication, too much control is centered in one person.

The hierarchical communication network is probably familiar to you. It is likely that your work group uses this type of communication pattern. The manager tells your supervisor what to tell you and your co-workers. Messages created and passed along in this way follow the hierarchy of the work group. You probably would not feel comfortable talking directly to the manager. Rather, you would pass along a message about vacation preferences through your supervisor. Although the hierarchical network can be efficient if it matches the type of work task or activity, it limits the development of group interdependence and group identity.

The spoke-and-wheel communication configuration is typical of many groups, especially those with elected leaders or one member who has higher status than other group members. In this communication network, the leader or high status member is at the center of the group's conversations. The leader directs messages to other members, and members direct their responses back to the leader. The conversations of most committee meetings occur this way. But the spoke-and-wheel is less centralized than the star or hierarchical networks because group members do talk to one another. In committee meetings, group members may not do this. But when the meeting ends, group members gather (without the leader present) to discuss and interpret what happened. Again, this is a two-tier communication network much like the relay network that occurs in an open network meeting.

The most centralized of all communication patterns is the linear chain. In this network, one person starts a message and asks that the message be relayed to another group member. This continues until all group members receive the message. This can be an efficient pattern for groups that need to pass along simple information. But it can also produce confusion and ambiguity. Messages that are relayed from one person to the next often become less specific. Unfortunately, it is difficult to know when details are lost along the chain because the last person to receive the message does not check with the initiator of the message. Let's see how easily this happens:

> WALT TO BARB: I'd like the group to meet on Wednesday, the 18th, at 3 P.M. in the employee lounge area. We're going to discuss the vacation and holiday schedule.
>
> BARB TO EVELYN: Walt wants us to meet next Wednesday afternoon to talk about vacation and holidays—something about the schedule.
>
> EVELYN TO STAN: Walt says we're going to meet Wednesday afternoon to talk about the schedule.
>
> STAN TO WOODY: Walt wants the group to meet one afternoon next week to talk about the schedule.
>
> WOODY HEARS: Walt wants to talk about the schedule.

When messages are passed along sequentially, it is easy for individual interpretation to change the original message. When all members together talk about the vacation and holiday schedule, consider how differently each member will approach the meeting based on the information they received.

Identifying Your Group's Network

Will the network of your group look exactly like those shown in Figures 3.1 and 3.2? Not usually. Unless communication among group members is severely restricted or controlled, you are likely to see patterns similar to each of the networks at some time in your group. Most groups think they use the decentralized all channel network where group members are free to talk to whomever they want. But roles and norms that develop in groups affect who talks to whom and who talks most frequently. Status and power differences among members also affect a group's communication network. As a result some group members will end up talking more and some will be talked to less, whereas other members will talk only to specific others.

Do not assume that where individuals sit during a group meeting accurately reflects which communication network is being used. To discover which network a group uses, you can make a simple diagram of the group and then track the flow of communication. Identify exactly where people sit around a table or in the meeting space. When a group member (Wallace) talks to someone (Marie), draw a line indicating that communication link; mark the link with an arrowhead to indicate the flow of the conversation. Each additional time Wallace talks to Marie, make a dash across the line. In Figure 3.3, Wallace talked to Marie four times (one time for the link; three times for the dashes).

Notice in Figure 3.3 that two arrows could link group members. Bren directs messages to Sandra, and Sandra responds to Bren. Notice that Aku talks to Bren, but Bren is either ignoring her or directing responses to her inquiries to other group members or to the group as a whole. Sometimes group member make statements or ask questions to the entire group. Indicate this type of interaction with a link to "group." In Figure 3.2, notice that Bren made comments to the group as a whole five times, whereas Donnie talked only twice to Aku.

What can this kind of diagram tell us? First, it tells us that the distribution of conversation in the group is unequal. More members talk to Bren and Sandra than anyone else while Wallace and Marie talk to others more frequently. Bren directs the most comments to the group as a whole. The figure also suggests that Bren, Sandra, Wallace, and Marie have formed a subgroup separate from the subgroup of Aku and Donnie. Also notice that Donnie only talks to Aku. Over time, this type of communication pattern reinforces the dominance of the four-person subgroup over the two-person subgroup. The communication network also suggests that Bren or Sandra is the leader or coordinator of the group. At this point, the group is using a hierarchical network centered around Bren or Sandra. To move the group into an open network, members will have to overtly help Aku and Donnie become more involved. More talkative group members also need to direct

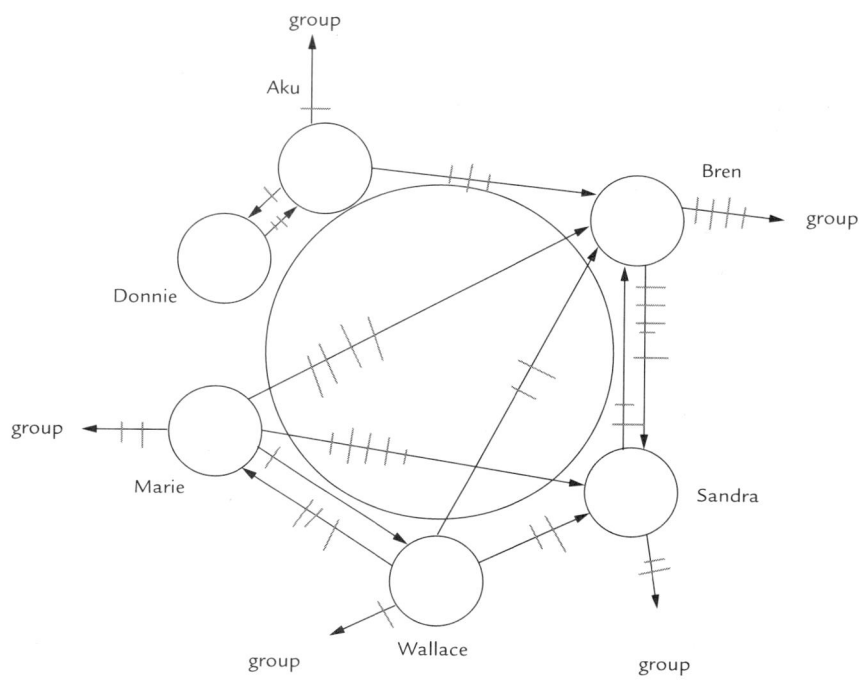

Figure 3.3 *Diagramming Communication in a Group*

some of their comments to Wallace and Marie, encouraging them to contribute more to the group as well.

Determining Which Network to Use

Which network should your group use? This depends on several factors. Although the task or activity of the group is often the primary determinant (Hirokawa, Erbert, & Hurst, 1996), do not forget about the effects of a communication network on a group's social or relational development. Most researchers agree that centralized networks like the spoke and wheel, hierarchical, and star are more efficient. Tasks are completed quicker and often with more accuracy. But these patterns also can create communication overload for the person in the central location. At the same time, these centralized patterns limit the opportunity for group members to get to know one another, to develop relationships within the group setting, and to create a group identity. So although centralized patterns may be better for the group's task, they may work against members' building strong interpersonal bonds that are important to the continued health of the group. The decentralized open communication network may slow the group's work on the task. Yet, members communicating in this fashion are generally more satisfied with the group and its activity and are more committed to the group. You can ask yourself these questions to determine which communication network would work best for your group situation:

1. What is more important to the group right now—working on this task, or developing relationships and commitment to the group?
2. How difficult is the task? Is it simple or complex?
3. To what extent do all group members need to develop leadership *and* followership skills? Or are roles and functions specifically set in this group?

Use Table 3.1 to help you decide which type of network will work best. If you find a conflict in network patterns, prioritize the needs of the group. For example, completing the task on time is important (centralized suggested), but you would also like members of your group to develop both their leadership and followership skills (decentralized suggested). In this group, you believe that developing skills is primary, and this particular task is secondary. Your group will be working together for a long time, and developing skills now will help your group throughout its life. So, choose a decentralized network.

Putting the Pieces Together reviews the material presented in this chapter. See if you can answer the questions it poses.

The Group's Structure and Its Impact on the Individual

Individual group members contribute to the group's structure, and the group's structure impacts individual members (Hackman, 1992). Once group structure is developed, it provides a context for members' thoughts and actions. For example, how you think of yourself in groups largely depends on your current membership in groups. Your interactions with other members provides cues about how to behave and how to evaluate ideas before the group. Group peer pressure affects the choices you make—both in how you communicate and in how you think. The mere presence of other members provides stimulation, urging you to communicate. This stimulation may be positive, causing you to perform better, or it may be negative, causing you to feel threatened. When you do choose how to behave, other members will reinforce behaviors they find positive and try to alter those

Table 3.1 *Choosing a Communication Network*

	Decentralized	Centralized
Task important		✓
Relationships important	✓	
Difficult task	✓	
Simple task		✓
All members need to develop skills	✓	
Roles specifically set		✓

> **PUTTING THE PIECES TOGETHER**
>
> *Group Structure, Interdependence, Group Goal, and Group Identity*
>
> Imagine you are a member of an advisory board for your health insurance provider. You, along with six others, represent different employers throughout your city. You meet once a month to provide information to the health insurance provider about its policyholders' needs. The group elected a leader at its first meeting. What kind of structure (other roles, norms to be developed, and communication network) would help this group accomplish its goal? Which of the three—roles, norms, or network—would be best to help the group develop its identity? What could prevent members from being interdependent as a group?

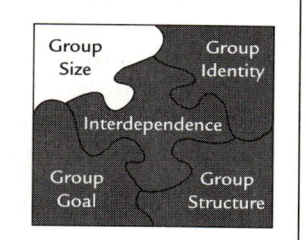

they perceive negatively. When your behaviors are reinforced by other members, you then evaluate those behaviors positively. If your behaviors are not reinforced, you are more likely to perceive them negatively and attempt to alter your behavior. So, the group influences how you think, how you communicate or behave, and how you evaluate that interaction.

Summary

When we send verbal and nonverbal messages to other group members, we are creating roles. A combination of formal and informal roles creates a structure for the group and its members. In turn, these roles shape group members' interaction. Formal roles are those that are required by the group—president, vice-president, secretary, and so on. Typically, group members are elected or appointed to these roles. Even when a group does not have formal roles, group members should consider selecting a leader, recorder, and critical advisor to help the group manage its communication and activities. Informal roles are those that emerge through group members' interaction. All group members take on some informal roles, whether those are task roles or maintenance roles. Too many members in the same informal role creates an imbalance and often competition. Group members should be flexible, not rigid, in assuming roles. Sometimes a group member will take on an individual role, which is counterproductive for the group. Because group settings should be learning experiences, rotating formal roles will help each group member learn the nuances of each role.

Norms are expectations group members have about their group experiences. Members may come to the group setting with expectations developed from previous experience. Additionally, a group's interaction establishes its own norms and expectations—positively or negatively. You should be able to recognize your role in setting and developing these expectations. Your interaction in the group—even if you take a quiet or submissive role—actively shapes what happens in the group. You have a responsibility to gauge your own interaction and its effect on the group. It is important, though, to remember that each group is different; thus different norms will guide your speaking and listening strategies. Your ability to be flexible within group situations and across different types of groups will increase your effectiveness as a group member.

Each group creates a communication network—a pattern or flow of messages among group members. Based on interpersonal relationships among group members or the group's task or activity, a decentralized network allows each group member to talk to every other group member. Alternately, centralized networks impose restrictions on who can talk to whom.

The structure of the group—roles, norms, and networks—has an impact on each individual in a group. This structure helps contextualize each group experience as a unique one. You will make choices on how to think, interact, and evaluate your interaction based on your experiences in the group's structure.

✓ Checklist

Group Knowledge

You should be able to:
- name and describe essential roles for a group.
- describe informal roles that develop through interaction.
- describe how a norm develops.
- describe the effects of norms on groups.
- distinguish between centralized and decentralized communication networks.

Group Skills

You should be able to:
- identify which roles are needed for a specific group.
- overcome using individual roles.
- help others in individual roles develop more constructive role identities.
- help your group identify its norms.
- initiate an effective norm in your group.
- help your group communicate in an open network.

Analytical and Assessment Techniques

You should be able to:
- assess informal interactions in your group to evaluate role balance.
- identify constructive and destructive norms in your group.
- select the communication network that would be most beneficial for your group.

- involve other members to make an ineffective communication network more effective.

Discussion Questions and Exercises

1. Many of the roles discussed in this chapter were developed for problem-solving or decision-making groups. What do you believe are the essential formal roles in a support or therapy group? in a group of friends who regularly play on the same football team?

2. Think back to one of your positive group experiences. Identify the formal and informal roles of each group member. How did the formal and informal roles of the group members interact? For example, did one member's formal role carry over into the group's informal role structure? Did the integration of roles differ when you think of a negative group experience? How so?

3. Groups frequently develop norms for the following group interaction elements: (a) specificity about meeting start times; (b) patterns of who talks to whom; (c) proportion of talk about the group goal or purpose versus talk about relationships or group maintenance issues; (d) how decisions are made; and (e) how necessary information is passed along to group members outside the group environment. Thinking of two specific but different groups, write an analysis comparing and contrasting these two groups on these five elements. Try to identify what led to the differences in norm development. What influences encouraged norm similarity?

4. Observe a group in action (for example, city council, advisory group, student council meeting) and diagram its communication network. Identify the type of network being used. Evaluate the strengths and weaknesses of the network. What suggestions would you make to the group and to individual members for changing the network structure?

4 The Environmental Context of Groups

What external factors influence my group?

Does my group have an influence on other groups or organizations?

Because I am a member of several groups, does that create any unique communication problems for me?

Do groups with different goals communicate in the same way?

Besides completing tasks, are there other types of group results?

How do I manage all of my group responsibilities?

Now that we have defined groups and examined the role of communication in developing the micro structure within groups and teams, it is time to turn our attention to a macro view of group communication. In this chapter, our attention focuses on the group and its relationship with its external environment. All groups are part of some larger system. A group's environment sets the foundation for its context. In return, a group's processes and interaction influence its larger environment. Let's examine these issues in more detail.

A Macro-System Perspective

A group's environment is the totality of physical and psychological influences and resources. This includes the influences of other individuals and groups as well as the task the group has been given or directed to do. As such, the environment in which group members interact has a profound effect on the group. Not only does it define the group it supports, but the environment provides limits or parameters for what the group can do and how the group can do it. In turn, the group influences the larger system that supports it. Thus the **macro-system perspective** provides the broadest view of a group. It includes everything in a group's environment—all physical and psychological influences, resources the groups uses, influences of other individuals and groups, and its tasks. For example, in your classroom group the environment includes your instructor and his or her requirements for your group activities as well as the required or elective nature of the course. Each of the factors contributes to the group's system—the structure or foundation in which the group operates.

Systemic influences operate in a reciprocal fashion. For every action in one part of the system, there is a reaction in another part of the system, which in turn creates yet another reaction somewhere else in the system. For your classroom group, how your group does on an assignment will affect your instructor's perception of how other groups perform and may influence whether that particular assignment is required for next term. Your group reacted to the instructor's requirements, which caused your instructor to react by rethinking the assignment, which caused another reaction of changing the assignment the next time the class is taught.

Social groups also have an external environment, or system, in which they operate. Even when a group is completing a task for its own enjoyment, group members' behavior is affected by the location and nature of its interaction. In a cookout in your backyard, for example, your friends are getting together because they enjoy one another's company and like to try new recipes on the grill. When the cookout is a casual gathering of friends, the larger system is the integrated relational network of each member's friendships. Hopper cannot ask Tia out on a date if Tia is with another set of friends at the cookout. By agreeing to go to the cookout, Tia is behaving in a way that affects the rest of her system and its members.

But if the same group of friends knew another from work, they would adopt different interaction strategies, the system would be changed as a result of how they know one another. Now two systems come together—the friend system and the work system. It is impossible for the two not to overlap. It is also impossible for what happens in one system not to affect the other system. While they are barbequing, work topics are likely to creep into the conversation even when the group swears it will not talk about work. Back at work on Monday, someone is likely to make a reference to what happened at the cookout, piquing the interest of other employees. Thus what happens in the group affects both systems.

In the following sections, we will explore how groups maintain relationships with their larger systems; the term *boundary spanning* captures this process. First, we will examine how groups impact the larger system and identify strategies for communicating to individuals in that system. Then we will discuss how boundary spanning creates system connections that link individuals across group and embed individuals in several groups simultaneously.

Boundary Spanning

Boundary spanning is the process of group members creating and maintaining relationships with individuals outside the group. For organizational groups, an important and primary boundary of the group is the relationship between the person responsible for the group and the group itself. Frequently this boundary spanner is the leader, or it could be a group member who holds membership in two different groups. If you are married, you are the boundary spanner between two family groups. By virtue of this dual membership, information can be imported from one to another. Boundary spanners represent the group to people outside the group. In this function they become sources of information and avenues for obtaining needed resources. Boundary spanners can also test ideas with others outside the group before the group commits valuable time and energy to an idea that others do not believe will work.

Group Impact on the Larger System Another boundary is the organizational culture and environment in which the group operates. Groups must consider people to whom their service, product, or output is intended and the organizational, communal, or societal context in which the group operates. A design group charged with the task of developing a new type of automobile fuel will not be successful if they spend their time pursuing fuel made from waste products. Consumer surveys have demonstrated that the public does not favor this type of fuel product regardless of its cost attractiveness. Legislative groups within the U.S. Senate and House of Representatives, for example, the Ways and Means Committee, consider what proposals the public will support when spending or cutting taxes. A group must be aware of its environment and of the elements in its environment that impact what they do or how they do it.

By using the macro-system perspective, we can examine the relationship between what a group does in its interaction and the effect of that interaction on a larger system. This perspective is well illustrated by the disastrous end of the *Challenger* space shuttle. In this case, faulty group interaction and the decision making process of one group was primarily responsible for the disaster (Gouran, Hirokawa, & Martz, 1986; Hirokawa, Gouran, & Martz, 1988). Analyses of the meeting transcripts and the events before and after decisions were made demonstrate how a group's output acts as feedback and input for the organizational system of which it is a part. This case also illustrates the complex relationship between a group and its larger environment.

In 1986 millions of television viewers tuned in to watch the first teacher participate in space exploration. But immediately after a normal lift-off, the shuttle exploded in a giant fireball, killing all seven crew members. The flight of the space shuttle *Challenger* lasted only 73 seconds. A presidential commission was charged with conducting an investigation of the accident. The commission discovered that the decision to launch the shuttle was made even though information concerning the safety of the launch had been discussed just days before the launch. A variety of negative and disruptive influences—both individual and systemic—were present in the decision environment. Cognitive and psychological factors influenced individual actions in the decision process while norms, social factors, and communication issues were the systemic influences of the group's larger organizational environment. Launching the shuttle was not a singular decision but was embedded in a complex decision environment of several groups and organizations that had direct implications on the long-term viability of the shuttle program. Unfortunately, this one decision that the shuttle was safe to fly profoundly influenced the lives of the astronauts and the future of NASA. The flawed group decision-making process failed to adequately take into account the day's colder-than-normal temperature and the lack of performance data about the pressure seal that was ultimately responsible for the explosion. In addition to underestimating the significance of the information before them, the group experienced extreme pressure to go ahead with the launch. Rather than insist on continued discussion or on collecting additional data, the group gave in to the pressures of other groups and other individuals in the decision-making system. Thus the group responsible for making the launch decision did not effectively manage its boundaries with the larger system environment.

As is frequently the case in policy-making groups, decisions made in determining policy and procedure affect others more than they affect members of the group. The engineers and managers responsible for the okay-to-launch decision were not putting their lives at risk. Government committees and caucuses, health care administrative groups, educational leadership groups, and community action groups are just a few of the types of groups that are often situated in the middle of such systems. Their decisions profoundly affect individuals who are not part of the decision-making group or the organizations they represent.

Strategies for Communicating Across Boundaries A group needs different types of strategies to effectively cross a group's boundary and impact its larger system (Ancona & Caldwell, 1992). One strategy—ambassadorial activities—involves group members purposely seeking access to the power structure of the larger system. By talking with those who care about what the group does or who control resources for the group, group members develop connections or relationships with important people outside the immediate group. This allows group members to promote the team and ask for and secure needed resources. Additionally, by keeping the macro system informed of its activities, a group may decrease the likelihood of excessive interference. A second communication strategy is task-coordination activities. Here group members actively try to provide a stronger bridge to other groups or to individuals in the macro system. Using coordination, negotiation, and feedback, group members are gaining entry at the same time they are bringing others into their group. By creating greater dependence among groups in the system, there is less likelihood that group members will be left out or that the group will be eliminated. Groups can also use scouting activities to pull resources from the macro system into the group. By making individual connections to other groups and individuals in the macro system, group members can provide useful information from parts of the system that would be otherwise unavailable to the group. Of course, groups can also use isolation as a strategy. Isolation from other parts of the macro system can create suspense and intrigue about what the group is doing. It can also create a sense that the group is not useful or necessary.

Each of these strategies are forms of **boundary management**—the process by which groups manage their interactions with parts of the system (Ancona & Caldwell, 1990). Boundary management communication may be directed vertically up the system or laterally to groups at the same level in the system. How much time will a group spend managing its boundaries? Overall, groups spend about

Ambassadorial

Task-coordinating

Scouting

Isolation

Groups use four types of strategies for communicating with their external environments. A group member using the ambassadorial strategy is purposely seeking others who control resources or information the group needs. Group members using the task-coordination strategy are developing and enhancing links with others through coordination and cooperation. A group member using the scouting strategy seeks out information that otherwise would not be available to the group. Isolation or seclusion is also a strategy.

15 percent of their time interacting with other parts of their system. However, some group members (often the leaders) spend up to 90 percent of their time in this activity on behalf of the group.

Systemic Connections

The system perspective allows you to locate where in the system the individual group member exists and where in the larger environment the group exists. Figure 4.1 demonstrates the relationships among individual group members, the

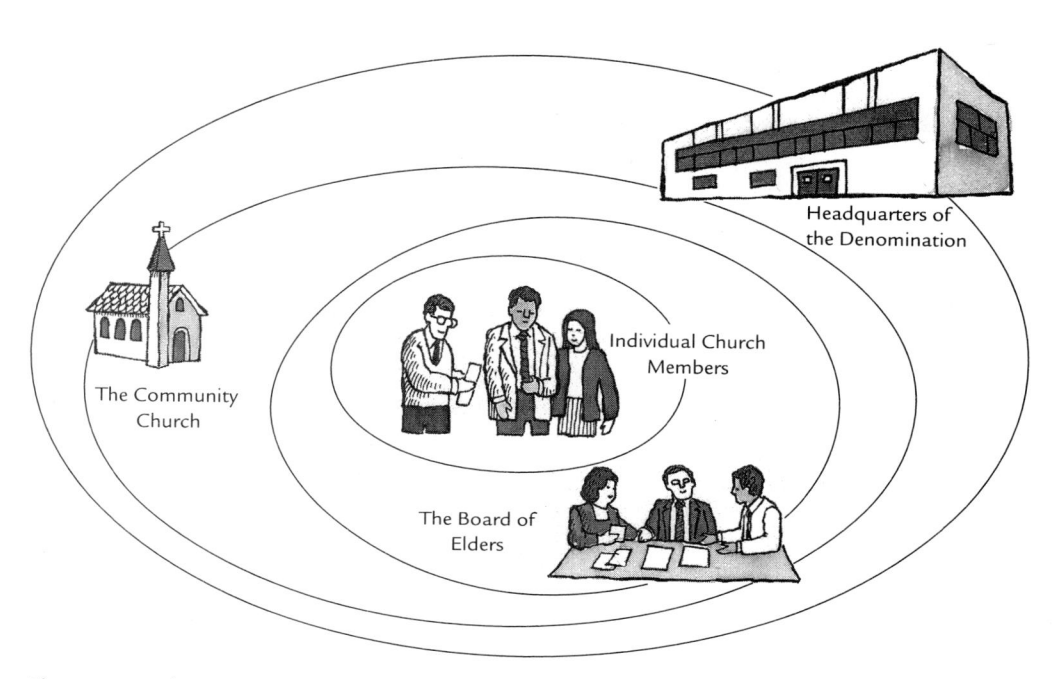

Figure 4.1 *The Systemic Interdependence of the Group's Individual Members, the Group, and the Group's System.*

group, and the group's system. This systemic interdependence creates a level of complexity in communication which the group must deal with to be successful. The board of elders is the group, or micro system, that directs the policy and activities of this community church. Their decisions affect other church members who do not have direct input into decisions and issues. However, members of the board of elders are also members of the church. Their frequent interaction with other members at Sunday services and other church activities influences the decisions made by the group. Notice, however, that the church is also a micro system; it is just one church of many that make up the denomination and are served by the organization at its headquarters. The systemic relationships work in both directions. Individual church members interact with and affect the board of elders, which affects what the group decides, which in turn affects the church, which affects headquarters. In the other direction, decisions made at headquarters provide guidance for new church policy, which the church passes to the board of elders, which activates the policy within the church, which in turn affects individual members of the church.

By identifying the parts of the group's micro and macro system, you will have a better understanding of how group decisions and actions are influenced. At the micro-system level, identifying parts of the system gives you a better understanding of why individual group members behave and communicate as they do. Understanding these influences helps you understand their motivations. At the macro-system level, identifying parts of the system helps you address the complexity of the group's environment and create more effective boundary spanning activities.

Connectivity and Embeddedness The systemic complexity of the church example is frequently found in bona fide groups (Putnam & Stohl, 1990; Stohl & Putnam, 1994). **Bona fide groups** are those with stable, yet permeable boundaries. The boundaries are generally stable because membership in the group is clearly identified, yet membership can change or be temporarily altered. The boundaries are permeable because members also participate in other groups that interact with and influence this group. Connectivity and embeddedness explain how a group interacts with its larger social environment in greater detail.

The **connectivity** of groups is the degree to which several groups share overlapping tasks or goals. The more tightly coupled the groups, the more likely that change in one group will alter activities in others. Going back to Figure 4.1, many churches have an education committee as well as a Board of Elders. It is likely that at least one elder is a member of the education committee. Although the groups have unique and specific goals, both groups function to meet the ultimate goal of the church—to provide religious and celebratory opportunities for the members. When change occurs in one group, it is likely to also affect the group to which it is most tightly connected.

Complexity increases when individuals serve as members in multiple groups. As a student taking several classes in your major, it is likely that during any one term, you are a member of several classroom groups. Although each group has unique membership and a goal specific to its particular course, it is likely that you use the information learned in one group in another. This information transfer is possible due to group members' multiple group membership. Although information transfer is often viewed as a positive characteristic of a group's systemic properties, it can be viewed negatively when information learned in one group is used to the detriment of another. For example, Bryce is not thrilled with being in another group with Katerina. In their statistics group, Katerina comes unprepared and seldom contributes anything meaningful. When Bryce finds out that both he and Katerina have been assigned to the same group in their persuasive campaigns class, he immediately tells other group members about Katerina's substandard performance.

Another factor in systemic complexity is embeddedness. **Embeddedness** reflects the centrality of the group to its larger organizational structure. A group's position within the informal power structure or formal hierarchical structure affects the ability of the group to get information and retain resources. Its position with respect to its environment also determines its degree of impact on the larger organization. For example, the student government group of your university is more deeply embedded within your university than any other student club or organization. Members of the student government have direct access to university officials; in fact, university officials may look to your student government as a primary source of student feedback and input. On the other hand, a club, such as

Lambda Pi Eta (the communication students' honor organization), is affiliated with the university as well as its national organization. To both the university and the national Lambda Pi Eta organization, it is just one student organization that competes with other organizations for attention and resources. Thus its level of embeddedness in both systems is shallower. In the university system, the student government group would deal with issues more similar to the university than the local Lambda Pi Eta chapter. In the Lambda Pi Eta system, this one chapter is not likely to have more influence than any other local chapter.

When a group is characterized by high connectivity and high embeddedness, its boundaries are fluid. Information flows easily in to and out of the group, making connections with other groups possible. Actually, it is the placement of a group within its environmental context that contributes to the challenges, conflicts, and stresses group members are likely to face (Lammers & Krikorian, 1997). The more connected and the more embedded the group, the more these system pressures and influences are heightened. When a group becomes highly embedded and connected, it may be difficult to clearly identify the group's membership. Boundaries separating the group from its system are ambiguous and in flux, which keeps membership in transition (Stohl & Putnam, 1994).

For example, think about your biology study group. Generally, you and four friends from school meet every Thursday night to prepare for Friday's biology test. But your interactions with one another as a group are not limited to just Thursday meetings. After biology class on Tuesday, you talk in the hallway about a problem that involves the use of a specific lab instrument. No one in the group is clear how to use the instrument. But Tommy overhears your conversation and offers his help. Because he is your instructor's lab assistant, Tommy is a reliable source of information. As the conversation about the lab instrument continues, Assaundra invites Tommy to join this Thursday night's study group. Getting nonverbal agreement from the group, Tommy says he will be there. Perhaps you are thinking that this is a group plus a visitor, but depending on how well the group interacts with Tommy, he may become a regular member of the study group. Let's say that group members generally like Tommy and his contributions and he does join the group, but by midsemester your involvement with the group is growing tiresome. In fact, each Thursday night you struggle to decide whether to meet with the group or to play in a basketball league with your fraternity. So although Tommy regularly joins the group, your attendance depends on when your basketball game is scheduled.

To clarify flux and ambiguous boundaries, let's continue with the example. By the end of the semester, only two of the initial group members are left. Tommy comes regularly now. You seldom study with the group, but you could use an extra night of study before the final. You join the group for this last session, but you arrive late. To your amazement, almost half of the class is there, sitting in small subgroups going over different parts of the test material. Who is in this group? Who is not? What boundary separates this group from its environment?

Although Putnam and Stohl (1990) were generally referring to organizational structures, these concepts also apply to community and societal systems. With respect to connectivity, it is common for civic and business leaders to be members of several boards of directors. Through membership on several community boards, information about community problems and grant resources is commonly shared.

Impact of the Group on the Individual Member Because of group embeddedness and connectivity, we should also consider the influence groups have on individuals. Group membership helps establish an individual's identity and also creates some complexities (Allen, Wilder, & Atkinson, 1983). Basically, you are who you are in groups. You learn about yourself through your interactions with group members. Through these group interactions, you find out that it is easy for silly arguments to irritate you. You know that you often end up as leader even when you really do not want that role. And, you know that you have a knack for asking questions to get the group started again. So, one impact that groups have on you is to help you establish your individual identity. As your identity is confirmed or changed, your self-esteem and self-confidence are affected. How strong are these effects of group membership on you? Fairly strong. Research that asks participants to respond to "Who are you?" finds that most people respond first with examples of group membership (I am a member of the Kilgore family, I am president of the nontraditional students' association, I am a member of Leadership Dayton).

Not only does group membership provide you with an identity, group membership also defines your abilities and the abilities of the group. There is a great deal of slippage between "I," meaning you as a group member, and "we," meaning you and all other group members together. If the group is effective and evaluated positively, you are effective and will receive similar positive evaluations. Your baseball team wins the season play-offs. Who is great? the team? we? you? Think back to a group situation in which you were a member of a winning team or another type of competitive group. How did you describe yourself and the team to individuals not familiar with the situation? More than likely, you had a positive evaluation of yourself because of your association with a winning team.

Individual group members are also influenced by role conflict. The greater the number of group memberships an individual holds, the greater the likelihood that conflict, ambiguity, or strain among multiple roles will occur. Although you are likely to communicate similarly in most of the groups, each group membership is unique, causing you to develop slightly different personalities and communication strategies for each group. Minor discrepancies among the many group roles you play will not cause much of a problem, but if major discrepancies develop you will experience role conflict.

During the day, Jay is a production team manager of an advertising agency. His job is to make sure that each print advertisement is properly prepared for publication—a task that requires the efforts of the typesetter, the proofreader, the account manager who conceptualized the ad, and the artist who drew the ad. During the production of an ad, the team meets regularly to discuss changes needed to meet production deadlines and changes requested by the client. Jay's job requires that he maintain control and stay focused but also be pleasant because he has to gain the compliance of four agency personnel and procure approval from the client.

Away from his job, Jay belongs to two groups: a group of weight lifters at the local gym and a ballroom dance company. Jay competes as an amateur ballroom dancer with a group that specializes in synchronized waltzes. He practices with the group three times a week. The four couples on the team have become close friends as they travel frequently to weekend competitions. Jay started ballroom dancing as a child through his parents' participation. He enjoys the competition team now because it gives him a place to be creative. He is also not the person in charge, so in this group Jay is a follower rather than a leader—a role he craves after 8 hours of staying on top of production issues. On the nights he does not practice with the ballroom team, Jay lifts weights with his friends. They do not know Jay is a ballroom dancer. Likewise, most of the dancers do not know Jay lifts weights. He has never tried to bring these two groups together; he believes members of the groups are just too different to mix easily. But Jay certainly sees the connection between the two groups: Ballroom dancing helps him stay flexible, and weight lifting has made him a stronger dancer.

So far Jay has been able to manage the various demands of the production team, the weight-lifting friends, and the ballroom dance company. He realizes that to each of those groups, he is a unique person—the communication strategies he uses at work would not be effective in either of his recreational groups. Jay feels that he must keep these identities and roles in their proper places. One day at work was particularly tense. Jay was pretty wound up when it was over and went straight from work to the gym. Working out with his friends, he found that he was barking orders, yelling at the guys to rack their weights, and generally trying to control the work out. Unconsciously, he was using his work behavior in place of his more typical low-key communication strategies for his friends. This role conflict created by communicating in an atypical manner confused them.

Another type of role conflict can occur if someone in one of Jay's groups negatively evaluates another of his groups. Jay has purposely kept quiet at work about being a member of a ballroom dance company. Some of his work colleagues know he lifts weights, but he has never told anyone that he is a ballroom dancer. He knows that many people would not understand his appreciation for this style of dance. Moreover, he worries that others might associate this activity with questions about his sexual orientation. One day during a production meeting, the conversation turned to outside topics while the team waited to hear from the client. The artist said, "Hey, I was flipping through the channels this weekend and saw that ballroom dancing thing . . . boy, what a bunch of losers!" Jay flinches, shrugs his shoulders, and grimaces but says nothing. The artist continues, "Why would guys want to dress in tuxes and dance like that?" How should Jay respond? Should he confront the artist and admit he is one of those "losers"? Or should Jay keep quiet and try to steer the conversation to another topic? Either way, Jay is experiencing role conflict because a member of one group is making a negative evaluation of another group to which he belongs. Jay feels the sting of the criticism because the group being attacked is a "we" Jay identifies with.

Expectations and Dependencies

As groups work toward their goals, group members have **expectations** about their potential performance—what to produce, how to produce it, and what they can or cannot expect from the larger system to help them accomplish their goals. Many times, expectations develop when group members consider the input of others outside the group. When expectations are present, **dependencies,** or reliances, upon the larger system are created. Together, expectations and dependencies help structure the environment or macro system in which a group operates.

Dependencies may be in the form of budgets; many groups can only spend as much money as they are allowed. A second type of dependency centers around issues of membership. Who is eligible for membership in this group? Most of the time, membership is a condition of the task. For example, a commission studying police brutality could only include citizens who live in that police jurisdiction. A third type of dependency exists when the group must rely on others to follow through or implement their decisions. The Board of Education may make policy decisions, but as a group, it relies on individual teachers in the school system to put the policies into action.

Both expectations and dependencies bind the group to its macro-system environment. Although most of our examples will be drawn from organizational groups, families also exist within a larger macro system. For example, your family (father, mother, sisters, and brothers) is part of two larger family structures (your mother's family and your father's family). The two sides of your family create competing expectations (Whose house do you go to for Thanksgiving dinner? Do you alternate holiday celebrations between the two families?) and dependencies (Do you spend the same amount of money on gifts for one family as you do the other? Which family hears important news first?). As in organizational groups, the same issues of connectivity and embeddedness exist for family structures. All groups have expectations and dependencies from their larger macro system. A small community nonprofit group serves clients within a larger macro system composed of the city where it is located, funding agencies that support it, and other nonprofits that compete or provide similar services. Groups simply do not exist in isolation.

The system in which the group exists has a great deal of influence on what the group expects to produce and on what group members believe are appropriate strategies for getting there. For organizational teams, the organization's culture provides the team with clues about how to perform and with guidelines for acceptable levels of performance. If the organization's vice-president expects innovative recommendations, the team is likely to develop new ideas and work in nontraditional ways. If the organization's culture expects groups to operate traditionally, groups are likely to produce outcomes that second-guess what the vice-president desires.

Issues like these affect how well the group believes it can perform. **Group efficacy** is the collective belief of group members that the group can be effective. This belief is created through interaction. If efficacy is high, group members will believe that they can coordinate their skills to perform well. As you might suspect, when efficacy is high, group members are more motivated to put effort toward the group task. Moreover, groups with high efficacy develop strong expectations for their continued success. As a result, these groups have higher goal aspirations because members believe that the group can perform. This, in turn, actually strengthens their ability to perform. This creates group performance that is self-fueling (Hackman, 1990). Unfortunately, groups can also develop poor performance spirals. The extent to which a group develops a positive or negative group efficacy is dependent on the support the group receives from its environment.

Hackman (1990) identified three organizational conditions that contribute to team effectiveness: group structure that promotes competent work on the task, an organizational context that supports and reinforces excellence, and coaching and process assistance. Notice that the first of these conditions is drawn from the innate resources of the group. The other two are drawn from the group's macro environment; they are not part of the natural resources of the group. Let's look at these three organizational conditions in turn.

First, it is likely that the group itself is the best arbiter of what structure promotes effective interaction. Unfortunately, individuals bring their past group experiences into new group experiences without challenging the effectiveness of importing norms about process and procedure. Group members are usually capable of deciding who in the group should fulfill certain roles and functions. Groups that are given the opportunity to develop their own structure are generally superior to groups that have a structure imposed upon them.

Second, we need to examine the role of individual and group reward systems. Organizations have long held on to the idea of individual rewards—traditional performance evaluations, pay raises, and promotions. Few organizations identify and reward group performance at the group level. Even when groups are recognized for outstanding performance, the group is identified as "Jack's team" rather than the "performance optimization team." Two types of rewards create an environment that supports and reinforces excellence: First, the group must be rewarded for its collective achievement; second, individual group members must feel that part of their reward is directed to them individually. A simple way to accomplish both types of rewards is to describe the group's accomplishments and then identify group members in alphabetical order. This is more random than identifying group members by department, seniority, or role within the group, which may artificially highlight some members over others.

Third, groups will perform better when they know they can turn to others in the organization for help when they need it. When groups want help with group process and procedures, or coaching help for individual members, they should be able to find it easily. Too often we assume that bright individuals will combine to make a great group. But Firestien (1990) found that groups trained in creative problem solving were more effective. Group members who were trained in group process participated more, were less critical of the ideas of others, provided more support for others' ideas, and generated more ideas. Three types of coaching or process assistance are frequently needed by groups. First, all groups need basic

> **PUTTING THE PIECES TOGETHER**
>
> *Group Structure, Group Goal, and Group Identity*
>
> Think of a recent group activity in which someone external to the group requested that the group be formed. How did that external influence affect the way group members identified with one another? Did all members agree upon the group's goal, or were there divergent views? If the external person decided who would lead the group, how did this affect group members' acceptance of and respect for the leader? What expectations did group members create? In what way was the group dependent on its macro system? How were these expectations and dependencies similar to or different from those of the external person?

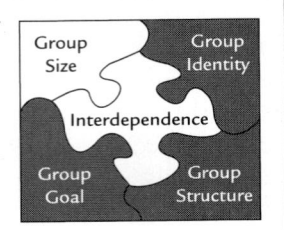

team effectiveness training. This creates a common knowledge base among all group members. It also gives members an opportunity to bring up questions before they start to work on the group's task. Second, group effectiveness can be maximized if individual or group coaching is available at the request of the group or its members. Just because Zack has always been the leader does not mean Zack is an effective leader. Just like your car needs a periodic tuneup, most of us would benefit from a periodic refresher course on group skills. Third, it may be necessary to bring in an outside facilitator to give the group the kind of feedback it needs to be effective. Facilitators can be particularly helpful when the group is frequently in conflict or is not moving forward in the decision-making process.

In complex macro systems, the expectations and dependencies groups create with their environments cause systemic influences that frequently go unnoticed or are accepted as inevitable facts of group life. Group members have identified several factors from the macro-systems environment as having a facilitating or inhibiting influence on group performance: Facilitating influences are compatible work schedules and adequate information resources; inhibitive influences are lack of available time, information resources, organizational assistance, financial compensation for group assignment and performance, as well as changing expectations from the larger organization (Hirokawa & Keyton, 1995). All of these result from groups' expectations and dependencies with their larger environment. Thus the relationship between the group and the macro system creates challenges and conflicts that ultimately influence group outcomes.

In another study (Broome & Fulbright, 1995), members of problem-solving groups identified many macro-system influences on group performance: lack of procedure and strategy for problem solving; cultural diversity issues; complaints about physical, technological, and other resources; pressure to give the boss the answer she or he wants; and pressure to provide immediate results. These complaints illustrate the strong influence of the group's macro system on group interaction and outcomes. The sophisticated methodology used by these researchers confirmed that it was the macro-system influences that caused the micro system (the group) to develop internal communication problems that resulted in negative individual attitudes and process failures.

The relationships between groups and their larger environment have been studied by researchers in other disciplines as well (Gladstein, 1984). Members of sales teams report that open communication and support from the organization increases satisfaction with their groups and produces higher sales. Training from the organization clarifies team members' expectations from the organization as well as what the organization provides (dependencies). This study also demonstrates that experience in the organization—a dependency—is associated with group members' levels of satisfaction. Team and group leaders can help manage the group's relationship with its larger environment by promoting group achievements to others in the organization. When the group-to-organization relationship is strong and visible, and the larger system is aware of what the group can accomplish, there will not be problems when group members ask for help or other resources. Try *Putting the Pieces Together* to see if you can recall a group experience that was influenced by the macro system.

The Group's Environment

Up to this point in our discussion, the type of expectations and dependencies a group has with its macro system result from the culture of the macro system. Another influence on group members and their interactions is the physical space and time a group occupies. A third influence on the group is the psychological environment created by members' relationships with the macro system. Both the physical and psychological environments are external influences of which group members may or may not be aware (Gouran, 1994).

Physical Environment and Material Resources

The **physical environment** includes meeting space and seating arrangements. In Chapter 2, we discussed the importance of finding a quiet meeting place where the group can have privacy. This type of setting promotes relational development because group members will feel more comfortable in negotiating differences of opinion in private. To the extent possible, seating arrangements should emphasize equality (equal status, equal conversational distance) among members. Circular tables are more likely to provide this perception. Circular settings also promote an open network of communication in which every group member can easily talk to every other group member or the entire group at once. When chairs are arranged in a lecture format (all chairs facing forward toward the leader or facilitator), it encourages one-way communication and reliance on the leader. A group member who is part of the "audience" will have to gain formal acknowledgment that it is okay and appropriate to speak. Other group members will not be able to see him or her easily. These physical conditions inhibit free-flowing

Group members are more likely to achieve effective communication and strengthen group member relationships if all members can easily see and hear one another during a meeting. The group's interaction will be further enhanced if the necessary equipment and resources are available in the meeting room.

interaction as well as the opportunity to develop relationships with other group members.

Besides needing meeting space, groups need time to meet. Time is a considerable resource for most groups and teams. When to meet and how long to meet are influenced by the number and length of other meetings group members must attend and other constraints on their lives. The higher the level of connectivity and embeddedness among group members, the more difficult it will be for a group to find a time to meet. As our organizations become more team-oriented, meeting time and meeting preparation time should be seriously considered. Groups that meet formally might also require time and space to meet informally in between regularly scheduled meetings. Informal interaction further anchors group member relationships and gives members opportunity to test ideas with others before presenting them to the entire group. You may think time is only a problem for organizational groups, but this is not so. Given the variety of demands on your schedule, your family, personal, and recreational groups may be even more pressed for adequate time.

The physical environment also includes the material resources needed by the group to complete its activities. Most organizational groups need office supplies (paper, pencils, chalkboards, flipcharts, and so on) and generally will need access to copy machines so documents can be distributed to all group members. When group members leave the group setting, they need time to accomplish individual tasks as well as access to information (in the form of data or other people) and technology (phones, fax machines, computers). Clubs and organizations need resources too. Minutes and notices need to be copied and distributed. Family groups meeting for recreational events need sports equipment and refreshments. The more loosely connected the members of the group, the more likely the group will not have the resources it needs. A group of friends planning a picnic may end up with too much potato salad and not enough buns for the hamburgers! Group management and planning are often overlooked; we will explore these concepts in more detail in Chapter 13.

Psychological Environment

Beyond the space, time, and material resources of a group's physical environment, each group communicates within a **psychological environment.** Those who review, support, or use a group's work heavily influence group members (Gouran, 1994; Hackman, 1990). The standards of quantity, quality, and timeliness set by others shape both the process and product of a group, and these external influences can create positive as well as negative expectations about the group experience. This is the psychological environment in which group members interact. For example, facilitators of the women's welfare-to-work ministry of a local church know that some of the public will question whether a church should be providing this type of public assistance program. Thus, these perceptions change how members of the facilitation team publicize their program. If everyone external to the group agreed with and supported the welfare-to-work program, the group would be more likely to succeed at its task. The support of the public would encourage and motivate them. Alternately, knowing that some of the public do not favor this type of program, the group facilitators must spend some of their time on public relations issues.

A negative psychological environment can also be created when someone who is not and will not be a member of the group has forced a group to convene or has volunteered members for the group. At a minimum, members of such groups are likely to spend some of their task time complaining. In a worse case scenario, group members may even resist the task activity. In particularly hostile situations, the group may try to subvert the external agent's authority and power.

It is likely that you have been a member of both types of groups—those with positive psychological environments and those with negative psychological environments. When the external agent is a positive force and a positive link to the resources needed by the group, group members work well together and take initiative and responsibility for creating both an acceptable and creative task outcome. However, when the external agent is a negative presence, group members can have difficulty making meetings effective. In these situations, group interaction is more likely to be negative than positive, and the topic of interaction may drift from the task to talking about the external agent. Let's consider two different extremes.

Olivia, Anthony, Reed, and DJ were volunteered by their supervisor to be the department's safety team in charge of safety procedures and training. To meet government standards, each month the team must present 60 minutes of training to everyone in the department.

> OLIVIA: Why did we get picked to do this? I don't know anything about safety or training.
>
> ANTHONY: We got picked because Walter "likes" us.
>
> REED: Yeah, right. He likes us because he knows we can't refuse to do what he wants. He does our performance reviews at the end of the quarter.
>
> OLIVIA: So, what do we do? How do we know what topic to pick for this month's meeting?
>
> DJ: Well, we've been having a lot of eye injuries. We could do something on that.
>
> ANTHONY: I've got a better idea. Let's get back at Walter by picking a really off-the-wall topic. As long as it's safety related, he can't complain.
>
> REED: Yeah . . . and we could do the presentation like a skit. We could have a supervisor named Falter . . . get it? . . . and whoever played Falter would act like Walter does—stomping around with his clipboard, shouting our names. This is going to be great!

This team is experiencing plenty of problems. First, it seems that most of the members are resentful that they were volunteered for the task without being asked. They realize that there is little to do about it. Complaining to Walter will probably just get them another undesirable assignment. However, rather than counteracting this negative psychological environment, the group maintains the negativity by making fun of Walter and selecting safety topics that are not relevant to their work environment. This safety team is more interested in getting back at Walter than in informing their colleagues about safe work practices.

Let's see the difference a positive psychological environment can make. This team has a positive relationship with the supervisor. And in this environment being on the safety committee indicates high status—co-workers vote for committee members.

> THAMES: Okay, let's get down to business. We need to select a topic for our next safety meeting.
>
> VIRGINIA: I've got the injury and illness list from last month. Looks like there were several back injuries, a couple of safety clothing violations, and a few unsafe equipment notations.
>
> THAMES: Good input, Virginia. Does someone want to take the lead on this next meeting?
>
> CARSON: I will. I think Jackson was more concerned about the safety clothing violations. There's really no reason that can't be corrected. The clothing is provided. It's up to us to put on the right clothing when we're working on specific tasks.

VIRGINIA: Okay, so safety clothing it is. Should I go get the procedure manual?

THAMES: Good idea, Virginia. Keep talking, Carson.

CARSON: Well, we probably need to review the safety clothing procedures—particularly emphasizing what tasks need special clothing. We've got so many new hires lately, they may not be adequately informed.

THAMES: Right. We should probably demonstrate how to put the equipment on and how to check for proper fit. I got my glove caught in a machine last month because I put on one that was too big.

VIRGINIA: Here's the procedure manual. I didn't realize there were forty-seven different situations in which safety clothing is required.

THAMES: Gosh, we should probably ask Jackson which ones he wants us to cover first.

This safety team is working in a completely different psychological environment. Rather than resentment, these members feel supported by their employer and their supervisor. From team members' comments, their relationship with Jackson, their supervisor, appears collegial and friendly. This team is not working against its macro system but working with it to better inform new employees and make their work setting a safer place. Notice how this safety team is actually making progress on their task compared to the team in the first example.

A group's psychological environment can also be affected by the organizational or community culture in a variety of ways. If an organization accepts group outcomes without giving them serious consideration and then make its own decisions, group members will not feel or act committed to their group and team tasks. If an organization rewards only individual performance, particularly emphasizing the performance of the leader, group members will withdraw physically or mentally from the group task, letting the leader finish the task and thereby diminishing the positive synergistic effects of group interaction. On the other hand, if a community or organization rewards group effort with sincere thanks and careful consideration of their outcomes, group members feel that their time and effort has been worth it. When organizations have a team approach to accountability and decision making, individuals want to be members of teams because they know their team efforts are supported and appreciated by others (Katzenbach & Smith, 1993). See "External Influences on the Group" to review how these factors may have shaped your group experiences.

Reacting to the Group's Environment

In the previous sections, we have identified ways in which the group is dependent upon its larger environment and how the group and its environment complete a system. Now let's turn our attention to how a group might react to its environment after it is formed.

> **THINK ABOUT IT**
>
> *External Influences on the Group*
>
> Think about the last group you were in that solved a problem that someone outside the group wanted addressed. How would you describe the physical environment in which the group met? How much control did the group have over this environment? Did this environment have all of the resources needed by the group? If not, what resources would you have added? How could the group have added these resources? How would you characterize the psychological environment of the group? Was the environment supportive or inhibitive? Explain.

A new group takes its initial cues from its environment before it develops an identity of its own. There are three response strategies a group can adopt as it reacts to and works with its environment (Ancona, 1990). One response strategy is informing. Once formed, a group using this strategy works on its own internal processes until it is ready to tell others outside the group what the group is doing. This strategy places a premium on developing a solid, cohesive group first, and then it deals with issues introduced through interaction with others. Although this strategy gives the group plenty of opportunity to develop its strengths and overcome its weaknesses without outside interference, it also limits the group's exposure to information in the larger environment. The disadvantage here is that a group that is out of sight may also be forgotten. By sequestering itself, a group may miss picking up important cues from outsiders. This can make it difficult for the group to know the standards to which it will be held.

A second response strategy is parading. A group using this strategy tries to work simultaneously on internal team building while making connections with outsiders. Juggling both types of tasks can create conflicting goals or stress for group members. It can also be confusing. A group using this strategy will appear eager and busy and, as a result, requires very committed members to keep up the pace. Unfortunately, the group itself may be underdeveloped and unable to deal with problems that occur among members because the group is spending half of its energy interacting with outsiders.

The third group response to its environment is probing. This strategy requires group members to actively seek information from its environment and then use that information to develop the processes and goals of the group. Although obtaining information from outsiders is important, it can cause delays in group formation that severely inhibit the development of strong member relationships. The leader of a group using probing will have to be directive in the absence of group cohesiveness. Due to the delay in building a strong internal group process, the impression can also arise that goals of individual group members must be incompatible as goal direction is generated externally rather than internally.

So, how do group members know which response to use? Group members must assess several issues to pick the strategy that is most appropriate for the situation. First, how quickly must the group react to its larger environment? Is a report, recommendation, or plan of action due within a short period of time? If so, parading might be the best strategy. Second, once the group interacts with its larger environment, will group members be able to reconvene to continue discussions or make alterations? In this case, probing may be the best strategy, but only if the group will meet over a period of time. Third, what expectations do individuals in the larger environment have for continued interaction with the group? Informing might be a good choice here as the group will be able to solidly form and create a positive impression for others. Of course, a combination of strategies may be appropriate, and certainly strategies may shift over time.

Denial of External Threats

Once formed, groups must balance their relationship with their larger system. A group's interdependencies with other entities make them vulnerable to external threats. External threats may take the form of unrealistic expectations of others, risks the group must deal with that were not generated by the group, or tenuous relationships with other entities. History has provided numerous examples of groups that have attempted to deny or avoid their connections with other groups and systems. Unfortunately, these cases have had disastrous outcomes. A primary outcome of denying external threats is the development of groupthink.

Groupthink

The **groupthink** hypothesis was originally conceptualized as the tendency of highly cohesive groups to adopt faulty solutions because members failed to critically examine and analyze options (Janis, 1982). Janis defined the conditions that lead to groupthink by describing and analyzing the historical case of President John F. Kennedy's invasion of Cuba's Bay of Pigs in 1962. Janis argued that groupthink occurs because three conditions are present. First, group members overestimate their power and invulnerability to risks. When groupthink occurs, group members do not question what they are doing or why they are doing it. Maintaining group harmony or building group identity is perceived by members to be more important than considering critical information that may temporarily decrease group cohesiveness.

Second, the group becomes closed-minded and rejects information that is contrary to its preferred course of action. By insulating itself from external threats and influences, the group, by its actions, isolates itself from its environment. Often this is accomplished by creating rationalizations that discount negative information. This can also occur when group members adopt a stereotype of the external agent or the macro environment that is inaccurate or negative.

Third, group members experience high pressure to conform because they have developed strong relationships with the leader or with one another. Thus members becomes overly sensitive to criticism or rejection from others in the group. Pressure and stress are heightened in the group when stakes are high or when the leader recommends a solution and group members fail to generate a viable alternative. This pressure to conform acts as a form of self-censorship, causing group members to believe that consensus exists in the group when it does not.

As Janis conceptualized groupthink, the conditions apply primarily to decision-making groups that are overly cohesive and in which group members have long and shared working histories, are deeply embedded in their macro organizational environments, and are insulated from the views of others. These conditions lead to full-blown groupthink. However, not all of these conditions need to be met for groups to make faulty decisions or to develop groupthink problems. We will examine groupthink again; here our primary concern is the impact of denying external threats.

Reread the three main characteristics of groupthink. When groups overestimate their power and invulnerability, they are no longer effectively interacting with their macro environment. By closing themselves off from receiving feedback messages about the group, the task, or the group's performance, the group is arbitrarily limiting needed information. The second groupthink characteristic identifies continued isolation from the group's larger environment as the group discounts or rationalizes negative information that it receives. The third characteristic identifies a complete systemic shutdown in the group. Because the group is no longer operating effectively and reciprocally at the macro level within its environment, information that could be critical to the success of the group is ignored, and all feedback systems within the micro system (the group) break down.

Even though Janis conceptualized groupthink by analyzing historical and political groups, you can probably recall one of your groups that suffered from groupthink as well. (Student classroom groups are notorious, according to my students, for allowing groupthink to develop.) How can your group avoid groupthink? One way is to bring decision-making procedures into the group. Groups that have high task commitment are more likely to search for and assess alternative courses of action than groups whose members are not committed to the group's task (Street, 1997). Adopting procedures to facilitate seeking information from outside the group is very helpful. This is a critical step because research has shown that groups tend to talk about what all members already know rather than acquire new information (Schittekatte & Van Hiel, 1996). When a group has high interpersonal cohesion and is more susceptible to the development of groupthink, a member with unique information may be unwilling to share that information because it does not fit with information possessed by other group members.

The Group's Charge

Part of the complexity of the group-to-environment relationship is created by the **group charge,** or the goal of the group. Agreement on one or several goals helps a group retain its groupness. The goal or charge of the group may come from its external environment. For example, most of your classroom activity groups have been given their assignments by the professor. She or he is external to your group. When your group receives its assignment, members interact to clarify or perhaps restructure the charge into goals. Groups can also create their own charge. For example, a group of friends decide to adopt a Salvation Army angel at Christmastime. Once they have agreed to support this community effort, they interact to make plans—these are the goals of the group.

Groups that do not have clear goals or who have not discussed their charge can wander aimlessly with members drifting apart or even becoming hostile. Interaction and an identifiable goal are necessary conditions to define and identify a group. Unfortunately, many groups are assigned to work as a committee without members having a clear idea of exactly what the group is supposed to do. A common complaint among group members is "I know we're supposed to do something—I just don't know what!" Whether the group is charged formally or informally, whether the group is given its charge or the charge is internally driven, a clear objective and mutual understanding about that objective by all group members is the first step to achieving group success.

It would be unrealistic to think, however, that groups have only one charge or goal. Most groups have a generally stated charge that can be restructured into several goals. It becomes even more complex when the group is trying to satisfy several different constituencies. For example, your university's student government association was asked by the administration to explore the idea of a student book co-op. This was the group's charge. From that charge, several goals can be derived. One goal is to provide a recommendation to university administration. A second goal is to develop a plan that makes buying used books less expensive for students. A third goal may be to structure the co-op in such a way that it does not compete unnecessarily with the university's bookstore. Notice how these goals may contradict one another. This happens because multiple goals exist to satisfy the multiple audiences or constituencies that are interested in the issue. Obviously, university administration is one audience, students are another, and the bookstore is a third. These constituencies are driven by different motivations and are likely to have their own ideas about how students should buy used textbooks. Thus one charge resulted in several goals and several parties who will be interested in the students' response.

If your group is not given its charge explicitly, then you and the group must develop your own. But, do not panic. There are several techniques that can help you develop the charge into goals or refine a general or ambiguous task. The first of these is to isolate the type of problem you are being asked to solve. This can be done by determining if the group is working on a question of fact, a question of value, or a question of policy.

Questions of Fact

Questions of fact are questions for which groups must analyze data to determine if the evidence is factual or probable. These are the types of issues juries face. They are asked to analyze the evidence presented to them to determine whether it is factual or probable. Other types of groups have to collect their own data and then arrive at a conclusion through analytical discussion. Not only must the correct set of data be collected, but the data should be unbiased and from credible sources. A student group at my university was concerned with the aesthetic appeal of the campus' urban environment. The main campus, which is spread over a 80-acre parcel, accommodates 20,000 students of which 40 percent are part-time. Like other universities, buildings have been added sporadically throughout the university's growth, and maintenance budgets are tight. Before attempting to develop recommendations to improve campus aesthetics, this group of students had to consider questions of fact: What did other students think about their campus environment? What university office or offices had jurisdiction over campus clean-up and maintenance? How much would more regular trash disposal cost? What would be the cost of designing and installing new signage? Answers to these questions would affect the recommendations that were ultimately made by the student group. Do not assume that questions of fact have one answer. In the case of campus aesthetics, some students thought the campus was beautiful; other students thought the campus was riddled with blight. These were the facts—conflicting perceptions by different sets of students. Also do not accept too quickly what appears to be a good or correct answer. Any information can be invalid or biased. Examining the source of the data is paramount in answering questions of fact.

Questions of Value

Questions of value are frequently posed as questions of right or wrong. Also in this category are questions that examine the desirability of an idea or the preference of a group of people, as well as questions of ethics. Questions of value cannot be answered by looking for an objective truth. Rather, they are explored by examining people's beliefs. Questions of value range from minor points ("Can we take the basic discussion from last year and repeat it in this year's report?" In other words, "Will anyone notice that we've repeated the worked turned in last year?") to larger ethical issues (a product design team weighing the consequences of short-changing product safety to balance increases in production cost and decreases in company profitability).

Questions of Policy

When groups respond to questions of fact and value, their outcome is likely to be a set of recommendations or policy. Many organizational or community and civic groups are assigned tasks for just such purposes. When a group is considering what should be adopted, what procedures should be enacted, or what programs should be implemented, they are responding to **questions of policy.** Developing this response is often built on responses to earlier questions of fact and questions of value. Another student group at my university was concerned about the information available to nontraditional part-time evening students (this is an urban campus). Before developing a recommended policy, they had to answer questions of fact: What information is available now? What hours are those offices open? How is information distributed? Once they had collected the necessary information, they moved to a critical question of value: Are we sure more information would attract additional nontraditional part-time evening students? Once that question was examined, the students moved to questions of policy; their recommendations for how, what, when, and where. After many hours of discussion, the group proposed a pamphlet developed specifically for the nontraditional part-time evening student population, containing office hours for various campus resources as well as basic information for registering and enrolling. The group had determined that procedures taken for granted by day-time and full-time students could be overwhelming and inconvenient to those less familiar with campus. Their product, the pamphlet, was delivered as a recommendation of what should be done to attract nontraditional part-time evening students.

Identifying the important questions of fact, value, and policy is a critical first step in developing the group's charge. Although some group members may want to proceed without these initial steps, isolating and identifying these critical questions will help the group focus and conduct their activities in a logical order. Too frequently, groups jump in to the problem-solving process without adequately examining their charge.

Where Do Opinions Fit In?

Facts, values, policies—juries make decisions about the facts, human resource executives decide which values their company will champion, and government officials determine policy. How does opinion play a part in these decisions? We all have opinions. Sometimes, our opinions are well thought out and based on personal experience or detailed information. Other times, our opinions are spur-of-the-moment reactions rattled off when an emotionally charged issue is raised. Do opinions count in decision making? Yes, especially when you can explain to others why your opinion is reasonable or why you hold your belief.

However, in group discussions, it is easy to substitute opinion for fact. For example, do you know that most traffic accidents occur after dark, or is your attention drawn to these accidents because you dislike driving at night? Most of us believe that our opinions are right, making it difficult for us to see that other group members hold different values or ethical standards. You may believe that spaying and neutering dogs and cats should be legislated, but can you understand why some animal owners might oppose such action? Questions of policy include both fact and value issues; thus opinions will surely surface. Because it is impossible not to have an opinion (even no opinion is an opinion!), the child-safety policies you believe should be implemented will reflect the opinions you have about parental responsibility, children's behavior, and manufacturer responsibilities.

So, should you withhold your opinions in group discussions? No. In fact, your opinions motivate people to work together to resolve issues. By revealing your opinions, you bring conflict out into the open so all group members can discuss the issues. Withholding your opinion is like withholding information: Doing so may keep your group from effectively accomplishing its charge.

Identifying Criteria

A second technique to help your group examine its charge or develop a more succinct and usefully stated objective is demonstrated in "Developing Criteria to Understand the Group's Charge." This exercise helps groups identify, isolate, and define what it is they are trying to do. Many groups shy away from this type of detailed analysis in the group's first meeting because the procedure may seem to lead away from the group's task. However, when a group faces a complex issue or objective, breaking the charge down into subgoals or minor objectives helps the group identify successes at intervals throughout a long project.

Discussion that moves you through the questions in the exercise will help your group identify what it wants to accomplish and the steps it must take to produce that goal. Although this amount of discussion may appear laborious, remember that a group is only effective when all members know what the group is supposed to do. Without this type of pretask discussion, group members are likely to have conflicting conceptualizations of the group charge or goal. As a result, each group member will work toward his or her individual conceptualization of the group goal rather than a mutually shared charge.

This method of developing and understanding the group's charge can also be used periodically to assess if the group is staying true to its charge. For groups working on long-term and complex problems, this technique will help the group identify any changes to the charge that may have occurred since the group began its work. If a critical element in the group's environment changes, it may impact what the group is working on. Or, a discovery of the group brought to the attention of the person who or the group which made the initial charge could alter the group's continuing course of action. This tool is an excellent group resource for groups which are actively defining their work as a group.

Goal Setting for Social and Support Groups

Many groups do not have problem-solving or decision-making tasks as their goals. Rather, the goal of these groups is to provide support or friendship for their members. These are affiliation goals. Social fraternities and sororities are primarily focused on affiliation goals. Many of these Greek groups also solve problems and make decisions as they determine who they will admit as members or which fundraiser they will support, but the primary group goal is to provide friendship and social support. Other groups may have entertainment as their goal.

Although it may appear that such groups do not need goals, unless all members are clear about the goals and direction of their group, problems are likely to surface in the group's interaction. Therapy and support groups also have affiliation goals as their focus. What exactly does this mean? A weight-loss group exists to support its members in their weight-loss activities. This is very different from a weight-loss group whose goal is to find the most effective weight-loss program. In that case, the goal has been redirected from an affiliative one to a problem-solving one. It is very important for affiliation groups to be clear in their goal statements so members know what and what not to expect from their groups. A clearly written goal or mission statement will help affiliation groups attract and retain interested members. In these types of groups, the leader must frequently assess the group's progress toward its goal.

Final Output

From a systems perspective, groups produce something. Most of us think of group outputs as things: reports, recommendations, decisions, and so on. But group output does not have to be a thing, and it does not have to have a finite beginning and ending. It may be the ongoing operations of a manufacturing facility, the continual service of clients or customers, or the support we receive from our friends.

Groups produce other effects as well. Relationships among group members are developed and made stronger or weaker by group interaction. Groups that work well together create cohesion, satisfaction, and commitment (Salazar, 1995), which influences the micro structures that exist between and among group members. New power alliances may be built, and old ones may be broken down. On the other hand, there may be some negative relational outcomes. Group members from groups that have difficulty in accomplishing their tasks are likely to develop **grouphate** (Keyton, Harmon, & Frey, 1996). This negativity can be internalized, and it can surface later as a bias against groups and group work, affecting the relationships among members in another group situation. When groups and teams are successful, group members grow personally and professionally as they learn new interpersonal, group, and organizational skills.

Organizations or the communities that support groups are altered as a result of a group's output. When the larger environment adopts the group's suggestions, it is changed by doing so. When a group's output is not adopted, the organization may not appear to change immediately or overtly. However, the effect is there: The organization may not ask that group of individuals to be a decision-making team again, it may decide to use teams in a different manner, or it may try an alternative to what was recommended. In any case, the larger external environment is changed to some extent.

To see how group outputs can vary, let's examine the outputs of a group of fire fighters who put out a blaze, saving lives and property. Typically, we count the things that were accomplished—the lives and property saved—and fail to examine the process of fire fighting as an output. If the team of fire fighters was successful, did they learn something about their group process? Sure, and they are likely to try to repeat those processes to save lives and property in the future. Did the group's emotional and relational quality change? Yes, it is likely that it did. Success would likely create greater cohesion and satisfaction. If the success of the fire fighting team did not meet their personal standards, they are likely to assess what happened to enhance their fire fighting effectiveness. A systems perspective would

BUILDING ANALYTICAL SKILLS

Developing Criteria to Understand the Group's Charge

Read through the steps and the example. Using a charge that you might like to work on with a group, work through every step in order. You may find that the answer to some questions is "nothing" or "not applicable," but think carefully before you accept these answers.

Step 1	Example	Your Example
Determine the broad goal that you wish to achieve through solutions to the problem.	Our group needs to develop a proposal for increasing nighttime safety on campus.	

Now, through group discussion, generate comprehensive criteria by answering the following questions.

Step 2	Example	Your Example
Identify the current status of the situation.	Students perceive that campus is not safe at night.	
What positive outcomes would it be desirable to preserve?	None identified.	
What negative outcomes would it be desirable to eliminate?	We'd like to change the security of campus, which would result in a change of students' perceptions. Some students won't come back to campus at night because they believe it is not safe	
What does the status quo require us to include?	We must focus on student perceptions. We must focus on safety on campus.	
What does the status quo deny us the ability to include?	We cannot include safety issues in the community surrounding campus.	

Create preliminary outcome statements by answering the following questions. Use complete sentences.

Step 3	Example	Your Example
What new outcomes must you create?	Campus should be safer at night.	
What new outcomes must you avoid?	We cannot recommend that the university hire more security personnel or campus police.	

Step 3	Example	Your Example
What new outcomes would you like to create?	We'd like to involve students in creating a safer environment. We could use existing student clubs and organizations.	
What new outcomes would you like to avoid?	By discussing safety issues, we don't want to make students more afraid to come to campus at night.	

Stop here and review what the group has decided.

1. Are any of the statements ambiguous, abstract, or vague? If so, rewrite them to be clear, concise, and specific.
2. Does each contain only one idea? If not, break into additional statements.
3. Do the criteria developed constitute a comprehensive set of standards by which you can evaluate ideas or potential solutions?
4. Do other criteria need to be included?
5. Add any other criteria needed for comprehensiveness; eliminate duplicates.

Step 4	Example	Your Example
Place the criteria into hierarchical order, with the first being those criteria that must be met; then order those that are desirable.	*Must Be Met* 1. Address night-time safety on campus. 2. Address perceptions of students. 3. Do not consider additional security personnel or campus police. *Desirable to Be Met* 4. Include student groups in recommendations. 5. Increase student activity on campus at night.	
Eliminate the criteria that are neither absolute or important.	Eliminate #5. This is different issue.	

Source: Adapted from Eldred (1996).

Positive Group Effects
Satisfaction
Commitment
Creativity
Alliances

Tangible Output
Reports
Recommendations
Decisions

Negative Group Effects
Aversion to groups
Unmanageable conflict
Frustration

Intangible Output
Service to others
Support received from others
Organizational skills
Knowledge

Group members often think of output, or outcomes, as being tangible, as in the case of the group's reports or recommendations. However, group outputs can also include the positive and negative effects of group interaction as well as the intangible elements like providing a service to others.

encourage them to examine both the things that they did and the relationships that provide a foundation for those activities.

In summary, a group's output can be analyzed on individual, relational, group, and organizational levels. Group output may be thought of as continual (as in processes), as finite (as in reports), or as relational (as in commitment). Whatever type of group output is achieved, it also affects the larger environment that supports the group, further embedding the group into the macro-system environment. In return, the larger environment is likely to be more reliant upon the group.

System Theory as a Foundation

Let's review how system theory can be a useful foundation for learning about groups. (These principles are adapted from Von Cranach [1996]). First, a group is an identifiable unit. Its membership and goal make it unique—unlike any other group, even those with similar goals or the same individuals as group members. Second, because of their uniqueness, groups also differ in their relationships and interactions with the larger systemic environment. Some groups will receive more favorable treatment from the sponsoring organization whereas others will have very loose connections with the organization and rarely report to another group. Some groups will only form weak and temporary relationships with other groups. Thus the uniqueness of the group (based on the type of group, the goal of the group, and the members of the group) influences what type of system is organized. Obviously, a work team is one of a collection of work teams in an organization. A city council is only one group of many in a city's bureaucracy. A dependency treatment group is sponsored in name by a hospital but otherwise has little connection with the hospital. A family is part of the neighborhood system or part of a school system. Some groups are embedded in several systems. For example, a classroom group is part of a course, which is part of a curriculum in a department, which is part of a university. Knowing what system the group is embedded in helps us understand the macro-systemic influences on the group as well as the group's influences on the system.

Third, groups are part of larger systems, but they also consist of smaller units and individuals, or micro systems. Group members form subgroups within a group. Perhaps these are temporary and based on the tasks or activities of the group. When a subgroup is based on friendships outside of the group activities, the subgroup may be long term, lasting for the duration of the group or longer. Each individual within the group is also a system—each with his or her unique characteristics, talents, skills, motivations, and personal goals. The individual micro system can be in conflict with the group's macro system. For example, you need to be at work in 15 minutes, but your study group has not divided up note responsibilities for the next study session. What do you do? Go to work (another system that depends on you) or stay to see what your assignment is so you do not let down members of your study group? Of course, either way you will not have time to stop and pick up your dry cleaning. Your individual system is in conflict with both group systems and the two group systems are in conflict with each other.

Fourth, even though we can identify smaller systems within a group and embed the group into a larger system, the group is still a group. It must act as a whole. Without all positions covered, the soccer team ceases to exist. If all players are present but goofing around rather than paying attention to the game, the soccer team is ineffective. Just as a car needs four wheels, an engine, and a steering mechanism, a group needs all of its members to operate effectively.

Fifth, as a group communicates to complete its activities or goals, many processes are occurring at once. Leaders are leading and followers are following. At the same time, conflict may develop if members do not like a leader's style. During the resolution of conflict, decisions are being made. While decisions are being made, relationships among members are being formed or destroyed. Many processes occur at once, and these are just the group-level processes. While the group is communicating, each individual's self-esteem is affected and communication styles are developed or confirmed. Simultaneously, the group is creating stronger or weaker relationships with its larger system. All of these processes occur together, creating influences within the group, influences on individuals, and influences back to the larger system. At the same time, the group is receiving influences from the larger system.

Sixth, the moment a group begins to communicate, it is creating history. This history is the key to understanding the influences noted above. How the group came into being, why the group came into being, and how individuals became members provide a reference point for interpreting what the group does. Groups with different histories make different choices. A family is a group in which individuals have little choice about membership. This is quite different from a group whose members were selected by the president of the company based on their sales quotas. Individuals who made their own decision to study together is a quite different group than a required study group for students with low grades. A neighborhood crime watch with members from the same neighborhood is different from a task force with members representing all sections of the city.

History also develops with the group. As a group meets challenges, additional history is being created. Group events create history for the interpretation of future events. At the same time, all group events are interpreted by the history before it. History creates a context for the group that is known only by group members. Beliefs and values held by group members are created or altered by group history.

Seventh, a group is not static but is a dynamic entity that is always in the process of development. That is not to say that all groups move forward or in a positive direction. Some groups evolve into ineffective systems. Development simply means that groups respond to interactions within their micro system and to interactions with their macro system. System responses create change—both positive and negative. Think of how a professional baseball team develops over a season. One team promises to be the wonder of summer. Just before midseason, they are winning two out of three games. Then they fall into a slump. The second team starts badly and only gets worse. In either case, the group is responding to macro- and micro-system challenges. Each group event changes the group in some way.

Eighth, the structure of the group—its roles, norms, and networks—result from the group's systemic interaction. All group structures are unique. Each structure is to some degree effective and to some degree ineffective. Members make corrections, additions, and alterations to group structure as they respond to systemic challenges. If members start coming late to meetings, a norm is developed about tardiness and absenteeism. If the leader is ill, other members step in to perform that role. One member likes to take notes and regularly performs that function for the group. Thus structure is created in response to what is happening to the group.

Ninth, because group structure is based on humans having relationships with other humans, issues of hierarchy, power, and status must be resolved. The role of leader is a role high in the hierarchy and generally has great power and high status, but not always. Some leaders have high formal authority but are detested by subordinates. Thus members afford this type of leader little status and low interpersonal power. In contrast, an otherwise quiet member may be responsible for identifying the key element in the group's success. Although this member had been previously ascribed low status and no power, now this member is perceived to be the group's informal task leader. Even when group members think their roles and positions are equal, personal idiosyncrasies create a hierarchy of power and status within the group.

Finally, communication is the force by which all of this is accomplished. Communication creates all of the micro- and macro-system relationships. Communication enhances, maintains, neutralizes, spoils, or destroys those relationships. Thus your communication is essential to each of the groups to which you belong at three levels: (1) Knowledge about how communication works in a group will help you understand your presence in group systems; (2) improving your communication skills will help you contribute positively to your groups; (3) with greater knowledge and enhanced skills, you can assess your group experiences, analyze what is going on, and intervene to make your groups more effective.

Summary

The advantage of using a system perspective is that it allows us to see the multiple layers to any group interaction. Although the group itself is a micro system, it exists within a larger environment or macro system. Boundary spanners in the group connect groups to their macro systems. Due to the connectivity and embeddedness of groups, the macro system influences what happens in the group, and the group's process and outcomes influence the larger environment.

Because groups are connected to elements in their system, group members must be concerned with the expectations about their potential performance and dependencies—or reliances—upon the larger system. Both of these bind groups to their macro system.

The environment the group operates in is also part of its macro system. The physical environment is composed of the group's physical meeting or activity location and the material resources the group needs to complete its activities. A group's psychological environment is created by those external to the group who review, support, or use the output of the group.

Groups actively react to their environments as they seek ways to minimize or maximize involvement with their macro system. Groups use three response strategies—informing, parading, and probing—to find out what is going on in the macro environment. Groups use these strategies to balance their relationships within their systems. Groups do run the risk of encountering threats from their external environment. When groups close themselves off from their external environment, groupthink may result. Groupthink is a reaction to the denial of an external threat that both further insulates a group and keeps it from making effective decisions.

A critical link between the group and its system is the charge of the group. Identifying and responding to questions of fact, questions of policy, and questions of value can help groups develop their charge or overall goal. Goals can then be broken into more succinct criteria against which to evaluate their performance. It may be helpful for groups whose goals are relational to write mission statements to help them clarify their purposes. As groups complete their tasks and activities, outputs or outcomes are produced. These may be relational outcomes or tangible outcomes.

System theory provides great utility for learning about groups. It helps us identify groups as units. It allows us to identify a group's relationship with its environment as it identifies the micro system that exists within each group. System theory also allows us to view the group as a whole, and we can view all of these processes at once. System theory provides for the history, present, and future of the group because a group is always in some state of development or retrenchment. Communication among and between group members creates all of these levels of systemic relationships.

✓ Checklist

Group Knowledge

You should be able to:
- describe how group members are boundary spanners.
- explain how a group's macro system affects the group and its individual members.
- explain how a group's macro system creates expectations and dependencies.
- differentiate among elements in a group's physical and psychological environment.
- describe how a group develops groupthink.
- differentiate among questions of fact, value, and policy.
- explain how a group's outcome or output creates new input for its macro system.

Group Skills

You should be able to:
- create a boundary management strategy for your group.
- act as a boundary spanner without creating negative implications for either group.
- maintain multiple group memberships and, at the same time, identify individually with each group.
- contribute to building a positive psychological environment for your group.
- help your group avoid groupthink.
- use questions of fact, value, and policy to develop your group's charge.

Analytical and Assessment Techniques

You should be able to:
- assess the effects of connectivity and embeddedness on your group.
- identify the impact of the group on individual members.
- help your group identify its expectations and dependencies.
- help your group adapt to its available physical environment and material resources.
- assess the psychological environment for both positive and negative attributes.
- use systems theory to provide your group a fuller understanding of its location in its macro system.

Discussion Questions and Exercises

1. Watch an episode of a current television sitcom or drama (for example, "Third Rock from the Sun," "ER," "NYPD Blues"). Identify the other groups with which the primary characters in the show are connected and embedded. In this one particular episode, identify the positive and negative as well as the short- and long-term aspects of those intergroup relationships. How would you analyze the connectivity and embeddedness of characters?

2. Think of the last decision-making or problem-solving group of which you were a member. What larger external environment supported your group? Specifically, to whom did the group report its findings, conclusions, or recommendations? What did they expect from your group? How did their relationship with the group hinder or help the group accomplish its objective? Finally, how did the group's outcome impact that external environment?

3. Think of one of your current social support groups. Within what larger environment does this group exist? Which has the most influence—the social support group or the larger environment? What is the outcome of this group? Is there more than one type of output?

4. Think of a time you were volunteered for a group by someone else. What skills do you possess that prompted this? Did something else prompt your being volunteered? Was this experience more or less rewarding than experiences in which you willingly joined the group? How did your feelings about being volunteered affect the group's interaction and its output?

5. Identify four different groups to which you belong. For each group, identify and describe the groups' charge. How did these groups come to understand their charge? Do group members hold conflicting interpretations of the groups' charge?

6. Use the front page of today's newspaper. For each group identified in each of the front-page stories, describe what output the group is creating. What group expectations and dependencies exist? How will these affect the group's ability to complete its task? How would these groups know if they are being successful?

7. Some people have difficulty in understanding the systems approach to group communication. What system analogies could you use to explain these concepts (for example, the food chain, ecology, the solar system)? Remember to include and explain both micro- and macro-system elements in your analogy.

5 Types of Groups and Group Activities

To what degree of effectiveness can group members work on different types of tasks?

How do work tasks differ from social tasks?

Do different tasks require different interaction strategies?

Can one group perform several types of tasks?

There are many types of groups, and there are many types of group tasks. Any one group may be responsible for several different types of tasks. Although decision-making tasks traditionally have been of primary interest to those in the communication discipline, we cannot ignore that groups also engage in social or relational tasks where the primary goal is to build, develop, and maintain relationships. Some group tasks are primarily mental or cognitive whereas others are physical or based on an activity. Understanding the different types of groups and the characteristics of different tasks will help you evaluate the group situation and prepare yourself for group interaction. Look at how Tatia described the tasks of the different groups to which she belongs.

Type of Group	Type of Task
Roommates	Agreeing to and maintaining living and household expenses; solving squirrel problem—get them out of the attic!
Statistics study group	Studying together; working problems together; sharing notes from class; making new friends
Student advisory group	Representing students to faculty and chair; providing input on new department initiatives; providing feedback from department meetings to students
Second-graders	Although my job, this is still a group; doing crafts and playing games with the kids; singing Russian folk songs with them

| Child care staff | Usually, discussing common problems and offering solutions; but today, talking about new director who starts next week |
| Family | Socializing and helping fix Slavic dishes for dinner; playing Scrabble to improve our English and spelling |

Types of Groups

We belong to many groups, and each is a unique experience. Three dimensions—formal versus informal, personal versus professional, and relational versus task—can help us identify their similarities and differences. Formal groups are those that have some type of regulated or predetermined structure. Most formal groups have formal roles such as elected or assigned officers. Informal groups tend to structure themselves through the group process as members communicate to pursue their goal. Personal groups are those that emphasize your family and friends and provide the social fabric of your life. Professional groups contribute to your occupation or job or provide a link to your community life. Although members of professional groups may socialize with one another and may develop friendships, that is not the primary purpose of their group. Groups that are relationally oriented meet your needs for affiliation—your opportunity to connect with others who have similar interests or needs. Groups that are task-oriented meet for some specific purpose that exists outside of group members' individual needs. However, groups can seldom be characterized by only one of these distinctions. You are most likely the member of many informal, personal, and relational groups—family, friends, and so on. You are also likely the member of many formal, professional, and task groups—committee at work, advisory task force for your university, and so on. Figure 5.1 illustrates the types of groups you might expect someone to belong to as we consider all of the possible combinations.

		Personal	Professional
Relational	Formal	A stop smoking support group	Lambda Pi Eta, the communication honors society
	Informal	A group of friends who play golf	A group of friends within a professional trade association
Task	Formal	Neighborhood crime watch group	The board of a civic organization
	Informal	A group of friends who help you move	A group of coworkers who meet regularly to solve common problems

Figure 5.1 *Types of Groups to Which an Individual Might Belong*

Communication in formal, task, or professional groups is usually more structured than communication in informal, relational, or personal groups. Formal, task, or professional groups are more likely to use procedures to guide or facilitate discussion whereas informal, relational, or personal groups tend to go with the flow. Look at the group activities in Figure 5.1. It is more likely that a group member's individual goals will be met in personal groups whereas the goals of professional groups will serve more people or a larger audience.

Another way to classify groups is to consider two dimensions: the span of time group members are together (long term or short term) and the scope of the group's activities (a variety of activities or a very specific activity) (McGrath, 1984). Families are **embedded groups,** a term used to describe groups with a very long time focus and groups that perform a broad base of activities. Contrast this to a **task force,** which is appointed for a specific project for a specific period of time. Commissions appointed by government bodies are common types of task forces. You may have served on a task force for your community, your professional association, or your church or synagogue. Other groups that have limited tasks to perform are **standing committees.** Sometimes these groups are called **teams** or **work groups.** Again, the tasks these groups address are limited, but group members expect to be together for an extended period of time. The last type of group is an **expedition,** a group responsible for a broad range of activities over a limited time. Perhaps you have been a member of this type of group on a camping trip. During that trip, you and other group members were responsible for all aspects of your living environment, safety, and social activities. Campers who are isolated from their regular living environment cannot rely on restaurants and motels for basic services; the group, like an expedition, must be self-sufficient.

One dimension that is missing from this typology is that of choice. Who chooses the group's membership? Do individuals form a group voluntarily? Or are individuals appointed or elected to the group? This is an important consideration, particularly for organizational groups. Group members who volunteer for a group assignment are likely to be more involved than disinterested group members who are selected by others or who are volunteered. When individuals feel forced to be members of a group, they often bring emotional baggage with them that can interfere with their interactions with the group and ultimately affect the group's interactions as a whole. Try "Identifying Groups and Their Characteristics" to uncover the groups to which you belong.

Group typologies tell us how groups are similar or different, but they tell us very little about what any particular group does. Realize that any type of group can perform any type of activity, and members join groups for a variety of reasons. For example, Aparnu belongs to Lambda Pi Eta, the communication discipline's student honor society. According to the model in Figure 5.1, it is a task-oriented, formal, and professional group. It has a formal internal structure (president, vice-president, secretary, treasurer). The group makes decisions about events it sponsors (bringing in speakers, holding a bake sale, and sponsoring a holiday party for faculty members). However, Aparnu's primary purpose for being a member is the support and encouragement she receives from other students with whom she has

GROUP ASSESSMENT TECHNIQUE

Identifying Groups and Their Characteristics

Use the chart below to identify the different types of group of which you are currently a member. After you have completed your chart, discuss your group memberships with several others in a small group. The discussion may remind you of your membership in other groups.

Name of group	Your role in group	Time span of group	Scope of group activities	Member by choice?
Example: scout troop	Assistant troop leader	Long-term; the group was together before I started helping out.	Weekly troop meetings, bi-monthly camp-outs, summer residence camp.	Yes
Example: my golf foursome	One of four players	We've just started playing together, but I hope we continue until my game improves.	Meet once a week to play golf.	Originally, no; this foursome was put together by the pro teaching golf lessons; now, yes.

Discussion Questions

1. Does the length of time a group is together affect group members' willingness to work together? their motivation to work together?
2. How broad is the scope of activities within your groups? What activities are common to several of your groups? Is it possible to take skills learned in one group and transfer them to another?
3. How does voluntary or involuntary membership affect interaction in your groups?
4. What is your favorite group? Why?
5. What is your least favorite group? Why?
6. In which group do you feel like you contribute the most? Explain your contribution. What would happen to this group if you left it?

much in common. Depending on what is going on in the group, Aparnu might describe the group as formal, professional, and task-oriented (such as when the group brings speakers to campus). At other times, she might describe the group as informal, personal, and relationally oriented (such as clowning around while cleaning up after the bake sale). Thus looking at the task and outcome characteristics provides a descriptive and useful way for identifying the type of group you are in and the type of interaction it will take to move the group forward to goal accomplishment.

Clearly, the type of group and type of group task make a difference in how members interact and participate. But in most every group, the task will have more influence on how members communicate because tasks have a direct impact on group performance (Goodman, 1986). At the heart of this chapter is the issue of interdependence. How much interdependence is required of group members to effectively complete their task? And as you have probably realized, any one group task is really many smaller tasks and activities. Although there may be a final group outcome, decision, or recommendation, the group is likely to have had many discussions, made many decisions, and rejected some alternatives and methods along the way. Few group tasks can be described by one single task. For example, in helping your friend move, you probably made decisions about where to start, how to load, when to stop, and how best to get the 8-foot sofa through the 7-foot door frame.

Most tasks can be broken down into subtasks. When this happens, it is likely that subtasks differ, even though they combine toward the same goal. So although groups develop for some purpose, that purpose or overall goal is more accurately described when it is broken into many tasks. Tasks are frequently interrelated, making it difficult to clearly identify where one task ends and another begins. From a systems perspective, one decision informs another as the output of one decision becomes the input or feedback for the next decision.

By using the taxonomies of group types and task types, and by analyzing the features of group tasks, we can make better decisions about how to proceed in our groups. At work you will be exposed to, and expected to participate in, many different types of groups. In organizations, there are teams that recommend things (task forces), teams that make, produce, or do things (production units, work teams, sales teams), and teams that run things (supervisory teams, executive management teams). Each team may face unique opportunities and challenges (Katzenbach & Smith, 1993); however, there are many similarities among decision-making tasks. It is the combination of subtasks within a group that creates novelty and uniqueness. The more we understand about the features of our groups and their tasks, the more equipped we are to contribute effectively as individual group members and to help the group develop effective process and procedures.

Types of Group Tasks and Activities

A good place to start analyzing group tasks is to ask two questions. First, can the task be broken into parts? In other words, is the task divisible or unitary? Second, will group members be held to deadlines or quality criteria in completing their task? Are there standards against which a group's work is evaluated? Using these two dimensions, we can create a typology of four different task results: disjunctive, conjunctive, additive, and discretionary.

Steiner's Typology of Group Tasks

In Steiner's (1972) typology, tasks are categorized by the demands they place or impose on groups. The first dimension of Steiner's typology—Is the task divisible?—is particularly helpful for deciding if a group or individual is better suited for the task. It also helps the group understand how member contributions are combined into the group's final product. The question that focuses attention on this task consideration is: How can the task be broken down? A task that can be broken into several parts is called a **divisible task.** It is easy to break some tasks into subtasks, allowing each group member to perform an activity that contributes to the group's outcome. When a division of labor is possible and useful, then the task is divisible. Preparing for your sorority's Valentine's Day dance is a divisible task. Three members work on the decorations while two members select songs from the DJ's play list. Two other members set up and check out the sound system. Sometimes it is impractical to break down a task even when it is possible to do so. For example, having several people alternately read sentences from a text would not contribute to anyone's understanding. In other words, the task is divisible, but it is not efficient or effective to do so. This type of task makes assistance from other group members impractical.

A task that cannot be broken down is called a **unitary task.** There are three types of unitary tasks. The first is a task in which there is one single outcome. A good example is a jury that must reach a single verdict. All jury members must agree on the verdict or the jury is deadlocked. The foreperson cannot report two separate and conflicting outcomes to the judge. A second type of unitary task is when the outcome of one group member can adequately represent the group. In this case, the group should select the most qualified member to complete the activity. You have seen this type of unitary task demonstrated on television game shows. Although all team members can contribute to the discussion beforehand, only one team member can represent and speak for the team. If this member misspeaks and gives the wrong answer—even if the team knew the correct one—the team loses. A third type of unitary task is when all members must succeed for the group to succeed. One football player cannot win while other players on the same team lose. All players succeed or fail together.

A second dimension considered in categorizing group tasks is whether or not criteria will be used for evaluating the group's output. Most frequently, groups are evaluated against criteria of timeliness and outcome quality (accuracy, quality, effectiveness, viability, and so on). On this dimension, there are two task considerations: (1) Did the team meet the deadline? (2) What standards must the group meet in completing the task? When a task or external system requires that a group accomplish a great deal or complete its task rapidly, it is a **maximizing task.** Here, force and speed are the characteristics a group needs to emphasize. How the group uses its time is the main consideration. Conversely, in an **optimizing task,** group members work together to meet a criterion of quality that has been set for them. In this case, how well the group's outcome meets a standard (for instance, accuracy, completeness) or quality objective (how well the proposed solution fixes the problem) is the main consideration. Beating a time deadline would be an example of a maximizing task, whereas achieving a perfect score would be an example of an optimizing task.

Using these two dimensions, we can identify four different types of tasks: divisible and optimizing, unitary and optimizing, divisible and maximizing, unitary and maximizing. Awareness of these task characteristics helps group members decide how to proceed in working on their task.

Disjunctive Tasks The **disjunctive task** type represents a task that is unitary and optimizing. It is difficult to break into subtasks, and it has a correct outcome that someone outside the group can use to evaluate the group's output. An example of this type of task would be a group being given their budget to examine for errors. When this task is presented to the group, the group should recognize that the task cannot be broken down easily into subtasks. It is probably more likely that one member has all of the receipts and that this member also holds the group's checkbook. It is probably easier for one member to efficiently add and subtract the columns. When this type of task is presented to the group, the group should first find out which member of the group has the ability to solve the problem or complete the task. Here, the group is responding to a situation in which only one group member's performance represents the group's efforts; the group product is really an individual product that is sanctioned by the group. But to ensure accuracy, another group member can check the completed task.

Another type of disjunctive task is when all group members believe they are capable of solving the problem. Unfortunately, each group member has a different answer, and the group does not know which answer is correct. In this case, it is best for the group to allow each member to work through the problem and then for group members to discuss which answer makes most sense. This often occurs in study groups that work together to develop answers to essay test questions. Each student develops his or her own answer. Then the group attempts to discover which answer best fits the professor's question. Here the group must make a selection of one member's solution over others. The selection of one member's answer represents the work of the group.

There are some interesting interaction conditions that can occur when a group encounters a disjunctive task. For example, a group is given a problem to solve; and, according to the person who charged the group with the problem, there is a right answer. Now, we would hope that the group member who knows the answer would step forward and offer the answer so the group could benefit. But, what if this member, George, is shy, apprehensive, or worried that his answer is wrong. He would not speak up. Someone else, Aria, who believes she has the right answer but does not, speaks up and offers her answer to the group. Because Aria is assertive, friendly, and has been right in the past, the group accepts her answer and announces the problem solved. Obviously, the group would benefit if its interaction climate were friendly, supportive of all members, and regularly enlisted the input all members. In this type of group climate, George would be more likely to feel comfortable about speaking up even when his solution is different from Aria's. In this type of task situation, one of the group members may possess the correct solution. But when the group member who has the correct solution is unwilling to share that solution with the group, everyone loses because of the unitary nature of the task.

There are three steps a group can use to help it deal with disjunctive tasks (Thomas & Fink, 1961). First, the group needs to determine if any member or members can solve the problem. Simply asking if there are members who know the answer may not be the best way to go about this. More assertive group members may overwhelm more submissive members. Second, the group has to analyze the proposed solutions to determine if they are actually correct or will work. Discussion is the process that helps group members reject faulty solutions and accept the best one. Starting the discussion with "what if" questions can help group members play out and evaluate the suggested solution. Finally, does the seemingly correct solution offer more support than incorrect solutions? Often, the most talkative group member can press for his or her solution whether or not it is correct. It is critical that other group members question and critically analyze the proposed solution. After all, the solution will represent them as well.

Conjunctive Tasks Once again, a single group member's performance determines the group's performance in a **conjunctive task** because it is unitary—for the task to be complete all members must succeed. In this case, however, it is the member who performs the poorest who exerts the most influence on the group task. You have heard the phrase, "A chain is no stronger than its weakest link." This describes a conjunctive task. Envision a team of mountain climbers who are linked together by safety ropes in their attempt to climb the face of the mountain to reach the summit. Every member of the team has to work together, yet the team can move no faster than its slowest member. You have probably experienced a conjunctive task as one of your classroom assignments. Perhaps you have been a member of a classroom group in which each member was responsible for preparing and then delivering one part of the group's presentation. You were worried that Ezra, the member with poor attendance, would not show up the day of the presentation. As it turns out, your worries were confirmed. Ezra does not show up, and your group cannot make its presentation because Ezra was to present the part that linked the beginning and the end of the presentation together. As a result, the group outcome and the impression others have of the group relies upon this one group member. Conjunctive tasks are unitary tasks because the group fails when one member fails. All members must succeed for the group to succeed.

To counteract problems faced in conjunctive tasks, group members need to take responsibility not only for themselves, but for other group members as well. When groups work on conjunctive tasks, extra care needs to be taken to motivate all group members. Sharing and assisting other members will help groups overcome the problems associated with conjunctive tasks. Some members may withhold important information or assume that specialized information is common knowledge among all members. Such assumptions artificially inflate the impact of the group's weakest member. Sharing information through discussion brings everyone up to speed and creates group commitment for all members.

Additive Tasks   Tasks can be identified by looking at the group's outcome as the sum of the group members' individual efforts. An **additive task** is divisible; it can be broken down into subtasks so that each member can contribute meaningfully to the group's outcome. In this case, the weakest member's input affects the outcome just as does the input of the strongest member. Let's say that a group is charged with the responsibility for selling tickets to a charity fundraiser. After the group decides on a design for the tickets and has them printed, the task of selling tickets can be broken down with each group member responsible for selling a certain number of tickets. Or the task of selling tickets can be broken down another way: One member is responsible for identifying potential markets for the tickets, another for designing and printing the tickets, three members for selling the tickets, and one member for keeping track of ticket sales. Which way should the group divide the task? It depends on what skills and interests group members possess and how much time the group has.

Discussion helps coordinate group members actions when working on additive tasks. In the ticket selling example, if group members do not coordinate their actions through discussion, it is likely that some potential buyers will be missed while several group members may unknowingly approach the same potential buyer. To most effectively accomplish an additive task, the group would need to plan a course of action. Decisions would include identifying potential ticket buyers, determining how many tickets needed to be sold, dividing ticket-selling regions to achieve maximum coverage, and choosing strategies to encourage people to buy tickets. Using group discussion to answer these questions, each group member will be better informed about the group's goal, which will help the group meet its target objective.

Discretionary Tasks   Finally, there are **discretionary tasks** in which group members are encouraged to combine their contributions in any way that they desire. The point here is that the group chooses its own method or process from among the many ways in which it can be done. To do so, the group needs to discuss which method might be better and then choose a method to use. Too frequently, groups that are given discretionary tasks follow the lead of the most talkative or assertive member rather than discussing other alternatives that could be used. Or, given a discretionary task, group members will simply do what they did last time. Group discussion is essential to weigh the advantages and disadvantages of each method. Doing so will help the group select the best method for effectively achieving its goal. The exercise in "Redesigning Tasks to Take Advantage of the Group" gives you some practice in categorizing various task types.

Chapter 5 Types of Groups and Group Activities   133

The extent to which a task is divisible or unitary will affect how a group interacts and completes its activity. The unitary nature of a disjunctive task requires that a group member performs the task to represent the group as a whole. A conjunctive task is also unitary, but this time, all group members must complete the task for the group to succeed. All group members can participate in an additive task. As a result, the group's outcome is affected by both its strongest and weakest members.

BUILDING ANALYTICAL SKILLS

Redesigning Tasks to Take Advantage of the Group

Break into small groups of five to seven members. Think about and discuss each of the following group tasks using the four primary task characteristics—disjunctive, conjunctive, additive, and discretionary. After you have categorized each group task, discuss the advantages and disadvantages of performing such a task as a group. How could you redesign the group task to make better use of group resources?

Task Description	Disjunctive? Conjunctive? Additive? Discretionary?	Advantages?	Disadvantages?	Redesign of Group Task?
The five-member campus entertainment committee of your student government wants to develop activities for nontraditional age students. After agreeing on ten possible activities, each group member is responsible for investigating two options and reporting back to the committee.				
Your civic group has agreed to help the local food drive. Each member has been asked to bring as many cans of food as possible to the next meeting. The group has committed to donating 100 cans of food.				

Task Description	Disjunctive? Conjunctive? Additive? Discretionary?	Advantages?	Disadvantages?	Redesign of Group Task?
Your math instructor has divided your class into teams to complete daily assignments. Each team member must complete the assignment before coming to class. In class, team members discuss their answers and decide which homework to turn in to represent them as a group for a grade.				
You are a member of a four-person relay team. In a track meet, your team is running well until the final runner (who complained earlier of a sore ankle) falls.				

McGrath's Group Task Circumplex

Steiner's typology helps us analyze the process by which group members work together to complete tasks. Another way to analyze tasks is to use McGrath's (1984) group task circumplex. In this typology, the emphasis is on what the groups do, or the content of the task. Here, the activities of groups are separated into four quadrants based on two dimensions: a communication dimension that ranges from conflicted to cooperative interaction and an activity dimension that ranges from conceptual to behavioral activities (Figure 5.2). These two dimensions combine to create four general types of group activities: generating alternatives, choosing among alternatives, negotiating, and executing.

Quadrant 1, Generate, represents tasks in which groups must generate ideas. Within this quadrant are planning tasks (task type 1) and tasks that require creativity from group members (task type 2) similar to the brainstorming process. Quadrant 2, Choose, represents tasks that are intellectual such as solving problems with correct answers (task type 3) and decision-making tasks where the solution chosen

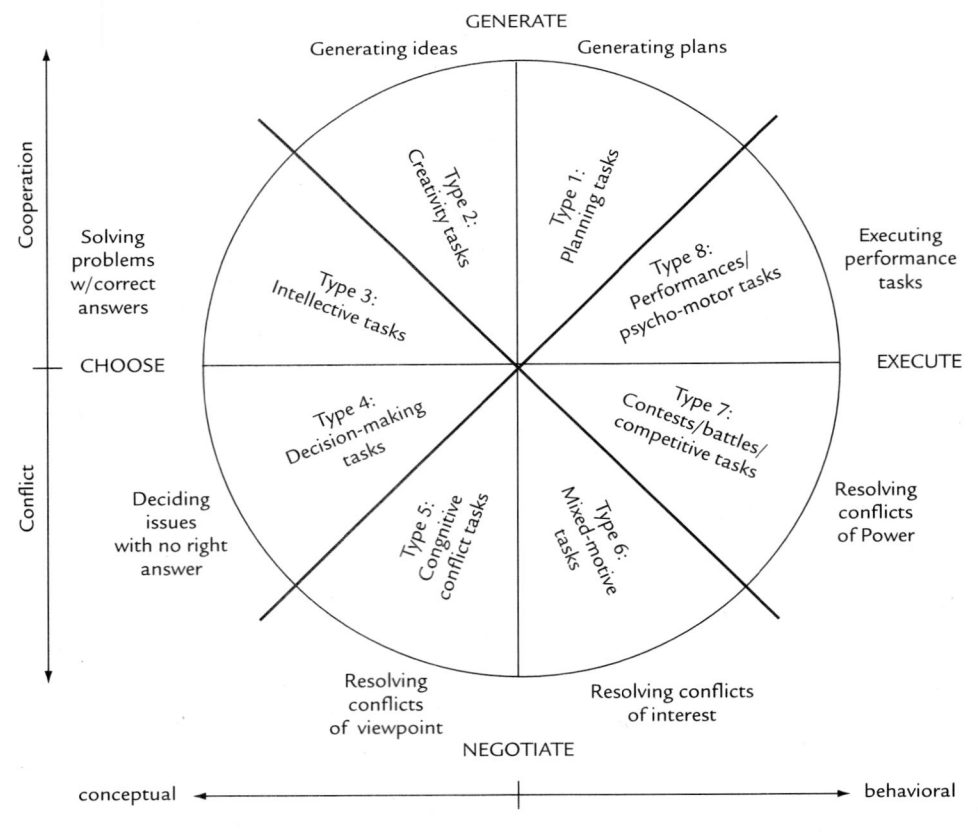

Figure 5.2 *The Group Task Circumplex*

is the answer preferred by the group (task type 4). Quadrant 3, Negotiate, represents tasks in which there is conflict within the group. Here, groups are engaged in cognitive conflict tasks where policy conflicts and viewpoints are resolved (task type 5) and mixed motive tasks where conflicting interests must be resolved (task type 6). Finally, Quadrant 4, Execute, represents tasks that are physical in nature. The two types of tasks here are competitive contests (task type 7) and performances of some physical task or sporting activity (task type 8).

Thus within the four quadrants, eight different group tasks are represented. The circumplex is useful because it demonstrates how groups tasks are both similar and different from one another. Using the two dimensions—type of interaction (conflict or cooperation) and type of activity (conceptual or behavioral)—it is easy to analyze the task. This will help you and your group members take the most effective steps in accomplishing the group goal.

Task Type 1—Planning Tasks In **planning tasks,** groups are responsible for generating plans to carry out previously made decisions or decisions made by others. Particularly in organizations, it is common for an executive group to make decisions while a task force carries them out. For example, my university has changed its registration process. This was a policy decision made at the university level. But the administrative group in each department is responsible for planning how best to communicate these changes to students, advise them, and get them registered. Here, a group at a higher level makes the initial decision while a group at a lower level decides how to implement or carry out the initial decision.

Task Type 2—Creativity Tasks In **creativity tasks,** the group is responsible for generating ideas or alternatives. When a group is charged with the responsibility of being innovative, it needs to use an idea-generation technique to enhance its group process. Two objectives must be considered: First, the technique should not create social influences that could inhibit individual creativity (for example, embarrassment); second, the technique should provide social support and reinforcement, or rewards, for participating and contributing. One technique that satisfies both objectives is brainstorming, which is discussed later in this book.

Groups that select or are charged with type 1 or type 2 tasks are generating plans and ideas. As the groups work in this capacity, members should be sensitive to generating values and goals that will aid cooperative interaction.

Task Type 3—Intellective Tasks Even though we have learned or practiced group decision making with activities that have correct answers, in reality there are few group tasks like this. Individuals would lose interest in being part of a group if their only charge was to find the correct answer. Why bring the group together when the answer is known? Groups are less effective when they are used to provide an answer that is known, easily found, or could be provided by an expert. However, we often assume that there is a correct answer even when there is not one. Group members who act in the critical advisor role can help their group identify this prevailing attitude if it arises.

For this type of **intellective task,** increasing the size of the group is advantageous. With more individuals involved in the group process, more expertise and a wider diversity of viewpoints are available from which group members can assess what might be correct. Additionally, more members make it more likely that someone within the group will be proficient in recognizing expertise within the group (Littlepage & Silbiger, 1992).

Task Type 4—Decision-Making Tasks **Decision-making tasks** are the most common group activities. In such tasks, the objective of the group's interaction is to reach conclusions through sharing information and group members' collective reasoning. This type of interaction focuses on choices; this is different from disseminating information, coordinating and organizing, motivating and encouraging, and developing affiliations (Scheerhorn, Geist, & Teboul, 1994).

Most decision-making tasks do not have one correct answer, but many groups behave as if one exists. Sometimes groups make the mistake of focusing on one solution as right rather than on which solution is better. False adherence to a correct outcome (or hope that one exists) consumes group interaction and keeps the group from moving forward in the discussion of viable alternatives. Groups that develop policy are more at risk for this type of false consensus. Rather than basing their decision on information that is unique to their task, they base their decision on the norms, values, and beliefs of the group's larger culture.

Groups involved in type 3 or type 4 tasks are choosing the correct or the preferred alternative. In these conceptual activities, group members' communication should balance agreement on values and goals to create consensus with asking questions to evaluate alternatives.

Task Type 5—Cognitive Conflict Tasks In **cognitive conflict tasks,** there are differing viewpoints that are difficult to resolve. Although there is agreement on goals and purpose, there is disagreement on the positions taken by group members *and* disagreement on how those viewpoints are reached. In other words, group members have difficulty understanding how other group members developed the position they express. In these cases, disagreement actually exists at two levels, making it difficult to untangle the conflict. The more personally involved group members are in the group task, the more likely this type of disagreement will develop. City council members disagreeing over where in the city's budget to increase and decrease spending are engaged in cognitive conflict. Even when council members finally agree, they still do not understand how or why other councilpersons support their preferred proposals.

Task Type 6—Mixed-Motive Tasks In **mixed-motive tasks,** not all group members share a common interest, goal, or motive. Group members typically believe that the group's decision affects them directly as individuals. In such a case, there is the attitude that the pay-off will benefit one group member at the expense of others. In this type of task, the interests of individual group members conflict because the best outcome for one group member is not desired by other group members. Will groups working on this type of task experience conflict? You bet. A good example of a mixed-motive task appeared in a local newspaper. A group of Hispanic businesspeople approached a local chamber of commerce hoping to establish a voice in their otherwise Caucasian and African American city. A group of chamber representatives agreed to meet with the Hispanic businesspeople, hoping to encourage them to join the chamber. Together they could not establish one goal that satisfied both parties. Rather, the motivations of the two groups were not compatible. One group wanted to be heard, to be recognized as a minority in the city. The other group wanted to increase membership by folding these businesspeople into their already existing minority business council. Nothing will be accomplished because they have not established a mutually satisfying goal.

Groups that are engaged in type 5 or type 6 tasks are resolving conflicts—conflicts of viewpoint or conflicts of interest. To help accomplish this, group members should develop norms to guide their behavior through these difficult negotiating processes. Group members should also focus attention on allocating roles and developing procedures that facilitate conflict resolution.

Task Type 7—Contests/Battles/Competitive Tasks You may have more experience with **contests/battles/competitive tasks** than with any other. During your childhood, you played dodgeball. Later in school, you played softball, volleyball, and other competitive team sports. In these types of tasks, one group wins, the other group loses. It is all or nothing. Your goal as a group and motivation as a group member is to beat the other team. Although the two teams may have to cooperate to play together, one team still wins in the end.

Other types of groups also operate in a competitive environment. You may be part of a sales team that is competing against sales teams in other regions. You may be in the military and regularly participate in exercises against other units. In these types of tasks, the most important group elements are how well the group performs and whether or not the group wins.

Task Type 8—Performance/Psycho-Motor Tasks Although the group tasks in this task type are also physical, there is no competition. Group **performance/psycho-motor tasks** are measured against standards of performance or excellence. Unlike a competition where the group's focus is the opponent, here the group's focus is on meeting a standard that is in place before the performance begins. A community theater group would be engaged in this type of task. Generally, this group receives good reviews from a local critic. Maintaining this standard is what motivates the members of the theater group to rehearse and perform.

Groups or teams engaged in type 7 or type 8 tasks are executing some physical behavior or activity. The environment in which the task is being executed helps make the distinction between contests and performances. In either case, the group is performing some action or task. To be successful, the group should focus their interpersonal energy on establishing and maintaining cohesion. This will help the group remain solidified until all task behaviors are executed.

> ### GROUP ASSESSMENT TECHNIQUE
>
> *Breaking Big Goals into Small Tasks*
>
> Before breaking into small groups, as a class identify several important issues that need resolving on your campus. Some issues you might consider are how to increase participation in volunteer activities, how to solve the parking problem, how to expedite class registration, or how to determine frequency and usage of student activity passes. Assign one issue to each group. Using the task circumplex, identify all of the types of tasks and activities that you believe the group will need to complete to provide a full recommendation for the identified problem. Remember that complex tasks are made up of many subtasks and subactivities. Some of your tasks will be decision tasks; others will be activities that must be performed by the group or some of the group members. Report back to the class on the types of tasks in which your group would likely engage.

If you are responsible for leading or facilitating a group, the group task circumplex can help you distinguish one type of group task from another so that you can make proper arrangements and be prepared for the type of interaction that will help the group accomplish its goal. Too frequently groups focus on identifying the task and not on analyzing the type of task for which they are responsible. Failing to do so may waste group time by trying interaction strategies that are not conducive to their task. For example, if your group is going to engage in a competitive task, someone needs to be the group's cheerleader and motivator. If your group needs to make a plan to carry out actions, some type of time or project scheduling process will be helpful to the group. Different group activities require different group processes.

Although decision making may be your group's primary concern, remember that most groups and teams will have different objectives at different points in their life cycle and will need to perform other functions in addition to decision making. A group whose main task is to make policy decisions will also need to coordinate schedules, inform others of the group's outcomes, and encourage others to follow newly developed policy. Often support groups focus on motivating and encouraging members, but occasions may arise when even support groups need to make a decision. For example, a weight control group may need to make decisions regarding meeting time, speakers, membership fees, and so on. Moving from one type of task to another can create confusion or conflict in a group that is unaware of the different demands new tasks create for members. The *Group Assessment Technique* will help you practice breaking down big goals into small tasks.

Task Characteristics

Regardless of the type of task the group takes on, the task or activity can be evaluated according to the following set of characteristics: task difficulty, solution multiplicity, intrinsic interest, population familiarity, acceptance level, area of freedom, and social complexity. You will want to analyze your group's task before you start. This helps the group thoroughly understand how to complete its charge. When you are responsible for supervising others in groups and responsible for making group charges, these task characteristics will help you design an appropriate group task.

Task Difficulty

Groups are usually given difficult tasks—tasks that require a sizable amount of effort, knowledge, or skill (Shaw, 1973). Having many individuals work together on difficult tasks spreads the workload and increases the chance that the group will find the best solution. Most tasks are complex; there is no right answer. Group members must pursue several avenues of solutions in solving difficult tasks. Think of the many paths investigators took in examining the crash of TWA flight 800 into the Atlantic Ocean off the coast of Long Island in May 1996. Many probable causes were proposed by the FBI and the National Transportation Safety Board. Each had to be examined. It would have been nearly impossible for one individual or for one group to effectively examine all of the proposed causes that downed the aircraft. Even if an individual were motivated enough to pursue all of the causes, it is unlikely that an expert on fuel tank vapors would also be an expert on mechanical failure and terrorist missiles. When tasks are difficult due to their complexity, teams are more likely than individuals to quickly and effectively resolve problems.

Another way of thinking about **task difficulty** is to ask three questions (Herold, 1978). First, is the task programmable? In other words, is it easily repeatable? Can it be mechanized? Is the decision routine? If you answer yes to these questions, the task is not difficult. Second, how much effort is required? The greater the number of skills needed to work on the task or activity, the greater the effort needed by team members. These two conditions generally mean that the task has a great number of subparts that increase the task's difficulty. Third, how diffused is information about the task? Can information be easily obtained? from one source? If you answer yes to these questions, the task is not difficult. On the other hand, if information from many sources is needed and it will be difficult for team members to obtain that information, the task is difficult. When knowledge is not centralized, the task is more complex.

Solution Multiplicity

A closely related feature is **solution multiplicity.** This refers to the number of alternatives available for solving the problem (Shaw, 1973) or to the number of ways in which the activity can be accomplished. Although there is one way to balance a checkbook (subtract debits, add credits, make sure there is enough money in the bank to cover the debits), there are many ways to create a community child care center. Consider all the child care centers you know. Now think of how they differ in services offered. Do they offer educational programs? What ages of children can enroll? What meal services are offered (breakfast, lunch, dinner, snacks)? What types of meals are available (vegetarian meals, nondairy diets)? Regardless of the differences you have identified, these organizations call themselves child care centers. Group members responsible for designing a child care center came to distinct and separate solutions for providing this service.

Intrinsic Interest

Some tasks and activities are more interesting than others. When they are, you are motivated to perform well and you are attracted to the group, the task, and its members. This is known as the motivating potential or **intrinsic interest** of the task (Shaw, 1973). But what is intrinsically interesting to you may be boring to someone else. Individuals are attracted to different types of group tasks based on their preferences, experiences, and desires to be challenged. Darci likes being on sports teams. In fact, she loves it that when anyone is planning an intramural, they think of her as a potential member. She enjoys demonstrating her athleticism and competing against others. Eugene, on the other hand, avoids physical activity. He would prefer to work on problem-solving tasks. Eugene likes developing alternatives to difficult problems with others. What is intrinsically interesting to Eugene is not interesting to Darci. If all group members are interested in the group task, it is more likely that they will participate and strive to be effective group members. Here is where choice comes in. It is hard to be interested in a group task when you are appointed to the group without being consulted.

Population Familiarity

Group members who are familiar with the task and one another, those who have **population familiarity,** are likely to work together effectively and quickly. Kate is a member of a steering committee that plans student research forums on her campus. At the first meeting, she did not know the other members and was not clear about what the group was trying to accomplish. As relationships developed and as the task became clearer, Kate's committee was able to plan a successful forum. When it came time to plan the second forum, the group worked together more effectively and efficiently because they were able to use what they had learned about the task and one another from their first experience. By the time the committee was planning the third and fourth forums, distinct group member roles had developed; each member was responsible for particular aspects of the forum planning.

However, when the committee was preparing for the transition to next year's committee, it became apparent that the group had become too specialized. Committee members who were returning for next year's committee did not know how to manage public relations for the forums because a member who was graduating had been doing it. Familiarity breeds interest and helps a group be effective. However, overfamiliarity can lead to the feeling of being in a rut or to exclusion from certain aspects of the group's task. Worse yet, overfamiliarity can produce the attitude that one member must do a task for the group without help from other group members. If a group member feels solely responsible for some group task, resentment may arise.

Acceptance Level

Groups can come up with great ideas, but a good idea is useless if it is not accepted or appreciated by others. A decision must be not only technically correct but usable by others; it must have a certain **acceptance level** to be useful. The practicality of a group's outcome should be considered not only from the frame of reference of group members but also from others who are involved with the group or who may use the group's decision. Others may consider the group decision to be ineffective if the decision is not acceptable to them.

Responding to budget cuts, the campus security team decided that security officers would no longer lock campus buildings at night. Rather, they announced that administrators in each building would be responsible for locking up at night and unlocking in the morning. This team forgot to assess the practicality of their new policy from the viewpoint of administrators who frequently travel in their jobs. Who would open the buildings while they were at conferences? Who would lock up after night classes when administrators went home at 5 P.M.? Although this decision was practical, it certainly was not appreciated by campus administrators.

Area of Freedom

How much authority or responsibility does your group have in its tasks? This is the group's **area of freedom.** For example, Katara is a member of the promotions committee at the department store where she works. The committee makes decisions about new merchandise promotions, in-store events, and public relations. But each decision her committee makes must be presented to the store's executive committee for its approval. Having to gain the approval of others before acting on their decisions limits the committee's area of freedom. Katara's committee cannot proceed with a promotion until it is approved by the executive committee.

On the other hand, a group of friends planning social activities has a much larger area of freedom. Their ideas for fun, entertainment, and socializing do not need approval from anyone outside the group. The group of friends carries out their decisions and accepts responsibility for their effectiveness. Many groups who work within a larger macro environment want larger areas of freedom within which to operate. But in taking it on, the group must also be responsible for its decisions and be accountable for its actions.

Social Complexity

Relationship effectiveness within groups, or the social demands placed on groups, are too important to overlook. In fact, relationship demands affect other task characteristics (Herold, 1978). Elements of **social complexity** include the level of ego involvement of the group members, group members' agreement on how to

> **PUTTING THE PIECES TOGETHER**
>
> ### *Interdependence and Group Goal*
>
> Focus on one of your current social groups. What kinds of tasks or activities does this group do? To what extent do the task characteristics—task difficulty, solution multiplicity, intrinsic interest, population familiarity, acceptance level, area of freedom, and social complexity—describe your group activities? Think carefully and creatively. Do not assume that your social group does not work on tasks or that social activities cannot be assessed with these characteristics. How could you use the characteristics to assess the surprise birthday party your group had for one of its members? How well do these characteristics describe the group goal—for example, throwing a surprise birthday party? To what extent does interdependence among group members create social complexity, acceptance level, and population familiarity in your social group?

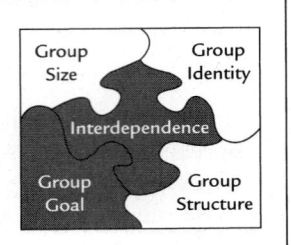

proceed, and group members' agreement on what should be accomplished. When relationships within a group are positive and strong, demands like these are easier to resolve. When relationships within a group are negative or weak, other issues surface. Groups with weak relationships require more interaction time to make effective decisions. Members often become more focused on healing poor relationships than on completing tasks. If group relationships cannot be mended, members will evaluate task outcomes negatively even when they are otherwise acceptable. A group that ignores the social demands that occur when individuals work together threatens the group's ability to effectively complete its task or activity. *Putting the Pieces Together* demonstrates how your group is influenced by its various task characteristics.

Task and Activity Constraints

Regardless of the type of group or type of task, four elements act as constraints and affect the group's ability to complete its task or activity. These constraints are time pressures, need to represent diverse views, degree to which the decision must be implemented, and outcome ambiguity (Wood & Phillips, 1990). The more these constraints are present, the more group members will have to work together to avoid or overcome their negative influence.

The first constraint is time pressure. The amount of time available for decision making or any task activity creates implications for group member interaction. When time pressures are high, groups are more likely to move quickly toward consensus. Sometimes this creates a **false consensus** where group members believe they all agree when they do not. Because group members know there is no additional time to gather information or debate issues, they keep silent when op-

"So, everyone agrees, right?"

False consensus is a common problem in group decision making. In this group, the Bartlett family is trying to decide on their vacation plans. Everyone believes that other family members agree with them on how to spend their time together. Unfortunately, it will be impossible for one vacation to satisfy the different vacation plans each family member prefers.

posing viewpoints have not been heard or adequately discussed. When time pressures are not as severe, group members have time to deliberate. However, when time is not seen as critical, groups often disregard the primary task and fill their time with other more pressing or interesting activities. Many of your classroom groups have been constrained by time pressures. Knowing you have six weeks to work on a group project, you encourage other members to put off meeting until the week before the project is due. When the group finally meets, it feels the pressure of performing well enough to get a decent grade. There does not seem to be adequate time to meet, find resources in the library, prepare the overhead transparencies and handouts, and practice the presentation. You may now wonder why you chose to wait so long to meet.

The second constraint is the need for representation of diverse views. When groups need to represent only the views that are held by group members, there is considerable freedom in how the group can go about their activities. Thompson family members deciding what activities to have at a family reunion are not concerned with individuals who are not family members. But a group making policy decisions must consider the impact of policy changes on a variety of people. Group members can act as subject matter experts when they represent their own issues. When views outside the group must be included, group members must rely on others for information, details, and facts. Individuals outside the group may or may not be powerful enough to persuade group members to bring divergent views into the group.

The third constraint is the degree to which decisions must be implemented by the group. It is easy to make decisions when the outcomes will not affect you personally or when you are not responsible for putting details into action. However, when the group's decision will have impact on the group members or when the group must implement the decision, group members are more likely to deliberate carefully—after all, their future is at stake. Members of the Thompson family must carefully consider what activities to suggest for the family reunion. If family members prefer card and board games, it may be useless to suggest more physically active sports like soccer or football.

Finally, **task outcome ambiguity** is the fourth constraint. When groups are asked to solve problems with known answers, ambiguity is low and group members are likely to have little interest in the problem and little interest in the process the group uses. In these situations, the group often defers to the member who can persuade other members that he or she knows the right answer. On the other hand, when a group starts on a task and members cannot predict the outcome, ambiguity is high. When a group is working on an ambiguous task, additional time and energy are required for group members to work through the uncertainty about their final objective. When such a condition exists, groups may be uncertain about which procedures and processes to use to help them solve their problem or complete their task. High ambiguity is common in decisions for which the determination of right or wrong is made when the solution is implemented (Jarboe, 1990). Unless your group is working on a disjunctive or intellective task, your task ambiguity is high because many possible outcomes can be effective and appropriate. The exercise in "Confronting Task Constraints" will help you understand how these obstacles have interferred with your group processes in the past.

Task and Activity Outcomes

Obviously, any decision made by a group is one type of outcome. But there are other outcomes that indicate how effectively group members are interacting. These are decision quality, members' satisfaction with the group's process, and group continuity (Hackman, 1990; Wood & Phillips, 1990). Researchers generally reserve these three characteristics for task groups, but they can apply to social or relational groups as well.

Groups make decisions, but not all of them are of high **decision quality.** One way to gauge group effectiveness is to monitor the quality of group decisions or activities. Standards of quality, quantity, and timeliness are commonly used to judge group output. Questions of quality include, Did the group make the best decision? Did the team play well enough? Questions of quantity include, Did the decisions made allow the group to accomplish all of its objectives? Did the team practice long enough to be in competitive form? Questions of timeliness include, Did the group use its time wisely? Was the project handed in on time? Individuals outside the group can also monitor or evaluate your group's decisions and activities. Were the group's recommendations acceptable to the vice-president? Did your team meet the early entry deadline? Did your ticket-selling team sell enough

> **THINK ABOUT IT**
>
> ### Confronting Task Constraints
>
> Think about your last group that solved a problem. What type of time pressures did the group feel? Were these pressures real or imagined? Were time pressures imposed by someone external to the group or by the group itself? To what extent did your group need to consider the opinions and view of others? If you did consider others' views, how well did you represent or introduce views different from those held by members of your group? Was the group responsible for implementing its decisions? If not, how did this affect the group's decision making? Finally, how much ambiguity characterized your task? Did group members know exactly what was expected of them? Or did the task lend itself to a number of potential outcomes?

tickets? In fact, the degree to which the group's output meets the standards of the people who receive, review, or use that output may be more important than how the group views its outcomes. Obviously, if a group generates an outcome that is unacceptable to others, it is one indication of the group's ineffectiveness. Particularly in organizational settings and in other situations where the group is tightly connected to its environment, the future of a group and its members may be more dependent on a subjective assessment from others than on any objective measure of the group's output.

In an ideal world, each group and each group member would want to strive for decisions and actions of the highest quality. Unfortunately, this is not always the case. Sometimes quality is not the most important issue. Time pressures may be so extreme that finding a solution—any solution—becomes the primary focus of the group. Quality is also diluted when member involvement in the group process is low or when group decisions do not directly affect group members. It is hard to be committed to a group decision when you are not responsible for it. If a quantity standard is imposed by others, group members may work to fulfill the standard without maximizing their abilities. Particularly when standards are imposed by others, developing group member agreement about the standards helps members identify the task and the standards as their own.

Member satisfaction with **group process** is a second outcome that groups should seek. When members do not trust or believe in the process the group is using, apathy develops, which distances group members from other members as well as the task. Members are more likely to be satisfied when their participation is encouraged, but those in groups with structure imposed on them may feel they are not in control of what happens. When the process of carrying out the group's work enhances the ability of members to work together, satisfaction with the task and satisfaction with the group increases. Although decision quality is more focused on task orientation, group process is relationally oriented.

Group continuity is the third outcome. Simply put, group members become more committed to the group, its members, the decisions or other tasks the group must perform, and the processes the group will use when group members know they will be together over time. This future orientation helps group members recognize that their current actions will affect their future as a group. Advocating a future orientation also helps a group focus on its goals.

Not every group achieves these three outcomes. Conflicts and disagreements create hostilities, which dampen group members' enthusiasm for working together. Ineffective information flow may create subgroups, hampering the sharing of information necessary to effective relationship building. Groups with more positive interaction strategies create effective interpersonal relationships, which strengthens the ability of group members to work together. Group members who work well together make complex or undesirable tasks easier to accomplish. Because effective interpersonal relationships are already in place, group members can move more quickly with the task or activity. This type of relationship resiliency is essential when groups are challenged by difficult tasks.

Chances for group continuity are increased when group experiences contribute to the growth and personal well-being of the group's members. This criterion focuses on the individual group member rather than on the task or the intragroup relationships identified in the other two outcomes. Group experiences should contribute to the skill development of each group member. Learning new meeting procedures, enhancing communicating abilities, or meeting some other individual need (for example, increased visibility in the organization) are a few examples of how group experiences contribute to the well-being of individuals. When group members feel that their individual needs are met through their group experiences, they are likely to be more satisfied with the group experience and more motivated to continue interacting with these group members.

The more involved each group member is in the group's task or activity, the more that group members will be motivated. Increased motivation should contribute to higher quality decisions and higher quality relational experiences. When group members experience cooperation rather than conflict, they typically will want to continue with their group. Group members whose tasks are always conflicted may grow weary of being in the group. Both cognitive and behavioral tasks can contribute to the growth and personal development of group members. Continuity and personal development increase a group member's identification with that particular group. When the group is seen as an opportunity for accomplishing both group and personal goals, desire to continue with that group is higher.

Summary

There are many types of groups, and there are many types of group tasks and activities. There are several ways to identify the type of group to which we belong. One way is to identify whether the group is formal or informal, personal or professional, and relational- or task-oriented. Communication in formal, task, or professional groups is usually more structured than communication in informal, relational, or personal groups. A second way to identify types of groups is to look at how long group members interact together and at the scope of the group's activities.

There is sometimes a link between type of group and type of group activity. But it is common for one group to be responsible for several different types of tasks. The typology of group tasks sorts tasks into those that are divisible or unitary and considers whether tasks or activities will be judged against some criteria. Using these two dimensions to identify groups, we can assess to what extent group members must work together.

The group task circumplex helps us identify tasks by looking at the amount of conflicted or cooperative interaction necessary and the degree of conceptual or behavioral activity required. These two dimensions result in tasks in which groups generate ideas, choose among alternatives, negotiate with others, and execute or perform some activity.

After the task type has been identified, tasks can also be evaluated for their task difficulty, solution multiplicity, intrinsic interest, population familiarity, acceptance level, area of freedom, and social complexity. By analyzing your group's task before you start, you will have a better understanding of how the task will challenge the group. Completion of tasks is hindered by four task constraints—time pressures, need to represent diverse views, degree to which the decision must be implemented, and outcome ambiguity.

Obviously, tasks are the outcome of group members' interactions. But there are other outcomes that indicate the effectiveness of group members' interaction. These are decision quality, members' satisfaction with the group's process, and group continuity.

✓ Checklist

Group Knowledge

You should be able to:
- explain the differences among formal and informal, personal and professional, and relational and task groups.
- differentiate between divisible and unitary tasks.
- describe how group tasks can be categorized by dimensions of conflict and cooperation and behavioral and cognitive activities.
- explain how task constraints can inhibit group performance.
- describe important outcomes for groups.

Group Skills

You should be able to:
- choose interaction strategies that optimize or maximize the group task.
- move easily among different types of group tasks.
- help your group identify and remove constraints affecting your task.

- use interaction strategies to help your group achieve positive group outcomes.

Analytical and Assessment Techniques

You should be able to:
- identify the type of task on which your group is working.
- redesign a task to take advantage of group members' skills, talents, and interests.
- recognize task constraints and point these out to other group members.
- identify the group's overall goal and break it into smaller goals of unique characteristics.

Discussion Questions and Exercises

1. In small groups of five to seven members, discuss what you would like to learn from this class (skills, processes, and so on). After this discussion, design a group task that will provide the opportunity to learn the skills and processes your group identified.

2. Reflect upon your recent group experiences, and write a short paper that answers the following questions: What types of group tasks and activities have been most frustrating to you? Why? What types of group tasks and activities do you find most exciting? Why?

3. Watch a situation comedy, drama, or film. Identify the types of groups and the types of group tasks portrayed. Are the portrayals positive or negative? Do the portrayals seem real to you? Why or why not? How well do the portrayals reflect your experiences with similar types of groups?

4. After your instructor gives you the parameters of a group task, put yourself in the following situation: You are responsible for helping the group with its task, but you will be out of town when the group meets. To help the group know what to do, write out instructions for completing the task. In class, exchange your written instructions with another student. Assess each set of instructions for completeness and clarity.

6 The Individual in the Group

Because I want others to like me, does that affect how I communicate in groups?

How does my personality affect my communication in a group?

What skills do I need to be an effective group or team member?

What should I do if I am apprehensive about communicating in groups?

What if my communication style does not fit with the styles of other group members?

Does the competence of individual group members make a difference in group settings?

Our focus in the previous chapters has been on the group—what defines a group, the communication within a group that creates micro systems, the external or macro environment of a group that impacts what a group does, and the types of groups and types of group tasks. Now our attention turns to you—the individual member in a group. We have seen that although individuals make up a group, effective group interaction and group productivity involve more than just people coming together. In this chapter, we will take a look at your communication role as an individual in a group. (The *Group Assessment Technique* illustrates the importance of communication skills in group interaction.) We will also explore issues of independence and identity that must be balanced with dependence on and interdependence with other group members.

When unique individuals come together to form a group, communication difficulties can arise. By assessing your personality and interaction style, you can find productive ways to work through the tensions that may develop in groups. We will begin the chapter with a discussion of your interpersonal needs that affect how you communicate in group settings. Then we will look at communication apprehension and how that anxiety may keep you from fulfilling group member obligations. Next we will discuss and evaluate the communication style you use in group settings. Knowing your current interaction style will help you develop more effective strategies to help your group achieve its goals. For instance, analysis of your communication style may reveal that you have the skills for diffusing tensions in the group or that you contribute to the tension.

GROUP ASSESSMENT TECHNIQUE

How Important Are Communication Skills?

Reflect for a moment on your present or past work group experience. In the job skills box, give yourself a score of 1 to 10 (1 is "no job skills," 5 is "moderate level of job skills," 10 is "all the job skills I need"). Job skills include all the technical knowledge and skills you need to be successful on the job. Now give yourself a score of 1 to 10 in the team/interactive skills box (1 is "no team/interactive skills," 5 is "moderate level of team/interactive skills," 10 is "all of the team/interactive skills I need"). Team and interactive skills include all of the communication skills needed at the interpersonal and group level to be an effective member of your work team.

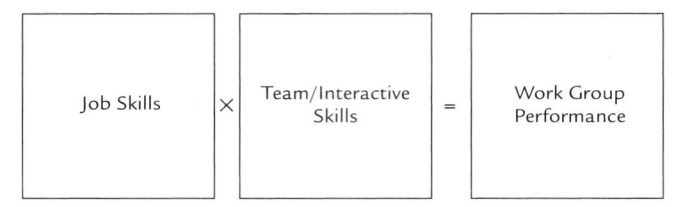

$$\text{Job Skills} \times \text{Team/Interactive Skills} = \text{Work Group Performance}$$

Now, multiply your score for job skills times your score for team/interactive skills. Scores should range from 1 to 100. How well did you score? This assessment should point out that regardless of how skilled you are at your job, your job performance is moderated by your level of team and interactive skills. Even if you gave yourself a 10 in job skills, that score multiplied by a 5 in team/interactive skills will diminish your overall effectiveness. Are you satisfied with your overall work group performance score? What steps could you take to enhance your score and your effectiveness in your work group?

Source: Adapted from Wellins, Byham, and Wilson (1991).

Your Group Interaction Style

Your interaction skills in group settings contribute to how others perceive you. How you present yourself and your ideas is a major factor in how others evaluate your worth as a group member. In fact, other members of your group are more likely to use your negative communication traits or lack of communication skills in developing impressions of you (Zimmermann, 1994). Thus how you communicate with other group members affects how your identity develops within the group and how well you work with others. You need two basic types of group skill competencies in group situations (Larson & LaFasto, 1989). First, you need to possess the necessary technical skills for group membership. These include the basic knowledge, skills, and abilities required for the group's activity. For example, to help your team win at a game of frisbee golf, you need a reasonable amount of skill in throwing and catching the frisbee as well as skills at motivating and cheering on other team members. Second, you need to possess personal characteristics that help you work with others. In a problem-solving group at work, for example, you need to demonstrate intelligence and creativity to help your group accomplish tasks that meet the standards set by your boss. The technical and personal skills needed will depend on the type of group and type of group task. Regardless of the type of group, members must display a desire to contribute and the capability of collaborating and cooperating with others (Larson & LaFasto, 1989).

Members of organizational work groups and those who participate in meetings overwhelmingly report that interpersonal problems and poor communication skills contribute most to unsuccessful group meetings (Di Salvo, Nikkel, & Monroe, 1989). Skills most frequently reported as contributing to group dysfunction were poor listening skill (for example, not paying attention when others are speaking), ineffective vocal quality (not speaking up so as to be heard by all group members), poor nonverbal presentation (fidgeting with notebooks while speaking), inability to clearly state the topic (taking an unnecessarily long time to describe a simple concept), and overuse of jargon or technical language (cool, stuff, you know, the ZBS, Form AE-100Z3-4).

Other communication behaviors that negatively affect group interaction include dominating conversations and demonstrating other behaviors designed to indicate one-upmanship or power, too much joking around, getting sidetracked during a group's conversation, and interrupting the speaker or talking over others. Participants in the research study also complained that some group members did not participate and that their lack of participation detracted from the group's success. There were three primary reasons given for why some members did not participate: lack of interest in the group, shyness, and wanting to avoid responsibility. Finally, group members reported that individuals who bring poor, defensive, or negative attitudes to their groups or meetings detract from the group's success. Thus a variety of negative group communication skills can hinder group progress. Are you guilty of any of these? Most of us are. Lack of motivation or commitment may have caused you to communicate ineffectively. Time pressures or role conflicts may have made you communicate differently than you would normally. For most of us, even if we believe we are effective group communicators, there are still a few skill areas that could be improved.

Each member brings a unique set of communication skills to the group setting. The more skilled you are and the more comfortable you are in displaying those skills, the more likely you will be perceived as an effective group member. It is important to increase your group skill level because skill deficiencies can obstruct the democratic process or create inequities in levels of participation. Often those perceived as having the most skill are given more opportunities to talk and more opportunities to direct discussion toward their concerns. When this happens, the skilled group member has a bigger impact on the group's overall interaction (Gastil, 1993).

Your group communication skills depend on three factors. The first factor is your need to associate with other individuals. Your level and type of interpersonal need fundamentally controls how you communicate in groups. Second, your level of anxiety or apprehension about working in a group or meeting with others may keep you from communicating often or well. If you are not apprehensive, it is more likely that you will join in the group's discussion as well as be a member of many groups. Third, your personality is largely responsible for the type of communication skills that you display. Personality-driven communication behaviors have been identified as communicator style. These factors—interpersonal needs, communication apprehension, and communicator style—are discussed in the next three sections.

Interpersonal Needs

Individuals have social needs—situations or conditions that can only be met by other people. This is what draws us to one another in groups to live, play, and work. FIRO-B (Fundamental Interpersonal Relationship Orientations-Behavior) (Schutz, 1966) describes three basic interpersonal needs—inclusion, affection, and control—that dictate your communication behavior in group settings. **Inclusion** is the need to establish and maintain satisfactory relations with others. We do this through interaction and association. Joining and communicating in groups allows us to work alongside those who have mutual interests. Identifying with other group members can help us satisfy this need. Each of these satisfies our need to be included and to include others. **Control** is the need to establish and share power and control with others and is often evident in group decision making. The degree to which we believe in our own competence and responsibilities is evaluated against the respect we hold for other members' competence and responsibilities. If we believe we are more competent, we take control. If we believe others are more competent, we let them take control. **Affection** is the need to establish psychologically close relationships with others. We do this through developing and maintaining close personal ties to others we meet in group settings. Affection is based on liking. Generally, we develop affection for those we like.

Each of these dimensions—inclusion, control, affection—is evident in group interaction in two ways. First, each dimension can be expressed or given by a group member. Expression of a dimension emphasizes the sender role. Each dimension can also be wanted, or desired, by a group member. Wanting dimensional needs from other group members emphasizes the receiver role. Thus a group member's communication behavior is affected by the degree of need on six variables: expressed inclusion, wanted inclusion, expressed control, wanted control, expressed affection, and wanted affection. Each group member has his or her own unique three-dimensional profile that is a mixture of expressed and wanted needs.

Each of the six needs and wants is also necessary in group interaction. If group members do not feel included, member identity with the group is likely to suffer. Thus members may drift away (physically or psychologically), hindering group member interdependence. If no one takes control, a group can easily get lost and not accomplish its goal. More submissive members may even desire that one group member help the group along. Although it is not necessary to develop intimate friendships with other members of a group, it is necessary for a moderate amount of affection to develop among group members. Trust among group members often

Table 6.1 *Wanted Needs and Expressed Needs in Group Communication*

	Wanted Needs	Expressed Needs Low	Expressed Needs High
Inclusion	High	Undersocial Social-compliant	Oversocial Social-compliant
	Low	Undersocial Countersocial	Oversocial Countersocial
		Low	High
Control	High	Abdicrat Submissive	Autocrat Submissive
	Low	Abdicrat Rebellious	Autocrat Rebellious
		Low	High
Affection	High	Underpersonal Personal-compliant	Overpersonal Personal-compliant
	Low	Underpersonal Counterpersonal	Overpersonal Counterpersonal

follows liking. Members of a group without any expressed affection may become suspicious or hostile, negating the opportunities to work together effectively.

Table 6.1 provides each dimensional possibility and demonstrates how expressed needs and wanted needs interact to predict behavior. A group member can represent any combination of expressed and wanted needs. For example, Yuichi has a high need to receive inclusion (undersocial, social-compliant) as well as a high need to receive control (abdicrat, submissive) from others. These are his wants, or the type of communication he desires from others. At the same time, he has a high need to give affection (overpersonal, personal-compliant) to others in the group. This is his expressed need and will influence how he communicates with other group members. If we examine the behaviors that characterize Yuichi's needs and wants, it is easy to see that Yuichi will not be a dominant member of the group. Rather, his needs and wants will probably result in communication that places him subordinate to other group members as he tries to make others like him and solicits inclusion and control cues from others. Will this make him an ineffective member? Not necessarily; it depends on how Yuichi's needs and wants interact with the needs and wants of other group members. In fact, Yuichi could be an extremely effective member if others in the group could provide the inclusion and control he desires. When this occurs, Yuichi will feel comfortable, which will create the opportunity for him to signal his liking (affection) for other group members.

The undersocial group member tends to be introverted and withdrawn. This group member avoids associating with groups in general and when she does join groups, is likely to say little. This group member may be late for meetings, schedule other activities to conflict with group sessions, or have reasons for leaving early. Conversely, the oversocial member seeks other people and wants them to seek him out. This person joins groups because he does not like being alone. Always seeking companionship, he may wait outside a meeting room for another member to arrive so they can walk in together.

The social-compliant group member is worried about fitting in. She constantly checks with other members to see if she is doing things correctly. She worries that if she performs poorly or makes a mistake, other group members will like her less. The countersocial group member does not seem to want anything from other group members. His lethargic or carefree manner may be disguising low self-esteem. The countersocial individual typically does not participate very much in group settings.

The abdicrat willingly takes on a submissive posture in groups to avoid being responsible for tasks and decisions. When someone else is in control, she does not feel responsible for problems the group experiences. The abdicrat willingly gives up responsibility in the group, hoping to also forgo accountability. The autocrat wants to control others and uses the group setting to gain status and power. An autocrat will likely emerge as a group's leader if other candidates are not present.

The submissive group member has such a high need to feel controlled by others that he is only active in the group if forced or pushed. Otherwise, the submissive member will say little and do little. The submissive member is often frustrating to other group members because they do not realize that the submissive is waiting for instructions from them. Conversely, the rebellious group member does not want to be controlled by other group members. Although the rebellious member believes that other group members should follow the norms and rules of the group, she also believes that the norms and rules do not pertain to her. These members are often mavericks with good ideas who bring creativity and innovation to the group, but sometimes at the price of cohesiveness.

The underpersonal group member appears detached from other group members. Others may interpret this detachment as lack of interest in the group's task or activity, but this is not necessarily the case. Although the underpersonal member may enjoy the group activity, he simply has little need to be socially demonstrative with others. On the other hand, the overpersonal group member uses the group setting as an opportunity to share her affection. This group member often agrees with everything others say. She does this because she does not want a disagreement between herself and another group member to detract from how much she likes the group.

The personal-compliant group member has a strong need to be liked. This need is so strong that he will do nearly anything another group member asks. This group member interprets interaction with him as a sign of affection, even when it is just an exchange of information. He will interpret others' initiations of conversation as a sign that they like him and want to develop a relationship. The counterpersonal group member is just the opposite. She has a very low need to receive affection from anyone. In fact, she may behave negatively in groups to confirm that others do not like her.

Achieving Need Compatibility

Compatibility in groups—and ease in communication—is achieved when there is a balance of group members who want to express a need and members who want to receive it. Generally, members whose interpersonal needs are compatible with other group members are more satisfied and effective as a group (Keyton, 1987). Compatibility should not be confused with liking; rather, it refers to how well group members are able to work together—especially groups that work together over a period of time. Compatibility is more a degree of how complementary group members are to one another. Can Sierra's high need for affection be met by anyone in the group? Ashton needs to be in control. Can the group give him a task for which he can be responsible? Tam needs to feel included. Perhaps she can partner with someone to work on activities rather than working by herself.

How much compatibility of needs must there be in a group for it to be effective? This depends on the type of group and type of task or activity. An effective social support group would have high compatibility on the inclusion and affection dimensions. A decision-making group would need compatibility on the control dimension. Must the numbers of group members who want a need be equal to the number of group members who express that need? No. Groups can very efficiently satisfy the expression and want of needs. A very dominant group member can satisfy several group members who need or want to be controlled. One very friendly member can satisfy the needs of several members who need a great deal of affection.

When a need incompatibility exists, however, the group will spend its time working out these differences. For example, each member of your car pool has a high need to control others. So when Bradley takes his turn at driving, he changes the route, affecting who is picked up first. Next week when Harris drives, he asserts control by changing the route to suit himself—once again, changing the time when car pool members are picked up. The third week when Bailey drives, she asserts control in a slightly different way. She keeps the route Harris established but insists that all group members follow her rules (no smoking in the car, silence during the newscast on the radio, wiping one's feet before entering the car), or she refuses to take her turn at driving. Conflict is likely to develop in this group of high controllers. And group members will have to spend time and energy sorting out their differences and coming to agreeable solutions.

Incompatibility can also create confusion. Let's use the election task force as an example. Five of the six task force members need to control others, but only Warren is willing to accept being controlled. As a result, Warren is unclear about how to proceed in setting up the voting booths because he gets several sets of conflicting instructions each time the task force meets. Lydia is one of four members of the task force with a high need to give affection to others. She is confused when Warren responds with a cold shoulder to her attempts to be friendly and personal. Lydia does not realize that with so many people trying to give Warren affection, he is afraid this group may become more personal and intimate than he desires or can handle. Thus when an incompatibility of needs exists within a group, anxiety is likely to develop. Once again, group members will need to work through these issues to effectively work on their task. "Finding Needs Embedded in Conversation" provides some practice at identifying needs that are expressed and wanted.

Communication Apprehension

Oral **communication apprehension** has been defined as fear or anxiety with either real or anticipated communication with other people (McCroskey, 1977). Viewed as a traitlike, personality-type variable, this communicative predisposition can influence how well you function as a group member (McCroskey & Richmond, 1987). Or, apprehension about communicating may only occur in certain contexts such as group meetings. Regardless of why you are apprehensive about communicating in groups, other group members typically perceive you as shy or reticent. In fact, communication apprehension may have greater negative implications in the small-group setting than in any other communication context (McCroskey & Richmond, 1992). It is almost impossible to avoid being in groups, and, in each group, several other members will evaluate your communication performance. What causes communication apprehension? Perhaps you had poor group experiences early in life, or you may have general communication anxiety—anxiety about speaking to others in many situations. Everyone experiences some group anxiety at some time. You may have been anxious about joining a particular group because you did not know the other group members. You may have felt anxious in a group meeting when your views were different from those being expressed. You may dislike groups because your experiences have taught you that being in a group means that you have to do the work of six, not the work of one.

Communication apprehension is most often thought of in public speaking situations, but many people express apprehension or anxiety about interacting in groups. Several studies (Burgoon, 1977; Heston, 1974; McCroskey, 1977) have demonstrated that those individuals who were reticent—or anxious about interaction in general—interacted less frequently in small groups than nonreticent individuals. More importantly, the contributions of group members who display anxiety to others are typically judged to be less relevant than the contributions of nonreticent group members. Apprehensive group members are also perceived by other group members as less credible, less effective, less likely to be sought for an opinion within a group, or less likely to emerge as the group's leader than nonreticent individuals (McCroskey & Richmond, 1976; McKinney, 1982). Why does this happen? The more apprehensive you are, the more likely it is that your voice is not powerful or forceful enough to be heard by other group members. Or your voice may express nervousness. You might even find that your apprehension is so strong that you remain silent even when you have something useful to say.

How other group members perceive you is important. Even though others make judgments about you before you even speak, evaluations of what you are really like as a person and a group member are made through how you communicate. High apprehensive group members even have lower opinions of themselves

BUILDING ANALYTICAL SKILLS

Finding Needs Embedded in Conversation

Let's join Kat, Patrick, Hanna, and JJ as they work on a new brochure for their university's department of communication. The department chair has asked members of the communication students' honor association to help design a new brochure. Let's see how they are doing.

KAT: Are you done?

PATRICK: Okay, I just want to work out the details on the last paragraph before I give it to Hanna.

KAT: Okay. I'm sorry.

HANNA: Our proposal is to consolidate information into a small pack, a pamphlet, that could easily incorporate deadlines, phone numbers, points of contact, and the like. This plan is to be the model for the remainder of the university while being the prototype for the communication department. I stop there.

PATRICK: I like it. Doesn't everyone like it?

HANNA: And I've also started a cover letter, but it's . . . it's just the normal basic stuff.

KAT: I have one small problem. The advising center repeatedly tells us that the goal of the university is not to educate us to graduate. If we keep emphasizing this in our copy . . .

PATRICK: I think Kat's right.

KAT: . . . if we keep emphasizing only graduation, I think we'll turn them off. Then they won't use the pamphlet.

PATRICK: Right.

KAT: That's my only problem.

HANNA: I don't believe it. It's impossible for you to have only one problem. Let's hear the rest.

KAT: It's not just the goal of the university I'm talking about; it's the goal of the pamphlet. Maybe we reword that . . .

PATRICK: Yeah.

KAT: No, I liked it. I just . . .

HANNA: I always like to do a rough and just throw it out. Okay, here, Kat. Fix it.

KAT: The advising center makes such a big deal about that, and I think that if we're selling it to the university, we really ought to broaden the goal statement.

JJ: Hmm, I made some possible goals . . . just wrote them out, and there are a whole bunch of them here. I'm just playing with words, but maybe you'd like it better if we could use the phrase "for students seeking a degree through the communication department," so our specific goal is to get students through the program with something, not just to graduate because they have the necessary hours.

PATRICK: Okay.

JJ: I don't know. It's your decision.

HANNA: Well?

KAT: Hold on. I just had a brief flash of inspiration that may not be worth mentioning. We were trying to come up with a phrase that could combine, you know, education and communication and graduating. Okay, I've lost them already. But something along the lines of, ummm, "information for students seeking to educate themselves in communication with the objective of graduating with a B.A. degree from the University of Wabash."

What needs do members express? What needs do members appear to want? What communication cues are you using to make those assessments? Does there appear to be need compatibility within this group? What needs aren't being met? What's the basis for your evaluation and opinions?

(Hawkins & Stewart, 1991). High apprehensive group members rated themselves as possessing and demonstrating fewer leadership skills. Other group members agreed with their assessments and rated them as being less socially and task attractive than people who were less apprehensive. This type of apprehensive behavior extends beyond the structured conversations of groups to the informal communication that precedes group interaction. Not wanting to engage in small talk may exclude high apprehensives from the informal interactions where relationships are built and maintained.

Talking less may seem like a good way to manage your apprehension, but in fact it may be interpreted by others as an unwillingness to communicate, which can further lead to the perception that you are unwilling to help the group. What can you do to overcome communication apprehension in groups? Initially, limit your group experiences to those with which you are most comfortable. As you gain group experience and have access to a greater repertoire of group skills, continue to broaden your participation in groups. Allowing yourself to experience group settings will help lessen your level of apprehension (Rubin, Rubin, & Jordan, 1997). When you do feel anxious in a group, find another group member and develop a one-on-one relationship with him or her. People are often more comfortable in dyadic interactions. Once you are comfortable communicating with this other group member, then you can use this relationship as a base for dealing with the group. Sit near this person in group meetings so you feel supported. Volunteer for group tasks you know you can accomplish (before you are assigned a task you are not comfortable with). This will build your confidence in speaking out in the group setting and contributing to the group's outcome. It is important to assess your level of group apprehensiveness and work to control or overcome those feelings (see "What Is Your Level of Communication Apprehension?"). Being anxious about communicating in group settings will affect how you interact with others and can result in them perceiving you as not caring about the group or its task.

Communicator Style

Another way to examine your interaction in groups is to assess your **communicator style.** When you communicate with others, you leave an impression, that is, your communicator style. Simply, it is your way of communicating both verbally and nonverbally (Norton, 1983). Your communicator style is observable and interpreted by others (Norton, 1978). Style messages are signals to others about how to process the content of your messages. Style adds the color, tone, and rhythm to your messages; it works to create a distinct signature of your communication. Thus style gives direction, form, or guidance to others about how the content of your messages should be understood. In effect, it is a message about content—a message about a message (Norton & Brenders, 1996).

Communicator style is characterized by ten constructs: **dominant, dramatic, animated, impression leaving, relaxed, attentive, open, friendly, contentious,** and **precise** (Bednar, 1981; Montgomery & Norton, 1981). The way you communicate content is inextricably part of any message. Thus not only should you be

> **? THINK ABOUT IT**
>
> ### What Is Your Level of Communication Apprehension?
>
> Think about two different groups: one social group and one task group. Did you feel apprehensive about communicating in either one? both? neither? What do you think caused you to feel apprehensive? Did you come to the group situations with that level of apprehension, or did something happen within the group to make you feel apprehensive? If you were apprehensive, what did you do to control or compensate for your anxiety? If you are seldom apprehensive in group situations, how could you help another group member who displays communication apprehension?

aware of the style, but you should also develop style flexibility to meet the changing demands of group interaction. One style profile (friendly, open, and relaxed) may work well in creating relationships, but you may need another style profile (dominant and precise) in defending your point of view when others question it. Use "Determining Your Communicator Style" to figure out your communicator style profile in group settings.

From "Determining Your Communicator Style" you should have a good sense of your predominant style. You may have scored 10 or above on several constructs. Let's see how these constructs work together to paint a picture of you as a communicator. For example, Virginia is contentious, dominant, and animated. Her forceful communicator style is effective for her as she leads her community group in political activities. But her style might be overwhelming for other group members when the group is working to establish trusting relationships. Anika is friendly, open, and relaxed. It is easy for her to engage others in conversation. However, she seldom starts a conversation; she almost always waits for other members to initiate the conversation. Others might interpret this type of style as being submissive or hesitant to take on responsibility. Each of the style characteristics can be effective or ineffective depending on the group situation. As you assess and interpret your style, be careful that you do not make assumptions about a particular characteristic, for instance, expecting that if you have a dominant style, your contributions are always constructive or effective. Quantity does not equal quality. You may talk a lot in the group but contribute little to the topic of the conversation (Hansford & Diehl, 1988).

How effectively does your style work for you? Is your style more effective in some group situations than others? The more scores you have of 10 or higher indicates the degree to which you can flexibly move among communication strategies. How would you assess your flexibility? Consider yourself to have well-developed flexibility if you scored 10 or higher on at least five characteristics. Effective communicators can flexibly respond to different groups and different types of group situations. With practice, you can increase your style flexibility and your ability to select the most effective style based on the communication situation.

GROUP ASSESSMENT TECHNIQUE

Determining Your Communicator Style

Thinking of how you generally communicate in groups, answer each question using the following scale:

0 = never   1 = infrequently   2 = sometimes   3 = frequently   4 = often

#	Statement	Scale
1.	I am comfortable with all varieties of people.	0 1 2 3 4
2.	I laugh easily.	0 1 2 3 4
3.	I readily express admiration for others.	0 1 2 3 4
4.	What I say usually leaves an impression on people.	0 1 2 3 4
5.	I leave people with an impression of me that they definitely tend to remember.	0 1 2 3 4
6.	To be friendly, I verbally acknowledge others' contributions.	0 1 2 3 4
7.	I am a very good communicator.	0 1 2 3 4
8.	I have some nervous mannerisms in my speech.	0 1 2 3 4
9.	I am a very relaxed communicator.	0 1 2 3 4
10.	When I disagree with others, I am very quick to challenge them.	0 1 2 3 4
11.	I can always repeat back to a person exactly what was meant.	0 1 2 3 4
12.	The sound of my voice is very easy to recognize.	0 1 2 3 4
13.	I am a very precise communicator.	0 1 2 3 4
14.	I leave a definite impression on people.	0 1 2 3 4
15.	The rhythm or flow of my speech is sometimes affected by nervousness.	0 1 2 3 4
16.	Under pressure, I come across as a relaxed speaker.	0 1 2 3 4
17.	My eyes reflect exactly what I am feeling when I communicate.	0 1 2 3 4
18.	I dramatize a lot.	0 1 2 3 4
19.	I always find it very easy to communicate on a one-to-one basis with people I do not know very well.	0 1 2 3 4
20.	Usually, I deliberately react in such a way that people know that I am listening to them.	0 1 2 3 4
21.	Usually, I do not tell people much about myself until I get to know them well.	0 1 2 3 4
22.	I tell jokes, anecdotes, and stories when I communicate.	0 1 2 3 4
23.	I tend to constantly gesture when I communicate.	0 1 2 3 4
24.	I am an extremely open communicator.	0 1 2 3 4
25.	I am vocally a loud communicator.	0 1 2 3 4
26.	In a small group of people I do not know very well, I am a very good communicator.	0 1 2 3 4
27.	In arguments or differences of opinion, I insist upon very precise definitions.	0 1 2 3 4
28.	In most situations, I speak very frequently.	0 1 2 3 4
29.	I find it extremely easy to maintain a conversation with a member of the opposite sex.	0 1 2 3 4
30.	I like to be strictly accurate when I communicate.	0 1 2 3 4

31. Because I have a loud voice, I can easily break into a conversation.   0 1 2 3 4
32. Often I physically and vocally act out when I want to communicate.   0 1 2 3 4
33. I have an assertive voice.   0 1 2 3 4
34. I readily reveal personal things about myself.   0 1 2 3 4
35. I am dominant in conversations.   0 1 2 3 4
36. I am very argumentative.   0 1 2 3 4
37. Once I get wound up in a heated discussion, I have a hard time stopping myself.   0 1 2 3 4
38. I am an extremely friendly communicator.   0 1 2 3 4
39. I really like to listen very carefully to people.   0 1 2 3 4
40. I insist that other people document or present some kind of proof for what they are arguing.   0 1 2 3 4
41. I try to take charge of things when I am with people.   0 1 2 3 4
42. It bothers me to drop an argument that is not resolved.   0 1 2 3 4
43. In most situations I tend to come on strong.   0 1 2 3 4
44. I am very expressive nonverbally.   0 1 2 3 4
45. The way I say something usually leaves an impression on people.   0 1 2 3 4
46. Whenever I communicate, I tend to be very encouraging to people.   0 1 2 3 4
47. I actively use a lot of facial expressions when I communicate.   0 1 2 3 4
48. I verbally exaggerate to emphasize a point.   0 1 2 3 4
49. I am an extremely attentive communicator.   0 1 2 3 4
50. As a rule, I openly express my feelings and emotions.   0 1 2 3 4

First, change your scores for items 8, 15, and 21: if 4, change it to 0; if 3, change it to 1; if 2, leave it a 2; if 1, change it to 3; if 0, change it to 4. After changing scores for these three items, transfer your scores to the following chart. Then add across the rows for a total score for each row. Your scores for each row should be between 0 and 16.

3 ___	6 ___	38 ___	46 ___	Total ___	Friendly
4 ___	5 ___	14 ___	45 ___	Total ___	Impression Leaving
8 ___	9 ___	15 ___	16 ___	Total ___	Relaxed
10 ___	36 ___	37 ___	42 ___	Total ___	Contentious
11 ___	20 ___	39 ___	49 ___	Total ___	Attentive
13 ___	27 ___	30 ___	40 ___	Total ___	Precise
17 ___	23 ___	44 ___	47 ___	Total ___	Animated
18 ___	22 ___	32 ___	48 ___	Total ___	Dramatic
21 ___	24 ___	34 ___	50 ___	Total ___	Open
28 ___	35 ___	41 ___	43 ___	Total ___	Dominant

(continued)

Determining Your Communicator Style *continued*

1. Circle your scores of 10 and above. These represent your predominant communicator style. This style is the one you use most often and the one you believe is normal for you. What are the advantages of such a style profile in a group setting? What are the disadvantages of your style profile in group interaction?
2. Read the descriptions of the styles that follow. Which styles do you believe you need to develop to be more effective in group settings?

Animated	This communicator uses expressive nonverbal behaviors such as facial expressions, eye contact, gestures, and body movements that reveal feelings; lively and expressive; emotional state is easy for others to read.
Attentive	This communicator attends to others in ways that let others know they are being listened to; closely related to friendly; considered a good listener, empathic, pays attention to the speaker; listens carefully and reacts deliberately.
Contentious	This communicator has a tendency to be argumentative and wants to debate points; is also quick to challenge others; demands that others back up their assertions with evidence.
Dominant	This communicator desires to take charge and control interaction; confident, forceful, active, and self-assured; talks more than others and more loudly; is less compliant.
Dramatic	This communicator has a tendency to dramatize points through exaggeration, emphasis, joking, story telling, and other dramatic devices; uses metaphor, rhythm, and voice to emphasize content.
Friendly	This communicator gives positive recognition to others through behavior that encourages and validates; closely related to attentive; affectionate, sociable, and tactful; encourages others, consistently acknowledging others' contributions.
Impression Leaving	This communicator is remembered by his or her manner of communicating; others remember what this person says and how he or she says it.
Open	This communicator is frank, approachable, and willing to disclose information about one's self; outspoken, gregarious, extroverted, and easy to read; readily reveals personal information about self.
Precise	This communicator reflects a concern for accurate and precise communication of ideas.
Relaxed	This communicator displays little anxiety and appears relaxed to others; calm, collected, confident; relaxed even when under pressure, not tense.

Source: Adapted from Norton (1978).

Examine these photos showing group members with different communicator styles. The styles are dominant and contentious (top left), animated and dramatic (top right), and friendly and open (bottom). Imagine being in a group with each of these individuals. How would their communicator styles contribute to or inhibit the group's interaction?

Group Communication Competence

Competent group communicators know how to communicate, when to communicate, and are able to communicate. Thus **communication competence** is the ability and willingness to participate responsibly in a communication transaction. The goal of a competent communicator is to maximize the outcome of shared meaning with other group members (Littlejohn & Jabusch, 1982). To maximize outcomes, group members must communicate with both appropriateness and effectiveness (Spitzberg & Cupach, 1984, 1989). **Effectiveness** is achieved when the goal of the interaction is achieved. If a group needs to make a decision, group members are only effective to the extent that an acceptable decision is made. **Appropriateness** is achieved when a group member communicates without violating behavioral expectations for that group context. Appropriate communication would not weaken relationships among communicators nor would it threaten any member's self-esteem. Appropriateness is synonymous with tact and politeness. Within a decision-making context, group members are appropriate when they do not shout at one another, make derogatory comments, or call one another names. Recognize, however, that behavior considered inappropriate for decision-making groups may be appropriate for sports teams—if the name calling is in jest and is a norm among players.

Three skills are needed to achieve competence as a group communicator (Littlejohn & Jabusch, 1982). First, competent communicators are able to comprehend the group situation and understand the dynamics of what is happening in the group. Group members who can describe and then analyze the process of the group are reflective. They think back to the group situation—think about what happened, why it happened, and what could have been changed to create a better group environment. To be reflective, you must be able to analyze your own behavior in the group as well as the behavior of other group members. Once you have trained yourself to reflect on your group experiences and analyze what happened, you will be better at selecting more appropriate and more effective behaviors in similar situations in the future. Ask yourself these questions to gauge your ability to reflect upon a past group experience: Can you identify the rules for communicating that the group is establishing? Do you know what informal and formal roles other members are performing? Do the roles with which you communicate fit effectively with the roles of other groups members and help the group accomplish its goals? The better you understand the dynamics of the group's conversation, the better you can choose how you will participate. The *Think About It, Group Assessment Technique, Putting the Pieces Together,* and *Building Analytical Skills* exercises can help you increase your ability to assess group situations.

Second, competent communicators are sensitive to the feelings of others. They watch for clues in the group's interaction to help them adapt messages to other group members. You notice that Nahini is being quiet; she looks troubled. During a break in the meeting, you ask if she is okay and do not pry when she says she does not want to talk about it. Back in the meeting, you sit next to her, giving her encouraging smiles and nodding when she does participate. In another classroom group, you know that today's discussion on affirmative action issues will require sensitivity. To help group members talk to one another without creating overly emotional responses, you initiate the conversation by tactfully asking how members prefer to identify themselves. Your attempt to be sensitive to others' feelings may keep another group member from using a label or identifier that makes half of the group angry. When you are sensitive to other group members and use situationally appropriate behaviors, your behavior will be interpreted as attentive and empathic. This contributes to a supportive environment for the group.

Third, competent communicators have verbal and nonverbal skills that contribute effectively to the group's conversation. A skilled communicator can give feedback, ask questions, answer questions, talk about an idea without getting sidetracked, and listen to others and to new ideas. The only way to increase your group communication skills is to participate, assess your interaction abilities, make adjustments, and try new communication strategies. The communicator style questionnaire in the *Group Assessment Technique* can help you describe your current communicator style. You might want to ask a group member whom you trust to complete the communicator style assessment for you. Receiving information about your style from another person's perspective will give you a broader picture of how you communicate. If the assessment reveals some weakness (for example, you have low relaxed and attentive scores), you can monitor your behavior in your next group situation and work consciously to be more relaxed and attentive (such as taking a few minutes before the meeting to concentrate on this group's task, removing distractions to avoid fidgeting, increasing eye contact with other members).

A competent communicator is both effective and appropriate. A group member can communicate appropriately but be ineffective. And an effective communicator may offend other members while achieving the group's goal. Thus, it requires both effectiveness and appropriateness to be competent. Group members need knowledge about effectiveness and appropriateness and need to be able to make decisions about which behaviors would be effective and appropriate in a group setting and then act on that decision. It is not enough to know how to communicate: Group members must demonstrate competence when they interact with others.

Being competent means that a group member demonstrates greater flexibility. This is especially important because communication competence is culturally bound. (We will explore diversity in groups in Chapter 7.) Group settings vary widely based on the task or activity of the group and the cultural diversity of the group's membership. Thus to be competent you must select the behaviors that fit this particular group situation. This characteristic is known as **responsiveness.** A responsive group member is someone who can communicate appropriately and effectively based on the parameters of a particular group situation. Generally, members who are apprehensive in group settings are more likely to have difficulty in being responsive, and members who are more responsive are more likely to be satisfied with their group experiences (Anderson & Martin, 1995). "How Competent Are You?" will give you a good idea of your communication competence.

Informal Interaction

Individuals engage in group interaction to accomplish some goal, perform some activity, or satisfy some need. Besides these outcomes, groups are also the setting for developing personal relationships—ones that extend beyond the group. Groups are a great place to get to know others. The **informal interaction** that occurs before most meetings or group sessions helps group members break the ice

GROUP ASSESSMENT TECHNIQUE

How Competent Are You?

Think about your most recent group situation. Read each of the following statements and rate yourself on the continuum from weak (little or no skill in this area) to strong (satisfactory skill in this area).

Is skilled at initiating and managing topics of conversation	weak __ __ __ __ strong
Is able to ask open-ended questions	weak __ __ __ __ strong
Uses complete sentences	weak __ __ __ __ strong
Avoids uses of nonverbal fillers (uhhh, ummm)	weak __ __ __ __ strong
Looks at others while speaking	weak __ __ __ __ strong
Nods to encourage others while they speak	weak __ __ __ __ strong
Avoids fidgeting while speaking	weak __ __ __ __ strong
Speaks clearly (tone and speed)	weak __ __ __ __ strong
Focuses body posture toward other group members	weak __ __ __ __ strong
Avoids irrelevant responses	weak __ __ __ __ strong
Describes ideas in detail	weak __ __ __ __ strong
Is able to express opinions without being overly emotional	weak __ __ __ __ strong
Provides clarifications	weak __ __ __ __ strong
Monitors talking time to create equality	weak __ __ __ __ strong
Laughs and smiles appropriately	weak __ __ __ __ strong
Uses gestures to emphasize conversation	weak __ __ __ __ strong
Shows appropriate facial expressions	weak __ __ __ __ strong
Expresses empathy to others	weak __ __ __ __ strong

How would you assess your communication competence as a group member? Did you notice any patterns in your responses? Were your verbal competencies stronger or weaker than your nonverbal competencies? Which aspect of your competency needs the most improvement? effectiveness or appropriateness?

---

and settle into the task; at the same time it provides an introduction of you to other group members. Informal interaction also occurs when groups split into subgroups to work on subtasks. Here the interaction is less formal, and you have the opportunity to establish a working partnership with someone as well as possibly a personal relationship.

Informal communication outside the group setting often provides additional opportunities for group members to discuss ideas, particularly sensitive ones. For example, Lainey belongs to a civic group that needs to raise $500,000 to stay in

> **PUTTING THE PIECES TOGETHER**
>
> *Interdependence and Group Goal*
>
> Think of your one favorite group. With which group member do you most often communicate informally? Do you talk to him or her during meetings and activities, or do you wait until after the group is finished? What do you talk about? something that happened in the group? other members in the group? things that have nothing to do with the group? How does this informal interaction affect your relationships with other members? Does it affect how well you work together? how well you communicate? Does your informal interaction ever interfere with the group's accomplishment of its goal?

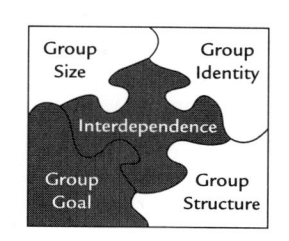

operation. She believes she has a great idea, but she is hesitant to bring it before the entire group membership. Lainey's a new member and not sure how others will accept her idea. But she is willing to talk privately with Harold, another group member, to test the viability of her idea. This type of off-side informal communication provides an alternative for introducing Lainey's idea into the group's discussion. Now that she has talked with Harold, she knows that he is in basic support of her idea. This supplementary communication channel can be advantageous when you need to build alliances, test ideas, or reduce interaction tensions. It is most likely that you will seek group members for whom you have the most trust and respect for this type of conversation.

Similarly, informal communication channels can serve as a check on what you think you heard in the group's discussion. Here, the informal communication acts to confirm or disconfirm what you took away from the larger group meeting. For example, earlier Lainey thought she heard that members of her civic group wanted to stay with tested methods of raising funds. But did she really hear that? Maybe Lainey heard others' frustrations with their previous experiences with half-baked ideas. The informal communication channels Lainey has established outside the formal group setting can provide her with additional information and clarification before she proceeds.

Be warned, however. Overusing informal communication channels or exclusively using informal communication channels may be perceived as strategic manipulation by group members who are outside your informal network. Also be careful of using your informal network for gossiping about other group members. Your informal network is linked to other informal networks, and any gossip is likely to reach unintended receivers. When it does, your informal interaction has weakened the group experience, not facilitated it. *Putting the Pieces Together* gives you a chance to see how informal communication works in your groups.

Maintaining Identity and Independence

Our society values groups, but more frequently we are rewarded for our individual achievements. In fact, your individual achievement, skills, or talents may be the very reason you were selected to be a member of a particular group. This is particularly true in team sports and organizational settings. When you join a group or team, it is important to build and maintain a group identity. But this does not mean you have to give up your individual identity. Besides identifying yourself as one of the group, you will want to maintain your uniqueness for several reasons. First, you are only valuable to the group if you continue to bring your unique skills, talents, and ideas to the group setting. If all group members have the same skills and talents and think alike, would it really be necessary to have a group?

Second, your connection to the many different groups you belong to helps create one part of your identity, and your identity helps others relate to you. Has something like the following happened to you? You walk into a classroom at the beginning of the semester. You are afraid that you will not know anyone in the class. But suddenly, another student recognizes you, saying, "I remember you, you were in my lab group."

A third reason for maintaining identity and independence from a group is to enhance your sense of fulfilling your own needs. We may elect to be a part of particular groups because it provides us with prestige or visibility. Joining a task force of the chamber of commerce may provide you with new leads to explore for sales. Joining a community or civic group when you arrive in a new town provides opportunities for creating personal relationships. Finally, you may join certain groups simply because you like the activity they provide. After all, you cannot play volleyball by yourself. When we voluntarily join groups, we have some personal motivation for doing so. This does not mean we cannot be effective group members. On the contrary, our motivation for joining makes us more effective in the group because we want to be accepted and liked by other group members. We join groups because we like the task or activity of the group, we like (or think we will like) the people in the group, or because the group is a means for accomplishing a personal goal or fulfilling a personal need.

Even when we are volunteered by someone for a group, we can often find ways to meet our individual needs. Next time you find yourself in this situation, look around at the other group members. Who is there that you do not know? Could this person be helpful to you—as a friend? as a colleague? as a connection or reference for a job you are seeking? When we find ways to make our group memberships fulfill our individual needs, we become more committed to the group. Not only does the group need us, we need the group.

Summary

To the extent that you want to appear to others to be effective, successful, and competent, group skills are important. In fact, your communication skills moderate everything you do in a group. In particular, your negative and lack of inter-

Maintaining identity with one group to which you belong is always balanced by your membership in other groups. Your identity—who you believe you are and how you represent that to others—is largely defined by the group memberships you maintain.

action skills contribute to how others perceive you. Group members frequently report that interpersonal problems and poor communication skills are the largest influence on unsuccessful group meetings.

At the most basic level, our communication in groups is based on our interpersonal needs. Needs are expressed on dimensions of inclusion, control, and affection. Reciprocally, we want to receive inclusion, control, and affection from other group members. Compatibility in groups—and ease in communication— are achieved when there is a balance of group members who want to express a need and members who want to receive it. When need incompatibility exists, a group will spend more of its time working out these relational differences than it will effectively working on the task.

Some individuals are communication apprehensive, particularly in group situations. Anxiety may result from earlier negative group experiences, or it may arise when you do not know other group members or you are unfamiliar with the group's task. The only way to overcome communication apprehension is to put yourself in comfortable group situations so you can practice talking with others.

Your communicator style is the impression you leave with other group members based on how you communicate verbally and nonverbally. There are ten communicator style characteristics: dominant, dramatic, animated, impression leaving, relaxed, attentive, open, friendly, contentious, and precise. You probably have a style profile of several of these characteristics that you routinely use in groups. The greater your flexibility using different style profiles, the more likely you will be successful in groups.

Evaluations of your group communication competence are based on how effectively and appropriately you communicate. Effective communicators achieve their goals, and appropriate communicators do so without damaging the esteem of others. Again, greater flexibility among communication styles will allow you to be responsive to individuals in all types of groups.

You probably engage in informal interaction while you are in groups. You do this to get to know other group members, break the ice, discuss sensitive ideas, or test out new ideas by introducing new topics to just a few of the group's members. This type of informal interaction helps you maintain your identity and independence from other group members because it highlights your unique talents and skills.

✓ Checklist

Group Knowledge

You should be able to:

- explain how communication moderates other task or job knowledge.
- differentiate between expressed needs and wanted needs.
- explain how the interpersonal needs of group members can be compatible.
- describe the effects of communication apprehension on group communication.
- define the characteristics that make up your communicator style.
- explain why being knowledgeable about group communication is only part of being communicatively competent.
- describe how the informal interaction of group members can contribute to a member's identity.

Group Skills

You should be able to:

- change your communication behavior to meet the interpersonal needs of other group members.
- minimize anxiety-causing elements for other group members.
- select the communicator style that is most effective and appropriate for several different group situations.
- maintain a suitable level of communication competence even when you are challenged or provoked.
- contribute to a positive informal environment within your group.

Analytical and Assessment Techniques

You should be able to:
- extract the needs of other group members by listening to the conversation.
- identify your own interpersonal needs in group settings.
- determine which needs of others are not being met and take steps to meet them.
- distinguish between the communication apprehension of other group members and their potential need to remain silent.
- assess the communicator style of other group members and then be flexible in your style.
- identify which components of communication competence are weak in your group.

Discussion Questions and Exercises

1. Think back to your favorite group situation. Write a short paper responding to these questions: How was the communicator style you displayed in the group different from or similar to how you generally interact in groups? How would you describe your interaction effectiveness? How would other communicator styles have helped your group complete its task or activity?

2. Watch a sitcom, drama, or film that features group interaction. Pay particular attention to the main characters. Do the characters display any evidence of communication apprehension? How do other characters react to the apprehension? What advice would you give to the character who was apprehensive? What advice would you give to the other group members about helping the apprehensive member?

3. In small groups of five to seven members, develop a communication profile of the ideal group member. Describe this member's interpersonal needs, level of communication apprehension, communicator style, and communication competence. How different are you from this ideal group communicator? Do you wish you had any of these attributes? What could you do to be more like this ideal communicator?

4. Think of three group members with whom you had difficulty communicating in the past. Using expressed and wanted needs, identify the interpersonal need structure for each individual. How did your communicator style meet or address the needs of these individuals? How could you have changed your communicator style to better meet their needs?

5. Sometimes people are unaware of their own needs. How would you help a group member understand the needs she or he expresses or desires from other members?

7 Communicating to Build Relationships in Your Group

How can I create closeness in a group?

Will being cohesive also make us satisfied with our task or activity?

Do cohesive groups perform better?

Why is power always an issue in groups?

What can I do to increase my power?

Why do some group members not play by the rules?

Do men and women communicate differently in groups?

Is diversity an issue for groups to consider?

The group is a social context. People come together to do some task or activity. This cannot be done without creating relationships among group members. Some relationships are characterized as positive, some as negative. This chapter will explore the communication relationships among group members that result in cohesiveness, satisfaction, and power dynamics. Tensions can develop within groups through a misuse of power or a lack of trust. Other tensions are caused by interacting with individuals who are different from you. Many groups are composed of both males and females and of members of many races and ethnic backgrounds. Because of these differences, each member contributes positive or negative energy to the group's micro system from which group member relationships are born.

Your Relationship to Others: Dependence

Some group tasks and activities force your dependence on other members within the group. **Dependence** may also be created with individuals outside the group when resources are only obtainable from external sources. Being dependent on another group member is different from being interdependent with others. At the interpersonal level, dependence means there is a connection between you and the group and its group members, but this connection has you in a subordinate position. Perhaps you are a new member and you have not quite found your role within the group. Or perhaps by nature you are more submissive than dominant. This is likely to put you in a more dependent relationship with other group members. In a dependent relationship, the reciprocity is imbalanced—one person gives more than another. This is not unusual in groups. However, you certainly would not want to be dependent on all other group members. In such a situation, you would not be perceived as contributing or as being a useful member of the group.

Jamal's classroom group was having a great deal of trouble dealing with an overly dependent member. Initially, Paula seemed to be an integral member of the group, contributing and bringing outside resources into the group. Gradually Paula's participation declined. Eventually, she was coming late to group meetings, failing to complete her assigned group tasks, and contributing very little to the group's interaction and output. Jamal believed that Paula considered other events in her life more important than this group. Other group members agreed with Jamal's interpretation. Interestingly, though, other group members *helped* Paula become dependent. As her contributions lessened, others took up her slack. They graciously brought her up to date when she was late. Jamal double-teamed her on many assignments so he was always ready to present her part if Paula did not pull through. In fact, Jamal and the other group members helped to create the overdependence as much as Paula did. When Paula perceived that the other group members were willing to help her out (she did not ask and she did not provide a reason for her lack of participation), she backed off even more. In this case, Paula's dependence on others was not because she was a new member. Initially, Paula's interaction style would not be characterized as submissive. The group simply reacted to her declining participation, and through their own behavior reinforced Paula's behavior as acceptable. In this case, dependence was unhealthy for both Paula and the group.

Your Relationship with Others: Interdependence

In contrast to dependence, interdependence is defined as equally balanced relationships within the group. It can also be defined as the extent to which your behavior in the group is influenced by other group members. Both of these concepts contribute to the group's ability to perform its task or achieve its goals. Remember that interdependence is one of the key elements in defining a group. Without interdependence a group fails to exist. There is a real advantage for group members to be interdependent on one another. Truly effective interdependence can only develop when group members have managed or resolved their problems. When interdependence exists, expectations develop about how group members will interact. Norms, or standards for behavior, become established. Having such a level of interdependence allows the group to focus more quickly on its task or work through relational issues when they arise.

A wonderful illustration of interdependence in groups is found in a description of the Detroit String Quartet, a subgroup of the Detroit Symphony Orchestra

(Hackman, 1990). The interaction of the 15-year-old group is described as smooth; group members knew their roles both as musicians and as task managers of nonmusical activities (each took on different responsibilities, such as scheduling performances, arranging music, scheduling rehearsals, and so on). It was apparent that this group knew how to work through its task and relational issues and did so. This was called "invisible management." You might also think of it as seamless management—everything fits together so well that it is hard to tell who does what. Interdependence in the group was so well developed, established, and accepted by group members that management of the group seemed invisible. A second characteristic of the group that contributed to its productive interdependence was each group member's commitment to excellence. The group had clear and elevating goals; each member and the group as a whole were clearly committed to performing well. As a result, the group had a shared sense of direction, and they experienced a strong collective responsibility to their work. And, their work was challenging: "Nobody ever has given a perfect performance of quartet music nor will that ever happen" (Hackman, 1990, p. 214). The group was self-managing; they alone decided who would be invited to fill vacancies and what norms would guide their behavior. All of this is astonishing for members of a part-time quartet who are not paid for performing. The level of interdependence achieved by the quartet is remarkable. Recognize that this depth of interdependence could not have been imposed on the group by others. Rather, it emerged from the quartet members' communication with one another. Thus, interdependence represents the culmination of each group member's contributions to the group.

Interdependent groups can be viewed through the application of social exchange theory (Thibaut & Kelley, 1959). Originally a theory about dyadic interaction, this theory can easily be applied to group communication. According to social exchange theory, all interactions have costs and rewards. A cost would be something you do not like to do or something that diminishes the value of the relationship or interaction. Alternately, a reward would be something you like to do or something that enhances the value of the relationship or effectiveness. For example, when you attend a parent-teacher association meeting, a cost to you is to sit through the formal part of the meeting before getting the chance to reap the reward of interacting informally with other parents. In a group, a cost from one member may be offset by a reward from another. It is not likely you will have equal exchanges with each group member but that overall you will end up with enough of a satisfying balance to keep you motivated and attracted to the group. The important thing to remember here is that what is a cost or reward to one group member may not be a cost or reward to another. As an example, Wanda really enjoys providing social support for her group members. She remembers birthdays and can tell immediately when someone is not feeling well. Don, on the other hand, really prefers to get down to business quickly in the group. From his perspective, the less informal interaction the better. In this group setting, celebrating a member's birthday provides positive feedback and social support as a reward for Wanda. Alternately, Don feels that these celebrations are a cost—they are forcing him to stop working on the task and acknowledge and celebrate

Groups with cohesiveness demonstrate this both verbally and nonverbally. Although cohesiveness is generally linked to friendly groups and positive group interaction, a cohesive group can sustain productive periods of conflict interaction.

someone's birthday. Group members like Wanda and Don who possess such different approaches to group interaction will develop different roles within the group.

Positive interdependence takes on many forms. Group cohesiveness and group satisfaction are terms you have probably heard before, and camaraderie may be familiar to you from your sports team experiences. We will look at each of these types of positive interdependence in the following sections.

Group Cohesiveness

When true member interdependence develops, cohesiveness among group members also develops. **Cohesiveness** is the degree to which members desire to remain in the group. When desires to be a group member are strong, members are more likely to be committed to the group's task. Cohesiveness is an illusive concept. We can sense when it exists within a group, but we cannot see it or touch it. Ask group members if they are cohesive—one might respond yes, another member no.

One group member cannot build cohesiveness alone, but one member's actions can destroy the cohesiveness of the group. Although we say that the group is cohesive, cohesiveness actually results from the psychological closeness group members feel toward the group. Cohesiveness can be built around interpersonal attraction to other members, attraction to the task, coordination of effort, and member motivation to work on behalf of the group (Golembiewski, 1962).

Sometimes people refer to cohesiveness as the glue that keeps the group together; others describe cohesiveness as the morale of the group. In either case, cohesiveness serves to keep group members together because of their attraction to the group. There are three specific advantages to building and maintaining a cohesive group. First, members feel that they are a part of the group. Second, cohesiveness acts as a bonding agent for group members. Members of cohesive groups are more likely to stick with the group throughout the duration of its task (Spink & Carron, 1994). This in turn creates more opportunities for norms to be developed and followed (Shaw, 1981). Third, cohesive groups develop a "we" climate, not an "I" climate.

A variety of factors can influence how your group develops cohesiveness. How a group is initially structured is one factor that can impact the cohesiveness of group members (Fuehrer & Keys, 1988). If too much structure is imposed on the group early in its history, members may become too concerned with meeting requirements imposed by the structure rather than building relationships with other group members. For example, if your group has too many rules, members can become lost learning and trying to follow the rules rather than spending time developing closeness with one another. On the other hand, groups without adequate structure can be frustrating for group members because they have too few guidelines to help them select appropriate behavior in the group. When this level of ambiguity exists, members are uncertain about what path to use for developing effective group relationships.

One method you can use to help develop cohesiveness in your task group is to give members frequent opportunities to talk about the task and about working with others. You might want to devote time at the end of each group meeting to building cohesiveness. This provides closure for this meeting and a bridge to the next. By giving group members the opportunity to share information and their feelings about the group's task and performance, you enhance the group's cooperation, cohesiveness, and future task performance (Elias, Johnson, & Fortman, 1989).

Researchers have demonstrated that some membership factors can affect the amount of cohesiveness a group is likely to develop. For example, a group whose members complement one another's need for interpersonal dominance are more likely to be cohesive than a group in which all members display high or low interpersonal dominance (Dyce & O'Connor, 1992). Groups whose members are all high in dominance would have more conflict, which would ultimately decrease cohesiveness. Members who display little dominance would not talk very much. This hampers their abilities in developing and maintaining relationships in the group. Cohesiveness cannot develop on its own. In some groups it never develops, and in others it requires persistent efforts by group members.

The degree of cohesiveness in the group can affect how well the group performs. The more cohesive the group, the more likely that the group will perform more effectively (Evans & Dion, 1991). This relationship between cohesiveness and performance is often reciprocal (Greene, 1989). When an ongoing group performs well, it is also likely that its members will generate additional cohesive feelings for one another or at least maintain the level of cohesiveness that was present in the group. Cohesiveness in a group can also affect individual group member performance. Members of groups with high task cohesiveness put more energy into working with and for the group (Prapavessis & Carron, 1997). In other words, individual members have greater adherence to the team task when the group's task is attractive to them. Thus group members are successful because they have helped the group become successful.

However, the relationship between cohesiveness and performance is not a straightforward one. The degree of interdependence needed to perform a group's task affects the cohesiveness-performance relationship (Gully, Devine, & Whitney, 1995). When a group task requires coordination, high levels of interaction, and joint performances from group members, the cohesion-performance relationship is stronger. But when task interdependence is low, the cohesion-performance relationship is much weaker. A surgical team of nurses and doctors is an example of a group that would require a high degree of interdependence to successfully complete its task. The coordination and communication efforts during an operation are very high. Thus the more cohesive the group, the more effective the team will be in its surgical tasks because high cohesiveness also motivates individual group members to perform well.

Alternately, tasks with low interdependence provide less opportunity for members to communicate and coordinate their actions. Even if cohesiveness develops, there is less opportunity for it to be demonstrated and affect group performance. A sales team is a good example of how low interdependence and low cohesiveness-performance interact. The salesperson approaches a client while the service manager makes the follow-up call. Back at the office, two administrative assistants talk the new client through the initial steps of filing forms and preparing documents. Once the goods have been delivered, the salesperson stops back to say hello. This task has low interdependence because the steps of the task are not done simultaneously and because team members are responsible for unique tasks. Thus cohesiveness is likely to be low among sales team members.

Our discussion to this point suggests that if a group is cohesive it will be successful. However, the processes that lead to cohesiveness are not sufficient to enhance group performance. In addition to being cohesive, effective group outcomes can be obtained in social and recreational groups when the group provides members the opportunity to be expressive, become more self-aware, and be creative. For task and work groups, effective outcomes are associated with a task orientation, order and organization, and leader control, as well as cohesiveness. Cohesiveness in your group in and of itself will not increase the performance quality of the group (Littlepage, Cowart, & Kerr, 1989).

What other benefits can cohesive groups expect? Members of cohesive groups are less likely to leave to join other groups. For groups with long-term goals, this can be an especially important benefit because group time will not have to be spent on finding, attracting, and developing new members. More cohesive groups also exert greater influence over their members. Thus norms are less likely to be violated because cohesiveness exists. This level of influence also encourages group members to more readily accept group goals and tasks. Generally, there is greater equality in participation in cohesive groups because members want to express their membership and identification with the group (Cartwright, 1968).

Can a group ever be too cohesive? Yes. Recall that cohesiveness can be based on the interpersonal attraction a group member feels toward other members or to the task. When cohesiveness is based on interpersonal attraction, groups are more susceptible to groupthink and to producing ineffective decisions. When cohesiveness is based on task attraction, groups are less susceptible to these deficiencies (Mullen et al., 1994). When your group has strong interpersonal relationships and cohesiveness is high, the group leader or facilitator may want to take extra precautions to prevent groupthink from developing.

Group Satisfaction

Closely related to cohesiveness is satisfaction with the group. **Satisfaction** is the degree to which you feel fulfilled or gratified as a group member; it is an attitude you express based on what you have experienced in the group. When your satisfaction is high, you are likely to feel content with the group situation. As an individual group member, you perceive some things about the group as satisfying (such as being assigned to the role you requested) but you may also perceive some group elements as dissatisfying (for instance, having to meet too frequently). The types of things that satisfy us in group settings are quite different from those that provide dissatisfaction (Keyton, 1991). As long as the group is moving along its expected path, group members are likely to be satisfied. This occurs, for example, when group members feel free to participate in the group, when they feel that their time is well spent, and when their group interaction is comfortable and effective. Dissatisfaction develops, for example, when group members spend too much time playing, when the group lacks organization, and when members display little patience. However, dissatisfaction does not necessarily result when the satisfying element is absent (Keyton, 1991). In most groups, if you perceive that your opportunities to participate in the group are adequate, you will be satisfied. But lack of opportunities to participate will not necessarily result in dissatisfaction, especially if you perceive that the group is making progress on its goal or task. Dissatisfaction is more likely to result from negative assessments you make about the group as a whole (such as, my group is in chaos), not from an evaluation of your individual interaction opportunities.

As with cohesiveness, your satisfaction with the group may be based on interpersonal elements, task elements, or a combination of both (Witteman, 1991). Generally, when you are satisfied with the activity of the group, you will try harder to communicate more effectively. As a result, you will be satisfied with communication within the group. How a group handles its conflict also affects member satisfaction. Members of groups that identified viable solutions to conflict reported higher satisfaction than members of groups that avoided conflict. Even groups that experience conflict can have a satisfying group experience. It is important to remember that how conflict is handled affects satisfaction levels, not whether conflict occurs. When conflict occurs, three types of behavior help create satisfaction with the group and the group process. First, make direct statements about the conflict rather than avoid it. Second, work to find a solution by integrating the ideas of all group members. Finally, be flexible. Flexibility is a constructive way to demonstrate goodwill toward other group members.

Building cohesiveness and satisfaction in your group cannot be accomplished alone. But there are some tactics you can undertake as an individual to help the process along. As a single group member you can adapt and monitor your communication so that your interaction encourages positive climate building in the group. Your interaction should be more supportive than defensive as discussed in Chapter 2. Encourage your group to celebrate its successes; this creates a history and tradition for the group. But do not wait until the project is over; each time the group accomplishes a subgoal, recognize the achievement. If you facilitate or lead the group, adopt a reward system that encourages each member, not just a few, to participate. Basing rewards on group output rather than individual output will build cohesiveness. To make this work, group goals must truly be group goals. Additionally, group members should have input into developing goals. Each time the group gets together, group members should be aware of how their communication and activities emphasize the pursuit of these goals.

There are three cautions about developing closeness in groups. First, groups that are not cohesive and in which members are not satisfied are unlikely to produce effective outcomes. But high levels of cohesiveness and satisfaction among group members do not always produce acceptable output (McGrath, 1984). Cohesiveness in a group can be so high that members overlook tasks in favor of having fun. Cohesiveness can also insulate a group, making it more difficult to fully explore its task or options. Refer to the discussion of groupthink in Chapter 4 and Chapter 9. Instead of making a group more vigilant, overly high cohesiveness among group members often makes the group susceptible to faulty thinking. With respect to satisfaction, group members may be satisfied because they like one another and as a result become focused on the relational aspects of the group while minimizing their attention to tasks.

Many people want to believe that cohesiveness and satisfaction are so tightly related that as one increases, so must the other. This is the second caution. If group members become overly cohesive, they may start to reject or ignore their task. If you are attracted to a genealogy group because you want to learn more about researching your family's history, you will probably not be very satisfied if the group regularly focuses its conversations on other topics. Although the cohesiveness of the group could increase the discussion of any topic, your satisfaction with the group may actually decrease because you are not accomplishing your goal.

The third caution involves group size. When a group grows too large, creating greater complexity than can be handled by the communication structure of the group, there will be fewer interaction opportunities among group members. This diminishes cohesiveness and satisfaction. Both cohesiveness and satisfaction develop from the opportunity for members to talk face to face on a regular basis. Just as you have probably drifted apart from your best friend in high school because you see each other less frequently, the same phenomenon occurs in groups. Frequency and quality of interaction are important to establishing cohesiveness and satisfaction.

Camaraderie

Closely related to both cohesiveness and satisfaction is camaraderie. **Camaraderie** assumes that group members are successful at both their task and their relationships. Keyton and Hirokawa (1997) began exploring this concept in groups based on their experiences with teams of medical residents and physicians who traveled into rural areas to deliver medical services. In interviewing medical teams with a high rate of success, the issue of camaraderie—esprit de corps, closeness, and intimacy—continually surfaced. Use the questionnaire in the *Group Assessment Technique* to score your level of camaraderie based on one of your recent group experiences.

Notice how many of the items on the camaraderie survey identify effective group process—for example, the group was characterized by the integration of members' abilities. This suggests that adequate procedures must develop in the group for camaraderie to exist. A dramatic story of four friends lost at sea helps us explore this concept. Enjoying a weekend fishing trip off the coast of Florida, the men's boat suddenly burst into flames. Thinking quickly, one fisherman picked up what he thought was water and threw it on the flames. Unfortunately, the can he picked up contained gasoline. The flames expanded quickly, destroying most of the boat. The four men were left with less than one-fourth of the boat, and they were in shark-infested waters! Now what? One man quickly organized himself and his friends. First, he took an account of everyone's injuries and instructed one friend in how to help another. Next, he took an account of what was left of their supplies. He persuaded the others to accept his method of rationing the precious water and clothing they had left. Another man created a way for them to use the shards of the fiberglass hull to fish. The third friend took the first watch for rescue boats and planes. The fourth man was too injured to help in any way. Did this group survive? Yes! Battling the elements at sea for three days, they were finally rescued.

To what did they attribute their survival? Camaraderie. In their television interview, the men explained how they first developed procedures and then shared tasks. They also told how they relied on the positive history of their friendship, which had developed through years of group sporting adventures, to overcome the obstacles of their ordeal. Thus, camaraderie is formed through positive and successful group interaction. Once established, it can provide the foundation for future group interaction even when a group encounters difficulty. Groups with high levels of camaraderie have strong group identities. The camaraderie in groups is evidenced through group members' behaviors toward one another.

Power Relationships

Anytime you bring people together in groups, there is going to be some element of stress. Intragroup relationships are power relationships. However, all power is not bad. Having access to power or knowing that others see you as powerful helps you feel confident in group settings. On the other hand, we are all familiar with the misuse of power in group settings and the relational damage it can cause. We will examine several aspects of power: power bases, control over resources, and situationally enhanced power. Role stress in groups also results in power imbalances. We will explore what happens when a group member uses his or her power to provoke the group so that the group feels powerless. Imbalances in power and equity are two related causes of relational stress in groups. Lack of trust among group members can also add stress to group situations. When group members feel stress, power inequities are more likely to develop.

Bases of Power

Power is a psychological commodity; it exists in relationships among group members. When a group member has power, she has interpersonal influence over other group members because they have accepted or allowed the attempt at power to be successful. Thus power exists because a group member perceives the influence of another group member and alters his behavior because of that influence. Although power was originally seen as residing primarily in group leaders (French & Raven, 1968), any member of the group can develop power and use it in relationships with other group members.

Five power bases have been identified (French & Raven, 1968): reward, coercive, legitimate, referent, and expert. You are probably most familiar with **reward power.** Rewards can be relationally oriented, such as attention, friendship, or favors. They can also take on tangible forms such as gifts or money. In contrast to the positive influence of rewards, threats represent coercive or negative power. In group settings, **coercive power** results from the expectation that you can be punished by another group member. Thus, you alter your behavior to avoid the punishment. Coercion can take the form of denying a group member the opportunity to participate or threatening to take something of importance away from a group member.

Legitimate power is the inherent influence associated with a position or role in the group. Leaders or facilitators often have legitimate power—they can call meetings and make assignments. Without another power base, however, a leader relying solely on legitimate power will have little influence in a group. **Referent power** is influence given by you to another group member based on your desire to build a relationship with him or her. In other words, you admire or want to be like another group member. Thus, you allow yourself to be influenced by this person. Larry admires Harvey and wants to be like him. Thus Larry is influenced by Harvey and follows his suggestions and recommendations. Anyone in the group can possess referent power, which is often based on charisma. And members can

GROUP ASSESSMENT TECHNIQUE

What Is Your Level of Camaraderie?

Think of a recent group interaction, and respond to each item by circling one number on the continuum.

1 = strongly disagree   2 = disagree   3 = slightly disagree
4 = undecided   5 = slightly agree   6 = agree   7 = strongly agree

1. The group was characterized by group members having mutual respect for one another.   1 2 3 4 5 6 7
2. The group was characterized by loyalty among people who were trying to reach the same goal.   1 2 3 4 5 6 7
3. The group was characterized by social harmony.   1 2 3 4 5 6 7
4. Group members showed concern for one another as people independent of the task.   1 2 3 4 5 6 7
5. The group was characterized by positive interaction whether the goal was achieved or not.   1 2 3 4 5 6 7
6. The group was characterized by emotional closeness that bound the group together.   1 2 3 4 5 6 7
7. Group members were mutually supportive.   1 2 3 4 5 6 7
8. The group created an atmosphere that was open to members' thoughts and ideas.   1 2 3 4 5 6 7
9. Group members demonstrated a helpful attitude toward others.   1 2 3 4 5 6 7
10. The group consisted of people who treated one another equally.   1 2 3 4 5 6 7
11. The group was characterized by positive relationships that could deal with stress as well as success.   1 2 3 4 5 6 7
12. Group interactions were based on trust.   1 2 3 4 5 6 7
13. The group was characterized by a partnership that felt like everyone contributed to a great extent.   1 2 3 4 5 6 7
14. The group was characterized by a pervasive trust that could withstand pressure.   1 2 3 4 5 6 7
15. Group interactions were smooth and comfortable.   1 2 3 4 5 6 7
16. Group members worked well together.   1 2 3 4 5 6 7
17. The group consisted of people who worked in sync.   1 2 3 4 5 6 7
18. Group members had similar convictions.   1 2 3 4 5 6 7

have referent power over others without intending to do so. A group member with a pleasant or stimulating communicator style often develops referent power with others, which gives her additional opportunities to develop further power bases with these same group members.

19. The group was characterized by the integration of members' talents. 1 2 3 4 5 6 7
20. Group members worked together to find a solution within the group. 1 2 3 4 5 6 7
21. Group members showed respect for one another's ideas. 1 2 3 4 5 6 7
22. Interactions were positive whether the goal was achieved or not. 1 2 3 4 5 6 7
23. Interactions were characterized by freedom and flexibility. 1 2 3 4 5 6 7
24. The group was characterized by feelings of members being accepted within the group. 1 2 3 4 5 6 7
25. Group members had a willingness to work together. 1 2 3 4 5 6 7
26. The group consisted of people who treated one another honestly. 1 2 3 4 5 6 7
27. The group was characterized by the integration of members' abilities. 1 2 3 4 5 6 7
28. The group coordinated varying personalities into action. 1 2 3 4 5 6 7
29. The group consisted of a positive gathering of easygoing, laid back people. 1 2 3 4 5 6 7
30. The group was characterized by feelings of members being comfortable within the group. 1 2 3 4 5 6 7
31. Group members came together to provide support for the team. 1 2 3 4 5 6 7
32. The group was characterized by a sense of teamwork. 1 2 3 4 5 6 7
33. The group consisted of members who were loyal to one another. 1 2 3 4 5 6 7
34. Group members were highly loyal to the task at hand. 1 2 3 4 5 6 7

Add your responses together to find your total score.

Discussion Questions

1. How close is your score to 166? If your group scores at this level or above, your group should be experiencing enough camaraderie to be successful. Below this cut-off, group members may not feel close enough to one another to work together effectively.
2. Do you believe your score reflects the level of camaraderie in your group? How is camaraderie you experienced similar to or different from cohesiveness and satisfaction?
3. Go back and circle each item on which you scored 5 or higher. Are any patterns evident among these high scores?

Finally, **expert power** is influence based on what a group member knows or can do. Group members develop expert power when they offer their unique skills to help the group, and their behavior matches the expectations they have created. Sheree says she can use computer-aided design software to lay out the team's new

> **PUTTING THE PIECES TOGETHER**
>
> *Group Structure and Group Size*
>
> Think of a recent group experience where you were not the person in charge, you were not the group's leader, or you took on a relatively minor role in the group. How did the member in charge or the leader create and sustain his or her power? To what extent was that use of power positive or negative? How did this use of power affect the structure of the group? If the leader held much of the group's power, did the group rotate around him or her? If power was more evenly distributed within the group, did this encourage participation among all group members? How did the number of members in the group affect power issues? Were there so many group members that it was easier to give most of the power to the leader to coordinate the group's activities? Or was membership small enough that each member could develop some bases of power?

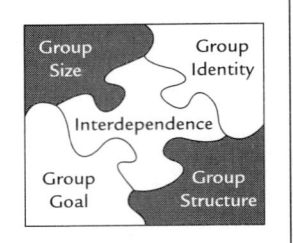

office space. Her team members will only reward her with this power, however, when she demonstrates this skill. Saying you can do something is not enough; your performance must match the expectations you create.

Of these five types of power, all except coercive power are essential for effective group process. Group members want someone to be in control (legitimate power); like it when others compliment them on their contributions (reward power); find it useful and comfortable when someone is the group's motivator, cheerleader, or contact person (referent power); and expect others to exert their knowledge and skills (expert power).

A group member can hold little power or can develop power in many areas. Although we often think that others give us power, that does not happen unless we act powerful. If Andy does not profess his expertise in creating computer graphics for the group's final report, other group members cannot create this power relationship with him. Andy's power only arises if the others are aware of Andy's knowledge and skill. Thus power emerges through interaction. Although typically the group leader or facilitator holds more power than other group members, each member should develop and demonstrate some base of power to augment his or her credibility and worth to the group. When power is distributed among group members, participation is more balanced and cohesiveness and satisfaction are enhanced.

How important is it that you develop a power base as a group member? Very. Power used positively creates attraction from other group members. We all like to be associated with powerful people. In fact, power, rather than status, has a greater effect on other group members (Bradley, 1978). This is because power is developed within relationships whereas status is generally brought into the group and is not critical to those relationships. You may have status because of where you live, what your parents do for a living, what car you drive, and so on. But these status issues are difficult to translate into communication relationships with other group members. Would it really matter to another group member that you drove an expensive car if you did not follow through with your group assignments? Would it matter if last semester you attended a prestigious private school if you did not share your knowledge with the group? Try *Putting the Pieces Together* to better understand the power bases of a group experience.

Analyzing Power Issues

You can analyze the impact of power dynamics in your group by examining power on two dimensions (Glaser, 1996). The first dimension is the degree to which power is structured. Highly structured power is defined or formalized by the group; often this is associated with specific roles. Unstructured power exists when power is not formalized or when a power base shifts from one member to another. The second dimension is the degree to which there is a struggle against the power dynamics that are emerging in the group. If members are actively contesting power relations, then struggle is high. If members accept the emerging power relations, then struggle is low.

These two dimensions of power dynamics interact to shape how the group deals with inequality. In the first power dynamic situation, power is unstructured and contested. In her statistics study group, Jacinthia repeatedly recalls her experience at her previous university to develop expertise power with her group members. But because the others have no experience with Jacinthia in that setting, it is difficult for them develop power relations with her based on knowledge and skills she has about another school's curriculum and activities. Jacinthia tries to create power for herself, but her power attempt is challenged by group members: "I can't believe she thought we would let her facilitate our study group when we don't have firsthand knowledge about her classroom performance."

In the second power dynamic situation, power is structured or defined as well as contested. In the same study group, Rod has created a great deal of coercive power with others as he tries to bully other members into doing the assignments he needs to complete. If a group member suggests that all members do the calculation and then compare answers, Rod makes mild threats in a joking voice: "The purpose of the group was to share the workload. Do you want to be a member of the group or not?" Thus the coercive power relationship is well defined, and the other group members are tired of Rod's attempts to control the group in this manner. Group members do not accept Rod's threats, and they want to change the power structure in the group. To do this, they plan a meeting after a midterm exam to discuss how the group will work together on the final. In this meeting, other group members purposely discuss procedures for sharing the workload. This discussion challenges Rod's view of sharing the workload and his attempts to dominate the group.

When power is defined and accepted, there is a third power dynamic situation. Once the study group has met and agreed to a new work-sharing procedure, the power dynamics have been redefined and accepted. Now the group is relying on

Belinda's referent power to keep group relations more positive and individual members' workloads more equitable. Belinda is pleasant with all group members, and she has a way of acknowledging their strengths and talents even when the group interaction becomes stressed. The group has decided to let Belinda coordinate each of the study sessions. In agreeing to do so, she points out each member's specific skills and talents she will be calling on. This is an example of successful power negotiations. The study group agrees that Belinda will have a certain degree of power, and Belinda agrees to take on those responsibilities for the group. Recognize, however, that Belinda did not *assume* these responsibilities for the group. Rather, this power relation results from the group's discussion of the issues. Also recognize that Belinda is chosen for this position because of the referent power she has demonstrated in past study sessions.

In the fourth power dynamic situation, power is undefined and accepted. Stefan, the fourth member of the study group, is also a member of a chemistry study group. Sometimes he feels torn between the two groups because it is difficult to be adequately prepared when his chemistry group meets only one day after this one. When Stefan comes to the statistics study group unprepared and gives the excuse that he has been studying with his chemistry group, the other group members do not hassle him very much. They know that as a pre-med major Stefan has to get good grades in both classes. Even when Stefan does not have his assignments done, he still contributes by explaining calculations the others do not understand. Thus other members accept his lack of preparation as a result of his competing interests. The group could challenge Stefan's involvement, but they do not. His presence in the group is valued.

Notice that the power dynamics of this study group are fluid. As the group confronts different relationship and task challenges, different power dynamics surface for the group to address. When members mutually define and accept the power dynamics within a group, a certain level of inequality can be tolerated. Yet when one member attempts to define the power dynamics for other group members without their consent, the degree of power inequality is enhanced. This usually backfires on the member who tries to impose his or her version of power dynamics.

Control of Resources

A power source that is often overlooked is control of resources—real or imagined. As groups work on their tasks, information and materials from outside the group are frequently needed. For example, when a group member volunteers to use her network of connections to obtain permission to use the dean's conference room for their meetings, or to use her roommate's computer to create the presentation graphics, she is exerting power over needed resources. At the same time, these powerful connections exclude other group members. Group members in control of outside resources are developing both expert power and referent power. Group members are often thankful someone in the group has access to these resources and impressed that the individual can obtain what they cannot. However, overusing these connections can create a defensive climate in the group. Here, power can be perceived as strategic manipulation. If Leatha volunteers to get the dean's conference room, then it is likely that she will see when its availability fits her schedule. If she volunteers to produce the presentation graphics on her roommate's computer and other group members are not there when Leatha finalizes the graphics, she can exert editorial control over the copy the group gave her. The following section will give you a better idea of how power can be framed in negative ways.

Situationally Enhanced Power

One way to conceptualize power in groups is to consider how group members frame messages and interaction to influence the outcome of the group's discussion. Consider a case study of a city council that illustrates power in action (Barge & Keyton, 1994). This type of power is described as overt attempts at compliance gaining aimed at influencing others to endorse or accept particular beliefs or actions (Frost, 1987). This conceptualization of power is greatly expanded over the power bases presented earlier because it takes into account the context in which power is demonstrated. The following example demonstrates how social influence can be employed by a group member to alter other members' existing beliefs and values. Such power is political because the power holder is serving her own interest in framing influential messages.

One group member, Judith, offers that she has had several classes with the professor who has assigned your group a difficult group project. "In fact," Judith continues, "she's my advisor, and I regularly meet with Dr. Peterson. She's the advisor to my Mortar Board group. She seems really cool." Judith is offering information that makes others believe that Judith really knows Dr. Peterson well. Other group members are likely to now look toward Judith's evaluations as being Dr. Peterson's evaluations. Judith continues, "I think our project should focus on a women's issue. I know Rebecca, sorry, I mean, Dr. Peterson does research in that area. I think that would impress her if we read her work and cite her." Now Judith has slipped information that attests to the personal level of her relationship with Dr. Peterson. Other group members are likely to be impressed and believe that Judith can help them obtain the grade they want. After all, it appears that Judith has the inside track on Dr. Peterson's preferences. Although this framing could be legitimate, it is also possible that framing messages in this way was designed by Judith to meet her own needs. She wants to impress Dr. Peterson. What the group does not know is that Judith has had several classes in women's studies; working on a women's issue means she will have less research to do if the group adopts this topic.

Judith is attempting to import referent and expert power from her purported relationship with Dr. Peterson. But do other group members know her motive for doing so? Not necessarily. How messages are framed create power. In reality, Judith does not know Dr. Peterson that well. All of the information she provided the group is readily and publicly available. Judith just perceived an opportunity to increase her power in the group and took advantage of it.

Primary provokers may initiate the role, but secondary provokers encourage that role development.

Primary Provokers Another type of negative power can be manifested by one member of the group who places undue stress and influence on how the group proceeds. Stohl and Schell (1991) first named this power-assuming group member a *farrago*. Interactions with a farrago result in confusion about responsibilities, group tasks, decision-making procedures, and so on. Further, these problematic interactions cause the entire group to become confused—also a farrago. Renaming the power-assuming group member the **primary provoker** and the group members who support this person's behavior **secondary provokers,** Keyton (1996) split the roles apart to study their interdependent communication roles. Case studies revealed that the primary provoker's dysfunctional behavior was dependent on other group members' willingness to play along. In these cases, the power the primary provoker wields is due to the active support provided by the secondary provokers.

You probably can identify a primary provoker from one of your previous group experiences. How did this person make trouble for the group? In what ways did the other group members—the secondary provokers—encourage or allow the primary provoker to dominate the group? The following interaction helps explain how secondary provokers consciously and unconsciously support the primary provoker in that role.

CHESU: Let's get started by hearing a report from each of you.

EUGENE: Okay, I'll go first. (pause) Just let me say . . . (relinquishes his speaking turn)

JORDAN: Maybe it would be better if I started out. I know that each of you will want to hear what I've got to say. (ah-hem)

(Chesu averts her gaze. She's angry at Jordan for once again interrupting. But rather than ask Jordan to wait his turn, she allows Jordan to continue.)

JORDAN: So, what I've found is that . . . well, that I was right all along! I'd like to take this opportunity to thank the other committee members for giving me the chance to meet with folks down at the chamber. As you know, I've had a long involvement with the chamber . . .

(Chesu and Eugene are still looking downward at their notes, not focusing their attention on Jordan. Other members, Lakesha and Samuel, have mentally checked out. Lakesha is checking her daily organizer for other things she needs to accomplish; Samuel is developing an outline for a presentation he must make later that week. Both are busy with their own thoughts and work.)

JORDAN: They seem to like me down there, so it was no problem getting the information I needed.

Notice how Jordan has taken over the meeting in his role as primary provoker and how the other group members have played the supporting roles of secondary provokers. By not taking back control of the meeting, Chesu has abdicated her leadership role. Eugene reacted submissively to Jordan's act of dominance. Lakesha and Samuel are ignoring Jordan, which allows him to continue his dominance despite the fact that he is not contributing anything substantive to the group at this point.

Why would a group member willingly play a supporting role to another problematic group member? First, the supporting group member, or secondary provoker, feels some need or is motivated to maintain some social relationship in the group with the primary provoker. Perhaps the secondary provokers believe that if they attempt to discredit the primary provoker they will be not be viewed as team players or will be discredited by their boss. In the example above, Jordan has long tenure with the company and opposing him only causes conflict they will have to later explain. Second, the deviance of other group members often highlights our own deviant tendencies, and, as a result, affects our ego. Secondary provokers try to distance themselves from problematic persons so they can keep their egos intact (Ferrari, 1990).

Two conditions encourage this dysfunctional power dynamic to emerge: habits of individuals involved and properties of the group's system. The first enabling condition—habits of individuals—can be viewed in three types of behavior. First, the primary provoker causes interactional tensions as he claims to be privileged to the correct meaning of the situation. Often the primary provoker alludes to some systemic connection other group members do not have. Second, the primary provoker causes interaction tensions when he claims to know what is best for the group. Not only can primary provokers cause problems, they believe they can fix them (and that they are not at fault)! Third, the primary provoker exhibits far more emotional energy and time than demanded by his group role. In other words, the primary provoker forces the group to direct attention toward him.

The second enabling condition—properties of the group's system—is evidenced in the following ways. First, dysfunctional group members are more likely to emerge in environments in which participatory decision making is expected. The primary provoker knows this and sets the stage for creating a power imbalance with which the group must deal if it wants to move on to decision making. Second, ambiguous connections to the group's macro system and ambiguous rules encourage dysfunctionality to emerge. If there are no rules, the primary provoker makes them. Third, high task interdependence among group members sets the stage for dysfunctional groups, and dysfunctional group members are more likely to emerge. High interdependence means the group cannot move on without the input of the problematic member.

How can you recognize primary provokers and secondary provokers and distinguish them from poor or ineffectively performing groups? This type of dysfunctional group can be identified by certain characteristics (Stohl & Schell, 1991): (1) complicating or compromising decision-making procedures that accommodate or avoid the primary provoker, (2) defining issues to reflect how the primary provoker sees things, (3) consuming a great deal of energy, both as a group and as individuals, talking about the primary provoker, (4) exhibiting confusing behaviors in response to the primary provoker's confusing interaction style, (5) being consumed with the underlying power imbalance rather than the task, and (6) displaying negative emotions toward both the group and the primary provoker. Thus the relational power of the primary provoker creates misdirected energies and negative emotions and consumes group time.

Confusion seems to be a key element to the primary provoker's power. Amazingly, this confusion exists on the friendly-unfriendly interaction dimension (Keyton, 1996). Secondary provokers generally do not believe anything is wrong in the group. As a result, they perceive their own behavior and the behavior of other group members as positive or friendly. Simultaneously, the secondary provokers perceive the behavior of primary provokers as negative or unfriendly. Even though confusion exists about what constitutes positive or effective behavior in the group, these issues are never brought up for discussion. These comments from a secondary provoker illustrate the depth of power this primary provoker has established:

> SECONDARY PROVOKER: If I don't agree with her (the primary provoker's) stand, I just let it drop or try to approach her later. Confronting her in a meeting doesn't do any good. Professional protocol requires that I accept her decisions, behavior, and treatment of subordinates; others usually don't even bother trying to give input into the group discussion. This is done to avoid being either ignored or intimidated.

Group members who find it difficult to confront a primary provoker in group meetings reinforce the situationally enhanced power of the primary provoker.

Primary provokers are not always individuals with high-ranking status and legitimate power. Case histories identify primary provokers in various hierarchical positions, dismissing the likelihood of positional, hierarchical, or legitimate power. Nevertheless, primary provokers wield a virtual stranglehold over their groups. However, primary provokers are not necessarily poor task performers. Frequently, primary provokers are held in high esteem by other group members for task abilities. In these types of relationship dynamics, the successful power attempt by the primary provoker allows group dysfunction to develop. Personality and communication differences create the power dynamics that dictate how the group interacts.

Power is relationally oriented. A group member cannot take power from anyone. Rather, it exists in relationships developed and established within and among group members. If attempts at influence are tried, but do not succeed, power has not been granted, and the person attempting such a power play does not become powerful in the eyes of the other group members.

How can your group deal with primary provokers? First, recognize that your behavior is supporting or allowing the primary provoker to redirect group energy away from the task and toward negative relationships that have developed in the group. Accepting some of the responsibility for this group dysfunction is the first step. Once the dysfunction has been recognized and accepted, the group has several choices (Wetlaufer, 1994). The first choice is to exclude the primary provoker from the group. But if this person's knowledge or connections are an asset to the group, then the group suffers from this decision. The next choice is to continue the group with the primary provoker present—making sure strong leadership can counter the negativity the primary provoker introduces. The leader should take steps to provide both structure and definition for the group. Giving precise directions, establishing intermediate goals, and keeping the group on a time schedule can help.

The most productive solution is to work with the primary provoker to harvest his contributions without allowing him to become a group menace. How can this be accomplished? One way is for the leader to talk privately with the primary provoker before meetings to discuss his input. Meeting individually again after group meetings would give the leader a chance to counsel and coach this group member. Another way to maintain or neutralize the negative effects of the primary provoker is to assign him special responsibilities that will take advantage of his talents and occupy the time and energy he would otherwise spend meddling with the group. Using one of the formal discussion procedures discussed in Chapter 8 is an excellent way to maintain or neutralize the negative effects of a primary provoker. This will help equalize and normalize all group members interactions, contributions, and reactions. Overall, the most important goal is to find a way for all group members to work effectively together.

Scapegoats Another role that develops from power imbalances and creates additional stress in a group is the role of scapegoat. A **scapegoat** is the group member to whom other members inappropriately direct their anxiety, aggression, or blame. Frequently, a member who represents a minority social or demographic group (such as the only female in a group of males, the only Hispanic in a group of African Americans) is inappropriately blamed for the group's problems. This is the group's candidate for a scapegoat. In this power imbalance, other group members have all of the power, the scapegoat has none. This person becomes the symbol of the group's stress and negativity as the scapegoat unconsciously represents the group's conflict for its members.

Group members do not volunteer for the role of scapegoat, but often one group member will unconsciously contribute to his or her selection to this powerless role. A group member who has been socialized to experience guilt at not fitting in is likely to become a group's scapegoat. The scapegoat role often develops when the group is unwilling or unmotivated to examine its own behavior and process. Too frequently, other group members direct negative attention toward the scapegoat to deflect attention from their own shortcomings. Because the group's dysfunction is left unexamined, it appears that the member in the role of scapegoat is creating and maintaining that role. When a scapegoat is present, other group members believe that if the scapegoat would only modify his or her behavior, then the group's problems would be resolved (Gemmill, 1989).

The scapegoat role is covert—one that is not discussed by group members. As long as the member in the scapegoat role allows other members to blame him or her, the group is likely to continue directing negative energy toward that person. If the negativity becomes too intense and the member in the scapegoat role leaves the group, another member is likely to be delegated into that role. By continuing to put a group member in the scapegoat role, the group can avoid discussing its real dysfunction and continue its power imbalance.

Equity

Equity in groups is similar to the costs and rewards mentioned earlier in this chapter's discussion of interdependence. Issues of equity, or more appropriately inequity, usually occur over rewards given to group members or effort demonstrated by group members. For example, two of the group members feel that their group performance was better than the other two members. Yet all four received the same grade. Defensive players on the basketball team are mad at the offensive players for not scoring enough points. Even though the defensive players kept the other team from running up the score, offensive players were cold—they simply were not hitting their baskets.

To combat feelings of inequity, groups may use an equity norm whenever possible (Forsyth, 1990). Groups using an equity norm reward members on a parity basis, in proportion to their group contributions. Alternately, groups using an equality norm reward group members by equally dividing the reward regardless of individual contributions. If all group members contribute about equally, the equality norm would promote a greater spirit of cooperation among group members. However, there are many groups where this simply does not happen. When group members' contributions are not equal (and the reasons for unequal participation are not accepted by the other group members), other group members resent the failing group member for receiving equal reward for unequal input. The issue of equity is of particular concern for group members when groups are externally rewarded for their work. Too frequently, these group members focus on the external reward system, and they fail to use an internal reward system to monitor and influence nonperforming group members.

It is particularly difficult for groups to deal with issues of inequity because they are perceptually rather than objectively based. A group member's effort on a subtask is largely invisible to other group members—particularly if they believe that the assigned task is not difficult or complex. When inequity in group contribution is perceived, other group members typically see the inequitable contributor as a deviant—someone who defies the work norms of the group. Too frequently, these issues are not discussed openly in the group setting. Rather, coalitions of group members, excluding the deviant, form to discuss and further perpetuate the perceived inequity and power imbalance. Inequity is also difficult to confront in group situations because it is unlikely that the group member who is not pulling her weight will openly admit her awareness of the inequity. In fact, she may not be aware of it at all. This is why it is so important for groups to have open and frank discussions about member expectations and work assignments.

Trust

You have probably heard that trust is not given, it is earned. Because we base trust on our previous experiences with people, it is particularly hard to develop trust with a group of strangers. Developing trust with other group members is difficult if your group is working under heightened time pressure or other severe external pressures. Trust develops over a period of time as relationships unfold and confidence builds. When you trust another group member, it helps you predict how this group member will behave or react. Establishing trust, then, usually occurs after a moderate level of rapport has been established in the group among all group members.

But here is the problem: You do not establish rapport with the group; rather, you establish rapport with each group member. That is why establishing trust in group settings takes such a long time. Trust is also extended slowly and incrementally. Ebon trusts you a little, you trust him a little in return. Ebon begins to feel comfortable with how your relationship is developing (and you are not doing anything to erode the trust you have established), so Ebon extends a deeper level of trust to you. Extending trust is risky, that is why we are unwilling to give full trust to new people in new settings.

Trust is also multifaceted. It is based on honesty, openness, consistency, and respect (Larson & LaFasto, 1989). As you might suspect, it would be difficult to trust a group member who was not honest. It is also difficult to trust a group member who was not open. Sharing part of yourself with the group by revealing personal or professional information will help others to know you and feel similar to you. Not only must you share with others, you must also be receptive to receiving personal and professional information about other group members. Openness cannot be one-sided. Being consistent in your group's interactions also helps others understand you. When you interact in an inconsistent manner, others will become hesitant around you because they are never quite sure how you will react. For example, let's say that you are normally very talkative in the group, but today you do not feel well. As a result you are quiet and subdued. A simple explanation that you do not feel well will prevent other group members from labeling your behavior as inconsistent and prevent them from making other negative attributions about your behavior change. Finally, trust is based upon respect. It is hard to trust someone who does not respect others or someone who cannot be respected. Your behavior and interaction are always being evaluated by other group members. If you tell off-color jokes about someone when that person is not present, other group members might assume that you would tell jokes about them when they are not around.

How can you build trust in groups? First, be aware of your communicator style in the group and minimize your apprehensiveness. This will increase your ability to develop positive interactions with others. Second, use the supportive climate interaction characteristics discussed in Chapter 2. If you interact in a defensive manner, it is unlikely that others will extend trust to you. Third, use appropriate self-disclosure. We have all met people who tell us more than we want to know in our initial meeting with them. Extend only the personal and professional information about yourself that you believe will be perceived by others as positive contributions to the group. As group members warm up to one another, self-disclosure often becomes more personal. Remember, however, that in decision-making and other task groups, revealing too much personal information may be considered unprofessional. Moreover, personal information can be used against you—once you have revealed it you lose power over the information. Fourth, focus on developing a positive and collaborative climate with all group members. Let's repeat that—you should attempt to do this with all group members. Jack may resist extending his trust to you because you treat Margaret more favorably than other group members. Finally, monitor your interaction behavior to ensure that you are not overusing power bases or becoming a primary provoker. Trust is seldom extended to group members who are perceived negatively. "How Fragile Is Trust?" explores the effect of lack of trust on group interaction.

Gender Influences in Groups

Most of the group communication literature focuses on gender effects as they relate to the role of leadership and group discussions of traditional college-age students. To date, research on gender differences has produced inconsistent findings about the ways in which male and female communication differs and affects groups. Stereotypical roles of males and females—such as males being more independent, aggressive, and task-oriented and females being more dependent, non-aggressive, and interpersonally oriented—dominated early research until the rise of the women's movement (Baird, 1976). Changes in society caused researchers to

> **THINK ABOUT IT**
>
> ### How Fragile Is Trust?
>
> Think about one of your recent group experiences where trust was an issue. How did you know that group members lacked trust for one another? Did a member not follow through on a commitment? Did someone break a confidence? Did you feel as if group members were withholding information from other members? Did a member say one thing and then do something else? How did your group respond to the erosion of trust? How did group members deal with this problem?

question, first, whether gender differences were actually present and, second, if they were present, whether differences confirmed stereotypical categories.

Clearly gender stereotypes exist in the discussion of group leadership (Andrews, 1992). Frequently, we expect that males will emerge as leaders of groups. But this is not always the case. Reviews of the leadership literature (Eagly & Karau, 1991) found that females are more likely to emerge as leaders when groups are dealing with relational issues. Alternately, males are more likely to emerge as leaders when groups are primarily task-oriented. Once the leader role is established, behavior for male and female leaders differs only very slightly (Chemers & Murphy, 1995; Eagly & Johnson, 1990). Yet stereotypes about gender and its affect on leadership ability persist despite research that demonstrates that both males and females can be effective leaders (Eagly, Karau, & Makhijani, 1995). Only one long-term leadership gender difference has been substantiated. That is, females are more likely to adopt a democratic or participative style of leadership whereas male leaders prefer an autocratic or directive style (Eagly & Johnson, 1990). Your use of effective communication strategies can help your group overcome stereotypical beliefs about leaders. For example, in decision-making groups, group members who communicate task maintenance messages to the group, regardless of their gender, emerge as leaders (Hawkins, 1995).

Our gender assumptions about leadership are firmly embedded in society. The male gender-leadership assumption is entrenched in our language. How can you avoid making the assumption that males are more likely linked to leadership roles? One way is to watch for usage of gender-specific language like "the person we elect as leader; well, he should be forceful, strong, and willing to work as hard as we do" and "the chairman will decide when the report will be due." Try to use gender-neutral language (for example, chairperson, not chairman; the secretary, not madam secretary) when talking about group roles.

Another focus has been on gender differences in groups in the workplace—particularly on conflict management strategies. Once again, the research results are confusing. Although gender was not the primary indicator of conflict management strategy selection, males were more aggressive and dominant whereas females were more submissive and pacifying (Gayle, 1991). This confirms the finding that males are predominantly "thinkers" and females are predominantly "feelers" (Sorenson, Hawkins, & Sorenson, 1995). Yet, these differences did not significantly influence the conflict style preferences of males or females.

Other studies have examined more broadly gender in groups (Taps & Martin, 1990). In otherwise all-male groups and in groups where females were underrepresented, females who gave internal attribution accounts (for example, giving credit to themselves by referencing personal expertise, knowledge, or skill) were regarded as negative and noninfluential in the group by male members. Conversely, females in these male-dominated groups who gave external attributional accounts (for example, made references to others in positions of authority or experts—particularly males) were seen as influential. But in all-female groups, females were able to make self-attributions without losing influence in the group. In gender-balanced groups, however, it seemed to matter little if females gave credit to themselves or others. This suggests that within gender-balanced groups a wider range of behaviors is legitimated for both males and females.

Unfortunately, males may still have more status than females in mixed-gender groups. Information introduced by a male group member is more likely to be used in a group's decision making than the same contribution made by a female (Propp, 1995). This type of gender bias can have profound effects on a group's ability to share and process information as members work on their task. Information held by females, even when it is critical to the group's task, may be accorded less status or importance. This study demonstrates the extent to which gender biases group members' ability to process information. Status is a natural outgrowth of group structure, but it would be better if status in groups were assigned to members based on individual ability or knowledge, not on gender or stereotypes.

Contrary to much of the past research that identifies males as the dominant group figures, one study (Mabry, 1989b) found that females dominated group interaction. Females also report preferring interaction with other females as their group members. All-female groups report more positive attributes about their groups than all-male or mixed-gender groups (Keyton, Harmon, & Frey, 1996). Likewise, participants in all-female groups report fewer negative group attributes than all-male or mixed-gender groups. These findings suggest that females may be more receptive to group situations in general or are better at maximizing positive while minimizing negative aspects of group interaction. We could raise many questions as to why females would choose to communicate with females rather than males. Could it be they use similar communication styles or could it be that females view their female colleagues as more effective in groups than their male counterparts? Such an attitude would likely affect females' attitudes toward and preferences for group work. There is some evidence to support this. Female students got along better with other group members and felt that classroom groups were a more effective context than did males (Freeman, 1996). "In the absence of men and the discrimination by men against women in mixed-gender groups, women are relieved of the expectation of defense to male leadership and are free to rely on their own strong feminine identity" (Gurman & Long, 1992, p. 397). Such gender-

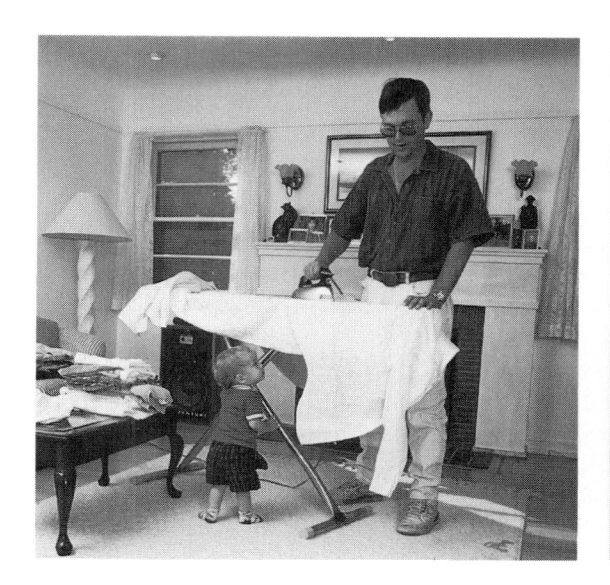

We often make stereotypical assumptions about group members based on gender. Doing so diminishes our ability to view group members as individuals and to recognize their unique talents and skills.

different approaches to group interaction may be based on attributional differences; females are more likely to credit other females for group success (Forsyth & Kelley, 1994).

It is important to remember that even when gender differences exist early in a group's meeting or history, these differences may dissipate over time. One study comparing all-female and all-male groups found that gender differences ceased to exist the longer the groups interacted (Verdi & Wheelen, 1992). Within the groups' first hour of meeting, all-female groups created more relational messages whereas all-male groups created more task statements. But as the groups continued to meet for another 4 to 5 hours, these differences evened out.

The degree to which members displayed masculine or feminine interaction characteristics is another way of examining gender influences on groups (Seibert & Gruenfeld, 1992). Group members who express more masculine characteristics (for example, are more task-oriented) are more dominant in group interaction regardless of their biological sex. Group members who express more feminine interaction styles (are more expressive) are more friendly in group settings regardless of their biological sex. These findings remind us not to overgeneralize about someone's group interaction style and to pay attention instead to how group members communicate.

With respect to the impact of gender composition on group interaction, no clear conclusions can be drawn. Early research provided mixed conclusions; more contemporary research is beginning to demonstrate a trend that females may be more group-oriented. Such an orientation may stem from the nurturing or collaborative tendencies of females. But when females and males are combined in team settings, as they are in organizational work groups, these effects are moderated by many other environmental variables. It is clear that if we rely on gender stereotypes, we will only perpetuate confusion and contribute to tension and stress in groups, as well as overlooking the unique contributions of individual group members.

Cultural Diversity in Groups

In addition to the stresses and power imbalances already mentioned, cultural or ethnic differences can also fuel stress in groups. Alternatively, cultural differences can create interesting variety and provide multiple perspectives from which to consider the group issue or problem. Individual differences and uniqueness make every group diverse. But as our society becomes more aware of the great infusion of cultural dimensions and as workers of all races and ethnic identifications are drawn into work groups, each of us will have a greater opportunity to work in a group with others who are unlike us in basic values, attitudes, beliefs, and assumptions. Certainly, this can create stress; but, these difficulties are not insurmountable.

Race and ethnic identification issues are much like gender issues in groups. It is pretty difficult to hide that I am a Caucasian female. You can see these attributes by looking at me. And if I were in a work group in Argentina, my language preferences and accent when I speak Spanish would further identify me as being different. As our organizations become more internationally oriented, it is likely that you will work in a group whose members represent several different cultures. As in the study of gender differences in group interaction, there is little research that can guide our way. Most research focuses on intercultural settings in which people from two different cultures interact. More commonly, however, groups are the sites of multicultural influences. Still, the advice generated by those studies can be used when your group is culturally diverse.

One of the biggest problems for members in groups like this is for individuals to recognize their own biases and come to terms with them. Most group members will be **ethnocentric.** This means that a person judges events and people as good or correct when they are similar to events and people in their own culture. This type of perceptual bias is natural as we grow up in cultures that teach us to differentiate between appropriate and inappropriate behavior based on similarities and differences. However, keeping biases and stereotypes under the surface (and continuing to rely on them without considering what is actually happening in the group's interaction) is harmful not only to the group but to your own personal growth and development. When we suppress our feelings and perceptions, we are more likely to choose interaction strategies based on perceived rather than real cultural differences. Even if cultural differences do exist, this is not necessarily harmful to the group. In fact, it may provide the group with additional variety and stimulation.

The extent to which a culture promotes individualism or collectivism is probably one of the most important dimensions of cultural difference. Individualistic and collectivistic cultures approach activities and communication differently (Hofstede, 1984; 1991; Oetzel, 1995). **Individualistic** cultures are those that value individual recognition more than group or team recognition. Because of this orientation, individuals are encouraged by social institutions and cultural values to self-actualize—"be all that you can be." As a result, group members from an individualistic culture are more likely to be task-oriented and to expect confrontation from others in groups. They also expect members to speak up, to say what is on their mind. Generally, people from the United States, Great Britain, and Australia champion this set of beliefs. Groups composed of individualistic members believe that high productivity or quality decision making is reflective of their group effectiveness.

Alternately, other countries promote **collectivistic** values in which work by groups or teams is valued over individual accomplishment. In this type of culture, "we" is more important than "me." People from collectivistic cultures are more relationally oriented and expect to have harmony in their groups. This heightens the tendency for group members to feel obligated to the group. Confrontation is perceived to be rude and impolite. When groups are composed of individuals from collectivistic cultures, group effectiveness is evaluated by group members' abilities to develop cohesiveness and commitment. Japan, China, and Taiwan value this orientation as do some Central and South American countries.

Three cautions: First, be careful of trying to identify a group member's culture as simply individualistic or collectivistic. Although the culture in the United States clearly supports individualism, look at how many groups exist and the ways in which our society is dependent on them. Second, be careful about similarly categorizing everyone from the same national culture. Research has demonstrated that individuals from the same culture do not always agree on basic values (Cox, Lobel,

& McLeod, 1991). For example, in a group setting, members from U.S. minority cultures preferred and engaged in cooperation rather than competition when working with similar others. Thus subcultures can pervasively influence majority cultures. Third, be cautious of overgeneralizing societal orientations to individuals. Differences in these cultural types are manifested in both verbal and nonverbal communication. Yet as a group member you cannot rely on simple guidelines that indicate that group members who are German will engage in frequent argument. This is because cultural differences do not consume individual differences. Remember that when you read about particular cultures, you are reading a generalized view of the culture. Within that culture, individual differences and individualized communicator styles still exist. Just because a group member looks different from you, you cannot assume that she will communicate differently from you. Similarly, just because a group member looks like you, do not assume that he will communicate in a group like you. Individual differences still predominate.

Perhaps a better way to examine the effect of cultural differences in groups is to look at the degree of self-construal in individual group members (Oetzel & Bolton-Oetzel, 1997). **Self-construal** is the degree to which individuals perceive themselves to be separate or connected to others and how these perceptions are evidenced in individuals' communication behaviors (Kim & Sharkey, 1995).

A group member with an independent construal of self would view himself as being distinct and unique from others. In making evaluations, this person would use his own skills and ideas as the referent rather than using a standard prescribed by others. A person with independent self-construal would value independence and individualism. This type of person would emphasize his internal abilities, thoughts, and feelings and strive to be unique or different from others. Individuals with independent self-construal prefer direct, clear, and nonambiguous communication. In groups, these individuals focus their energies on tasks, believing that working together toward goal achievement will help group members develop cohesiveness.

A group member with an interdependent construal of self would place value on feeling connected to others. Interdependent self-construals stress belonging and fitting in—issues of harmony; that is why they try to meet the needs and goals of others. They place greater value on roles and relationships; thus they prefer group settings to fulfill their needs to communicate conformity and cooperation. In a group, these individuals want to create relational harmony that will enable the group to work effectively on its activity.

Individuals with an independent self-construal are more likely to come from individualistic cultures whereas individuals with an interdependent self-construal are more likely to come from collectivistic or pluralistic cultures. How would these differences surface in group interaction? Group members with differing self-construals would bring different meanings, value assumptions, and communicator styles into the group, which could threaten achieving a common group goal. The degree to which group members' self-construals are independent or interdependent will affect their choices of conversation strategies and tactics in the group setting.

A group with cultural differences can create similarities by focusing on the group's goal or task.

Two other dimensions of interaction—power distance and uncertainty avoidance—can also create differences in interaction style (Hofstede, 1984). Power distance captures how an individual feels or responds to issues of inequality. Inequality based on social status and privilege, wealth, real or perceived power, or society-based rules can surface in interaction. Thus **power distance** is the measure of influence one group member has over another based on these attributes. It can also be perceived as the degree of inequality in power among group members. A common communication tension develops when power distance is present among group members. The more powerful group member attempts to maintain or increase power; at the same time, the less powerful group member attempts to reduce the power distance between them. Some cultures value power distance (for example, Mexico, India), supporting obedience to authority and autocratic decision-making style. Group members from cultures without a strong power distance influence (such as the United States, Germany, Israel) are more likely to resist conformity. Thus, when group members represent different degrees of power distance, there is often difficulty in establishing leadership in a group (Bantz, 1993).

Uncertainty is common to all people regardless of where they live, as individuals cope with changes in technology, law, religion, or societal rules. How one copes with uncertainty is termed **uncertainty avoidance.** Ways of coping with uncertainty are part of our cultural heritage. Cultures seem to tolerate uncertainty differently. For example, the Greek, Portuguese, and Japanese cultures are high in uncertainty avoidance. This means that change is viewed as risky and stressful. In relation to this high level, the United States, India, and Sweden are low in uncertainty avoidance. Generally, this is evidenced in an individual's willingness to take risks. Another way uncertainty avoidance is evidenced is in group members' search for the truth. Group members from high uncertainty avoidance cultures prefer certainty or depend on experts whereas group members from low uncertainty avoidance cultures prefer a practical approach and will seek usable information from any source. Thus groups with members from different culturally bound methods of dealing with uncertainty are likely to experience problems in establishing group norms, especially those about conflict and leadership (Bantz, 1993).

The differences brought to a group discussion by group members from different cultures can have significant impact on the flow of conversation. One study (Watanabe, 1993) looked at how conversation differed in process and how conversation was framed by Americans and Japanese. Americans entered and exited discussion promptly whereas the Japanese began and ended gradually. Japanese members also provided a gradual entrance into discussion topics as they talked about how they would proceed with the discussion. When the discussion was over, they continued to talk to assure themselves that the conversation was complete. Another difference surfaced in how group members presented arguments. Americans provided arguments as reasons or reports. Their voices had little intonation as they provided one reason for each argument in a matter-of-fact tone. A completely different style was used by the Japanese. They gave arguments by telling stories that were organized in a chronological order. Their detailed multiple accounts allowed for some contradiction as details from one story sometimes disputed details in another. From the stories, Japanese members would draw a conclusion rather than using the argument-as-statement-of-fact strategy of Americans. With these differences revealed, it is easy to see how cross-cultural communication can be perceived as miscommunication rather than as differences in communicator strategy and style.

Beyond Cultural Diversity

Diversity issues go far beyond gender, race, and ethnicity to include diversity on social and professional attributes and other demographic categories. Not all of these types of diversity are equal, yet one type cannot be isolated from another. **Cultural distance** is the degree to which you differ from another group member on dimensions of language, social status, religion, politics, economic conditions, and basic assumptions about reality (Triandis, 1995b). When cultural distance is pronounced between two group members, they will have greater difficulty working together.

However, the type of group and group activity create a unique context for each group in which diversity issues become salient. For example, your work group may be more sensitive to diversity in education, organizational tenure, and department than to diversity in race and gender. The cultural distance created by differences in race and gender may be minimized if all work group members are from the same department and have similar lengths of service with the organization. On the other hand, the cultural distance created by race and gender differences may be maximized if work group members represent different departments and different levels of education.

Especially in organizational work teams, diversity can be identified on a number of attributes: organizational tenure, department or unit membership, formal credentials (for instance, CPA or other certifications), and educational level. These attributes can be especially important to the task of the group. Other cultural indicators—gender, race, ethnicity, national origin, age, religious and political affiliations, sexual preference, and physical features—have more impact on relationships among members in the group. The first set of cultural attributes is more likely to affect information processing and power within a work group. The second set of cultural attributes is more likely to affect attraction to the group and feelings of anxiety or frustration associated with the group (Sessa & Jackson, 1995). Try "What Is Your Diversity Filter?" to see how you bring your own cultural values into groups.

Dysfunctional Reactions to Cultural Differences

When members perceive that their group is diverse, they are likely to react in one of several ways (Larkey, 1996; Thomas, 1995). The first response is generally one of inclusion or exclusion. Group members who are of the majority group (for example, gender, ethnicity, socioeconomic class) usually exclude members of any minority group by not including them in conversations. Exclusion can occur in two ways. One type of exclusion occurs when majority group members start conversations only with other members who are similar to them. A second type of exclusion occurs nonverbally or verbally. Nonverbally, you can see exclusion when a majority group member physically turns away from minority group members as if to direct his interaction only to certain group members. Verbally, you can hear exclusion being practiced when majority group members direct the topic of conversation away from the interests of minority group members. By not participating in group conversations, the excluded members lose information, contacts, and opportunities they need to help the group be successful.

A second behavior response to diversity in groups is the continued use of divergence in place of the use of convergence. Divergence occurs when a majority group member uses the communication style or dialect rules of her own group although others in the group are more comfortable with other communication practices. Convergence occurs when group members adjust their way of speaking to match or accommodate another group members' communication style. When a group member retains her own communication style even when other styles are present in the group, she may be calling attention to the power and status she believes she has over others in the group. This type of behavior threatens a group's solidarity and ability to develop cohesiveness. For example, Del, who is from the Midwest, starts every meeting with the phrase "you guys." When Del was growing up, "you guys" meant everyone—males and females. However, Del now lives in the deep South, and he continues to use "you guys" even when females are present in the group. According to his current group members, he is ignoring half of the group. A co-worker told him that this phrase was offensive and generally not used in the South, but Del shrugged off his suggestion and now uses the phrase to playfully irritate others.

A third response is for group members to deny that diversity exists in the group. When members negate that diversity matters, they may be offending other

BUILDING ANALYTICAL SKILLS

What Is Your Diversity Filter?

Use the following chart to identify your diversity filter: the values and assumptions that you bring to group settings. For each dimension of diversity, describe yourself and then think how your membership in that group would affect the values and rules you uphold and their potential impact on a team.

Dimension of Diversity	Values and Rules	Potential Impact on Team
Example: nationality: American	Work hard, play hard.	My work-first-then-play attitude may make others think I'm too task-oriented.
Age:		
Race:		
Gender:		
Occupation or profession:		
Marital status:		
Educational background:		
Geographic home:		
Current geographic location:		

Source: Adapted from Gardenswartz and Rowe (1994).

group members who want their diversity to be recognized. Denying diversity occurs when majority group members try to suppress minority group members with put-down statements. "How long have you been a member of this group?" is meant to remind minority group members of their minority status. Practicing segregation within the group is also a denial tactic. When majority members cluster together at one side of the meeting table, their behavior is a reminder to minority members that they are not welcome or that they are not seen as equals in the group.

A fourth behavioral response to diversity is to artificially limit the variety of ideas the group generates by adhering to one identity or one cultural characteristic—for example, national, ethnic, or occupational allegiances. When this happens, the group will generate greater conformity or uniformity in their ideas. This severely limits the potential of the group. Diverse groups can produce greater diversity of ideas and be more creative. Usually, the greater the diversity of ideas to choose from, the better the idea selected. How well group members allow themselves to understand other group members is the fifth behavioral response to diversity in groups. To create understanding, the expectations of one group member must match the meanings of other members. Misunderstandings can occur when language patterns are different or when language is used in different ways. For example, one member's understanding of a group's work ethic is based upon the Protestant work ethic that hard work pays off. Misunderstanding occurs when another member's work ethic is centered around the concept that work is play and should be enjoyed. It will be difficult for these two group members to agree on how group members should work together and toward what goal until they have reached understanding on this issue.

The sixth behavioral response to diversity is the degree to which negative evaluations are present in the group. Majority group members often consider themselves the in-group while considering minority group members the out-group. Such perceptions foster positive evaluations of one's own group that encourage negative evaluations of others who are dissimilar in some way.

Typically, unequal participation occurs when multiple cultures are represented in groups (Kirchmeyer, 1993). There is still some debate about why this happens. The easy answer would be to say that group members from the majority culture dominate the group's interaction over members from minority cultures. A second explanation is that team members typically overestimate their similarity to members of the same culture and at the same time overestimate their differences from members of other cultures (Northcraft et al., 1995). Thus subsequent information processing about majority and minority group members is often biased to confirm our over- and underestimations of others. We talk more to people we perceive to be more like us and less to people we perceive to be dissimilar.

Another explanation is that minority culture members may be less comfortable with the language of the majority culture that is typically the language used in a group. When a group member has difficulty interacting in the language of other members, she often demonstrates less communication competence. This group member may be hesitant to ask questions or to speak for long periods. She fears that the more she talks, the more likely she will make mistakes in selecting the words or phrases to appropriately describe her ideas.

We should not overgeneralize and expect that minority culture members will be less competent in group settings. Remember that we help create differences among people by categorizing people by cultural identifications. Using those identifications, we judge which group members are more similar to us and which are less similar. This often disguises the real differences and real similarities that can exist among group members, which are not based on cultural identifications. Personal characteristics can also account for differences in group interaction style.

Overcoming Diversity Problems

One way to overcome conflict in multicultural groups is to focus on goal interdependence or cooperative goals (Triandis, 1995a; Wong, Tjosvold, & Lee, 1992). Groups that have cooperative goals are groups whose members have a common vision and who believe that each member will share in the rewards of the group's activity. Even when individuals hold individual goals in addition to the group's goal, a group with a cooperative goal outlook will find ways to ensure that one member's success contributes to the successful goal attainment of other group members. Focusing on long-term rather than short-term goals can also provide group members a path to goal consensus (Bantz, 1993). Short-term goals focus on the here and now, which causes conflict over goal differences that are misattributed to diversity within the group. Long-term goals, however, focus the group on the future—its future—a vision in which all group members can participate. Although conflict is often expected to occur in diverse groups, group members who can communicate to other members that their primary interests are cooperative and group goal-oriented will be able to move through conflicting periods more easily.

Another way to decrease diversity problems is to increase similarity while decreasing dissimilarity among group members (Triandis, 1995a). Even though group members may come from different cultures, they may share certain beliefs and values based on their race, gender, age, occupation, and so on. Taking time to explore the bases of similarities can help the group overcome perceived differences due to cultural diversity. For differences that are real, address them in a group discussion. Find a way to make the differences an advantage for the group. Do not automatically jump to the conclusion that differences are always negative. For example, recognize that diversity often helps a group become more creative. Use the diverse backgrounds of group members to help the group view the problem in alternative ways. In this way the diversity becomes an advantage rather than a drawback.

Another strategy is to emphasize learning about the cultures represented in the group (Triandis, 1995a) and about members as individuals. Establish time in the early development of the group to learn about both. Have members tell about their language, customs, food, and use of nonverbal symbols. Do not assume that group members who are not from the United States know and understand all of the American customs, language, and nonverbal symbols. Take time to share information about each of the cultures represented in the group; all group members will benefit from this. Also take time to learn about individual group members. This will help overcome any stereotypes that have developed that may negatively affect the group interaction.

Still, another method is to emphasize equal status by using group discussion procedures to equalize the amount of talking in the group. It is easy for members who do not feel comfortable to refrain from talking and for those who do feel comfortable to not recognize they are monopolizing the conversation. Building social cohesiveness as well as task cohesiveness can help group members feel more comfortable with one another. When group members feel comfortable, it is more likely that all will participate in group discussions (Bantz, 1993). Emphasizing the team's own unique culture helps develop group unity and promote equality.

Another idea is to focus on the collective mixture of cultural influences in the group rather than on a standoff created by two subgroups. For example, Caucasian and African American members may clash over racial issues occurring outside the group. If the problem is prominent enough to be brought into the group's interaction, all members of the group must be involved in the resolution. Bringing the conflict to the attention of one subgroup or both will do little to solve the problem when other races are represented in the group (Thomas, 1995). When groups adopt a collective cultural focus, mutual adaptation is necessary from all group members (Thomas, 1995). Mutual adaptation requires that majority as well as minority members assess their behaviors and communication styles and work to create a group system that is satisfying to all.

Finally, emphasize personal identity not social identity (Oetzel, 1995). Rather than seeing yourself and others as belonging to categories (for example, Caucasian, American, male, manager), view yourself and other group members as individuals—each with an unique identity and personality. Doing so helps to eliminate attitudes that are based on social identities and then imported into the group (for instance, males are better than females attitude). When group members are viewed as individuals, more equal participation results.

Culturally diverse groups have many issues to sort out in addition to working on the group task. Thus groups composed of culturally diverse members may need additional time (Northcraft et al., 1995; Oetzel & Bolton-Oetzel, 1997). Different orientations are brought to group work by individual differences in self-construal. Thus individual group members need time to adjust to the alternative perspective, and then the group needs time to develop a process that meets the needs of all group members. Although monocultural groups generally perform better initially, over time heterogeneous groups catch up and can even surpass the performance of homogeneous groups (Watson, Kumar, & Michaelsen, 1993).

Diversity can provide a group with advantages when the team takes time to develop its own culture from the combination of cultures brought to it by group members. By establishing its own norms and procedures, members' group-related values, beliefs, and attitudes are likely to converge. When convergence occurs,

> ### ❓ THINK ABOUT IT
>
> *Are You Ignoring Diversity?*
>
> Put yourself in the following situation. You have been asked to serve on a neighborhood action group. You are surprised you were asked to join the group as you recently moved into the neighborhood, and you do not even know everyone on your block. Your neighbors believe that your neighborhood lacks some important city services and wants the action group to draw this to the attention of the city's action council. Imagine that this situation existed in your neighborhood. What types of diversity would be represented in the neighborhood action group (gender, race, nationality, age, religious affiliation, occupation, and so on). To what degree would diversity facilitate or inhibit the group from working well together?

members enhance their sense of group identity and build greater cohesiveness with other group members. Although convergence can create similarity in group-related attitudes, diverse groups can still draw upon its differentiation—the specialized skills and knowledge of its members (McGrath, Berdahl, & Arrow, 1995). Achieving congruence or integration does not mean that everyone gets everything their way. Rather, it means that the group has negotiated among all of the differences present in the group to find a positive fit among apparently conflicting positions, values, and beliefs (Northcraft et al., 1995).

Effective and ineffective groups differ more in how they manage their diversity than in the extent to which diversity is absent or present. When a group is composed of diverse individuals, the group needs to take proactive steps to create a supportive climate in which integration and congruence can occur. By creating a team culture from the diversity of its members, the group can take advantage of diversity by making it a resource for the group (Adler, 1986; Cox, 1995). Try the exercise in "Are You Ignoring Diversity?"

Summary

Working in groups means building relationships with others. You will develop dependent relationships with other group members in addition to dependencies on individuals outside your group. Be careful. Dependent relationships create superior-subordinate interaction. Alternately, interdependent relationships are those that are equally balanced. When group members perceive interdependence with one another, communication can be used to resolve differences. Interdependence also creates a seamless flow among group members.

Group cohesiveness contributes to the development of interdependence. When a group is cohesive, members want to remain in the group, whether they are attracted to the group's task or group members. Cohesive groups often perform more effectively; but, cohesiveness does not ensure good group performance. Too much cohesiveness can actually interfere with the group's ability to critically examine alternatives.

Like cohesiveness, satisfaction develops from interdependent relationships. Members are satisfied when they are fulfilled or gratified by the group, particularly when the group is moving along its expected path. Dissatisfaction can also occur, but when the elements that create satisfaction are not present, dissatisfaction may not increase. Rather, dissatisfaction is more specific and created by group members wasting time or failing to use effective procedures. When group members are satisfied, however, they are willing to work harder and be more committed to the group.

Camaraderie is another element that demonstrates closeness among group members. Camaraderie focuses on both group task and group relationships. Primarily based on the use of effective procedures, camaraderie promotes task sharing among group members.

When relationships and interdependence develop among group members, power issues are inevitable. Power is created through communication and can be based upon rewards, coercion, role or position, charisma, or expertise. Power is best analyzed contextually. The extent to which power develops may be based on formalized power structures and the degree to which struggle over power occurs. Power is fluid, not static; power in relationships changes frequently. Power can also be created when a group member has control over real or imagined resources.

Power can also be misused. Two extreme cases result in the development of two specialized roles: the primary provoker and the scapegoat. The primary provoker is a power-assuming member who creates problems and confusion for other group members. This high level of ambiguity actually causes the other members—the secondary provokers—to help the primary provoker sustain his or her power grip over the group. Group dysfunctionality results as the group spends more time on dealing with its relationship with the primary provoker than it does working on its task. The scapegoat represents another misuse of power. In this instance, group members inappropriately direct their anxiety, aggression, or blame to one member who then becomes blamed for the group's problems.

Equity and trust also result from interdependent relationships in groups. Equity is different than equality. Equity occurs when group members are rewarded proportionally for the work they do in the group. Inequity occurs when all group members receive the same reward even if the distribution of effort is uneven. Trust is based on honesty, openness, consistency, and respect. Group members must earn trust with one another through their interactions. Trust is fragile; once broken, it is hard to reinstate.

Working in groups will put you in contact with people who are dissimilar to you. These differences may be based on gender or cultural issues. Research on gender differences has produced inconsistent findings. However, many people still hold stereotypes about males and females in leadership roles even when females demonstrate effective leadership capacity. There is some evidence that females may be more group-centered than males.

Issues of cultural diversity are most often linked to race and ethnicity but can also be based on age, profession or occupation, geographic home, organizational tenure, religion, politics, socioeconomic status—any category that identifies differences among people. Diversity creates difficulty for groups because all group members are ethnocentric to some degree. Individuals also rely upon their home cultures for cues about how to behave in groups. Group members from individualistic cultures will view the group setting differently than group members from collectivistic cultures. How group members construe themselves in relation to the group is also a diversity issue. Members who feel independent and separate from the group will communicate with different strategies than members who feel interdependent and who prefer harmony, conformity, and commitment. Individuals are often uncomfortable communicating with dissimilar others; their dysfunctional reactions create a higher degree of confusion, confirming their anxiety. But there are many ways to overcome diversity problems. Focusing on long-term and cooperative goals, identifying similarities even when diversity is present, learning about others' cultures, using discussion procedures to equalize talking turns, and emphasizing personal over social identity are just a few ways to overcome diversity problems.

✓ Checklist

Group Knowledge

You should be able to:

- explain the difference between dependence and interdependence.
- describe how cohesiveness affects group interaction.
- explain three ways to help a group develop cohesiveness.
- name the bases of power in groups.
- explain how power can be misused in groups.
- explain the impact of gender differences and cultural diversity on groups.

Group Skills

You should be able to:

- assist your group in developing cohesiveness.
- maximize your satisfaction in a group.
- use power in a group effectively and positively.
- refocus the negative effects of a primary provoker or the group's use of a scapegoat.
- minimize stereotypical assumptions about gender and cultural differences.
- maximize the advantages of gender and cultural differences in a group.

Analytical and Assessment Techniques

You should be able to:
- explain how group members can create interdependence with one another.
- identify what is contributing to camaraderie among group members.
- determine which power base is being used and evaluate its effectiveness.
- select strategies for minimizing the development of primary and secondary provoker roles.
- assess the level of equity and trust in a group.
- suggest strategies to help a group overcome cultural differences.

Discussion Questions and Exercises

1. Think back to a group where trust was high and to another group where trust was low. Write a short paper responding to these questions: What accounted for the difference in level of trust? How did the level of trust affect the group's communication? How did the one group build trust? What happened in the other group to erode trust?

2. In your most recent group experience, identify the power bases that you held. Explain how the power relationships were developed. Assess the effectiveness of holding and using such power. Explain why you avoid or ignore other bases of power.

3. Watch a sitcom, drama, or film that features group interaction. Pay particular attention to the gender roles of the main characters. Were the roles realistically portrayed? What gender differences did you notice? Have you noticed these same gender differences in your own group interaction?

4. In small groups of five to seven members, discuss the group experiences you have had in which cultural differences surfaced. Although ethnic, racial, and national cultures create some of the more obvious cultural differences, other cultural differences exist. Allow yourself to think broadly about cultural differences. What types of cultural differences have you experienced? Try to assess whether cultural or individual differences were the main focus.

PART 2

Meeting Group Challenges

8 Using Groups to Make Decisions and Solve Problems

Why do we spend so much time on decision making?

Is there a difference in decision-making procedures?

Is one decision procedure better than another?

How do I know which decision procedure my group should use?

How do I know when my group is making effective decisions?

When groups need to solve problems or make decisions, they can choose from a variety of strategies. One strategy is for a group to deny or hide the problem. This option is likely to be chosen when the problem seems severe but impossible to solve. Another option is to take a wait-and-see attitude. This delay tactic may initially seem prudent because group members think the problem is not severe enough to warrant their attention. The strategy can backfire, however, when unattended problems increase in intensity or frequency. A third option is for one group member to work on the problem or make the decision independently of the group. This option seems attractive when there is a member with the expertise to deal with the issue or when group time and energy are already stressed. Yet solo problem solving or decision making may generate negative returns with respect to commitment to the decision and group cohesiveness. Another option is to involve others outside the group. Rather than having the group resolve the issue, group members shift the problem to another person or another group. This strategy minimizes the group's responsibility, but again, negatively affects commitment to the decision. Collaborative problem solving and decision making is the preferred alternative in group settings. Let's examine why.

Using the Group's Strength to Solve Problems

Why are groups better at decision making than individuals? For complex decisions or problems, it is unlikely that any individual would possess or have access to the knowledge and resources necessary to make an effective decision. Second, groups generally bring a greater diversity of perspectives to the situation. It is too easy for one person to become locked on to an idea that lacks merit. Third, and probably most important, when more people are involved in decision making and problem solving, the group has the opportunity to check out ideas before one is selected and implemented. This opportunity to try out ideas allows groups to be more confident than individuals in making similar decisions (Sniezek, 1992).

Groups produce better decisions through communication. Communication is central to group members' ability to work together to select high-quality solutions (Salazar et al., 1994). Even when group members have high potential (are highly skilled or highly knowledgeable), the communication among members is the process that allows the group to do its best. Groups that spend their time on goal-directed communication to evaluate task-relevant issues and generate ideas create superior group outcomes.

Decision making is also a social process. The presence of others creates a context of social evaluation that motivates us to find the best possible solution (Kameda, 1996). For decisions that affect many individuals, involving them will increase their commitment to upholding the decision as it is implemented. To carry out some decisions, the cooperation of many people is needed. Including those people in the decision-making process helps to ensure their cooperation as well as overall satisfaction with the decision. (People do not like it when someone in authority makes decisions that affect them without asking their opinions.) Moreover, involving them in the decision making increases their understanding of the solution so that they can perform better in the implementation stage.

To take advantage of these strengths, however, groups need some structure to the decision-making discussion (Van de Ven & Delbecq, 1971). Using a procedure to structure group discussion and decision making helps groups in four ways. First, the content of the discussion is more controlled and on task than when discussions are left unstructured. Second, group member participation in the discussion is more equal when some type of procedure is used. Alternative viewpoints from group members do not help the group unless those viewpoints are revealed during discussion. Third, the emotional tone of a group's discussion is less likely to become negative or out of control. Finally, groups make better decisions when structure is used. Think of a procedure as a map to follow or a guidebook to lead the way. You could get there from here—but it is easier with some help.

When a decision needs to be made, generally one of two conditions exists: Either there is some type of disagreement among group members about what is best or group members do not know how to fix the problem. Your group can proceed in several different ways (Laughlin, 1996). If the group is aware of its choices or alternatives, members could randomly select from among the choices. Or the group could use each of the alternatives in some turn-taking fashion. You could vote to establish a preference or use discussion to demonstrate preferences and then choose from among them. If the group does not know how to resolve the problem, members can use discussion to generate or create alternatives from which to make a selection.

Voting is a popular decision procedure in the United States. We will discuss voting procedures and its weaknesses and strengths. However, our main focus will be on group discussion and how it can be used to analyze preferences, create alternatives, and make final choices. Most groups are faced with complex decisions, few of which have correct answers (for example, mathematical problems and jigsaw puzzles). When decisions are complex, many different alternatives could be satisfactory. This creates a dilemma for groups: How do you decide among several acceptable options?

We should recognize, however, that there is a great deal of variety in decision-making procedures (Schweiger & Leana, 1986). Procedures can vary according to how group members participate in decision making (style) and according to how much group members participate (quantity). Procedures also differ according to whether participation is voluntary or forced. Some procedures are formal, others more informal. To maximize their effectiveness, groups should be able to use a variety of decision making procedures. *Putting the Pieces Together* will help you understand the decision-making procedures in which you have participated.

Groups are frequently asked to find solutions for problems. Whether these are problems in your organization (such as a task force assigned to reduce shoplifting) or problems in your community (how to reduce juvenile delinquency), most problems have multiple outcomes or solutions that could be acceptable. The job of the group is to find the solution best suited to solving the problem. Research has shown that groups that accomplish five functions in their discussion perform better. These five functions are thoroughly discussing the problem, examining the criteria of an acceptable solution before discussing solutions, proposing a set of realistic alternative solutions, assessing the positive aspects of each proposed solution, and assessing the negative aspects of each proposed solution (Gouran & Hirokawa, 1983; Hirokawa, 1982, 1983a, 1983b, 1988; Hirokawa & Pace, 1983, Hirokawa & Scheerhorn, 1986). Your group can accomplish these functions by using one of the formal discussion procedures described in the following section.

Using Decision Procedures

You may be thinking that all groups use procedures. But one study found that most group members are unaware of the rules their group uses to make decisions (Johnson, 1991). Groups benefit from the use of procedures—guides in the form of a person or a process to help the group with its decision making. Without procedures to follow, a group typically defers to the preference of the group member who is perceived to be the expert or to the group member who seems to care the most about the problem (Johnson, 1991). The procedures that follow—standard agenda, critical advisor, consensus, voting, ranking, brainstorming, and nominal group technique—vary widely in the amount of control and the type of help they provide to groups. Think of a decision procedure as a framework for guiding the group's interaction. Procedures help groups overcome limitations that routinely arise when groups make decisions, such as the following problems:

- All group members do not speak up, or the opportunity for all members to speak up is not present.
- The group has trouble staying focused on what it needs to accomplish.
- The group has difficulty sticking to the meeting agenda.

> **PUTTING THE PIECES TOGETHER**
>
> ### Group Goal and Interdependence
>
> Think about the last decision you made in a group. How did the decision relate to the goal of the group? Was the decision made by everyone? Or were just a few members really involved in making the decision? In what way did the decision-making activities increase or decrease the amount of interdependence among group members? Do you believe that group members took the decision-making process seriously? If not, what factors contributed? If your group had the chance to make that decision over again, would you recommend a different approach to decision making?

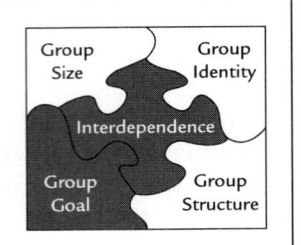

- The group performs cursory rather than detailed analyses of alternatives.
- Members of the group are pressured to conform.
- The group tends to give way to premature convergence to avoid conflict.
- The most talkative few take up the group's talking time.
- The group has low motivation for working on this decision, or the group has fallen into a rut.

Groups that use procedures generally outperform groups that do not. Each of the procedures described in the following sections provides process or ground rules for members to follow. Although the use of procedures does not guarantee group effectiveness, using procedures maximizes opportunities for groups to achieve the results they desire. One procedure that is not discussed here is parliamentary procedure, which is a highly formalized procedure to help medium and large groups (for example, parent-teacher organizations) with both discussion, decision, and business activities. If you are an officer in an organization that uses parliamentary procedure, you will want to become familiar with its many protocols. However, small or informal groups rarely follow these procedures. We will start with the standard agenda.

Standard Agenda

The **standard agenda,** also known as reflective thinking, is a procedure with a strict linear process that groups follow in considering decision alternatives. A group using this procedure would pass through a series of six steps—each focusing on different aspects of the problem-solving process. Each step must be completed before going on to the next.

The first step is problem identification. Here the group must clarify what it wants to do or what it is being asked to do. A good way to start is to ask the question, Is the problem before your group a question of fact, value, or policy (see Chapter 4 for a discussion of each), or some combination of these? Too frequently, groups overlook this step. Rather, each group member knows what the problem is and assumes that other group members have the same problem in mind. For example, a student group selected for its class project finding a solution to not having food available on north campus. All of the food outlets were at least a mile away from this part of campus. What is the problem? Students, faculty, and staff do not have access to food for lunch and dinner. Are you sure? This group canvassed students and staff to examine the problem from their point of view. This helped them be certain that they were on track before going ahead with the rest of the project. Before going on to the next step, each group member should be able to state what the problem is.

The second step is problem analysis. Here group members should be gathering information, data, even opinions to help them examine the history and cause of the problem. Group members need to decide how serious or widespread the problem is. Considering solutions to resolve a problem for a few isolated people is quite different from considering solutions to resolve a problem that affects many. Continuing with the food on north campus problem, the group again surveyed students for the type of food they would like access to. Their next step was to contact the food services department on campus to discuss any difficulties in making food available on north campus. With both sets of information, the group was able to compare the foods that were easily accessible from food services with the foods students wanted. And, although the general focus was on problems, group members also needed to think of any issues that were hidden by the problem. One hidden issue—and the real reason food was not available on this part of campus—was that custodial staff was limited on this part of campus, meaning that there would not be enough custodians to clean the classrooms and keep the food areas up to health department standards.

The third step is identifying the minimal criteria for the solution. In the food problem, criteria involved issues of money. How much were students willing to spend for the convenience of eating near their classes? How much money could food services allot in their budget to establishing food service on north campus? How much money would be required for extra custodial help? The group stopped at this point, but then they found other criteria needed to be considered. For example, where would these new food services be located? Who would give permission to install food outlets in classroom buildings? Because space was so tight, the only place that reasonably could hold a food outlet was the theatre department's ticket office. The group did not pursue what would happen to the ticket office if it was moved to accommodate food outlets. The more criteria group members can think of for evaluating solutions the more complete and the more useful their decisions will be.

In the fourth step, group members generate solutions. As you might guess, it is hard to keep from doing this throughout the discussion procedure. But groups that generate solutions too quickly will prematurely conclude that they are done without fully investigating all potential solutions. The group studying the problem of food on north campus failed to generate other solutions like independent food cart vendors that would not require permanent space. It is a good idea to allow at least two meetings for idea generation. This way, group members have the opportunity to think and reflect about the problem individually before coming back to the group.

Evaluating solutions and selecting one as best is the fifth step. If the group has followed the standard agenda, this step will be relatively easy because the group has access to all needed information. Using the criteria generated in the last step, the group should evaluate the advantages and disadvantages of each solution separately. What about the food on north campus group? Unfortunately, they got stuck early on in the process. They became so focused on moving the ticket office and installing a Mexican fast food outlet that they did not have other options to evaluate at this step. As a result, they forced themselves into recommending a solution that would not be approved.

The sixth step of the standard agenda is solution implementation. Follow-through is often a weak area for groups because the charge of the group often does not include implementation, so group members get little practice in this area. Other times, a group has used all of its energy in decision making and has little left over for implementing the decision. Thus they simply stop after selecting a solution. Because implementation is a common weakness for groups, we will explore this step further in Chapter 9.

The standard agenda maximizes group communication because it provides equal opportunity to all proposals, no matter who makes them. Highly cohesive groups will benefit from using the standard agenda procedure. Members of highly cohesive groups may feel inhibited about criticizing an idea or proposal before the group (Pavitt, 1993). Thinking that any criticism may ruin the closeness of members, a group member may refrain from saying something that seems to question someone else. Following the steps of the standard agenda allows group members to question ideas and ask for clarification. Although the standard agenda is often seen as the ideal procedure for most decision-making activities, it is not always practical (Jarboe, 1996). Some groups may find it difficult to follow the steps of the standard agenda, and, certainly, this procedure takes time.

The other procedures that follow can be used in the various steps of the standard agenda. Each procedure can contribute to the group's decision making in different ways. In practice, groups may use several different procedures throughout their decision-making activity.

Critical Advisor

Often referred to as the devil's advocate, the critical advisor consciously becomes the group's critic. In this role, the critical advisor suggests disadvantages to alternatives posed, reveals hidden assumptions by offering analyses of the problem that the group has not discussed, and questions the validity or reliability of information used as evidence for selecting the solution. The critical advisor helps the group see errors in its logic and thinking. By asking questions, asking for clarification, or challenging data, the critical advisor forces the group to provide support for its decision. (This technique is a modified version of the more complex and time-consuming procedure suggested by Schweiger, Sandberg, and Ragan [1986].)

Only one group member is assigned to the critical advisor role. Over time, different group members should assume the role. Group members may find that the critical advisor interjects unexpected and alternative reasoning when the group is on a roll. This is an advantage for the group because it keeps the group from falling into traps of agreement. However, negativity can surface because the critical advisor interjects questions into the discussion. Sometimes the negativity is directed to the person playing the critical advisor role. Rotating the role among group members minimizes the likelihood that a single group member is accused of slowing down the group. Role rotation also strengthens members' skills as each member has the opportunity to fulfill the critical advisor role.

When should a group use the critical advisor role? Group members who have had experience working with one another will probably get the most out of the critical advisor role. Because this procedure has little structure, it can be used when other procedures would consume too much time. This procedure is also useful when a group must present and support its decision to an external audience. Having responded to the questions of the critical advisor, the group should be able to respond more effectively to outside challenges. The constructive conflict allowed in the critical advisor procedure helps groups produce high quality decisions. Let's see how the role of critical advisor works in a group.

TIM: Jody, do you think we can move on the proposal?

JODY: I'm not sure, Tim, we've still got a lot to think about.

NICK: (in the role of the critical advisor) Maybe it would be a good idea to stop and consider what we have left to do.

SELA: Okay, we've got to finalize the budget, draw the timeline, get someone to draw the graphs, and write the cover letter.

JODY: I said I'd do the graphs. Did everyone turn in their sketches?

TIM: Sorry, Jody. I forgot. How about tomorrow?

SELA: You've got mine.

NICK: Mine too. Do we need to look at all of the graphs as a group?

JODY: That's a good idea. I don't want to spend time on the computer and then have someone disagree with what I've done. Let's do that at our next meeting.

NICK: Tim, let's come back to your comment about needing to move on the proposal. Is there some other pressure we don't know about?

TIM: Well, I saw Mr. Campbell at lunch yesterday. He asked about our proposal. Gave me the pep talk, you know.

NICK: Did he say anything to indicate that the deadline was moved up?

TIM: Not exactly, I just got that feeling, you know, that he was waiting on us.

> **? THINK ABOUT IT**
>
> ### Could You Be a Critical Advisor?
>
> Think of one of your recent group experiences when a critical advisor would have helped the group's decision discussion. How would the group have reacted to your volunteering to be the critical advisor? How could you have persuaded them that a critical advisor is needed? Think about the most effective way to play the critical advisor role in this particular group. What communication strategies would you have needed to make this role effective for the group?

NICK: Maybe we should confirm the deadline for the proposal with Campbell. I'll send him an e-mail just as soon as we're through. Tim, anything else?

TIM: Well, I didn't want to mention it, but I also saw Ms. Rhoades. She also asked when we'd get the proposal done.

NICK: Is she waiting on our proposal? Or on Campbell's decision, Tim?

JODY: Good question, Nick. Before she's pushed me to finish something I had to do for Campbell because Campbell takes longer than she likes in making a decision.

NICK: Is that a concern of this group then?

SELA: Well, it could be. Rhoades is watching what we're doing because I think she has something else planned for us when this is finished.

TIM: I got that feeling, too, Sela.

JODY: Well, maybe we need to get moving, then.

NICK: That could be. But let's confirm the deadline with Campbell. And let's not move so quickly that the proposal we turn in will fail.

Nick's role as critical advisor is to watch the group's process and ask questions that clarify what the group is talking about. When someone plays this role in a group, the intent is to be the ideal group member, not an antagonist. Try "Could You Be a Critical Advisor?" to see how this role could help your group.

Consensus

Consensus means that each group member agrees with the decision or that group members' individual positions are close enough that they can support the group's decision (DeStephen & Hirokawa, 1988). In the latter case, even if members do not totally agree with the decision, they have chosen to support the group by supporting the decision. Why would members agree to support a decision they do not fully accept? Consensus is achieved through discussion. To the extent that group members feel that they have participated in the decision-making process, they develop satisfaction with the group's interaction. That satisfaction is then extended to the consensus decision. Thus when all group members can give verbal support, consensus has been achieved (Hoffman & Kleinman, 1994).

A group with consensus uses discussion to combine the best insights of all members to find a solution that incorporates all points of view. Juries that award damages in lawsuits must make consensus decisions—everyone must agree on the amount of money to be awarded. Too frequently, consensus is thought of as a freewheeling discussion without any sort of process, plan, or procedure. But there are procedures that a group can use in a consensus discussion (Hare, 1982). These procedures are particularly helpful when a group must reach a consensus decision that is a subjective judgment falling along some continuum (for example, a panel of judges meets to discuss which contestant will best represent the university; the local United Way board of directors meets to decide how much money will be allocated to which community service agencies).

To develop consensus, the leader or another group member takes on the role of coordinator to monitor the group's process, not the group's decision. The leader or coordinator does not express his or her opinions or argue for or against proposals suggested by the group. Rather, the leader uses ideas generated by members to formulate proposals that can be acceptable to all members. Another group member should act as a recorder to document each of the proposals made. When the group feels it has reached consensus, the recorder should read aloud the decision so members can give approval or modify the proposal.

In using consensus, group members first need to agree to follow the basic rule of consensus; that is, the group is to look for a solution that incorporates all points of view. Group members should give their opinions on the issue as well as seek out differences of opinion from other members. In this step, the coordinator should make extra effort to include less talkative members in the discussion. When a group member gives his or her opinion, remarks should be addressed to the group as a whole and not addressed to the coordinator. Throughout the discussion, the recorder should read back statements that reflect the initial agreements of the group. This step ensures that the agreement is real.

During consensus, group members should avoid calling for a vote or other procedures that could shorten the discussion. Consensus can only be reached through interaction. Although each group member should be encouraged to give his or her opinion, group members should avoid arguing for their personal ideas. It is better to state your ideas and give supporting reasons. Arguing about whose idea is better or whose idea is more correct will not help the group achieve consensus. If other group members express opinions that differ from yours, avoid confrontation and criticism. Rather, ask questions that can help you understand the others' point of view.

As the group works toward consensus, it can be tempting to change your mind just so the group can reach consensus and move on to other activities. Be careful! Changing your mind only to reach agreement will make you less satisfied with the process and the decision. If the group has trouble reaching consensus, it is better to postpone the decision until another meeting or to use another decision-making procedure. Pressing for a solution because time is short will not help group members understand and commit to the decision. If a decision is postponed, making assignments to gather more information can help the next discussion session.

Groups can realize some advantages from using the consensus procedure, especially as an alternative to voting (Hare, 1982). Discussion leading to consensus allows more viewpoints to be discussed so members are made aware of issues and facts they did not know. Group members also like consensus because they feel like they are part of the group action. Consensus discussions involve everyone; a high degree of integration can be achieved when at least part of everyone's point of view is represented in the final decision.

Consensus discussions can take longer when groups rely on free-flowing conversation instead of the consensus procedures above. Groups may reach consensus more quickly, but often the decision is a false consensus—agreeing to a decision just to be done with task. When consensus discussions are short, some alternatives may be left unaddressed. Thus the extent to which consensus is effective is reliant on the voluntary and effective participation of group members. When controversial or complex decisions must be made, a group is likely to make a better decision with a more standardized approach that structures group inquiry.

One way to maximize consensus decision making is to consider the decision rule orientation of each group member. A **decision rule orientation** is the manner in which you process information (Beatty, 1988, 1989). You could say that a decision rule reflects a group member's philosophy about making decision choices. Group members who have a **maximax decision rule** orientation are optimists who assume a best-case scenario and search for the solution that promises the biggest pay-off or positive outcomes. In other words, individuals focus on the positives or the rewards and accept the risk in their decision choice. Being able to accept or even ignore failure is necessary in this orientation in order to make large gains. The complete opposite of the maximax orientation is the **maximin decision rule** orientation. Group members who have this decision rule orientation—the most conservative of all orientations—search for the largest pay-off that at the same time would minimize the losses. This orientation is characteristic of group members who try to avoid failure or loss and who hold a pessimistic view of the situation. But most experts recommend a **maximum expected utility decision rule.** This orientation is a middle ground between large gains and large losses because choices are made to reflect consistency and stability. Using this orientation, group members would search for the alternative that provides the highest average pay-off across many conditions or situations. A group member with this orientation would estimate the value for or utility of each alternative and then multiply that number by the probability of occurrence for each alternative. This calculated orientation would not be the choice for entrepreneurs!

Let's see how your decision rule orientation would affect decision making. Imagine that you are a member of committee charged with the responsibility for planning a party for your retiring sales manager, Sonjay. You are fond of Sonjay, and you want to have a nice party, but because the company is not paying for it, you need to consider the expenses involved. Together, the committee has narrowed

A group member's decision rule orientation is the manner in which he or she processes information in decision making. In fact, different information is enhanced by different decision rule orientations. Even though all group members have access to the same information, differences in their decision rule orientation allow each member to arrive at a different outcome.

down the choices in caterers to three: Italian Catering Company can provide an Italian food buffet for $6.50 per person; Deli Dining has proposed a cold meat sandwich with vegetable and fruit trays for $8.00 per person; and the Steak Shop has proposed a sit-down steak or fish dinner for $18.50. If you just consider price as the deciding criterion, then obviously you pick the Italian Catering Company. But you know that out of these three choices, Sonjay would prefer a grilled tuna steak served on a bed of rice. Which option would you choose? If the meal is too expensive, fewer people will come to honor Sonjay, but the least expensive option is not Sonjay's favorite food. In terms of utility, the best choice to satisfy both meat eaters and vegetarians is Deli Dining. With the utility evaluated, how do you think price will affect the number of people who come to Sonjay's retirement celebration? What do you think of first? price? Sonjay's food preferences? the number of co-workers who will help celebrate Sonjay's retirement? A person with a maximax decision rule orientation would select the Steak Shop because it is Sonjay's favorite food. Being an optimist, she would believe that co-workers would not mind paying more money. A committee member with a maximin decision rule orientation would select the Italian Catering Company because his pessimistic orientation would indicate that expensive prices would deter people from coming to the celebration. Finally, a member with a maximum expected utility rule orientation would choose the Deli Dining option because everyone would be able to find something to eat, and the price is not much more than the price of a restaurant lunch.

Even when group members have the same information decision rule orientation focuses the decision maker on different aspects of the information. When

228 Part 2 Meeting Group Challenges

> ### GROUP ASSESSMENT TECHNIQUE
>
> ### Can Consensus Work?
>
> An often-debated issue is to what extent men and women should live and work together while they are members of the U.S. armed forces. Since 1993, combat jobs have been open to women. Generals and admirals have generally been opposed to this change, which was initiated by the White House. In recent years, the armed forces have been plagued with sex scandals (rape, sexual assault, sexual harassment), and one service branch even had to admit that sexual harassment and mistreatment of women in uniform was quite prevalent. As an example of some of the problems that exist, during the U.S. presence in Bosnia, every three days a woman soldier had to be evacuated due to pregnancy. But one fact that seldom makes the news is that there are far more single fathers in the military than there are single mothers (Armed forces, 1998).
>
> Choose one of the following questions for your group's discussion:
>
> Goal 1: To what extent should men and women be housed together in the same barracks while they serve in the U.S. armed forces?
>
> Goal 2: To what extent should men and women train and work together while they serve in the U.S. armed forces?
>
> Use consensus as your group's decision-making procedure. After coming to a decision, use the following scale to answer each question about your group and its decision making.
>
> 1 = strongly disagree   2 = disagree   3 = undecided   4 = agree   5 = strongly agree
>
> 1. The group reached the right decision.   1 2 3 4 5
> 2. I believe that our group's decision/solution is appropriate.   1 2 3 4 5
> 3. I support the final group decision.   1 2 3 4 5
> 4. I believe we selected the best alternative available.   1 2 3 4 5
> 5. I would be willing to put my best effort into carrying out the group's final   1 2 3 4 5
>   decision.

orientations are mixed in a group, the group is likely to draw contradictory conclusions about the preferred course of action or the direction of the discussion. When group members share a decision rule orientation, they share intuitive and implicit agreement about how to process information and what constitutes an acceptable choice. Thus, consensus is higher in groups where members have similar decision rule orientations. "Can Consensus Work?" gives you a chance to test the consensus of your group.

Voting

Voting in groups requires group members to cast written or verbal ballots in support of or against a specific proposal. Many organizational groups rely on the outcomes of majority voting to elect officers or pass resolutions. A group that votes

6. I believe we approached our task in an organized manner. 1 2 3 4 5
7. This group used effective decision-making techniques. 1 2 3 4 5
8. This group was a place where people could feel comfortable expressing themselves. 1 2 3 4 5
9. I like the members of my group. 1 2 3 4 5
10. I would like to work with members of my group on another similar project. 1 2 3 4 5
11. I believe I contributed important ideas during the decision-making process. 1 2 3 4 5
12. I believe I had a lot of influence on the group's decision making. 1 2 3 4 5
13. I contributed important information during the group's decision-making process. 1 2 3 4 5
14. During group meetings, I got to participate whenever I wanted to. 1 2 3 4 5
15. I believe that the other members of the group liked me. 1 2 3 4 5
16. Other members of the group really listened to what I had to say. 1 2 3 4 5
17. I felt that I was a genuine member of the group. 1 2 3 4 5

Total Score _____

If your score was between 68 and 85, you believe that your group demonstrated high consensus. How does your score compare with the scores of your group members? If your score was below 68, what could you have done to help the group achieve consensus?

Source: DeStephen and Hirokawa (1988).

needs to decide on three procedural issues before a vote is taken. The first decision is how the vote will be taken. When sensitive issues are voted on, it is better to use a written ballot. Similar ballots or pieces of paper are given to each group member. This way group members can vote their conscience and retain their anonymity. Two group members should count and verify the decision before announcing it to the group. A verbal vote, or a show of hands, is more efficient when it is necessary only to document the approval or disapproval that was apparent in the group's discussion. For example, your communication students' association has several items of business to take care of at the next meeting. The association needs to elect officers, approve the budget, and select a faculty member for the outstanding professor award. The budget was read to members at the last meeting and then discussed. Although members will ask some questions before the vote, the group basically needs to approve or disapprove the budget. Because there is nothing out of the ordinary about the budget and little controversy is expected, it is okay to use a show of hands in this case. However, electing officers and voting for one professor to receive an award can bring up conflicting emotions among group members. Both of these matters are better handled with written ballots. This way group members can freely support the candidates and the professor they desire without fear of intimidation or retaliation.

The second procedural issue that needs to be agreed on before taking a vote is how many votes are needed to win or decide an issue. Most of the time, a simple majority vote (one more than half of the members) is satisfactory. However, if a group is changing its constitution or taking some type of legal action, a two-thirds or three-fourths majority may be preferable. Both the method of voting and the majority required for a decision need to be agreed upon before any voting takes place.

The third procedural issue centers on the discussion the group should have before members vote. You would not just walk into a meeting and vote. Voting should be based on clear proposals and plenty of group discussion. Here is a suggested procedure to follow in voting (Hare, 1982). Members bring items to the attention of the group by making proposals in the form of motions. Let's say that your communication students' association is making decisions about their budget. Karen says, "I move that we set aside part of our budget for community activities." Discussion among group members would reveal two ambiguities. What does Karen mean by "part of our budget"? twenty percent, forty percent? What are "community activities"? teaching junior high students how to give speeches? With other members' help, Karen's proposal is made more specific: "I move that we set aside 20 percent of our budget for community intervention activities that help children appreciate the value of communicating effectively." Now with a specific motion, Karen can argue for her proposal by stating its merits. Even with a specific proposal, she is going to receive some opposition or more questions. That is okay because it helps all group members understand her motion more clearly. During this discussion, the group leader makes sure all those who want to be heard get a chance to talk. However, the leader does not argue for or against any particular motion. To do so would put undue influence on the group. The group's secretary or recorder keeps track of the motions and identifies which ones received approval from the group.

Voting can be efficient, but it can also arbitrarily limit a group's choices. Many times motions considered for a vote take on an either/or position that limits other alternatives. For example, if you vote against using 20 percent of the budget for community intervention activities, it may be unclear what you voted against. Are you not in favor of using only 20 percent of the budget? Or are you against using any of the group's monies for community activities? just these community activities?

Ranking

When a group uses **ranking** with a set of decision alternatives, each member individually assigns a numerical value to each available position (1 is assigned to the most valued choice, 2 to the next most valued choice, and so on). These rankings may be based on a rating evaluation (0–100) performed by each group member on a set of criteria developed by the group (for instance, How well does this alternative fix the problem? Is the alternative possible within the time frame allotted the project?) The alternative with the highest score would receive the rank of 1. After individual rankings are completed, they are summed and totaled. The alternative with the lowest total receives the group's number 1 ranking. This procedure can be done publicly where group members can see or hear the ranking of one another's alternatives, or the process can be done on paper so individual rankings are anonymous.

Although ranking decreases group members' feelings of personal involvement or participation, groups using this procedure report little negativity in making decisions. Fewer arguments or conflicts are reported when ranking is used because it is more difficult for one or two individual members to alter a group's decision process. Each member gets to indicate his or her preference, and all preferences are treated equally. Thus group members report feeling satisfied with the outcome (Green & Taber, 1980).

Brainstorming

Brainstorming is a group discussion and decision technique with a long history. Developed to improve productivity and increase creativity, it is based on five principles (Osborn, 1963). First, group members should state as many alternatives as possible to a given problem. Second, ideas do not have to be traditional or those tried in the past. Actually, the wilder and crazier the ideas, the better. Third, ideas that have been presented can be improved upon or combined with other ideas. Fourth, all ideas should be accepted without criticism—verbal or nonverbal—from other group members. Evaluation of ideas is reserved until the idea generation phase is complete. Finally, all ideas are recorded for future consideration, even those that are initially discarded. A group member can act as the facilitator of the brainstorming session, but research has shown that someone external to the group may be more effective in the facilitator role. The facilitator helps the group continue its momentum and helps members remain neutral by not stopping to criticize ideas (Offner, Kramer, & Winter, 1996).

These principles were developed to help groups generate as many ideas as possible to provide the group with the greatest number of ideas from which to select an effective solution. Generally, as the number of ideas increases, so does idea quality. Members may experience periods of silence during idea generation, but research has shown that good ideas can come after moments of silence while members reflect and think individually (Ruback, Dabbs, & Hopper, 1984). So it may be premature to end idea generation the first time all members become quiet.

Brainstorming can help groups accomplish other goals. Brainstorming can help increase cohesiveness because it ensures that all group members participate. It also helps group members realize that they can work together productively (Pavitt, 1993). Members of brainstorming groups are positive about their group experience. Group members report that they like the opportunity to be creative and to build upon one another's ideas (Kramer, Kuo, & Dailey, 1997).

When should a group use brainstorming? Brainstorming is best used when the problem is specific rather than general. For example, brainstorming can be effective to find a new way to attract minority employees to your organization. But the problem, What kind of organization do we want to be? is too broad. If the problem is broad, use a brainstorming session to break it down into subproblems, and then devote a further session to each one. A brainstorming session could answer the question, In what areas does our organization want to improve? Having identified several areas in the brainstorming session, the group could rank the areas to select the first area to address. Now a more specific brainstorming session could consider how the organization will improve in a specific area.

Group members usually find brainstorming fun. However, groups do better if they have had a chance to warm up or practice the process (Firestien, 1990). The practice session should be unrelated to the subject of the actual brainstorming session. Practice sessions are beneficial because they reinforce the procedure as well as reassure participants that the evaluation and idea generation steps will not be integrated. Posting the first four brainstorming principles so they are visible during the session will help remind participants of the procedure's rules.

Nominal Group Technique

The same basic principles of brainstorming are also applied in **nominal group technique (NGT)** except that group members work independently without interaction. So how is this a group technique? NGT refers to a "process in which individuals work alone with the results of their efforts later combined and viewed as if the individuals had worked together in a group" (Green, 1975, p. 63). For the time that NGT is being used, the group is a group in name only (Delbecq, Van de Ven, & Gustafson, 1975). Group members temporarily suspend interaction to take advantage of independent thinking and reflection before coming together as a group to discuss the ideas generated.

NGT is a linear process; a pseudo-group passes through a series of steps. Each focuses on different aspects of the problem-solving process. This is how a NGT session would work. In step 1, group members are silent as they independently generate as many ideas as possible in writing. If there are no relationship problems in the group, members can be instructed to simply write down as many ideas as possible. If relationship conflicts do exist, it would be better for members to write down ideas on an index card without identifying themselves. Before moving on to step 2, make sure that all group members have finished writing. Give members a few minutes after everyone appears to be finished as some of our best ideas occur to us after we think we are finished.

In step 2, the ideas are recorded on a flip chart by a facilitator. Generally, it is best to invite someone outside the group to help facilitate the process so all group members can participate. Members take turns giving one idea at a time to be written on the flip chart. Duplicate ideas do not need to be recorded, but ideas that are slightly different than those already posted should be posted as well. Ideas are not discussed during this step. The person capturing the group's ideas on the flip

Using brainstorming procedures, group members alternately generate ideas, post ideas, and discuss ideas. Each group member has the opportunity to contribute ideas, to ask questions about ideas, and to vote for his or her top choices.

chart should summarize lengthy ideas into a shortened phrase. The person summarizing the idea should check with the member who originated the idea to make sure that editorializing did not occur. When a member runs out of ideas, he or she simply says "pass," and the facilitator moves on to the next group member. When all members have passed, the recording step is over. If members wrote ideas on index cards, the cards are collected and each idea is written on the flip chart for everyone to see. If the group is not experiencing relationship problems, one group member can facilitate this process.

In the third step, group interaction resumes. Taking one idea at a time, group members discuss each idea for clarification. If an idea needs no clarification, then the group moves on to the next one. Rather than only asking the group member who contributed the idea to clarify it, the facilitator should ask if any group member has questions about the idea. By including everyone in the clarification process, group ownership of the idea increases.

In the fourth step, group members vote on the ideas they believe are most important. If your group generated forty ideas, consider asking group members to vote for their top five. By not narrowing the number of choices too severely or too quickly, group members get a chance to discuss the ideas they most prefer. If time permits, let group members come to the flip charts and select their most important ideas themselves. This helps ensure that members select the ideas that are important to them without the influence of peer pressure.

Step 5 of NGT is a discussion of the vote just taken. From the forty ideas presented, eleven have received two or more votes. Now is the time for group members to further elaborate on each of these ideas. Direct the discussion by the order of ideas as they appear on the flip chart, rather than starting with the idea that received the most votes. Starting the discussion in a neutral or randomly selected place encourages discussion on each item, not just on the one that appears most popular at this point in the procedure.

With that discussion over, the sixth step of NGT requires group members to repeat steps 4 and 5. Once again members vote on the importance of the remaining ideas. With eleven ideas left, you might ask members to select their top three choices. After members vote, the group discusses the three ideas that received the most votes. Now it is time for the final vote. This time, group members select the idea they most favor.

The greatest advantage of NGT is that the independent idea generation steps encourage equal participation of group members regardless of power or status. The views of more silent members are treated the same as the views of dominant members (Van de Ven & Delbecq, 1974). This characteristic of NGT can be very positive for group members as they feel more satisfied and more effective than group members who did not use any specific procedure (Kramer, Kuo, & Dailey, 1997). Typically, NGT groups develop more total proposals and higher quality proposals than groups using other procedures (Green, 1975). Another advantage of NGT is that its specified structure helps bring closure and accomplishment to group problem solving (Van de Ven & Delbecq, 1974). When the meeting is finished, members have a firm grasp of what the group decided and are satisfied because they helped the group reach that decision.

When is it best to use NGT? Several group situations can be enhanced by the NGT process (Pavitt, 1993). NGT is most helpful when proposal generation is crucial. For example, your softball team must look for new and creative ways to raise funds. Your team tried most of the traditional approaches to raising money, and their enthusiasm for going door to door is low. Using NGT would help the team identify alternatives without group members surrendering to the ideas of the player/coach or the best players. Second, NGT can help groups that are not very cohesive. When a group's culture is unhealthy and cohesiveness is low, but the group's work must be done, NGT can help the group overcome its relationship problems and allow it to continue with its tasks. The minimized interaction in the idea generation phase of NGT gives everyone a chance to participate, increasing the likelihood that members will be satisfied with the group's final choice. Finally, NGT is particularly helpful when the problem facing the group is particularly volatile—for example, when organizational groups have to make difficult decisions about which items or projects to cut from the budget. Conflict that would likely occur through more interactive procedures or unstructured process could be destructive. The structured process of NGT helps group members focus on the task because turn taking is controlled.

Comparing Procedures

Procedures help the group by managing its discussion and decision process. In turn, this enhances the quality of decision making in the group by coordinating members' thinking and communication, providing a set of ground rules all members can and must follow, balancing member participation, and revealing and managing conflicts (Jarboe, 1996; Poole, 1991). Most importantly, procedures help groups avoid becoming solution minded too quickly. But which procedure is best? Often, the group leader or facilitator will select a procedure. Other times, the group will rely on familiarity—selecting the procedure it used last time regardless of its effectiveness. Rather than select a procedure arbitrarily, groups should select a procedure that best suits their needs.

Procedures differ on five dimensions (Poole, 1991). Reviewing these can help your group select the most effective one. The first dimension is scope, which is the extent to which the procedures are general purpose procedures and not procedures that are only effective for a specific discussion or decision task. Critical advisor, consensus, and standard agenda have the highest ratings on scope because they can be used in many decision-making functions whereas brainstorming and NGT are only used for the generation of ideas. Voting and ranking are also low in scope because these procedures are used only for ranking preferences or making final decisions. Procedures also differ in their degree of restrictiveness—that is, the degree to which they limit or control the group members' activities. Brainstorming and NGT are high in restrictiveness because they give precise instructions about how group members are to communicate. Ranking and voting are low in restrictiveness because they apply to only one part of a group's decision discussion. Consensus is low in restrictiveness because only the discussion facilitator has procedures to follow; otherwise group members are encouraged to talk until they can come to an agreement. Standard agenda has moderate restrictiveness because it provides steps for group members to follow but does not specify which group member contributes to each step. Critical advisor is low in restrictiveness because only one member's behavior is affected.

Third, procedures differ in their comprehensiveness or in how general or specific the rules appear. NGT and brainstorming are rated high in comprehensiveness because each specifies exactly what steps the group should take. Voting and ranking are moderate in comprehensiveness because the rules are specific but only apply to one aspect of the group's decision discussion. Standard agenda has moderate comprehensiveness; although it provides a general script for group member behavior, it also allows considerable variation within those steps. Critical advisor and consensus have low comprehensiveness.

The fourth dimension is group control, which is the degree to which the group can manage the procedure by itself without help from a facilitator. Critical advisor, consensus, standard agenda, voting, and ranking are high in group control because group members can facilitate these procedures by themselves. Brainstorming and NGT vary from moderate to high group control. Group members can facilitate these procedures themselves or ask a facilitator to help the group. Last, procedures differ in their degree of member involvement. Member involvement is the number of the members who must cooperate in order for the procedure to work. Brainstorming and NGT are high in member involvement because all members must agree to and participate in the procedure. Consensus, voting, and ranking are high in member involvement because they encourage the democratic principle of all members participating. Standard agenda is moderate to low in member involvement. To work effectively, all members must agree to using the discussion and decision procedure, but the procedure itself does not ensure that all members will participate. Critical advisor is low in member involvement as only one group member takes on the questioning role.

To these five dimensions, we add a sixth—face-to-face interaction—to help clarify how the procedure works in a group setting. In using the critical advisor or brainstorming procedures, face-to-face interaction among group members may be less than optimal because free-flowing communication is punctuated by the advisor asking questions or the silent periods of idea generation. And face-to-face interaction is greatly minimized in NGT due to its strict structure for idea generation and idea sharing. However, if group members are highly emotional about the task or decision, these techniques may prove useful. Voting and ranking have moderate to low degrees of face-to-face interaction. Although we assume that voting and ranking will be preceded by general group discussion, nothing in these procedures ensures that discussion will take place. The greatest degree of face-to-face interaction will occur using consensus or standard agenda as all group members can share in the group's use of this procedure.

Before you select a procedure, you should analyze the type of task before your group. If the task is easy—groups members have all of the necessary information to make effective choices—the type of procedure you select will have less consequence on the group's ability to resolve the problem or make decisions. However, if the group task or decision is difficult (for example, members' decision-making skills vary, the group needs to consult with others outside the group, the decision has multiple parts), the decision procedure selected will have greater impact on the group's decision-making abilities. Generally in these situations procedures "that encourage vigilant and systematic face-to-face interaction tend to result in higher-quality outcomes" (Hirokawa, Erbert, & Hurst, 1996, p. 176). Recognize, however, that the use of any discussion or decision procedure that encourages a group to analyze a problem thoroughly by evaluating both the positive and negative qualities of possible alternatives will lead to higher quality decisions (Hirokawa, 1985). Also recognize that, in practice, a group may use several of these procedures (Jarboe, 1996). The procedures and their ratings on the six dimensions are shown in Table 8.1. After analyzing the characteristics of your group's decision task, use the table to help your group decide which procedure would best fit the needs of your group; see also "Which Procedure Would Help Your Group?"

Preference for Procedural Order in Groups

Besides considering procedures based on the type of task situation, you should also consider your **preference for procedural order (PPO),** or your desire to have the activities of your groups ordered (Putnam, 1979, 1982). Although procedural order is more tightly linked to task groups, social groups also experience procedural order. A group of friends spends time in small talk even though they know one another well, and they understand that this meeting of friends is to make decisions about Bonita's wedding. This small talk before making decisions about

Table 8.1 Analyzing Tasks

Dimension	Standard Agenda	Critical Advisor	Consensus	Voting	Ranking	Brain-storming	NGT
Scope	high	high	high	low	low	low	low
Restrictiveness	moderate	low	low	moderate to low	low	high	high
Comprehensiveness	moderate	low	low	moderate	moderate	high	high
Group Control	high	high	high	high	high	moderate to high	moderate to high
Member Involvement	high	low	high	high	high	high	moderate to low
Face-to-Face Interaction	high	moderate to high	high	moderate to low	moderate to low	moderate to high	low

the primary topic provides order for the group. Order in group conversations provides expectations about appropriate behavior. Group members would think Mandy rude if she jumped directly from "Hello" to "What color will our dresses be? Do I get to help pick them out?"

With respect to task or decision-making groups, those high in procedural order prefer to establish norms for working as a group. Behaviors that help provide structure and order for the group discussion include using planning and sequencing to organize task activities, being concerned about time management, placing emphasis on predictable procedures, clarifying group procedures, and reminding members to stick to the task. Order can also be achieved through the use of agendas or decision procedures. In other words, group members with high PPO like their group tasks to be orderly and organized in some manner that is easily accessible to the group. Members with a preference for low procedural order let the group develop its own structure, retain flexibility in establishing and changing plans, and balance the task and relational needs of members. Although individuals may have a high or low preference for procedural order, this characteristic is moderated by other factors such as the difficulty of the task, the time parameters for completing the task, and leadership development within the group. Read the situation of the group in "Identifying Your Preference for Procedural Order" and imagine that you are going to be a member of the group. Take the survey to discover your preference for procedural order.

If you have a high PPO, you have strong expectations about how a group should operate. High PPO members prefer systematic order; thus they often prefer to use formal discussion procedures. In fact, group members who have a high preference for procedural order make higher quality decisions using a formal

> ### THINK ABOUT IT
>
> ### *Which Procedure Would Help Your Group?*
>
> Think of one of your recent group experiences where decision making was the focus of the group's activity. Which procedure do you believe would have been most beneficial for the group? Why? Could the group have benefited from using more than one procedure? How would you have initiated the use of procedures in your group? Would group members have welcomed procedural assistance or resisted it? What strategy or strategies would you have used to move your group into one of these procedures? Who else in the group could have helped you accomplish this?

discussion procedure than when using free discussion. They like the deductive method that discussion procedures provide—working first with the more general issues and then moving to more specific issues. Alternately, if you scored higher on the low PPO scale, you prefer a loose and inductive structure. When several low PPO group members are together, free association among topics occurs as group members jump from the middle of one topic to another. As suspected, group members who prefer less procedural order have greater effectiveness in free discussion groups (Hirokawa, Ice, & Cook, 1988). Both types of group members—those with a high preference for procedural order and those with low preference for procedural order—have structure in their group interactions; the structures are simply different.

The Paradox of Using Procedures

Research has demonstrated that groups using formal discussion procedures generally develop higher member satisfaction and greater commitment to the decision. Although the standard agenda procedure helps groups pay greater attention to detail, NGT and brainstorming groups generally produce more ideas and higher quality ideas. Yet many groups try to avoid using procedures. This is because discussion and decision procedures take time, and the group must plan their meetings accordingly. Another disadvantage to using procedures is that group members often are reluctant to use them. A group unaccustomed to procedures may initially find them too restrictive. Group members may be more willing to try a procedure when they find out that one of the most frequent mistakes made by groups is to plunge into their task without adequate discussion and thorough review of alternatives. Remember the student group who tried to find a solution to the problem of food not being available on north campus?

It is often difficult for groups to stick with a procedure once it has been initiated. For example, members may find it difficult to refrain from nonverbal evaluation of ideas in brainstorming. Groups using NGT may believe they have found the best idea on the initial voting and discussion steps. They stop without pursuing the rest of the process. Groups find that the standard agenda is difficult to stick with because it requires the diligence of all group members. One group member can successfully dislodge others from using the process. But it is exactly these difficulties that procedures guard against. In each case, the group avoids the procedure to move along more quickly, but efficiency is generally not a characteristic of effective groups.

Procedures help group members resist sloppy thinking and ineffective group habits (Poole, 1991). When procedures seem unnatural, it is often because group members have little practice with them. If members have not used a particular procedure before, it is best to hold a practice session on a nonrelated topic. Practice can help document that the use of a procedure keeps groups from falling into traps of ineffectiveness or faulty thinking. Procedures help groups manage their discussion and decision conversations. This helps them become more effective by providing a set of objective ground rules. All group members know the procedure, and this helps keep the leader from assuming too much power and swaying the decision process or from having to make the decision for the group. Procedures help coordinate members' thinking and interaction, making it is less likely that a group that needs to make a decision about the current budget will end up discussing next year's officer elections. By capitalizing on the strengths of groups, member participation becomes more balanced. More voices are heard, and more ideas are deliberated.

To help your group gain experience with procedures, use these seven guidelines (Poole, 1991). First, motivate your group to use a procedure. Provide positive feedback to group members when a procedure is used. Look for discussion and decision problems that occur in your group and then suggest a procedure to help the group overcome that specific difficulty. Second, champion the procedure process. Know and advocate the value of the procedure; remind the group to use it; and provide advice and help when the group uses the procedure. Train yourself in several procedures so you can help your group use them effectively. Third, help other group members learn the procedure technique. The more members who know and who can use the procedure, the more likely the procedure will be used because it will be familiar to several members of the group. Fourth, if needed, tailor the procedure to the group's needs. Perhaps your group works so fast at brainstorming that two facilitators are needed to write down members' ideas. This modification helps the group use the procedure more effectively. Tailoring a procedure to a group's particular needs will give the group ownership over the process.

Fifth, suggest that your group spend time analyzing its discussion interaction with and without procedures. Getting members accustomed to talking about the group's strengths and weaknesses will help them realize that procedures can become a natural part of the group's activities. Sixth, when conflicts are high or cohesiveness is low, use a neutral facilitator who can ensure that a procedure is fairly administered. Using an outside facilitator also provides a role model and new norms when a procedure is new to the group. Finally, help the group set reasonable expectations with respect to using procedures. Using a procedure cannot solve all

GROUP ASSESSMENT TECHNIQUE

Identifying Your Preference for Procedural Order

Think ahead to what you believe will be your next task group at work or your next student group assignment. Thinking of that situation, identify each of your preferences by using the scale to respond to each of the items below.

1 = do not prefer   2 = little preference   3 = unsure
4 = some preference   5 = great deal of preference

1. You want your group to use an agenda to keep the meeting tightly organized.   1 2 3 4 5
2. You prefer the group kick around ideas without a specific purpose.   1 2 3 4 5
3. You want group members to list tasks that need to be completed before the deadline.   1 2 3 4 5
4. You like it when the group jumps from point to point before coming to any decisions.   1 2 3 4 5
5. You like it when a group member suggests the group follow a procedure.   1 2 3 4 5
6. You prefer a group where brainstorming is used for the fun of it.   1 2 3 4 5
7. You like it when your group lists its ideas on paper.   1 2 3 4 5
8. You like it when the group develops a norm of moving quickly from one idea to another.   1 2 3 4 5
9. You prefer one group member to identify relationships between the contributions of group members.   1 2 3 4 5
10. It is okay with you if the group suddenly switches from working on its task to talking about a social event.   1 2 3 4 5
11. You prefer to be in a group where one member helps the group rank-order the alternatives they have discussed.   1 2 3 4 5
12. You do not mind when group members revisit topics that have already been discussed.   1 2 3 4 5
13. You like it when one group member keeps an eye on the time and reminds the group how much time is left.   1 2 3 4 5
14. You do not mind when the group resets deadlines because the first deadline was missed.   1 2 3 4 5
15. You prefer a group that sets clearly defined goals.   1 2 3 4 5
16. You do not mind when the group meets for seemingly no reason.   1 2 3 4 5
17. You like it when your group sets deadlines for the completion of tasks.   1 2 3 4 5

18. You do not mind when your group starts with a procedure and then forgets about it. 1 2 3 4 5
19. You like group meetings that have been carefully planned so everyone knows what is expected. 1 2 3 4 5
20. You like it when group members socialize and kid around even when there is work to be done. 1 2 3 4 5
21. Before you finish a meeting, you would prefer to set the time, place, and date of the next meeting. 1 2 3 4 5
22. You do not mind groups where one member cracks jokes or makes funny comments even when others are trying to work. 1 2 3 4 5
23. You like group meetings when someone summarizes the group's discussion to provide a sense of closure to the group's interactions. 1 2 3 4 5
24. You prefer groups where several lively conversations can go on at the same time. 1 2 3 4 5
25. You would prefer that a group member remind the group what needs to be accomplished during this meeting. 1 2 3 4 5
26. You prefer groups where socializing is as important as completing the task. 1 2 3 4 5
27. You like it when the group leader moderates the discussion so that the group sticks to its agenda. 1 2 3 4 5
28. You do not mind if four reports are scheduled, and the group spends all of its time on the first one. 1 2 3 4 5
29. You would prefer for someone to help the group return to the task when members begin to discuss nontask issues. 1 2 3 4 5
30. You do not mind when someone interrupts the group to bring up an interesting but completely different idea. 1 2 3 4 5
31. You do not mind when one member wants to write everything down in clear outline form to help the group stay on track. 1 2 3 4 5
32. You do not mind when a member makes long contributions even if they do not pertain to the point being discussed. 1 2 3 4 5

Total for odd items _____   Total for even items _____

Odd items indicate a high preference for procedural order. Even items indicate a low preference for procedural order.

Source: Adapted from Putnam (1979).

> ### BUILDING ANALYTICAL SKILLS
>
> ## Was Your Decision Effective?
>
> After a decision-making activity and the initial decision procedure assigned by your instructor, use the following scale to assess the quality of your decision-making discussion. Respond to each question by circling the number that best reflects your answer on the response dimension.
>
> 1. The overall quality of the discussion was
>   poor   1 2 3 4 5 6 7   good
> 2. The discussion, on the whole, was
>   ineffective   1 2 3 4 5 6 7   effective
> 3. The outcome of the discussion was
>   unsatisfactory   1 2 3 4 5 6 7   satisfactory
> 4. The discussion was
>   incompetently executed   1 2 3 4 5 6 7   competently executed
> 5. The issues explored in the discussion were
>   trivial   1 2 3 4 5 6 7   substantial
> 6. The content of the discussion was
>   carelessly developed   1 2 3 4 5 6 7   carefully developed
> 7. The manner in which the participants examined issues was
>   nonconstructive   1 2 3 4 5 6 7   constructive
> 8. The group's movement toward reaching a conclusion on the discussion question was
>   insignificant   1 2 3 4 5 6 7   significant
> 9. The behavior of the group was
>   not goal directed   1 2 3 4 5 6 7   goal directed
> 10. The participants initiated discussion on
>   irrelevant issues   1 2 3 4 5 6 7   relevant issues

of a group's problems, but it can help a group discuss alternatives and make decisions more effectively. Make sure the procedure fits the group need. This will ensure that the group achieves greater success and will encourage group members to view the procedure as a tool, not as a panacea for all of the group's troubles.

Decision-Making Effectiveness

No one person, procedure, or process will make group decision making effective. Generally, decisions are said to be effective if the decision is correct, the decision is of high quality, the decision has utility—high rewards and low costs—or the decision is acceptable to group members or others who will use or implement the group's decision (Gouran, 1988). Of course, not every decision can be evaluated against all four criteria. Refer back to the discussion in Chapter 5 about the types

11. The participants' contributions were
     poorly amplified   1 2 3 4 5 6 7   well amplified
12. The participation in the discussion was
     unevenly distributed   1 2 3 4 5 6 7   evenly distributed
13. The positions taken in the discussion were
     undocumented   1 2 3 4 5 6 7   documented
14. Ideas expressed in the discussion were
     uncritically examined   1 2 3 4 5 6 7   critically examined
15. The participants dealt with issues
     unsystematically   1 2 3 4 5 6 7   systematically
16. The interpersonal relationships among the participants appeared to be
     unhealthy   1 2 3 4 5 6 7   healthy
17. The functions of leadership in the discussion were
     poorly served   1 2 3 4 5 6 7   well served

Now look back at each item. How did your communication contribute to each of your responses? For example, look at item 6 regarding the content of the discussion. What input did you have into the content of the discussion? Did you contribute effectively? Or did you withhold information for some reason? Look at item 16 regarding interpersonal relationships. How effective were you in developing and maintaining healthy relationships with other group members? If the quality of group members' relationships inhibited decision making, did you suggest using a decision or discussion procedure?

Source: Gouran, Brown, and Henry (1978).

of tasks and task characteristics to help your group decide the type of task it is working on, and thus which tests it needs to meet: the test of correctness or accuracy, the test of quality, the test of utility or the test of acceptability.

One way to help your group make effective decisions is to monitor how well your group is performing its decision-making or problem-solving activities. Here is a checklist you can use while you are in group decision-making settings to gauge how effective your group will be (Hirokawa, Erbert, & Hurst, 1996). First, did the group have access to all of the information it needed? Generally, the more informed members are about the problem or decision, the more likely the group will reach a quality decision. Second, how would you evaluate the effort of group members? Is their effort of high quality? Or do group members simply put in their time? High quality effort is characterized by examining and reexamining information on a single topic, not by sitting together for long periods and talking about several different topics off the agenda. Third, what is the quality of group members' thinking? High quality thinking is characterized by using logic and reason to reach opinions, not simply relying on surface opinions like "because I like it." Fourth, is your group using some system of reasoning, or a **decision logic**? Most groups use either a rational or a political decision logic (Senge, 1990). A **rational decision logic** is one in which the group considers both the positive and negative qualities of all choices and then selects the choice with the most positive and least negative qualities. This type of logic maximizes the strengths of a decision while minimizing the risks associated with it. In a **political decision logic** group members rely on factors not intrinsic to the decision. If group members look to others—want to please the boss or some other external person or want to build power bases—a personal rather than group agenda is being served. Thus the logic is political rather than rational. As you might guess, effective decision making is more likely to occur when groups employ a rational decision logic over a political decision logic. Try "Was Your Decision Effective?" to assess your group's decision-making process.

Summary

Groups often need to make decisions. To a large extent, our society depends on groups to make decisions—decisions that affect governmental and organizational policies, long-term policies, and day-to-day activities. Generally, groups are better decision makers than individuals when the problem is complex, when the problem requires input from diverse perspectives, and when people need to identify with and commit to the decision.

Decision procedures can help groups stay on track, equalize participation among members, and balance emotional and social aspects with task issues. Groups can choose from a variety of decision or discussion procedures. The standard agenda, or reflective thinking, is a strict linear process that helps groups focus on different stages or aspects of the problem-solving process. By moving through each step, group members can first identify and then evaluate each of the potential alternatives in complex problem solving. Using a critical advisor is suggested for groups that will be challenged from an external audience. By responding to questions and requests for clarification, a group can maximize the strength of its decision before presenting it to others. Consensus is a technique with wide application in group decision making. In this procedure, one group member helps facilitate the discussion and makes sure that all members have the opportunity to give their point of view. Voting is a popular procedure used when groups must make their final selection from a set of alternatives. Like ranking, voting allows each member to equally affect the outcome. Brainstorming is an idea generation procedure that can help groups be creative in thinking of alternatives. Nominal group technique also assists the idea generation process, but it strictly controls the amount and type of communication among group members.

Each procedure can help groups be more effective, but some procedures are better suited to different aspects of the decision-making process. Groups can compare procedures for their fit to the task by assessing each procedure's scope, restrictiveness, comprehensiveness, group control, member involvement, and amount and type of face-to-face interaction. Group members should also assess their preference for procedural order in groups. Members who have a high need for structure or order will more easily adapt to the more structured decision procedures.

No one person or procedure will make group decision making effective. It is the effective selection and combination of people, talents, procedures, and structures that strengthens group decision making. By monitoring your own performance and the performance of the group as a whole, you will be able to select the most appropriate decision or discussion procedures.

✓ Checklist

Group Knowledge

You should be able to:
- explain why and when groups are better than individuals at making decisions.
- describe how each of the decision-making procedures work.
- explain how decision-making procedures create a paradox for groups.
- explain how your communication in group decision making affects the group's effectiveness.

Group Skills

You should be able to:
- select the best procedure for a group decision-making situation.
- lead your group through the use of at least three decision-making procedures.
- adapt your preference for procedural order to the procedure that would most help the group.
- assist your group in enhancing its effectiveness.

Analytical and Assessment Techniques

You should be able to:
- assess decision procedures and select the one that would be most helpful to your group.
- identify your preference for procedural order and know how your preference will impact your performance in group decision making.
- analyze the effectiveness of your group's decision-making process.
- analyze your contributions to your group's decision-making process.

Discussion Questions and Exercises

1. For one week, keep a diary or journal of all the group decisions in which you participate. Identify who in the group is making the decisions, what the decisions are about, how long the group spends on decision making, and any identifying strengths or weaknesses of the decision-making process. Come to class ready to discuss your experiences and to identify procedures that could have helped your group be more effective.

2. Using the data from your diary or journal above, write a paper that analyzes your role in group decision-making effectiveness.

3. Select someone you know who works full-time in their chosen career or profession and ask this person to participate in an interview about group or team decision making at work. Before the interview, develop a list of questions to guide the interview. You might include questions like: How many decision-making groups or teams are you a part of? What is your role and what are your responsibilities in those groups and teams? How would you assess the effectiveness of your decision making? Is there something unusual (good or bad) that helps or hinders your groups' decision-making abilities? If you could change one thing about how your groups make decisions, what would it be?

9
Theoretical Lessons for Group Decision Making

What do I need to know before I suggest changes to my group's decision making?

How can I have more influence on my group's decision making?

How do I avoid the influence of others?

What can I do to help my group avoid poor decisions?

What happens after our decisions have been made?

The previous chapter examined different procedures groups can use in making decisions. This chapter moves into more theoretical territory and explores why groups do what they do in making decisions. Using lessons from these theoretical explorations of group decision making, this chapter reviews the advantages and disadvantages of using subgroups, how groups should function during decision-making periods, how influence is created and used during decision making, why groups make faulty decisions, and how groups should implement and monitor decisions.

Group Decision Principles

Before giving advice about how groups should make decisions, let's review what is known about the group decision-making process. There are four assumptions that seem to fit most group decision-making situations (Hirokawa & Johnston, 1989). First, group decision making is an evolutionary process. The final decision of the group emerges over time as a result of the clarification, modification, and integration of ideas that group members expressed in their interaction. A good analogy for this evolutionary nature of group decision making is sculpture. The sculptor may have an idea about what he wants the sculpture to look like, but the final product is a result of the molding and merging of clay over many days in the studio. A student government group may know that it needs to make a decision about how to provide child care for university students, but the final decision results from the group bringing new information to meetings and other group members asking for clarification and extension of proposed ideas.

The second assumption is that group decision making is characterized as a circular rather than a linear process. Even when they try, it is difficult for group members to follow a step-by-step approach to group decision making. The circular nature of group decision making occurs because group members seldom bring all the needed information into the group's discussion at the same time. Your group may need to make a primary decision (for example, when to hold a fundraiser) before you can consider secondary decisions (what type of event the fundraiser may be). In this case, your group was constrained more by when the event should be held than by what type of event it should be. But let's extend this example to demonstrate the circular nature of decision making. Let's say that your group decides to hold the fundraiser on June 3, close to the end of the spring semester. Your group needs to make this decision first to secure a date on your university's student activities calendar. Now that the date is settled, your group can concentrate on what type of fundraiser might do best. But you have to take into consideration that it is late in the spring semester: Not only will students have limited time because of due dates for final papers and exams, but it is also likely that their funds will be depleted. That information will affect the type of fundraiser you will plan. But wait! At that time of the semester, students really enjoy having coffee and doughnuts available in the early morning, after all-night study sessions. And your group can sell lots of coffee and doughnuts to many students for very little money. Do you see how information about the date and type of event moved back and forth to integrate into a final fundraising decision?

You have probably already recognized that many different types of influences affect your group's decision making. This is the third assumption about decision making. Group members' moods, values and beliefs, motivations, and communication skills are individual-level variables that affect the group's final decision. These are individual-level variables because each member brings a unique set of influence to the group. One type of system-level variable is the influence that is generated by forces outside your group. An example of this type of system-level variable is the generally accepted societal rule to make decisions quickly and cost efficiently. Another type of system-level variable is one that group members create for themselves. An example of this is when group members agree to select the presentation format that requires the least amount of work. A third type of system-level variable is the dynamics of the interpersonal relationships among group members. The nature of group member relationships affects the group's level of cohesiveness and group member compatibility. Finally, the communication structure adopted by the group is a system-level variable. How information flows among and between group members defines the structure of the group.

The fourth assumption about group decision making is that decisions are made within a system of external and internal constraints. Few groups have as much freedom of choice as they would like. Groups are constrained by external forces such as deadlines or budgets imposed by outsiders and the preferences of the people who will evaluate or use the group's decision. Internal constraints are the values, morals, and ethics that individual members bring to the group setting. These values guide what the group does and how it does it.

Advice from Functional Theory

The functional perspective of group decision making (Gouran & Hirokawa, 1983, 1996; Gouran et al., 1993; Hirokawa, 1982, 1988; Hirokawa & Scheerhorn, 1986) suggests that group members perform five critical functions in their decision-making activities. A function is not just a step or a procedure, but an activity required for the group to make a decision. When the five functions are not addressed, a group diminishes its chances for identifying an effective solution or making a good decision.

First, group members need to achieve understanding of the problem they are trying to resolve. The group should deliberate until it believes members have an accurate or valid understanding of the nature of the problem, the seriousness of the problem, the possible causes of the problem, and the consequences that could develop if the problem is not dealt with effectively. For example, parking is generally a problem on most campuses. But groups addressing the parking problem without having an adequate understanding of the problem are likely to suggest solutions that will not really solve the problem. The parking problem on your campus may be that there are not enough parking spaces. Or it may be that on your campus there are not enough parking spaces where students want to park. Or perhaps the parking problem exists at only certain times of the day. Another type of parking problem exists when students do not want to pay for parking privileges and park their cars illegally on campus and in the surrounding community. Each parking problem is different and would require different solutions. When group members address this function—understanding the nature of the problem before trying to solve it—their decision-making efforts result in higher quality decisions (Hirokawa, 1983a).

Second, the group needs to develop an understanding of what would constitute an acceptable resolution of the problem. In this critical function, group members need to accurately understand the objectives that need to be achieved to remedy the problem or specific standards that must be satisfied for the solution to be acceptable. This means that the group needs to develop criteria by which to evaluate each proposed alternative. Let's go back to our parking problem. In this step, group members would need to consider how much students and employees would be willing to pay for parking. Group members would also need to find out and discuss the type of solutions campus administrators and campus police would find acceptable. The group probably also needs to consider if community police need to agree with their recommendation. In other words, the group has to decide on the objectives and standards that must be used in selecting an appropriate solution. Any evaluation of alternatives must be based on known and agreed upon criteria (Graham, Papa, & McPherson, 1997).

Third, the group needs to seek and develop a set of realistic and acceptable alternatives. With respect to the parking problem, students groups frequently stop generating alternatives when they generate a solution they like. Let's look at the following dialogue:

MARTY: Okay, I think we should think about building a parking garage.

LINDSEY: Where would it go?

MARTY: I don't know. But there's all kinds of empty lots around campus.

HELEN: What about parking in the church parking lots?

LINDSEY: That's an idea, but I like the idea of our own parking garage better.

TODD: I like that too. It would be good to know that whatever time I go to campus, a parking spot would be waiting for me.

MARTY: Any other ideas, besides the parking garage?

LINDSEY: No, I can't think of any. I think we need to work on the parking garage idea.

TODD: Me too.

HELEN: Shouldn't we consider something else in case the parking lot idea falls through?

MARTY: Why? We all like the idea, don't we?

If a group gets stuck in generating alternatives, like our parking group does, a brainstorming or NGT session (described in Chapter 8) may help. A group cannot choose the best alternative if all the alternatives are not known.

Fourth, group members need to assess the positive qualities of each of the alternatives they find attractive. This step helps the group recognize the relative merits of each alternative as compared to one another. Once again, back to the parking problem. Students on campus would probably cheer for a solution to the parking problem that did not cost them money. Certainly, no-cost or low-cost parking would be attractive to everyone. But if this is the only positive quality of an alternative, it is not very likely that this is the best choice. For example, to provide no-cost or low-cost parking, your recommendation is that students park in the parking lots of churches that do not use their parking lots during the daytime, and, at night, in the parking lots of office buildings. Unfortunately, these organizations can be up to 2 miles away. Although the group has satisfied commuters' concerns about cost, it is doubtful that many students would find this alternative attractive.

The fifth critical function is for group members to make assessments of the negative qualities of alternative choices. Had the group considering parking in church and office building parking lots discussed the negative quality of distance, this alternative probably would not be one for serious consideration!

When group members communicate to fulfill these five functions, they increase the chance that their decision making will be effective. This is because group members have worked together to pool their information resources, avoid errors in individual judgment, and create opportunities to persuade other group members (Gouran et al., 1993). First, participants in our example group brought different information to the discussion because three of them came to school at different times of the day. Those who came early in the school day or for evening classes had a harder time finding a place to park than those who came early in the afternoon. By pooling what each participant knew about the parking situation, the group avoided becoming biased or choosing a solution that would resolve only one type of parking problem. Second, as the group discussed the problem, members could identify and remedy errors in individual judgment. It is easy to think parking is not a problem when you come in for one class in the early afternoon and leave immediately after. From your perspective, you see the parking lot as having some empty spaces because you come at a time when others have left for lunch. When you leave 2 hours later, the lot is even more vacant—making you wonder what the fuss is about in the first place! Third, discussion provides an opportunity to persuade others or be persuaded. Discussion allows alternatives to be presented that might not occur to others and allows for reevaluation of alternatives that, at first, seem unattractive. Let's go back to the group discussing the parking problem:

MARTY: Okay, where are we?

HELEN: Well, I think we've pretty much discussed parking alternatives. I'm not sure.

LINDSEY: What about using the bus?

TODD: You've got to be kidding.

LINDSEY: Why not? The bus line goes right by campus and the fare is only 50¢.

MARTY: Well, it's an idea.

HELEN: Well, what if the bus doesn't have a route where I live?

LINDSEY: Well, that may be the case for you, Helen, but I bet many students live on or near a bus line.

MARTY: I wonder how many?

LINDSEY: Why don't we call the bus company and get a copy of the entire routing system.

MARTY: Good idea, Lindsey. We were looking for parking alternatives and hadn't thought about other modes of transportation.

Groups that successfully achieve each of the five critical functions of decision making make higher quality decisions than groups that do not (Hirokawa, 1988). (Try "Identifying Decision-Making Functions" to get firsthand practice at analyzing group decision making.) But the functional perspective is not a procedure for making decisions because there is no prescribed order to the five functions. Rather, it is the failure of the group to perform one of the five functions that has a profound

> ### BUILDING ANALYTICAL SKILLS
>
> *Identifying Decision-Making Functions*
>
> Select one of your favorite television shows (hour-long dramas would be a good choice for this exercise). Step 1: Watch the show and jot down what characters say as part of the decision-making process. Pay particular attention to statements or questions you believe are important. Step 2: Now check your list for the following. Can you identify:
>
> 1. statements or questions that helped the group understand the problem or decision? If not, how did characters know and agree upon what the problem or decision was?
> 2. statements or questions that helped the group understand what would constitute an acceptable choice? Did the characters identify any criteria against which the decision would be evaluated?
> 3. statements or questions that identified alternatives the group would consider?
> 4. statements or questions that indicated that the group was assessing the positive qualities of the alternatives?
> 5. statements or questions that indicated that the group was assessing the negative qualities of the alternatives?
>
> Step 3: Watch the show again to see if you can fill in any of the categories. Step 4: Answer the following questions:
>
> 1. Specifically, what was the decision or problem on which the group was working?
> 2. Did the characters make a final decision or resolve the problem?
> 3. What was the decision or how was the problem resolved?
> 4. How many alternatives did the group consider?
> 5. To what extent did the characters apply the five functions of group decision making?
> 6. To what extent do you believe the group's decision making was effective?
> 7. In what areas does the group need to improve?
> 8. If the situation were replicated in real life, what recommendations would you give to the group about their decision making?

effect on the quality of the group's decision making. For example, if no one had brought up the fact that the churches and office building parking lots were a good distance from the campus, this alternative might have been chosen.

Many factors can keep groups from doing what they know they should do. Group members may feel time pressures, or undue influence from one particularly powerful group member may be enough to distract the group from its course. Because effective decision making should not be left to chance, groups should consider asking one group member to act as a reminder (Schultz, Ketrow, & Urban, 1995).

In the role of the reminder, one group member is appointed to assess the group's process and to ask questions that help steer the group back on course. The reminder role is similar to the critical advisor role discussed in Chapter 8. The goal of the reminder is not to interfere with what is happening in the group, but only to ask questions to ensure that four conditions have been met (Schultz, Ketrow, & Urban, 1995). First, the reminder assesses the group's interaction to determine if the group has enough evidence to support its choice or solution. Second, the reminder can ask if the group examined a sufficient number of alternatives. Third, the reminder checks to see if the group reexamined alternatives rejected earlier by the group. Finally, the reminder asks questions to make sure the group has avoided stereotypical thinking or premature judgment. By using a friendly yet serious communication style, the reminder might say, "Why do you think this proposal might work?" or "Maybe we shouldn't decide on our choices until we have spent a little more time analyzing other choices." Does using a reminder work? Yes! Groups using trained reminders made higher quality decisions, especially when the role of the reminder was taken on by someone other than the group's leader (Schultz, Ketrow, & Urban, 1995).

Influences on Decision Making

When we enter group decision-making situations, we expect there to be influence—from ourselves, from others—and we expect the influence to affect both the topic and the process. Sometimes we accept influence from other members; at other times, we reject or repel their influence. But rather than just having the expectation that influence will occur, effective group members know how to make influence a valuable and favorable aspect of group decision making. Influence, which occurs through communication, helps group members change their minds or make choices among alternatives. Influence occurs in all types of group decision-making settings, but it is especially important when decisions involve a high level of risk (juries deciding on a verdict, executive teams developing organizational strategy). There are several complementary explanations for how influence affects group decision making (Seibold, Meyers, & Sunwolf, 1996). We will explore five of them—prediscussion influence, social comparison theory, persuasive arguments theory, social identity theory, and social-interactional perspective. We will also explore how social and contextual factors influence decision making.

Prediscussion Influence

One source of influence arises from the position of individual group members at the beginning of the conversation (Propp, 1997). Individuals generally do not enter group discussions belief-free. Even if they have not thought that much about the group's problem or decision, members will form some beliefs or generate some ideas to bring to the group. Actually, groups whose members start a discussion with conflicting prediscussion preferences use more information in coming to a final decision than groups that begin a discussion with similar preferences. This occurs because a group member is likely to only introduce information into the group that supports his or her alternative or idea. This strategy creates salience for the group member but limits the information and options before the group. When prediscussion preferences differ among group members, the group must use information relating to all alternatives, making it more likely that the group will evaluate both positive and negative attributes of each alternative. On the other hand, if all group members come to the discussion supporting one alternative, only information about that alternative will be given.

Social Comparison Theory

When you come to a group to work on a decision task, you are often aware that others hold points of view different from your own. **Social comparison theory** is based on two principles (Seibold, Meyers, & Sunwolf, 1996): The first is that being part of a decision-making group drives you to reevaluate your own preference when presented with the preferences of other group members; the second is that being part of a group decision involves some pressure to conform. We may react to an internal pressure like feeling afraid that others will not want to work with us in the future if we do not go along with their ideas, or we may react to external pressure. For example, as a child you may have felt pressured to play the games your older siblings wanted to play because you felt intimidated by them.

Decisions always represent choices, and choices are associated with values. So, when you are in a group decision setting, you want to know where other members stand—especially on choices that involve risk. If others support the risky choice, you are more likely to support that choice as well. According to social comparison theory, the function of group discussion is to allow group members to compare their positions. This is how groups create a **risky-shift**—the tendency for groups to select a higher risk alternative than any member would favor individually (Clark, 1971). This phenomenon is particularly pronounced when groups are making decisions in support of values, attitudes, or opinions (Myers & Bishop, 1971). Group members who independently view themselves as risk takers consider themselves more risky than others, and the group discussion would only increase that evaluation. Thus the group's decision would be even riskier than members' initial individual positions. Think of yourself as a member of a jury. You are in favor of nailing the defendant because he raped someone. Your sister was raped many years ago, and you know firsthand the trauma such a crime creates for the victim and her family. As the discussion among jury members continues, you find that three other jurors have also known rape victims. Even though a life term or the death penalty cannot be considered in this case, before you know it, the jurors are saying that they would give him life if they could.

Risky-shift can also arise from being in a group because of the illusion that others will share in the responsibility of the decision (McGrath, 1984). Thus group members can create and accept a more extreme solution if they have adopted the belief that others will take some of the burden or responsibility for the decision. Another explanation is that our society, particularly in business communities, values risk (McGrath, 1984). When group discussion reveals risk or the potential for supporting a risky solution, other group members are more likely to assume and support risky positions.

These same effects also occur in the reverse and is known as a **cautious-shift.** Group members who believe they are cautious decision makers or who believe they hold cautious positions will only magnify that caution in group decision making. Thus the dominant values of individual group members influence the flow of information in the group and its final decision (Stoner, 1968). The cautious-shift appears to have occurred in the Terry Nichols Oklahoma City bombing trial. The jury forewoman was more conservative than other jury members, and her position to not invoke the death penalty, which was supported by two other jurors, was at odds with seven who favored the death penalty and two who favored acquittal. As forewoman, she maintained her position, forcing the jury to an inconclusive position, even though other jurors claimed to be ready to restart deliberations. In the end, the cautious-shift that occurred with some jury members prevailed. The jurors did not make a final recommendation; the judge dismissed them and took Nichols' sentencing into his own hands.

Persuasive Arguments Theory

Another view of how influence works in group decision making is offered by **persuasive arguments theory.** This theory suggests that influence is generated by how group members process arguments (Seibold, Meyers, & Sunwolf, 1996). Often before you join others in making a decision you mentally go over some alternatives on your own. During that evaluation, you create arguments, or reasons and considerations, that influence how you view each alternative. Other arguments may be culturally or socially driven. For example, before his video production team meets to finish shooting, Dylan thinks of arguments for why the team should reshoot an earlier scene. Dylan is the producer of the video so this position helps him create some unique arguments—after all, he is responsible for the look of the video. In addition to these arguments, Dylan also considers the shared culture and values of production team who are union members. Thus Dylan also develops the argument that reshooting the scene is okay because everyone welcomes overtime pay. Remember that according to the theory all group members go through this process, meaning that the production team probably shares Dylan's argument that overtime pay is welcomed. But the other group members also develop their own unique set of arguments. As a result, no one group member has access to all of the arguments that individuals have generated.

How does this affect group decision making? Just prior to or during the production meeting, each member will evaluate his or her own set of arguments and select the alternative for which he or she has developed the best or most arguments. During the group's discussion, members share the alternative they find most attractive—usually the alternative for which they have the most arguments. While other team members are talking, Dylan is reexamining his own set of arguments, checking them against the arguments of others. Researchers have shown that generally the alternative chosen by the group is the one for which members hold the most arguments (Myers & Bishop, 1971). The *Group Assessment Technique* will show you what arguments you bring to a group.

GROUP ASSESSMENT TECHNIQUE

What Arguments Do You Bring to the Group?

For each of the following two situations, identify at least two safe or cautious choices as well as two more attractive but riskier choices. Think about the reasons, considerations, or arguments you will bring up in support of your choices.

	Less attractive but safer choices	*More attractive but riskier choices*
You are going on spring break with a group of five friends. Three friends do not drink; two members do not drive; one is afraid of flying. Money is not an issue. Identify at least two locations and two modes of travel to discuss with your friends.		
Tonight your fiancé and you are meeting with your family to tell them you are getting married in 6 months. Your parents are not particularly fond of your fiancé. You have little or no money to spend on the wedding; your fiancé has been saving money and can finance some of the wedding. Identify at least two options to obtain funds for the wedding and two types of wedding ceremonies to discuss with your family and fiancé.		

Compare your arguments with the arguments of other students. How much similarity or difference is there in the choices and arguments you proposed? Which choice and which argument do you think would have the most influence on others? If these situations were real, which choices would you really make? Why?

Social Identity Theory

A different explanation of how influence works in groups is provided by **social identity theory.** According to this theory, influence, or social identification, occurs in three steps (Mackie, 1986; Seibold, Meyers, & Sunwolf, 1996). As a member of a group, you identify yourself with other group members to create a group identity. This is known as the **in-group,** and it creates the first step of influence. Knowing that you are a member of the 31st Combat Wing Drill Team allows the possibility for influence to occur. As a member of the drill team, you share beliefs and values with other members that are different from other drill teams and different from other units of the 31st Combat Wing. This is the second step of influence. Not only do you identify yourself with your drill team, you distinguish the team from other units (these are known as **out-groups**). The third step of influence is created as you adopt the beliefs and values of other members of the drill team. To summarize, first you identify with the group; second, you distinguish between your group and other groups; and, finally, you adopt the characteristics of other members of your in-group.

As you participate in discussions with members of your in-group, you hear the opinions of other in-group members. Changes in decision alternatives occur as you judge how similar or dissimilar your opinions are to others in your group. Wanting to be like other group members, you adopt the opinion of the majority of group members. According to this theory, group membership indicates what information is important to you as well as how that information is interpreted and why it is valued by the group (Mackie, 1986). Thus your willingness to identify with a group creates the opportunity for influence to occur.

Social-Interactional Perspective

A view that supports the proposition that communication is central to how arguments affect decision making is **social-interactional perspective** (Meyers & Seibold, 1987). This theory argues that the messages one sends and receives in a group discussion, not the cognitive arguments developed, produce the influence that can change members' prediscussion choices to the choice supported in the final decision making. You are more likely to influence other group members to change their mind if you can successfully weave into the conversation a number of different arguments supporting your choice (Meyers, 1989). "Where Does Influence Come From?" helps you to see this process and how influence operates in groups.

Social and Contextual Influence

Because groups are tied to some larger environment—three teenagers are a subgroup as part of a family, a sales team is part of a large retail organization, a city's planning commission is part of the larger city government—influence is also created by the context in which the group is situated. The context into which groups are embedded biases how group members perceive their tasks, what they believe are acceptable and effective decisions, and how the group decision-making process works. In groups, influence is generated by group members' perceptions of connections to the external environment. One way to influence others is to alter how group members view that context (Barge & Keyton, 1994).

> **THINK ABOUT IT**
>
> ### Where Does Influence Come From?
>
> Think about a group with which you closely identify or associate. How does being a member of that group influence what you think? what you value? how you communicate? Do you communicate differently in this group than in other groups or in team settings? How would you characterize the decision-making activity of this group? Do you feel that your presence in the group helps to generate influence over other group members? Which explanation of influence best describes your experience in this group?

This type of influence is strategic and is sometimes manipulative in a negative way. By getting the group's activities to be viewed in a particular way, a group member gains control over the situation and the decision-making process. This type of political activity restructures the surface or immediate environment of the group in order to favor the self-interests of one group member (Frost, 1987). If the group member is successful at these reframing attempts, then he or she has altered the context of the group, which will ultimately affect the group's decisions.

Let's look at a transcript of a city council meeting for evidence of this type of social and contextual influence. First, however, you need some background information to understand the context and the type of influence in this discussion. In the fall of 1990, the Waco, Texas, City Council met to discuss when to schedule its meetings. Five council members elected by their districts and the mayor are members of the group. Mayor Reed is in a unique situation because he is the first elected mayor in Waco. Prior to this election, council members selected one member as mayor pro tem. The following transcript was printed by the local newspaper:

COUNCIL MEMBER JOHNSON: I suggest that we have on the agenda a resolution on time.

MAYOR CHARLES REED: Why do we need a resolution on times when we have a resolution and we've completed the . . . ?

CITY ATTORNEY EARL BRACKEN: Uh, Mr. Mayor . . .

JOHNSON: We can place it on the agenda, and if there's some opposition to it, we could discuss it at that point, but will you at least give me an opportunity to discuss it? As a councilman, I'm requesting that it be an agenda item.

REED: What, what, what, what is the purpose of the resolution? I would, I would like to know.

COUNCIL MEMBER LaNELLE McNAMARA: I think we currently have a resolution that has no time in it. Is that correct?

REED: We have a resolution that does not contain times, but the council has by motion approved time that uh, that uh, supplements the resolution.

COUNCIL MEMBER SAM JACK McGLASSON: I think you at least need to afford Councilman Johnson the courtesy of putting it on the agenda. He has requested it. He's within his right to have done it.

REED: He has a right to request putting it on the agenda, and he did. What I'm asking is, for what purpose? What purpose would it serve to put it on there?

McGLASSON: It's his business.

REED: Well, I think as mayor it's my business to have something to say about what's on the agenda, and I don't see any purpose in having that on the agenda.

JOHNSON: Is it your position that I have to explain it and justify it to you?

REED: Yes, that's my position.

McGLASSON: God almighty.

JOHNSON: So, in that case you're saying you have the control over what's on the agenda?

REED: You're absolutely right I have control over what's on the agenda.

McGLASSON: I think you're as wrong as you can be, Mayor.

REED: Well, I'm sorry, I disagree with you.

McNAMARA: Mr. Bracken, may we have a ruling as to whether or not we as council members have a right to place items on the agenda?

REED: Well, I don't know where, uh, uh, I don't know what purpose you're seeking an opinion from the city attorney on this, because as the mayor I believe it is clearly my job to do this, and I'm not asking for any opinion on it.

BRACKEN: Since this has come up, it is my opinion that the charter describes what the mayor's areas of responsibility are, and it does not include the controlling of the agenda. Preside at the meeting, as provided by the charter, and one vote. That's my interpretation of the charter.

REED: I disagree with the city attorney's opinion there.

McNAMARA: Who sets the agenda under the charter? How is it set?

REED: The charter does not say, and as such it is clear that the mayor—it says the mayor is the presiding officer of the council and as such the presiding officer is the person who controls the agenda. That's the way I see it.

JOHNSON: Okay then, Mr. Mayor, I would like to make a motion. I move that a resolution with respect to our meeting schedule be placed on the agenda.

REED: (bangs gavel) The motion is out of order!

Although at first glance the meeting appears to be about scheduling meeting times for council meetings, a closer examination of the discourse suggests powerful influence attempts by both the mayor and council members. First let's look at the context or environment, of this city council. Although each council member is elected, he or she only represents voters in a specific district. On the other hand, the mayor is elected by a popular vote across districts. Being the first elected mayor, Reed is in a unique situation. Also, Reed's professional career has some bearing on when he can be available for council meetings; the council members appear to be more flexible in this regard.

So although the dispute concerns what time the council will meet, the discourse also reveals the influence the mayor is trying to establish over council members. By framing the rights and responsibilities as mayor in his particular way, the mayor will have more power than other council members. As you can see, there appear to be distinct interpretations of his role: the mayor's interpretation and council members' interpretation. Added to that is the city attorney's interpretation of the roles and responsibilities of mayor.

This meeting was not the first one in which differences of opinion about the city charter had surfaced. Earlier, Reed had tried to change the council's meeting times by arguing that as mayor his vote counted more than the votes of the council members. It may not be obvious here what controlling the time of the meetings really means. If the mayor is successful in framing the discourse his way, he will control the time the council meets. If council members concede to this interpretation, it will be easier for him to also control the agenda. Controlling the agenda means that the mayor's issues will have priority over issues council members want to address. So if the mayor's reframing of what constitutes the mayor's roles and responsibilities is successful, in practice his one vote will carry more weight than the single vote of any council member.

This play for influence has a long history in the interactions between the mayor and the council members. In the first citywide election for mayor, Reed, who held no previous elected office or position on any city board, beat Council Member McGlasson. In campaigning for mayor, Reed accused McGlasson, then a council member, of being inaccessible to Waco's citizens. Reed indicated he wanted to open up council meetings so citizens could attend; that meant having evening meetings. But Reed's hidden and personal agenda about time did not surface until the council meetings began. Although other members were fairly flexible, Reed could only attend evening meetings. To meet during the day, he would have to take vacation time from his job—something he did not want to do.

These influence attempts were a strong force on the city council. At the next meeting, members discussed the time issue for 2 hours and could only conclude that they needed to reach an agreement on time. Again, another meeting was scheduled to decide on meeting times. After 2 months of debate, the council finally agreed on a meeting schedule. Thus the time discussions were attempts "to reframe the discussion over who has power within the council, and what constituency groups outside the council will be heard" (Barge & Keyton, 1994, p. 102). Although Reed did not succeed in advancing his agenda, he did successfully steer the discourse over trivial matters in such a way that it precluded the discussion of valid city business.

Faulty or failed decisions are more prevalent than many of us believe. Making assumptions about facts, using faulty logic, and being pressured by someone external to the group are just a few of the factors that can contribute to faulty decision making.

Reasons for Faulty Decisions

Generally, research has shown that groups make better decisions than individuals when decisions are complex. Yet, groups can make faulty or ineffective decisions. Eight factors contribute to faulty group decision making (Gouran, Hirokawa, & Martz, 1986; Hirokawa, Gouran, & Martz, 1988). First, some faulty decisions result when group members make assumptions about the facts of a case. When members assume they know the facts, or assume they have all of the knowledge needed to make a decision, the decision-making base is flawed. For example, recall from our parking example earlier in the chapter that students usually believe that there is not enough parking on campus. This belief becomes a fact and affects the type of solutions the student group develops to combat the problem. However, when students investigate the issue, they find that it is not a question of how many parking spaces are available but of where or when the parking spaces are available. This additional information changes the type of solution they propose. Questioning one another and asking for clarification even when everyone believes it is a fact can help a group overcome making faulty assumptions.

A second factor contributing to faulty decision making is the breakdown in the group's reasoning process. Even when group members have all of the needed information, they can still make a poor decision if they allow themselves to jump to conclusions or use faulty logic. Drawing unwarranted inferences is one example of faulty reasoning. Unwarranted inferences are not based on facts, data, or information; rather, they are based on what group members think to be true. What they believe to be true enters the discussion as fact before anyone checks the validity of the inference. As group members continue to interact, the unwarranted inference becomes a fact—now, no one thinks it needs to be checked out. Here is an example of how this happens:

PAULA: I think we're not having an awards ceremony because the president of the university will be out of the country.

ALTHEA: How do you know that?

PAULA: I heard my dad talking on the phone. He went to a chamber of commerce breakfast and our president was the guest speaker. My dad said the president talked about traveling to central Europe.

LOREN: But when?

PAULA: I don't know. But don't you think it's unusual that the university canceled an event that's been a tradition for 25 years?

LOREN: Well, maybe there's some other reason.

ALTHEA: I think she's right, Loren. Why else would they cancel the awards ceremony?

Using one of the discussion procedures in Chapter 8 can help group members overcome this problem by critically examining the ideas before them.

Third, faulty or ineffective decisions are more likely to occur when the group is under pressure to make a quick decision or when a group believes that it has to pick one particular solution to please someone outside the group. In both cases, group members perceive that no other choice is available them. Such a belief, even if the pressure is imagined, curtails the group's discussion and prevents it from exploring the negative consequences of the choice. Once this type of perception crystallizes in the group, it can become so salient that it seems impossible to move from this position. You have probably been a member of a class group in which this happened. The teacher tells the groups they can pick whatever topic they want for their presentations. But instead of focusing on topics of interest to your group members, you try to figure out what topic your teacher would like to hear about. Somebody mentions that he was in the Marines. Before you know it, your group is planning a presentation on why military service should be a requirement rather than voluntary.

Incomplete decision rules or decision criteria is the fourth factor contributing to faulty decision making. Many groups work to resolve problems that are time or budget sensitive. Groups frequently use a time or budget criterion as the primary or only criterion. By focusing on this one issue in the exploration of alternatives, a group overlooks other potential negative consequences. For example, a group working under the budgetary pressure to purchase the cheapest available product will select the cheapest alternative. Believing they have satisfied their budget constraint, group members may have overlooked the long-term costs or the costs to implement the decision. Buying the cheapest copy paper may cause the copier to continually jam. How would you evaluate the lost time to unjamming the copier in comparison to the pennies saved on the paper?

Fifth, faulty decision making occurs when group members are unable to persuade or convince one another that another decision is better. For example, Kedrick believes that adopting the neuter-spay/reduced animal license fee program will increase pet owner responsibility. But in conversations with others, he has difficulty first presenting and then defending this point of view. His inability to persuade others that some pet owners will be lured by the financial incentive to neuter or spay their pets allows the group to reject this alternative. Thus your persuasive ability as a group member can help your group accept a high quality alternative and reject low quality ones.

The sixth factor contributing to faulty decision making is the use of ambiguous and vague language (for example, "Do you remember what we were talking about?" "Yeah." "Sure." "Okay, then, here's what we're going to do . . ."). When group members are vague and indirect, other group members may misread the intended meaning. In discussing alternatives, clear and concise language is needed to explore the positive and negative consequences.

Seventh, rigid adherence to role boundaries can create conflict for group members. When role conflict exists, group members rarely venture outside their ascribed roles to collect other information or to pursue additional alternatives. This occurs more often when roles and prescribed channels of communication are closely aligned. For example, a female secretary who is a member of an otherwise all-male executive committee knows that her primary role is to serve as the group's recorder. In a policy-making discussion about maternity benefits, however, she wants to offer the group her beliefs about what women in the organization want. The information she possesses could really help the group in its decision making, but she feels hesitant to change roles from passive recorder to active participant. Feeling pressure to remain in her formal role, she remains quiet while the men discuss maternity benefits.

Finally, failure to ask relevant or obvious questions creates assumed understanding. Frequently, the most obvious question goes unasked because a group member is fearful that he or she will be penalized or humiliated by other members for not knowing the answer. Asking questions that appear to be already answered gives groups another opportunity to explore details that are often taken for granted. For example, a student group had been preparing a graphic presentation of its final project. Wanting to impress their instructor and classmates, they spent extra time together just to build the computer slide presentation and practice with it. All members assumed, and no one asked, if the computer in the presentation room could run the slide presentation program. Minutes before their presentation, the leader popped in their disk and waited for the computer to demonstrate their creativity. Nothing happened. Finally, a message appeared on the screen: "Powergraphics cannot open the presentation." Failing to ask obvious or relevant questions can waste a group's time and render other decisions ineffective.

Constraints on Decision Making

In general, there are three types of constraints that produce faulty decision making (Gouran & Hirokawa, 1996; Janis, 1989). **Cognitive constraints,** or difficulties and inadequacies in processing information, occur when there is little information available, limited time for making a decision, or when the decision is more difficult than group members can comfortably or normally handle. When decision making occurs under these conditions, group members may feel unable to handle the situation and fall back on how others made similar decisions.

For example, a member of your family unexpectedly dies in an automobile accident. Members of the immediate family fly in to provide support for one another but also find themselves faced with many decisions that need to be made immediately. When and where will the funeral take place? Will the family have visitation, a funeral service, and graveside services? What type of funeral arrangements would best honor the deceased family member? As often happens in these situations, the desires of the deceased are unknown because she or he did not leave a will. Thus family members have limited information on which to base their decisions. The decision situation is further complicated because time is very limited. Funeral service decisions must be made quickly so that other relatives and friends can be notified. More than likely, this family group has had little experience in working together. Coupled with not knowing the preferences of the deceased, family members rely on their memories of how the deceased reacted to the funeral arrangements of other family members. This decision situation is severely influenced by cognitive constraints.

A second type of constraint—**affiliative constraints**—are those that are based on the relationships among members of the group. When relationships, or the fear that relationships will deteriorate, are the dominant concern, some group members will exert undue influence on other group members. Affiliative constraints are often present in family decision making, but they can also occur in work teams.

For example, Tamika has just joined Physician Services, a company that helps employers manage their workers' compensation claims. As a recent college graduate, Tamika is fully aware that she has much to learn and that how she performs in this first job will either make or break her career with Physician Services. Other members of Tamika's claims management team include Roth, the team leader who has been with the company for 7 years; Mel, a friend of Roth's and an expert claims manager; and Cicely, another claims manager, but also the daughter of the company's founder. In the few weeks Tamika has worked at Physician Services, she has established good working relationships with the other team members. She is particularly fond of Mel; they went to the same university where Tamika's brother currently plays basketball with Mel's brother. Mel has gone out of his way to help Tamika understand the claims process and how to secure new claims business for the company. In a team meeting one afternoon, the group is discussing aggressive marketing strategies. To Tamika, the conversation is interesting, but she is wondering how she will handle her claims management responsibilities and meet the goal of ten prospective client visits per week that is being discussed by the team:

ROTH: Okay, great idea, Mel. Ten new visits per week sounds reasonable to me.

MEL: Right! If we visit a prospective client before we come in to the office in the morning and then visit another one right after lunch each day, we'll each have ten visits locked up in a week.

CICELY: That sounds like a great plan, Mel. If we all use the same schedule, we could meet as a team, say at 9:30 A.M., to discuss how well the visits went and what follow-up strategies we want to employ.

ROTH: Okay. Then maybe we should meet again as a team immediately following the after-lunch appointments. Some companies may be more likely to join our service if our follow-up with them is within the next day. Okay, Tamika?

TAMIKA: Sure.

Even though Tamika has been with the company just a short time, she recognizes that visiting a prospective client and then meeting as a team will occupy most of the morning, leaving her little time to manage claims before lunch and another round of client and team meetings. She wonders why no one else sees this as a problem. She is sure that other team members also have claims management responsibilities, but their eagerness to attract new business seems to overshadow managing their existing work. Tamika does not speak up because she has so little experience. She believes that if she challenges the new plan, other team members might believe she is not a team player. This type of affiliative constraint hinders group decision making because group members are reluctant to challenge relationships with others upon whom they rely to complete their work.

The third type of decision-making constraint is egocentric constraints. **Egocentric constraints** occur when one group member has a high need for control over the group or its activities or when this group member has a personal or hidden agenda. It is likely that Marshall Herff Applewhite, the leader of the Heaven's Gate cult, created egocentric constraints on that group's decision making. Said to be both charismatic and funny, Applewhite had led his followers around the country for more than two decades. Members abandoned their families, belongings, and even their sexuality to join the cult. Both male and female members emulated Applewhite's appearance by getting buzz cuts and wearing shapeless clothes. Applewhite's egocentric needs seem to have had undue influence on the decision-making abilities of the cult's members.

Recognizing Constraints It is not always clear that cognitive, affiliative, or egocentric constraints are operating and affecting group decision making. Often these constraints reveal themselves to group members over time as patterns start to develop in group conversations. There are, however, some signs that signal the presence of a constraint and some strategies that can help minimize these constraints (Gouran & Hirokawa, 1996). For example, a group member may make the complaint, "How do they expect us to deal with this problem in only 2 weeks?" or "Here we go again—another case of hurry up and wait." These complaints are an indication that cognitive constraints have taken hold. Or, if a group feels pressured by the urgency of the task at the expense of pursuing a thorough understanding of the problem, cognitive constraints are likely. Affiliative constraints are indicated when unusually unequal participation occurs in group discussions. Affiliative constraints are also involved when a group member feels extreme pressure (favorable or unfavorable) to go along with the majority sentiment. Finally, egocentric constraints are present when one member bolsters his or her own views while being overly critical of the views of others. Frequently, egocentric constraints are framed as win-lose or "are you in or out?" If one group member constantly reminds others of his or her past achievements, egocentric constraints are likely operating.

Responding to Constraints When cognitive constraints are present, group members should not deny similarities between this decision and other decision events, but they should also analyze how the two situations are different. No matter how similar decisions appear on the surface, "rarely are two situations so alike that what applies to one necessarily applies to the other" (Gouran & Hirokawa, 1996, p. 68). Group members can also minimize the effects of cognitive constraints by recognizing the resource deficiencies with which the group must deal. Perhaps the urgency attached to a decision is perceived, not real. Finally, group members should voice the weaknesses or costs associated with making ineffective or inappropriate decisions.

In response to the presence of affiliative constraints, group members can ask for clarification about what the group is trying to accomplish. After agreeing with her team members that calling on new clients is important, Tamika could have asked how they suggest she balance the responsibility of calling on prospective clients with her claims management responsibilities. Not only would her input bring an important point into focus for the group, but her team members could also tell that Tamika is carefully listening to the group's conversation. Rather than weaken her relationships with other group members, this should strengthen them as she demonstrates commitment to the group's goals. In other situations where affiliative constraints are apparent, group members should try to separate personalities from the issues being discussed. Using reflective feedback ("I understand that you want to attract new clients. I look forward to those challenges. With the time we're setting aside for that function, I wonder how it will affect our abilities to manage our present claims?") will help make it clear that you are addressing ideas rather than attacking people.

Egocentric constraints are probably the most difficult to handle. Remember the discussion of primary provokers in Chapter 7? If the person presenting egocentric constraints has no more power than others in the group, then it is up to other group members to not yield compliance. Making statements that support equality among group members ("We're all in this together; what we come up with represents the group") can heighten this awareness. If the individual with the high need for control continues to dominate, group members may suggest using one of the decision procedures described in Chapter 8 that help equalize participation. If egocentric constraints come from a group or team member who does have more power than other members, different tactics need to be tried. Because fears of reprisal may be real, group members have to use more subtle and nonconfrontational strategies; for example, "You've been clear in outlining the strengths of this proposal; what weaknesses did you consider or what weaknesses do you want us to consider before we vote on it?" It is important to not confuse egocentric people with those who lack good judgment. Their judgment may be sound, but their presentation of ideas may not be effective, or they may be overreacting to the fear that others might not go along.

To overcome or minimize the effects of constraints on decision making, group members should: "(1) make clear their interest in arriving at the best possible decision; (2) identify the resources necessary for making such a decision; (3) recognize possible obstacles to be confronted; (4) specify the procedures to be followed; and (5) establish the ground rules for interaction" (Gouran & Hirokawa, 1996, pp. 75–76).

Process Loss

Faulty decision making also occurs when there is a process loss in the group. Communication in the group is probably the most important influence on the success of a group's decision making (Hirokawa, Erbert, & Hurst, 1996). But the communication of group members is not always on target. Often the communication of group members does not help the group complete its task or achieve its goal. This is known as **process loss.** Process loss is the difference between actual group productivity and potential group activity (Steiner, 1972). When what the group accomplishes does not add up to what the group could do, the process of communicating is said to be faulty. You probably can recall group conversations that added nothing to the group's goal or parts of conversations that kept the group from making a decision. Although group and team members should want to maximize their time and effort together, everything we say or do in a group rarely helps the group make choices and accomplish its goal.

Groupthink

The groupthink concept was first introduced in Chapter 4 as one consequence that can occur when groups feel pressures from their external environments. Groupthink is faulty decision making. Groupthink occurs regularly and deserves our attention in this chapter as well. Let's review the conditions that precede the development of groupthink:

- The group develops an extraordinarily high sense of cohesiveness.
- The group uses language to detach itself from ethical or moral considerations associated with finding a solution.
- The group is not vigilant in its thinking and artificially narrows what it considers to be an acceptable solution.
- Group members feel that the group is infallible—that the group can do no wrong.
- Group members protect one another from any criticisms or new knowledge that might demonstrate that the group is wrong.

A group would not intend to let groupthink occur, but it does because effective face-to-face communication is not taking place. The absence of disagreement may be the primary contributor to groupthink (Courtright, 1978). Groups that are cohesive are less likely to allow discussion that criticizes the group, its activity, or the ideas it generates. As a result, the group develops premature concurrence that shelters the group from critical thinking. Thinking that they have arrived at a unanimous decision, group members terminate deliberations prematurely (Cline, 1994). Yet cohesive groups can guard against groupthink by assigning a member to the critical advisor role or adopting a standard agenda procedure to help them overcome their inability to discriminate between satisfactory and unsatisfactory solutions.

The groupthink hypothesis was originally conceptualized by Janis (1982) as the tendency of highly cohesive groups to adopt faulty solutions because members failed to critically examine and analyze options. Groupthink occurs because three conditions are present. First, group members overestimate their power and invulnerability. Group members do not question what they are doing or why they are doing it. Maintaining group harmony or enhancing the desire to build an identity with the group is perceived by members to be more important than considering information that may temporarily decrease group cohesiveness.

Second, the group becomes closed-minded and rejects information that is contrary to its preferred course of action. By insulating itself from external threats and external influences, the group, by its actions, is taking itself out of its own environment. Often this is accomplished by creating rationalizations that discount negative information. This can also occur when group members adopt a stereotype of the external agent or the macro environment that is inaccurate or negative.

Third, group members experience high pressure to conform because of strong leader-group member relationships or because of the role the group plays relative to its environment. Pressure and stress are heightened when stakes are high or when the leader recommends a solution and group members see no viable alternative. This pressure to conform acts as self-censorship, causing group members to believe that consensus exists in the group when it does not. In these cases, members view pleasing the leader to be more important than considering other options.

These conditions create a working climate for a group that rewards closeness and cohesiveness and punishes members for being different. When time pressures and high-risk or high-consequence decision making also characterize a group's environment, these difficulties are amplified (Neck & Moorhead, 1995). These types of groups often fail to use decision procedures to help them think of and then analyze alternatives.

With this conceptualization of groupthink (Janis & Mann, 1977), the conditions apply primarily to decision-making groups that are overly cohesive. When cohesiveness is high, group members are more psychologically dependent on one another and less willing to challenge ideas. Groupthink is also more likely to occur in groups in which members have long and shared working histories, are deeply embedded in their macro-organizational environments, and are insulated from the views of others. These conditions lead to full-blown groupthink. However, not all of these conditions need to be met for groups to make faulty decisions or to develop groupthink problems.

Reread the three main characteristics of groupthink. When groups overestimate their power and invulnerability they are no longer effectively interacting with their macro environment. They are closing themselves off from receiving feedback messages about the group, the task, or the group's performance. Remember that from a macro-systems perspective, influences are reciprocal, meaning that the group influences the larger environment *and* the macro environment influences the group. The second groupthink characteristic identifies continued isolation from the group's larger environment as the group discounts or rationalizes negative information it receives. The third characteristic identifies a complete systemic shutdown in the group. Because the group is no longer operating effectively and reciprocally at the macro level within its environment, information that could be critical to the success of the group is ignored, and all feedback systems within the micro system (the group) break down.

How can your group avoid groupthink? One way is to bring decision-making procedures into the group (Neck & Moorhead, 1995). Decision procedures help focus a group on the task; groups that have high task commitment are more likely to search for and assess alternative courses of action than groups whose members are not committed to the group's task (Street, 1997). Adopting task procedures helps the group be open to information that exists outside the group's expertise because decision-making procedures require that members seek out information that is not currently known. Research has shown that groups tend to talk about what all members already know rather than identify information that is unique to one individual (Schittekatte & Van Hiel, 1996). When a group has high interpersonal cohesiveness and is more susceptible to the development of groupthink, a member with unique information may be unwilling to share that information because it does not fit with other information possessed by the group.

If you are the leader of a group suffering from groupthink, you may want to alter your leadership behavior to influence changes in members' behavior (Neck & Moorhead, 1995). A leader who encourages member participation and divergent opinions and who emphasizes the importance of reaching an effective decision will promote greater depth in the group's discussion. As leader, avoid stating your opinions at the beginning of the meeting. Your opinion is one of many that group members should deliberate. When a group is converging on groupthink behaviors, the leader has the additional responsibility of developing a norm of spirited inquiry.

Implementing Decisions

Once a decision is made, groups must implement that decision. This is where payoff occurs for group members. The decision is put in place, and the process of embedding it in the group or organization, in a family or a society, becomes the central activity (Nord & Tucker, 1987). How does a group evaluate its implementation? You might just want to ask, Did it work? but there are multiple criteria against which to judge the success of a decision implementation (Nord & Tucker, 1987).

Criteria for Successful Implementation

The first question to be addressed is, Did the group reach its goal? If the executive board intended to generate, evaluate, and rank projects for the humane society, then the first success criterion is met if in fact these activities took place and the humane society now has a list of projects to guide it through the next year. A second criterion of success is achieved when the group's output (in this case, the list of projects) have utility or value for the humane society. If the projects will help publicize the mission of the humane society, increase donations, and increase membership as well as pet adoptions, then the second criterion of success has been achieved. As the year progresses, another success criterion will be used to measure the effectiveness of each project in addressing one of the goals. In this case, the group would assess the long-term consequences of the group's decisions. For most decisions, there are costs involved. Thus another criterion of successful implementation is if the decision stayed within budget in terms of costs of supplies, personnel, time, and money. Decisions that use a lot of an organization's resources, require more personnel, take longer than expected, or go over budget are not successful implementations. One success criterion that is less obvious is how the process of decision making affected those who made the decisions. If the executive board found that they could work effectively together and they are enthusiastic about their relationships with one another, another measure of success has been achieved. Thus when the decision-making process contributes to the growth and personal well-being of team members, another type of success is achieved (Hackman, 1990).

Another aspect of decision implementation is to consider whether the decision is routine or radical. If the executive board of the humane society simply decides to repeat last year's project in the coming year, the decision and what is to be implemented are routine. People who will implement the decisions and those who are affected by them have a good idea of how the board's decisions will affect their actions. But if the executive board decides to recommend unique projects, board and organizational members will face uncertainty as they implement the decisions. Generally, the more innovative the decisions, the more the board will have to rely on communication to make sure that everyone understands what they are to do: "The more radical the innovation, the greater the disruption of the status quo and, other things being equal, the more changes there will be in information, values, incentives, power, and other elements" (Nord & Tucker, 1987, p. 11). So, if the board decides to try something different for a fundraiser—say, an adult overnight party at the zoo—the implementation is more complex. Board and organizational members will be dealing with new tasks; thus they will not be able to rely on how things were done in the past. This type of implementation requires greater levels of communication than implementation of standard or routine decisions.

Figure 9.1 *Decision Implementation Using PERT*

Decision made; ready for implementation —— three weeks —— All implementation activities completed

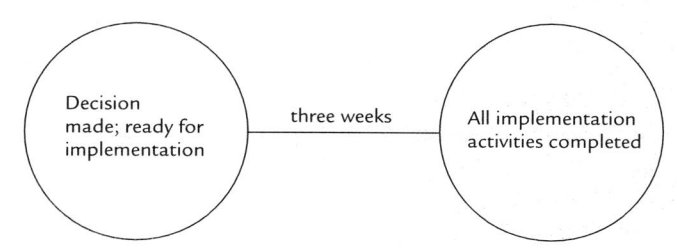

Designing the Implementation with PERT

The implementation stage may create a new series of decisions or problems for the group to consider. One technique that help groups with the implementation stage is **PERT** (program evaluation and review technique), a technique that helps group members order the activities that must be completed to implement a decision (Fourre, 1968). With PERT, group members plan the actions that will be needed and how long it will take for each action. PERT is especially useful when implementation is believed to be complex because it encourages group members to consider which, if any, activities can overlap or be completed simultaneously.

A PERT network is composed of events (points on the diagram) that are connected by one or more lines. The events are diagrammed against a time line so that deadlines are visually prominent and logically thought out. Using PERT, a group is only through with a decision when all activities are done and implementation is complete. Look at the PERT diagram in Figure 9.1. The diagram flows from left to right; the time line can be calculated in days, weeks, or months. Few decisions would be as simplistic as the one diagrammed in Figure 9.1. To implement most decisions, actions can be broken into smaller activities that are also represented by an event. For example, in planning a family reunion "food purchased" is an event, "purchasing food" is the activity leading up to the completion of the event. Generally, group members are responsible for some activities but not all. There may be a time in the implementation process that all group members need to meet again to coordinate their activities before going back to continue their implementation activities.

Using a PERT diagram can help a group identify which activities must be completed first, second, and so on, which activities can overlap or be completed simultaneously, and how long it will take for activity completion. PERT visualizes the full implementation process, which helps group members recognize that many small but significant steps must be taken before other activities can occur.

The following steps will help you develop a more complex PERT diagram (Applbaum & Anatol, 1971; Phillips, 1965). First, identify the final event or activity that will mark the completion of implementation. As an example, we will use the Bundschu family reunion, an annual event that draws together over 100 family members from 13 states. This event goes in the circle at the far right of the diagram (Figure 9.2). Second, with all group members working together, make a list of all the other events that must happen before the final event. In this step it is not

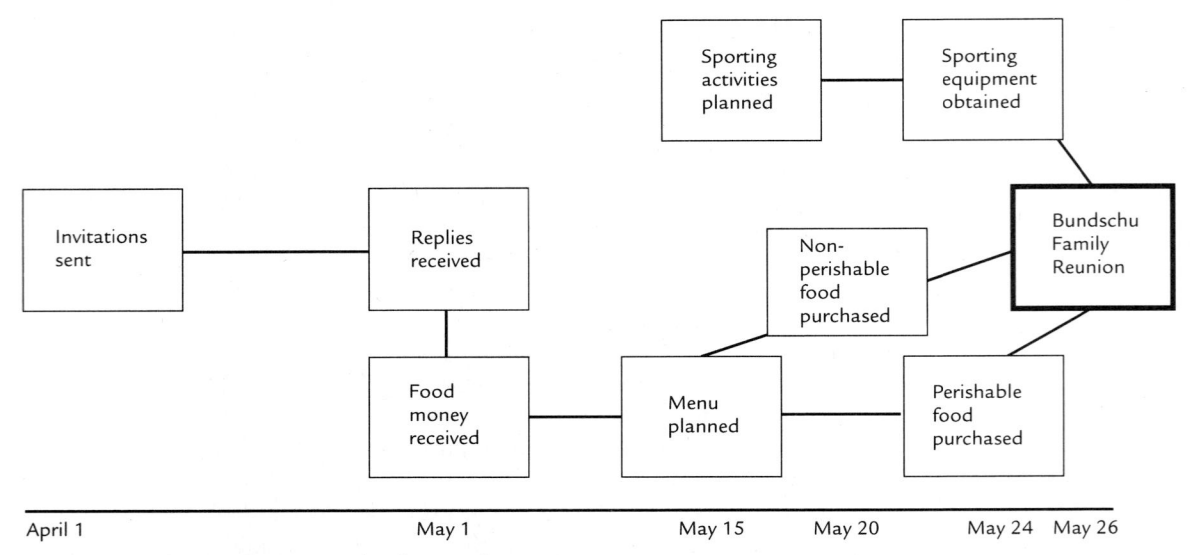

Figure 9.2 *The PERT Diagram for the Family Reunion*

necessary to list the events in order, but it is essential that the list of events is as complete as possible. Third, review the list of events and start to order the list. This should lead to the discovery that some events can occur simultaneously. For example, in planning the family reunion, food can be purchased by one committee while others are gathering sporting equipment. Ordering the events should also help the group recognize which events are dependent on other events. In planning the family reunion, the food committee cannot purchase food until the menu has been planned and the money has been obtained. Buying food is dependent upon completion of two events: menu planned and money obtained.

The group is now ready for the fourth step—to start developing its PERT diagram. Because PERT is a planning and scheduling process, it is unlikely that your group will develop the best flow of events and activities on the first try. Have plenty of paper available. Visualizing the events and activities will help you identify any errors in your planning logic in the third step. Let's look at the PERT diagram for planning the family reunion (Figure 9.2).

The critical first step in planning the reunion is sending the invitations. Without knowing how many people will be attending, planning for food and activities will be difficult. Notice that family members have been asked to send their money back with their reply. Without knowing how many people and thus how much money there is to spend, the food committee cannot plan the menu. Also notice that the food committee starts planning the menu before the sports committee starts their activity. Menu planning is more difficult as committee members must take into account differing diet preferences among the wide age range of family members. The food committee will also want to take advantage of sales at the grocery story on nonperishable items. So this committee begins its work first.

In the fifth step, group members assess how much time will be needed for each of the activities. Be realistic here. The group should consider (1) the optimistic time—the time it would take under ideal conditions with no complications, (2) the pessimistic time—the time it would take if every possible delay has been encountered, and (3) the most likely time—the time it would take under normal conditions. By looking at time in this way, the group will calculate the expected time—a reasonable estimate of the time involved. How would these conditions apply to planning the family reunion? From the optimistic point of view, no invitations would get lost in the mail, and every family would return their notices (with their money) on time. Further, every time the planning committee gets together, each member shows up and has completed his or her assignments. From the pessimistic perspective, invitations would be mailed late and then come back requiring extra postage, and families would not return their notices (or their money) on time. And, by the way, you quit your job and are now working as a temporary until you can find a new job! The most likely time can be calculated by asking each group member to make individual estimates of the time needed. By talking through committee members' different points of view, you will find a time allotment that seems reasonable. Having completed these three discussions, you will have a better assessment of the time it will take to plan and carry out the reunion. These discussions may also focus your attention on other events and activities that are not on your PERT diagram. For our family reunion planning committee, these discussions helped identify April 1 as the deadline for invitations to go out. The date allowed enough time to receive the replies and the money to make the reunion a reality. It also helped the planning committee recognize that they had not thought of alternative places for holding the reunion in case of bad weather. As a result of this discovery, another committee was formed to search for and select a backup location. When each group member is satisfied with the logic of events and activities and the time allotted for completing activities, then your PERT analysis and diagram are complete.

Dealing with the Pressures of Time

Time can be a group's worst enemy. Some groups work under very defined and nonchangeable time deadlines. The deadlines are set, and the group must meet those deadlines. For example, a committee to elect a local businessperson to your state legislature must meet, conduct its business, gather the needed signatures, and fill out the proper forms by a specific time and date to enter him as a candidate in the primary election. In this case, the deadline is not movable under any circumstance. The decision to support this candidate had to be implemented according to firm deadlines. Failing to meet the deadline would mean that the candidate would not be a candidate.

When a group's deadlines are absent, fuzzy, or constantly changing, groups invariably encounter problems (Hackman, 1990). Ambiguity about deadlines encourages group members to believe they have more time than they really do. Your vocal group wants to enter the talent competition at the regional fair. The group

Groups never seem to have enough time! Establishing your group's time frame for decision making and decision implementation is a crucial first step in the decision-making process.

asked you to call to see when applications were due and when the preliminary rounds of competition would be held. You call and you are told, "Applications are due sometime in the spring; preliminary rounds start after we get all the applications. The deadlines are always printed in the Sunday newspaper." You are not particularly happy with the answer, but pressing for more information does not reveal more specific information. You report back to other members of the group, and you decide to practice once a week until the applications are due. At that point, the group plans to practice at least three times a week to get ready for the competition. This sounds okay, but what if you do not see the application deadline published in the newspaper? What if the application deadline is only 2 weeks before competition starts, and your group pulls the first round of preliminaries? In this case, initially you did not get the information you needed to help the group implement its decision (its rehearsal schedule). What could you have done? You could have called another time and asked to speak to someone else, visited the fair office in person, or asked someone at the fair office or someone who competed previously how much time there was between the application deadline and the preliminary competitions. You could and should have done more to help your group identify a specific deadline. Deadlines can serve as a powerful and motivating force (Gersick & Davis-Sacks, 1990).

People react differently to time pressures and deadlines. Student groups in classroom assignments usually take one of the following two paths. Ideally, when given the assignment, group members would get together, decide what they want to do, design an implementation plan (a PERT chart would work well here), and do it. This type of group makes steady progress. There is time for members to meet regularly to check in with one another so any difficulties or issues of coordination can be addressed. This group finishes its project on time, feeling confident about what they have accomplished. Other student groups meet when initially given the assignment, decide who is going to do what, and schedule a future meeting—oh, say, the day before the group project is due! Groups like this are procrastinating and have fallen into the "it's a long time before the project is due" trap. If the assignment is given 7 weeks before the assignment is due, this group meets on the assignment day and waits almost the entire 7 weeks before meeting again. When group members come to the second and final meeting, they realize that the different parts of the project will not work together. Worse yet, one group member has dropped the class, and now there is not time to finish his part. Group members stay up most of the night working on the project and slide into class just before the assignment is due. They are glad the assignment is done, but they are not confident of what they are turning in.

Groups like in the first example develop a regular cycle of activity that becomes a rhythm. Over time, this rhythm becomes part of the group's character and climate (Hackman, 1990). In the second example, the students have paid little attention to time—both in terms of deadlines and in terms of how long it will take to pull the group project together. Of which kind of group would you rather be a member?

Additional Implementation Considerations

When implementation of decisions is complex or the decision to be implemented is novel or risky, there are other factors to consider. First, are those who have to implement the decision motivated and willing to try or learn new things? A great decision will fail if those who must implement it are unwilling or unable to take on the tasks. Thus motivation and knowledge are two things groups should consider when making a final selection from among alternatives. Second, does the organization in which the group operates have the capacity for allowing its members to try new things? By their very nature, some groups and organizations are open to new ideas. For example, a theatre group, because of its creative nature, will be more willing to implement novel ways of attracting subscribers. On the other hand, other groups—like some families or church groups—that allow history and tradition or norms to set the standards may be reluctant to allow group members to use creative or new approaches. Thus the flexibility of group members who will implement the decision and the flexibility of the group's organization are important to consider. Some groups and types of organization are slower to accept change than others.

Groups that expect their members to learn from their experiences will want to document the implementation process. Doing so creates a record of what worked, what did not work, and why. The work of many groups continues even though leadership changes yearly. Your university's student government association carries on with many of the same activities year after year. If the implementation process is not documented, each new set of officers will have to re-learn the same lessons or make the same mistakes all over again. Keeping budgets, a PERT time line, and other essential records will help document the group's activities and the success of the implementation.

Monitoring and Evaluating Decision Outcomes

While the decision is being implemented, group members should constantly be monitoring the decision for its presumed effectiveness. After implementation, a final evaluation should take place. There are three basic questions groups can use to structure these evaluations (Gouran, 1990). The first question is, Did the decision have the effect group members intended? In other words, was the group's goal consistent with what happened? Let's go back to the executive board of the humane society. In making decisions about projects to be carried out in the next year, the board intended to publicize the mission of the humane society, increase donations, and increase membership as well as pet adoptions. The set of projects the board approved had good potential, and at the year-end evaluation session board members were pleased with what they accomplished. By implementing the projects, the humane society had a more visible image in the community, donations were up 15 percent, membership was up 23 percent, and 97 percent of all the animals the shelter took in were adopted.

The second question groups can use to guide their evaluation is, Was the decision reached responsible for the observed effects? How can the board know that it was their set of projects that helped them to accomplish their objectives? Could it be that people in this community suddenly became more sensitive to the plight of unwanted pets? Could the national campaign for the humane treatment of animals that appeared in the media over the last 9 months be partly responsible for the success of the projects? Frequently when groups achieve favorable outcomes group members will attribute those outcomes to the group's effective decision making. On the other hand, when the outcomes are not favorable, group members are likely to ignore them or attribute the failures to factors outside the control of the group. One way for the humane society board to be more confident that their projects indeed created the positive outcomes would be to conduct a follow-up survey. By asking potential adopters how they found out about the shelter, or asking new members what encouraged them to join, the board would more fully understand the impact of their decision making.

The third evaluation question is, Did the decision have any unintended consequences that outweigh or offset the intended or positive consequences? Despite their hard work, the board's projects created an unintended consequence. With the additional publicity and public outreach, the humane society drew considerable scrutiny from the media. Reporters frequently came to the animal shelter to check on the conditions of the kennels. One television news program tried to expose the shelter, claiming that the shelter would not take in stray dogs. In reality, the shelter was full, and accepting more animals would have violated state animal control regulations. Even so, this news report created negative publicity for the shelter during one of its major donation drives. Increasing media scrutiny and potentially negative press and media coverage were not the board's intended goals. In the final evaluation, the positive outcomes of the many projects had to be balanced by the negative publicity. *Putting the Pieces Together* will help you understand the decision-making process and implementation in your own group experience.

> **PUTTING THE PIECES TOGETHER**
>
> *Group Goal, Group Structure, and Group Identity*
>
> Identify a recent group experience where your group followed the decision or task completely through to its implementation. How did the goals of the group differ in the initial stages of working on the task, through the decision making, and through the implementation stages? As the goals changed, how did the structure of the group respond? Did members keep strictly to their assigned roles? Did members offer to help in areas outside of their responsibilities? Finally, what happened to the group's identity as the group moved through the various stages of the project? Did its identity weaken or become stronger?

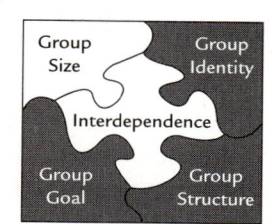

Summary

Group decision making is complex. The procedures discussed in Chapter 8 can help groups move effectively through their decision-making tasks, but we gain additional understanding about decision making from considering different theoretical perspectives. Acknowledging that group decision making is evolutionary and circular and that there are multiple influences on decisions made within a larger context of constraints allows us to embrace rather than fight the process.

Functional theory advocates five functions as necessary for effective decision making: understanding the problem, understanding what constitutes an acceptable choice, generating realistic and acceptable alternatives, assessing the positive qualities of each alternative, and assessing the negative qualities of each alternative. Groups whose communication fulfills all five functions will be more effective in their decision making because information has been pooled and evaluated. One way to help your group achieve each of the five functions is to appoint a member as a reminder. The reminder helps the group pay special attention to the group process and asks questions to steer the group back on course.

There is always influence when people come together to make decisions or solve problems. Group members should understand how they are influenced by others and how they can favorably influence others as well. Influence is generated by a variety of factors. Even before discussion begins, you have prediscussion positions that influence how you receive and evaluate information. Social comparison theory argues that being in the presence of others forces you to evaluate yourself and your positions against others. Persuasive arguments theory suggests that individuals rehearse their strongest arguments and then share them with others. Social identity theory holds that group members make decisions based on whether or not they are in the in-group. Social-interactional perspective argues that it is the messages group members reveal through communication that influences others. Group members also experience influence from their larger environments. If others accept how you frame the environment in which the group operates, you will influence others and the group's decision making.

Understanding how groups can make faulty or poor decisions may help you avoid these failures. Faulty decision making occurs for several reasons: when assumptions are made, when there is a breakdown in the group's reasoning, when there is a time pressure, when the group uses incomplete decision rules or criteria, when group members are unable to persuade one another, when group members adhere too rigidly to roles, and when group members fail to ask relevant or obvious questions. By paying attention to the group's process, each of these problems can be overcome.

Group members are more likely to contribute to faulty decision making if the group faces constraints. Cognitive constraints, or difficulties in processing information, hamper group discussion. Affiliative constraints also pose a problem as relationships among members become strained. Egocentric constraints occur when one group member needs to control the group or its activities. All of us have experienced these constraints in our group activities.

Process loss is another type of interaction problem. When the group's productivity does not add up to the group's potential, this is known as process loss. All groups suffer from some level of process loss.

Groupthink is the phenomenon that occurs when groups are pressured by external environments, high sense of cohesiveness, sense of vulnerability, and sense of infallibility. When these characteristics combine with a charismatic and powerful group leader, the group retreats from vigilant discussion about decision alternatives and adopts the alternative suggested by the leader with little or no critical evaluation.

Too frequently, groups spend a great deal of time on making decisions, forgetting that their time and effort is also needed in the decision implementation and monitoring stages. Implementation is where the pay-off for groups occurs if the group achieved its goal, if the outcome had utility, and if the project stayed within the resources budgeted. Implementation is a success if a group can confirm these objectives and indicate that the group developed as a unit throughout the experience. PERT is a technique that can help groups plan the sequencing of implementation activities. Working on a time line, PERT allows group members to specifically identify which steps of implementation must occur first, second, and so on. PERT is particularly useful when time deadlines are rigid, when time is limited, or when multiple tasks must be accomplished.

Monitoring the decision outcomes is the final step in decision making. Groups should ask three questions: Did the decision have the effect group members intended? Was the decision responsible for the observed effects? And did the decision have any unintended consequences?

✓ Checklist

Group Knowledge

You should be able to:
- describe how a reminder helps a group in meeting the five critical functions.
- explain how influence occurs in groups from at least three different perspectives.
- define cognitive, affiliative, and egocentric constraints on group decision making.
- describe why groupthink occurs.
- explain what a group is responsible for in the implementation and monitoring stages of group decision making.

Group Skills

You should be able to:
- help your group in implementing the five critical functions of decision making.
- play the role of the reminder for your group.
- favorably influence others in your group.
- avoid or respond to unfavorable influence from others.
- maintain vigilant communication to avoid groupthink.
- develop a PERT diagram.

Analytical and Assessment Techniques

You should be able to:
- identify the five critical functions and adapt your communication to meet any unfulfilled function.
- assess from where influence in the group is coming.
- address social and contextual influences without being rigid or egocentric.
- distinguish between discussion that is vigilant and discussion that is leading toward groupthink.
- logically think through all of the necessary steps in the implementation stage.
- identify appropriate and reasonable criteria against which to measure the success of your group's decision.

Discussion Questions and Exercises

1. Keep a journal or diary of your group experiences for the next week. Pay particular attention to influences on you in these situations. You may want to review parts of this chapter that discuss influence before keeping your journal. At the end of the week, what or who had the strongest influence on you in

group activities or tasks? How was that influence developed or sustained? How did you react to influence attempts? Did these influence attempts result in favorable or unfavorable outcomes?

2. Write a short position paper on the importance of communication in group decision making. Be sure to specifically identify the role you believe communication plays in decision-making activities. If you believe other elements besides communication are important to group decision making, identify those and explain any connection those elements have to communication.

3. Keep a journal of the decisions you made in groups for a two-week period. Identify the three decisions that are most important to you. How did social influence change the decisions? How would you describe the social influence that occurred? What was your role in influencing others? in being influenced by others?

4. Think about one of your classroom group experiences in which groupthink occurred. How was your classroom situation similar to or different from the conditions of groupthink explained in this chapter? Give a full explanation of how groupthink developed and who or what in the group allowed it to continue. Try to draw what happened in a model. Looking back on that experience, what did you learn about the groupthink phenomenon? What can you do in future classroom groups to prevent groupthink from occurring?

10
Leadership in Groups

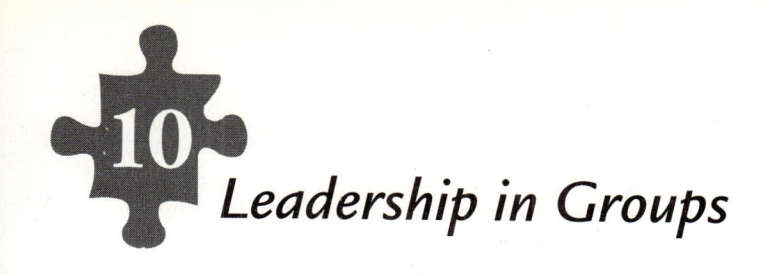

Why do groups need leaders?

What does a leader do?

Does a leader take on all of the responsibility for the group?

What different styles of leadership are there, and which one is most effective?

What do group members expect out of a leader?

Leadership is a process of influence. The person who influences other group members is the leader of the group even though he or she may not be appointed or elected to the formal leadership role. Leaders influence what groups do or what groups talk about. They also influence how groups perform their activities and achieve their goals. Society's conceptualization of what a leader is has changed over time, and those changing attitudes are reflected in developments in leadership theory. More recently, leadership theory has focused on the leader as a motivator—someone who can provide the group with energy. Many of the older theories initially may not seem useful to you, but each one provides information about why certain group members are frequently looked to as leaders and why certain leadership strategies are more effective than others. There is one thing you should keep in mind as you read about leadership: Research on leadership has focused almost exclusively on groups that make decisions in formal or hierarchical settings. So some of the findings presented here may seem out of place for friendship or other less formal groups or groups where initiating, developing, and maintaining relationships are the goals for the groups.

Defining Leadership

We could define leadership in a number of ways. In its broadest sense, leadership is the use of positive interpersonal influence to help the group attain a goal. More specifically, **leadership** is both a process and a property: "The process of leadership is the use of noncoercive influence to direct and coordinate the activities of the members of an organized group toward the accomplishment of group goals. As a property, leadership is the set of qualities or characteristics attributed to those who are perceived to successfully employ such influence" (Stogdill, 1974, p. 7). This definition encourages us to view leadership not as residing in one person—

the leader—but as a series of transactions between the leader (or leaders) and followers (Jago, 1982). By defining leadership as process—something one does—as well as a property—something one possesses—communication becomes central to the discussion. Leadership is a social phenomenon: "Leader and follower together create the social phenomenon we know as leadership (Fisher, 1985, p. 171). Because leadership is a process that occurs between and among people, leadership vividly demonstrates the type of interdependence found in group situations. Recall that one of the defining elements for a group in Chapter 1 was that members must have agreement about a goal. The interdependence created by group members sharing a collective goal forces issues of leadership to surface (Hollander, 1985).

Four caveats are worth mentioning here. First, you are not exhibiting leadership if others are not following. If group members do not respond to your leadership attempts, you are not the leader. Second, being appointed as head, chair, or leader does not guarantee that you will influence others. Group members will follow the member or members who exhibit influence in a positive manner to help them achieve their group and individual goals. Thus leadership influence is not necessarily consistent with position. In most cases, nearly all members perform some leadership functions (Hamblin, 1973). Third, leadership and power are not synonymous. Leadership may be infused with power (Hollander, 1985), but other group members also control power in the group. Finally, the leader cannot do everything (Hollander, 1985). There are limits to everyone's capacity, knowledge, skills, and motivation in performing this role. As a result, many followers will perform leadership roles in a group. Thus the distinction between leader and follower may not be as clear as you might initially believe.

Group members bring with them expectations about how leaders should behave (Pavitt & Sackaroff, 1990). First, group members expect the leader to encourage participation by others. The second expectation is that the leader will keep the group organized by talking about the procedures the group will use, summarizing the group's discussion, and facilitating group discussion. The third expectation is that the leader will work to develop and maintain harmony in the group by managing group conflicts. Finally, members expect the leader to play the role of the devil's advocate or critical advisor.

Generally, leadership behavior can be divided into three types: procedural behavior, analytical or task behaviors, and social or relational behavior (Chemers, 1993; Ketrow, 1991). Effective leaders are adept at all three types of leadership behaviors. Procedural leadership behaviors are those that coordinate the group and help members function as a group. Procedures often help a group achieve its goal, and group members look to others in the group for procedural help. The person who does this best will likely be selected as the group's leader (Ketrow, 1991). Thus leaders provide team coordination. This means that leaders successfully coordinate the skills, abilities, and resources available in the group.

Analytical or task leadership behaviors are those that help the group assess and evaluate their discussions. Group members recognize the need for someone to display task behaviors and believe that the member who displays this type of behavior is the most influential person in the group. However, this person will not be chosen as the leader over another member who displays procedural behavior (Ketrow, 1991). Somewhere between procedural and task behaviors is the expectation that the leader will provide image management. This means that the leader must establish credibility by behaving and communicating consistently with group members' expectations. If a group desires task direction, then to appear effective to the group, the leader must be task-directed with them.

Social or relational leadership behaviors are those that help the group express cooperation and support for one another. Effective leaders also need to address relationship development. In this function, leaders develop and maintain relationships with group members to foster interpersonal relationships, increase motivation and goal activity, and create perceptions of fairness within the group. Thus a leader must be able to demonstrate a wide repertoire of behaviors. Try *Building Analytical Skills* to test your leadership potential.

Becoming a Leader

You may have wondered how a person becomes a leader. When we enter a new group situation, one of the first things we want to know after identifying the group's task is who is going to be the leader. Leaders come to their positions in one of three ways: They are appointed, they are elected, or they emerge from the group's interaction.

Appointed Versus Elected Leaders

If a leader's authority comes from an appointment by individuals outside of the group, the group environment for both leader and group members differs from the environment of an elected leader (Hollander, 1978, 1985). When leaders are elected by group members—usually by a simple majority vote—members have a stronger investment in and more motivation to follow the leader than when the leader is appointed by outsiders. Each manner of leader selection validates one person as leader, and each creates a different reality for testing a leader's legitimacy. Elected leaders can face some difficult times. When things are going poorly for the group, elected leaders are more likely to be rejected by group members. Thus elected leaders may face a greater sense of responsibility as well as higher expectations for leader success than appointed leaders. For example, you elected Jason as chairperson. You expect him to take responsibility for the group; yet, you will blame him if he fails. One way to interpret this is to think of the group electing someone as leader the same as the group giving a reward to one group member in advance. Group members, then, expect the elected leader to pay back the group by producing favorable outcomes (Jacobs, 1970). Now let's examine what happens if Jason is appointed leader of your group. Your evaluation of Jason as a leader depends on his performance as leader and your confidence in the person or persons who appointed him. If he does not perform well, you may attribute the group's failure to Jason. But you can also attribute the group's failure to the person who appointed him, and you will do so especially if Jason is well liked in the

BUILDING ANALYTICAL SKILLS

What Is Your Leadership Potential?

Leaders are responsible for many different functions in a group. Identify your leadership potential by using the following scale to respond to each leadership behavior.

1 = no skill or motivation   2 = weak skills or low motivation
3 = adequate skills or motivation   4 = strong skills or motivation

1. Do you prepare yourself for meetings and teamwork?	1 2 3 4
2. Have you established credibility in the group?	1 2 3 4
3. Do you convey enthusiasm, involvement and commitment?	1 2 3 4
4. Can you adapt to other members' communicator styles?	1 2 3 4
5. Are you able to monitor your communication behavior during group meetings?	1 2 3 4
6. Do you consider the ethical implications of your behavior as leader?	1 2 3 4
7. Are you willing to improve your communication skills?	1 2 3 4
8. Can you create a supportive group climate?	1 2 3 4
9. Can you represent the group's interests to others?	1 2 3 4
10. Can you motivate or coach others?	1 2 3 4
11. Can you focus group members' attention and organize the group's work?	1 2 3 4
12. Can you plan agendas and manage meetings?	1 2 3 4
13. Can you work through problems with others?	1 2 3 4
14. Can you help quieter group members contribute to the group?	1 2 3 4
15. Can you help group members reach mutual understanding when there is a conflict?	1 2 3 4

How did you score? If your score is less than 45, you may have some difficulty effectively performing in the role of group leader. What steps can you take to enhance these skills or functions?

---

group. Generally, a leader who is elected by the group after a process of allowing leaders to emerge and be tested is in the strongest position to get things done (Hollander, 1978).

Emergent Leaders

Some groups rely on **emergent leadership**—a leader who is not appointed or elected but who emerges over time as a result of the group's interaction. Emergent leadership is most likely to occur in leaderless groups, or in groups with ineffective leadership. For some groups that are initially leaderless, a leader finally emerges while the group is completing its task. At the start, group members assess the trustworthiness and authoritativeness of members to see who might possibly be

Any one of these group members could be the group's leader. Although early leadership theories focused on traits stereotypically related to Caucasian males, the contemporary view of leadership is based on how well one group member meets the needs and expectations of other group members.

leader-worthy (Baker, 1990). The group member most likely to gain influence from other group members is the member who

- is not hesitant to speak
- uses nonverbal movement to create dynamism, alertness, involvement, and participation
- is supportive of and concerned with the welfare of others
- says and does the things that others in the group want to hear
- is charismatic
- does not control resources to demonstrate power

Those members who take an active role and talk frequently in the group are most likely to end up in the leadership role (Anderson & Wanberg, 1991; Baird, 1977; Hollander, 1985). The reverse has been confirmed as well (Baker, 1990). Group members who do not contribute ideas for the group task or do not contribute organizing help for the group are eliminated from leadership consideration. Those members who remain quiet and who are vague and tentative will effectively be passed over. Thus your behaviors and actions act as a test because leadership must be attempted before you can judge the success of your ability to influence other group members (Bass, 1981).

Emergent leaders are generally those group members who can use their social intelligence to monitor the situation and to modify their behaviors as required by the task and other members (Ellis et al., 1988; Ellis & Cronshaw, 1992). This type of person is good at monitoring social cues to assess whether their leadership behavior is appropriate and wanted (Cronshaw & Ellis, 1991). When one group member possesses this type of social and task awareness, other group members are likely to look to this person as being the natural leader of the group. In fact, the greater the degree of behavioral flexibility displayed by the potential leader in response to situational changes, the more likely that person will take on leadership roles within the group.

Although emergent leaders tend to have similar characteristics, one member cannot emerge as a leader of the group unless other members allow that emergence to occur (Hollander, 1978). Leadership emergence can be supported in two different ways. Let's use Ava as an example. First, group members willingly support the emergence of Ava as leader, and they encourage her to take on the leadership role. Or, they allow Ava to emerge as leader because they are passive and do not assume any of the group's leadership functions. In either case, a leader can only emerge through the sanctioning behavior of other group members. Either way, a leader has emerged when other group members perceive and act as if Ava is leading them and when Ava's attempts to initiate action or structure the group's interaction are successful (Bormann, Pratt, & Putnam, 1978).

Are men more likely than women to emerge as leaders? Not necessarily. Although biological sex is not a good predictor of who will emerge as leader, a group member with a masculine communication style—male or female—is likely to become the group's leader (Kolb, 1997). Members who are self-reliant, independent, assertive, and willing to take risks or take a stand possess a masculine communication style. How you communicate within a group is important because other group members are evaluating your potential for leadership by assessing your communication (Schultz, 1986). In particular, your ability to communicate clear goals, give directions, and summarize will either identify you as a potential leader or eliminate you from consideration. If several members are competing for the leadership role, the degree to which you communicate in a self-assured manner contributes to your selection as leader. The person most likely to emerge as the group's leader will be the member who can identify sources of differences or conflicts within the group and then develop and present a compelling rhetorical vision that can transcend those differences (Sharf, 1978). Let's see how these principles are revealed in the following group:

NANCY: I'm glad I'm in your group. This should be fun.

QUINTON: Me, too. It'll give me a chance to know Andrea better.

JOEL: Yeah.

ANDREA: Uh . . . what's your name, again?

NANCY: I'm Nancy, and that's Quinton and Joel.

QUINTON: Can we get started? I've got another meeting in an hour.

NANCY: Sure. Where should we start?

ANDREA: I'm not sure I know enough at this point to really help out.

JOEL: Me either.

QUINTON: Let's try getting started by identifying what each of us knows about the registration problem.

NANCY: Good idea, Quinton. For me, it's the standing in line. I don't understand why we stand in line to register on computers.

QUINTON: Joel, what do you think the problem is?

JOEL: I, uh . . . don't really know. I just know it doesn't work.

QUINTON: Andrea?

ANDREA: Well, it seems that . . . maybe I shouldn't say since this is my first semester.

QUINTON: Okay. This is my fourth time to register this way. I agree with you Joel that it doesn't work. One thing I've noticed is that the registration form we fill out doesn't follow the registration prompts on the computer.

NANCY: Right. That sure makes it confusing.

QUINTON: And, I've had trouble trying to give another option when my first course selection is closed out. Well, it sounds like we've had different problems, but it also seems that we believe a different system for registering could be developed. Do you agree?

Who do you believe will emerge as leader of this group? Nancy and Quinton are certainly more assertive, and both are contributing ideas for the group to consider. Joel is both vague and tentative. Andrea bases her hesitancy to help the group on her limited experience at the university. But does that mean she would not be a good leader? If the conversation continues in a similar way, we could expect that Nancy or Quinton would emerge as leader.

It can be detrimental to a group if a leader does not emerge; groups with emergent leaders outperform groups without leaders (De Souza & Klein, 1995). Group members who emerge as leaders tend to have high task ability and high commitment to the goals of the groups. This ability and attitude apparently influences other group members, helping them be successful. When leaders do not emerge, groups spend more time on procedural issues, incompletely discuss alternatives, and spend more time on irrelevant topics (Larson, 1971).

Universal Approaches to Leadership

The explanations of leadership that follow are loosely organized chronologically. Generally, universal approaches to leadership were followed by contingency approaches. Transformational leadership is the most contemporary of leadership theories. We will explore each type of leadership theory separately. Let's turn our attention to universal approaches to leadership. In this perspective, people are seeking the "one best way" to lead.

Leadership Traits

One of the earliest leadership theories, **trait leadership,** identified personal characteristics that allowed individuals to assert leadership in group settings. The trait approach assumes that leaders are born, not developed. So, unless you were endowed with a certain set of characteristics at birth, it would be nearly impossible for you to be a leader! Not a very comforting view, is it? Initially, leadership traits were discovered by reviewing the experiences of successful leaders in history. Unfortunately, this approach provided a list of characteristics solely associated with Caucasian males. In the time frame that this approach was popular, generally only White men were public or government leaders. Traits such as physical appearance (height, weight, physique, and looks), intelligence, self-confidence, sociability, initiative, persistence, ambition, dominance, talkativeness, enthusiasm, and alertness were all identified as characterizing leaders from nonleaders (Stogdill, 1948). Table 10.1 identifies all of the traits that have been identified with leadership. Do you agree that effective leaders would possess or demonstrate these traits?

Not only was it popular to identify leaders by certain characteristics or traits, but research also documented that certain traits would be perceived negatively by group members (Geier, 1967). When group members demonstrated negative traits—in particular, being uninformed, nonparticipative, or extremely rigid; using authoritarian behavior or an offensive communicator style—they were eliminated from consideration as a group's leader.

More recent research finds that group members still expect their leaders to exhibit some of these same traits (Pavitt & Sackaroff, 1990). In terms of personality traits, members expect that leaders will be enthusiastic, understanding, supportive, and friendly toward others. Leaders are expected to demonstrate intelligence and creativity. Being organized is also an expectation. Finally, leaders are expected to be forceful. More directly related to communication, group members expect leaders to listen to what others have to say as well as respond to the input of group members. Group members also expect leaders to possess and disclose the information they hold on the group's topic. And group members expect leaders to demonstrate an ability to influence others in the group (Weinberg, Smotroff, & Pecka, 1978). Although these traits may be some of the first things members look for in potential leaders, how leaders behave over time is more important to group members in their evaluation of a leader's effectiveness. "What Do You Want a Leader to Be?" helps you understand your own expectations of leadership.

Table 10.1 *Traits Identified with Leadership*

Physical and Constitutional Factors	Personality Characteristics
activity, energy	achievement, drive, ambition
appearance, grooming	adaptability
height	adjustment
weight	aggressiveness
	alertness
Skills and Abilities	antiauthoritarianism
	dominance
administrative ability	emotional balance, control
intelligence	enthusiasm
judgment	extraversion
knowledge	independence, nonconformity
	initiative
	insightfulness
Social Characteristics	integrity
	objectivity
cooperativeness	originality
interpersonal skills, sensitivity	persistence
popularity, prestige	responsibility
sociability	self-confidence
socioeconomic position	sense of humor
talkativeness	tolerance of stress
tact	

Source: Adapted from Jago (1982).

Autocratic and Democratic Leadership

Autocratic or authoritarian leaders control a considerable portion of a group's process and generally control all of the group's decision making (Lewin, Lippitt, & White, 1939). Typically, an autocratic leader's use of power is negatively received by group members because this type of leader will make decisions by him- or herself and simply announce them to group members. Autocratic leaders use more task statements, are more concerned with achievement, and are less likely to use procedures that promote the participation of group members (Sargent & Miller, 1971).

Often considered the opposite of autocratic leadership is democratic leadership. In a group setting, **democratic** means that all members participate within a structure that is relatively equal in power and status (Lewin, Lippitt, & White, 1939).

The most elaborate description of democratic leadership focuses on five separate issues involving leaders, followers, and the leadership situation (Gastil, 1994a). First, democratic leaders are not necessarily authorities. Likewise, authorities are not necessarily democratic leaders. Democratic leaders gain authority by being responsible for both individual and group decisions and by keeping power issues

> **THINK ABOUT IT**
>
> ### What Do You Want a Leader to Be?
>
> Think back to your group experiences and imagine that you could construct an ideal leader. What characteristics would that leader possess? Do you believe that these characteristics could be acquired through experience, education, or training? Or do you believe that people are born with some of these characteristics? Are there any traits or characteristics that you believe all leaders should possess? Why?

open and visible to group members. In democratic leadership, the group confers authority to the leader who manages the process of the group. To uphold that authority, the leader frequently checks the power structure within the group to make sure that any power inequalities that surface are necessary. The democratic leader also tries to provide procedures to the group so that concentrations of power do not develop. In other words, the group gives the democratic leader authority to watch out for inequities in power and status in the group.

Second, the democratic leader acts to sustain the democratic process of the group. This is done by distributing responsibility among group members, empowering members to take responsibility and be accountable for group activities, and helping the group use procedures that support the democratic process. When responsibilities are distributed, all members are participating. This also serves to equalize power relationships within the group. Empowering group members helps develop individual members' personal and professional capacities. The democratic leader aids deliberation through his or her own constructive participation, facilitating the group, and helping to maintain healthy relationships within the group. When the democratic leader is successful at sustaining the democratic process of the group, individual members are strengthened, and, as a result, the group is strengthened.

You are probably realizing that it would be very difficult for one person to perform all of the functions of democratic leadership. Thus, the third component of democratic leadership is that leadership is diffused. This means that more than one member can serve in each leadership role, no one individual performs an inordinate amount of leadership, and each group member performs some leadership function. One way to accomplish this is to rotate leadership functions among group members. As a result, individual members become capable leaders and can contribute to the overall democratic nature of the group.

Fourth, even groups practicing democratic leadership have followers. Democratic followers have responsibilities as well. Democratic followers are willing to take on responsibility and agree to be accountable for their actions. Because equality in participation is the most widely guarded principle of democratic leadership, democratic followers are responsible for maintaining autonomy from the leader. Thus democratic followers would not give in or be overly compliant to all leader requests, nor would democratic followers wait for the leader before attacking a problem they could handle on their own. The diffuse quality of democratic leadership requires that followers identify ways in which they can function as leaders in the group. Yet followers are also required to work willingly with others when others are leading.

The fifth issue focuses on what types of groups or group tasks can effectively support democratic leadership. Obviously, the problem must involve more than one person, and the problem must concern the group members. To be effectively implemented, group members must be considered equals and must be the best representatives to work on the problem. Finally, members must be committed to the democratic process or at least want to build the skills in the democratic process. It is not enough for the leader to demand that democracy exist. Democratic leadership is enacted by both leader and followers.

A leader needs to work hard to maintain democracy in a group setting, but the advantages that accrue from democratic leadership make it worthwhile (White & Lippitt, 1960). The primary advantage to democratic leadership is that it fully involves all group members. When this occurs, satisfaction and commitment are increased. Productivity gains are made as well. Democratic leadership also helps groups achieve spontaneous cooperation. That is, cooperation results naturally from the friendly and productive environment created by the group's use of democratic principles. By demonstrating friendliness and consideration, the leader promotes a healthy environment that supports open-mindedness and receptive listening in group members. Although democratic leadership promotes consensus seeking, it also protects the individuality of group members, which, in turn, promotes creativity. Knowing that your ideas will be considered and that your participation will be welcomed, your energies turn creatively to the task, and you are not burdened by dysfunctional group relationships. Groups led by democratic leaders also produce high quality decisions. In this group climate, individuals work together and feel comfortable identifying risks in the suggestions of other group members. Thus faulty ideas can be tested and eliminated by the group's interaction.

Generally, democratic leadership is believed to be superior to autocratic leadership (Barge, 1994). This is due to two reasons. One, in democratic leadership, group members can express their views; in autocratic, they would likely not be given that opportunity or would not take it if it were offered. Two, groups working under democratic leadership make better decisions than groups working under autocratic leadership. In Chapters 8 and 9, we found that when members participate in decision making, higher quality decisions and higher levels of member satisfaction are achieved. Democratic discussions allow differing viewpoints to be heard—another factor that we know enhances decision-making quality.

However, democratic leadership does not work in some situations. If the group is not interested in the problem, members will be unwilling to take on the responsibilities required of them as followers or as diffused leaders. Democratic leadership does not work if there is great disparity among group members in terms of power, status, or knowledge. This style of leadership requires that individuals perceive and feel a sense of equality. This is what ensures the democratic principles.

Democratic leadership is useless if there is a predetermined goal or solution and the group merely reaffirms a choice already made. Finally, democratic leadership does not work if all members are not committed to the democratic process or prefer that the leader take on most of the responsibility and accountability associated with the decision.

Which is a more productive leadership style for groups? Generally, we like democratic leadership better because relationship issues as well as task issues are considered by the leader. But both autocratic and democratic leadership can be productive in helping groups accomplish their tasks and in satisfying group members (Gastil, 1994b). Autocratic leadership is effective when group goals must take precedence over individual goals. Autocratic leadership is also more effective when a group's goal is obscured by ambiguity (Korten, 1962). Realize, however, that groups led by autocratic leaders have higher levels of dissatisfaction.

Functional Leadership

Using a roles approach, **functional leadership** proposes that leadership occurs when the duties and responsibilities of leadership are performed by any member of the group so that objectives are achieved. The functional view takes a universalist approach by proposing that the same set of behavioral functions are required regardless of how members or their personalities differ, or how groups or their tasks differ. Research has not demonstrated one set or combination of task and social functions that satisfies each leadership situation (Gouran, 1970).

Still, to be effective, leaders need to be able to tap into at least two different broad categories of functional behavior: task functions and relational functions. Recall the task and maintenance roles (Benne & Sheats, 1948) described in Chapter 3. Initially, these roles were identified as the types of task and relational functions needed by leaders. Take a moment to review those two role categories. Do you agree that leaders need to be able to perform those functions for their groups? Are there other roles you believe leaders should be able to perform? To what extent do you believe other group members should also perform those roles?

The functional view of leadership has been helpful in predicting who will be the leader in an emergent leader situation. Generally, a member who takes on the functions of orienting his or her group to the problem, suggests procedures for organizing discussion, and provides summaries of the group's progress will be the leader (Knutson & Holdridge, 1975; Schultz, 1974, 1986). Thus when a group does not take immediate steps to select a leader, you could encourage group members to perceive you as their leader if you fulfill those two functions for the group.

Leadership Styles

Another universal approach to leadership is to evaluate the communication and behavioral style of a leader. This perspective moves from identifying specific leadership traits to viewing leadership as an observable process or activity (Jago, 1982). Researchers believed that different **leadership styles** had varying impacts on group members and group outcomes. Yet, the different leadership styles did not always result in positive differences in group performance. This perspective on leadership began in the 1950s and is commonly referred to as the Ohio State leadership studies. These researchers believed that leadership could be identified by two dimensions: the leader's consideration of others, or the relationship dimension, and the leader's ability to structure group activities, or the task dimension. A leader high on the relationship dimension would communicate warmth and friendliness toward group members; a leader high on the task dimension would communicate strategies for how the group could best complete its goal. Generally, it was thought that leaders who were high on both dimensions—high relationship and high task—would be the most effective leaders.

Another way of identifying leadership styles is found in the managerial grid (Blake & McCanse, 1991; Blake & Mouton, 1985). By turning the relationship dimension into a concern for people and the task dimension into a concern for production or task and then adding a dimension that distinguishes between positive or negative motivations, seven different leadership styles were identified. Each style—impoverished, country club, authority-compliance, middle-of-the-road, paternalism, opportunism, and team—represents a unique set of assumptions leaders use to link issues of relationships to issues of production.

Impoverished is a style leaders use to exert minimum control over group members. Members are left alone to work with little direction from the leader. Leaders using a country club style focus on keeping people happy by creating an environment in which group members have favorable relationships with one another as well as the leader. The leader expects that the positive relationship will be sufficient to motivate them toward task accomplishment. The middle-of-the-road style emphasizes both a concern for people and a concern for production, but both to a moderate degree. The primary goal of a leader using the authority-compliance style is to get the task done with a minimum of discussion. To do so, the leader is very directive; he or she describes exactly how members should perform, with little awareness or interest in how members are affected by the directions.

Paternalism combines the high production focus of the authority-compliance style and the high concern for people of the country club style. A leader using this style displays contradictory behaviors. At one time, the paternalistic leader acts like a parent and is overly concerned with the welfare of his or her subordinates; at another time, the leader is demanding and expects subordinates to do exactly as he or she desires. As a result, subordinates begin to feel that they cannot win no matter what they do. Opportunism is characterized by the leader shifting among the other styles depending on what will serve him or her best when working with a particular subordinate. This type of leader selects an interaction style based on who the interaction target is and what he or she believes can be gained from that target for his or her own selfish needs.

Team leadership is believed to be the most effective, or best, style. This leader emphasizes concern for people and concern for production—both at extremely high levels. For a group, this means that the leader and members work together to create an environment that supports and promotes high standards of excellence and fulfilling relationships. Because members' concerns have been addressed, together the leader and group members can create strong task interdependence to accomplish group goals. The team leader promotes participation, involvement, and commitment to teamwork. You can identify team leaders by their candid and forthright comments, confidence, decisiveness, determination, and enjoyment of work. Team leaders are usually open-minded, positive, reflective, innovative, spontaneous, and unselfish. Interaction traits you might observe in this type of leader include focuses on real issues, follows through, is able to get concerns out in the open, promotes high standards, is able to uncover underlying problems, clarifies priorities, sets challenging goals, speaks his or her mind and stands his or her ground, and stimulates participation.

Contingency Approaches to Leadership

A contingency is a situation. With respect to leadership, the contingency approach advocates that leaders select the style that best fits the situation. There are a variety of leadership theories or perspectives that can be included under the broad heading of contingency approaches to leadership.

Contingency Model of Leadership

The first of the situational approaches is the **contingency model of leadership** (Fiedler, 1967, 1968). This approach centers on three contingencies. The first and most important is leader-member relations. When followers respect the leader and are attracted to him or her, the leader is rewarded with considerable power over them. Thus, the degree of confidence and trust followers place in their leader gives the leader power. In any leadership situation, leader-member relations can be described as being good or poor. Next in importance is task structure. If tasks are structured, what is required from members is clear. Task completion can be verified, and groups tasks have a best outcome or solution. However if the task is unstructured, the leader must rely on his or her own resources to inspire and motivate followers. Thus, on this second factor, tasks are considered structured or unstructured. The third contingency is position power, or the amount of power inherent in the formal position irrespective of the person. For example, it does not matter who fulfills the role of manager or leader. Whomever is manager has the same rights, responsibilities, power over subordinates, and control over rewards and punishments. Power is inherent in the position, not in the person who occupies or holds the position. Thus position power is seen as being either strong or weak.

Using these three contingencies as situational dimensions, we can locate the best leadership style. Several assumptions drive this theory. First, leaders with good leader-member relations have little need for position power or other power from the organization. Members follow the leader because they like him or her. A second assumption is that someone leading a highly structured task needs little position power. This assumption allows that even a low-ranking person can easily lead

Leadership Style	Task	Task	Task	Relationship	Relationship	Relationship	Relationship	Task
Leader-Member Relations	Good	Good	Good	Good	Poor	Poor	Poor	Poor
Task Structure	Structured	Structured	Unstructured	Unstructured	Structured	Structured	Unstructured	Unstructured
Leader Position Power	Strong	Weak	Strong	Weak	Strong	Weak	Strong	Weak

Figure 10.1 *Three Situational Dimensions of the Contingency Model of Leadership.* Source: Fiedler (1968).

others when the task is ordered or programmed (for example, a lead cashier can teach her new team member how to run the cash register). Use Figure 10.1 to see how the three situational dimensions are integrated. Notice how task-oriented leadership is most effective when the group situation is either very favorable or unfavorable. On the other hand, relationship-oriented leaders are more effective in situations with moderate favorableness. This is when the task is structured, but the leader is disliked and must be diplomatic and concerned with the feelings of his or her followers. Or, this occurs when a liked leader leads an unstructured task (such as creating a new computer software interface) that requires the leader to depend upon the creativity and willing cooperation of subordinates. Thus this theory assumes that if the leader is well liked and considerate, relationship-oriented leadership is unnecessary and probably inappropriate.

The contingency model contends that leadership effectiveness is contingent, or dependent, upon the appropriateness of the leader's style to the group-task situation. If a leader's style does not fit the group-task situation, there are two remedies: The leader can change his or her behavior to the most effective style, or the group-task situation can be changed to fit the leader. How can this be done? A leader's position power can be changed by giving him or her more or less authority. The group-task situation can be improved by assigning unstructured tasks to one type of leader and structured tasks to another. Leader-member relations can be improved by isolating troublemakers. Society's current approach to groups, however, favors empowering the group rather than the leader. Thus the contingency model may be more useful today for considering how leader behavior should be adjusted to the conditions and environment of the group.

Situational Leadership Model

The next development in leadership is the **situational leadership model** (SLM) (Hersey, Blanchard, & Johnson, 1996) that bases leadership on (1) the amount of task direction a leader gives, (2) the amount of relational support a leader provides,

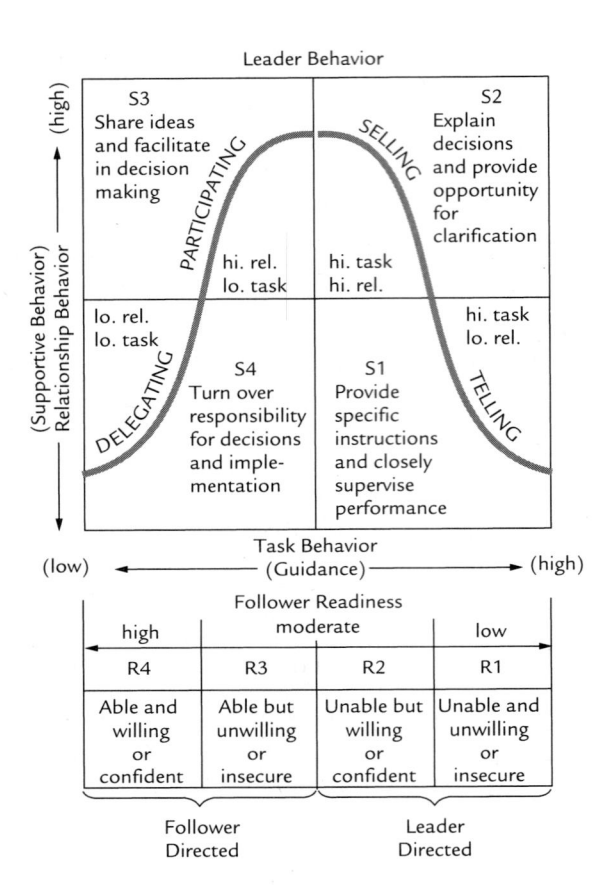

Figure 10.2 *Situational Leadership Model*

Source: Hersey, Blanchard, and Johnson (1996).

and (3) the readiness level of group members in performing their tasks. Task direction and relational support are very similar to the task and relationship dimensions of the managerial grid. However, SLM proposes that each leadership style can be effective depending on how well the leader selects a style based on the contingencies created by the situation. This view directly opposes the earlier view that leadership is a constant, or universal, regardless of who the group members are, what help they might need, what the task is, or in what environment the task is being pursued.

Readiness of group members is the key element in SLM. **Readiness** means ability and willingness and has nothing to do with age or tenure. A member with high readiness is someone who is knowledgeable and able to complete a task as well as someone who is motivated toward task completion. Thus, readiness is task dependent. Let's explore this concept more fully by looking at Figure 10.2.

Telling, or the high task and low relationship leadership style, is best for group members who are both unable and unwilling to take responsibility for group tasks. By providing clear and specific directions with low readiness group members, leadership has a good chance for being effective. Selling, or the high task and high relationship leadership style, is best for group members who are unable but willing to take responsibility for group tasks. Group members at this readiness level (low to moderate readiness) are enthusiastic and motivated but lack the abilities or skills to complete group tasks. By offering increased levels of emotional support and acting as a role model, this leadership style can be effective. You are selling because, by your actions, you are trying to get group members to buy into what needs to be done.

Participating is for moderate to high readiness members—members who are able but unwilling. By increasing levels of relational concern, the leader can overcome any insecurities or anxieties group members may have. This nondirective leadership style includes members in the decision making; the leader's role is to facilitate and communicate. Delegating is most effective with group members who express high task readiness; they are both willing and able to take responsibility for group tasks. In this case, the leader takes a low profile, delegating as much of the group's tasks as he or she can to group members.

Let's examine how these different styles would be applied. On the first work shift, Malique is responsible for four relatively new nurses who are, of course, new to this particular hospital as well as to nursing in general. So he will use a telling style. His team members are technically competent, but they have not been around the hospital long enough to fully know hospital procedures. They are also somewhat unwilling. They are not trying to be uncooperative, but they are hesitant because they are new both to nursing and to this hospital. Kia is supervisor of the second work shift, and her team members have between 1 and 3 years of nursing experience; most have been with the same hospital for that length of time as well. Recent changes to nursing procedures, however, have made them more excited about their jobs, but they do have to be checked out for some new procedures. So Kia will use a selling leadership style to overcome that obstacle. The third nursing shift is led by Deanna. Members of her nursing team have long tenure with the hospital—in fact, many of them help train some of Malique's new hires. Their reaction to changes in the nursing procedures, however, is not favorable. They believe that nursing administration is making them change to avoid litigation not because the nursing procedure needs improvement. Deanna will use the participating leadership style with them. Finally, Aaron is the leader of the floating nurse team. He and his team members cover all shifts when extra staffing is needed or when other nurses are out sick or on vacation. The nurses on this team are the most flexible because they have to be able to fit in with nurses on the other three teams. Aaron feels lucky to lead such an experienced team, and to a great degree, he can rely on a delegating leadership style. Let's see how each nursing team leader would use his or her leadership style to inform and then convince the teams about the procedural change:

> MALIQUE: (using the telling style) Before you start your shift, I need to explain a change in a pharmacy procedure. When people come in to the emergency room with their own medication, we must do three things:

(1) find out why they're taking that particular medication, (2) find out how often they're taking it, and (3) check the pill against the picture in the *Physician's Desk Reference*. The first one to get a case like this today should let me know. We'll use your patient as a learning case. Okay?

KIA: (using the selling style) Last thing before you go to the floor, there's a change in pharmacy procedures. This is a new one—thanks to Felicia. Her suggestion earned her a $50 bonus. Thanks for making us look good. Felicia, do you want to lead us through the procedure? I'll back you up if you need it.

DEANNA: (using the participating style) I know you don't need one more thing to relearn, but we've got a change in pharmacy procedure. I've heard the gossip, but I don't think this change has anything to do with lessening hospital liability when you handle patient medication. I think this new procedure has some merit. (Deanna hands out the new procedure.) After shift tonight, let's discuss how the new procedure went.

AARON: (using the delegating style) Okay, I just want to remind you of one notice on your update sheets. We've got a new pharmacy procedure. Let me know what you think. Nursing administration will want to hear your opinions. Check in with me if you need anything.

One way to distinguish among leadership styles is to assess the degree to which the leader helps the group structure its discussion (Jurma, 1979). A structuring leader would help the group by making sure the relevant issues of the task were understood, providing information to the group, helping to stimulate and motivate group members, making constructive criticism, and reminding the group of any time limits. This would be characteristic of a telling or selling leadership style. Nonstructuring leaders would allow a group's discussion to develop on its own. This type of leader would also be vague if members asked for structuring assistance. Group members who have a high task orientation may be able to work without a structuring leader as they are capable of directing and structuring the task on their own. This would be more in line with a participating or delegating leadership style. Thus one contingency or situation that leaders should address is the degree of task orientation among group members. If task orientation is high, the leader can encourage group members to take on some of the structuring responsibilities. If the task orientation of members is low, the leader should perform these responsibilities for the group.

How do you determine which leadership style is best? First, take an assessment of the group activities your group must accomplish. Second, evaluate the level of readiness of group members. Third, select and employ one of the four styles of leadership. If, after observing group members, you believe that their readiness level can be increased, use training to enhance their ability or knowledge and use restructuring of tasks to motivate them to try new behaviors or tasks. Another responsibility of leaders is to develop the readiness levels of group members to the extent that they desire such development.

Leader-Member Exchange Model

The **leader-member exchange (LMX) model** suggests that leaders may develop different types of relationships with different members of the same work group to accomplish goals (Dansereau, Graen, & Haga, 1975; Graen & Scandura, 1987; Liden & Graen, 1980). Why would leaders do this? One explanation is that leaders have limited time and energy. These limitations cause leaders to develop different types of relationships with each group member. This leadership theory is particularly interesting in the group context because it explains how members develop and sustain different relationships with the leader. The focus here is not so much on the group as it is on the individual leader-member relationships. This is what makes it situational or contingent. The perceived differences among group members act as the catalysts for the unique relationships that develop within the same work group.

One way to distinguish among the different relationships the leader has with group members is to categorize each relationship as being an in-group exchange or an out-group exchange. An in-group exchange means that the leader perceives the group member as a valuable group resource. There is a high level of interaction between the two, which is accompanied by a high level of trust. An out-group exchange means that the leader is less trusting and less supporting of the group member. As a result, in-group members have more input in decision making and more informal influence than out-group members. As you might guess, interactions between the leader and out-group members are more limited.

These differences are particularly pronounced in the **negotiating latitude,** or the degree to which the leader will use his or her position power to help the group member solve work-related issues. Group members who develop high negotiating latitude (most likely in-group exchange members) with the group's leader take on additional responsibilities toward the group and have higher commitment to ensuring that the group is a success (McClane, 1991). Leaders are more likely to develop negotiating latitude with group members who demonstrate similar power motives. This suggests that the leaders and group members are more comfortable with each other when power similarities exist between them. Trust and delegation seem to be pivotal in these relationships (Bauer & Green, 1996). The more a leader trusts a group member, the more she or he will delegate group responsibilities to the member. If those responsibilities are fulfilled, more trust is extended, along with a greater willingness to delegate even more responsibility.

How do these differing leader-member relationships affect the group? Let's say, for example, that you have an in-group relationship with the group's leader, Orin. Other members of the group become aware of the differential treatment you receive as they observe you interacting cooperatively with Orin or gaining control over resources. The more cooperatively you interact with Orin, the more likely other group members will try to cooperate with you (Lee, 1997). By being in a position of positive influence with the team leader, you have established positive influence with other group members. However, your differential treatment by Orin might not always receive positive reactions from other group members.

Other group members might talk about why you are being treated differently and analyze the fairness of the treatment, particularly if they feel they are treated unfairly (Sias & Jablin, 1995). This does not mean that your group members are negatively evaluating you, but it does mean that the leader's treatment of you has generated a discussion that others are using to make sense of the group's climate and issues of equity (Sias, 1996).

Another effect also occurs: You and other group members have the opportunity to observe your team leader, Orin, with his superior, Maria. You perceive that Maria and Orin have established an effective working relationship. In fact, the relationship Orin has with Maria can be characterized as an in-group relationship. You and other group members support Orin's views and perspectives on things and trust his ability to send information up and down communication channels. As a result, you and your group members feel supported by Orin and are able to work cooperatively together (Anderson & Tolson, 1991; Pelz, 1952; Jablin, 1980a, 1980b; Lee, 1997). If Orin is seen and regarded positively, then, you believe, your group will be seen and regarded positively; after all, Orin is your leader. Notice here how the relationship, Orin, the team leader, has with his superior, Maria, links the group to its external environment.

Understanding group members' expectations of leadership behavior can help us understand why different styles of leadership are preferred. Not only are there different styles of leadership, but group members prefer different leadership behaviors. These differing expectations held by members can explain why leaders need to be flexible in how they interact with group members. Some group members prefer leaders who are task-oriented whereas other members respond favorably to leaders who are relationship-oriented. We each have established a prototype of how we think an effective leader behaves. When the person in the leadership role acts in a way that is consistent with our prototype, we evaluate the leader more favorably (Nye & Forsyth, 1991). This suggests that, for greatest effectiveness, leaders need to take some time talking individually with group members to establish their individual leadership needs and preferences.

Criticisms of Early Leadership Approaches

One criticism that applies to universal approaches to leadership is that these approaches imply that there is only one effective style of leadership. This assumption has been regularly refuted (Downs & Pickett, 1977), just as has the assumption that a leadership style that demonstrates a high concern for people and a high concern for task has been challenged (Hunt & Liebscher, 1973). A criticism directed toward the style approaches, like the managerial grid, is that situational variables are not taken into consideration (Kerr et al., 1974). As you can imagine, it would be nearly impossible to identify and then classify all of the individual member, group task, group process, and organizational variables that affect a leader's influence on a group.

These early foundations of leadership—universal and contingency—share several common problems (Gouran, 1970). First, they focus on individuals as leaders, ignoring leadership behaviors that are shared formally and informally among group members. Second, they undervalue the messages or communication patterns that members recognize as leadership. Certainly, communication is acknowledged, but they do not emphasize its creative, motivational, and empowering aspects (Barge, 1994). Thus, up to this point, we have described **transactional leadership** theories. This means that they focus on the transaction or exchange between leaders and group members (Bass, 1985). Such approaches to leadership can only create first-order change—change that is task or situation dependent. This is not to say that transactional leadership strategies should not be used. Leaders should, however, recognize that higher order, or second-order change, can be achieved. Second-order change occurs when group members have revolutionary changes in attitudes, values, and beliefs. In the next section, transformational leadership is introduced and explained. You will find that transformational leaders are masters of assessing the situation and then using a wide repertoire of communication skills to inspire group members. Hence, members are transformed by the leadership.

Transformational Leadership

More recently, **transformational leadership** has become popular. A transformational leader is one who sets an example for group members to follow. This type of leader uses rhetorical skills to build a vision with which members can identify and use as a guiding force toward goal completion (Bass, 1985, 1990). Transformational leaders do not rely on their position of power or the use of organizational rewards. Rather, they communicate a sense of urgency and utility—a group vision—that members find appealing. Transformational leadership occurs when leaders broaden and elevate the interests of group members, when they generate awareness and acceptance of the group's purpose and mission, and when they encourage group members to look beyond their own self-interests and work for the good of the group (Bass, 1990). Thus group members are encouraged to take on more challenges and greater responsibility.

Although many of the other leadership theories imply that a leader use organizational rewards or sanctions to maintain power over group members, a transformational leader creates power through the use of dramatic and inspirational messages. Thus you are likely to find transformational leaders at lower levels of organizations and in group settings where motivation and providing service are more important than monetary rewards. Your son's soccer coach could be a transformational leader. Your church group may be empowered by a transformational leader. Many civic and community groups, particularly grass roots organizations, are led by transformational leaders. As you might guess, transformational leaders have greater success in recruiting group members and helping them achieve high quality performance.

Transformational leaders have charisma. This means that they have a great deal of confidence in their own competence and a great deal of conviction in their beliefs and ideals. Such a spirit generates faith, trust, and respect with other group members. Transformational leaders can inspire others by communicating high expectations. These leaders are animated, which arouses others and heightens their motivation. Transformational leaders are intellectually stimulating, helping group members to pay more attention to problem awareness and problem solving. Most importantly, and the reason for their success, transformational leaders give special attention to each group member, treating members as individuals. Thus each group member is treated differently according to his or her needs and capabilities.

Transformational leaders are particularly good at getting group members to perform the extra work that is often necessary to achieve performance goals (Avolio, Waldman, & Einstein, 1988). Group members may feel pressure from other sources that keeps them from contributing energy, effort, or time to group activities. Transformational leaders are typically able to persuade group members to give what it takes to achieve group goals. Even when more traditional rewards are available, the charismatic personality of a transformational leader augments and extends the leader's effectiveness (Waldman, Bass & Yammarino, 1990). The confidence and inspiration of transformational leaders are the motivating factors for group members.

To learn transformational leadership behaviors you must be willing to, first, withstand the scrutiny of your group members, and, second, accept their views of your performance. You cannot learn transformational leadership by watching someone else—although there is nothing wrong with selecting a role model to emulate. Learning transformational skills is best accomplished by doing thorough assessments of your current leadership behavior and the effects it creates. Do your group members appear bored with their group tasks? If so, to move to a transformational level, you would need to consider how you might inspire or motivate them. You could also consider how you might rearrange or restructure work on group tasks to provide more stimulating activities. By knowing the current state of affairs in your group, you can then address what you would like the group climate to be like. Knowing that, you can analyze a variety of alternatives to help you meet that goal. Ultimately, these assessments will lead you to strategies that can help group members recognize their individuality, creativity, and responsibility to the group. What you will find as a transformational leader is that you are valuing group members differently. Together, your group members will have transformed from "what is" to "what is desirable" and "what ought to be" (Rosenthal & Buchholz, 1995). "Evaluating a Transformational Leader" will help you recognize transformational leadership behaviors.

A Communication Competency Approach to Leadership

The **communication competency approach to leadership** is based on three assumptions (Barge & Hirokawa, 1989). First, leadership is action that helps group members overcome the barriers or obstacles they face in achieving the goal or completing their task. The leader takes active steps to reduce ambiguity and manage the complexity faced by the group. In other words, the leader helps the group create a system for working together and accomplishing its goals. Second, leader-

The passion of a transformational leader is often the characteristic to which group members identify and respond. Communicating both a sense of urgency and utility, transformational leaders use the power of communication to reach and empower group members.

ship occurs through interaction and communication. Thus, relationships established and maintained between leader and group members through verbal and nonverbal communication are central to defining the nature of leadership. Third, there are a set of skills or competencies that individuals use to exercise leadership in groups. Thus a certain level of communication competency is required for a leader to be effective.

Effective leaders must be able to demonstrate two sets of competencies—task and relational. Task competencies are skills that help manage the group's task. Relational competencies are skills that help manage relationships among group members and the group's overall communication climate. The competency approach is similar to functional leadership described earlier in this chapter. However, the competency approach requires that leaders know which competencies their group needs and requires that leaders be flexible, changing to other competencies when the group needs it. Which set of competencies will be required by your group? It depends on two factors: (1) the type of goal your group is working toward and (2) the situational complexity of the group's environment. When the group's goal is primarily relation-oriented (for example, maintaining sorority or fraternity solidarity), the leader will probably need more relational competencies.

BUILDING ANALYTICAL SKILLS

Evaluating a Transformational Leader

Reflect on one of your group experiences in which you believe the leader was a transformational leader. For each statement, use the following scale and judge how frequently this leader displayed the behavior described.

0 = not at all   1 = once in a while   2 = sometimes   3 = fairly often   4 = frequently, if not always

1. It makes me feel good to be around him/her.	0 1 2 3 4
2. He/she is satisfied when I meet the agreed-upon standards for good work.	0 1 2 3 4
3. He/she makes me feel we can reach our goals without him/her if we have to.	0 1 2 3 4
4. I earn credit with him/her by doing my job well.	0 1 2 3 4
5. He/she finds out what I want and tries to help me get it.	0 1 2 3 4
6. I can count on him/her to express his/her appreciation when I do a good job.	0 1 2 3 4
7. He/she commands respect from everyone.	0 1 2 3 4
8. He/she gives personal attention to members who seem neglected.	0 1 2 3 4
9. He/she is a model for me to follow.	0 1 2 3 4
10. In my mind, he/she is a symbol of success and accomplishment.	0 1 2 3 4
11. He/she has provided me with new ways of looking at things that used to be a puzzle for me.	0 1 2 3 4
12. I am ready to trust his/her capacity and judgment to overcome any obstacle.	0 1 2 3 4
13. He/she is an inspiration to us.	0 1 2 3 4
14. He/she makes me proud to be associated with him/her.	0 1 2 3 4
15. He/she has a special gift of seeing what it is that really is important for me to consider.	0 1 2 3 4
16. His/her ideas have forced me to rethink some of my own ideas that I have never questioned before.	0 1 2 3 4
17. He/she enables me to think about old problems in new ways.	0 1 2 3 4

When the group's goal is primarily task-oriented (such as a sales team developing a marketing plan), the leader will need more task competencies. The degree of situational complexity—goal complexity, group climate, and role ambiguity—also affects the degree to which the leader will need to demonstrate competencies. Greater depth and breadth of skill is needed as the group's goal becomes more complex, the group's climate becomes more negative, or roles within the group are ambiguous. Effective leaders are competent in each of these areas and flexible enough to demonstrate all of these skills.

18. He/she inspires loyalty to him/her.   0 1 2 3 4
19. He/she increases my optimism for the future.   0 1 2 3 4
20. He/she inspires loyalty to the organization.   0 1 2 3 4
21. I have complete faith in him/her.   0 1 2 3 4
22. He/she excites us with his/her visions of what we may be able to accomplish if   0 1 2 3 4
    we work together.
23. He/she treats each group member individually.   0 1 2 3 4
24. He/she encourages me to express my ideas and opinions.   0 1 2 3 4
25. He/she encourages understanding of points of view of other members.   0 1 2 3 4
26. He/she gives me a sense of overall purpose.   0 1 2 3 4
27. He/she has a sense of mission that he/she transmits to me.   0 1 2 3 4
28. He/she makes everyone around him/her enthusiastic about assignments.   0 1 2 3 4

Charismatic/inspirational leadership is total for items 1, 7, 9, 10, 12, 13, 14, 15, 18, 19, 20, 21, 22, 24, 25, 26, 27 and 28 = _____ out of a potential 72.

Individualized consideration is total for items 2, 3, 4, 5, 6, 8, and 23 = _____ out of a potential 28.

Intellectual stimulation is total for items 11, 16, and 17 = _____ out of a potential 12.

How did the leader you select measure up to the characteristics of a transformational leader? How effective was this person in leading your group? If you could suggest one leadership change to this person, what would that be? What leadership lessons have you learned from working in a group with this person? Could you apply these same leadership strategies in your group activities? Why or why not?

Source: Adapted from Bass (1985).

Task Competencies

To help the group accomplish its tasks or activities, a leader should be able to (1) help the group establish operating procedures, (2) analyze problems facing the group, (3) help the group generate criteria to evaluate potential solutions, (4) help the group identify those criteria for solutions or actions under consideration, and (5) help the group select the best solution or activity. These task or procedural competencies are required in most group situations.

Relational Competencies

As individuals work together to accomplish the group task or activity, it is natural that miscommunication and conflicts will surface, challenging interpersonal relationships among group members. Effective leaders provide four types of relational assistance—interaction management, expressiveness, other-orientation, and relaxation—to help group members maintain, manage, and modify the relationships within the group. Effective leaders help the group manage its conversations by clarifying and summarizing the comments of group members. Interaction management is also visible when the leader balances participation among group members. Managing conflicts and building consensus are also examples of interaction management assistance leaders can provide.

Although interaction management helps the group with the flow and balance of communication, assistance with expressiveness helps groups avoid ambiguity. Effective leaders can help group members express themselves clearly by identifying undocumented opinions and irrelevant remarks. In providing other-orientation, the leader displays concern for and interest in other members, which helps the group develop a climate of trust and respect. Anxiety is a natural state in a group and occurs because individuals are often hesitant to express their ideas for evaluation. An effective leader reduces the amount of social anxiety in the group by creating an atmosphere of involvement and participation.

Technical Competencies

A third type of competency—technical competency—should not be overlooked. Leaders must demonstrate technical competence in relation to the technical demands of the group's activity (Bass, 1981). Leaders who cannot express or share their expertise, or who are unwilling to learn new skills on the behalf of other group members, will be disregarded by group members. This does not mean that the leader of a softball team must be the best fielder and hitter, or that the chairperson of the budget and finance subcommittee must be a gifted accountant as well as understand tax laws. It does mean, however, that the leader must possess enough competence to help other group members and to know when outside expertise is needed. Generally, we expect leaders to be qualified or technically competent in at least one area relevant to the group's problem or activity.

Leading Through Communication

Regardless of which theory you believe has the most utility for leading small groups and teams, you should recognize that "leadership is an interactional process" that helps members of groups in three ways (Barge, 1994, p. 13). First, leadership helps organize and manage a group's environment. Second, leadership facilitates members' understanding of the obstacles they face in completing their tasks and activities. Third, leadership helps groups plan and select the actions to help them achieve their goals. In each case, it is the communication of the leader and the communication relationship that the leader and members establish together that are the primary influencing forces behind group accomplishment.

As we have seen through the varying descriptions of leadership presented in this chapter, the complexity of a leader's communication varies with the way one views the complexity of the group's environment. For simple group tasks with relatively few obstacles, perhaps a simple and single style of leadership will work. However, when groups attempt complex tasks or encounter many obstacles on their way to goal completion, leadership becomes more complicated. Not only may a variety of leadership styles be warranted, but perhaps different people will need to fulfill some of the group's needed leadership functions.

In task, decision-making, and problem-solving groups, the role of leader is especially important as the leader is often the individual who connects the group with its environment. The connection has two purposes. First, the organization expects the leader to positively influence group members and the task. Second, group members expect the leader to represent them to others in the organization. The connection the leader provides between the organization and the group is so important that often a leader's effectiveness is measured by the team's performance. Likewise, group members assess the leader's effectiveness based on the degree to which the leader helps the group manage that connection by tolerating uncertainty and gaining support from outside sources (Kolb, 1996). Use *Putting the Pieces Together* to review your understanding of effective leadership.

Your Leadership Evaluation

Effective team leadership is critical to a group's success (Hirokawa & Keyton, 1995; Larson & LaFasto, 1989). To be an effective leader you must be in control of three factors—knowledge, performance, and impression. These three factors constitute an evaluation of competence (Spitzberg, 1983) that is useful in evaluating your leadership ability. First, are you knowledgeable about leadership issues? Do you understand a variety of leadership theories, and can you explain why different types of leadership may be needed? Second, can you perform a variety of leadership behaviors and leadership functions? Or, are you stuck—having to rely on one type of leadership behavior? Third, what kind of impression do you leave as a leader? Do you receive favorable comments from group members, even though the group has difficulty completing its work? Or do your group members despise you and complete the group's goal in spite of you? Impression has two levels. The first is the impression you leave as a person; the second is the impression you leave because you were able or unable to help the group. Frequently, the two different factors become confused. A likable person can be a lousy leader. And someone who is disliked by the group can lead the group to goal accomplishment. Thus the most effective leader gets high evaluations on both factors, which, is more likely if you are knowledgeable about leadership and can demonstrate a wide variety of leadership behaviors.

> **PUTTING THE PIECES TOGETHER**
>
> *Group Goal, Group Structure, and Interdependence*
>
> After reading this chapter, you have developed some idea of your leadership effectiveness. Think about one of your group leadership experiences. How would you describe or characterize your leadership? Specifically, what communication strategies did you use? To what extent did these strategies help the group achieve its goal? In what ways did your leadership enhance or inhibit interdependence among group members? Did other group members find it easier or more difficult to work together? How did your leadership affect or alter the group's structure or the group's use of decision procedures? Were you the only leader? Were additional leaders required? Did additional leaders emerge? If so, why were other leaders needed? To what extent did each group member exhibit leadership to help the group?

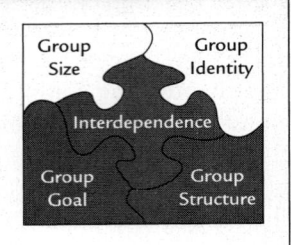

In this chapter, we have explored many different explanations of what constitutes effective leadership. So you might be wondering if there are any behaviors that leaders should avoid. The answer is yes. Leaders should avoid giving their opinions (Hill, 1976). Groups whose leaders are deliberately opinionated in group discussions report being further from consensus at the end of their discussions than leaders with more moderate or no opinions. A leader who consistently expresses her or his personal feelings or beliefs inhibits the group's ability to seek alternatives and to reach agreement. As for other group members, factual information or reasoned arguments do more to move a group's discussion forward than highly opinionated statements. Opinionated group leaders are also rated as being less competent and less objective.

Multiple Leaders

Although most of the leadership theories treat leadership as being the province of one person, generally it is not. One consistent finding of leadership studies is that leadership in real settings is far more complex than leadership in the research lab. This is why few leadership theories address the need for multiple leaders. But when a group needs both high relationship and high task orientations, two group members can effectively split these leadership functions. Certainly, groups with formal leaders are also influenced by informal leaders—group members who produce positive influence for others even though they do not hold a formal leadership role. You have probably been in a group in which an informal leader emerged when the formal or appointed leader could not satisfy all group members' needs.

A Group's Need for a Leader

After reading the descriptions of the many leadership theories presented in this chapter and the information about emergent leaders, you might think that groups always need leaders. Before you assume that, let's examine **substitutes for leadership** factors, which mediate the influence between leaders and group members (Kerr & Jermier, 1978). In some cases, individual, task, and organizational characteristics act as substitutes for leadership because they negate or replace the leader's ability to influence group members regardless of which leadership style or which leadership behaviors are used. Let's look at some of these.

Some group member characteristics, like ability and experience, will neutralize leader task attempts. This makes sense, particularly if you reread the section on SLM. Remember in SLM if members are ready—both able and willing—leadership is low on the task dimension. Thus group member ability and experience can substitute for leadership. In some groups, members want to and are able to exert their independence. If members also have a professional orientation and are generally indifferent to organizational rewards, both task and relational leadership attempts will be rebuffed. A group of physicians, for example, may demonstrate high levels of independence and professional orientation and may be less sensitive to the rewards that organizations or external environments can provide. Even if the group desperately needs leader influence, attempts to lead this type of group may fail.

Certain types of tasks may also encourage group members to ignore the leader's influence attempts. When tasks are unambiguous and routine, or when task completion is the only feedback needed to know if the group was successful, task attempts by a leader will be negated. A manufacturing team who weekly manages the same production schedule on the same products is facing generally unambiguous and routine tasks. The members of this type of team do not need a leader to tell them they have been successful. They know they are successful if the tonnage produced meets or exceeds company goals and if the quality of the product produced meets or exceeds manufacturing standards. Alternately, a task that is intrinsically satisfying can negate the effects of a leader's relationship influence. For example, a group of performers who love acting and would act even if they were not being paid would not perform better just because the leader—the director—tries to create a strong relationship orientation with the cast.

Finally, we need to consider factors from the group's larger environment, in most cases, this is the organization that sponsors the group. Groups in very formal organizations with plans, goals, and rigid procedures will not need as much task management from the leader. Rather, the culture of the organization with its rules and procedures takes the place of the leader. On the other hand, groups whose members are closeknit and cohesive will need relatively little relational leadership and maybe little task leadership. Members draw relational support from one another, and if relational outcomes are positive enough, the cohesiveness of the group may provide its own task influence. Two other organizational factors negate both relational and task leadership attempts: When leaders do not control organizational rewards or when there is great physical or psychological distance between the leader and group members, most leadership attempts will be refused.

What should a leader do in these cases? First, being in charge or being appointed or elected leader does not automatically make you an omnipotent force in the group. Just as respect and trust are earned from others, so is leadership. If you want to be an effective leader, you must listen to group members and respond to their needs—not your own. Second, part of the analysis you need to do as leader is to evaluate the individuals in the group, the type of group task to be completed, and the environment in which the task is to be done. Sometimes factors such as those mentioned above will act as substitutes for your leadership. In other words, these factors or characteristics will render your leadership unnecessary. Of course, if any of the factors or characteristics change (for example, suddenly your organization gives you the responsibility of rewarding group outcomes with monetary incentives), you must be willing and able to fulfill that leadership function. Leadership is like walking a tightrope. You must balance task and relational concerns with demands of the task as you move from a beginning to an ending point. You must be able to anticipate and deal with unexpected problems and regain control if the situation warrants it. Thus the greater your balance, sense of control, and confidence, the more successful your journey.

Summary

Leadership is a process of influence that occurs when a leader and group members interact. Leadership can also be considered a property, as in the leadership qualities one possesses. Because leadership requires followership, interdependence is created among group members through this social and communicative phenomenon. To be effective, leaders need to demonstrate procedural leadership behaviors, analytical or task behaviors, and social or relational behaviors.

Leaders are appointed, elected, or emerge from the group's interaction. Elected leaders generally face a greater sense of responsibility and accountability than appointed leaders. Emergent leaders are usually group members who are active and dominant in the group's conversation, are trustworthy and authoritative, and can monitor the group situation to meet the task and relational needs of members.

Universal approaches to leadership attempt to find the "one best way" to lead. Trait leadership, a universal approach, seeks to identify those personality and physical characteristics that separate leaders from nonleaders. Autocratic leadership promotes the use of control and power to subordinate individual needs to group needs. This approach can be useful when a group's task is vague or ambiguous. Democratic leadership, an alternative to autocratic leadership, promotes group members' full participation in the decision-making process. People generally respond favorably to democratic leadership because it allows open expression of all members' views.

Functional leadership, also a universal approach, takes a slightly different perspective. Here leadership is not concentrated in one person but is diffused among group members who fulfill the variety of leadership functions. The managerial grid advocates team style leadership—a style that is high on concern for production and high on concern for people—as the most effective style regardless of group situation.

Contingency approaches to leadership view the group's situation as a primary factor in selecting the best leadership style. The contingency model uses leader-member relations, task structure, and leader position power to determine the choice between task or relational leadership. The situational leadership model (SLM) evaluates group situations based on the readiness of group members. By examining both the ability and willingness of group members, leaders can select one of four styles that best meets members' needs. Leader-member exchange (LMX) promotes a micro-level view of leadership by examining each group member's relationship with the leader.

Although each of the universal and contingency approaches tells us something about why certain group members are frequently looked to as leaders and why certain leadership strategies are more effective than others, transformational leadership is a more contemporary leadership theory. A transformational leader communicates a sense of urgency and utility, which creates motivation for group members. Group members report that transformational leaders are charismatic, inspiring, intellectually stimulating, and treat each group member as an individual. Thus this type of leader can empower group members to accomplish more than they originally thought possible.

Regardless of which approach or style you prefer, leadership occurs through communication. The communication competency approach to leadership is based upon a leader's competency in both task and relational skills. A third competency, technical skills, enhances these other areas. In the role of leader, he or she helps organize and manage a group's environment, facilitates members' understanding of obstacles they face, and helps members plan and select the most effective actions. The more complex the group activity, the more complex the leader's communication needs to be.

Some groups find that one person cannot possibly handle the many leadership responsibilities. Thus in some groups leadership responsibilities are split along task and relational lines. Groups with formal leaders can be assisted by the informal leadership of others. At times, some individual, group, and organizational factors act as substitutes for leadership. In these cases, leadership is negated or neutralized by the presence of other forces.

✓ Checklist

Group Knowledge

You should be able to:
- define leadership.
- explain why some group members would emerge as leaders while other members are passed over for this role.
- describe how leadership is viewed according to at least three different leadership theories.
- explain why groups prefer democratic leadership.

- explain how group readiness can affect leadership style choices.
- explain how transformational leaders empower group members.
- identify the task and relational competencies needed for effective leadership.

Group Skills

You should be able to:

- help your group by fulfilling some leadership functions.
- identify the traits of group members that may encourage others to perceive them as leaders.
- favorably influence group outcomes using democratic leadership.
- select the most effective leadership style based on group member and task variations.
- develop the qualities needed to be a transformational leader.
- provide adequate leadership for your group.

Analytical and Assessment Techniques

You should be able to:

- assess your leadership potential.
- match leadership styles with task concerns, relational concerns, and readiness levels of group members.
- distinguish among the different relationships you have as leader with each group member.
- assess a group for the need for multiple leaders.
- assess a group's situation to determine if factors will act as substitutes for leadership.

Discussion Questions and Exercises

1. Select at least two people you know who lead or direct groups, and ask them to participate in informal interviews on their views of leadership. You might select someone who (1) chairs a task force or project team in a for-profit organizational setting, (2) leads a not-for-profit group of volunteers, (3) chairs a committee for an educational or government organization, or (4) leads a religious study or self-help group. Develop at least five questions to guide your interaction with your two leaders. For example, how do they view their role as leader? What functions do they perform for the group? How did they come to be in that particular leadership role? How do they believe other members of the group perceive them and evaluate their leadership? If there were one thing they could do to improve their leadership, what would that be?

2. Think of a community, regional, or national leader who is a transformational leader. What evidence do you have to support that claim? Do others agree with your assessment?

3. To help you review the types of leadership to which you have been exposed, complete the chart below:

Group Situation	Leader	Type of Leadership Used	Type of Group Task or Goal	Leadership Effectiveness

4. Identify the leadership behaviors that you feel comfortable using in groups. Are there leadership behaviors that you could use, but that you think need development? What are those behaviors? What leadership behaviors do you currently lack? What could you do to develop those behaviors you identified?

5. Set a timer for 3 minutes. In that time, think of as many labels as you can for "leader." In addition to your own experiences, also think about what leaders may have been called at different points in history, in organizations, in families, in friendship groups, in community and civic groups, and so on. Compare your list with other students' lists. How did your lists differ? What labels did you overlook?

11 Managing Conflict in Groups

How do I get myself into so many conflicts?

Can conflict ever have a positive outcome?

Why is it that others in my group do not see conflict in the same way?

How can I respond to a conflict to really make a difference?

How can I manage conflict?

Should we use a mediator for important conflicts?

Defining Conflict

Conflict heightens emotional responses in group interactions. Few of us like to be in conflicts, but most of us have. To the extent that your group is a collection of diverse individuals or is experiencing difficulty managing its activity and its external environment, conflict will occur. Conflict can range from disagreements—the types of conflict most groups experience—to physical violence (Thomas, 1977). Conflict is a natural form of expression in groups, and most groups experience it on occasion.

In this society, we use the word *conflict* regularly, often not thinking about what it really means. Although conflict is often defined as incompatible activities (Deutsch, 1969), it is more complex than that. To be in a **conflict** means that at least two parties (individuals or groups) capable of invoking sanctions oppose each other. In other words, you believe that the other party has some real or perceived power over you or can threaten you in some way. Conflicts occur because parties have mutually desired but mutually unobtainable objectives. An interdependency exists in such a way that both parties want what only one can have. This does not mean that the desired outcome is the same for both parties but simply that both parties cannot simultaneously realize their objectives. Your family cannot take its only vacation simultaneously in Canada as well as Mexico. Generally, conflicting parties have different value systems or perceive the same issue differently. You believe a vacation should be on the beach, enjoying the sun and the ocean. Your brothers believe that vacation should be filled with adventure, hiking, canoeing, and camping in the wilderness.

Conflicts can result in four types of action. Each party may want to obtain the objective or may just want to end the dispute. Each party may want to invoke sanctions or get even with the other party or simply communicate something to their opponent. Fortunately, most conflicts have an end. This occurs when each party is satisfied with what it won or lost or when those involved believe that the costs of continuing the conflict outweigh the advantages of continuing the conflict, hoping to win (Watkins, 1974).

Conflict is a process that occurs over time or in a sequence of events (Thomas, 1992). Conflict also occurs in a context. As a result, the conflict and the response of the conflicting parties are in part determined by the environment in which the conflict occurs. For example, how long the conflict over vacation plans lasts depends partly on when your reservations need to be made. Generally, we choose the responses or strategies we believe will help achieve the outcomes we desire. Outcomes are the consequences affecting the task and those affecting the maintenance of the social system between the two conflicting parties.

At its worst, conflict interferes with coordination and creates opportunities for dysfunctional power attempts. At its best, conflict can help groups find creative solutions to problems and increase rationality in decision making. Most conflict research focuses on conflict between two people, or dyadic conflict. Much of the research has focused on conflict in organizational settings, particularly conflict between superiors and subordinates. Certainly, conflict between two group members is a regular occurrence in group settings, and issues of power and role status are prevalent, but very little is known about the situation in which all or most of the group members are engaged in conflict. In these cases, the issues surrounding conflict are more complex, and thus more difficult to manage, because the conflict is not just with one other person. Still, research findings about dyadic and organizational conflict can provide basic principles about dealing with conflict in groups.

Ways of Thinking About Conflict

One way of thinking about conflict is to consider the past, the present, and the future (Hawes & Smith, 1973). Generally, we say that conflict occurs when people have incompatible goals. The underlying assumption is that goals direct your behavior. Thus goals in the present motivate your future behavior. If goals of group members are in conflict (present), then so must be their subsequent behavior (future). Your goal is to finish the group project before spring break. Michael wants to finish the project after spring break. And the other group members will be glad as long as the project gets done. As you, Michael, and the other group members interact, these goals will drive your communication. Before long, it will be apparent that there is conflict in the group about finishing the project.

Now let's turn that logic around and look at the past. Some argue that goals only become meaningful after you behave. If you made the jump shot, then your goal to do so is meaningful. If you did not make the jump shot, then it was "no big deal." From this viewpoint, we realize we are in a conflict when the communication episode takes place, as if after the conversation you said, "Our goals don't agree; therefore, we must be in conflict." This is not as far-fetched as you might think. During group discussions, there is a great deal going on to which we must pay attention. In a group discussion, you mention that Starr is not your first choice for

Conflict can escalate quickly when each group member views the conflict in his or her own way. To avoid escalation and the emotional responses it invokes, group members should recognize that they are all in the conflict together. Achieving this recognition will help group members manage their conflicts productively.

leader; you prefer Peter and give your reasons. The discussion continues and you start to realize that everyone else is supporting Starr; after a vote, Starr is elected. After the meeting, Tony says, "Way to go . . . you sure made a big impression. Now the group thinks you're not going to work well with Starr." Now you realize that a conflict existed between you and the other group members. Your goal of supporting Peter created a conflict because everyone else supported Starr. You were not trying to start a conflict, but it is clear now that others think you were.

Which way do you identify conflict? You probably do so in both ways. Someone using the present-future tense for defining conflict knows that they are in the conflict whereas someone using the past tense for defining conflict must reflect on what has happened to define a conflict episode.

Is Conflict Always Disruptive? Conflict can be productive for groups (Deutsch, 1969). When conflict exists, people are engaged and talking with one another, stagnation is prevented, interest and curiosity are stimulated. Conflict provides an opportunity for you to test and improve your abilities. Solutions are created. This is not to say that a group seeks conflict. Rather, conflict is not something that should be avoided. Conflict about the group's task can keep members from prematurely accepting or agreeing on solutions. In fact, conflict increases the likelihood that the group will engage in effective problem solving (Baxter, 1982).

Although conflict can help groups generate creative and innovative solutions, many groups try to avoid conflict at all costs. Other groups deny that conflict exists and continue with their interactions as if nothing is wrong. Still other groups believe that conflict is disruptive and detrimental. Why would groups be hesitant to engage in conflict if positive outcomes can be achieved? One answer lies in the anxiety that is associated with conflict. When you compare the language and interaction of groups in conflict with interaction when they are not in conflict, there is a distinct difference between conflict and nonconflict interaction. Group members in conflict actually change their verbal patterns. Group members become more repetitive and use simpler forms of language in the conflict interaction. During conflict, anxiety rises, which affects our ability to take the perspectives of others in the group. As a result, we begin to speak in a habitual way, repeating phrases without adding anything new to the conversation. Let's look at the following example:

LUCY: Can we just get on with it?

JIM: Sure, I want us to vote for the incorporation.

ELLA: Right, as if the incorporation will do us any good.

JIM: Well, it will . . . the incorporation, I mean.

LUCY: Can you explain more about the incorporation plan, Jim?

JIM: Well, as you know, the incorporation plan will incorporate all of the surrounding towns into Plainview.

ELLA: If we incorporate, we'll be just like Plainview. No different, but just like Plainview.

LUCY: I've figured out you're against incorporation, Ella. But could someone please tell me what incorporation means?

It may be that low levels of language diversity or redundancy—like the repeated use of the word *incorporation* with no explanation of what it means—reinforces the negative reaction many people have toward conflict (Bell, 1983).

Is Conflict Inherent? Conflict occurs because one of three things happens (Smith & Berg, 1987). One, individuals with different skills, interests, and values are brought together for a purpose. Group tasks and activities often need people who are different to accomplish the goal. "This means that differences must be brought into the group and then integrated in a way that provides unity while preserving difference" (Smith & Berg, 1987, p. 65). Thus difference alone can create conflict. How those differences are integrated may create the conflict as well. Although group member difference is necessary, it can also threaten a group's capacity to function effectively.

Two, groups have a natural tendency to polarize themselves as a way of ordering and defining reality. If a group member suggests that a group of friends consider going to dinner and a movie, the next person is likely to suggest going to the theater. Although the suggestions may seem similar, they really are polar opposites—the movie option is informal and spontaneous whereas the theatre option means getting dressed up and planning ahead. Although the friends may, in fact, enjoy either option, the polarization or difference between the two options can cause a conflict. Groups can also polarize themselves in terms of how they communicate (Bales & Cohen, 1979). Friendly group members will feel that they are in conflict with group members who are negative and unfriendly. Submissive members will feel opposed to members who are dominant, outgoing, and assertive.

> **? THINK ABOUT IT**
>
> *Did I Do That?*
>
> Think about one of the last group conflicts in which you were involved. At what point did you know that a conflict had developed? What cues led you to this conclusion? What was your role in helping to develop or establish the conflict? Did you say something that someone found offensive, inaccurate, or personal? Or, did you neglect to say something when you should have spoken up? Did you behave in a way that demonstrated lack of interest in the group or in what the group was doing? Could you have changed your communication or behavior in any way to help the group avoid or minimize the conflict?

When differences in group member dominance are great, conflict is likely to occur (Wall & Galanes, 1986). Shareece and Joe are both talkative, bold, and expressive. They usually initiate group conversations and occupy most of the group's talking time. In comparison, Marcel and Wendy are more submissive. They really do not like to talk much, preferring to follow Shareece and Joe's lead. But that does not mean Marcel and Wendy will go along with anything and everything they suggest. Wendy, in particular, becomes angry—but does not show it—when Shareece and Joe decide what the group will do. As in this example, differences in ideas are often exacerbated when there are differences in group member dominance. More dominant members take responsibility for the group, often without asking other members for their input or for agreement. More submissive members are less likely to take a vocal or overt stand against ideas, making it appear that they agree with more dominant members.

Conflict is also likely to occur when there are differences in group members' task orientation (Wall & Galanes, 1986). Some members are eager to complete the group's task; other members prefer to socialize. When these two types of group members come together, there is a high likelihood that destructive conflict will occur. This difference in orientation affects how individuals perceive their group membership and the primary function of the group. The high task-oriented members think the socializing members are slowing them down. The socializing members think the high task-oriented members need to chill out. Frequently these group members will find themselves locked in a distributive conflict where one side will win and the other will lose. Try "Did I Do That?" to reveal your role in a group conflict.

Thus group life is "filled with 'oppositional forces' that exist as an artifact of members' perceptual processes. This means that individuals in groups and groups as a whole will always be managing differences even as they are seeking a certain level of homogeneity" (Smith & Berg, 1987, p. 66).

Three, group members experience an ambivalence about their group membership. They want to identify with others and be part of a group, but they also want to retain their individuality and be different. Thus each group member feels both drawn toward the group and pushed away from it: "I'm like them; I'm not like them." The desire to be separate from and connected to the group can result in individual-to-group conflict. Jones is a member of a fraternity and likes his affiliation with his fraternity brothers. He wears their logo proudly on a cap and a sweatshirt. He even moved from his apartment into the frat house. He is active on their soccer team and captains their softball team each spring. But Jones's fraternity brothers are notorious for waiting until the last minute to fulfill their service work as campus escorts. Because Jones lives in the frat house, he is called on frequently to take shifts when others do not show up. Lately, he has become resentful of others relying on him to take their shifts. "After all," Jones snarls, "don't they realize I have a life of my own?"

When issues and problems are discussed in group situations, some level of conflict may be inherent. For example, one researcher coded the ideas that naturally occurred in work group discussions. The results encouraged him to propose the **law of inherent conflict** (Warfield, 1993). Each group averaged sixty-four ideas per session—that is, group members produced sixty-four unique ideas for the group's consideration. When group members voted on their top five ideas, thirty-three different ideas received at least one top-five vote. Is conflict present? Yes, particularly when we see conflict as differences in perceptions and values. In this situation, then, who is right and who is wrong? No group member is completely right, and all group members are wrong to some degree. Thus, "no matter what the complex issue, and no matter what the group involved in its study, there will be significant inherent conflict within the group stemming from different perceptions of the relative significance of the factors involved in the complex issue" (Warfield, 1993, p. 73).

The Importance of Communication

Communication—verbal, nonverbal, written, and electronic—is the key to moving from disruptive to constructive conflict. In conflict situations, we often look for cues—both positive and negative—in the other party's communication. Thus we must consider all of the communication that occurs when conflict exists. The briefest glimpse of a smile may convince you that the other person is as tired of the conflict as you are and is ready to find an agreeable solution. By communicating with those with whom you conflict, you can exchange information, coordinate efforts, resolve differences, vent feelings, reason together, bargain, exercise influence, and thus find a way to manage the problem (Johnson, 1974).

How group members communicate in a conflict situation has a large impact on conflict outcomes (Pood, 1980). Groups that confront conflict by focusing on the content of the conflict without attempting to injure or eliminate the conflicting parties create more accurate decisions. Members are also more satisfied with the interaction and the amount of influence they were able to exercise. Power struggles are avoided because group members focus on the content of the problem, not on attacking one another. In this case, conflict is interaction that productively supports and defends alternative points of view.

Types and Sources of Conflict

Conflict is not necessarily destructive. It may seem that way when you are involved in a conflict situation, but actually conflict can be productive for the group. Conflict is destructive if it completely consumes the group's energy and time, tears the group apart preventing members from working together, or escalates into violence. Alternately, conflict can be productive if it exposes new ideas, helps clarify an issue, or alerts the group to a concern that needs to be addressed.

It may appear that when conflict erupts in a group all group members will view the conflict similarly, but that is not always the case. Frequently, group members disagree about what the disagreement is! To be effective, groups must express some agreement about the type of conflict that is occurring (Pace, 1990). One distinction that must be made is the personalized or depersonalized nature of the group's conflict (Guetzkow & Gyr, 1954). **Personalized** or **affective conflict** is that which is rooted in interpersonal relationships, emotions, or personalities whereas **depersonalized** or **substantive conflict** is that which is rooted in issues or ideas. For example, members disagreeing about the appropriateness of two alternatives and members disagreeing about the scope of their responsibilities are substantive conflicts. Managed effectively, substantive conflicts help groups improve their problem-solving abilities as well as generate member satisfaction with decision making (Witteman, 1991). When Ankar refuses to listen to what Scott has to say because Scott makes it clear that women could not possibly understand the importance of continuing the tradition of bachelor parties, the conflict is affective. Affective conflict is based on social or relational issues, and it generally increases emotional responses. Effective groups are those that can view conflict over ideas without tying the conflict to particular group members. When conflict is linked to a particular group member, it is personalized. This type of conflict is likely to be more dysfunctional.

Another distinction concerning conflict is whether the conflict exists in a competitive or cooperative environment. **Competitive conflict** is polarization with one side winning and the other side losing. When this happens groups are likely to escalate the conflict and become defensive or even hostile toward each another. **Cooperative conflict** occurs when the disagreement actually helps move the group along with its task or activities. In this case, the climate surrounding the conflict is supportive or positive. As a result, the group is more likely to find a mutually beneficial resolution to the conflict.

A third distinction is the centrality of the conflict to the group. How important is the issue to the members who are in disagreement or to the group as a whole? If the conflict is about a trivial matter (for example, what type of paper to copy the agenda on), then the conflict is not salient, or important, to the group's objective.

If group members are arguing about a critical feature of the group's project, then the conflict is salient, or more important, and has the capacity to create more dysfunction in the group.

As you reflect on your group experiences, you are likely to identify three different types of group conflict (Knutson & Kowitz, 1977). One type is conflict over information or data or the analysis of that information. This is known as **judgment** or **cognitive conflict.** For example, you say that the university could return professor evaluations to students earlier. Another student government senator says, "No, they've got to go to the professors first, and they don't get them until the middle of the following semester." "But," you argue, "that's not what the Dean of Students told me." You are having a conflict about what constitutes the real scenario of delivering results of professor evaluations. One of you has judged the information incorrectly or made an incorrect assumption about the data you collected. In most cases like this, the conflict can be resolved when group members get more or better information. Conflict over information could result in a higher quality solution or in more severely polarized positions (Knutson & Kowitz, 1977). Thus this type of conflict might best be resolved with evidence or data from a credible and valid source that could be examined by others. It does not work to say "because I say so." To resolve an informational-type conflict, data must be available for all group members.

A second type of group conflict can occur over procedural issues. Your group may find itself in disagreement about the type of leadership it needs or about the size of the majority it needs to finalize your group's plans. **Procedural conflicts** like this occur when procedures were not discussed beforehand or when the group encounters a situation for which there is no precedent. So conflicts about goals, tasks, or any other actions or activities of the group are also procedural conflicts. Procedural conflict impedes a group's work. It would be difficult for a group experiencing procedural conflict to work effectively on its task. Let's say that a group is having difficulty picking a leader. At least three members are qualified to be the group's leader; two have even said they would like the chance to lead the group. But now, the group's membership is evenly divided in support of the three members. This conflict could resolve itself by the group selecting the best leader candidate, or the worst!

A third type of group conflict—**interpersonal conflict**—occurs when the attitudes or perceptions of group members do not match. Some group members may feel that they must defer to the group leader. Interpersonal conflicts revolve around status, power, perceived competence, cooperation, and friendliness. Interpersonal conflict is like a deep current running through the group, and it is often subtle. You know it exists, but you are not exactly sure why. Erin and Carl never sit next to each other and always dispute what the other one says. Dennis says this has been going on between them for years. Depending upon the roles and responsibilities Erin and Carl have in the group, this interpersonal conflict could be devastating to the group or could be just a side show for other members to speculate about.

Conflicts can also occur because goals or interests differ. This means that each party favors his or her own goal, but to accomplish the goal, another's goal cannot

> ### PUTTING THE PIECES TOGETHER
>
> #### Group Goal, Group Structure, Group Identity, and Interdependence
>
> Can you remember the last conflict you and your group members dealt with? Was the conflict personalized or depersonalized? If it was personalized, how did this conflict over relationships or personalities affect the interdependence of the group? Did the group work well together when the personalized conflict was evident? Was the conflict competitive or cooperative? In what way did this affect the group's goal activity? Was the group able to make progress toward the goal while the conflict was apparent? In what way did the group's conflict affect your willingness to identify with the group? Did the conflict make you more or less interested in being a member of the group? Finally, did the conflict affect the group's structure? Did members change roles or take on additional roles because the group was in conflict?

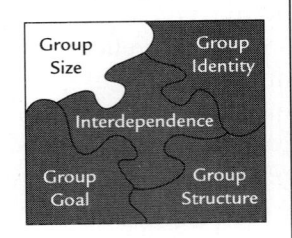

be achieved. Two group members cannot be elected chair of your work team. Only one person's goal can be satisfied; the other person's goal is defeated.

Another type of conflict is **normative conflict** (Thomas, 1992). Normative conflict occurs when one party has expectations about another party's behavior. In other words, conflict occurs when someone evaluates your behavior against what the person thought you should have done. Sororities and fraternities are notorious for dealing with normative conflict. One sorority sister turns another in because she violated sorority house rules. Normative conflict can evoke an emotional response like blame, anger, or disapproval, and it is usually followed by sanctions intended to produce conformity to the formal rules or implied standards.

When group members disagree about how personalized or depersonalized the conflict is, how competitive or cooperative the conflict is, or how central the conflict is to the group, then these issues will need to be addressed before the group can resolve the primary conflict. The more disagreement there is about the nature of the conflict, the more strain there will be on the group's interpersonal relationships. Group members who can come to agreement through interaction on the nature of conflict are more likely to build consensus and cohesiveness (Pace, 1990). *Putting the Pieces Together* will help you understand how conflict affected one of your group experiences.

The Origin of Conflict

Conflict is a sequence of events (Thomas, 1992). Let's examine each part of the process shown in Figure 11.1. Conflict begins with awareness—when one party becomes aware that another party is, has, or will negatively affect something that

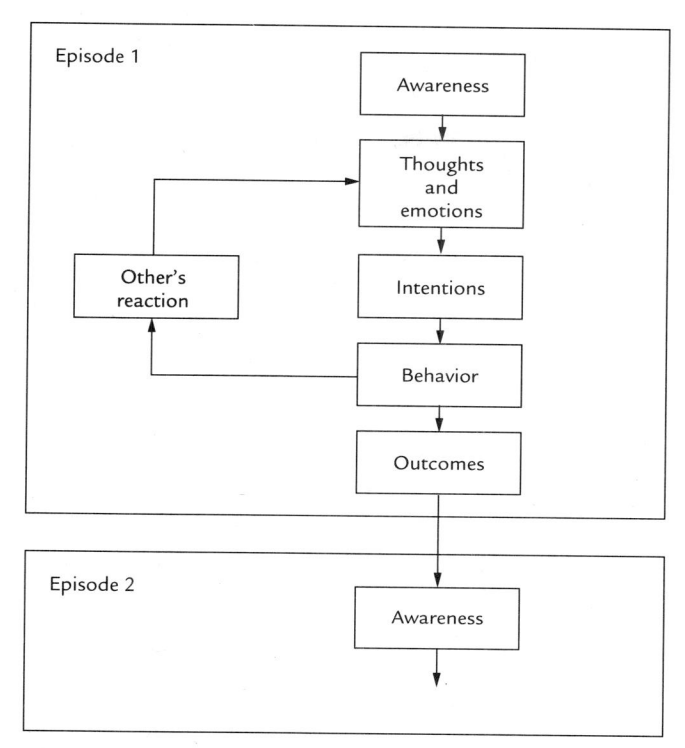

Figure 11.1 *Conflict Process Model*
Source: Adapted from Thomas (1992).

the first party cares about. Usually, this awareness follows a triggering event, like a co-worker blowing up at you unexpectedly or you realizing that you offended your friend when you misspoke.

The next stage of the process is the thoughts and emotions you experience. How you think helps you make sense of the conflict, and, certainly, emotions cause you to interpret the event in a particular way. In this step, you create your subjective reality of the situation. Thus your cognitive and emotional reaction to the conflict can both predict and explain what you will think about doing. How you frame the conflict influences how important you believe the conflict is. If you believe the conflict is a life-or-death situation, your reactions will be intensified. If you frame the conflict as just a minor irritation, you may want to wait to see how the other person reacts before you say or do anything. During this stage, you will also make some assessment about what you believe your odds are for winning the conflict. You will examine different potential outcomes and evaluate their desirability. A great deal is going on here, and little of it is obvious to the person or party with whom you are in conflict.

The third stage is where your intentions are more clearly developed and organized. You also try to guess the other person's or party's intentions because what you think the other person meant is an important motivator in deciding what to do next (Thomas & Pondy, 1977). What did he mean? Why did she say that? What does he want? How you read the intentions of others will guide you in how you plan your strategy. Reading the other person's intentions also provides a basis from which you make emotional decisions. If you believe that another's intention is to harm you, your emotions are different than if you believe that the other person's intention is to find an equitable solution. Unfortunately, you do not always evaluate other people's intentions accurately, nor do your intentions and behavior always match.

The next stage focuses on your behavior—what you say or do. You may use integrative behaviors like pursuing problem solving instead of competition. You may try to accept the other's viewpoint instead of rejecting it. Alternately, you may select distributive behaviors like threats, put-downs, arguments, or demands. We will discuss integrative and distributive behaviors further a bit later in this chapter. Notice that according to the model you are also reacting to the other person's or party's behaviors at the same time you are trying to implement your intentions. This is why there is slippage between your intentions and your behavior. No matter how well you think out a conflict strategy or how well you rehearse what you are going to say, you can never fully predict what the other person will say or do. Thus in this stage you are sizing up the other person, responding to him or her, and adjusting your intentions and behaviors.

Finally, you are at the outcomes stage. Outcomes occur when you are done talking. If a decision has been reached, this is an outcome. Your emotional reaction to the decision is an outcome as well. Thus your favorable or unfavorable attitude toward the vote to incorporate constitutes an outcome. The nature of relationships among group members is also an outcome. If you are able to leave the conflict with a better understanding of Ella and Lucy and the relationships among the three of you are stronger, you have realized a positive relational outcome. Of course, negative relational outcomes can also occur.

Now notice that one conflict episode is connected to the next one. How you evaluate the outcome of the first conflict episode will affect your awareness of the next, or potential, conflict. Suppose you believe that the two of you reached an agreeable decision. The next time you engage in conflict with that person, or a similar type of person, you will expect to again reach an agreeable outcome. On the other hand, if you believe the decision to be totally unfair to you, the next time you become aware of a conflict you will bring these emotions into the interpretation that a conflict exists. In other words, your awareness for conflict in the second episode has been heightened by your loss in the first one.

Conflict aftermath is the feelings that group members have developed as a result of the conflict episode (Pondy, 1967). Conflict episodes are connected to one another. The outcome of one episode affects how, and even if, another conflict will begin again. In other words, each conflict leaves a legacy or an aftermath. If the conflict is settled with an integrative strategy, members are likely to feel motivated and enthusiastic about the group as they understand that conflict does not necessarily destroy group relationships. However, if the conflict is resolved with a distributive strategy, some group members have lost, and their feelings are negative, maybe even hostile, toward the group and other group members.

How important is conflict aftermath? Conflict aftermath affects group members' perceptions of the group's ability to work together. When aftermath is negative, members are less likely to embrace conflict in the future. After all, they feel that they lost this time and do not want to lose again. Theo is distraught over his group's recent conflict episode. Not only was the conflict settled distributively, but Theo felt like he really did not get a chance to express his viewpoint while all of the arguing was going on. "Man, that wasn't a good situation," he concludes. "Now nobody in the group gets along, and we were just given another project to complete." Theo's feelings—his conflict aftermath—will affect his interaction in the group. His motivation to work with group members, his ability to trust other members to work for the good of the group, and his interpersonal relationships with other members are negatively affected.

But conflict can also create positive outcomes (Wall, Galanes, & Love, 1987). A moderate amount of conflict increases the quality of group outcomes. Conflict, in this case, has stimulated members to participate and pay attention and has strengthened the group's ability to solve problems. Furthermore, when group members manage the conflict by satisfying their own concerns in addition to the concerns of others, group outcomes are also of higher quality (Wall & Galanes, 1986; Wall & Nolan, 1986).

Conflict Between Groups

Conflicts can also occur between groups. "Since groups belong to a world populated by other groups, they tend to be forever banging into each other, each struggling to find its own place and identity" (Smith & Berg, 1987, p. 183). For example, if you are married, the two sides of your family may be in conflict with each other over which side will host the Thanksgiving celebration you and your spouse will attend. Each family is a complete group by itself, but when you come home for Thanksgiving, the two families are brought together by your presence. Forcing this type of interdependence can create competition over your family loyalty. Your basketball team competes with other teams. Your project team at work competes against teams from other organizations for a prospective client's business. How well your group deals with conflict from external sources can affect the internal interaction of your group.

Within a group, members communicate with one another to develop the image of the other group as the enemy or the competitor, as well as how the two groups are in conflict with each other and what actions should be taken to resolve the conflict (Johnson, 1975). In other words, your group creates other groups as the enemy through communication. Until someone in your group identifies a conflict with another group and other members agree with that vision, conflict with the other group does not exist. Think back to high school. How is it that your football team became rivals with one of the many high schools in your city or region? The conflict or competition between the teams was generated through

Conflict between groups often results from communication practices within groups. Group members can create competition with another group by labeling that group as the enemy. This type of rhetorical force is responsible for creating intergroup competition.

communication. Even before you entered high school, you probably knew who your rivals were. In high school, there were pep rallies, announcements over the loud speakers, and banners in the hallways encouraging your team to "Tromp the Wildcats" or "Make the Cats Meow!" You developed a vision that an enemy or competitor group existed because people communicated that message to you. This rhetorical force is very strong in groups. It only takes a thread of a conversation to construct the reality among group members that another group is competing with them.

Generally, as a sense of competition with another group builds, the level of cohesiveness within your group also builds (Johnson, 1975). Because your group has identified an out-group (a group different from yours in some way), your in-group becomes closer and more meaningful to you. Often, a group can work itself into conflict with another group through verbal statements. Later this conflict is overtly expressed to others outside of the group, and, before you know it, the other group has accepted the fact that it is in conflict with your group.

Conflict Management Strategies

Conflict resolution or conflict management? Which is more appealing to you? Resolution means to solve, to fix, to end, to settle. Can we really do that with conflict? Conflict management may be a better way of expressing our need to deal with conflict. For you, there may be little difference between conflict resolution and conflict management, but the two terms represent widely divergent views of conflict (Hawes & Smith, 1973; Pood, 1980). Resolving conflict requires that we view conflict as destructive or as a disruption that we need to eliminate. Thus the only kind of good conflict is a dead conflict. Managing conflict, on the other hand, means that conflict is a normal and inevitable situation that groups must handle. When groups are able to manage their conflicts, groups can take advantage of conflict situations to see alternative views not before addressed. Managing conflict results in creative and innovation solutions.

There are three general types of conflict management strategies: integrative, distributive, and avoidance. Although you probably prefer one strategy or have a primary orientation for managing conflict, you should know that you can change your strategy as the conflict interaction progresses (Conrad, 1991; Nicotera, 1994; Putnam & Poole, 1987). And certainly your conflict management strategy should vary across different conflict settings (Thomas, 1988). Before reading further, try "What Conflict Strategy Do You Prefer?" to determine which strategy you prefer.

Conflict Management Alternatives

A group member who uses an **integrative conflict management strategy** uses problem solving or collaboration to manage the conflict. This helps the group achieve a win-win outcome—or an outcome with which everyone can agree—because information sharing and collaboration are promoted. Integrative management strategies attempt to maximize the gains of all conflicting parties. This promotes rather than inhibits relationships among group members (Canary & Spitzberg, 1989). To initiate the integrative conflict management strategy, you can ask other members how they feel about the problem or let others know that something about the group or its task is bothering you (Jarboe & Witteman, 1996). Or, you can self-disclose—a good way to get others to self-disclose and open channels of communication (Sillars & Wilmot, 1994). These cooperative strategies help motivate both parties because they understand that one outcome objective needs to satisfy both sets of concerns. Groups that can achieve integrative conflict management produce higher quality outcomes (Wall, Galanes, & Love, 1987) and generate higher group member satisfaction (Wall & Galanes, 1986). We should not be surprised that an integrative approach is the preferred conflict management strategy (Thomas, 1992).

In **collaborating,** the parties share the superordinate goal of solving the problem even though their initial ideas for how to solve the problem differ. Thus communication is the process parties can use to "redefine the situation so that they both perceive it as a shared predicament to be solved jointly" (de Reuck, 1990). Besides sharing the goal, the opposing parties must develop or build a common language in order to create a shared frame from which to view the problem. Ultimately, this means that opposing parties who see each other as enemies must be able to move from that framing device into one that views the other as analysts of

GROUP ASSESSMENT TECHNIQUE

What Conflict Strategy Do You Prefer?

Think about the last time you perceived a problem in one of your groups. If a similar problem arose in one of your groups in the future, how do you think you would respond? Using the following scale, respond to each item to indicate how likely it would be for you to use these behaviors.

1 = not likely at all   2 = not very likely   3 = unsure   4 = somewhat likely   5 = very likely

1. I pointed out to the group what I thought the problem was. 1 2 3 4 5
2. I talked to the group about my feelings and thoughts about the problem. 1 2 3 4 5
3. I simply stated what I thought the problem was. 1 2 3 4 5
4. I asked the group about their thoughts and feelings about the problem. 1 2 3 4 5
5. I talked to the group about how the problem could be resolved. 1 2 3 4 5
6. I let the group see something was bothering me. 1 2 3 4 5
7. I demanded that the group deal with the problem. 1 2 3 4 5
8. I shouted at one member of the group. 1 2 3 4 5
9. I shouted at the group. 1 2 3 4 5
10. I insulted one member of the group. 1 2 3 4 5
11. I cursed at the group. 1 2 3 4 5
12. I insulted members of the group. 1 2 3 4 5
13. I expressed negative feelings to members of the group. 1 2 3 4 5
14. I demanded that someone in the group change his or her behavior. 1 2 3 4 5
15. I did not say anything about the problem. 1 2 3 4 5
16. I avoided talking about the problem. 1 2 3 4 5

Total items 1 through 7 and divide the sum by 7 _____
Total items 8 through 14 and divide the sum by 7 _____
Total items 15 and 16 and divide the sum by 2 _____

The first score is your preference for integrative conflict strategies. The second score is your preference for distributive conflict strategies. The third score is your preference for avoidance strategies. Which strategy are you most likely to choose in your next conflict situation? Can you predict the effectiveness of such a strategy?

Source: Jarboe and Witteman (1996).

---

the problem and then later as partners. To effectively work in the problem-solving mode, a new "we" must be created to include all parties to the conflict. This process of reframing adversaries into partners may be easier if you think of it this way: You see the other party as holding a position different from yours; they are your adversaries. But let's turn the tables: They see you as holding a position different from theirs; you are the adversary from their point of view. "But I'm not an adversary," you say. That is what the other party is saying as well. Acknowledging this type of mirror logic can help you move from self-perception to "we" perception.

Integrative conflict management is a constructive way of managing intragroup differences. Open discussion of differences, having access to a variety of opinions, and carefully critiquing assumptions help create commitment to the group, as well as trust and respect for group members (Thomas, 1992). Thus constructive conflict management can offset problems caused by initial differences or unequal participation caused by diversity within the group (Kirchmeyer & Cohen, 1992). Not only does this integrative strategy help produce higher quality decisions and solutions, it also helps parties master effective conflict management for future situations (Thomas, 1992).

Are there any disadvantages associated with the integrative strategy? Primarily, the only disadvantage is the time it takes to achieve an integrative solution (Thomas, 1992). Thus the integrative conflict management strategy may not be appropriate or feasible when time is limited. Digging into the underlying issues and trying to meet both parties' concerns take more time than fighting for one side of the conflict. However, this extra time is worth it as an integrative solution is more likely to resolve the problem for good, keeping the group from wasting time and energy on the same or a similar conflict in the future.

A **distributive conflict management strategy** is competitive and antagonistic and is characterized by a win-lose orientation, or an outcome that satisfies one party at the expense of the other. Conflicts managed this way are characterized by someone trying to control the group's interaction or activities to satisfy his or her own issues at the expense of others. Using a distributive strategy of conflict management promotes you and your individual goals over the needs of others and your relationships with them. In distributive conflicts, group members show anger and sarcasm. Group members who use this strategy typically have negative feelings for the group. They are likely to yell or shout at the group, and they might even insult others or demand that others change their behavior (Jarboe & Witteman, 1996). Groups that use distributive conflict management may settle the conflict, but the relational aspects of the group will be damaged. When conflict is managed distributively, groups reduce the amount of conflict allowed, perhaps because some members simply give in because they are tired of losing. When win-lose strategies are used, the quality of the outcome is also lower (Wall, Galanes, & Love, 1987).

Two types of distributive strategies are competing and accommodating (Thomas, 1992). Both emphasize one party winning while the other party loses. **Competing,** or forcing, emphasizes you winning at the other person's expense. In a sense, you take from the conflict and give very little. Using a competing strategy and using your power over others, you are assertive and uncooperative. So, it is likely that you would force the issues and dominate the interaction. You believe that you are right and the other person is wrong.

Competing also closes down communication channels (Deutsch, 1969). In fact, you might go out of your way *not* to talk to other group members because

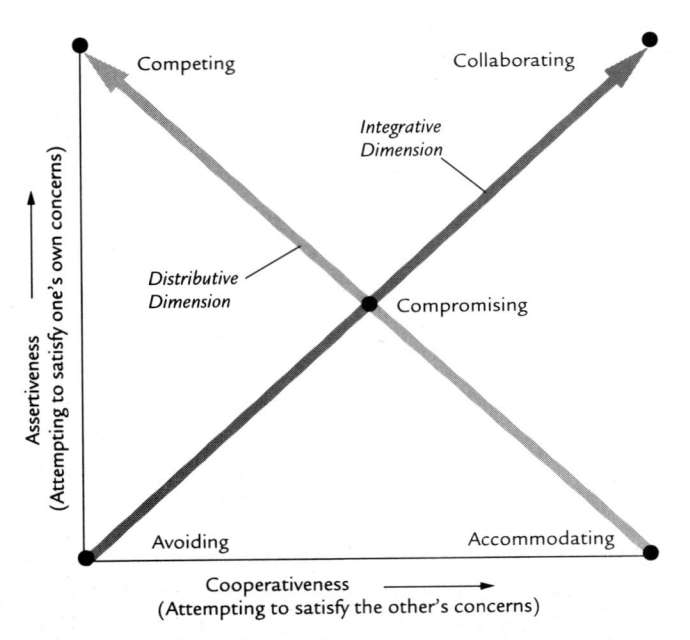

Figure 11.2 *Five Basic Approaches to Managing Conflict.* Source: Adapted from Thomas (1992).

[Figure 11.2: A diagram with two axes. Vertical axis: Assertiveness (Attempting to satisfy one's own concerns). Horizontal axis: Cooperativeness (Attempting to satisfy the other's concerns). Five approaches are plotted: Competing (top-left), Collaborating (top-right), Compromising (center), Avoiding (bottom-left), Accommodating (bottom-right). The Distributive Dimension runs from Competing to Accommodating; the Integrative Dimension runs from Avoiding to Collaborating.]

communication in competing is intended to mislead or humiliate. Even when communication is taking place, you are suspicious of the information you receive from other parties. Thus error and misinformation abound. Competing also stimulates the view that the solution to the conflict can be of only one type—the type that is imposed by one side on the other (Deutsch, 1969).

Accommodating is at the other end of the distributive continuum. In this conflict management strategy, you give everything and take very little from the conflict. Here you would be cooperative, yet unassertive. You would focus on trying to satisfy the other's concerns rather than your own. You would try to smooth over issues and relationships by being obliging and yielding. Nell is great at accommodating Henry. Each time Henry starts to bring up a sensitive issue, Nell becomes submissive and quiet. Even when Henry tries to force Nell to talk about the problem by screaming at her, Nell holds her head down and says something like, "Whatever you say, Henry. I'm sure you must be right. You've never led us down the wrong path before."

The **avoiding conflict management strategy** is nonconfrontive. Group members choosing this strategy try to sidestep the conflict by changing the topic or shifting the focus to other issues. Group members simply hope that if they ignore it or do not draw attention to it, the conflict will disappear. By allowing only minimal discussion about the conflict, events take their own course without members' input. Avoiding is not only verbal withdrawal; it can take physical and psychological withdrawal forms as well. College roommates are exemplar avoiders (Sillars & Wilmot, 1994). One roommate will acknowledge a problem he has with his roommate, then back off. For example, "I get pretty ticked off sometimes but it's not really a problem." This type of denial is to be expected, given the awkwardness of most roommate pairings. The decision to live together is financial, and, many times, roommates are initially strangers. This type of forced intimacy (which also occurs in some work groups) can be characterized by nervous tension and denial.

Thus there are four basic approaches to managing conflict: the integrative strategy of collaborating or problem solving, the distributive strategies of competing and accommodating, and the nonconfrontive strategy of avoiding (Figure 11.2). A fifth strategy, compromising, also deserves our attention (Putnam & Wilson, 1982; Thomas, 1977). **Compromising** is an intermediate strategy somewhere on the middle ground of both cooperativeness and assertiveness. Although compromising may settle the problem, it also will offer incomplete satisfaction for both parties. You have given up something, but you are still holding out for something better. Although a compromise may be easier to obtain than collaboration, at best, it is a temporary fix. You have probably compromised with a roommate over who will perform household tasks such as taking out the trash. These compromises are okay at first because they solve the immediate problem—they ended the fighting on trash day. But over the long term, your roommate will forget to take out the trash when it is his turn, you will blow up and start looking for a new apartment.

Which Strategy Do You Pick? In conflict situations, you are managing three views of the situation—your view of the conflict, what you believe the other person's view is, and your evaluation of the relationship between you and the other person. When conflicts occur, it is not unusual to start with a management strategy that emphasizes your view of the problem. Even if you enter the conflict with little concern about your view, that quickly changes. You would not be in the conflict if your own view of the problem was not important to you. And, as you might expect, your attention to the other person's view is lower or becomes lower throughout the interaction. Thus a pattern dominates most conflict situations: Most people enhance their own view of the situation while minimizing the view of the other person (Nicotera, 1994). Such attributions are common during conflicts. People tend to attribute positive behaviors and outcomes to themselves and negative behaviors and outcomes to the conflict partner (Bradbury & Fincham, 1990).

If we consider just your behavior in a conflict situation, this pattern seems reasonable. We would not be in a conflict if our own view on the issue was not important to us. Attempts to minimize the view of the other person seem reasonable given that we seldom want to lose in conflicts. And we generally have conflicts with people who matter to us. But remember that your conflict partner has the same orientation to the conflict. Both of you are trying to maximize your view while minimizing the view of the other. Thus even our attempts at managing conflict create a greater distance between us and the other person. Yet, neither one of you want to disrupt the relationship!

How you manage conflicts provides others with a screen for evaluating your communication competence (Canary & Spitzberg, 1989, 1990). Your conflict messages are assessed according to their appropriateness and effectiveness. In turn, these assessments act as a filter through which evaluations of your competence are made. Generally, you will be perceived more negatively and as having lower competence if you manage conflicts with distributive or avoiding strategies. Group members who use an integrative strategy and focus on the issue or content of the conflict are perceived more positively by others than members who use distributive strategies (McKinney, Kelly, & Duran, 1997).

Conflicts can create critical turning points in relationships. One conflict episode can influence how your relationship with someone develops. And, certainly, a pattern of conflict over time will influence your ability to maintain relationships with others.

Which conflict management strategy is best? It depends upon you and your involvement in the conflict situation (Thomas, 1977). Usually, the integrative strategy of collaborating or problem solving will return the best long-term gains, but it takes time and commitment from all conflicting parties. Collaborating should be used when concerns are too important to compromise, when you have a long-term relationship with the other party and other conflicts are inevitable, when you could learn from merging your insights with the insights of others, and when you need to build community and commitment. Although the other strategies may seem effective in certain situations, they also have costs or risks associated with them.

The distributive strategy of competing can be used when decisive action is vital, as in an emergency, or when you need to implement an unpopular action. Competing can be effective when the conflict is with others who would take advantage of your using a noncompetitive strategy or when you know you are right (just be sure you are!). Accommodating, the other distributive conflict management strategy, is especially effective when you find that you are wrong. By accommodating, you demonstrate that you are willing to learn from others. Accommodating can also be effective when you need to satisfy others to maintain their cooperation; in other words, the issue is more important to them than it is to you. And, because you value the long-term nature of the relationship, it is important to be reasonable and demonstrate harmony as well as loyalty to the relationship.

Avoiding is only effective when the issue is trivial and you can let go of it or when other matters are more pressing. Sometimes it just makes sense to walk away from a conflict. Avoiding can be an effective strategy when you perceive no chance of satisfying your concerns. Why fight over something you cannot have? As a teenager, you probably used avoiding with your parents to let everyone cool down and gain perspective before dealing with an important but sensitive issue again.

Compromising may be effective in some situations, especially if you and the conflicting party are willing to accept a temporary settlement. Also, compromise may be all you can achieve when both sides are adamantly fixed on opposing or mutually exclusive goals. For example, in a face-off between pro-choice and pro-life groups, the only type of settlement likely to be achieved is a compromise.

Generally, these two groups are fundamentally opposed to each other's view, so it is unlikely that anything more than a compromise can be achieved. Recognize, however, that the resolution is only temporary. Parties with fundamentally conflicting views are likely to reinitiate the conflict or start another one. Try "Identifying Conflict Strategies" to test your analytical skills.

Symmetry in Conflict Management Strategies So far, our focus has been on your strategy, but what about the strategy of those with whom you are in conflict? Generally, we pick the strategy that matches the strategy of the other party. Thus symmetry is the extent to which parties match strategies of conflict (Sillars & Wilmot, 1994). For example, you are more likely to avoid conflict if others are avoiding it. You are more likely to use a competing strategy if others are confronting you. Although there are times when you will compensate—choose the strategy opposite the other party's—most of the time, you will select a symmetrical strategy. This is because if you are given compliments, you are likely to compliment back, and if you are given criticism, you give criticism back. This type of reciprocity is common in conflict management.

Across time and group history, patterns of symmetry tend to develop. This can be problematic if the pattern favors one of the distributive conflict management strategies or avoiding. When group members settle into an inflexible manner of dealing with conflict—any conflict, every conflict—group members have lost the capacity to deal constructively with conflict (Sillars & Wilmot, 1994). Unless group members are matched in using collaborating or problem solving, managing the group's conflict is going to be very difficult. Being locked in symmetrical patterns of avoiding, competing, or accommodating is not likely to move the conflict along.

Let's look now at compensating or asymmetric patterns of conflict management. Sometimes when one member confronts or competes, others will avoid. This type of "hit-and-run" conflict management (Sillars & Wilmot, 1994) will lead to dissatisfaction among the group members who feel they are being taken advantage of. And a destructive pattern can develop. The more confrontive one member becomes, the more other group members avoid him or her, the group, and its task. Over time, this pattern can escalate into one of aggression-withdrawal—clearly a dysfunctional mode for group communication.

Balancing Conflict and Problem Solving

Recall that the integrative conflict management strategy is collaborating or problem solving. Let's see how these two processes are integrated with the decision making discussed in Chapters 8 and 9. When conflict occurs in groups, members have choices for how to handle it. They can select any of the five strategies described earlier. But when group members have long histories of working together, when they expect to work together in the future, and when their working

BUILDING ANALYTICAL SKILLS

Identifying Conflict Strategies

For each of the following items, identify and list the strategy suggested: competing, avoiding, accommodating, compromising, and collaborating.

Communication	Strategy
1. Prolong the discussion of the issues until the other person tires and gives in to your approach for handling the problem.	_____
2. Downplay the seriousness of the problem and suggest that you not waste further time on the matter.	_____
3. Go along with whatever the other person wants rather than get into the difficulties of direct confrontation.	_____
4. Point out that if the disagreement is to be resolved, some sacrifices must be made by both of you.	_____
5. Try to sort out where each of you stands and identify options available to meet all parties' needs.	_____
6. Make the first move in the conflict and get command of the situation to maximize your chances of getting your demands accepted.	_____
7. Let the other person determine how the problem should be handled and offer to support whatever decision others make.	_____
8. Solicit others' assistance in helping meet both of your needs in settling the conflict.	_____
9. Tell others that the problem does not concern you.	_____
10. Offer to handle the problem any way the others want to.	_____
11. Express your concern for the differences between the conflicting parties and let the other party know that you want a resolution that satisfies you both.	_____
12. Explain that there is no point in trying to resolve a conflict between two different people with such basically different personalities.	_____

relationships are important, collaborating or problem solving is the best choice. Let's see why.

Problem solving—for example, using the standard agenda or making sure that the group's discussion uses the five critical functions—provides many opportunities to logically and rationally discuss the issues for which there are conflicting

13. Suggest that you take your ideas and the ideas of others and put them together to make an even more workable idea. _____
14. Try to win your own position by pressing your own points very firmly. _____
15. Try to keep the matter calm by adapting to the wishes of others. _____
16. Explain to others that there is little point in fighting because your personality differences would prevent the group from reaching a satisfactory solution. _____
17. Suggest that the two opposing parties integrate all of the concerns and develop a combined solution to the problem. _____
18. If the conflict gets too unpleasant, let the others know that you do not want to be bothered with the matter. _____
19. Explain exactly what you want done to resolve the conflict and firmly pursue that objective throughout all discussions. _____
20. Suggest that each of you define your perceptions of the problem and see if a combined view can be developed to reach a solution. _____
21. Point out to the others that if everyone will make some concessions, the conflict can be solved quickly. _____
22. Offer to negotiate a settlement of the major issues with everyone involved in the conflict. _____
23. Pursue your own goals with determination regardless of the concerns of others. _____

Items 1, 6, 14, 19, and 23 are competing. Items 2, 9, 12, 16, and 18 are avoiding. Items 3, 7, 10, and 15 are accommodating. Items 4 and 21 are compromising. Items 5, 8, 11, 13, 17, 20, and 22 are collaborating.

Source: Adapted from Riggs (1983).

opinions. By framing the discussion as one of problem solving rather than one of conflict, more productive communication is likely to take place. The decisions made or solutions developed will manage the conflict that prompted the problem-solving session in the first place. Moving from conflict management to problem solving emphasizes that all group members are in this together, that everyone's

BUILDING ANALYTICAL SKILLS

A Case Study in Conflict Management

Redford, Sonya, and Len have been friends throughout high school. Now the three of them attend the same college. They meet frequently for lunch and to catch up on what the others are doing. Sonya mentions that there was an announcement in the student newspaper for applications for an honorary organization and encourages Redford and Len to apply. At their next lunch, Redford shyly announces that he was accepted for membership in Omicron Delta Kappa. Somewhat to his surprise, so were Sonya and Len. After their initiation, the initiate class had to elect officers, and Sonya and Redford both found themselves nominated for president of the initiate class. When the vote was tallied, the outgoing president announced that there had been a tie between Sonya and Redford and asked them both if the loser of the next vote would take the position of vice-president. They looked at each other, shrugged their shoulders, and responded, "Okay." When the vote was tallied, the president announced that Redford would be the next president and Sonya would be the vice-president. Other elections were held, the meeting ended, and the three gathered outside to talk about the night's events.

LEN: Congratulations, you two! That's great!

SONYA: Thanks, Len. By the way, who did you vote for?

REDFORD: Sonya, let's not go there. Don't put Len in the middle.

SONYA: Well, I want to know. After all, it must have made the difference in who was elected president.

LEN: Please, Sonya . . .

REDFORD: Does it really matter, Sonya?

SONYA: Of course it does. You're president; I'm only vice-president. Doesn't that matter?

REDFORD: Len, do you want to say who you voted for?

LEN: Come on, is this really necessary?

Their discussion ends unproductively; Len does not reveal who he voted for. Sonya stomps off to her car while Len and Redford go get something to eat. Since then Sonya has been acting aloof, not talking like she usually does with Redford and Len. Her lack of communication has, in fact, drawn the two of them closer as they try to figure out how to deal with Sonya's uncharacteristic behavior. At the first Omicron Delta Kappa meeting, Redford calls the meeting to order and introduces the other officers. Sonya sits by and only coolly acknowledges Redford's introduction of her. During the meeting, the new members discuss service projects they want to pursue, and a heated debate

---

input is desired and needed, and that the group, not an individual, is responsible for the decision or solution. *Building Analytical Skills* presents a case study on which you can practice analyzing conflict situations.

Conflict and Cultural Differences

Conflict often intimidates people, making them lose confidence in their abilities to effectively negotiate the situation. Conflict that includes cultural differences can

starts to take place. Sonya is leading some members who want to work on a Habitat for Humanity project; Len is leading other members who prefer to perform their service work closer to campus. As the discussion continues, it becomes evident that Sonya's position on the project is directed more toward her anger at Len than to Len's service suggestion.

SONYA: I think, and these other members agree, that Habitat for Humanity is the project we should support.

LEN: I agree that Habitat would be a good project. I think what the rest of us are trying to say is that we'd like our service work to have an impact closer to the college campus.

SONYA: And, Habitat isn't a part of our community?

LEN: Well, of course it is. But could we use our energy to help those who live in the college neighborhood?

REDFORD: Do we have a motion for the group to consider?

SONYA: Habitat would give us more publicity . . . everyone knows about Habitat.

LEN: Is publicity what we're seeking?

SONYA: (She looks at members supporting the Habitat project and then turns back to Len.) Well, a little publicity wouldn't hurt. Who's going to publicize us picking up trash around here?

REDFORD: Is there a motion?

SONYA: Redford, what do you think?

REDFORD: I believe my position as president doesn't allow me to enter the discussion here. Do we have a motion to vote on?

SONYA: Oh, so you're taking up with Len again?

LEN: Sonya, please. Can we discuss this later?

REDFORD: A motion . . . ?

ANOTHER MEMBER: I move that . . .

What is this conflict about? Who are the parties to the conflict? Has the conflict among Sonya, Len, and Redford spread to Omicron Delta Kappa? To what extent is the communication among Sonya, Len, and Redford effective or ineffective? To what extent is the communication within Omicron Delta Kappa effective or ineffective? Take the role of another member of this organization. What would you say or do in this situation? What conflict management strategy would you recommend to Sonya? to Len? to Redford? Using the diagram of conflict presented in Figure 11.1, can you diagram this conflict from Sonya's point of view? from Len's point of view? from Redford's point of view?

---

heighten that anxiety. One way to minimize that anxiety is to think of the cultural differences that permeate every conflict (Avruch & Black, 1993). Even a group of culturally homogeneous members represents a wide variation of cultural beliefs. Remember that cultural values, beliefs, and attitudes are not evenly distributed across members of a cultural group. Not every female, Italian, Republican, prolifer, teenager, or African American profess the same values, beliefs, and attitudes. Thus in one way cultural differences are present in every conflict, not in just those where cultural differences are heightened, such as a conflict between Arab and Israeli students. Viewing culture this way encourages us to recognize that a person's culture creates that person's perception-shaping lens, which in turn shapes how that person sees each and every conflict.

Having said that, we still need to realize that cultures—even subcultures—vary in how conflict is perceived. In U.S. society, competition is generally pursued and conflict is expected. We assume we will have conflicts with one another because the First Amendment guarantees our freedom of speech, which in reality means that we believe others have the "right" to hear our opinion! Still African Americans and Whites approach conflict differently (Kochman, 1981). These differences are apparent in how the two groups view confrontation and argument, the appropriateness of emotionality in discussions and negotiations, and what constitutes valid arguments, truths, or evidence. Cultural differences are even more pronounced between America and Japan. The American view of "What is in it for me?" is quite different from the Japanese perspective of "What is good for the group, is good for me." As you can imagine, these cultural perspectives would resonate differently with American and Japanese members in conflict.

Because cultures treat conflict differently, we should also do a cultural analysis besides analyzing the conflict. Even if we try not to, we are going to analyze the conflict based on our cultural view of the world. Supplementing the conflict analysis with a cultural analysis will help us see how others culturally different from us may be perceiving the conflict. What might seem bizarre to us may be normal from another culture's point of view. Be wary of trying to explain or rationalize something that appears odd to you. Be careful of accepting gross evaluations of a culture (for example, the English are cold). Instead try to view the conflict from the other's point of view. Above all, do not pile cultural differences on top of any conflict that already exists.

Because much of our communication is habitual, we need to be especially mindful about our communication in intercultural settings (Gudykunst & Hall, 1994). This means that we need to acknowledge the scripts or patterns in our communication on which we rely, and we need to analyze them for their usefulness in this particular situation. In intercultural conflicts, it would be effective to allow different or alternative ideas to be presented, to be open to new information, and to be aware that others bring different perspectives to the conflict.

In conflict, description, interpretation, and evaluation are especially important to our understanding of the conflict and to our understanding of others' interactions in the conflict discussion. Remembering these five principles will help you minimize the misunderstandings that can occur.

1. Remember that you can never fully know the attitudes, thoughts, and feelings of other people.
2. You depend on signals to code the information others provide. Many of these signals or cues are ambiguous or have a variety of interpretations.
3. You have no choice but to use the coding system you know, and this coding system may be defective when trying to decipher signals from other cultures.

4. Your state of mind in a conflict (for example, mine is generally agitated) will bias your interpretation of other people and their positions.
5. You may believe you are correct in determining or attributing another person's motivations and attitudes, but you are probably wrong.

You can decrease the level of misunderstanding you create by knowing that these five principles guide how you describe, interpret, and evaluate the actions and communication of others.

Most intercultural conflicts take place in shared linguistic settings—typically French or English (Avruch & Black, 1993). Diplomacy meetings, interethnic disputes, and international trade are typical sites of group and intercultural conflicts. Because a language is shared, it is easy to assume that views and values are shared as well. Just because the German engineer speaks English does not mean that he shares American perspectives and attitudes. It is easy to think that intercultural conflicts are simply that—cultural differences. However, intercultural conflicts are real conflicts. Yet, intercultural differences rarely account for all of the conflict between or among people who are culturally diverse (Avruch & Black, 1993).

Minimizing Ineffective Conflict In Your Group

In addition to the conflict management strategies described above, there are some communication strategies that can help minimize the negative effects of conflict. Of course, not all conflicts will work out as we desire. When that happens, you might want to use a mediator. Both of these are explained in the following sections.

Communication Strategies

One way to minimize conflict is to emphasize the goals that are shared among group members. When members perceive that they have goals in common with others in the group, group members develop more positive feelings for the group. Then when conflict occurs, members are more likely to use integrative conflict management or problem solving to resolve the issue (Jarboe & Witteman, 1996). Think back to the student group in Chapter 9 that wanted to find an alternative to the parking problem on campus. The shared goal was finding a low-cost alternative to the present parking situation. If the group could keep this shared goal in front of them, their discussions would be less splintered and more productive.

When substantitive conflict occurs in groups, evidence or data can help your group reach a resolution (Knutson & Kowitz, 1977). Thus use factual information or opinions of valid and credible sources to help support your position. Once conflict develops in your group, try to steer the conflict to substantive issues and away from affective, or emotional, issues. Group members who introduce statements about the task or content of the conflict will encourage other members to do the same (Bell, 1974).

When conflict occurs, communicate! It is difficult to resolve a conflict when group members will not talk about the problem. When there is no or little communication about a problem, you must make assumptions about others' positions. Discussion about the problem lets you know where others stand. In fact, your positions may not be as far apart as you think.

Another way to minimize or manage conflict is to focus on the relationships among group members rather than the positions group members hold (Broome, 1993). Attempting to create shared meaning with other group members will help you view different ideas as alternative ideas. An idea that is viewed as a difference is odd or unknown to you, and generally you will oppose it. An idea that is viewed as an alternative deserves your consideration and attention. Shared meaning is created through communication, and shared meaning can best be created by trying to understand the other person fully and without reservation. This means that you must give up the notion that his or her ideas oppose you and communicate to get a full description and analysis of those ideas. When you do this, you develop understanding and shared meaning. The ideas are no longer his or hers; they are yours together. Let's see how this happens.

BRENDA: Do you guys agree with me?

STEVE: I don't think so, Brenda. Manny, what do you think?

MANNY: Sorry, Brenda, your proposal seems at odds with our goal.

BRENDA: Okay, let me try to restate it. I'd like . . . I'm sorry, we'd like to start a neighborhood patrol. The goal of the patrol would be to check in on elderly residents who live alone, to check on homes when people are on vacation, and to . . . uhhh . . . help me here.

MANNY: . . . to have a visible presence in the neighborhood. That's good—what you said in the first two parts.

STEVE: Yes, I'd like to add . . .

MANNY: I just want to remind you, Steve, that anything you add must adhere to the goals of the patrol.

STEVE: Right. How about adding that another one of our goals is to act as a welcoming committee for people who move into the neighborhood.

BRENDA: But that takes us back to where we started arguing, Steve. Our patrol can't be all things to all people.

MANNY: I think she's right, Steve. Can you restate that part so it can be integrated with the neighborhood patrol?

STEVE: No, I guess I can't.

BRENDA: So, then the goal of *our* neighborhood patrol would be to check in on elderly residents who live alone, to check on homes when people are on vacation, and to have a visible presence in the neighborhood.

MANNY: I agree. Do you, Steve?

STEVE: Yes, I can live with that.

When conflicting parties cannot come to an agreement, a mediator can help them talk about their problem in a more effective manner. Mediators do not suggest solutions; rather, they help group members avoid personal attacks and use discussion procedures that encourage equal participation.

Mediation

A relatively new technique—the use of mediators—has been successful in family, community, and landlord-tenant and labor-management disputes. Mediation has been so successful that many primary and secondary schools are training students to be peer-mentors to resolve disputes rather than relying on parental or teacher authority. **Mediation** is an intervention performed by a mediator, a person who is an impartial third party who has no authority or decision-making power in the situation. When a mediator helps two people talk about their problem, the three people become a group with the mediator acting as an intervenor.

The goal of the mediator who is selected by the disputing parties is to help conflicting parties build a cooperative context for negotiation. The mediator does not help the disputants develop an agreement, nor does the mediator address the content of the conflict. Rather, the mediator helps the parties through the process so they can formulate an agreement themselves. A secondary objective of mediation is to teach disputants how to resolve their own conflicts by creating collaborative solutions (Burrell, Donohue, & Allen, 1990).

Generally, people come to rely on the help of a mediator when all parties agree that they cannot reach an agreement or a solution. In some cases, conflicting parties are sent to mediation to avoid legal dispute resolution. By monitoring turn taking, allocating how long each party talks, and assisting parties manage conversation topics, the mediator helps disputants find an equitable solution. Conflicting parties use mediation as a way to avoid escalating a disagreement into dysfunctional conflict.

Mediators may also be labeled facilitators or counselors. But, in all cases, to be effective, mediators require training. Mediators need training in at least three specific areas: They need to be able to interrupt group members as soon as they begin verbally attacking one another, they need to maintain control of the discussion by enforcing the rules of the session, and they need to help disputants formulate proposals for consideration (Burrell, Donohue, & Allen, 1990). As you might guess, the ability to listen effectively and to develop feedback messages are key mediation skills. With your knowledge of group communication and other communication contexts, you could act as mediator for a dispute at work, at your child's school, or at the mediation center in your community.

Message Feedback If you are going to use mediation, a good way to start is to explain how message feedback works (Keltner, 1995). Next ask one party to describe the conflict. The mediator then asks the other party if he or she needs to make any clarifications, ask any questions, or state any additional information. Here is where **message feedback,** a type of message reflection, is used. As the two disputing parties start to develop their conversation with each other, at any time one can stop the conversation and ask the other party to summarize or rephrase what he or she is talking about. Using message feedback in this way lets the mediator know exactly what the dispute is about. In disputes, emotionality further confuses any existing communication problems. Message feedback will help the mediator untangle emotion from content.

When disputing parties communicate, they often resort to attacking one another. Message feedback can also be used here (Keltner, 1995). The mediator can stop an attack session and ask each party to repeat what the other party said. When they cannot do this, the mediator repeats what both parties just said. This proves to the disputants that attacking, rather than communicating, is taking place. Now as the conversation continues, the mediator uses message feedback as a model for the parties to follow. Let's see how this works:

KENNETH: I can't believe you dragged us here for this! I've got better things to do with my time than this!

MARY: Right! And what am I supposed to be doing in the meantime? I mean, who's feeding, clothing, and taking care of our kid?

KENNETH: Can she force me to this mediation thing? I'd rather just let the judge settle it. She's going to get it all anyway.

MARY: I knew this would happen.

MEDIATOR: I'd like to try something with you. I'm going to ask Mary first to describe what she wants and then I'll ask you, Kenneth, to do the same thing. Okay?

MARY: Okay.

KENNETH: If we have to.

MEDIATOR: Mary, tell Kenneth in a calm voice what you want from him. Be specific.

MARY: Okay . . . umm . . . Kenneth, I want you to provide child support that's adequate. I want our child to have the benefit of knowing two parents.

KENNETH: Just like I said, she wants everything I have.

MEDIATOR: Kenneth, did she say that?

KENNETH: Not exactly, but that's what she means.

MEDIATOR: Kenneth, try repeating what Mary asked you for.

KENNETH: Mary's mad at me because I don't love her, and she wants to get even.

MEDIATOR: I thought Mary said that she wants adequate child support from you and that she wants your child to benefit from having two parents involved in her life. Kenneth, do you agree?

KENNETH: I guess so.

MEDIATOR: Can you put what Mary said into your own words?

KENNETH: I'll try . . . she, uh, Mary wants for me to pay child support. I think she also said that I can have visitation rights.

MEDIATOR: I agree with the first part of your statement. Do you agree, Mary?

MARY: Yes, but about visitation rights . . .

MEDIATOR: Yes, let's go to that. Kenneth, did Mary say anything about visitation rights?

KENNETH: No, I guess I thought that's what she meant, though, by having me be a part of our child's life.

MEDIATOR: Mary, what did you mean?

MARY: I meant that I would agree to co-parenting with Kenneth as long as he paid child support.

KENNETH: Oh.

By using message feedback, the mediator was able to model for Kenneth and Mary the technique encouraging them to listen to each other well enough to repeat what the other had said. Message feedback is an excellent technique for mediation, or in any type of conflict, because it helps clarify what is happening. It also gives disputing parties some variety in describing and dealing with their differences (Sillars & Wilmot, 1994). When disputing parties know each other, they often confuse knowing each other for a period of time with understanding what the other person is saying.

Message feedback has several advantages (Keltner, 1995). First, it allows the person who originates the message to check on how the message is received. By hearing what the other person thinks you said, you can adjust or modify the message. Second, message feedback also allows receivers to test their listening ability. There is simply no sense in continuing to argue if the two disputing parties hear one message in two different ways. Third, a mediator can introduce message feedback as a model for disputing parties to follow. Done effectively, the technique may be adopted by disputing parties and used in conversations outside the mediation. Thus this technique provides a way to teach others how to paraphrase, reflect, or ask content-related questions.

Working on Problem Solving Once disputants can satisfactorily exchange information, parties can move into a problem-solving mode. When mediation helps disputants move from a competitive stage to a cooperative one, problem solving can begin in earnest (Jones, 1988).

Thus effective mediation has some natural phases (Jones, 1988). First, the mediator helps disputants reestablish effective communication using techniques like message feedback. Then the mediator leads the parties into an information-exchange phase to discuss substantive conflict issues. This agenda-building stage helps disputants agree on what the conflict is about. Third, the mediator helps each side explain their side in the dispute. To achieve resolution, each party's position must be known so a phase is necessary for parties to differentiate their views. Finally, the mediator introduces the parties to problem solving or negotiating behaviors so the disputants can begin discussing potential solutions.

Summary

The word *conflict* generally conjures up negative emotions. However, in our society and in working groups, conflict is a normal part of day-to-day activities. When parties are in conflict, they have mutually exclusive goals. Because the parties are interdependent, all parties cannot have things their way simultaneously. Conflict can be productive for groups by stimulating interest and providing opportunities to evaluate alternatives.

Conflict is inherent in group interactions because different skills, values, and talents of members are needed to complete complex activities and goals. These differences, although necessary, also allow conflict to occur. Effective communication can help groups manage their differences and find solutions to conflict problems.

Conflicts can be over personal issues or substantive issues. They can be cooperative or competitive. Conflicts can occur over judgment or cognitive tasks, over the use of (or lack of) procedures, or over incompatible personalities. Conflicts can arise over differing goals or interests, and they develop when one party evaluates another concerning what should have been done or accomplished.

Conflict is a process that occurs through a sequence of events. First, your awareness of the conflict is developed. Then you have thoughts and emotions about that awareness. Next, you develop your intentions and then move to communicate and behave according to those intentions. Unfortunately, there is generally slippage between these two stages because you cannot fully predict what others will say or do. As a result, you are adjusting your behavior (and what you think about the conflict) while you are interacting with those you oppose. When the talking is done, an outcome or decision has been reached. But besides this outcome, conflict also produces emotional and relational outcomes. This is known as conflict aftermath, and it will affect how you become aware of and how you will interact in the next similar conflict situation.

Conflict between groups is common in our society. We create enemies by talking about our adversaries. We belong to multiple groups and sometimes find ourselves caught in the middle. When our group is in conflict with another, intragroup cohesiveness and commitment build as we distinguish ourselves from the out-group members.

There are three general types of conflict management: integrative, distributive, and avoiding. Collaborating, or problem solving, is an integrative strategy that can produce high quality solutions and decisions for the group. Through discussion, all parties contribute their ideas to find one solution that satisfies everyone's concerns. Distributive conflict management is characterized by a win-lose orientation. In competing, you win and the other party loses. In accommodating, you allow yourself to lose to let the other party win. Avoiding, the third general type of conflict management, is characterized by verbal, physical, and psychological withdrawal from the conflict situation.

Usually, you will select a conflict management strategy that emphasizes your view over others. But as the discussion continues, you are likely to change your strategy. Recognize that the strategy you use will affect how others judge your communication competence. Although each strategy has advantages and disadvantages, most people prefer the integrative strategy of collaborating.

Frequently in conflicts there is symmetry in the choice of conflict management strategies. If one party starts with competing, the other party will compete back. Patterns of symmetry tend to develop in group settings, so it is important to view conflict from a shared goal perspective rather than from your own goal perspective. When you can see the common ground between you and the other parties, you are more likely to try collaborating.

The collaborative conflict management strategy is very much like problem solving discussed in Chapters 8 and 9. Shifting the interaction from a conflict perspective to a problem-solving perspective emphasizes that all group members are in this together, that everyone's input is desired and needed, and that the group, not any individual, is responsible for the decision or solution.

Conflicts can be heightened when cultural differences come into play. Not every culture views conflict or competition in the same way. However, most cultural conflicts involve real differences. The conflicts do not exist simply because members of the group are from different cultures.

You can minimize conflict in your group in two ways. First, you can adopt communication strategies that help emphasize the shared nature of goals. Second, you can increase the communication among conflicting parties. Frequently, when groups are in conflict, communication decreases as members withdraw. If you still need help, you might want to consider a mediator. Mediation is an intervention by an impartial third party who has no authority or decision-making power. The mediator helps conflicting parties talk about their problem in an effective way.

✓ Checklist

Group Knowledge

You should be able to:
- explain the advantages and disadvantages of group conflict.
- identify types and sources of conflict.
- describe how conflict episodes start and affect group member interactions.
- explain the importance of conflict aftermath.
- describe the five conflict management strategies.
- explain how conflict and problem solving can be integrated.
- explain why cultural differences and conflict are not synonymous.
- explain the value of mediation and message feedback.

Group Skills

You should be able to:
- help your group view conflict as a natural part of the group process.
- identify potential sources of group conflict.
- use communication strategies to manage conflict in your group.
- favorably influence the outcomes of intergroup conflicts.
- avoid or respond to nonproductive conflict management strategies.
- help your group move from conflict management toward problem solving.
- develop your mediation skills.

Analytical and Assessment Techniques

You should be able to:
- address the role of conflict in our society in a positive or productive manner.
- analyze how you perceive a conflict to better manage group interactions.
- view conflict from other group members' points of view.
- determine potential conflicting points between groups.
- tell when symmetrical or asymmetrical patterns of conflict management are positive or negative.
- integrate the assumptions between the collaborative strategy of conflict management and group problem solving.
- assess cultural differences for their potential to cause group conflict.
- identify when mediation is needed.

Discussion Questions and Exercises

1. Most television shows revolve around conflict—even situation comedies. As you watch television this week, make a list of the conflicts you see and note how the conflicts are managed. What conflict management strategies did characters use? What conflict management strategies should they have used?

2. Keep a journal for one week of your conflicts. Describe and analyze the following characteristics of each conflict: Who was involved in the conflict? When did you become aware that you were involved in the conflict? What were your intentions about the conflict? How did you communicate with the other person(s)? Did your plan for managing the conflict change as you communicated with the other person(s)? How long did the conflict last? What was the outcome of the conflict?

3. You probably can remember at least one conflict that did not turn out as you expected or wished. Think back to that conflict and how you communicated during that interaction. Was your conflict substantive or affective? What part did emotion play in this conflict? Who was most emotional—you or other group members? Now that you have had a chance to think about and reflect on that interaction, how do you wish you would have communicated? Write down what you should have said. How can you avoid an overemotional reaction in conflicts like this in the future?

PART 3

Developing and Facilitating Your Group

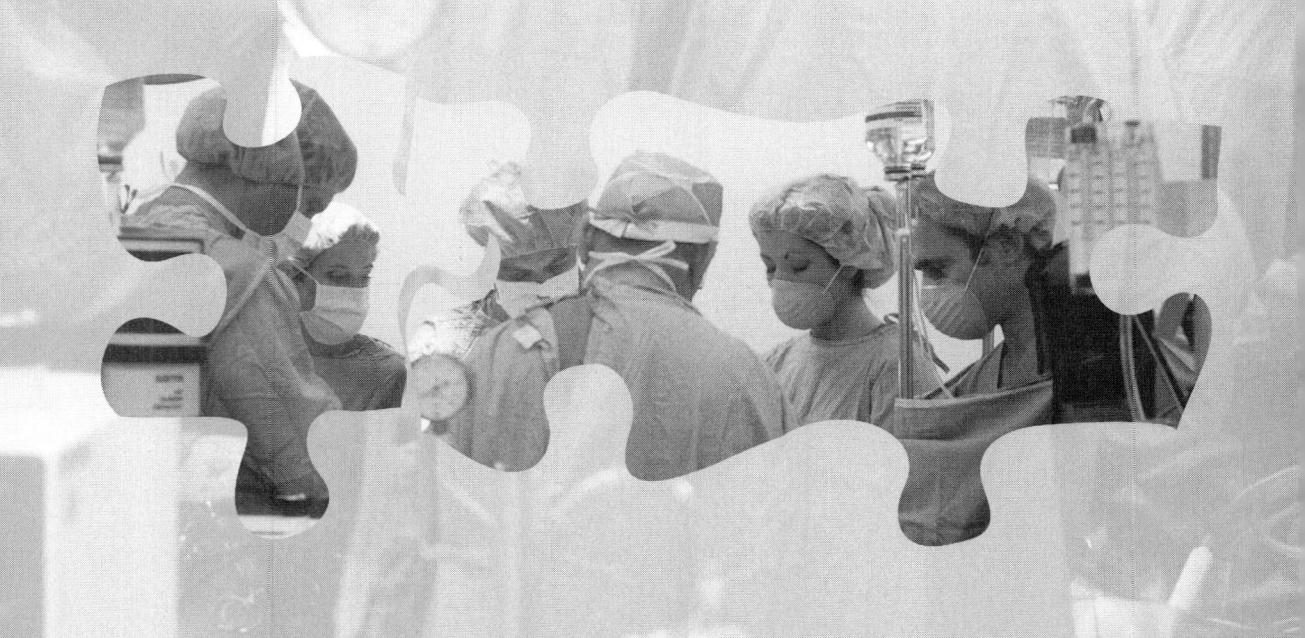

12 Group Development and Evolution

Why do some groups develop differently than others?

How does group member selection affect group development?

How do I determine which stage of development our group is in?

How should a group manage member turnover?

What should we do at the conclusion of the group's activities besides just end the group?

Why do some groups taper off whereas others end abruptly?

Once you have mastered the basic principles of group interaction (decision making, leadership, and conflict management), it is time to turn your attention to issues of group development and evolution. Groups are not alike in this regard. Groups form, members come together and accomplish some tasks or activities, and then groups end. The life cycle of each group is unique. To some extent, you can manage a group's life cycle positively if you are aware of the influences member selection has on your group and if you can identify which stage your group is currently in. Both issues are addressed in this chapter.

The Origins of This Group

Some groups form deliberately; others form through spontaneous interaction (Cartwright & Zander, 1968a). When groups form deliberately (for example, work groups), someone decides that a collection of individuals can effectively accomplish a purpose or goal. Often it is the assumption that a group must be formed because it would be impossible for fewer people to accomplish the goal. Most problem-solving or decision-making groups (such as city councils) and social action groups (for instance, Mothers Against Drunk Driving) are examples of deliberately formed groups.

Some groups are formed spontaneously. Generally, individuals come together in these groups because of the satisfaction they expect to gain from associating with one another. A group of friends at work is a good example of a spontaneous group. In these cases, group membership is by mutual consent—each member wants to be in the group and each is accepted as a group member. Proximity and frequency of interaction are required for these individuals to become acquainted and to develop into a group. Thus group membership is based on attraction. In comparison, members of a deliberately formed group may only meet occasionally. Their assignment or selection to the group, or their desire to be associated with a certain group, establishes their membership.

Group Member Selection

How one identifies individuals for group membership depends on whether the group is deliberately or spontaneously formed. If a group is deliberately formed, group member selection is key to the success of the group. In initial selection or in member replacement, groups should generally look for individuals who possess two types of competencies: (1) technical skills and ability and (2) the personal characteristics necessary to work well with others (Larson & LaFasto 1989). Technical requirements are those knowledge, skills, and abilities group members need to perform the activities of the group. Personal or relational characteristics are the personal qualities or skills and abilities people need to work well in a group environment. For example, a group of activists (for example, NOW) needs members with the technical skills of recruiting new volunteers and seeking and obtaining funding. Members also need the relational skills of motivating members to continue to work on behalf of the organization and the ability to create a supportive environment for members. The challenge is to find the appropriate balance between the two sets of skills. The balance will vary depending on the type of group or its activities and goals.

A group deliberately formed for a short period of intense work on a complex project may prefer members with a balance favoring technical skills over relational skills. For example, the technical skills needed in the team of doctors, nurses, and medical technicians delivering sextuplets are more important to the success of the group's task than how well team members get along. The team is together for a very short period of time and then disbands. Roles and responsibilities within the team are highly defined, which helps the team in the absence of well-developed personal relationships. On the other hand, a team that expects to stay together for a long period of time may initially favor a balance toward personal and relational skills. This is because over time, group members can help one another increase their technical proficiency if the relationships among group members are strong and well developed. For example, a multifunction project team representing different aspects of a food manufacturer are given the assignment to develop prototypes for new market initiatives. Representing manufacturing, marketing, quality control, and food sourcing, the new product development team is given a 6-month time frame for developing at least four products for consumer testing. If members possess the ability to work well with one another, they can also rely on one another to help fill in the technical expertise they may lack as individuals. Jerry, the representative from manufacturing, knows very little about marketing. Initially he relies heavily on Shanita's marketing expertise. Jerry asks Shanita lots of questions, requests marketing reports to read, and talks with her over lunch about marketing initiatives that have worked for other products. As the team works on product

The balance of relational and technical skills needed in a group will depend on the type of group task and how long group members expect to be together.

development, Jerry learns enough about marketing from Shanita to give informed opinions and ask appropriate questions. This process is enhanced because Jerry finds it easy to approach Shanita, and Shanita likes Jerry's willingness to learn about marketing.

A spontaneously formed group is likely to favor relational over task skills. Because group membership is based primarily on personal attraction to one another, relational skills are more important. If group members cannot get along and form a cohesive group, attraction will decrease and members will leave the group voluntarily. This does not mean that task proficiency is not important. Rea's golf foursome started over lunch when the four women discovered their common hesitancy in taking golf lessons. The decision to first take lessons together and then practice together one day a week was a natural outgrowth of the women liking one another; forming the group was not based on anyone's technical skill in playing golf. As the group completes its lessons and starts to practice at the golf course, members become confident enough to give one another friendly advice about club selection, teeing up, and reading the green. If one member starts to consistently give poor advice or advice that detracts from one member's ability to achieve par, this member's technical skill or motivation is questioned and may in fact disturb the relational balance of the group.

Regardless of how group members come together, the fit among group members is important. Each group determines what constitutes fit. A group of friends may decide their fit by assessing the extent to which they enjoy doing the same types of activities. It is unlikely that a group of friends will remain as friends if one member wants to go to the movies, one member wants to visit historical sites, one member wants to party on the town all night, and one member enjoys playing bridge. A group of friends could also determine fit by assessing the extent to which members are comfortable with how often they are called on the phone or visited by one another. Many family groups would use this aspect of fit in determining which members of the extended family are inside or outside the family group. A task group may determine its fit by how well group members' knowledge and expertise cover the task requirements. A business group that needs someone knowledgeable in profit and loss statements has not achieved its fit, regardless of how well group members work together, if not one among them has this specific knowledge.

Group Startup

However a group or team comes together, its initial interactions have an enduring effect on the group (Hackman, 1990). Thus it is essential that a group get off to a good start. If the initial meetings are effective, the group has established a solid base on which to draw if it meets a crisis. If the initial meetings are ineffective, group members may not be able to draw on the resources of the group to survive a crisis later on. Thus a group's startup should include time for establishing its boundaries and identity. The group needs to define its tasks and decide on the level of interdependence needed. Group members need to feel both accountable to and responsible for the group. This happens when group members are involved in the group's process as well as the group's task. Thus taking time to create a supportive group environment will help the group develop a self-fueling positive spiral.

Another factor affecting group startup is the degree to which group members bring expectations and norms with them from their other group experiences. When individuals come together as a group, they step into a preexisting "shell" (Ginnett, 1990). This means that the roles of group members are predefined or that the roles carry certain expectations about what one is to do in a role. In some groups, the roles of the group remain constant even though different individuals could, and do, fulfill those positions. For example, a flight crew is composed of the captain, the first officer, the engineer, and the flight attendant staff. These roles are fixed; individual airline employees rotate in and out of these roles on a daily, even hourly, basis. Who selects the group members of a flight crew? A personnel director for the airline does, and these selections are made on individuals' schedule availability and ability to perform certain skills. This type of member selection is common for groups whose activities are highly routinized (such as nursing units, police units). Regardless of the group to which you are assigned, you can expect the routine to be much the same from group to group.

How, then, can a flight crew develop into a team so quickly? Not only does a shell for the group exist, but a shell for each individual role in the group also exists. Thus, captains know how to act like captains and how captains should interact with

During group startup, group members need to define themselves as a group by identifying their roles, norms, and values. Group members bring ideas for roles, norms, and values from their previous group experiences. But these cannot be directly imported into the new group. Rather, group members must negotiate these for this group.

other flight crew members. Likewise, other members of the flight crew know the specific job responsibilities of their positions and how those positions are supposed to interact together. Will these expectations about group performance necessarily create an effective team? No, but the role expectations do provide a blueprint for how the group should interact, which allows group members to come together quickly.

Group Member Assimilation

When a deliberately formed group is new, or when several new members are added to an existing group, it is useful to take some time to welcome these individuals to the group. If you are the new member, there are many ways to introduce yourself to other group members. If you get there early, you can greet the other members when they arrive. If you are apprehensive about walking into a group of strangers, this can be an especially effective strategy in reducing your anxiety. Always be sure to introduce yourself to anyone you do not know well. When you do this, you help establish a friendly and supportive climate and create an openness to which others will respond.

One way to get to know others in the group is to sit next to someone you do not know at all or you do not know well. You can start a conversation by bringing up an easy topic (weekend activities, hobbies, how long you have worked for this organization). The objective here is create an opportunity for interaction that will help you get to know the other person. But the topic of conversation must not be threatening or invading. In fact, if you ask a stranger if they have met their quarterly goals, you will be perceived as creating distance rather than closeness in the relationship.

> **PUTTING THE PIECES TOGETHER**
>
> *Group Structure, Group Identity, and Interdependence*
>
> Can you remember how your group of friends started? On what was your friendship based? Who approached who? How did the group add new friends? How was the group structured? Did one friend take on the role of calling others? Did one friend come up with ideas for what you would do together? How do you believe your group of friends would identify themselves? Would others outside the group agree that you were a group of friends? To what extent were individuals in this group interdependent? How could you observe or explain this interdependence to others?

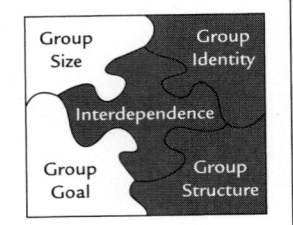

During a meeting, you can assimilate new group members by asking them to comment on what the group is talking about ("Mary, what do you think of this plan?"). This is especially important if new members are brought into an existing group. They may believe that their opinions are not welcomed because they have little or no history with the group. Of course, bringing food or other snacks to a meeting generally helps to decrease tension. *Putting the Pieces Together* will help you recall how some of your groups got started.

Group Development

Throughout this book, we have emphasized the dynamic nature of groups and teams. The behavior of individual group members as well as the performance of the group will vary depending on many characteristics. This is the reason the textbook emphasizes an analytical approach to understanding group process. Earlier, we said that no two groups were alike. Not only are groups not alike, but it is unlikely that any two groups would develop in exactly the same way. Group development examines how groups develop over time. In assessing group development, we should consider two factors: a group's history and a group's level of maturity (Mennecke, Hoffer, & Wynne, 1992). A group's history is based on how much time it is has spent together as well as the quality of its interactions. What group members have shared or not shared impacts a group's development. We also must consider the degree of cohesiveness that reflects the group's maturity. A group that worked well together in the past is more likely to work well together in the future. A group with some successes and some failures may find it more difficult to succeed in the future.

In this chapter, our focus is on looking at a group as a process over time. In one sense, you could think of a group as similar to shooting a movie. First the director and producer conceptualize what the film is going to be about and how it will be shot and edited. But during production, things happen that change the direction or dialogue of the film. The director finds that the leading man can create jokes on the spot, which actually adds to the humor of the dialogue. The director starts to use his quips and insights, inserting them for scripted dialogue. After shooting the film, the director realizes that he did not get quite the scene he visualized. Rather than capturing the two young lovers against a picturebook sunset, they are framed on the film by rolling clouds and birds in the distance. Now he must make other changes to accommodate using this footage and make it vital to the continuation of the storyline. Although the director and producer had an idea of what was going to happen while shooting the film and how these events would play out as they viewed the footage, they could not predict exactly what would happen.

Likewise, every group you are in has its own life and destiny. Even though you may know in advance what group members want to accomplish, you are only one member of the group with input to the group process. There is no way for you to be absolutely certain of what will happen or for you to be in absolute control of how the group will develop. Thinking of a group as a movie—a process—is preferable to viewing the group as a snapshot—something you can capture and hold in time. Certainly, you could take hundreds of snapshots over the course of the group, but even piecing those pictures together would not give you the processes that unfold in a group over time.

We will explore two ways of looking at group development. First we will examine stages of group development, which is the perspective that groups develop along a progression of stages. Then we will examine an opposing view of progressive group development, which is the multiple-sequence perspective.

Stages of Group Development

According to this perspective of group development, groups are a systemic entity and, as such, have a life cycle complete with a beginning, a middle, and an end. Many researchers believe that groups develop through five stages or phases (Tuckman, 1965; Tuckman & Jensen, 1977; Wheelan & Hochberger, 1996; Wheelan & Kaeser, 1997). Communication within the group during these phases is distinct (Moosbruker, 1988; Wellins, Byham, & Wilson, 1991). Let's look at each of the stages: forming, storming, norming, performing, and termination.

Forming When the group first becomes a group, issues of inclusion and dependency are explored. Members ask themselves, "Will I be accepted by others in the group?" and "What will I have to do in this group?" Often, group members express anxiety because they are unsure about their roles in this particular group or have concerns about how well the group will function. Because group members are focusing on "I" questions instead of "we" questions, a group has not really become a group yet. This first phase of group development is called **forming**. In this phase almost all comments are directed toward the formal leader or the person group members perceive will become leader. Members include comments that provide cues to their identity and status outside of the group because the connection to the group is not strong. There is little basis for trust at this stage because most members take a wait-and-see attitude. Most of the time, the discussion is superficial because the issues are tentatively addressed until members discover where others stand. Little effective listening is occurring as group members are trying to establish who they are and what they will agree to do in this group. As you can see, in this stage the group is new and the group's process is new and unfamiliar. Thus individuals may actually be confused as they try to frame this new group in the experiences of their previous groups. Let's see how one student project group working on recommendations for a revised professor evaluation system interacted in this phase:

CYD: Okay, I'm ready to get started. What do you want me to do?

PEARL: I want to work on the questions on the form. Is that okay?

TAL: (says nothing, looks down to avoid eye contact with others)

DARCY: If no one wants to be leader, I could . . .

CYD: Have you been leader of a group like this before? I haven't.

DARCY: Yes, I know what we need to do. I'm the president of the Student Honors Association and I'm vice-president of the Panhellenic Council. Anybody else want to be leader?

PEARL: Can I work with somebody on something since I'm new to campus?

CYD: I could introduce you around to my friends in my sorority.

PEARL: Thanks, let's talk after class; I belonged to Delta Delta Delta at my other university, but there's not a chapter here on this campus.

DARCY: Tal, do you have anything to say?

TAL: I've got another class after this one—a test; I need to study.

DARCY: (ignores his comment and continues) I suggest we brainstorm a list of issues that need discussion and then let's divide up the work before today's session is over. Agreed?

PEARL: What about the timeframe for delivering results back to the students? Don't you think students should get feedback on how well the professors are doing?

DARCY: Okay, that's two issues: questions and time frame for feedback. Anything else?

TAL: (sits reading his chemistry textbook)

This group is in the initial stages of forming. Little trust is being demonstrated toward others in the group. Most comments are self-oriented, not group-oriented. Very quickly the group allowed Darcy to take on the leadership role. From that point on, she dominated the conversation without including the less talkative Tal.

Certainly, this group is moving in uncharted territory; they have not developed a sense of "we-ness" to any extent. And at this point, there is no strong consensus about the group's task or how it will proceed.

What can help groups move through this first stage? One way to help the group find its purpose is to ask the group to write its charter or mission statement (see Chapter 13). By identifying its purpose, group members will get to know one another while building commitment toward a larger unifying goal (Wellins, Byham, & Wilson, 1991). Once a group can identify its goal, it can be helpful to develop an implementation plan—a roadmap—of how the group will get where it's going. Although the group may not be able to identify all of the specifics or the associated timeframes at this point, developing something like a PERT chart (see Chapter 9) will give the group an idea of how it can accomplish its goals.

Group members can help their group move through this stage of the group's development in the following ways (Wellins, Byham, & Wilson, 1991). First, group members should increase their one-to-one communication with one another. Everyone should get to know other group members and be able to identify them by name. If you sense conflict with other group members—especially conflict in reaction to the ambiguity of the group's task—recognize that all group members will feel some tension during this stage. Try to relax, use a calm voice, and attempt to view activities from others' points of view. Participate in group meetings so other members can get to know you. Sitting back and taking it all in will only increase the tension in this development stage.

Storming The second phase is typically a period of conflict or of **storming**. Now in the group members are asserting their individual preferences; thus conflict occurs as part of the group's natural development. As individuals bring their talents, skills, and knowledge to the group, group members may find themselves competing with one another for roles and for attention from other group members. In this phase, group members will also struggle over issues of status and power. Members may also feel individual conflict because they are being asked to handle tasks or activities that are new to them. They may also feel time pressures as they try to fit these new activities into their schedule.

Generally, participation by all members is high in this phase. As a result, conflicts arise, which further encourages members to use assertive and dominant styles. As group members express their positions on issues, subgroups and coalitions begin to form. As a result, allegiances and commitment are stronger toward the subgroups than toward the group as a whole. This can dampen the cohesiveness of the group. Because of the natural outbreak of conflict in this stage, group members must pay attention to their conflict management skills. If a group cannot learn to manage its stresses in this stage, it is unlikely to manage them well later on. Let's take a look at the professor evaluation group now:

DARCY: Okay, you presented your viewpoint, Pearl. Let's move on!

TAL: I don't think I can agree with Pearl.

DARCY: No one can, Tal. Let's move on!

CYD: What about the questions? Has anyone looked at the questions I've developed?

DARCY: We can't deal with the questions just now, Cyd. We've got to figure out the time frame for reporting results back to professors.

TAL: Professors should get their own results first.

PEARL: Why can't they go to the library and look them up like students have to do?

TAL: That's humiliating. Would you want to do that if you were a professor?

PEARL: I wouldn't mind.

TAL: I'm telling you they'll mind and turn down our proposal altogether!

DARCY: Ladies! Gentleman! I'm going to make an executive decision here. Let's table all evaluative comments until we can agree on a time line.

CYD: You know, Darcy, you're not always right.

DARCY: But right enough to move us along. Okay, let's draw the time line on the board . . .

This group is definitely storming. There is conflict over what task deserves the most attention, and there is conflict over Darcy's portrayal of the leadership role. Members are not listening because they are too focused on competing with one another. And, still, it is not clear that all members would agree that they are working on the same task.

What can help a group through the storming stage? There are both group and individual strategies that can help stabilize a group during this stage (Wellins, Byham, & Wilson, 1991). To maintain group unity in light of the conflicts that arise during this stage, group members should review their charter or goal statements. Knowing that there is an ultimate outcome or goal can help members more productively manage their conflict. At each meeting, the group should review its performance as compared to its implementation plan developed in the first stage. Storming can also be a stage of learning because when conflicts arise, group members learn more about individual opinions and positions. Group members should try to manage their conflict through problem-solving strategies (see Chapter 11). Getting members to agree to meeting management procedures (Chapter 13) and helping group members see the value of feedback and observation (Chapter 14) can help a group overcome problems encountered in this stage. In the storming stage, individual group members should become accomplished at leading and participating in meetings as well as at supporting other members in their group roles. Doing so provides integration with other members and can decrease conflicts. Because many ideas will surface in this stage of group development, members should be open to diversity—valuing differences rather than rejecting them. Faith and patience are the keys to moving through storming to the third phase, norming.

Norming Once the conflicting issues are resolved, the group enters the third phase—**norming**—the phase in which trust is developed and acceptance occurs. Now knowing their roles and how the group will proceed with its activity, group members can openly negotiate differences while maintaining positive social relationships. The conflicts and diversity the group struggled with in the storming phase are now integrated effectively into the group. Group members feel like "we're all in this together" (Wellins, Byham, & Wilson, 1991). The group's communication structure becomes more flexible. Members are likely to report high levels of satisfaction, cooperation, and commitment to the group. Group members are able to laugh together (Moosbruker, 1988). "We" is used more frequently than "I." Let's see how our group has made the transition from storming to norming:

TAL: We've got a plan now. Good!

DARCY: Okay, let's review. We've decided on the time frame for returning feedback to professors and students. Cyd, tell us about how the revisions to the questions are coming along.

CYD: Well, of the thirty questions, we've made changes to about half. It really helped putting the questions on everyone's e-mail and having you send your comments back. That way I could synthesize everyone's ideas. I'll have a final version to show you next meeting. I'm meeting with the president of the Faculty Senate to get her input before I finish it all up. She said she would be glad to meet with us.

DARCY: Pearl, with the time line done, what's the next task you want to take on?

PEARL: As I review our original plan, there's only the computer coding to consider. I'd be happy to go see the analyst in Information Systems to discuss what we'd need.

DARCY: Thanks, Pearl. That would be great.

TAL: Can I help you, Pearl?

PEARL: How about meeting with me after I go to Information Systems? At that point I'll need some help figuring out how to meet their guidelines.

TAL: Sure!

This certainly is a different group now. Personal and task conflicts are minimized and the group seems to be working effectively toward one goal that all members agree on. Members appear to be integrating their tasks and are open to sharing information with one another. If it continues with this type of communication, the group will likely finish its project on schedule and be proud of its accomplishment.

But caution should be exercised at this stage. Just because the group is more cohesive at this stage does not mean that the group can ignore its processes. Groups can become myopic, or their vision can narrow, during this stage. Because the group is working well, it can become vulnerable to making wrong choices.

Procedures that seemed overwhelming in the beginning may now help the group be more productive (for example, using the standard agenda for decision making). This is also a good stage to introduce or continue feedback and observation. Now that the group is working well together, group members will be able to use feedback information to make it work even better.

Performing The fourth phase—**performing**—is where the task activity of the group is accomplished. Now that both procedures and relationships have been developed and are stable, there is clarity and agreement on the group's goals. It is during this phase that the group works on its task or activity. Problem solving or decision making is more easily accomplished because open discussion is promoted and supported, and group members have expectations that they will be successful as a group. Trust among group members is at its highest level. During this performance stage, group members are so tightly integrated with the team that they find it difficult to distinguish themselves from the group. How does our group communicate now?

> DARCY: Pearl, will you help Cyd proofread our report one more time? Thanks.
>
> TAL: I've got to paste in these graphics and then we're ready to print.
>
> PEARL: When you get done, Tal, let me know, and I'll look over that as well.
>
> TAL: Sure.
>
> CYD: Oh, problem here. Look at page 14. Is this a mistake in the sentence or a mistake in our logic?
>
> DARCY: Pearl, you worked on this part with Tal. You two take a look at it.
>
> PEARL: (after conferring with Tal) No, just a problem in our grammar. The computer logic is fine. I think we wrote this section fairly fast. Must be our mistake. But, we can fix it.
>
> TAL: Okay, let me know when you're ready to print that page again. We're about ready to put this project to bed.

Our group has settled into effective role sharing in the performing stage. Trust is high, and the likelihood that anyone would be blamed for the grammatical mistake is quite low. This group is now successful (and satisfied with) using open discussion and problem solving.

How can a group maintain this stage? Groups that want to stay together and take on new activities must actively work to maintain the positive characteristics and attributes found in this stage (Wellins, Byham, & Wilson, 1991). By now, the group should be regularly involved in feedback and observation, rotating this responsibility among members.

Termination Finally, the group reaches its ending point or point of adjournment or **termination**. Most groups have a specific ending point or a point at which members are removed or remove themselves from the group. Some groups find it a relief that their tasks are finished. But this stage can also create anxiety for group members as they become unsure about their future participation on this task or with these members.

Different types of groups have different types of endings. Some groups are formed for a specific purpose and terminate when the project or task is completed. For example, your friends joined together as a softball team in a summer league. When the softball season is over, the team is finished. On the other hand, your group of friends from high school who did everything together probably dissolved over time as one member after the next left for college, the military, or to work full-time. The ending to this group was gradual and not planned in advance.

When groups end, it is typical for members to have emotional reactions to the group's finish. Some members may have enjoyed the group experience so much that they do not want the group to end. Thus they feel happiness and pleasure at having a good group experience, but they also feel sadness and loss that the group is finally over (Rose, 1989). This type of group member may try to involve other group members in another group. When group members have had less positive experiences, they may be glad the group is over and demonstrate this emotion by distancing themselves as completely and as quickly as possible from the group activity and other group members.

Groups that are part of a larger organizational structure (your softball team plays in the same league each year; your project team at work) need to pay attention to how the group dissolves or terminates (Keyton, 1993). The interaction climate during the period of dissolution will affect the willingness and motivation of individuals when it comes time for the team to regroup or renew its activities or when group members are once again asked to be a member of a team.

Groups that plan to work together again should review and summarize what the group accomplished, review and evaluate the effectiveness of procedures used for the task activity and group discussion, and assess the quality of relationships developed within the group. Additionally, differences and conflicts that were not fully resolved during the group's interaction should be addressed and finalized. In taking these steps, groups learn lessons about past group performance. In addition, the identities of individuals within the group are strengthened. This helps members maintain a connection to the group even when the group is inactive. Encouraging members to recognize the ending of the group and giving them opportunities to say goodbye to one another reinforces and recognizes the existence of the team (Adato, 1975).

Celebrating success is an excellent way to solidify the individual's connection to the group even though the group is done with its activities. Many groups conclude their work in a frantic or harried fashion, devoting little time to relationships or to individual or group reflection. Setting aside a time to celebrate helps group members bring closure to the group activity while strengthening group relationships. Sports teams often celebrate the end of the season with a banquet or picnic. This is a good time to review highlights of the season (such as beating the Wildcats, your team's perennial foe). It is also a good time to thank people who helped support the group's activities. Awards can be given to recognize the best performances.

Work groups usually are less formal about their conclusions. Some will celebrate the ending with a special meal in a favorite restaurant. Groups should be encouraged to formally recognize this ending stage. It gives members an opportunity to make sense of their experiences, to compare mental histories, and to relive stories. Work groups or other groups connected to larger organizations (the new building task force at your church) need to address substantive issues as well as symbolic ones in the termination stage (Keyton, 1993). The group should review what was accomplished and assess those accomplishments against their original objectives or goals. In these situations, group members generally prepare a formal report. The group also needs to decide who will be responsible for further inquiries about the group's outcome after the group is dissolved.

Progressing Through the Stages

When the stage progression model of groups was first introduced, it was assumed that all groups developed through each stage in similar fashion. However, that assumption has been challenged (Cissna, 1984). Today, we can use the stage progression model to examine how groups develop without assuming that all groups develop the same way. Some groups move steadily through each phase of group development, but this does not mean that a group will spend equal time in each phase. The degree to which group members know one another before this group opportunity and members' level of task familiarity affect how long a group stays in each phase. For example, a group composed of members who do not know one another are likely to spend considerable time in the first three phases as the group works out the structure of their group. This is frequently the case with your classroom groups. You must spend time getting to know one another before you can work effectively on the assigned task. On the other hand, individuals who find themselves frequently together in groups will import their previous experiences with one another into a new group and move quickly through the first three phases, getting to the performing stage earlier.

Other groups move through the phase cycle for each activity and then recycle themselves through the phases for each subsequent task. This is particularly true of groups with stable membership that are given different types of tasks over long periods of time. Group membership does not change, but the type of task presented to or generated by the group creates new challenges to which the group must adapt its roles, structure, and relationships. A group responsible for the startup of an organization is an example of a group with stable membership and a wide variety of tasks. To create The City Zoo, a store that sells gifts for pet owners and animal lovers, the management group had to design the layout of the store, select and order merchandise, create its marketing plan, interview and hire employees, stock the store, and operate it. These tasks are varied in their complexity and difficulty and draw differently upon group members' talents, skills, and knowledge. Thus the group found itself repeating the group development cycle as it encountered these different activities.

Groups can slip backward instead of progressing forward through the stages (Wellins, Byham, & Wilson, 1991). Why does this occur? Sometimes groups acquire new members, and this causes the group to revisit the forming and storming phases until the new member is integrated into the group. A team's progression can also be upset by a trauma or another critical event. If the event is significant enough to cause emotional upheaval among group members, the group may find itself back in the storming stage. This is likely to happen if the trauma upsets or makes useless what the group had accomplished. Now, once again, the group has to move through conflict to refocus on their goal. Finally, groups can move backward in the stages if group members fail to pay attention to issues of group development. Length of time together does not ensure steady progression through the stages of group development Try the *Group Assessment Technique* to discover how far your group has developed.

Multiple-Sequence Views of Group Development

An alternative view of group development argues that groups develop in different ways on different issues. From this multiple-sequence perspective, the phases a group finds itself in are generated by factors within the group itself. We will examine two in this chapter: the contingency model and the punctuated equilibrium model.

The Contingency Model The contingency model suggests that rather than following a set pattern of phases or stages, a group develops in a series of interlocking threads over time (Poole, 1983). One thread focuses on task activities, another thread on relationships among group members, and the final thread on the topics of the group's conversation. When groups develop all three threads or tracks, the group may actually seem to be progressing as if moving through the forming, storming, norming, performing, and termination stages. But other progression patterns can occur as well. A group could make great progress on one track, adequate progress on another, yet fail to make any forward movement on the third. This model presents group development as progression through a series of breakpoints.

A **breakpoint** is a discontinuity in the group's interaction, and it represents transitional periods for the group. A breakpoint can be normal, like scheduled meeting adjournments or obvious shifts in topics of conversation (moving from talking about the budget to talking about which contractor does the highest quality work). Or a breakpoint can be an adaptation or reflection. This means that the group cycles back to revisit work or issues previously discussed. For example, no matter how hard group members try, a conversation develops in each budget meeting about the limited funds with which the group has to work. Doubling back to this conversation topic is a reflection as group members once again try to figure

> **GROUP ASSESSMENT TECHNIQUE**
>
> ## How Far Has Your Group Developed?
>
> Circle the numbers of the statements that best describe the current activity of your group.
>
> 1. We keep asking what we are doing and why.
> 2. Team members do not know one another.
> 3. We are unclear about what we are supposed to do.
> 4. We are having trouble getting along.
> 5. Members are jockeying for power.
> 6. We disagree about how to proceed.
> 7. We are seeing the progress of our work.
> 8. Team members are open and honest in asking questions and giving feedback.
> 9. As we get to know one another better, we are working more smoothly together.
> 10. We feel pride in our accomplishments.
> 11. We are really "cookin'."
> 12. We all do what it takes to get the job done.
>
> If most of your circles are for items 1 through 3, then your group is forming. If most of your circles are for items 4 through 6, then your group is storming. If most of your circles are for items 7 through 9, then your group is norming. If most of your circles are for items 10 through 12, then your group is performing.
>
> *Source:* Adapted from Gardenswartz and Rowe (1994).

out how to get more money. Another type of breakpoint is a disruption. This occurs when the group encounters a major conflict or fails at one of its intermediate goals. For example, the U.S. Olympic baseball team suffered a disruption breakpoint when it failed to win one of its medal-round games. Thus the group's goal of winning the gold medal was thwarted.

Recognizing and dealing with breakpoints are essential for a group to continue its development as a group. If the baseball team failed to learn from its medal-round loss, it would affect the team in its post-Olympic play. The inability of the budget team to move toward how to most effectively spend its fund rather than argue about why its budget is so limited will certainly affect the effectiveness of this group.

The Punctuated Equilibrium Model The punctuated equilibrium model (Gersick, 1988, 1989, 1990; Gersick & Hackman, 1990) argues that group development is characterized by periods of stable or habitual routines that are abruptly disrupted about halfway by a transitional period. According to this model, group members

Most group members are unaware of how much time they spend together as a group. Yet, you have probably experienced the dramatic transitional period when you and other group members realize that time has gone by and that you are not working on the group's activity or task.

interact according to an internal group clock based upon how long group members expect to be together. When the group approaches the midpoint of its existence, it gears up for action and makes abrupt changes in behavior and focus. This dramatic change occurs in the transition period sandwiched between periods of routine behavior. Patterns of behavior adopted in the first half of the group disappear, and the group searches for new ways of working together to accomplish their tasks. Once a group adapts to the transition, it once again finds a routine way of performing.

In its initial routine period, it is unlikely that the group makes any significant progress because group members have difficulty finding an effective way of dealing

> **? THINK ABOUT IT**
>
> *Identifying Group Breakpoints and Transitions*
>
> Think about the group on which you are most dependent right now. This may be a group of friends, another social group, a sports group, or a work group. Think back to recent events in the group. Can you identify a breakpoint in the group's development? Was there some event that now defines the group, that recast the group in a different light, or that had a significant impact on group membership or group activities? How did group members handle the breakpoint? Did they see the breakpoint as a challenge and move ahead positively? Did group members perceive the breakpoint negatively or fail to acknowledge the change at all? Do you think this breakpoint represents a midway point in the group? Why or why not?

with their task. The midpoint transition acts like an alarm clock and creates a shift in how group members approach their work, enabling them finally to make advances on their tasks. Typically, a group experiences only one transition in its life cycle together. So if the group does not make good use of the transition, it misses the opportunity to positively alter the course of its interaction.

This model suggests that groups pace themselves and that group activity changes dramatically when the group senses its time together is nearly done. You have probably noticed this phenomenon in classroom groups. You and the other group members spend time initially getting to know one another or talking about social topics. This is the first habitual or routine phase. Then someone glances at their watch and sees that you have only 30 minutes left in your hour-long assignment. This is the dramatic transition phase. With that recognition, the group changes gears to work on its task, but again settles into another, and hopefully more effective, routine for doing just that. Thus your group's interaction was punctuated by a transition phase that led you out of and then into a period of routine behavior.

Why do groups do this? One explanation is that group members have a tendency to maintain an interaction style until they are forced to alter their practices. Usually this alteration occurs because of some dramatic or critical event: For example, the group's goal is changed by information introduced by an external agent—your work group thought it was supposed to be considering applicants for an administrative secretary position and then the boss announces that the position was downgraded to that of a clerical assistant. Too frequently, groups become entrenched in habitual behavior that is ineffective or dysfunctional. Group members are unable or unwilling to challenge the status quo. After the group is challenged in its transition phase, it attempts to reengage using different behaviors, but now the group has limited time in which to complete its activities. Try the *Think About It* box to test your recognition of group breakpoints and transitions.

Membership Changes In Groups

The theories of group development assume that group membership is fairly stable, that most group members remain in the group throughout the group's history. But this is not always the case. Some groups, like nursing units in hospitals, have high turnover. As a result, group members may face ambiguity adjusting to new personalities and to changes in how members take on roles in the group. Sometimes membership changes are temporary, as when a nurse takes a 2-week vacation and is replaced by a nurse who floats among assignments at the hospital. At other times, membership changes are permanent. Members may leave the group when they quit or retire from the organization, or members may be transferred to other units. Also, members may simply grow tired of the group and drop out. Each of these membership changes are member-initiated.

Membership change in groups can be critical because a change in the composition of the group also changes the cluster of knowledge, skills, and abilities within the group (McGrath, Berdahl, & Arrow, 1995). Let's explore some of the issues surrounding membership change to assess its impact on groups (Arrow & McGrath, 1993). First, when membership change increases or decreases the number of members in the group, other aspects of the group must change as well. Kara's honors study group meets with her honors advisor to work on a research project. For over a year, the group—the professor and four students—has met in the professor's office. After much discussion about the necessity of adding other students, the group decides that adding one more student would help in sharing the workload of running the experiments. Unfortunately, the group does not think ahead to how an additional group member will affect the group's meetings. The professor's office is crowded with stacks of books and computer printouts. There is a couch that can only hold three people, a chair, and the professor's chair. When the group with its new member gather to meet for the first time, someone has to sit on the floor. This seating arrangement creates awkward dynamics among group members and impedes the group's ability to work together on coding data. Certainly, the group could move to a new meeting location, but that would cause another disruption in the group. Although adding a member seems to be a gain for the group because it will lighten the workload, it also creates an unexpected consequence.

Second, it is important to know why there is a change in group membership. Group members react differently to situations in which membership change is member-initiated versus controlled by someone outside the group. You are more likely to accept a new member who persuades you to let her join than a member who joins because your boss says she must. Sometimes groups actually expel or recruit members themselves. Nonproductive members or members who have difficulty getting along may be asked to leave the group. Also, an individual who has skills other group members lack may be recruited for the group.

The timing of change in group membership is also important. We expect, for example, that the president of the United States will make changes in his cabinet after being reelected. Many second-term presidents choose this natural break to make personnel adjustments; or cabinet members may believe that this natural break provides an opportunity for them to move on. Cabinet changes in the middle of a president's term, however, are more dramatic, and many of these occur because of unexpected personality differences or political scandals. Thus it is predictable that a president would make changes in cabinet membership as one term draws to a close and another term begins. Changes in midterm are unpredictable and are likely to cause more disruption in the cabinet as a group.

The frequency with which groups change membership also reflects on the stability of the group, on the group's ability to chart a course for itself, or on the group's leadership. An executive group that cannot hold any person in the position of administrative assistant for longer than 6 months makes you wonder more about the executive group and less about the individuals rotating through the administrative role. Groups that have regular turnover like this are often questioned about their ability to work together. The assumption is that their inability to work together effectively drives off the administrative assistants. Questions about the group's ability to function legally and ethically are also raised. Do the administrative assistants leave because they are unwilling to participate in the group in the manner the executives wish? Regular change in group membership affects our interpretation of the group and its performance.

Fourth, it is important to know who is changing. Group members are not necessarily interchangeable. A group with a charismatic leader may be at a loss if the leader leaves the group. Most group members develop fixed roles within their groups. When a member leaves, a vacancy is created. Sometimes another group member can assume that role and its additional responsibilities. Other times, the group literally has a hole that must be filled. Your relay swim team relies on the swimmer who can assess how the other teams are doing in relationship to your team and then really kick in for a quick finish. Thus if you lose the member who normally swims in this position, your group has a loss to fill.

What is affected by changes in membership (Arrow & McGrath, 1993)? First, it should be obvious that membership dynamics will change. Any change in group membership will alter to some degree the interactions among group members. Not only does the structure and the process of the group change, performance is also likely to be affected. The more interdependence among members of the team, the more the team will feel the effects of membership change. The more central the member to the team, the more the team will feel the effects of membership change.

Group members develop a history together, and each group develops a memory of how and why it does certain things in certain ways. At the very minimum, a new group member will be unfamiliar with a group's habits and routines (Gersick & Hackman, 1990). These will need to be explained, or the new group member will feel left out. And the new group member will not be able to share in the memory of the group—there is simply no way for the new group member to know what it feels like to be a part of this group (McGrath, Berdahl, & Arrow, 1995). Assumptions or old knowledge that other group members use in making decisions are not available to or do not make sense to the new group member.

> ### BUILDING ANALYTICAL SKILLS
>
> *Reflecting and Remembering*
>
> Identify two different groups that are among your favorites. Write a short story using pictures, words, or both for each group that tells the story of the group's development from beginning to end. In your story (or series of pictures), be sure to address the following:
>
> 1. How did this group begin?
> 2. Did members know one another before being in this group? If so, in what way? How did that previous history affect interaction in the group?
> 3. What were the goals or activities of the group?
> 4. Describe how the group developed using either the stages of group development or one of the multiple-sequence theories. Give a specific example for each phase/stage you believe the group experienced.
> 5. What happened to individual group members after the group terminated?
> 6. How is the group remembered? by you? by other group members? by individuals outside the group?

Also, there is no guarantee that current members will be able to make the behavioral adjustments needed when a new group member enters. However, a group can overcome these effects by realizing that membership change actually creates a new group. Members must allow the group time to resocialize and reidentify its role structure. The challenges of membership change are (1) to initiate the new members into the team, (2) to learn from the new member's fresh perspective, and (3) to not sacrifice the pace and focus on the team (Katzenbach & Smith, 1993).

Would a group ever purposely change members? Yes. Sometimes a group member creates a logjam, making it difficult for the group to accomplish anything (Cohen, 1990). Groups can get stuck when strong self-oriented individuals are in the leadership role, or groups can fail to meet their potential if there is a weak link. Changes to replace ineffective leadership or poorly performing members are made purposely to help the group out of its entrenched patterns. We expect professional sports teams to use this strategy. We should want our groups to do the same. Try "Reflecting and Remembering" to review the development of one of your groups.

Summary

Some groups are deliberately formed; others are formed spontaneously. Members of deliberately formed groups are selected for their technical skills and ability and the personal characteristics necessary to work well with others. The balance of these two sets of skills vary depending on the type of group and its activities. This balance helps the group identify the fit among members.

A group's initial interactions have an enduring effect on the group. Thus groups need to get off to a new start. Taking time to define tasks and build member relationships will help the group develop a positive self-fueling spiral. One factor that affects a group's initial interactions is the degree to which a shell exists for group members' roles and responsibilities. Welcoming new group members and introducing yourself are two ways to assimilate group members. Talking with others about nonthreatening topics is a useful strategy for decreasing initial tensions in the group.

There are two perspectives on group development: stages of group development and multiple-sequence views of group development. There are five recognizable stages of group development: forming, storming, norming, performing, and termination. In the forming stage, group members maintain a strong self-orientation because trust is not high in the group. As members state their individual preferences and opinions, the second phase, storming, occurs. In this phase, conflict occurs as a natural part of the group's development. Members may compete for attention from one another as well as for roles. Once the conflicting issues are resolved, a group enters the norming stage. Here group members are comfortable with their roles and responsibilities and work well with others. The group finds that it is a "we" rather than a collection of "I's." The fourth stage is performing. In this stage, the group completes the task activities of the group. The group has reached clarity and consensus on its goals, and group members are tightly integrated. Finally, a group reaches termination, the ending point of the group. Depending on the quality of interaction among group members, this may be an anxiety-producing stage, a stage full of regret, or a stage of loss over the group's conclusion. Celebrating the success of a group with a party is an excellent way to solidify group members' connections to the group and to recognize collective and individual achievements. Although there is the assumption that groups progress steadily through the five stages, not all groups spend equal time in each phase. And groups may doubleback and revisit previous stages when new members enter the group or when the group encounters new tasks or crises.

Multiple-sequence views of group development argue that there is no universal sequence to group development. Rather, groups develop based on internal factors. For example, the contingency model suggests that groups develop simultaneously, but differently, on three tracks: task activity, group member relationships, and conversation topics. The punctuated equilibrium model argues that group development is characterized by periods of stable or habitual routines that are abruptly disrupted about halfway by a transitional period. According to this perspective, each group has an internal clock that recognizes the group's midpoint. This transition provides groups an opportunity to shift their work patterns to more effective patterns.

The theories of group development assume that group membership is fairly stable. However, this is not always the case. Some groups face regular turnover issues. In other groups, turnover may be less frequent or may be temporary. Regardless, membership change can affect important group factors. Membership change can either increase or decrease the amount of work a group member must accomplish, be voluntary or forced upon a group, occur at a natural breakpoint in the group or be unexpected and dramatic, or may affect members in central or peripheral roles. These changes will affect interaction and performance dynamics in the group, the group's history, and the ability of group members to rely on a group memory.

✓ Checklist

Group Knowledge

You should be able to:
- distinguish between the interaction differences likely to occur when groups are deliberately or spontaneously formed.
- explain the necessity of group member assimilation.
- describe the five stages of group development.
- distinguish between stages of group development and multiple-sequence group development.
- explain why not all groups develop in the same way.
- state three reasons why groups should celebrate their successes.

Group Skills

You should be able to:
- select appropriate communication behaviors to help assimilate new group members.
- use appropriate communication strategies to help your group move through the five stages of development.
- design and implement a group celebration.
- help your group move forward when it is stuck in one stage of its development.
- manage membership change in your group.

Analytical and Assessment Techniques

You should be able to:
- identify the stage of development of your group.
- recognize breakpoints or transitions in your group's development.
- assess the impact of membership change on your group.

Discussion Questions and Exercises

1. Assume that you are the supervisor of a newly formed team at your place of employment. How would you design the startup and group member assimilation activities of the group? What would you hope to accomplish during these activities?

2. Watch the final episode of "M*A*S*H," "Seinfeld," or any of your favorite television shows. How did the group of characters in the show terminate their

group? To what degree do you think the termination was successful or effective?
3. Think of a group you are in currently. How would you celebrate its ending? Why? Why would this type of ending be suitable for this particular group?
4. Interview two individuals about their group experiences. Did they volunteer information to suggest that the groups experienced a breakpoint or transition during group development? Or, do their descriptions fit better with the five stages of group development?

13
Meeting Management and Group Facilitation

Because my group has regular meetings, do we need to follow some meeting procedure?

Is the group leader the one who is most responsible for the group's effectiveness?

If I am not the leader, what can I do to help my group be more effective?

How can I help my group save more time and be more efficient?

How can my group become a team?

Can a group have ethics?

Why should groups be concerned with how they meet or with the procedures they use? Procedures, even simple agendas, can provide structure for groups and can keep meetings running smoothly (Poole, 1991). Procedures help coordinate members' thinking and provide a set of objective rules all group members can follow. Similarly, group facilitation strategies can help groups guard against their own bad habits. You have probably been a member of a group that did not accomplish what it wanted to because a more interesting topic was introduced into the discussion. As a result, the group spent most of its time on this new topic, forcing you and other group members to make important decisions in the last 10 minutes without much discussion.

Meeting management procedures and group facilitation strategies capitalize on the strengths of groups because they balance member participation. Using these procedures and strategies increases the opportunity for each group member to contribute. When all group members share their input, higher quality decisions are made and members are more supportive of the group's output. There are many other advantages to using meeting management and group facilitation strategies. These techniques help to uncover and then manage conflicts that can steal valuable resources and time from the group. They provide structure that can be revisited if a group takes a temporary detour, and they encourage group members to reflect on their meeting process and progress.

This chapter will show you how meeting management procedures and group facilitation strategies help teams develop more effectively and overcome obstacles;

this chapter also explores issues of ethical group membership. Being able to help your group manage its meetings, providing your group with facilitation expertise, helping your group develop as a team, and understanding the ethical responsibilities of group membership are responsibilities that go along with group membership. Each of these responsibilities allows you to participate in the group to the best of your abilities. At the same time, you are helping your group's interaction become more effective and efficient. You might think that the leader should bear these responsibilities, but when all group members participate in helping the group's interaction develop effectively, the group's process is smoother and more efficient.

In this chapter we will take a look at some ways you can help a group be successful. First, we will explore formal meeting planning. You have probably used some of these procedures in the past, but just because your group developed an agenda does not necessarily mean that your group effectively managed its time together. There is more to formal meeting planning than simply listing out items of business.

Formal Meeting Planning

Meetings should not just happen, but many do. Taking a needs assessment (Johansen et al., 1991) before the meeting will help you organize the meeting in such a way as to achieve the group's goal—or help you realize that a meeting is not needed at all.

Premeeting Planning and Preparation

When a meeting is called, most of us put the time and date on our schedule and show up. But that is really not enough. The group's leader or facilitator should do premeeting planning, and every group member should do some premeeting preparation. If you need some motivation to do this extra work before your next group meets, think of this: A typical group meeting generates somewhere between 100 and 600 speaking turns or opportunities for individuals to talk (Scheerhorn, Geist, & Teboul, 1994). Can you imagine trying to make sense out of so much information without at least an agenda to guide the way?

Leader Premeeting Planning Before calling any meeting, the leader should decide, first, if there is enough business to hold a meeting, and, if so, what the meeting's purpose should be. If there is not enough business, or if a clear purpose does not emerge, do not hold a meeting. One way to make these decisions is to make a list of the business items or what you want the group to consider or accomplish during its next meeting. Now look at the items. Can they be organized in some fashion that will make sense and move the group forward? If not, are these issues really ones that the entire group needs to discuss? Could talking individually with some group members take care of these issues? It may seem obvious to consider the overall purpose of the meeting, but answering this question can force you to consider why you need a meeting in the first place. Perhaps you are going to call a meeting because your boss told you to. She wants the vacation schedule for your department. Is a meeting the best way to collect and coordinate this information? If you cannot identify a purpose for the meeting, do not have a meeting!

Now consider the participants. You need to sort out who should be invited to the meeting and who should be informed about the meeting. The two lists are not always the same. If a key person cannot attend, should the meeting be canceled or rescheduled? Should the meeting go on regardless of who shows up? Answering these questions can help you determine the importance of those attending the meeting as well as the importance of the meeting itself.

Once you have decided that there is a real reason for the group to meet, you need to consider how long the meeting needs to be. Everyone identifies a start time, but few groups know when they can expect to be finished with the group's meeting or activities. Identifying a stop time is important because it can help a group focus on its work. Knowing that time is limited is a motivator and can keep group members from delaying action or decision making. Group members appreciate knowing when a meeting should be finished. This actually increases attendance because it allows group members to schedule around the meeting and avoid time conflicts. This is important because many employees belong to several work teams, and time devoted to meetings must be integrated with their other responsibilities.

Time limitations make an agenda that much more important. An **agenda** lists what the group needs to consider in detail and the order of consideration. Group members should receive a copy of the agenda before the group meets. This way, group members can be thinking about what they want to say and can collect data or information to support their point of view. When group members have an agenda before the group meets, they are better prepared to contribute effectively and efficiently. The agenda should list the meeting's starting and stopping times, the location of the meeting, who is expected to attend, the overall goal of the meeting, as well as the specific goal of each agenda item (for example, to share information, item for discussion, decision items). (Figure 13.1 shows a sample agenda.) Additionally, the agenda should identify or describe any preparations that group members should make, such as, "Come to the meeting with ideas on how to make sure our department can pass its accreditation assessment."

Once an agenda is complete and distributed to all group members you are done, right? Wrong! Now, as the group's leader you still have some work to do. First, given the items on the agenda, what leadership style should you use? What decision procedures will be most appropriate? Will the group meeting require any equipment? Have space and equipment been reserved? Are there enough seats? Can the participants fit comfortably around the table? Does the table and the configuration of the room allow for all participants to see and speak to one another easily? Is the room available when you need it? Do you need to make a reservation?

Agenda
Project Development Work Group
Thursday, January 29, 1:00 to 2:00 p.m. Conference Room A
Participants: Cynthia, Dan, Lu, Marquita, Tyron
Purpose: Project Update Tracking

Welcome

Introduce any guests

Preview agenda; ask for additional agenda items

Information sharing
    Review developments since January 15th meeting
    Dan, report on final numbers for December's project activity
    Cynthia, tell group about presentation to Federal Express

Discussion items
    Progress on planning of telephone service cut-over
    Evaluation of new project tracking board

Decision item
    Need decision on feasibility of switching to digital networks (bring cost estimates)

Suggestions for next meeting's agenda

Set next meeting date/time

Adjourn

Figure 13.1 *A Sample Agenda*

Will you need refreshments? What level of documentation is needed? What agendas, minutes, or reports will the meeting require? How many copies will be needed? Who will make them? Will it be necessary to have overheads, flip charts, chalk boards, or electronic meeting assistance present during the meeting? Do you have to make an equipment reservation?

After your needs assessment, you are ready to plan the meeting and invite or inform those you identified in step 2. Make sure to give adequate lead time and send along the agenda and any other documentation they will need prior to the meeting. If you want participants to prepare in some special way for the meeting (for example, bring lists of budget requests), make sure to tell them that. The more

> **PUTTING THE PIECES TOGETHER**
>
> ### Group Identity and Group Goal
>
> Identify a recent formal group experience in which you prepared for or helped prepare for the meeting. To what extent did your preparations help the group achieve its goal? Are you sure? Would the group have taken the path it did even without your preparations? What could you have done before the meeting to increase the likelihood that the group would meet its goals? Now think of how your preparations may have helped or hindered group identity. Did the agenda include all group members? Or, did the agenda focus attention on one or two group members who did most of the talking during the group meeting? How would this affect group members' willingness to identify with the group and be motivated to complete the group's activities? What preparation steps would you recommend to someone preparing for a group meeting?

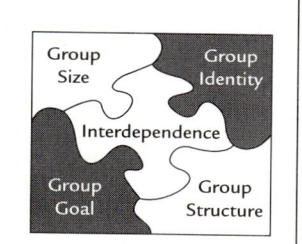

completely you prepare for the meeting, the more quickly the group will be able to work on its business and complete its activities.

Group Member Premeeting Preparation You have just put your next work group meeting on your calendar. Now what? To be an effective contributor, you should review the agenda (or ask for one if it is not provided) to determine if you need to prepare anything before the meeting. (Try *Putting the Pieces Together* to uncover how premeeting preparation operated in one of your groups.) By looking at the agenda, Dan sees that his group is going to begin considering alternative work schedules at their next meeting. He has not been asked to prepare anything, but he knows that these discussions will be sensitive and emotional. Even though his group members complain frequently about the schedule they work, changing the work schedule will also cause problems. First, Dan reviews the overtime records to see how much overtime each member has worked. Then he reviews the project record to see if there is any pattern to how projects flow into the department. He notices that only a few projects come in the first few weeks of the month and then work picks up steadily until many projects must be worked on simultaneously and completed by month-end. This gives him an idea. Why not propose that everyone work flex-time the first two weeks of the month and take some additional time off? This would balance out the overtime needed during the final two weeks of the month. Now, Dan has an alternative based on data to be presented to the group for their consideration.

Preparing for a meeting may require that you talk with other group members. After reviewing her agenda, Marquita believes that she should talk with Dan about the scheduling issues. As a single mother who depends on child care, changes in

> **THINK ABOUT IT**
>
> ### Making Plans Count
>
> Think about one of your last formal group meetings in which you received an agenda. Did you receive the agenda prior to the meeting or when you came to the meeting? Did the use of an agenda help the group communicate more effectively? Did the group stick to the agenda? What would you have added to or changed about the agenda to help the group? As the meeting progressed, did it become obvious to you that some of the group members were not well prepared for the meeting? What would you recommend as adequate preparation in a similar situation? Now, thinking about your own preparation, were you adequately prepared? What else could you have done to contribute more effectively to the group? Would your plans change if you were the group's leader?

schedules are particularly critical. She must get to the child care center by 6 P.M. or face a stiff late penalty and an anxious child. Marquita talks first with other parents in the group to see how they manage their child care arrangements. Cynthia tells her about one child care center that is open until 8 P.M., and Karen tells her that the company is scheduled to have an on-site child care center within a few months. At the meeting, Marquita suggests that the work team lobby the company's executive board about the importance of an on-site child care center. With that benefit, employees like Marquita would be willing to work unusual schedules. Although the child care center issue is not on the agenda, child care issues affect the group's discussion of work schedules. Without talking beforehand to Cynthia or Karen, Marquita would not know of any alternative child care arrangements or of the company's plans for an on-site child care center. Without this knowledge, Marquita could easily steer the group off its primary topic to more emotional issues. "Making Plans Count" will help you recall how your groups have used agendas.

Conducting the Meeting

The group's leader or facilitator should arrive at the meeting site early to make sure everything is ready. When it is time for the meeting to start, the meeting should be called to order. The leader should preview the agenda with the group and ask if other topics need to be added to it. By presenting the agenda as tentative rather than firm, the leader gains group member support when together they agree that the agenda has all of the important items listed (Schwarz, 1994). Posting the agenda so everyone can see it will help keep the meeting moving along. Before starting the meeting, the group should agree on the ground rules (when the meeting will stop; what will happen if there is a tie vote). Finally, the group should review developments since the last meeting. These should be brief reports to bring group members up to date.

Now you are ready to move ahead with new business. Taking each agenda item, in order, announce the item and then ask what process would be most appropriate for this item of business. The leader may make suggestions but should be open to the ideas of other group members. For example, for the agenda item concerning new ways of meeting the production schedule, a group member suggests using PERT (see Chapter 9). If other members agree that this is appropriate, this procedure should be used. With the item of business described and the process decided upon, the leader proceeds with the discussion or action item. Generally, the leader's role is to initiate and structure discussion, not to control the discussion content. It is normal for group members to look to the leader for approval. One way to break this pattern and encourage input from everyone is, for example, to ask Karen to respond to what Dan has said. This keeps the group discussion from developing into a spoke-and-wheel pattern in which the leader says something each time a group member speaks.

Sometimes members complain, taking up valuable group time unnecessarily. For complaining members, your job as leader is to listen carefully to the complaints for their relevance to the agenda item. If a complaint is really about another topic, ask other group members to respond so you can gauge the extent to which this is a group rather than an individual concern. If it is a group concern, suggest that this issue be made another agenda item for later in the meeting (if there is time) or for a future group meeting. If it is an individual issue, let the complaining group member know that you will speak with him or her about it after the meeting. Besides controlling complaining speakers, you may also have to encourage less talkative members to contribute. You can do this by asking open-ended questions (such as, "David, you've worked at other companies with rotating schedules. What can you tell us about your experiences?").

When different ideas are presented, summarize these in a compare-and-contrast format. Ask group members if your summaries are complete and accurate. If group members are quiet, do not assume their apparent consensus. Ask questions until you believe that group members really do agree on the substance of the issue. When an argument or conflict begins, do not take sides. Rather, ask group members to clarify their comments and probe for alternative viewpoints. Only reveal your viewpoint if it differs from those already expressed. To help clarify what the conflict is really about, ask group members to write down their response to the statement "I believe our conflict is about . . ." This technique allows each group member to identify the conflict individually. Then ask group members to read their statements to the group. You may find that there is disagreement over what the conflict is about. Once the conflict is identified and agreed upon by all group members, encourage joint problem solving through discussion. When it is time for the group to make a decision, consider the advantages of each of the decision-making procedures described in Chapter 8. Be sure to let group members know if the decision they are making is a binding decision or if a vote is simply an opportunity to see how group members are currently thinking about an issue.

Part of the leader's responsibility is to make group members feel welcome. This indirectly invites them to participate in and contribute to the group's activity.

Managing Relational Issues Besides conducting the meeting and helping the group accomplish what is on the agenda, the leader or facilitator is also responsible for developing and maintaining a supportive group climate. Greeting group members as they arrive and engaging them in social conversation can help establish a friendly meeting environment. If group members do not know one another well, brief self-introductions, name badges, and table tents will help members learn names more quickly.

If the meeting is long, suggest taking a break. This gives people time to take care of personal needs or get a snack, but it can also break the tension that develops in some groups when they meet or work together. Another way to help group members be more comfortable is to ask for volunteers for assignments. When someone volunteers, ask others who know and like this member to work together as a team.

As the leader, you are also the primary person for establishing and setting group norms. Group members will follow your lead. As the meeting progresses, analyze norms for their effectiveness. Just because your group has always done it a certain way does not mean that it is effective. When you speak, try to use "we" and "our team" rather than "I" language. These subtle cues help create a team atmosphere other members can accept and adopt.

Because conflict is a natural outgrowth of group discussions, watch for cues from group members that conflicting positions or hidden agendas are developing. Conflict cues include escalating voices as conversation goes back and forth between group members and the use of more dominant nonverbal behaviors—such as visible tightening of the arms and face, strong movements with arms and hands, turning body away from potential conflict partner. Some group members become silent and retreat from a group's conversation when conflict arises. Watch for these signals as well. A hidden agenda may be developing when one group member dominates the conversation with his or her own input while dismissing input from others. A person with a hidden agenda will frequently ask loaded questions—"So, you don't think I would be a good chairperson?"—to which other group members will either retreat or respond with the answer the person is looking for just to keep peace in the group. When you see cues that conflict or hidden agendas are developing, deal with them now. The longer you wait, the more entrenched they will become, making them more difficult to manage for the group and the group less effective. See Chapter 11 for strategies for managing conflicts.

Using Space Four principles should guide the selection and use of meeting space (Schwarz, 1994). First, all group members should be able to see and hear one another. Many different room configurations can accommodate this goal, but generally round or rectangular tables are best for groups of less than ten. A U-shaped table configuration can work well for groups of twenty or so. Second, if your group will be using visuals (see the next section), the seating arrangement should allow each member to easily view the flip chart or other visual aids. Third, if nonparticipants are invited to the meeting to provide information or to just observe, they should not sit with the meeting participants who will discuss or vote on issues before the group. Nonparticipants can easily participate when called upon if they sit in a ring outside or just beyond the meeting participants. This seating arrangement keeps nonparticipants from invading the psychological or relational space of group members. As a final consideration, the space for the group meeting should fit the needs of the group but not be so large as to allow for empty seats among participants. Group members may need space to bring notebooks or other materials, and members should not feel crowded. But allowing for too much extra space among members may increase the psychological distance among them and impede group progress.

Using Visuals Even the best meetings and the best groups can profit from using visual records of what is happening in the group. Although a secretary or recorder may be taking minutes, minutes generally reflect only the outcomes or the final decisions made by group members. Graphics or visuals can be used to keep track of the group's process (Sibbet, 1981). By keeping and then posting a running record of the key ideas and central themes of what happens in the group, several positive things occur. First, group members know immediately if others are accurately hearing them. As a group posts its ideas on a flip chart, it is easy to determine whether another group member accurately summarized your 4-minute statement. You can correct misperceptions immediately. Second, writing what people say makes members feel acknowledged and part of the group process. When this type of validation occurs, group members are more likely to continue to contribute to the group discussion, which increases members' participation, cooperation, and involvement. Third, visualizing or graphing what is going on in a group helps to spark the creativity of group members. Providing a visualization of the interaction helps group members both analyze and synthesize ideas before the group. Finally, visualizing the group's interaction provides a graphic memory for the group, helping to reinforce group decisions. In this case, seeing is believing. The visuals can also be used for making minutes more detailed. The graphic memory can be referred to in future meetings when a group needs to revisit something it has already addressed.

What does it take to visualize a group meeting? Markers and flip chart pads are the best tools, although chalk and a chalkboard can be used. You might be thinking, "I couldn't do this. I'm not an artist!" It does not require artistic talent, but it does require that you be interested in what is happening in the group and are able to follow the interaction. Most group members can visualize or graph a group with just a little practice. Here is how the process works.

The leader or any group member can be the group's visualizer. In either case, the role of this person is to capture what people say, not to evaluate ideas. Record everything, as accurately as you can, in group members' words. Your job is to provide some structure or organization to what people say. You might want to use different colors—say, green for positive attributes and red for negative attributes and then use purple for questions that still need to be explored. When you have filled one flip chart, hang it up and start another. As you put charts up, hang them close together so you can draw arrows from one to another. Periodically stop and ask other group members if you have captured everything accurately and clearly. Use stars (*), boxes, and underlining to indicate important items or to indicate what has been decided upon. Use forms (stick people, smiling faces, dollar signs, check marks, question marks—any visual form you feel comfortable drawing) to help structure or organize the conversation.

Group graphics can take several forms. The one with which you are probably most familiar is making lists when groups use the brainstorming procedure (Chapter 8). As group members contribute ideas, the facilitator writes them one by one on a flip chart. Putting the group's agenda up on a flip chart also helps the group keep moving. It is more difficult to stay stuck on one item when you can see that the group has twelve other things to discuss. Both of these are lists because they focus group members on the sequence of ideas.

Another type of graphic with which you are familiar and that can be used in group interactions is mapping. You have probably drawn a map to your house for someone. Maps can also be made of group meetings. Where did the conversation start? What other topics did the group address? Which ideas did the group support? What needs to be done now? Look at Figure 13.2. Can you tell what this group discussed?

Other visual techniques that can assist your group include clustering, matrixes, organizational diagrams, and flow charts. In the clustering technique you place comments together as themes start to emerge in a group's discussion. Starting with just a few spread out circles helps you cluster items together. And you can draw lines out to other ideas or connect circles (themes). Clustering helps groups separate and integrate ideas. A matrix helps groups find relationships in a systematic way. Let's say that your group is proposing ways to raise funds. Look at Figure 13.3. By identifying options for making money and then comparing them against criteria the group developed, members can analyze which money-making strategy is best for them. When a group has data to analyze, using a matrix is a good idea.

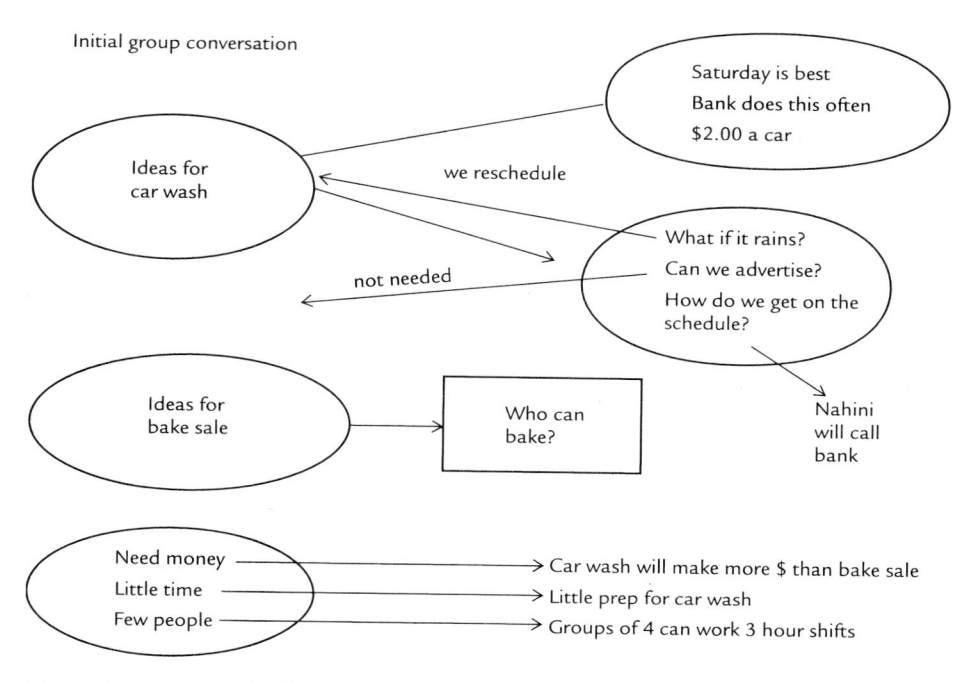

Figure 13.2 *A Sample of Mapping a Group Meeting*

Another type of visual is an organizational diagram, which is really a treelike sketch. Although most often associated with people and their roles or responsibilities, organizational diagrams can be useful with any type of hierarchical information. For example, your fraternity is trying to develop a new structure for the group's many social roles. By drawing the existing structure and then editing the structure on paper as group members discuss what is missing, needed, or redundant, you will soon have a new hierarchical structure to present to the fraternity's board. The PERT diagramming discussed in Chapter 9 is a form of flow chart. In a PERT chart, the diagram acts as a planning tool. It flows from left to right, indicating what needs to be completed first, second, and so on. But your chart can start anywhere and go anywhere as long as it imitates the process and makes sense to group members.

When a group gets stuck on an idea, it can be very useful to give every group member markers and paper. Have each person diagram the problem or graph out where they want the group to end up. Hang up the visualizations and let everyone review them. By comparing the visualizations of all group members, it will be easy to find points of agreement and disagreement.

Whatever visualizing or graphing technique your group uses, do not throw them away. The group's secretary or recorder can use them to write more detailed minutes. Group members might want to refer back to them between group

	need money	little time	few people
Car wash	Can charge up to $3 a car	Only takes about 10 minutes to wash a car	Two people can wash the same car
Bake sale	Items generally sell for $1 or less	Must bake the night before	Would need more people to bake
Magazine subscriptions	Only get 5% of sales	Would have to go door-2-door	Can 8 people do this

Figure 13.3 *A Sample of a Matrix of a Group Meeting*

meetings to see if an idea was discussed. And because the visualizations are a pictorial memory of the group's process, they can even be used to settle disputes. The *Group Assessment Technique* presents some scenarios of group meetings for you to practice your preparation techniques.

Making Assignments Most group meetings reach a point at which additional information is needed. The leader may assign individual members these responsibilities or group members can volunteer. In either case, you need to develop action statements and get agreement about what is to be completed. For example, it becomes obvious to Terry that his group needs more information on how to use the company's e-mail system before this group will agree to adopt its use for between-meeting communication. Being comfortable with computers, Terry offers to find information about e-mail training for the group. Sounds good, right? But what exactly is Terry going to do? Will Terry find out when the training is scheduled? Will he explore what is covered in the training? Will he see if there is a quick-guide group members can keep near their computers once they have received the training? When should he report back to the group? and how? by e-mail? By specifying what should be accomplished, Terry's expectations will parallel what others expect of him. When assignments are made or taken in meetings, this action should immediately be noted for inclusion on the next meeting's agenda. It helps create continuity in the group when group members report back on what they have accomplished, and it keeps all group members informed of progress toward group goals.

GROUP ASSESSMENT TECHNIQUE

How Would You Plan and Conduct These Meetings?

Break into small groups and select one of the following meetings. Develop a specific and detailed plan for preparing and then conducting the meeting. Use the questions to aid your planning. Compare your preparations with other groups preparing for the same meeting. How do your preparations differ? Did other groups think of items you forgot?

Meeting 1

Your boss asked you to get a task team together to develop next year's sales department budget for his review. You have two weeks to prepare the budget. In your work unit, there is Richard, a popular salesperson who has been with the company 15 years; Gina, the department's relatively new administrative assistant; Brian, a salesperson with 5 years experience, but recently he has been in a sales slump; Elaine, the sales department's marketing manager who has been with the company 2 years; Dana, the top salesperson for the last three consecutive years; John, the department's accountant who has been with the company 20 years and with this department for the last 5 years; and Althea, a new salesperson who is training with Richard.

1. How would you describe the purpose of the meeting? What specifically do you want to accomplish?
2. Who do you invite and why? What would you ask each to contribute?
3. How will you conduct the meeting? Be specific. When? Where? Why? What outside interferences will you try to plan around?
4. How many meeting sessions will it take to develop a budget to present to your boss?
5. What obstacles do you expect to encounter? What planning or preparation can you do to avoid them?

Meeting 2

Neighbors in your community have been talking about developing a neighborhood watch group (a formal program exists in your community and is supervised by the police). You decide to take the lead on this issue and invite neighbors to your home for the initial meeting.

1. How do you extend meeting notices to neighbors? Where do you draw the lines of your neighborhood?
2. Do you invite others to the meeting? the police? members of other neighborhood watch programs?
3. Where would be an appropriate place to hold the meeting? Can this place accommodate all of the neighbors who will want to come?
4. What relational issues do you think will have to be managed during the meeting?
5. What is the specific purpose of your meeting?
6. What will be your role during the meeting?

Ending the Meeting At the end of the meeting, the group should perform two steps. First, the group should review decisions and plans for action. Taking this step helps everyone understand the decisions that were made and who is responsible for following through for the group. Second, if the group does not have a regular meeting time, the next meeting should be scheduled and a tentative agenda should be discussed. This step helps group members view the meetings as having continuity rather than each meeting being an independent activity.

Taking Minutes Groups need a record, or **minutes,** of what they did at each meeting. Minutes should capture who attended the meeting, the content of what was discussed, what was decided, who agreed to take on what responsibilities, and what the group plans to do next. Generally, the secretary or the group's recorder takes the minutes, finalizes them, and then presents them to the group at the next meeting. Many groups prefer that the minutes be prepared and distributed before the next group meeting. This gives members ample opportunity to review the record for accuracy. At the next group meeting, the minutes should be reviewed and corrected, if needed, before being accepted by the group as its formal record of activity.

Postmeeting Follow-Up

Most leaders consider their job done when the group concludes its meeting. However, to make meetings more effective, a few follow-up steps should be performed. First, review the minutes with the person who took them, and distribute them to each group member. This should be done as soon after the meeting as possible. This serves two functions: (1) Other group members are able to review the minutes for completeness and accuracy; corrections should be made as soon as possible, and the minutes should be redistributed. (2) Because the minutes include action statements for which group members agreed to be responsible, this reminds them of their commitment to the group. Second, if a group's actions will have impact on other groups or individuals, the leader should share the group's decisions with those parties. And, third, as the leader reviews the actions to be taken from this agenda, he or she should begin preparing the initial framework for the group's next agenda.

The leader has another responsibility toward the group. After each meeting, the leader should analyze what went well and what did not work. To a great extent, the leader is responsible for making sure that the group realized its goals during the meeting. Did that occur? If not, why? The leader should also think back over the meeting's interaction to assess whether individual group members' goals appear to be in alignment with the group's goals. If not, what could the leader do to encourage or motivate group members?

After important group business is conducted, the leader should also analyze to what extent inequality was an issue in the group. Some inequalities may stem from the leader's influence attempts. Some leaders are too assertive or dominant in their communicator style, which effectively shuts down reciprocal communication in meetings. This influence pattern almost diminishes the need for a meeting as the leader is the only group member talking, giving input, and making decisions. Another ineffective influence occurs when a leader always looks to and speaks to the same group members. By consistently relying on some group members to answer questions and take on responsibilities for the group, the leader is implicitly saying to the others "You don't count" or "I don't trust you to do this for us." In either case, the leader's influence creates subgroups—the dominant subgroup that performs most of the group's work and a subordinate subgroup whose members are just expected to follow along. A leader can avoid these problems by making eye contact periodically with all group members, encouraging more silent group members to give their opinions, deferring the input of more dominant group members, and using decision procedures to help equalize any undue influence in the group. Taking these steps will help you improve the effectiveness of your role in leading your group through its meeting.

Group members also have postmeeting responsibilities. If you were assigned or took on a responsibility to the group, do it. If you believe the group forgot to cover something important, tell the leader so he or she can make sure it is part of the next meeting's agenda.

Overcoming Obstacles

There are six general obstacles to group discussion (Gastil, 1993): (1) long meetings, (2) unequal member involvement and commitment, (3) formation of cliques, (4) different levels of communication skills, (5) different communicator styles, and (6) personal conflicts. You have probably been a member of a group that had several of these problems. Let's examine each obstacle and consider how you could help your group overcome each one.

Long Meetings

No one likes long meetings, but actually lack of preparation by group members contributes to this dilemma. It is easy to be prepared for your group's meeting. Review what happened at the last meeting and review what the group wants to accomplish at this meeting. At the meeting, try to speak in a clear but concise manner. Do not ramble and do not let other group members ramble on and on. If a group member gets off track, ask him or her to clarify the point. If your group has several long-winded talkers, you might want to consider asking group members to establish a time limit for individuals to contribute to the discussion. This can quicken the pace of the meeting. During the meeting, take notes and be attentive so that you do not take a mental vacation. Keep side conversations to a minimum because one side conversation seems to escalate into several more side conversations. Finally, if possible, schedule the meeting for a time of day when everyone is alert. Having definite start and stop times for your meetings can help.

If you cannot cover all of the agenda items in your meeting, ask members for their commitment to continuing the meeting or schedule a follow-up.

Unequal Member Involvement and Commitment

It is easy to say that you should interact in such a way as to make others feel more involved and hope that their increased commitment will follow. However, you cannot be directly responsible for another member's level of involvement. What you can do is tie the interests of each member back to the goal or activity of the group. Consider what each individual group member can gain from the group's activity. Pointing out these personal-group relationships to others may help them identify with the group more strongly. Generally, when members identify with the group, they become more committed. Another strategy for increasing involvement and commitment is to allow the group to create and develop its own goals. When members help direct the activities of the group, their involvement and commitment should follow. Finally, if involvement and commitment are not being demonstrated, you may want to consider changing the membership of the group. Perhaps a group member does not want to belong or feels out of place in the group. Private conversations with this member may help identify resolutions for these problems.

Formation of Cliques

Cliques, or subgroups, develop when there is a reason or need to communicate outside the group setting. When cliques develop, all group members will not have access to needed information. You probably cannot entirely avoid the formation of cliques based on long-term friendships, but you can reduce the impact of cliques on the group by having an alternative means of communicating with all group members. Perhaps you could post the group's minutes, activities, or agenda on the computer system or a bulletin board. If it is going to be a long time until the next group meeting and group members do not have access to a common area, send information about the group to all members. Ask group members to communicate important developments that occur between group meetings to all other members before the start of the next meeting. Finally, be sure to recognize personally each group member early in the group's discussion. Using their names and asking each a question that personally involves them in the group's discussion will increase each member's involvement in the full group.

Different Levels of Communication Skill

You may think there is not much you can do to enhance another group member's lack of communication skill, but there is. First, establish a procedure that allows everyone to speak early in the group discussion. You might begin a group session by asking each member to report on what he or she accomplished while away from the group or to give reflections about what happened in the last group meeting.

Subgroups, or cliques, develop from the communication networks that group members establish. Cliques often form when group members have relationships together outside a particular group and when group members do not feel comfortable expressing themselves in the group's meetings.

The important element here is to give each group member an opportunity to speak freely. You can help other members improve their skills by asking them questions that you know they can answer easily but that still contribute to the group. For example, you know that Marianne did a great deal of work checking out three sites for the festival. But you have recognized that Marianne has some difficulty in giving detailed descriptions. Here is how you can help. Ask Marianne to tell the group about the three festival sites. When Marianne pauses, ask her a question about the site she seems to prefer. What did she particularly like about that site? What criteria did she use in selecting sites? By asking Marianne questions you know she can answer, you are helping her overcome her anxiety as well as providing detail for other group members so that they can appreciate the work Marianne did.

Usually, each group member could improve his or her communication skills. Even members with typically good skills can find some aspect of their group performance that can be enhanced. Here is one way to encourage all group members to work on their interaction skills. In addition to working on the group's activity or task, have the group identify a particular skill as the practice skill for that meeting. For example, in one group meeting the group may decide to work on asking good questions of one another. In another meeting, the group could work on not interrupting members when they are talking. By selecting one skill for all group members to work on, you are enhancing everyone's skills without paying undue attention to one group member.

Different Communicator Styles

As people are different, so are their personalities and their communicator styles. But as we discussed in Chapter 6, the more aspects there are to your communicator style, the more flexibly you can interact with others who favor different styles. What can you do to decrease differences among communicator styles in your group? The first thing is to remain flexible and accepting of other styles. If everyone had the same communicator style, the group's interaction would be boring and less productive. Think about maximizing the opportunities that differences bring to the group rather than negating others who communicate differently.

Personal Conflicts

Personal conflicts and personality conflicts are likely to happen particularly if the group is feeling other pressures (such as time, resource, or deadline pressures). Rather than panic when these conflicts occur, use them as opportunities to learn more about other group members. Help group members maintain mutual respect for others by not contributing to gossip. If you work to build a strong and positive personal relationship with each group member, it is less likely that group members will gang up on somebody. Another way to avoid personal conflicts is to create a supportive climate in which members can express their feelings with the group. Sometimes conflicts occur simply because we think someone said something other than what they did. When a conflict does arise, help members work through it by having each side express themselves clearly. Finally, if an intense conflict develops, direct the group's attention to the primary conflict issue before continuing with other group activities or business. Failing to deal with the conflict when it arises will likely escalate the conflict later. "What Would You Do?" gives you some practice at overcoming obstacles in group meetings.

Building A Team

Groups that meet for extended periods of time often consider themselves teams. But it takes more than calling your group a team to ensure that all members view the group with enthusiasm. *Teamwork* and *teambuilding* are terms we often hear, but what do they mean? **Teambuilding** means that a group strives for effective meetings by addressing both task and process issues on the agenda (Weisbord, 1988). Teambuilding works best when all group members agree to participate in both the task and process activities of the group because they want to improve their group performance. For teambuilding to be successful, each member must have the opportunity to influence what goes on the agenda. Teambuilding cannot be directed or mandated by the leader; all members must willingly participate. The real motivation for building a team comes from the problem or activity on which the group is working. When the issue is complex and group members have an interest in the outcome, the recognition that they must rely upon one another to accomplish the task can motivate members to pursue teambuilding activities.

A group that wants to build itself as a team has four objectives (Burke, 1988). First, the group must be able to set clear goals or priorities. Second, the group must analyze how the group's work should be done and then perform that work within group members' roles and responsibilities. Third, the group must examine how it is working as a collective. Group members must examine processes like norms, decision making, and so on. Finally, to be a team, group members must be concerned with and actively pursue positive relationships with one another.

Teams are groups that can accomplish tasks effectively because the group is simultaneously pursuing positive member relationships and efficient work process through self-examination. It is the self-examination activities that set teams apart from groups. Where does a group start its teambuilding process? The first step of group examination should be its goals or priorities. Having clear goals can keep other problems from occurring. To accomplish this first step in teambuilding, all group members must understand, acknowledge, and accept the group's goals. There is not any room for assumptions here. What about one of your current groups? Are you sure that everyone understands and accepts the group's goals? Or, do you assume that is the case?

The second step in teambuilding is to clarify the roles and responsibilities of group members. By doing so, ambiguity is decreased and members have a better idea of what is expected of them in a particular role. Labeling a role with a title is not enough. Group members must know what their roles require of them, be able to perform adequately in those roles, and have acceptance and support for those roles from other group members. The third teambuilding step is to examine the processes the group uses in its task activities. These include the processes we examined in Part 2 of this book—decision making, problem solving, leadership, and conflict management. Are group members skilled in several different decision-making procedures? Is the leadership style or strategy used in this group appropriate for the group's task and its members? Does the leadership style facilitate or inhibit the group's activities? Can group members effectively manage conflicts, allowing communication to continue within the group? These are difficult questions to answer. They are also difficult questions to bring before other group members. A good way to introduce these topics into the group's conversation is to set aside a time at the end of each group meeting to discuss how well the group worked together. This is also a good time to discuss alternative procedures and processes for the next meeting.

The final step in teambuilding is to examine relationships among team members. This step is purposely left for last because interpersonal problems among

BUILDING ANALYTICAL SKILLS

What Would You Do?

The following presents several common problems experienced in groups and teams. Read each problem and decide what you would do to facilitate your group or team.

Problem	What I Would Do to Facilitate the Group?
1. People did not do their homework. They were not prepared for the meeting.	
2. We did not have the right people at the meeting.	
3. There was not enough time to finish the task.	
4. The space we had was too small and members were uncomfortable.	
5. We did not have the support we needed from upper management.	
6. There was no agenda.	
7. We did not know exactly what we were supposed to do.	
8. People kept straggling in after we had started.	
9. I was never sure how we would make our decision.	
10. I could never figure out if there was a plan for the meeting.	
11. We never seemed to follow a set sequence or logic.	
12. Everything was confused; it was hard to tell where we were going.	
13. We just started talking about the problem without figuring out how we should go about the whole thing.	

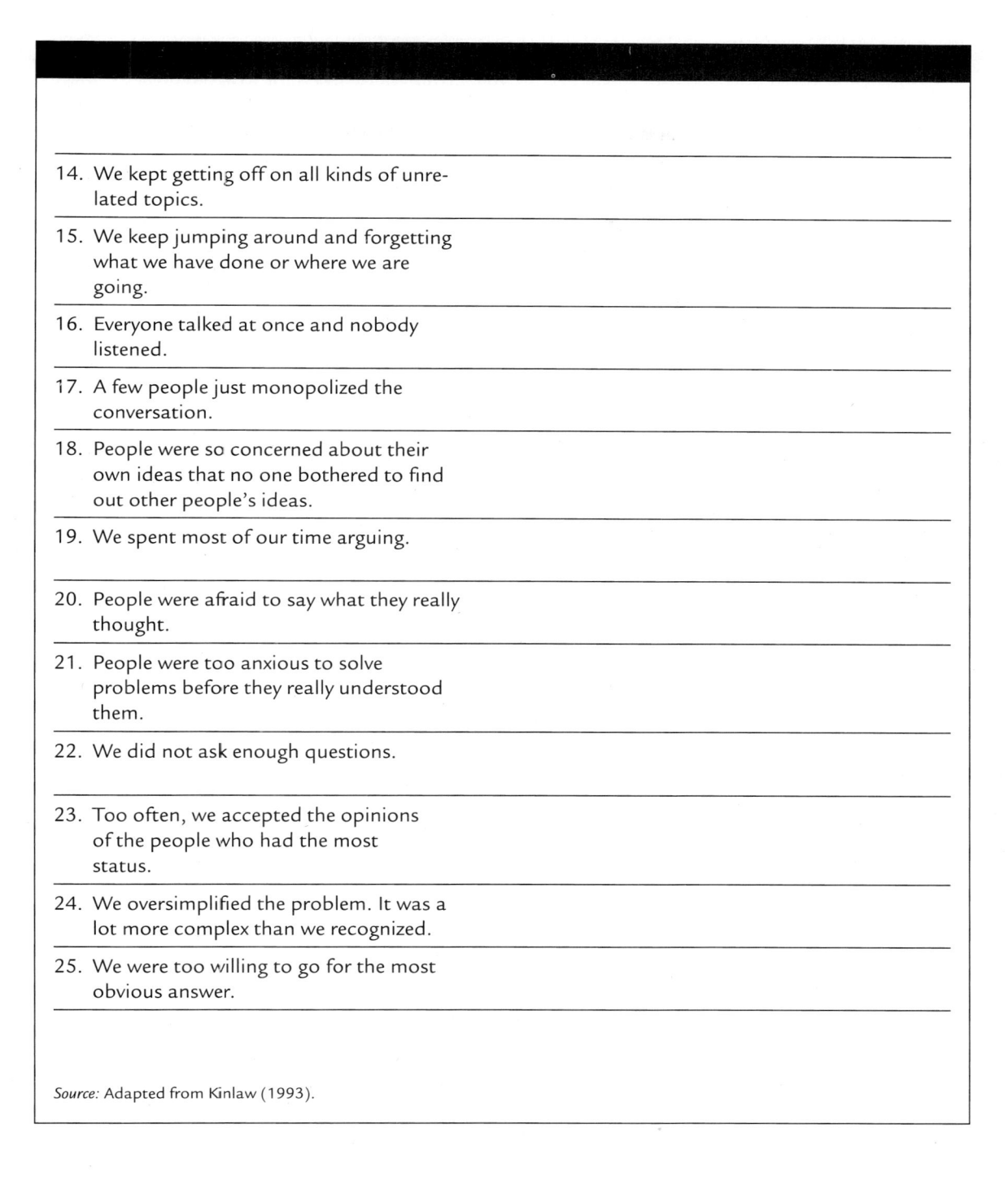

14. We kept getting off on all kinds of unrelated topics.

15. We keep jumping around and forgetting what we have done or where we are going.

16. Everyone talked at once and nobody listened.

17. A few people just monopolized the conversation.

18. People were so concerned about their own ideas that no one bothered to find out other people's ideas.

19. We spent most of our time arguing.

20. People were afraid to say what they really thought.

21. People were too anxious to solve problems before they really understood them.

22. We did not ask enough questions.

23. Too often, we accepted the opinions of the people who had the most status.

24. We oversimplified the problem. It was a lot more complex than we recognized.

25. We were too willing to go for the most obvious answer.

Source: Adapted from Kinlaw (1993).

group members may be caused or exacerbated by unclear goals or problems with procedures or processes. Frequently, group members want to avoid directly talking about interpersonal problems although they are more than eager to talk about these issues with others outside the group context. When this happens, negativity surfaces in the group, compounding the initial emotional reaction. Examine the following list of emotions. Can you recall a group meeting in which you had these feelings?

intimidation or frightened of others	afraid of looking silly or awkward
embarrassment	afraid to violate norms
overstating your views	afraid of appearing naive
hostilely responding to others' inquiries	becoming the target of jokes or unwanted humor
losing control of your behavior	appearing flirty or seductive

If you have felt any of these, it is likely that one of your relationships with one or more group members needs attention (Bocialetti, 1988). Generally, we would not say anything or behave in such a way as to make others feel uncomfortable. But when one of these emotions surfaces during group interaction, we are reacting to something, and often we are reacting to someone in the group with whom we have a poor relationship. Here is a rule of thumb that can help your group effectively manage its interpersonal relationships: If a personal issue is problematic enough to motivate you to talk to others about how to handle it, the issue is worth addressing face to face with other group members directly involved in the situation. Group members are more likely to receive feedback about interpersonal relationships if feedback about group goals, procedures, and processes are a regular part of group's teambuilding activities.

Does teambuilding really make a difference? Yes. Over time, group members will recognize an increased ability to raise issues and manage their own conflict. Members who are committed to their teams are more eager to give other members praise and support and are more willing to engage in cooperative efforts. The roles and responsibilities of team members become clarified and allow group members to work more efficiently because there is less role conflict and competition. As a result, team members develop greater commitment to the team (Glaser, 1994). *Think About It* provides a brief exercise to help you understand how emotions affect group interaction.

Identifying the Effectiveness of Your Team

Groups that work effectively as teams still have problems, but group members are open and honest with one another when problems occur and they take steps to manage the task or group processes more effectively. Let's review the characteristics of an effectively functioning team (Hanson & Lubin, 1988). You can use these characteristics as standards or goals for your group's performance.

> **THINK ABOUT IT**
>
> ### The Power of Emotions in Groups
>
> Think about one of your favorite and one of your least favorite group experiences. Select at least three emotions from the following list that describe your emotions in each of those experiences.
>
> | | | | | |
> |---|---|---|---|---|
> | pleasure | sadness | satisfaction | pride | boredom |
> | frustration | jubilation | remorse | fear | disgust |
> | daring | depression | jealousy | happiness | excitement |
> | repulsion | loneliness | love | elation | gratitude |
> | silliness | incompetence | hesitation | guilt | surprise |
> | guilt | envy | hopelessness | eagerness | hate |
> | weariness | spite | anger | adventurousness | gladness |
> | inspiration | grief | joy | contentment | confidence |
> | amazement | anxiety | helplessness | solemnity | rejection |
> | apathy | motivation | hope | overwhelmed | ecstatic |
>
> How did these emotions facilitate or inhibit your groups becoming teams? To what extent were these emotions shared by other group members? How did others react when you displayed these emotions? What is your position on sharing emotion in group settings? Should you conceal your emotions or let other group members know how you feel? Why?
>
> *Source:* The list of emotions is from Bocialetti (1988).

- Members of effective teams share a sense of purpose and have common goals; moreover, group members are willing to work for those goals.
- Effective teams have members who are aware of and interested in how well the group is operating as a system.
- The team can identify the resources available among its members and can use them appropriately; this means that all group members have influence in the group.
- Group members listen to one another and clarify their statements; they value communication with one another by showing interest in what others say and feel.
- Differences of opinion are encouraged; no one feels hesitant to say what they think.
- The team can effectively manage conflicts and, as a result, operate more effectively because differences have been aired and integrated.

- The team uses its energy to solve problems rather than using energy to resolve interpersonal disputes or competitions among members.
- Roles among members are balanced and shared, which leads to high levels of group cohesion and morale.
- The team encourages members to take risks and be creative; mistakes are treated as a source of learning rather than as failures.
- The team can respond to changes; members are flexible and open to new ideas and experiences as well as open to the changing demands of those external to the group.
- Team members periodically review how well the team is doing; allowing time in the group's agenda to talk about process and procedures, evaluation is built in to the team's interaction.
- An effective team is built on a climate of trust; group members recognize and regard this element as crucial to achieving the other elements of effectiveness.

Understanding the Problem of Your Team

Everyone seems to agree that their group has some problem, but you are likely to get a variety of responses if you ask group members to identify the problem. You can use the *Group Assessment Technique* to determine if you perceive the group's problem as a task issue, a relational issue, a group process or procedural problem, or a teamwork problem.

Developing a Group Charter and a Code of Conduct

One way to help a group in its initial stages is to suggest that the group develop a charter and code of conduct. A **group charter** describes the goals or mission of the group (Shea & Guzzo, 1987). A **code of conduct** describes behaviors that are appropriate in this particular group. Developed early in the group's history, both documents will help the group move effectively toward its goal. To develop a group charter, the group must discuss and agree upon what members view as important and what members hope to accomplish in this group experience. Groups goals are generally the primary component of a group charter. Each goal should be listed individually. Both task and relational goals should be included. What individual members can expect to learn or obtain from the group can also be included. The group may also wish to include a vision or mission statement to outline the overall objective of the group. Figure 13.4 provides an example of a group charter. As you can see, the charter is specific and clear and provides direction for the group. But it does not dictate how the group will meet its objectives. This allows the group to use its creativity and work on its own to meet its objectives.

Check your charter by answering the following questions (Goodstein, Nolan, & Pfeiffer, 1992): Is the statement understandable for all group members? Is it brief

GROUP ASSESSMENT TECHNIQUE

Diagnosing Team Problems

To help diagnose the type of problem your team is having, respond to each question by putting a check mark under the most appropriate answer.

	almost always	sometimes	almost never
1. We are clear about the goals of our group.	_____	_____	_____
2. We help each other out when needed.	_____	_____	_____
3. I can count on my teammates to pull their share of the load.	_____	_____	_____
4. We have processes that help us get past obstacles when they occur.	_____	_____	_____
5. Work is organized in a way that helps get the job done efficiently.	_____	_____	_____
6. People on the team are clear and direct in communicating with one another.	_____	_____	_____
7. I need to work with others to get my job done.	_____	_____	_____
8. We spend time talking about how we are working together.	_____	_____	_____
9. We spend time working on ways to increase our productivity.	_____	_____	_____
10. We have effective methods of dealing with conflicts when they arise.	_____	_____	_____
11. I have responsibilities and tasks that are shared with other team members.	_____	_____	_____
12. We spend time learning how to work together more effectively.	_____	_____	_____

Total your scores for each of the four areas by using the following scale:

almost always = 3   sometimes = 2   almost never = 1

Task: items 1, 5, 9   Task total: _____
Relationships: items 2, 6, 10   Relationship total: _____
Process/procedure: items 3, 7, 11 Process/procedure total: _____
Teamwork: items 4, 8, 12   Teamwork total: _____

Your lowest score identifies the type of problem your team is experiencing.

Source: Adapted from Gardenswartz and Rowe (1994).

> **Group Charter**
>
> Group's Mission Statement: To work interdependently as team members to identify relevant issues, resolve problems, learn new skills, and have fun.
>
> Our group will develop a strategic plan for our organization for the next five years. The plan must: 1) be accepted by the executive committee to which this group reports, 2) be implemented by the rest of the organization, and 3) meet a set of conditions given to us by the executive committee.
>
> In working on the strategic plan, each group member should develop skills in group facilitation, organizational forecasting, and team member effectiveness.
>
> Our goal is to complete the first objective in six months from our start date.

Figure 13.4 *A Group Charter*

enough that team members can remember it and keep it in mind? Does the charter clearly specify the activities of the team? Does the charter reflect realistic goals? Is the charter in line with members' values and beliefs? Is the charter inspiring or motivating to members?

A code of conduct (Figure 13.5) lists those behaviors that members feel are appropriate and will help group members be effective in the group. Too frequently, group members do not discuss what they expect from other members in terms of behavior. Left undiscussed, members are unsure of what is appropriate or inappropriate behavior. Thus they use behavioral norms from other groups to guide their behavior. Of course, norms from previous groups are not always transferrable to other group situations. Attendance and preparedness are examples of individual behavior to be included in the code of conduct. Group-level behaviors—role sharing within the group, decision-making rules, election procedures, and group structure—can also be described and included (Shonk, 1992). Specifying both individual and group behaviors ensures that all members are aware of what is expected of them in this group.

A code of conduct provides a set of guidelines—much like rules provide the guidelines by which you participate in any sport. Guidelines provided by the code of conduct create equity in the group process because all group members share in their creation. By developing a group charter and a code of conduct, members in the group are more likely to share perceptions about what constitutes effective group membership. Developing these documents also helps a group crystallize its identity and culture.

> **Code of Conduct**
> **created and agreed to by all group members,**
> **August 14, 1998**
>
> As a team, we expect all members of the team to support the team's charter. Our communication, actions, and decisions should emphasize teamwork, not individual accomplishment. Each group member is responsible for being involved in the day-to-day business of the team. Each group member expects to receive information and influence from all other group members.
>
> As a group, we will elect a leader for each month we are together as a team. By rotating the leadership role, we will help to develop each member's leader and follower skills. The leader is to provide overall direction and support for the team. Followers are to carry through their assigned responsibilities and inform the leader if they encounter any obstacles.
>
> We expect to make decisions as a team using the majority vote rule. In cases where a minority vote member is so uncomfortable with the decision outcome that he or she cannot support the group's decision, he or she may ask the group to re-consider the issue.
>
> Group members are expected to attend all meetings. When a member cannot attend, other members will expect his or her assignments to be completed and handed in to the leader before the next meeting. In the event any member finds that he or she cannot fulfill the responsibilities of being a member of this team, he or she may ask the group for a reduction in, or termination of group responsibilities.

Figure 13.5 *A Code of Conduct*

Ethical Group Membership

What is ethical behavior? How is it important to group situations? How do group situations affect an individual member's ethical behavior? These questions and others like them are gaining in importance as we increasingly rely on groups, particularly in work settings. Ethical group membership is based on two dimensions of interaction—caring and responsibility (Littlejohn & Jabusch, 1982). The first dimension—caring—means that an ethical group member is concerned about the well-being of all participants. This is evident when a member is more interested in promoting group goals than in promoting individual goals. The good of the group comes before the good of the individual. The second dimension—

responsibility—means that group members share in the responsibility for the outcome of the group's interactions. You can demonstrate responsibility by monitoring the quantity and quality of your interactions. Perhaps more importantly we must realize that being a member of a group creates responsibilities beyond those normally assigned to individuals. Because groups can act collectively, allowing for actions that could not occur individually, new moral or ethical responsibilities surface (May, 1987). As a member, you represent the group. Your actions alone can affect how others think and react to other members of your group. Thus as a member of a group, your moral or ethical responsibility has increased. You are no longer merely responsible for yourself; now you are responsible for and to every other member of your group.

Defining Ethical Behavior

Beyond individual choice over behavior, group settings allow other moral and ethical issues to surface. In particular, issues of deception (such as lying, not revealing all that you know) can hamper the development of group member relationships as well as the group's ability to proceed effectively with its task or activity. In developing a list of guidelines, however, it is easy to see that ethical behavior is situational. In groups, one ethical guideline may conflict with another because there can be competing claims on the group. Should group members always tell the truth? Should group members withhold some information if it can potentially harm relationships among group members? Let's take a look at a list of ethical guidelines for group interaction (Johannesen, 1983).

First, be candid and frank when you state your personal beliefs and feelings. "I don't think so" should mean just that—not, "I'd like to tell you but don't feel that I can right now." Not only should disagreement be direct and supported with a rationale, but so should agreement. This kind of direct and straightforward communication will keep other group members from assuming how you think and feel about a problem before the group. Second, and sometimes in opposition to the first guideline, when social relationships among group members are valued, it is better to maintain those relationships rather than completely divulge what is on your mind. For example, in your family, you may have information about your brother-in-law, and you believe that telling your sister that information would hurt her. Here you will have to decide if you should tell your sister what you know, causing her some short-term pain but preparing her for dealing with her husband later, or if you should remain silent and let her discover the information on her own. Thus ethical behavior is situational: You will find you have to make choices between being candid and harming others.

Third, when you share information in group settings, that information should be communicated accurately without distortion or exaggeration. For example, you took on the responsibility to check on availability dates at the clubhouse for your group's party. After checking several ideal dates, you are frustrated: The only date available is one for which you have another obligation. Reporting back to the group, you claim, "The clubhouse isn't going to be available. They're booked all

> **THINK ABOUT IT**
>
> ### Who Is Responsible?
>
> Think about one of your recent group experiences in which you were troubled by the final decision of the group or troubled by what some of the group members did. How effectively did the group discuss the decision or these actions? Did you participate in these discussions? Did you express agreement or disagreement with any part of the discussion? Did you remain silent? How did your actions contribute to selecting the final decision that you could not support? How did your actions encourage others to behave in a way with which you did not agree? If you could go back in time to the group deliberations, what would you change about your own behavior? How do you believe the group outcomes would differ?

the way through June!" You probably did not intend to exaggerate your claim to make it appear that the clubhouse was not available, but that is the message you delivered to your group. If you do this intentionally, this is unethical. The ethical way to handle this is to report back what you found out *with* the information that you want to attend the party but cannot on the only date the clubhouse is available.

Fourth, in group settings it is easy to cut someone off from speaking or to change the subject. This is unethical if you do this intentionally. Each group member should have the opportunity to speak as well as the opportunity to fully explain him- or herself. The fifth ethical guideline concerns trust. Although trust is rarely offered explicitly without a relationship history, you should be willing to extend your trust to others in the group and to act in a trustworthy manner. This means that you are open and willing to listen to what other members have to say; you are not closed-minded, refusing to accept others' points of view. This means that you can be trusted with information or responsibilities given or assigned to you. Trust is created among group members, but you must be willing for trust to develop.

Sixth, particularly in decision-making situations, each group member should be allowed to make up his or her own mind without coercion or manipulation. Consensus or agreement is best developed through discussion rather than force. Likewise, in advocating for one alternative over others, group members should be encouraged to provide their reasoning or their rationales. Seventh, because group members represent the collective, each should be responsible for defending the decisions of the group to others. If you cannot do this, say so during the group's decision-making deliberations. *Think About It* explores ethical dilemmas in group experiences.

Groups often must make ethical choices during their decision making, and complex decisions deliberated in group settings often center around ethical dilemmas. Frequently, the ethical choice has other negative consequences or is not the popular choice. For example, your marketing team is developing an advertising campaign for a new headache remedy. The dilemma facing the team is the report from the independent testing service. Their results show that only six out of ten doctors surveyed thought your product superior to others on the market. Your team realizes that without doctors' recommendations, your product will not have a chance. The dilemma centers on how your team will make use of the information available in a persuasive ad campaign introducing the product. Several alternatives are available to your team, each with different ethical problems.

You could give the data as it is—six out of ten doctors agree—but that type of claim is not likely to sell much of your product. Another choice would be to imply say that doctors recommend your product, but that is not the complete truth. What if a consumer group wants the data for your claim? Or, you could skip this data all together and return to the initial studies in which three out of four doctors preferred your product and then not tell consumers that only four doctors were in the initial test. You would probably sell more product with the third option, but it is the most misleading. If your team chooses the first option, honesty would be maintained, but you probably would not attract customers. Each of these choices has ethical consequences—for the product, for the team, and for the organization. Why would a group risk making an unethical decision? The environment in which decisions are made can create additional demands or pressures on a group (Street, Robertson, & Geiger, 1997). For example, if group members feel hopeless or incapable of making a decision, they may opt for an unethical alternative because they feel defeated. Or group members may feel that they have invested so much time and energy in the project that the selection of any alternative, regardless of its ethical implications, will do. A group may start out wanting to do what is best and what is right, but as time, risks, and costs to the group increase, moral intent and moral behavior can become confused. In this type of pressure environment, an unethical alternative can be regarded as viable. Careful problem solving and the use of decision-making procedures can help groups avoid these problems.

Group Impact on Individual Ethics

Can a group have a positive influence on individual members' ethical behavior? Yes. Just as a group can help identify weaknesses in solutions that individual members propose, a group can help individuals see ethical situations from new perspectives (McDonald & Zepp, 1990). Group discussions about problems and issues can cause individuals to reevaluate their positions and select a more ethical response (Nelson & Obremski, 1990). Discussing an ethical issue in a group causes members to examine their own moral reasoning process (Peek, Peek, & Horras, 1994). In discussions, not only do members revisit the pros and cons of the problem, but they may be exposed to pros and cons they had not considered earlier. In fact, discussions in a group with one or two members with high levels of moral reasoning can actually raise the moral reasoning of other members (Nichols & Day, 1982). This means that if you have a moral or ethical argument for doing or not doing something, you should openly discuss your position with other group members. You may be able to influence their reasoning and help the group avoid selecting an unethical course of action. Group discussion about ethical issues also forces group members to justify their positions to others. In most cases, this makes individual members think through their position more thoroughly and carefully before exposing their reasoning to the group.

Summary

Meeting management procedures and group facilitation strategies capitalize on the strengths of groups because they balance member participation. Formal meeting planning includes premeeting planning and preparation by group members as well as by the group leader. An agenda, identifying both start and stop times and all matters the group will consider, should be prepared and distributed before any group meeting. Remember: If you cannot identify a specific purpose and goals for a meeting, do not have one.

The group's leader conducts the meeting according to the agenda. However, the leader's role is to initiate and structure discussion, not to control the discussion content. Besides helping the group move through its business issues, the leader is also responsible for developing and maintaining a supportive group climate. Introducing members, establishing norms, and managing conflict are some of these responsibilities.

The space in which a group meets is important. All group members should be able to see and hear one another easily. The size of the space for the meeting should fit the needs and size of the group. Members should not feel too crowded nor too distant from others in the group. Using visuals and graphics can help a group record what is happening in the group. Listing topics of conversation, drawing a diagram of the group's conversation, clustering ideas together, creating data matrices, and drawing organizational charts are just a few forms of visualization that help a group capture a pictorial memory of its interaction.

In most meetings, group members volunteer for or are given assignments to be completed before the next meeting. These actions should be noted in the minutes and on the next meeting's agenda as well. At the end of a meeting, the group should review decisions and plans for actions, schedule the next meeting time, and discuss future agenda items. A secretary or recorder should take minutes at each meeting. Minutes should include what was discussed or decided, who agreed to take on what responsibilities, and what the group plans to do next. Minutes should be distributed and revisions made as soon as possible.

Most groups experience some obstacles. Long meetings, unequal involvement, the formation of cliques, differing levels of communication skills, different communicator styles, and personal conflicts are common obstacles groups must overcome. Any group member can help a group remove these barriers.

Groups that meet for extended periods of time consider themselves a team. But it takes more than calling your group a team to ensure that a team exists. Teambuilding means that a group strives for effectiveness by addressing both task and process issues. Teambuilding is an activity for all group members to participate in. To help your group become a team, you need to help the group set clear goals or priorities, clarify members' roles and responsibilities, examine how well group members work together, and strengthen the relationships among members.

One way to help your group is to develop a group charter and a code of conduct. A group charter describes the goals or mission of the group; a code of conduct describes behaviors that are appropriate for this particular group. Both can provide direction and clarity for group members.

Finally, all groups need to consider what constitutes ethical group membership. An ethical group balances caring, or the well-being of all participants, with responsibility. Ethical issues to be considered are deception, lying, considering whether all information should be shared, speaking without exaggeration or bias, trust, and coercion and manipulation. To avoid making unethical decisions, groups should use careful problem solving and use decision-making procedures. Just as individuals influence the ethics and integrity of a group, a group can influence an individual group member's ethics. Group discussions can help members reevaluate their positions and select a more ethical response. Group discussions can also help members justify their position to others.

✓ Checklist

Group Knowledge

You should be able to:

- explain the importance of premeeting planning for both group leaders and members.
- describe how a group can use visualizations.
- state at least five different factors the leader should consider in conducting a meeting.
- name three obstacles that groups must typically overcome.
- explain how groups become teams.
- describe what goes in a group charter and a code of conduct.
- explain the importance of ethical group membership.

Group Skills

You should be able to:

- design and lead an effective group meeting.
- participate effectively in a group meeting.
- select and prepare appropriate visuals to help the group record what is happening.
- follow up on assignments given in a group meeting.
- take effective minutes for your group meeting.
- assist your group in overcoming obstacles.
- act ethically in a group.

Analytical and Assessment Techniques

You should be able to:
- assess the strengths and weaknesses of your group's meeting.
- detect relational problems that could adversely affect group meetings.
- assess the extent to which obstacles occur in your group.
- analyze the team potential of your group.
- figure out how to deal with unethical group member behavior.

Discussion Questions and Exercises

1. Think of your most recent group experience—one where the group will meet again. Write a three- to five-page paper analyzing your group by using the following four issues as a guide. First, acknowledge the successes of your group. Describe at least two things the group did well. Second, identify and describe one aspect of the group process or procedure that was effective and one aspect that was ineffective. Third, if you could redo this group experience, what would you do differently? What do you think the outcome would be now? Fourth, what did you learn about yourself as a group member that you can carry forward to the next group experience? What did you learn about the group that you can apply in the next group session? (adapted from Gardenswartz & Rowe, 1994)

2. You have been charged with leading your team at work. The team is responsible for planning this year's achievement banquet—an off-site dinner party to reward employees and their groups for meeting or exceeding established goals. The manager to whom you report has only been on the job for six months. Develop three arguments to convince others to join your team. Be specific about what they can achieve as individuals by being a member of your team.

3. Interview at least three people who have been members of formal teams. Ask each how would they describe their team. Does their description sound like an effective team or a group in trouble? Do any questions of ethics surface in their descriptions of the group's activities or member responsibilities? Are task, relationship, process/procedure, or teamwork issues more prominent in their descriptions?

14 Making Observations and Giving Feedback

Why do groups need feedback?

Do groups need a feedback process beyond their face-to-face interaction?

Is feedback given to individual group members or to the group as a whole?

Because I feel awkward telling group members how I feel about our interaction, is there another technique we could use?

How can I create feedback for myself?

When groups develop into teams, group members have additional responsibilities toward the group. Primary of those responsibilities is to monitor one another's performance in the group (McIntyre & Salas, 1995). This means that each group member is responsible for monitoring or assessing how well the group is doing, as well as for providing feedback to other group members. Feedback can be information about the quantity or quality of a group's work, an assessment of the effectiveness of the group's work, or an evaluation of individual performance. **Feedback** is information about individual group members' actual performance or the actions of a group (Nadler, 1979). Observing other group members' communication and performance to provide feedback is not spying on one another. Rather, each group member knows and expects that other group members will be checking on one another to offer assistance and feedback. Nor is the type of feedback described here part of a formal performance evaluation system.

Feedback, as we are interested in it, is a group process that serves as an error detection device to help a group identify and begin to solve its interaction problems. Thus feedback is generated by group members themselves. In this additional role, group members are both participants and observers. Observations are aboveboard and apparent to other group members. Group members who trust one another can effectively take on these additional group roles. Perhaps you are thinking that feedback should be a responsibility of the leader, but the most effective leader is one who can help the group develop to the point where members themselves are the primary source of feedback information (Keltner, 1989). When trust develops among group members, there is a safety net to help each group member perform as effectively for the team as he or she can. When individuals are drawn this tightly into a group, their interdependence is extremely high. By investing in one another through observation and feedback, their interdependence is strengthened.

Refer back to the description of a system in Chapter 2. The type of feedback described here is synonymous with the feedback described there. The information provided through group and individual feedback is a reflection on or evaluation of the group's output; it also creates new input for the group's system. Is feedback necessary? Without it, the group would be unable to adapt and eventually would find its ineffectiveness overwhelming. Because groups do not automatically correct for these problems, group members must pay conscious attention to feedback and then interpret and act on it (Nadler, 1979).

There are three feedback systems groups can use. The first is the most common and perhaps the least obvious—that is, your message feedback to other group members. Throughout a group meeting, you are constantly providing feedback to others—both about what they say and how they say it. You may not have thought of group conversation as feedback, but many messages we send have feedback implications. The second feedback system is more formalized but can still be managed by group members themselves. This is the use of questionnaires or surveys—much like the ones that appear throughout this book as *Group Assessment Techniques* or *Building Analytical Skills*. These can be used by group members during breaks in group interaction or at the end of a group meeting. The third type of group feedback and observation requires access to either audio- or videotaping equipment or the use of one member in the formal role of group observer. All three will be discussed in this chapter.

Why Groups Need Feedback

Listen to the weekend sports news during football, baseball, or basketball season. When a team wins and the sportscaster asks an athlete what contributed to the team's win, the player is likely to say something like, "We just went out there and did what we had to do." You are thinking, that is pretty admirable. A basketball player who scored 21 points and had 10 assists is giving credit to his teammates; he is not hogging the win for himself. Now listen to the feedback of a player whose team lost: "Our defense was weak tonight. We weren't getting inside the way we need to do with Orlando."

What is the difference between the winning and losing players' explanations? You may not notice it at first, but the winning player's feedback is ambiguous and generalized. Reread the winning athlete's statement. What exactly did this player say contributed to his team's winning the ballgame? There is nothing specific enough in his comments that his team could use to repeat their success. Now look at the feedback from the losing player. What specifically did this player say contributed to his team's losing the ballgame? Notice how this feedback is more specific. Defense was weak, and players were unable to get to the inside of the Orlando defense. These are specific things the losing team can work on to better its record.

Many of us are biased about our responsibility to groups. If the group succeeds, we tend to believe that the group's success should be attributed to us personally. If the group fails, we blame the group and avoid taking responsibility for the group's failure. We are more effective group members and a greater asset to our groups when we recognize this type of attribution bias.

This type of general-if-it-is-good and specific-if-it-is-bad bias fits many feedback situations. As a child you were probably told to "sit still," "cover your mouth when you cough," or "stand straight." Each of these messages is specific; you knew exactly what to do to change the poor impression you were creating with your parents. On the other hand, when you were good you were likely told, "that's a good girl," "aren't you a nice young man," or "very good." Although you were basking in the praise, it was still unclear to you exactly what you did to earn these praises and positive distinctions. This same bias happens in groups (Nadler, 1979). We are more likely to give detailed feedback when the information is negative or the team has suffered a loss and general feedback when the information is positive or the team is glowing after a success. Initiating a feedback system can help your group overcome this bias; having a feedback system in place can help your group develop more effectively.

Let's continue our examination of bias in feedback. When asked how you contributed to a group's success, most of us would reply that we were personally responsible. But ask how we contributed to a group's failure, and we would probably avoid taking that responsibility. This attributional bias is common in group members. Virtually without exception, members of successful groups will claim personal responsibility when their group is successful and deny personal responsibility when their group fails (Forsyth & Kelley, 1994). This type of self-serving bias may cloud our judgment, keeping us from truthfully recognizing our impact on the group. Another factor figures in here as well. Some of us are optimists—

we expect things to generally go well. Conversely, some of us are pessimists—we expect things to generally turn out poorly. Personality traits like these can also cloud our judgment of our impact on group interaction. Feedback—or information that evaluates or judges our communication performance—is one type of tool or intervention that can help overcome this bias and improve our abilities as group members. Feedback also improves the functioning of the team. In successful teams, everyone is accountable all of the time (Larson & LaFasto, 1989). Thus each team requires some system of checks and balances—both at a team level and at an individual group member level. If you are still wondering if a group really needs feedback about how well its members are communicating, consider this: Nearly 75 percent of all group problems are linked to interpersonal problems and poor communication (Di Salvo, Nikkel, & Monroe, 1989).

Initiating a feedback system in a group provides several advantages. Group members who believe that their input to the group will be evaluated are less likely to become social loafers (Comer, 1995). **Social loafers** are those group members who do not perform to their maximum level of potential contribution. Rather, they know that the group context provides a shield they can hide behind and still reap the same benefits as other group members who work to make the group a success. Groups that develop and provide opportunities for evaluation of group members automatically decrease the likelihood of social loafing. Even if the group is not comparing itself to other groups, the presence of evaluation and potential feedback about individual performance is enough to motivate potential social loafers to take on other more productive roles in the group.

Second, most group members identify with their group more strongly than they identify with their group's supporting organization (Barker & Tompkins, 1994). A feedback system can further enhance that identification with the group. The more a group member identifies with his or her group, the more committed he or she will be, creating stronger interdependence among group members. Communication will also be more effective among group members who identify with their group.

A third advantage results when groups implement feedback systems and increase group efficacy. Group efficacy is the collective belief among group members that the group can and will be effective (Gist, 1987; Shea & Guzzo, 1987; Spink, 1990). Individual group members are more likely to develop the attitudes that support this belief if they know that their group is working to its maximum potential. A belief in group efficacy directly influences the extent to which group members are willing to mobilize and coordinate their skills, the amount of effort they are willing to put into the task, and their persistence when faced with challenges (Bandura, 1986). Knowing that evaluation and feedback are a regular part of the group's interaction will strengthen a group member's group efficacy belief. Group success fuels higher expectations about group performance whereas group failure lowers efficacy expectations (Silver & Bufanio, 1996). Groups wanting to maintain group success need feedback to identify their strengths so they can capitalize on them. Groups wanting to turn failure into success need feedback to identify their weakness so they can make improvements.

Message Feedback to Group Members

Feedback is information group members give to other members about their performance, behavior, or communication displayed in the group setting. Effective feedback is relatively factual, and it works best when group members agree to use feedback as a mechanism for improving group performance (Keltner, 1995). Good feedback is not just advice about how a member *should* communicate in a group but is a description of how a member *does* communicate in a group. Feedback to group members improves role clarity (Kopelman, 1986), which in turn generally improves group performance for the individual and the group. Feedback reminds members of how they are communicating—something that is difficult to track when group meetings become emotional or conflict-laden or when time or other external pressures increasingly challenge the group. As a result, feedback reduces role ambiguity and prompts competent communication behaviors.

Feedback will come naturally to a group when it develops rules for constructive controversy (Tjosvold, 1995). A group member will only want to provide feedback to and receive feedback from other group members when a norm of openness is established. When openness is encouraged, group members feel comfortable expressing their opinions, doubts, and ideas. Groups that champion openness know that tentative ideas are worth being listened to as they develop form and structure in the group conversation. Feedback is also more easily received when group members regularly use individuals or subgroups in the role of the critical advisor (see Chapter 8). Groups comfortable with hearing constructive criticism are more likely to receive feedback in the spirit it was given. Feedback is more easily received when group members respect one another. This means that group members have risen above petty or personal insults to providing feedback about ideas rather than personalities.

Who gets the feedback? is a question you are probably asking. Although there can be times when feedback about the group as a whole is given to all group members simultaneously, feedback about communication performance is best given to group members individually (Archer-Kath, Johnson, & Johnson, 1994). Let's look at why this is. Your food design team has just met an important deadline. Everyone worked hard to make sure that the prototype meals for the new restaurant your company is opening were tasty, pleasing to the eye, within reasonable costs for a family-style restaurant, and on time. After the successful presentation of the meals to the executive board, the vice-president of development met with your food design team to discuss the apparent success of your team's work. After glowing praise about the unique and creative approach your team took to developing family-oriented meals not already in the marketplace, Ms. Ferguson then turned to some criticisms. Although the meals met their budget estimates, there was little variety in the color schemes of the meals, and most of the meals centered on meat dishes despite the guideline to incorporate more vegetarian dishes.

Although generally pleased, Ms. Ferguson cautioned the design team members about the need to adhere to all of the relevant guidelines in the next design project. Who should take responsibility for these problems? the team leader? the member of the group most responsible for checking the meals against the guidelines? another member of the team who suggested that yellow squash and yellow peppers were cheap vegetable accompaniments? This type of feedback focuses on the group's output, and it is appropriately directed to the entire group because all team members contributed to and were responsible for creating the meal plans.

But Ms. Ferguson gave another type of feedback. In working with the team one day, she noticed that some members were rude and impolite, which, in turn, created a negative climate in the group. In this same feedback meeting she said, "And I encourage you to work on your interaction skills. Last Thursday when I met with the team, it was very unsettling to find that some of you treated others with such negativity. I'm sure that negativity affected your ability to work together. But, in spite of it all, I'm glad the team performed so well." Who is Ms. Ferguson talking to? all group members? the group members who are impolite and unfriendly? If so, what if these team members do not think her comments apply to them? When feedback is about specific communication issues, the feedback should be given to those group members individually. In this case, the feedback about the group's success with the meal designs and the feedback about the team being able to pull together despite some ineffective interaction should have been delivered to the team as a whole. The feedback about impolite and rude behavior should have been given to Kaitlin and Elliott, the two members Ms. Ferguson observed communicating in that way. Let's see how she might do this:

MS. FERGUSON: And I have some specific comments about interaction skills. Last Thursday when I met with the team, it was unsettling to find a great deal of negativity.

CHRISTIAN: Thanks for bringing it up. I didn't like what was happening.

MS. FERGUSON: I felt that Kaitlin and Elliott were rude and impolite. Now, I wasn't there for the entire meeting, so I don't know what motivated this behavior. Can either of you explain?

KAITLIN: Okay, I admit . . . I was getting mad. I probably was rude.

ELLIOTT: (jumping in) Right, and I was rude, too. But Kaitlin and I felt pretty stressed. We did yell at each other, but we're used to talking to each other that way.

CHRISTIAN: They were yelling, I heard it!

MS. FERGUSON: Christian, how did your communication as a member of the group contribute to this problem?

CHRISTIAN: Me?

MS. FERGUSON: I ask because you seem to know quite a bit about the situation.

CHRISTIAN: With me? Things were just normal.

KAITLIN: Actually, Christian, your refusals to rerun the graphics set up on the computer is what put us behind. I don't know how to run the program, neither does Elliott . . . and we needed to revise the graphics.

CHRISTIAN: So, it's my fault?!

MS. FERGUSON: It's not any one person's fault. Together you work as a team. Every person's actions contribute to the group's output. Did you refuse to rerun the graphics, Christian?

CHRISTIAN: (meekly) Yes.

MS. FERGUSON: (to all) It doesn't matter why, I just want to point out that rude and impolite behavior won't help you work together. Christian, if you can help Kaitlin and Elliott out, you need to do so. Likewise, Kaitlin and Elliott need to minimize reruns at the last minute. But yelling at each other won't help anyone.

Group members who work together over a long period of time are more able to accept individually directed feedback. Successful and effective groups are likely to be based on strong and favorable group member relationships. If this is the case, group members can handle individually directed feedback in front of other team members. In fact, when a group is open to individually directed feedback that is both positive and negative, acceptance among group members can actually increase (Archer-Kath, Johnson, & Johnson, 1994). Another advantage to giving individually directed feedback with the entire group present is that other group members will know of the problem and may be able to help facilitate the group more effectively. However, group members should be asked, and all should agree, that it is okay for individually directed feedback to be given in group meetings. Remember that in a group no one group member can work independently, each member's performance is confounded by the actions of other group members (Nadler, 1979). Although we might agree that Kaitlin was rude, her behavior was likely prompted by Christian's refusals to help.

There are limitations to the power of feedback, however (Kopelman, 1986). First, its effects are limited to the specific setting in which group members' communication is observed. Observing Kelly initiate a conflict in her work group and later providing feedback to her about the incident is not likely to reduce her initiation of conflict in her family group. And giving Kelly feedback about conflict will not reduce her disruptive nonverbal behaviors. Feedback must be specific to a behavior and to a setting.

Second, feedback is also limiting to the extent that it is motivating. Simply giving information about a group's member performance may not in itself be motivating. Feedback given in pejorative or negative terms may also increase the distance between the offending group member and others. Recall from Chapter 2 that descriptive words are more effective than evaluative words in creating a supportive climate. A good way to increase the effectiveness of feedback is to describe the consequences that occurred after the behavior display. "Kelly, your comments upset me. It makes me not want to talk to you." Feedback is limited to the extent it does not mention consequences. When consequences of a group member's communication behavior are described, it reminds them of the social relationships in which their communication is interpreted and evaluated. Feedback about consequences helps create anticipation about gaining (or losing) rewarding behavior from others. To be effective, feedback must be specific, motivating, and mention consequences.

Let's continue with Kelly as an example. You observe Kelly initiate a conflict with Grey. Kelly likes to make jokes, and she frequently teases Grey about his name. "Couldn't your parents think of a real name? What's it like being named after a color?" Kelly perceives this as friendly teasing; Grey feels anger and humiliation. Generally, Grey is nonconfrontive. Rather than ask Kelly to quit making fun of his name, Grey simply removes himself from these interactions. His reaction reinforces Kelly's perception that she is getting the best of him. What feedback would you give Kelly?

Your feedback to Kelly must be specific along several dimensions. First, what specific incident did you observe? How would you describe her behavior? How would you describe Grey's reaction? What was the consequence of her behavior to Grey? on other group members? After your feedback, Kelly should know that she initiated a conflict with Grey, how she initiated the conflict, what the probable consequences were to her relationship with Grey, and what the probable consequences were to her relationships with other group members. Only when Kelly has this specific information can she make better choices about how to communicate.

How can your feedback motivate Kelly to change her communication? Which statement would work best? "Kelly, if you keep talking to Grey like that—well, it's no wonder he hates you." Or, "Kelly, it's good you include Grey in the group's conversation. I wonder how he really feels, though, when you make fun of his name. In yesterday's meeting, I heard you call him 'halfway between black and white.' I saw him turn around and leave the room. Is that really the response you wanted?"

Most important, feedback should not limited to negative behaviors. Sometimes we get focused on providing feedback to group members who are the least competent. These behaviors and their consequences are likely to stick out in the group. However, good performance also deserves feedback. This type of feedback provides motivation to continue with the positive communication behaviors until they become norms for the group. When Kelly talks to Grey about how they will monitor the group's progress on the computer program—and does not make fun of Grey's name—she should be given feedback that reinforces that positive communication behavior. "Kelly, I overheard you and Grey discussing the monitoring system after the meeting was over. Looks like the two of you are working well together." In summary, feedback can have a tremendous impact on members' behavior in groups (Ammons, 1956). Generally, feedback increases our understanding and learning, and it creates motivation. The more specific feedback is, the greater its impact. However, the longer the delay between performance and feedback, the less effective it will be.

Giving feedback effectively is easier said than done. Think about the times you have received feedback about your performance in a group or team. How did that feedback affect you? To what extent did you agree that the feedback was accurate and helpful? Many people believe that blurting anything out is feedback. Maybe so. But for feedback to be effective, it has to be delivered carefully with the intent to help, not hurt.

One way to assess the effectiveness of feedback is to evaluate the ability of the other person to follow your directions (Keltner, 1995). This is known as **behavior feedback.** Behavior feedback occurs when Kyoko tells Ron that the group needs to review its budget at the next meeting. Kyoko will receive feedback that her message was effective if Ron shows up at the meeting with the budget and is ready to review it with other group members. Many of us rely upon behavior feedback. Unfortunately, think of the many other interpretations Ron could have given to Kyoko's message. Ron might have thought Kyoko meant that: (1) she would bring the budget to review it at the next meeting, (2) the two of them would review the budget separately from other group members, (3) the budget needed to be reviewed at some time in the future when they had time, or (4) he was to review the budget and if everything was okay, then he simply needed to tell the group that everything was okay. The problem here is that the behavior that provides the feedback may occur at some time in the future. There could be a period of hours, days, or even weeks before Kyoko knows if her message was received completely and as she intended.

Reflective feedback occurs when one group member reflects back exactly what was said to him or her so the other person can check the message for accuracy (Keltner, 1995). Reflective feedback is a form of copying what the other person says. This is one step better than behavior feedback, but it is not error-proof. For example, Kyoko says to Ron, "The group needs to review its budget at the next meeting." Ron responds to Kyoko by saying, "I agree, the group needs to review the budget at the next meeting." Seems like the message was sent and received accurately, right? Are you sure? Could Kyoko and Ron be bypassing each other? **Bypassing** occurs when two group members use the same words but individually attribute different meanings to the words or phrases. What exactly does "review the budget" mean? Kyoko may mean a detailed line-by-line examination of the budget. Ron may mean a simple examination of the bottom line to make sure the group has not overspent the total monies allotted. Who is right? Both interpretations can be. Unfortunately, Kyoko and Ron have not shared their differing interpretations so they both falsely believe that they have communicated and that the communication was effective.

Closed-Loop Communication as Feedback

Closed-loop communication is one way to deliver feedback effectively. There are three parts to **closed-loop communication** (McIntyre & Salas, 1995). First, the sender delivers the message. Second, the receiver accepts the message and provides feedback to the sender indicating that the message has been received. Finally, the sender double-checks to ensure that the intended message was received. Let's see how this works:

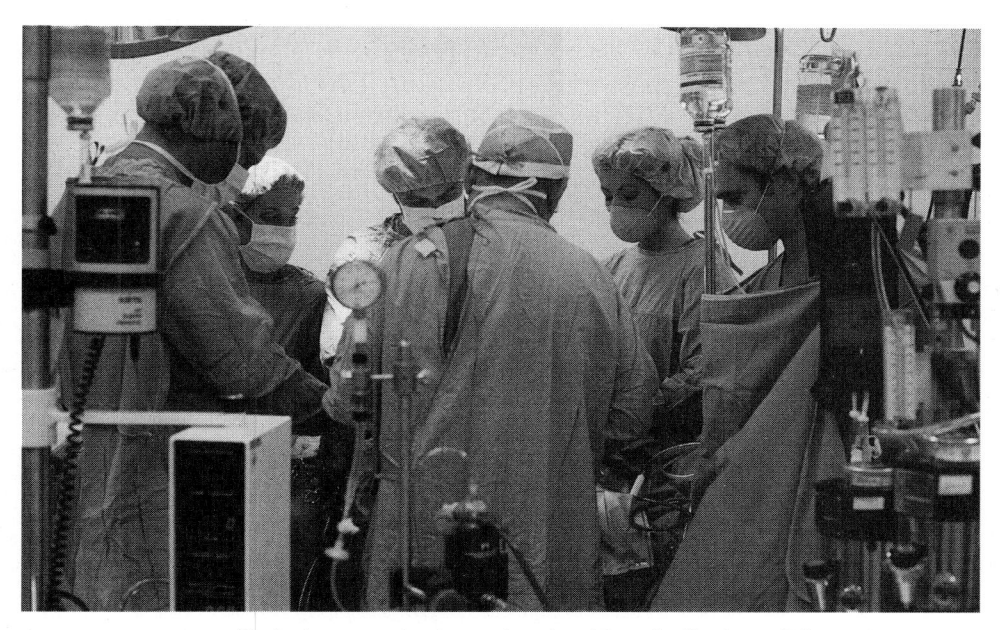

Some groups cannot afford miscommunication. Using closed-loop feedback can help group members communicate effectively and avoid communication failure.

NICOLE: This is frustrating. I can't find the information we need.

MOHAN: Have you tried the online databases at the library?

NICOLE: Yes, but I didn't see what I thought we needed.

JOLENE: Did you say you were having trouble finding information for our project on the online databases?

NICOLE: Yes.

JOLENE: If you're having trouble with the online databases, perhaps I can help out. I worked at the library during the summer and learned some neat tricks for finding information I thought was impossible to find.

MOHAN: That would be great, Jolene. Can you meet Nicole and I at the library at 10 A.M.?

Jolene provides feedback when she says, "Did you say you were having trouble finding information for our project on the online databases?" Her feedback in the form of a question asks for Nicole to respond; this is the first step of closed-loop communication. Then Nicole agrees with Jolene's feedback or assessment; this is the second step of closed-loop communication. In the third step, Jolene repeats the feedback and offers her help: "If you're having trouble with the online databases, perhaps I can help out. . . . ." As you can see from this example, feedback does not have to be formalized or always set aside to a specific time during a group's meeting. Feedback can be spontaneous and a natural part of a group's conversation. But you can also see from the example that effective feedback is that which is double-checked for its accuracy and intent.

Being able to use feedback informally throughout a meeting will make members more agreeable to more formal feedback and evaluation at the end of a meeting. Let's take a look at a more formalized feedback session at the end of a meeting:

NICOLE: Okay, let's end the meeting with our feedback session. Why doesn't everyone take a few minutes to jot down notes?

—after a pause—

MOHAN: I'd like to comment on our ability to work together. I think we're doing much better. Personally, I feel less stress. And I feel like we're working together better as a team.

JOLENE: Can you explain why you feel less stress, Mohan?

MOHAN: Sure. I feel more open to the group and feel that group members are accepting me and the information I provide. That indicates to me that we've developed a more supportive climate and that we're working better as a team.

NICOLE: I agree with Mohan's assessment to some degree . . . but not completely. I'm not sure that we're as open as we should be with one another. For example, I'm still a little uncomfortable talking to you like this at the end of the meeting.

JOLENE: I heard you say two different things, Nicole. First you said you agreed with Mohan that we've become more open, developed a more supportive climate, and are working better as a team. Then I heard you say that you're still uncomfortable with the feedback part of our meeting.

NICOLE: Right. . . . I mean that I agree with the first part. I mean, I'm, me, I'm still uncomfortable giving feedback . . . well, maybe that's receiving feedback from the rest of you. But look at me—I'm talking to you now, aren't I?

JOLENE: Is it the giving feedback or receiving feedback that's most troublesome for you?

NICOLE: I guess it's the receiving of feedback. I'm still scared of what you'll say about me.

MOHAN: Sometimes I sense this too. Maybe we all are more critical of Nicole because she's the newest member of the group.

NICOLE: You may be right, Mohan. I've seen you give personal feedback to other group members, and I'm not sure I could handle it right now.

JOLENE: Well, what's the worst thing we say to you right now, Nicole?

NICOLE: You could say that I didn't do my part and that I'm not contributing to the team. That would really hurt my feelings.

MOHAN: But we wouldn't give you that feedback. You *are* doing your part, and you *are* contributing to the team.

JOLENE: How could we help you overcome the fear of receiving feedback?

NICOLE: Could I go first at the next feedback session? I think that might give me more confidence.

MOHAN: But you went first today, Nicole.

NICOLE: No, no I didn't! I suggested we jot down notes. But you gave the first real feedback. It may seem like I went first, but I didn't.

JOLENE: Okay, let's make a procedural rule for giving and receiving feedback. We'll rotate the role of who initiates the feedback session. Whoever initiates the session will also be the first to give feedback. Okay by everyone?

MOHAN: Sure.

NICOLE: Okay, can I start at the next session?

Can you find examples of closed-loop communication in this dialogue? Members of a group that regularly rely on feedback are more likely to have a collective view of the group. Knowing that feedback is a regular part of the group's interaction will motivate them to be prepared for and contribute to the group's interaction (McIntyre & Salas, 1995).

Feedback Style

Besides the procedure for giving feedback, the style in which feedback is given is also important. The group member who receives your feedback will make evaluations about its helpfulness based on both what you say and how you say it (Ogilvie & Haslett, 1985). Dynamism, or your ability to be direct and frank but helpful, plays a major role in how your feedback is interpreted. Closely related to dynamism is trust. If the receiver perceives that you are being fair in your assessment, then your feedback is more likely to be received and acted upon.

The mood you are in when you give feedback is also important. Providing feedback in a relaxed and pleasant manner demonstrates to the receiver that you are supportive and positive. Thus the receiver is more likely to listen to what you have to say. But giving feedback from a defensive or closed-minded position will only increase the distance between you and other group members. It appears that group members do not mind getting constructive criticism as long as the criticism is clear. Refer back to your communicator style assessment in Chapter 6. Which dimensions of communicator style do you believe are most appropriate for giving feedback in a group? Are these among your strengths? Which dimensions of communicator style should you avoid or minimize in feedback sessions? Feedback is more likely to be accepted when the sender of the feedback uses a style that is assertive yet responsive and relaxed (Ogilvie &

> **PUTTING THE PIECES TOGETHER**
>
> *Group Goal, Interdependence, and Group Identity*
>
> How group members give and receive feedback can help a group achieve its goals or weaken relationships among group members. Feedback should always be grounded in the group's goal or be task-directed. Reflect on your last group meeting. What feedback do you believe would have helped the group? specific group members? you? If you had the opportunity, how would you have constructed and delivered feedback to help the group become more effective? Would it have been difficult or easy to persuade everyone to participate in both giving and receiving feedback? How do you think giving and receiving feedback would affect group members' interdependence and identity? What fears would you have with giving and receiving feedback? What about the fears of other group members?

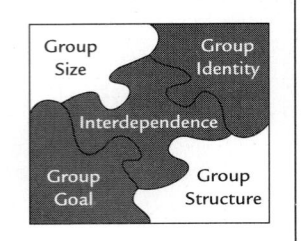

Haslett, 1985). The *Putting the Pieces Together* box will help you explore the feedback process.

Types of Feedback

Now that you understand some of the basics of using messages as feedback, let's explore feedback more closely. There are three types of feedback—descriptive, evaluative, and prescriptive. Each has a different intent and carries different inferences.

Descriptive Feedback

Descriptive feedback merely identifies or describes how a group member communicates. You may describe someone's communicator style, or you may note that someone's verbal communication and nonverbal communication suggest different meanings. For example, you say to Yelena after a meeting, "You asked me to comment on how you communicated with others in the group. From my perspective you were very dominant; you talked a lot and seemed very active in the group. I also felt that you argued each point introduced. Someone once told me that I was contentious when I did that. And, you were precise. You said exactly what was on your mind. Everyone got the message!"

Evaluative Feedback

Evaluative feedback is that which goes beyond mere description and provides an evaluation or assessment of the person who communicates. After describing Yelena's communicator style as dominant, contentious, and precise, you follow up by saying that this style causes other group members to avoid talking with her. Yelena asks what you mean by that. You let her know that others with a more submissive style find Yelena's style overwhelming, making it difficult for some members to feel equal to her in the group. Not only did you describe Yelena's style, you evaluated her style as negatively affecting group member interaction. However, extreme levels of evaluative feedback can elicit defensive reactions from group members. Too much negative evaluative feedback will decrease motivation and elicit defensive coping attributions, like attributing the feedback to others. At the extreme, it can destroy group members' pride in their group. In these cases, group members are likely to spend additional time rationalizing their failures (for example, finding a way to see a loss as a win) (Nadler, 1979).

On the other hand, favorable feedback generates motivation and increases feelings of attraction among group members (Nadler, 1979). Let's go back to Yelena. After your feedback, Yelena has toned down her dominance and has quit arguing minor points. "Great job today, Yelena. I thought today's meeting went much better. That's due to you, of course." Naturally, we assume that positive evaluative feedback will have positive effects on a group. Could a group receive too much favorable feedback? Yes. A group inundated by positive remarks, particularly in the absence of negative evaluations, will start to distrust the feedback as information and perceive the feedback as insincere.

Prescriptive Feedback

Prescriptive feedback is that which provides group members with advice about how they should act or communicate. After your description and evaluation of Yelena's communicator style, she asks you how she might change her style to be more accepted by other group members. You suggest that she tone down the dominance and try to be more friendly and open. You also suggest that her being precise is only a problem because of her overly direct style based on dominance and contention. Other group members will probably appreciate her precise and exact way of communicating if she is friendlier to them and more open to what they have to say. Try *Think About It* to learn how you responded to feedback in one of your group experiences.

Levels of Feedback

Feedback can occur on many levels. Feedback may focus on how the group is working with procedures, how an individual is handling a specific group role in working with others, how one member sits silently saying nothing, how the group is dealing with a conflict, or how the organization is using the information the group provides.

Task and Procedural Feedback

Feedback at the task or procedural level usually involves issues of effectiveness and appropriateness. Issues of quantity and quality of group output are the focus of

> ### THINK ABOUT IT
>
> #### How Do You Respond to Feedback?
>
> Think back to an experience when you received feedback in a group. Did you know how to correct or enhance your behavior when the feedback was only descriptive? How did it feel when another group member evaluated your communication without adequately describing the behavior being evaluated? How did you feel when you received prescriptive advice from others? Did it matter to you who gave the feedback? How comfortable did you feel in receiving feedback in front of others?

task feedback. Did the team win? To what extent did the group's presentation satisfy the judges? Likewise, two primary questions drive procedural feedback: Is the procedure effective for the group? Is this the procedure the group should be using? These questions capture the spirit of feedback at this level. Groups need this level of feedback, especially after trying a new group procedure or after a major milestone in the group's development.

Relational Feedback

Relational feedback is information about group climate or environment or interaction dynamics within a relationship in the group. Relational feedback focuses group members' attention on how well they are working together rather than on how they are working together (task/procedural feedback). It is most effective when it is both descriptive and prescriptive. Relational feedback seems to work as a cueing function (Nadler, 1979). For example, a group that meets regularly could benefit from relational feedback, particularly when the group has succeeded where it normally is inefffective. Allison comments, "We did a better job today at letting everyone talk. For me, it created a greater sense of group unity—even when we were expressing different ideas." "I agree," says David. "Let's try to recapture this at our next meeting." This means that group members receiving relational feedback are made aware that something is wrong and are more likely to be on the lookout for similar trouble in future interactions.

Individual Feedback

Individual feedback focuses on a specific group member. Feedback may address the knowledge, skills, or attitudes the group member demonstrates or displays. What specifically might you address about one another as group members? Your potential to be an effective group member centers around the following seven characteristics (Larson & LaFasto, 1989). The first is intellectual ability. Can the person secure relevant information and relate and compare data from different sources? A group member who is analytical or creative is especially helpful to his or her group. The second factor is results orientation. A group member who can demonstrate the ability to work toward outcomes and complete activities started will help further the progress of the team. The third factor—interpersonal skills—encompasses a group member's ability to relate to the feelings and needs of other group members. The fourth factor is the ability to plan and organize. An individual who is able to schedule personal time as well as work within the time schedules of others is important to a group accomplishing its goals. Typically, group members must handle several activities at once and have the ability to meet competing deadlines.

The fifth factor is the individual's ability to demonstrate a team orientation. Can the person work collaboratively with others on complex issues? If so, the individual is demonstrating a commitment to the team on which others can depend. The sixth factor is maturity. The individual group member is considered mature when he or she acts responsibly when dealing with people or difficult situations. Finally, the seventh factor is presence or image. The person's willingness to present a friendly impression reflects positively on the individual as well as on the team.

Feedback can cover any or all of these issues. But, in general, group members are going to respond to three main issues (Larson & LaFasto, 1989): Do you demonstrate the essential skills and abilities needed by the team? Do you demonstrate a strong desire to contribute to the group's activities? Are you capable of collaborating effectively with other team members? Remember that while you are being evaluated on these dimensions, you are evaluating other team members as well.

Group Feedback

At this level, feedback focuses on how well the group is performing. Have team members developed adequate skills for working together? Does the role structure or hierarchy of the group support the group's task and activities? Has the team developed norms for communicating that help it accomplish its goals? Does the group possess adequate skills, knowledge, or motivation for the task it must complete? Feedback at this level can have a dramatic impact on members' attraction to the group, as well as their feelings of involvement and esteem. Certainly, feedback to the group about its performance on its task increases group members' motivations to improve their performance. The more interdependently group members work together, the greater the impact of group feedback concerning the task (Nadler, 1979). The *Building Analytical Skills* box, "Topics for Group Feedback" will give you some ideas for applying feedback in your groups.

Over time, it is important that a group receive both **taskwork feedback**—feedback about the technical competencies or the functional task activities of the team—and **teamwork feedback**—feedback about the group's interactions and members' relationships, cooperation, communication, and coordination (McIntyre & Salas, 1995). Using both taskwork and teamwork feedback, a group can actually improve its development over time.

> **BUILDING ANALYTICAL SKILLS**
>
> ## Topics for Group Feedback
>
> Although each group is different and unique, most groups will benefit from reflecting on the following questions. How would you answer these questions for one of your current groups?
>
> ### Goals of the Group
>
> 1. Are members committed to the goals of the group?
> 2. Are members' personal goals in alignment with the group's goals?
>
> ### Roles in the Group
>
> 1. Are roles and responsibilities within the group clear to all?
> 2. Who in the group is providing leadership?
> 3. Is the group responding well to this leadership?
> 4. Are other necessary roles covered by someone in the group?
>
> ### Procedures and Processes
>
> 1. Are group members communicating effectively together?
> 2. Are decision-making procedures used appropriately?
> 3. Is conflict managed?
> 4. Does the group spend its time together effectively?
>
> ### General
>
> 1. What are the strengths and weaknesses of our group?
> 2. Is someone or something outside the group hindering us?
>
> Using these questions to guide a feedback session at the end of a meeting could uncover issues that need to be addressed or resolved. Even if no difficulties are uncovered, the group will benefit from reviewing its positive direction and successes.

Organizational Feedback

We often do not think that we are able to give feedback to the organization or supporting environment of the group, but we can and should if we are interested in how well the group is performing. Questions that drive feedback at this level include: Is the group receiving adequate support in terms of resources or supervision? Does the organization reward the group and its members appropriately and adequately? Can information pass easily between the group and its larger environment?

Certainly, group members can receive feedback from their supporting organization. Members may have conversations with others in the organization who are depending on the group. These conversations create feedback for the group. For example, Craig talks to Nkemjika about processing the group's travel claims. "Thanks, Nkemjika. I know your group is traveling a lot these days. But it really does help when one team investigates these problems. We're getting consistency now in how to fix the audit problems." When the investigation team meets again, Nkemjika shares this praise for the team with everyone.

In formal organizations, some groups are required to collect data and create reports for the organization. Then feedback is received from the organization in the form of group rankings, such as when the performance of sales or production is compared to other similar groups. Knowing that your group is in first place or last place will certainly have an impact on your group. The *Building Analytical Skills* box, "Specifying Feedback" provides practice in understanding types of feedback.

Questionnaires and Surveys as Feedback

Throughout this book, you've been encouraged to complete the exercises in *Group Assessment Techniques* or *Building Analytical Skills*. Many of these can be used to provide feedback to your group. Table 14.1 reviews those that can accomplish this function most effectively.

Other Feedback Techniques

Talking to others in the group and using questionnaires or surveys are two traditional ways of providing feedback to group members. In this section, we will explore two other types of feedback—interaction diagrams and taping the group. Both require more preparation but can provide information not available from other feedback techniques.

Interaction Diagrams

A very simple way to provide feedback for a group is to construct a diagram of who talks to whom. In Chapter 3, we discussed group interaction networks. Figure 3.3 visualizes the interaction of one group. In the role of formal observer, one group member can collect the data to construct the **interaction diagram** for the group. Sitting just outside the group's interaction circle, the observer first makes a diagram that corresponds to how group members are seated. The first time each group member participates in the conversation, the observer draws an arrow to the person to whom the message is directed. If the message is directed to the group as a whole, an arrow should be drawn away from the group (for ease in seeing the data). A hashmark across the arrowed lines represents subsequent interactions. At the end of the interaction, the observer can tally the interactions and create a matrix like the one in Figure 14.1 (page 429); this matrix uses data from the example in Chapter 3.

The matrix helps the observer organize feedback for the group. Let's look at the total number of messages sent. There is a great deal of disparity in the activity of group members. Donnie only sent three messages in comparison to the more talkative Bren and Marie. Remember, however, that the diagram only captures quantity of interaction, not quality of interaction. Donnie may not talk much, but what he has to say is important to the group and helps move the group toward completion of its activities. Let's also look at the total number of messages directed

BUILDING ANALYTICAL SKILLS

Specifying Feedback

Learning to give effective feedback takes practice. Listed here are examples of feedback statements taken from transcripts of group meetings. The examples show both the intent of the feedback and the actual feedback given. After considering the intent of the feedback, evaluate the feedback given. If you think it is lacking in any way or likely to be ineffective, rewrite the feedback to be more effective.

Intent of Feedback	Feedback Given	Your Feedback Suggestion
Individual, Positive	"I think Connor did a great job helping us focus on the real arguments when he asked each of us to describe why we felt the way we did."	
Group, Positive	"We did a great job, guys."	
Individual, Negative	"I think we all could do a better job of managing our tempers."	
Descriptive, Prescriptive, Group	"We wasted our time today. We've got to do better."	
Evaluative, Relational	"Mark, next time, why don't you just bring a gun and shoot Darius? You were mad at him the entire meeting."	
Descriptive, Group, Task/Procedural	"In my observations, I saw the group use four different decision-making strategies."	
Negative, Group, Relational, Prescriptive	"Let's see. Together we successfully squashed any attempt at creating a supportive or positive group climate. We have to get along better."	

to each member. Donnie received the fewest messages in comparison to the many messages sent to Bren and Sandra. Coupled with his low sending profile (both the group and individual members), we can determine that Donnie is participating far

Table 14.1 *Exercises for Feedback*

Chapter/Page: Exercise	Use as a Feedback Tool
2/pp. 40-41: *Group Assessment Technique:* Rating Verbal and Nonverbal Interaction	This tool can be used throughout a group's history to observe and analyze group interaction. Focusing on verbal and nonverbal interaction, group members can rate themselves and other group members after a group meeting to determine the group's interaction dynamics. This tool provides effective feedback if the group has interacted for at least 30-45 minutes.
3/pp. 69-71: *Group Assessment Technique:* Identifying Informal Role Behaviors	This questionnaire can be used to identify the roles played in the group. It is most effective if each group member thinks of his or her own behaviors. After all group members have completed their assessments, group members should discuss which roles are covered and which are not.
6/pp. 162-163: *Group Assessment Technique:* Determining Your Communicator Style	This questionnaire is especially effective early in a group's development. Each group member should use the questionnaire to identify their communicator style. After all group members have completed their assessments, group members should discuss how effectively the communicator styles of group members work together. As the group continues to develop, this questionnaire can be used to ascertain if style changes are needed as group tasks and activities change.
6/p. 168: *Group Assessment Technique:* How Competent Are You?	This survey helps to identify the critical skills group members need to work effectively together. Group members can rate themselves as well as other group members on each item. The results can be used to stimulate more specific descriptive, evaluative, and prescriptive message feedback. This feedback should help group members develop individual goals for improving their group performance.
7/pp. 184-185: *Group Assessment Technique:* What Is Your Level of Camaraderie?	This questionnaire is used most effectively after a group has had a chance to develop or in groups that expect to have an enduring history together. At the completion of a substantial group goal, each group member should use the questionnaire to identify their level of camaraderie. A discussion about similarities and differences in group members' scores should uncover if and why group members vary in their perceptions of how the group has developed. After the discussion, group members should identify at least three action steps to take to maintain or reactivate group development.
8/pp. 228-229: *Group Assessment Technique:* Can Consensus Work?	After a major group decision achieved through consensus, group members should use this survey to test their satisfaction with their decision and this decision procedure. After comparing their results, group members should discuss what other decision-making procedures could have been effective.
8/pp. 242-243: *Building Analytical Skills:* Was Your Decision Effective?	This questionnaire can be used to test a group's decision-making effectiveness regardless of which decision-making procedure is used. This tool tests basic decision-making effectiveness dimensions and can be used after decision-making interactions at any point in the group's development.

(continued)

Table 14.1 *Exercises for Feedback (continued)*

Chapter/Page: Exercise	Use as a Feedback Tool
9/p. 252: *Building Analytical Skills:* Identifying Decision-Making Functions	The questions in this exercise can be used by one group member serving in the formal role of group observer. Using two columns to track the group's conversation, the group should be able to generate feedback about its ability to satisfy critical group decision-making functions. Groups who choose to use this technique should rotate observers at each meeting. Sitting just outside the group's interaction circle, the observer would listen to the group's interaction, keeping track of *what* the group discussed in the left column and keeping track of *how* the group discussed issues in the right column. At the end of the interaction, the observer could use these notes to answer the questions in this exercise. This technique is most effective with groups who have a substantial history together and who can afford to allow a group member to assume the formal observer role.
12/p. 366: *Group Assessment Technique:* How Far Has Your Group Developed?	This questionnaire can help a group identify its stage of group development. This can be particularly useful if members feel that the group is stuck. By knowing at which stage the group is stuck, members can develop strategies for moving the group forward.
13/p. 399: *Group Assessment Technique:* Diagnosing Team Problems	This questionnaire can help a group identify if its problems are task, relationship, process/procedure, or teamwork oriented. This tool is best used with groups that have been together for some time or for groups that are stuck because their members cannot identify the problem.

less than other group members. And we can determine that Bren is the most active group member. Not only does she send many messages, she is also the target of a good portion of others' messages. But remember that talkativeness does not always equal high quality participation. This type of feedback can help groups recognize if there is a pattern of unequal communication flow.

Taping the Group

A powerful way to demonstrate the effectiveness of group process or group member relationships is to audiotape or videotape a segment of a meeting. After the meeting, or in a separate one, listening to or viewing the tape and then discussing it can motivate group members to improve their performance (Walter, 1975). Many sports teams do this after every game—win or lose—to enable the team to review its mistakes and to see in what situations they performed effectively.

Before you suggest taping your group, let's explore the effect taping could have on your group. Some group members may be hesitant for their performance to be captured on tape. Thus they may become less talkative in the taped meeting. Conversely, some may use the taping as an opportunity to show off for others by clowning around, making jokes, or talking more than usual. Usually these effects diminish as the meeting progresses if others avoid drawing attention to the taping

This person talks to →	Aku	Bren	Donnie	Marie	Sandra	Wallace	The Group	Total number of messages sent
Aku	---	4	1	0	0	0	2	7
Bren	0	---	0	5	6	0	5	16
Donnie	3	0	---	0	0	0	0	3
Marie	0	5	0	---	6	2	3	16
Sandra	0	3	0	0	---	0	3	6
Wallace	0	3	0	4	3	---	2	12
Number of messages directed to →	3	15	1	9	15	2	15	

Figure 14.1 *An Interaction Diagram Matrix*

process. Once the camera or tape player is set up, check to make sure it is working correctly and then leave it alone until the end of the meeting or until a group member asks that the recording device be turned off. If a group member makes this request, it should be honored without discussion or explanation.

Taping your group's interaction is a strong reminder of what you did or did not say. It also shows you *how* you said something. Hearing how you communicated in the group can help you determine which of your communication skills need improvement. Taping a group's interaction also helps the group as a whole determine how well its members work together. Taped interactions are undeniable testaments to who talked and who did not, to whose ideas were listened to and whose were not, and to what decision procedure worked and what did not. Groups, just like individuals, can fall into patterns of communication. Periodically, you need to take an assessment of both.

When the group is ready to listen to or view the taped proceedings, it is best to focus on one aspect of the group's communication. For example, you could suggest that your group count the number of times talking turns were interrupted or assess the degree to which group members used the decision-making functions described in Chapter 9. Analyzing taped proceedings will be more effective if you avoid focusing on specific group members. For example, it would be better to analyze how the group maximized use of its leadership rather than to focus on Brooke's leadership style. In the former, group members could listen to or view the tape to assess which leadership roles were distributed among group members and whether the group successfully avoided a spoke-and-wheel pattern in which the leader talks after every member contributes. These are issues for which the entire group is responsible.

Principles for Designing a Group Feedback System

Teams are commonplace today in organizations. As a result, teams are expected to be measured for effectiveness like other parts of an organizational system. Let's look at some principles that can guide you as you set up your group's feedback system (Meyer, 1994). More than anything else, the feedback system should be set up for the group, not for nonmembers to gauge the progress of the group. Teams that are developing and maturing need a system for self-correction when they run into problems. If there is fear that someone else is watching over the group, members will focus their actions on satisfying the external agent and withhold energy from their interactions in the group. Thus groups should design their own feedback system. Team members know best the type of feedback they need and the type of feedback with which they will feel most comfortable. Feedback systems should not be forced on teams.

When groups mature, they can become more sensitive and responsive to feedback that tracks outputs with which others are interested. Feedback systems can be developed to satisfy others as well. Although the group may be more focused on teamwork and taskwork during their feedback sessions, others may put more value on how many goals are met or how many cases have been examined. A memo to the person to whom the team reports detailing what the team accomplished, its action plans, and its agenda for the next meeting can go a long way toward satisfying someone who was not at the meeting. The person external to the group can see via the memo that the group did make progress and is working toward its goals. Simple feedback systems like memos or short reports can create a safety zone between a group and others interested in what the group is doing. Graphs and charts can be especially helpful in informing others of the group's progress, particularly when data can be quantified like budgets or number of weeks to project completion.

How many measures should a group use? The answer to that question depends on the group, its task, and the environment in which the group works. However, a group generally should only adopt a handful of dimensions for evaluating itself. When teams take on too many evaluative dimensions at once, the meeting becomes focused on producing the feedback instead of accomplishing tasks.

Getting Started

It can be difficult to initiate a feedback system in your group. Often, this will be group members' first experiences with feedback and observation techniques. Here is one way of developing a feedback system that increases incrementally over time until a fully developed system is operating in the group. First of all, recognize that groups and members do not just want to hear **negative feedback**—feedback that tells the group what it is doing that is not working. If a group hears only negative feedback, eventually its ability to function is seriously damaged (Smith & Berg, 1987). Groups and members are more likely to accept negative feedback when positive feedback is also included.

For groups that have not used feedback systems before, start by introducing and explaining the concept of feedback at the end of one meeting. Individuals are often hesitant to disclose what they think or feel to others. To ease the group into the feedback process, ask each group member to write down three things that went well in the group session and three things that did not work so well. Focus their efforts on the task and procedural or the group level of feedback—how well the group worked together, how conflict kept the group from making a decision, how well group members shared the leadership function, or to what extent the group was able to work through its agenda. The idea here is to get group members started thinking critically about the group's process. Starting with yourself, ask group members to alternate reading first a positive and then a negative comment until all of the comments are before the group. You may want to ask someone to write these down on a board or flip chart. Even if every group member chooses the obvious positives and negatives, the concept of feedback has been introduced in the group. Now with the positives and negatives before the group, ask group members to select one positive that they will remember and use at the next meeting and to select one negative that they can work on together at the next meeting. Before adjourning, ask each member to write down specifically what he or she will do to help the group overcome the negative the group selected. Using this procedure, you have called attention to the feedback process and have stimulated members' thinking about how well the group is operating.

At the end of the next meeting, ask group members to repeat the process described above and also write down three things they did that contributed to the group's success and three things that they could improve upon to help the group. Once again, repeat the round robin disclosure of the task/procedural or group level positive and negatives. Again, select a positive and a negative for the group to work on at its next meeting. If you feel the group is mature enough to handle more personal self-disclosure, start with yourself and reveal one thing you believe you could improve upon to help the group. For example, let's say that you reveal that you found yourself talking just to fill the silences between other members' talking. Now state what you intend to do about it. "So, at the next meeting, I'll try to limit my talking to times when I have something important to say that contributes to the conversation. If you think that I'm just talking to be talking, would one of you remind me? Thanks." Now you have modeled for other group members a process of revealing a personal issue you would like to work on, your idea for improvement, and your commitment to bettering your communication within the group. When you are finished, ask the next group member to continue this process.

If your group decides to use questionnaires or surveys, interaction diagrams, or taping the group as feedback, be sure to set aside time for the group to collect data and to hear the feedback reports. Groups who do this regularly are often more satisfied with their group experiences. Not only do group members have the opportunity to contribute to the group's decisions and actions, they have the opportunity to actively and positively influence the group's process. Do not be surprised if your group needs two or three sessions to feel comfortable with the feedback and observation process. To help create acceptance for using feedback, also set aside a few minutes to discuss the effectiveness of the feedback tools used. Perhaps the feedback is not accepted because group members are uncomfortable with the questionnaire or do not understand how an interaction diagram can help them.

Feedback Advice

The feedback process is not a blaming process. Rather, the feedback process should be used as a goal-setting strategy, as an awareness strategy, and as a learning tool. Many groups use feedback to help them determine and set goals. In this case, feedback is a motivational tool. Task groups frequently use feedback in this way. Feedback can also be used to help members become more aware of their group interaction performance. When group members have higher awareness, they are paying more attention to their communication and its effects on others in the group. If you have been a member of any type of self-help or therapy group, you are familiar with using feedback in this way. For example, the group's leader notices that you frequently reference your mother when talking about how you feel: "Noah, I noticed that you again said your mother made you feel that way when you were talking about your feelings of inadequacy. Can you restate how you feel without relying on your mom?" Noah responds, "I'll try. I just feel inadequate about being able to quit smoking. I need someone else to help me. I guess I'm just used to relying on her. Sorry, I wasn't supposed to say that." In this case, the leader's comment about Noah relying on his mother created an awareness for Noah. It was unlikely that he even realized the extent to which she appeared in his comments. Feedback can also help group members learn new skills. For example, after your softball team comes in from the field, your coach yells, "You have to have your glove up to catch the ball." Next time you are in the field, you are sure to keep your eyes on the ball and to get your glove up before the ball is thrown by the pitcher.

In giving feedback, be sure to use specific examples from the group's interaction. This will focus group members' attention on what needs to be improved or what needs to be repeated. Also, use words that are concrete. Words like *great*, *poor*, or *okay* are vague and ambiguous. Using these in your feedback are not likely to help group members very much. More concrete words and phrases like "better than last meeting," "disruptive," or "we are maintaining the same level of effectiveness we achieved at the last meeting" are more meaningful and helpful to others. Finally, when giving feedback, be sure to explain the reasons behind your statements, especially when delivering evaluative or prescriptive feedback. Simply telling a group that it needs to improve how group members share the leadership role does not provide enough detail for the group to understand how sharing the leadership role failed to be effective or how to better utilize members in that role.

When groups use feedback, disagreement should be welcomed and expected. It is not likely that every group member will agree with every one of your perceptions and views. One reason for integrating feedback into a group is to raise critical issues with the group. If you raise issues but do not give group members the opportunity to explore them, you have wasted your energy and the group's time. If after giving feedback, other group members are silent, invite their questions and comments. At the minimum, ask others if they agree with your view. If they do not or are expressing their disagreement nonverbally, ask questions to solicit their reactions. Statements like "Some of you may disagree with my assessment. If you feel differently, I'd like to hear what you think" may open the floor for discussion of the feedback.

Do not rely on one person as the observer. Doing this can weaken or completely destroy group members' motivation for engaging in the feedback process. The feedback process should be jointly owned and operated by all group members. At some meetings, the observation process may be in the hands of one group member in the role of observer. Pass this responsibility around. At other group meetings, use one of the survey or questionnaires so each group member can participate. Feedback can only become a regular part of the group's interaction if the group as a whole is involved in the process. Not only should all group members take responsibility for observing and giving feedback, but all group members should understand that everyone is expected to participate in the discussion after feedback is given.

At its best, the feedback process should allow the group to discuss undiscussable issues. An undiscussable issue is one that is relevant to the group's task but is perceived to have negative or political ramifications if discussed openly in the group (Schwarz, 1994). What issues are undiscussable? In groups, typical undiscussable issues include poor member performance (especially when it is the leader), lack of trust, and personality conflicts. Too frequently, group members deal with these issues by not talking about them or by talking about them to others outside the group. One way to overcome the problem of discussing the undiscussable is to acknowledge to the group that the issue may be considered undiscussable (Schwarz, 1994). "I realize what I'm about to say may be difficult for us to deal with" is an excellent way of raising an undiscussable issue.

What should a feedback system do for your group (SYMLOG Consulting Group, 1986)? Using feedback regularly, group members should be able to discover and correct misperceptions that cause communication failures. Group members should discover that some aspects of their communication can be improved. Also, as group members learn to express their dissatisfactions honestly and tactfully, they will actually come to like one another more. This happens because feedback provides opportunities to develop a greater understanding of why people communicate or behave the way they do. In addition, after using feedback systematically, group members should be able to express their appreciation for and satisfaction with the things they like about their group. This reinforces their ability to work together as a team. Also, using feedback allows group members to develop a clearer picture of their behavior and communication expectations of one another. And, after using feedback, group members should be able to make decisions more effectively and efficiently. Finally, feedback systems help raise group members' awareness about how groups actually operate.

Summary

An additional responsibility group members have toward the group is to monitor their own and others' performance in the group. By giving feedback, members provide others in the group with information about the actions of individuals as well as the performance of the group. Feedback serves as an error detection device to help a group identify and begin to solve its interaction problems. Feedback is part of a group's system. It provides an evaluation and serves as input.

Three types of feedback can be used in groups: message feedback, questionnaires and surveys, and interaction diagrams or audio- and videotaping of the group. Groups need feedback to overcome common evaluation biases and to help group members communicate and perform more effectively. Advantages of initiating feedback in groups include discouraging social loafing, increasing group member identification, and increasing group efficacy.

Message feedback occurs as a part of a group's interaction. When groups maintain an open and trusting climate, feedback acts like constructive criticism. However, there are limits to feedback, and the time and place for feedback should be considered. Feedback must be specific both to a behavior and to a setting. If feedback is too negative, it can be offensive or rejected. However, the overuse of positive feedback will be interpreted as insincere. The effect of feedback is also limited if it does not mention the consequences that result from the behavior.

Behavior feedback is effective if the person receiving the feedback is able to follow your directions. Reflective feedback is effective if the person receiving the feedback can repeat back what was said. Closed-loop communication is also an effective way to deliver feedback. To deliver this type of feedback, the sender delivers the message, and the receiver accepts the message and provides feedback to the sender. Finally, the original sender double-checks to ensure that the intended message was received.

The style in which feedback is delivered is important. The ability to be direct, frank, and helpful will help others accept and use the feedback you provide. Being open-minded, supportive, and positive will help others listen to you.

Feedback can be identified by one of three types—descriptive, evaluative, or prescriptive. Descriptive feedback describes how a group member communicates. Evaluative feedback goes a step beyond description by providing an assessment of how the person communicates. Prescriptive feedback provides group members with advice about how they should communicate.

Feedback can also be identified by its level—task/procedural, relational, individual, group, or organizational. Task/procedural feedback focuses on quality and quantity issues and should be used anytime a group tries a new procedure. Relational feedback focuses on issues of group climate or environment. Individual feedback focuses on a specific group member. Group feedback focuses on how well the group is developing and maintaining communication processes. Organizational feedback is given by a group to the larger environment that supports it. The reverse can happen as well.

The questionnaires and surveys throughout this textbook can also be used by groups as feedback tools. Interaction diagrams provide feedback about who talks to whom and how much. Capturing the group's interaction on audio- or videotape is very powerful feedback. These techniques are strong reminders of what you did or did not say, as well as how you said it.

Groups should design their own feedback systems based on their needs and their comfort level with the different techniques. A group should use only one or just a few techniques at a time. A good way to initiate a feedback system is to start slowly and gradually add additional types and levels of feedback as the group becomes comfortable with the process. Regardless of which type of feedback is used, a group should set aside time to hear the feedback reports. Doing so increases group member satisfaction.

Remember that feedback is not a blaming process. Rather, feedback should be used as a goal-setting strategy, as an awareness strategy, and as a learning tool. Feedback is more effective if specific examples from the group's interaction are used. Use concrete rather than vague words in describing members' interactions. When groups use feedback, disagreement should be welcome. Not everyone will agree with all of your views or perceptions. If one or two group members must assume the role of a formal observer, be sure to rotate this responsibility among everyone. At its best, everyone contributes to the feedback process. Feedback allows a group to discuss undiscussable issues. Used effectively, feedback systems raise group members' awareness of their individual contributions to a group as well as to the overall performance of the group.

✓ Checklist

Group Knowledge

You should be able to:
- explain the importance of feedback.
- describe how to use closed-loop communication.
- distinguish among descriptive, evaluative, and prescriptive feedback.
- identify the five levels of feedback.
- explain how a group could use questionnaires or surveys as a feedback tool.
- identify the type of feedback an interaction diagram can provide.
- name two advantages of capturing a group on audio- or videotape.
- explain how a group can start its own feedback system.

Group Skills

You should be able to:
- use message feedback during a group meeting.
- design a closed-loop message as feedback.

- select and use descriptive, evaluative, and prescriptive feedback appropriately.
- identify the situations that require task/procedural feedback versus relational feedback.
- apply individual, group, and organizational feedback appropriately.
- select an appropriate questionnaire or survey as a feedback tool.
- help your group use a questionnaire or survey as feedback.
- complete an interaction diagram and its matrix.
- persuade your group to try audio- or videotaping as feedback.
- help your group design a feedback system.

Analytical and Assessment Techniques

You should be able to:
- analyze your feedback style.
- determine the impact of message feedback on your group.
- assess the impact of descriptive, evaluative, or prescriptive feedback before you give it.
- identify the appropriate level of feedback to be given.
- recognize barriers your group might have to using feedback.
- assess questionnaires and surveys for their appropriateness and effectiveness as feedback.
- analyze an interaction diagram.
- detect group strengths and weaknesses from an audiotape or a videotape of a group interaction.
- assess the group's climate for using feedback.

Discussion Questions and Exercises

1. Watch a television situation comedy or drama. Identify the main characters and their roles and responsibilities. If you could design a feedback system for this group, what would you recommend?

2. Many of us are dissatisfied with the communication in our work groups or work units. Knowing that your colleagues would likely be resistant to suggestions for implementing a feedback system, how would you convince them that developing a feedback system would be an important step in the group's development?

3. Talk with friends and relatives about their work, social, and community groups. To what extent do these groups integrate feedback into their communication?

Glossary

abstract A type of word that paints a broad generalization.

acceptance level Criterion for evaluating a decision; decision must be not only technically correct but usable by others.

accommodating A win-lose conflict management strategy exemplified by trying to satisfy the other's concerns.

action-oriented listening style A style of listening in which a receiver concentrates on the task and helps others in the group stay on the task.

active listening A style of listening and feedback in which a receiver paraphrases what the speaker has said and asks questions to confirm what was said.

additive task A task that is divisible; it can be broken into subtasks so that each member can contribute meaningfully to the group's outcome.

affection The need to establish psychologically close relationships with others.

affective conflict A type of conflict based on social or relational issues.

affiliative constraints A constraint to decision making based on the relationships among members of the group; fearing that relationships will deteriorate, some group members will exert undue influence on other group members.

agenda List of activities or topics to be considered at a group meeting; should also include starting and stopping times, location of the meeting, who is to attend, and overall goal of the meeting as well as the specific goal of each agenda item and any preparations that group members should make.

animated A dimension of communicator style exemplified by expressive nonverbal behaviors and easy-to-read emotional state.

appropriateness A criterion of communication competence that is achieved when communication does not violate behavioral expectations, does not weaken relationships among communicators, does not threaten any member's self-esteem.

area of freedom The degree of authority or responsibility a group has in completing its tasks or activities.

artifacts Objects used to convey nonverbal messages.

attentive A dimension of communicator style; exemplified by letting others know they are being listened to; empathic.

autocratic leadership A type of leadership based on an authoritarian leader's control over group process and decision making.

avoiding conflict management strategy A nonconfrontive strategy for managing conflict; based on verbal, physical, or psychological withdrawal.

behavior feedback Information that evaluates the ability of the other person to follow directions.

bona fide groups Groups with stable yet permeable boundaries; membership in the group is clearly identified yet membership can change or be temporarily altered.

boundary management The process by which groups manage their interactions with other parts of their macro system.

boundary spanning The process of group members creating and maintaining relationships with individuals outside the group.

brainstorming A group procedure designed to help groups generate creative ideas.

breakpoint A discontinuity in a group's interaction representing transitional periods in the group's development.

bypassing A misunderstanding; occurs when two group members use the same words but individually attribute different meanings to the words or phrases.

camaraderie A feeling of closeness that exists among group members when they believe they are successful at both the task and with their relationships.

cautious-shift A phenomenon based on members who believe they are cautious decision makers or who believe they hold cautious positions; as a result, caution is magnified in group decision making.

certainty A dimension of defensive communication climate that emphasizes a group member's belief that he or she has all the answers or knows in advance what another group member is going to say or do.

chronemics The use of time; conveys nonverbal messages.

closed-loop communication A process of feedback in which the sender delivers the message, the receiver accepts the message and provides feedback to the sender, and the sender double-checks to ensure that the intended message was received.

coalition formation Occurs when one member takes sides with another against yet another member of the group; creates an imbalance of power; can only occur with at least three group members.

code of conduct   A group document that describes behaviors that are appropriate for a group.

coercive power   A type of power resulting from the expectation that one group member can be punished by another.

cognitive conflict   A type of conflict; disagreement over judgment about information, data, or the analysis of information or data; also known as *judgment conflict*.

cognitive conflict tasks   Group tasks in which differing viewpoints or positions taken by group members create disagreement.

cognitive constraints   Constraints to decision making based on difficulties or inadequacies in group members' abilities to process information; occur when information or time is limited or when the decision is more difficult than group members can comfortably or normally handle.

cohesiveness   The degree to which members desire to remain in the group.

collaborating   A conflict management strategy based on parties sharing a superordinate goal of solving the problem even though their initial ideas for how to solve the problem differ.

collectivistic   A type of culture in which groupwork or teamwork is valued over individual accomplishment.

communication apprehension   The fear or anxiety associated with either real or anticipated communication with other people.

communication climate   The result of group members' use of verbal and nonverbal communication and listening skills; can be defensive or supportive.

communication competence   The ability and willingness to participate responsibly in a communication transaction exemplified by maximizing shared meaning with other group members and communicating with both appropriateness and effectiveness.

communication competency approach to leadership   A model for leadership based upon three principles: (1) leadership is action that helps a group overcome barriers or obstacles; (2) leadership occurs through interaction; (3) there are a set of skills or competencies that individuals use to exercise leadership in groups.

communication network   The interaction pattern or flow of messages between and among group members; creates structure for the group from patterns of who talks to whom.

communication overload   Communication that is too much or too complex from too many sources; causes stress and confusion.

communication underload   Communication is infrequent and simple, causing group members to feel disconnected from the group.

communicator style   The impression one leaves with others after communicating; includes the following dimensions: dominant, dramatic, animated, impression leaving, relaxed, attentive, open, friendly, contentious, and precise.

competing   A distributive conflict management strategy exemplified by forcing; emphasizes one party winning at the other party's expense.

competitive conflict   Polarizations; one side winning with the other side losing.

compromising   A conflict management style; an intermediate strategy in the middle of cooperativeness and assertiveness; compromising may settle the problem but will also offer incomplete satisfaction for both parties.

concrete   A word that is specific and clear.

conflict   At least two interdependent parties capable of invoking sanctions on each other oppose each other; based on real or perceived power; occurs because parties have mutually desired but mutually unobtainable objectives.

conflict aftermath   The feelings that group members have developed as a result of a conflict episode; the legacy of the conflict interaction.

conjunctive task   A group task in which the group member who performs the least well determines the group's performance.

connectivity   The degree to which several groups share overlapping tasks or goals.

consensus   A decision procedure in which each group member agrees with the decision or in which group members' individual positions are close enough that they can support the group's decision.

contentious   A dimension of communicator style exemplified by argumentativeness; wants to debate points.

content-oriented listening style   A style of listening in which a receiver carefully examines everything he or she hears.

contests/battles/competitive tasks   Group tasks that pit two or more teams against one another; only one team can win.

contingency model of leadership   A type of leadership based on leader-member relations, task structure, and position power of the leader; a style of leadership based on the interrelationships among these three factors.

control   The need to establish and share power and control with others.

controlling behavior   A dimension of defensive communication climate in which the sender assumes to know what is best for others.

cooperative conflict   A type of disagreement that actually helps move the group along with its task or activities.

creativity tasks Group tasks in which the group is responsible for generating ideas or alternatives.

critical advisor A role in a group exemplified by suggesting disadvantages to alternatives posed, revealing hidden assumptions, and questioning the validity or reliability of information used as evidence; helps the group see errors in its logic and thinking; devil's advocate; constructively criticizes ideas brought before the group.

cultural distance The degree to which group members differ on dimensions of language, social status, religion, politics, economic conditions, and basic assumptions about reality.

decision logic A system of reasoning used in making decisions.

decision-making task The most common of group activities; the objective of the group's interaction is to reach conclusions through the sharing of information and the use of group members' collective reasoning.

decision quality The criterion for judging group output; based on issues of quality, quantity, and or timeliness.

decision rule orientation The manner in which an individual processes information in making decisions; reflects a group member's philosophy about decision choices.

defensive climate A communication climate based on negative or threatening group interaction.

democratic leadership A type of leadership based on the premise that all members participate within a structure that is relatively equal in power and status.

dependence A relationship created with or accepted from other group members that puts the individual in a subordinate position.

dependencies Group reliance upon its larger macro system.

depersonalized conflict A type of conflict rooted in issues or ideas; also known as *substantive conflict*.

description A dimension of supportive communication climate that occurs when a group member responds to the idea instead of evaluating the group member who offered the idea.

descriptive feedback Feedback that identifies or describes how a group member communicates.

discretionary tasks Group tasks in which members are allowed and encouraged to combine their contributions in any way that they desire; a group chooses its own method or process from among the many ways in which the task can be done.

disjunctive task A group task that is difficult to break into subtasks; has a correct outcome that someone outside the group can use to evaluate the group's output.

distributive conflict management strategy A win-lose conflict management strategy exemplified by competitiveness and antagonism; an outcome that satisfies one party at the expense of the other.

divisible task A group task that can be broken into several parts.

dominant A dimension of communicator style exemplified by taking charge and controlling interaction; confident, forceful, active, and self-assured.

dramatic A dimension of communicator style exemplified by talking more often and more loudly than other group members; uses exaggeration, emphasis, joking, story telling.

dyadic interaction Interaction between two people (a dyad); interpersonal interaction.

effectiveness A criterion of communication competence that is achieved when the goal of the interaction is satisfied.

egocentric constraints Constraints to decision making based on a group member's high need for control over the group or its activities or on a group member's personal or hidden agenda.

embedded groups Groups with a very long time focus; groups perform a broad base of activities.

embeddedness The degree to which the group is central to its larger organizational structure.

emergent leadership A group member is not appointed or elected to the leadership role; rather, leadership develops over time as a result of the group's interaction.

empathy A dimension of supportive communication climate that expresses genuine concern for other group members; conveys respect for and reassurance of the receiver.

equality A dimension of supportive communication climate in which trust and respect for all group members is expressed.

ethnocentric A culturally based bias allowing a person to judge events and people as good or correct when they are similar to events and people in his or her own culture.

evaluation A dimension of defensive communication climate in which a group member uses language to criticize other group members.

evaluative feedback Feedback that goes beyond mere description to provide an evaluation or assessment of how a person communicates.

expectations Objectives about a group's potential performance (what to produce, how to produce it) as well as what a group can or cannot expect from its macro system to help it accomplish its goals.

expedition A group responsible for a broad range of activities over a limited time.

expert power A type of influence based on what a group member knows or can do.

false consensus A belief among group members that

they all agree when they do not; agreeing to a decision just in order to be done with the task.

feedback (1) Asking questions, restating the message, or agreeing or disagreeing with a message sent by another group member; (2) one element of the communication system; system output that generates new inputs for the group's system; (3) information about individual group members' actual performance or the actions of a group.

formal roles Roles expected in most groups; easily labeled (leader or chair, vice-chair, secretary or recorder, program planner).

forming The first phase of group development exemplified by group members directing comments toward the formal leader, members relying on identity and status outside the group, and little trust.

friendly A dimension of communicator style; gives positive recognition to others through behavior that encourages and validates; is affectionate, sociable, and tactful.

functional leadership A type of leadership based on the premise that the duties and responsibilities of leadership can be performed by any member of the group; a universal set of behavioral functions regardless of how members, their personalities, the type of groups, or their tasks differ.

group Three or more members who identify themselves as a group and who can identify the interdependent activity of the group.

group charge A group's goal, often given or assigned to the group by agents outside the group.

group charter A group document that describes the goals or mission of the group.

group continuity A belief that group members will be together over time.

group efficacy The collective belief of group members that the group can and will be effective; created through interaction.

group goal An agreed-upon task or activity that the group is to complete or accomplish.

grouphate A negative predisposition toward groups and group work.

group identity Members identify themselves with other group members and the group goal.

grouping People identified as a group when they have little or no expectation that interaction will occur with one another.

group maintenance roles Informal group roles that help define a group's relationships and develop a group's climate.

group process The interactions among group members and the procedures or activities the group uses to complete its goal.

group role Interactive positions within a group; the micro components of a group's structure.

group size The number of members in the group; the minimum number of members is three; the maximum number of members depends primarily upon the complexity of the task or activity.

group structure The patterns of behavior that group members come to rely on; develops with or emerges from group rules and norms.

groupthink A type of faulty decision making based on the tendency of highly cohesive groups to adopt faulty solutions because members failed to critically examine and analyze options while under pressure from the external environment.

haptics The use of touch; conveys nonverbal messages.

impact The effect or result of a message on other group members.

impression leaving A dimension of communicator style; remembered by his or her manner of communicating.

inclusion The need to establish and maintain satisfactory relations with others.

individualistic A type of culture that values individual recognition more than group or team recognition.

individual roles Informal roles that are typically counterproductive for the group by focusing attention away from the group and its goal.

informal interaction Nontask-related communication with other group members that helps them get to know one another and establish relationships.

informal roles Roles that emerge naturally through group member interaction.

in-group A type of influence based on group members' identification with other group members.

input One element of a communication system; information or messages that contribute to the group's system of interaction.

integrative conflict management strategy A win-win conflict management strategy based on problem solving or collaboration; produces an outcome with which all parties can agree.

intellective task A group task, normally a decision-making task, that has a correct answer.

intentionality A sender purposely communicates with a receiver.

interaction diagram A diagram identifying which group members talk to other group members and how frequently.

interdependence Both group and individual outcomes are influenced by what other individuals in the group do; group members must rely upon and cooperate with one another to complete the group activity.

interpersonal conflict A type of conflict exemplified by differences in members' attitudes or perceptions; typically based on issues of status, power, perceived competence, cooperativeness, and friendliness.

intrinsic interest   A task characteristic; the motivating potential of the task; based on group members' motivation to perform well and members' attraction to the group, task, and members.

judgment conflict   A type of conflict; disagreement over information, data, or the analysis of information or data; also known as *cognitive conflict*.

kinesics   The use of facial expressions, eye contact, hand gestures, or body posture; conveys nonverbal messages.

law of inherent conflict   The premise that no matter the issue or group, there will be significant conflict stemming from different perceptions of relative factors.

leader   A formal role; a group member who plans for and facilitates meetings, encourages and motivates group members, and acts as a group's link to its external environment.

leader-member exchange (LMX) model   A theoretical explanation of leadership based on the premise that leaders may develop different types of relationships with different members of the same work group.

leadership   A process of influence in groups; a property of the person who holds the primary influential role.

leadership style   A type of leadership based on the premise that one universal style of leadership is preferred over others.

learning dimension   The process of learning or acquiring information through group experiences; learning can be content knowledge, relational, or process knowledge.

legitimate power   A type of power based on the inherent influence associated with a position or role in the group.

macro-system perspective   One of the systemic levels of a group; the totality of a group's environment including all physical and psychological influences, resources, the influences of other individuals and groups, and the task a group has been given or directed to do.

maximax decision rule   A decision-making orientation that assume a best-case scenario; individuals focus on the positives or rewards and accept the risk in decision choice.

maximin decision rule   A conservative decision-making orientation that assumes that the search for the largest pay-off will minimize losses.

maximizing task   A group task that requires members to accomplish a great deal or complete its task rapidly.

maximum expected utility decision rule   A decision-making orientation reflecting consistency and stability by searching for the alternative that provides the highest average pay-off across many conditions or situations.

mediation   An intervention performed by a mediator, a person who is an impartial third party who has no authority or decision-making power in the situation.

message   Information sent by a sender through verbal, nonverbal, written, or electronic channels to a receiver.

message feedback   A type of message reflection used in mediation; at any time one party can stop the conversation and ask the other party to summarize or rephrase what he or she is talking about.

micro system   One of the systemic levels of a group; interaction within the group (among group members); more micro systems exist in the subgroups or dyads of the group.

micro-system perspective   One of the many levels of a group's system; at this level, the focus is on the communication among group members and between subgroups or dyads in the group.

minutes   A record of what the group did or accomplished at a meeting; should reflect who attended the meeting, the content of what was discussed, what was decided, who agreed to take on what responsibilities, and what the group plans to do next; usually taken by the group's secretary.

mixed-motive task   A group task in which not all group members share a common interest or goal; group members believe that the benefits of the group's decision affect them directly as individuals.

multichannel   Group members use verbal messages, nonverbal messages, or both; some groups also use written or electronic channels; channels may be used singly or simultaneously.

negative feedback   Information about the group or its members exemplified by what it is or what they are doing that is not working.

negotiating latitude   Associated with the leader-member exchange theory of leadership; degree to which the leader will use his or her position power to help the group member solve work-related issues.

neutrality   A dimension of defensive communication climate expressed when a group member reacts in a detached or unemotional way; a lack of warmth or caring for other members making them feel as if they are not important.

nominal group technique (NGT)   A decision-making procedure in which the group temporarily suspends interaction to take advantage of independent thinking and reflection before coming together as a group to discuss the ideas generated.

nonverbal communication   Meaning derived from

how words are said or the use of behaviors to replace or substitute for verbal messages; occurs in many forms—vocalics, kinesics, proxemics, haptics, chronemics, and artifacts.

norm An expectation about behavior; an informal rule adopted by a group to regulate group members' behaviors.

normative conflict A type of conflict that occurs when one party has expectations about and evaluates another party's behavior.

norming The third phase of group development exemplified by trust, role development and acceptance, and open negotiation of differences.

open A dimension of communicator style; frank, approachable, and willing to disclose information about oneself.

optimizing task A task in which group members work together to meet a criterion of quality.

out-group A group against which the in-group distinguishes itself.

output One element of a communication system; the outcome of the interaction.

people-oriented listening style A style of listening in which receivers are attuned to the emotional aspects of the conversation and to relationships with other group members; demonstrates care and concern about others; is nonjudgmental.

performance/psycho-motor tasks Physical tasks in which a group is being judged against predetermined standards of performance or excellence.

performing The fourth phase of group development exemplified by task or goal accomplishment.

personalized conflict Affective conflict that is rooted in interpersonal relationships, emotions, or personalities.

persuasive arguments theory A theoretical explanation for how influence is generated in groups; the degree to which each member creates unique arguments to be introduced into a group's interaction.

PERT Program evaluation and review technique; a decision technique that helps group members order the activities that must be completed to implement a decision.

physical environment The setting in which a group meets; includes meeting space and seating arrangements.

physical noise Noise from a group's environment that can affect the degree to which messages are heard within a group.

planning task A group task in which members are responsible for generating plans to carry out previously made decisions or decisions made by others.

political decision logic A type of reasoning used in making decisions; relies on factors not intrinsic to the decision.

population familiarity A task characteristic; degree of member familiarity with the task and other group members.

power distance The measure of influence one group member has over another; the degree of inequality in power among group members.

precise A dimension of communicator style exemplified by a concern for accurate and clear communication of ideas.

preference for procedural order (PPO) The degree to which a group member desires to have the activities of his or her groups ordered.

prescriptive feedback Information that provides group members with advice about how they should act or communicate.

primary provoker The power-assuming group member who places undue stress on how the group proceeds; is supported by secondary provokers.

problem orientation A dimension of supportive communication climate that strives for answers and solutions to benefit all group members and to satisfy the group's objective.

procedural conflict A type of conflict that occurs when procedures are not discussed beforehand or when the group encounters a situation for which there is no precedent; conflicts about goals, tasks, or any other actions or activities of the group.

process The continuous sequence of communication events; difficult to identify where communication starts and stops.

process advisor A group role; a member who monitors the effectiveness of the group's listening.

process loss The difference between actual group productivity and potential group activity.

provisionalism A dimension of supportive communication climate that is committed to solving the group's problems by hearing all of the ideas; encourages the experimentation and exploration of ideas in the group.

proxemics The use of space; conveys nonverbal messages.

pseudo-listening A style of listening in which group members respond with cliché phrases such as "right," "yeah," and "I know what you mean" without listening to the actual content of the message.

psychological environment The positive as well as negative expectations held by group members about a group.

psychological noise Attitudes or other mental disruptions of group members that can affect the degree to which a group member hears messages within a group.

questions of fact Questions for which the group must analyze the data and evidence presented to determine the probability that the evidence is factual or probable.

questions of policy Questions for which the group must develop recommendations for further action.

questions of value Questions of right or wrong; questions that examine the desirability of an idea or the preference of a group of people; ethical questions.

ranking A decision procedure in which members assign a numerical value to each available position; rankings are then ordered.

rational decision logic A system of decision reasoning based on consideration of both the positive and negative qualities of all choices.

readiness Ability and willingness to perform group activities.

receiver The person to whom a message is sent.

referent power A type of influence given by a group member to another member based on a desire to build a relationship with him or her.

reflective feedback When one group member reflects back exactly what was said to him or her so the other person can check the message for accuracy.

relational dimension Group interaction that provides social and emotional support as well as a mechanism for developing and maintaining role identities within a group.

relaxed A dimension of communicator style exemplified by little anxiety; calm, collected, and confident.

responsiveness The degree to which a communicator selects the behaviors that fit a particular group situation; communicates appropriately and effectively based upon the parameters of a particular group situation.

reward power A type of positive influence; relationally oriented such as attention, friendship, or favors, or materially oriented and based on tangible influence such as gifts or money.

risky-shift The tendency for groups to select a higher risk alternative than any member would favor individually.

satisfaction The degree to which a group member feels fulfilled or gratified based upon experiences in the group.

satisficing Settling for less than what can be maximally produced by the group.

scapegoat The group member to whom other members inappropriately direct their anxiety, aggression, or blame.

secondary provokers The group members who support through their interactions a primary provoker's influence on the group.

secretary/recorder A formal role; a group member who takes notes to capture what happened in the group's interaction.

selective listening A style of listening in which receivers have a frame of reference making it difficult for them to hear or understand what other group members are trying to say.

self-construal The degree to which individuals perceive themselves to be separate or connected to others.

sender The person who is the source of a message or information.

shared meaning The degree to which group members agree upon the interpretation of a message.

situational leadership model A type of leadership based on (1) the amount of task direction a leader gives, (2) the amount of relational support a leader provides, and (3) the readiness level of group members in performing their tasks.

social comparison theory A theoretical explanation for how groups make decisions; based on the principle that being part of a decision-making group drives group members to reevaluate their preference when presented with the preferences of other group members and the principle that being part of a group decision also presents some level of pressure to conform.

social complexity A task characteristic; degree to which group members are ego-involved; group members agree on how to proceed, and group members agree on what should be accomplished.

social identity theory A theoretical explanation for how groups make decisions; based on group members' identification with the in-group; distinguishing between this group and out-groups; and adopting the characteristics of other members of the in-group.

social-interactional perspective A theoretical explanation for how groups make decisions; based on the proposition that communication is central to how arguments affect decision making; argues that the messages one sends and receives in a group discussion, not the cognitive arguments developed, produce the influence that can change a member's prediscussion choices to the choice supported in the final decision making.

social loafers Group members who do not perform to their maximum level of potential contribution; the group context allows them to contribute minimally but still reap the same benefits as other group members.

social loafing Individual efforts decrease as the size of the group increases; a detachment from the group that occurs when group members feel as if they are not needed to produce the group's outcome or as if their individual efforts are not recognized by other members.

solution multiplicity A task characteristic; the number of alternatives available for solving the problem.

spontaneity A dimension of supportive communication climate exemplified by a group member who is open and honest with other group members; creates immediacy with other group members.

standard agenda A decision-making procedure with a strict linear process for groups to follow in considering decision alternatives.

standing committee A type of group; the tasks are limited, but group members expect to be together for an extended period of time.

storming The second phase of group development exemplified by members asserting preferences, conflict, and competition among group members over status and power.

strategy A dimension of defensive communication climate in which the sender manipulates others by placing him- or herself above the group or its task.

substantive conflict A type of conflict rooted in issues or ideas; also known as *depersonalized conflict*.

substitutes for leadership Individual, task, and organizational characteristics that act as substitutes for leadership because they negate or replace the leader's ability to influence group members regardless of which leadership style or which leadership behaviors are used.

superiority A dimension of defensive communication climate exemplified when a group member continually reinforces his or her strength or position over others.

superordinate goal A task or goal too difficult, time-consuming, and burdensome be completed by one person.

supportive climate A communication climate based on positive group interaction.

synergy Exists when the performance of a group goes beyond the capabilities of group members as individuals; communication among group members allows synergy to occur.

system An organized set of interrelated and interacting parts that attempts to maintain its own balance with the influences from its surrounding environment; the structure or foundation in which the group operates.

system perspective A theoretical paradigm in which a group's communication can be explained as a set and series of interrelated interactions on three levels: (1) in relationships among group members, (2) within the group as a whole, and (3) between the group and its environment.

task difficulty A task characteristic; the degree to which a task requires a sizable amount of effort, knowledge or skill.

task dimension A group's interaction that focuses on its task, activity, or goal.

task force A group appointed for a specific project for a specific period of time.

task outcome ambiguity The degree to which group members cannot predict the outcome.

task roles Informal roles that help the group move forward with its task or goal.

taskwork feedback Information about the technical competencies or the functional task activities of the team.

team A group that performs a specified and limited number of activities.

teambuilding A process of a group striving for effective meetings by addressing both task and process issues.

teamwork feedback Information about the group's interactions and members' relationships, cooperation, communication, and coordination.

termination The ending point or point of adjournment for groups.

throughput One element of a communication system; using interactions to make sense of the information or input into the system.

time-oriented listening style A listening style in which the receiver values time and encourages other group members to do the same.

trait leadership A type of leadership based on the identification of personal characteristics that allow individuals to assert leadership in group settings.

transactional Group members communicate to create mutual meaning and understanding.

transactional leadership A type of leadership based on the interaction or exchange between leaders and group members.

transformational leadership A type of leadership based on the premise that the leader sets an example for group members to follow; uses rhetorical skills to build a vision that members can identify with and use as a guiding force toward goal completion.

uncertainty avoidance A cultural bias for coping with uncertainty.

unitary task A task that cannot be broken into subtasks.

verbal communication Meaning derived from what we say.

vocal activity The amount of time a member talks in a group.

vocalics A form of nonverbal communication; meaning derived from how the voice is used; includes inflection, tone, accent, rate, pitch, volume, number of vocal interrupters, and quality of voice.

voting A decision procedure in which group members cast a written or verbal ballot in support of or against a specific proposal; generally, a majority or two-thirds vote is needed to support a proposition.

work group A group, often an organizational group, that has specific tasks to perform over an extended period of time; also known as *teams* or *standing committees*.

References

Adato, A. (1975). Leave-taking: A study of commonsense knowledge of social structure. *Anthropological Quarterly, 48,* 255–271.

Adelman, M. A., & Frey, L. R. (1994). The pilgrim must embark: Creating and sustaining community in a residential facility for people with AIDS. In L. R. Frey (Ed.), *Group communication in context: Studies of natural groups* (pp. 3–22). Hillsdale, NJ: Erlbaum.

Adler, N. (1986). *International dimensions of organization behavior.* Boston: Kent.

Allen, V. L., Wilder, D. A., & Atkinson, M. L. (1983). Multiple group membership and social identity. In T. R. Sarbin & K. E. Scheibe (Eds.), *Studies in social identity* (pp. 92–115). New York: Praeger.

Ammons, R. B. (1956). Effects of knowledge of performance: A survey and tentative theoretical formulation. *Journal of General Psychology, 54,* 279–299.

Ancona, D. G. (1990). Outward Bound: Strategies for team survival in an organization. *Academy of Management Journal, 33,* 334–365.

Ancona, D. G., & Caldwell, D. (1990). Improving the performance of new product teams. *Research Technology Management, 30,* 25–29.

Ancona, D. G., & Caldwell, D. F. (1992). Bridging the boundary: External activity and performance in organizational teams. *Administrative Science Quarterly, 37,* 634–665.

Andersen, P. A. (1992). Nonverbal communication in the small group. In R. S. Cathcart & L. A. Samovar (Eds.), *Small group communication: A reader* (6th ed., pp. 272–286). Dubuque, IA: Brown.

Anderson, C. M., & Martin, M. M. (1995). The effects of communication motives, interaction involvement, and loneliness on satisfaction: A model of small groups. *Small Group Research, 26,* 118–137.

Anderson, L. R., & Tolson, J. (1991). Leaders' upward influence in the organization: Replication and extensions of the Pelz Effect to include group support and self-monitoring. *Small Group Research, 22,* 59–75.

Anderson, S. D., & Wanberg, K. W. (1991). A convergent validity model of emergent leadership in groups. *Small Group Research, 22,* 380–397.

Andrews, P. H. (1992). Sex and gender differences in group communication: Impact on the facilitation process. *Small Group Research, 23,* 74–94.

Applbaum, R. L., & Anatol, K. (1971). PERT: A tool for communication research planning. *Journal of Communication, 21,* 368–380.

Archer-Kath, J., Johnson, D. W., & Johnson, R. T. (1994). Individual versus group feedback in cooperative groups. *The Journal of Social Psychology, 134,* 681–694.

Argyle, M., & Kendon, A. (1967). The experimental analysis of social performance. In L. Berkowitz (Ed.), *Advances in experimental social psychology* (vol. 3, pp. 55–98). New York: Academic Press.

Armed forces: Too close. (1998, January 5). *Newsweek,* p. 17.

Arrow, H., & McGrath, J. E. (1993). Membership matters: How member change and continuity affect small group structure, process, and performance. *Small Group Research, 24,* 334–361.

Avolio, B. J., Waldman, D. A., & Einstein, W. O. (1988). Transformational leadership in a management game simulation. *Group & Organization Studies, 13,* 59–80.

Avruch, K., & Black, P. W. (1993). Conflict resolution in intercultural settings: Problems and prospects. In D. J. D. Sandole & H. van der Merwe (Eds.), *Conflict resolution theory and practice: Integration and application* (pp. 131–145). New York: Manchester University Press.

Baird, J. E., Jr. (1977). Some nonverbal elements of leadership emergence. *Southern Speech Communication Journal, 42,* 352–361.

Baker, D. C. (1990). A qualitative and quantitative analysis of verbal style and the elimination of potential leaders in small groups. *Communication Quarterly, 38,* 13–26.

Bales, R. F., & Cohen, S. P. (1979). *SYMLOG: A system for the multiple level observation of groups.* New York: Free Press.

Bandura, A. (1986). *Social foundations of thought and action: A social cognitive theory.* Englewood Cliffs, NJ: Prentice-Hall.

Bantz, C. R. (1993). Cultural diversity and group cross-cultural team research. *Journal of Applied Communication Research, 21,* 1–201.

Barge, J. K. (1994). *Leadership: Communication skills for organizations and groups.* New York: St. Martin's.

Barge, J. K., & Hirokawa, R. Y. (1989). Toward a communication competency model of group leadership. *Small Group Behavior, 20,* 167–189.

Barge, J. K., & Keyton, J. (1994). Contextualizing power and social influence in groups. In L. R. Frey (Ed.), *Group communication in context: Studies of natural groups* (pp. 85–105). Hillsdale, NJ: Erlbaum.

Barker, J. R., & Tompkins, P. K. (1994). Identification in the self-managing organization: Characteristics of target and tenure. *Human Communication Research, 21,* 223–240.

Bass, B. M. (1981). *Stogdill's handbook of leadership: A survey of theory and research.* New York: Free Press.

Bass, B. M. (1985). *Leadership and performance beyond expectations.* New York: Free Press.

Bass, B. M. (1990). From transactional to transformational leadership: Learning to share the vision. *Organizational Dynamics, 18*(3), 19–31.

Bauer, T. N., & Green, S. G. (1996). Development of leader-member exchange: A longitudinal test. *Academy of Management Journal, 39,* 1538–1567.

Baxter, L. A. (1982). Conflict management: An episodic approach. *Small Group Behavior, 13,* 23–42.

Beatty, M. J. (1988). Increasing students' choice-making consistency: The effects of decision rule-use training. *Communication Education, 37,* 95–105.

Beatty, M. J. (1989). Group members' decision rule orientations and consensus. *Human Communication Research, 16,* 279–296.

Bechler, C., & Johnson, S. C. (1995). Leadership and listening: A study of member perceptions. *Small Group Research, 26,* 77–85.

Bednar, D. A. (1981). Relationships between communicator style and managerial performance in complex organizations: A field study. *The Journal of Business Communication, 19,* 51–76.

Bell, M. A. (1974). The effects of substantive and affective conflict in problem-solving groups. *Speech Monographs, 41,* 19–23.

Bell, M. A. (1983). A research note: The relationship of conflict and linguistic diversity in small groups. *Central States Speech Journal, 34,* 128–133.

Benne, K., & Sheats, P. (1948). Functional roles of group members. *Journal of Social Issues, 4,* 41–49.

Berteotti, C. R., & Seibold, D. R. (1994). Coordination and role-definition problems in health-care teams: A hospice case study. In L. R. Frey (Ed.), *Group communication in context: Studies of natural groups* (pp. 107–131). Hillsdale, NJ: Erlbaum.

Bettenhausen, K. L. (1991). Five years of groups research: What we have learned and what needs to be addressed. *Journal of Management, 17,* 345–381.

Bettenhausen, K., & Murnighan, J. K. (1985). The emergence of norms in competitive decision-making groups. *Administrative Science Quarterly, 30,* 350–372.

Biddle, B. J. (1979). *Role theory: Expectations, identities, and behaviors.* New York: Academic Press.

Blake, R. R., & McCanse, A. A. (1991). *Leadership dilemmas—grid solutions.* Houston: Gulf Publishing.

Blake, R. R., & Mouton, J. S. (1985). *The managerial grid III.* Houston: Gulf.

Bocialetti, G. (1988). Teams and the management of emotion. In W. B. Reddy & K. Jamison (Eds.), *Team building: Blueprints for productivity and satisfaction* (pp. 62–71). San Diego: NTL Institute for Applied Behavioral Science and University Associates.

Bormann, E. G. (1994). Response to "revitalizing the study of small group communication." *Communication Studies, 45,* 86–91.

Bormann, E. G., & Bormann, N. C. (1988). *Effective small group communication.* Edina, MN: Burgess.

Bormann, E. G., Pratt, J., & Putnam, L. (1978). Power, authority, and sex: Male response to female leadership. *Communication Monographs, 45,* 119–155.

Bradbury, T. N., & Fincham, F. D. (1990). Attributions in marriage: Review and critique. *Psychological Bulletin, 107,* 3–33.

Bradley, P. H. (1978). Power, status, and upward communication in small decision-making groups. *Communication Monographs, 45,* 33–43.

Brewer, M. B. (1995). Managing diversity: The role of social identities. In S. E. Jackson & M. N. Ruderman (Eds.), *Diversity in work teams: Research paradigms for a changing workplace* (pp. 47–68). Washington, DC: American Psychological Association.

Broome, B. J. (1993). Managing differences in conflict resolution: The role of relational empathy. In D. J. D. Sandole & H. van der Merwe (Eds.), *Conflict resolution theory and practice: Integration and application* (pp. 97–111). New York: Manchester University Press.

Broome, B. J., & Fulbright, L. (1995). A multistage influence model of barriers to group problem solving: A participant-generated agenda for small group research. *Small Group Research, 26,* 22–55.

Burgoon, J. K. (1977). Unwillingness to communicate as a predictor of small group discussion behaviors and evaluation. *Central States Speech Journal, 28,* 122–133.

Burgoon, J. K. (1980). Nonverbal communication research in the 1970s: An overview. In D. Nimmo (Ed.), *Communication yearbook 4* (pp. 179–197). New Brunswick, NJ: Transaction.

Burgoon, J. K. (1985). Nonverbal signals. In M. L. Knapp & G. R. Miller (Eds.), *Handbook of interpersonal communication* (pp. 349–353). Beverly Hills: Sage.

Burgoon, J. K. (1996). Spatial relationships in small groups. In R. S. Cathcart, L. A. Samovar, & L. D. Henman (Eds.), *Small group communication: Theory & practice* (7th ed., pp. 241–253). Madison: Brown & Benchmark.

Burke, W. W. (1988). *Team building.* In W. B. Reddy & K. Jamison (Eds.), *Team building: Blueprints for productivity and satisfaction* (pp. 3–14). San Diego: NTL Institute for Applied Behavioral Science and University Associates.

Burrell, N. A., Donohue, W. A., & Allen, M. (1990). The impact of disputants' expectations on mediation: Testing an interventionist model. *Human Communication Research, 17,* 104–139.

Canary, D. J., & Spitzberg, B. H. (1989). A model of the perceived competence of conflict strategies. *Human Communication Research, 15,* 630–649.

Canary, D. J., & Spitzberg, B. H. (1990). Attribution biases and associations between conflict strategies and competence outcomes. *Communication Monographs, 57,* 139–151.

Cartwright, D. (1968). The nature of group cohesiveness. In D. Cartwright & A. Zander (Eds.), *Group dynamics: Research and theory* (3rd. ed., pp. 91–109). New York: Harper & Row.

Cartwright, D., & Zander, A. (1968a). Groups and group

membership: Introduction. In D. Cartwright & A. Zander (Eds.), *Group dynamics: Research and theory* (3rd. ed., pp. 45–62). New York: Harper & Row.

Cartwright, D., & Zander, A. (1968b). Pressures to uniformity in groups: Introduction. In D. Cartwright & A. Zander (Eds.), *Group dynamics: Research and theory* (3rd. ed., pp. 139–151). New York: Harper & Row.

Cathcart, R., & Cathcart, D. (1996). Group lifetimes: Japanese and American versions. In R. S. Cathcart, L. A. Samovar, & L. D. Henman (Eds.), *Small group communication: Theory & practice* (7th ed., pp. 345–355). Madison: Brown & Benchmark.

Chemers, M. M. (1993). An integrative theory of leadership. In M. M. Chemers & R. Ayman (Eds.), *Leadership theory and research: Perspectives and directions* (pp. 293–319). San Diego: Academic Press.

Chemers, M. M., & Murphy, S. E. (1995). Leadership and diversity in groups and organizations. In M. M. Chemers, S. Oskamp, & M. A. Costanzo (Eds.), *Diversity in organizations: New perspectives for a changing workplace* (pp. 157–188). Thousand Oaks, CA: Sage.

Cissna, K. N. (1984). Phases in group development: The negative evidence. *Small Group Behavior, 15*, 3–32.

Clark, R. D., III. (1971) Group-induced shift toward risk: A critical appraisal. *Psychological Bulletin, 76*, 251–270.

Cline, R. J. W. (1990). Detecting groupthink: Methods for observing the illusion of unanimity. *Communication Quarterly, 38*, 112–126.

Cline, R. J. W. (1994). Groupthink and the Watergate cover-up: The illusion of unanimity. In L. R. Frey (Ed.), *Group communication in context: Studies of natural groups* (pp. 199–223). Hillsdale, NJ: Erlbaum.

Cohen, S. G. (1990). Hilltop Hospital top management group. In J. R. Hackman (Ed.), *Groups that work (and those that don't): Creating conditions for effective teamwork* (pp. 56–77). San Francisco: Jossey-Bass.

Comer, D. R. (1995). A model of social loafing in real work groups. *Human Relations, 48*, 647–667.

Conrad, C. (1991). Communication in conflict: Style-strategy relationships. *Communication Monographs, 58*, 135–155.

Courtright, J. A. (1978). A laboratory investigation of groupthink. *Communication Monographs, 45*, 229–246.

Cox, T., Jr. (1993). *Cultural diversity in organizations: Theory, research, and practice*. San Francisco: Berrett-Koehler.

Cox, T., Jr. (1995). The complexity of diversity: Challenges and directions for future research. In S. E. Jackson & M. N. Ruderman (Eds.), *Diversity in work teams: Research paradigms for a changing workplace* (pp. 235–253). Washington, DC: American Psychological Association.

Cox, T. H., Lobel, S. A., & McLeod, P. L. (1991). Effects of ethnic group cultural differences on cooperative and competitive behavior on a group task. *Academy of Management Journal, 34*, 827–847.

Cronshaw, S. F., & Ellis, R. J. (1991). A process investigation of self-monitoring and leader emergence. *Small Group Research, 22*, 403–420.

Dabbs, J. M., Jr., Ruback, R. B., & Evans, M. S. (1987). "Grouptalk": Sound and silence in group conversation. In A. W. Siegman & S. Feldstein (Eds.), *Nonverbal behavior and communication* (2nd ed., pp. 501–520). Hillsdale, NJ: Erlbaum.

Daly, J. A., McCroskey, J. C., & Richmond, V. P. (1977). Relationships between vocal activity and perception of communicators in small group interaction. *Western Journal of Speech Communication, 41*, 175–187.

Dansereau, F., Graen, G., & Haga, W. J. (1975). A vertical dyad linkage approach to leadership within formal organizations: A longitudinal investigation of the role making process. *Organizational Behavior and Human Performance, 13*, 46–78.

DeLamater, J. (1974). A definition of "group." *Small Group Behavior, 5*, 30–44.

Delbecq, A. L., Van de Ven, A. H., & Gustafson, D. H. (1975). *Group techniques for program planning: A guide to nominal group and delphi processes*. Glenview, IL: Scott, Foresman.

de Reuck, A. (1990). A theory of conflict resolution by problem-solving. In J. Burton & F. Dukes (Eds.), *Conflict: Readings in management and resolution* (pp. 183–198). New York: St. Martin's.

De Souza, G., & Klein, H. J. (1995). Emergent leadership in the group goal-setting process. *Small Group Research, 26*, 475–496.

DeStephen, R. S., & Hirokawa, R. Y. (1988). Small group consensus: Stability of group support of the decision, task process, and group relationships. *Small Group Behavior, 19*, 227–239.

Deutsch, M. (1969). Conflicts: Productive and destructive. *Journal of Social Issues, 25*, 7–41.

Deutsch, M. (1973). *The resolution of conflict*. New Haven, CT: Yale University Press.

Di Salvo, V. S., Nikkel, E., & Monroe, C. (1989). Theory and practice: A field investigation and identification of group members' perceptions of problems facing natural work groups. *Small Group Behavior, 20*, 551–567.

Downs, C. W., & Pickett, T. (1977). An analysis of the effects of nine leadership group compatibility contingencies upon productivity and member satisfaction. *Communication Monographs, 44*, 220–230.

Dyce, J., & O'Connor, B. P. (1992). Personality complementarity as a determinant of group cohesion in bar bands. *Small Group Research, 23*, 185–198.

Eagly, A. H., & Johnson, B. T. (1990). Gender and leadership style: A meta-analysis. *Psychological Bulletin, 108*, 233–256.

Eagly, A. H., & Karau, S. J. (1991). Gender and the emergence of leaders: A meta-analysis. *Journal of Personality and Social Psychology, 60*, 685–710.

Eagly, A. H., Karau, S. J., & Makhijani, M. G. (1995). Gender and the effectiveness of leaders: A meta-analysis. *Psychological Bulletin, 117*, 125–145.

Eldred, J. P. (1996). A procedure for teaching criteria generation. *Speech Communication Teacher, 10*(2), 9–10.

Elias, F. G., Johnson, M. E., & Fortman, J. B. (1989). Task-focused self-disclosure: Effects on group cohesiveness, commitment to task, and productivity. *Small Group Behavior, 20,* 87–96.

Ellis, D. G. (1979). Relational control in two group systems. *Communication Monographs, 46,* 153–166.

Ellis, R. J., Adamson, R. S., Deszca, G., & Cawsey, T. F. (1988). Self-monitoring and leadership emergence. *Small Group Behavior, 19,* 312–324.

Ellis, R. J., & Cronshaw, S. F. (1992). Self-monitoring and leader emergence: A test of moderator effects. *Small Group Research, 23,* 113–129.

Evans, C. R., & Dion, K. L. (1991). Group cohesion and performance: A meta-analysis. *Small Group Research, 22,* 175–186.

Feldman, D. C. (1984). The development and enforcement of group norms. *Academy of Management Review, 9,* 47–53.

Ferrari, A. (1990). Social complexity, threat, ego defenses, and labeling the other a deviant: A "racial" incident in the development of a small group. *Small Group Research, 21,* 538–553.

Festinger, L., Schachter, S., & Back, K. (1968). Operation of group standards. In D. Cartwright & A. Zander (Eds.), *Group dynamics: Research and theory* (3rd. ed., pp. 152–164). New York: Harper & Row.

Fiedler, F. E. (1967). *A theory of leadership effectiveness.* New York: McGraw-Hill.

Fiedler, F. E. (1968). Personality and situational determinants of leadership effectiveness. In D. Cartwright & A. Zander (Eds.), *Group dynamics: Research and theory* (3rd ed., pp. 362–380). New York: Harper & Row.

Firestien, R. L. (1990). Effects of creative problem solving training on communication behavior in small groups. *Small Group Research, 21,* 507–521.

Fisher, B. A. (1971). Communication research and the task-oriented group. *The Journal of Communication, 21,* 136–149.

Fisher, B. A. (1985). Leadership as medium: Treating complexity in group communication research. *Small Group Behavior, 16,* 167–196.

Fisher, B. A., & Hawes, L. C. (1971). An interact system model: Generating a grounded theory of small groups. *Quarterly Journal of Speech, 57,* 444–453.

Forsyth, D. (1990). *Group dynamics.* Pacific Grove, CA: Brooks/Cole.

Forsyth, D. R., & Kelley, K. N. (1994). Attribution in groups: Estimations of personal contributions to collective endeavors. *Small Group Research, 25,* 367–383.

Fourre, J. P. (1968). *Critical path scheduling: A practical appraisal of PERT.* New York: American Management Association.

Freeman, K. A. (1996). Attitudes toward work in project groups as predictors of academic performance. *Small Group Research, 27,* 265–282.

French, J. R. P., & Raven, B. (1968). The bases of social power. In D. Cartwright & A. Zander (Eds.), *Group dynamics: Research and theory* (pp. 259–269). New York: Harper & Row.

Frey, L. R. (Ed.). (1994). *Group communication in context: Studies of natural groups,* Hillsdale, NJ: Erlbaum.

Frey, L. R. (Ed.). (1995). *Innovations in group facilitation: Applications in natural settings.* Creskill, NJ: Hampton.

Frost, P. J. (1987). Power, politics, and influence. In F. M. Jablin, L. L. Putnam, K. H. Roberts, & W. Porter (Eds.), *Handbook of organizational communication* (pp. 503–548). Beverly Hills: Sage.

Fuehrer, A., & Keys, C. (1988). Group development in self-help groups for college students. *Small Group Behavior, 19,* 325–341.

Gardenswartz, L., & Rowe, A. (1994). *Diverse teams at work: Capitalizing on the power of diversity.* Chicago: Irwin.

Gastil, J. (1993). Identifying obstacles to small group democracy. *Small Group Research, 24,* 5–27.

Gastil, J. (1994a). A definition and illustration of democratic leadership. *Human Relations, 47,* 935–975.

Gastil, J. (1994b). A meta-analytic review of the productivity and satisfaction of democratic and autocratic leadership. *Small Group Research, 25,* 384–410.

Gayle, B. M. (1991). Sex equity in workplace conflict management. *Journal of Applied Communication Research, 19,* 152–169.

Geier, J. G. (1967). A trait approach to the study of leadership in small groups. *Journal of Communication, 17,* 316–323.

Gemmill, G. (1989). The dynamics of scapegoating in small groups. *Small Group Behavior, 20,* 406–418.

Gersick, C. J. G. (1988). Time and transition in work teams: Toward a new model of group development. *Academy of Management Journal, 31,* 9–41.

Gersick, C. J. G. (1989). Marking time: Predictable transitions in task groups. *Academy of Management Journal, 32,* 274–309.

Gersick, C. J. G. (1990). The students. In J. R. Hackman (Ed.), *Groups that work (and those that don't): Creating conditions for effective teamwork* (pp. 89–111). San Francisco: Jossey-Bass.

Gersick, C. J. G., & Davis-Sacks, M. L. (1990). Summary: Task forces. In J. R. Hackman (Ed.), *Groups that work (and those that don't): Creating conditions for effective teamwork* (pp. 146–153). San Francisco: Jossey-Bass.

Gersick, C. J. G., & Hackman, J. R. (1990). Habitual routines in task-performing groups. *Organizational Behavior and Human Decision Processes, 47,* 65–97.

Gibb, J. R. (1961). Defensive communication. *Journal of Communication, 11,* 141–148.

Ginnett, R. C. (1990). Airline cockpit crews. In J. R. Hackman (Ed.), *Groups that work (and those that don't): Creating conditions for effective teamwork* (pp. 427–448). San Francisco: Jossey-Bass.

Gist, M. E. (1987). Self-efficacy: Implications for organizational behavior and human resource management. *Academy of Management Review, 17,* 183–211.

Gladstein, D. L. (1984). Groups in context: A model of task group effectiveness. *Administrative Science Quarterly, 29*, 499–517.

Glaser, H. F. (1996). Structure and struggle in egalitarian groups: Dimensions of power relations. *Small Group Research, 27*, 551–571.

Glaser, S. R. (1994). Teamwork and communication: A 3-year case study of change. *Management Communication Quarterly, 7*, 282–296.

Golembiewski, R. T. (1962). *Making decisions in groups*. Glenview, IL: Scott, Foreman.

Goodman, P. S. (1986). Impact of task and technology on group performance. In P. S. Goodman (Ed.), *Designing effective work groups* (pp. 120–167). San Francisco: Jossey-Bass.

Goodstein, L. D., Nolan, T. M., & Pfeiffer, J. W. (1992). *Applied strategic planning: A comprehensive guide*. San Diego: Pfeiffer.

Gouran, D. S. (1970). Conceptual and methodological approaches to the study of leadership. *Central States Speech Journal, 21*, 217–223.

Gouran, D. S. (1988). Group decision making: An approach to integrative research. In C. H. Tardy (Ed.), *A handbook for the study of human communication: Methods and instruments for observing, measuring, and assessing communication processes* (pp. 247–267). Norwood, NJ: Ablex.

Gouran, D. S. (1990). Evaluating group outcomes. In G. M. Phillips (Ed.), *Teaching how to work in groups* (pp. 175–195). Norwood, NJ: Ablex.

Gouran, D. S. (1994). The future of small group communication research: Revitalization or continued good health? *Communication Studies, 45*, 27–39.

Gouran, D. S., Brown, C., & Henry, D. R. (1978). Behavioral correlates of perceptions of quality in decision-making discussions. *Communication Monographs, 45*, 51–63.

Gouran, D. S., & Hirokawa, R. Y. (1983). The role of communication in decision making groups: A functional perspective. In M. S. Mander (Ed.), *Communications in transition* (pp. 168–185). New York: Praeger.

Gouran, D. S., & Hirokawa, R. Y. (1996). Functional theory and communication in decision-making and problem-solving groups. In R. Y. Hirokawa & M. S. Poole (Eds.), *Communication and group decision making* (pp. 55–80). Thousand Oaks, CA: Sage.

Gouran, D. S., Hirokawa, R. Y., Julian, K. M., & Leatham, G. B. (1993). The evolution and current status of the functional perspective on communication in decision-making and problem-solving groups. In S. A. Deetz (Ed.), *Communication Yearbook 16* (pp. 573–600). Newbury Park, CA: Sage.

Gouran, D. S., Hirokawa, R. Y., & Martz, A. E. (1986). A critical analysis of factors related to decisional processes involved in the Challenger disaster. *Central States Speech Journal, 37*, 119–135.

Graen, G. B., & Scandura, T. (1987). Toward a psychology of dyadic organizing. In L. L. Cummings & B. Staw (Eds.), *Research in organizational behavior* (vol. 9, pp. 175–208). Greenwich, CT: JAI.

Graham, E. E., Papa, M. J., & McPherson, M. B. (1997). An applied test of the functional communication perspective of small group decision-making. *Southern Communication Journal, 62*, 269–279.

Green, S. G., & Taber, T. D. (1980). The effects of three social decision schemes on decision group process. *Organizational Behavior and Human Performance, 25*, 97–106.

Green, T. B. (1975). An empirical analysis of nominal and interacting groups. *Academy of Management Journal, 18*, 63–73.

Greene, C. N. (1989). Cohesion and productivity in work groups. *Small Group Behavior, 20*, 70–86.

Gudykunst, W. B., & Hall, B. J (1994). Strategies for effective communication and adaptation in intergroup contexts. In J. A. Daly & J. M. Wiemann (Eds.), *Strategic interpersonal communication* (pp. 225–271). Hillsdale, NJ: Erlbaum.

Guetzkow, H. (1968). Differentiation of roles in task-oriented groups. In D. Cartwright & A. Zander (Eds.), *Group dynamics: Research and theory* (3rd. ed., pp. 512–526). New York: Harper & Row.

Guetzkow, H., & Gyr, J. (1954). An analysis of conflict in decision-making groups. *Human Relations, 7*, 367–382.

Gully, S. M., Devine, D. J., & Whitney, D. J. (1995). A meta-analysis of cohesion and performance: Effects of level of analysis and task interdependence. *Small Group Research, 26*, 497–520.

Gurman, E. B., & Long, K. (1992). Gender orientation and emergent leader behavior. *Sex Roles, 27*, 391–400.

Hackman, J. R. (Ed.). (1990). *Groups that work (and those that don't): Creating conditions for effective teamwork*. San Francisco: Jossey-Bass.

Hackman, J. R. (1992). Group influences on individuals in organizations. In M. D. Dunnette & L. M. Hough (Eds.), *Handbook of industrial and organizational psychology* (pp. 199–267). Palo Alto, CA: Consulting Psychologists Press.

Hamblin, R. L. (1973). Leadership and crises. In R. J. Ofshe (Ed.), *Interpersonal behavior in small groups* (pp. 466–477). Englewood Cliffs, NJ: Prentice-Hall.

Hansford, B. C., & Diehl, B. J. (1988). Verbal comments, ideas, feedback, and self-assessment during small-group discussions. *Small Group Behavior, 19*, 485–494.

Hanson, P. G., & Lubin, B. (1988). Team building as group development. In W. B. Reddy & K. Jamison (Eds.), *Team building: Blueprints for productivity and satisfaction* (pp. 76–87). San Diego: NTL Institute for Applied Behavioral Science and University Associates.

Hare, A. P. (1976). *Handbook of small group research* (2nd ed.). New York: Free Press.

Hare, A. P. (1982). *Creativity in small groups*. Beverly Hills: Sage.

Hare, A. P. (1994). Types of roles in small groups: A bit of history and a current perspective. *Small Group Research, 25*, 433–448.

Hawes, L. C., & Smith, D. H. (1973). A critique of assumptions underlying the study of communication in conflict. *The Quarterly Journal of Speech, 59,* 423–435.

Hawkins, K. W. (1995). Effects of gender and communication content on leadership emergence in small task-oriented groups. *Small Group Research, 26,* 234–249.

Hawkins, K. W., & Stewart, R. A. (1991). Effects of communication apprehension on perceptions of leadership and intragroup attraction in small task-oriented groups. *Southern Communication Journal, 57,* 1–10.

Herold, D. M. (1978). Improving the performance effectiveness of groups through a task-contingency selection of intervention strategies. *Academy of Management Review, 3,* 315–325.

Hersey, P., Blanchard, K. H., & Johnson, D. E. (1996). *Management of organizational behavior: Utilizing human resources* (7th ed.). Upper Saddle River, NJ: Prentice-Hall.

Heston, J. K. (1974). Effects of personal space invasion and anomia on anxiety, nonperson orientation and source credibility. *Central States Speech Journal, 25,* 19–27.

Hill, T. A. (1976). An experimental study of the relationship between opinionated leadership and small group consensus. *Communication Monographs, 43,* 246–257.

Hirokawa, R. Y. (1982). Group communication and problem-solving effectiveness I: A critical review of inconsistent findings. *Communication Quarterly, 30,* 134–141.

Hirokawa, R. Y. (1983a). Group communication and problem-solving effectiveness: An investigation of group phases. *Human Communication Research, 9,* 291–305.

Hirokawa, R. Y. (1983b). Group communication and problem-solving effectiveness II: An exploratory investigation of procedural functions. *Western Journal of Speech Communication, 47,* 59–74.

Hirokawa, R. Y. (1985). Discussion procedure and decision-making performance: A test of a functional perspective. *Human Communication Research, 12,* 203–224.

Hirokawa, R. Y. (1988). Group communication and decision-making performance: A continued test of the functional perspective. *Human Communication Research, 14,* 487–515.

Hirokawa, R. Y., Erbert, L., & Hurst, A. (1996). Communication and group decision-making effectiveness. In R. Y. Hirokawa & M. S. Poole (Eds.), *Communication and group decision making* (pp. 269–300). Thousand Oaks, CA: Sage.

Hirokawa, R. Y., Gouran, D. S., & Martz, A. E. (1988). Understanding the sources of faulty group decision making: A lesson from the Challenger disaster. *Small Group Behavior, 19,* 411–433.

Hirokawa, R. Y., Ice, R., & Cook, J. (1988). Preference for procedural order, discussion structure, and group decision performance. *Communication Quarterly, 36,* 217–226.

Hirokawa, R. Y., & Johnston, D. D. (1989). Toward a general theory of group decision making: Development of an integrated model. *Small Group Behavior, 20,* 500–523.

Hirokawa, R. Y., & Keyton, J. (1995). Perceived facilitators and inhibitors of effectiveness in organizational work teams. *Management Communication Quarterly, 8,* 424–446.

Hirokawa, R. Y., & Pace, R. (1983). A descriptive analysis of the possible communication-based reasons for effective and ineffective group decision making. *Communication Monographs, 50,* 363–379.

Hirokawa, R. Y., & Scheerhorn, D. R. (1986). Communication in faulty group decision-making. In R. Y. Hirokawa & M. S. Poole (Eds.), *Communication and group decision-making* (pp. 63–80). Beverly Hills: Sage.

Hoffman, L. R., & Kleinman, G. B. (1994). Individual and group in problem solving: The valence model redressed. *Human Communication Research, 21,* 36–59.

Hofstede, G. (1984). *Culture's consequences: International differences in work-related values* (abridged ed.). Newbury Park, CA: Sage.

Hofstede, G. (1991). *Cultures and organizations: Software of the mind.* London: McGraw-Hill.

Hollander, E. P. (1978). *Leadership dynamics: A practical guide to effective relationships.* New York: Macmillan.

Hollander, E. P. (1985). Leadership and power. In G. Lindzey & E. Aronson (Eds.), *The handbook of social psychology* (3, vol. II, pp. 485–537). New York: Random House.

Homans, G. C. (1950). *The human group.* New York: Harcourt, Brace.

Hunt, J. G., & Liebscher, V. K. (1973). Leadership preference, leadership behavior, and employee satisfaction. *Organizational Behavior and Human Performance, 9,* 59–77.

Infante, D. A., Rancer, A. S., & Womack, D. F. (1997). *Building communication theory* (3rd ed.). Prospect Heights, IL: Waveland.

Jablin, F. M. (1980a). Subordinate's sex and superior-subordinate status differentiation as moderators of the Pelz Effect. In D. Nimmo (Ed.), *Communication yearbook 4* (pp. 327–347). New Brunswick, NJ: Transaction.

Jablin, F. M. (1980b). Superior's upward influence, satisfaction, and openness in superior-subordinate communication: A reexamination of the "Pelz Effect." *Human Communication Research, 6,* 210–220.

Jackson, J. (1965). Social stratification, social norms, and roles. In I. D. Steiner & M. Fishbein (Eds.), *Current studies in social psychology* (pp. 301–309). New York: Holt, Rinehart & Winston.

Jacobs, T. O. (1970). *Leadership and exchange in formal organizations.* Alexandria, VA: Human Resources Research Organization.

Jago, A. G. (1982). Leadership: Perspectives in theory and research. *Management Science, 28,* 315–336.

Janis, I. L. (1982). *Groupthink: Psychological studies of policy decisions and fiascoes* (2nd ed.). Boston: Houghton Mifflin.

Janis, I. L. (1989). *Crucial decisions: Leadership in policy making and crisis management.* New York: Free Press.

Janis, I. L., & Mann, L. (1977). *Decision making: A psychological analysis of conflict, choice, and commitment.* New York: Free Press.

Jarboe, S. (1990). What we know about individual performance in groups: Myths and realities. In G. M. Phillips (Ed.), *Teaching how to work in groups* (pp. 13–49). Norwood, NJ: Ablex.

Jarboe, S. (1996). Procedures for enhancing group decision making. In R. Y. Hirokawa & M. S. Poole (Eds.), *Communication and group decision making* (pp. 345–383). Thousand Oaks, CA: Sage.

Jarboe, S. C., & Witteman, H. R. (1996). Intragroup conflict management in task-oriented groups: The influence of problem sources and problem analyses. *Small Group Research, 27*, 316–338.

Johannesen, R. L. (1983). *Ethics in human communication* (2nd ed.). Prospect Heights, IL: Waveland.

Johansen, R., Sibbet, D., Benson, S., Martin, A., Mittman, R., & Saffo, P. (1991). *Leading business teams: How teams can use technology and group process tools to enhance performance.* Reading, MA: Addison-Wesley.

Johnson, B. M. (1975). Images of the enemy in intergroup conflict. *Central States Speech Journal, 26*, 84–92.

Johnson, D. W. (1974). Communication and the inducement of cooperative behavior in conflicts: A critical review. *Speech Monographs, 41*, 64–78.

Johnson, V. (1991, June). Group decision making: When trying to persuade others, knowledge is power. *Successful Meetings, 40*, 76–77.

Jones, T. S. (1988). Phase structures in agreement and no-agreement mediation. *Communication Research, 15*, 470–495.

Jurma, W. E. (1979). Effects of leader structuring style and task-orientation characteristics of group members. *Communication Monographs, 46*, 282–295.

Kameda, T. (1996). Procedural influence in consensus formation: Evaluating group decision making from a social choice perspective. In E. H. Witte & J. H. Davis (Eds.), *Understanding group behavior: Consensual action by small groups* (pp. 137–161). Mahwah, NJ: Erlbaum.

Katzenbach, J. R, & Smith, D. K. (1993). *The wisdom of teams: Creating the high-performance organization.* New York: HarperBusiness.

Keltner, J. (1989). Facilitation: Catalyst for group problem solving. *Management Communication Quarterly, 3*, 8–32.

Keltner, J. W. (1995). Message feedback in work groups. In L. R. Frey (Ed.), *Innovations in group facilitation: Applications in natural settings* (pp. 119–147). Cresskill, NJ: Hampton.

Kerr, S., & Jermier, J. M. (1978). Substitutes for leadership: Their meaning and measurement. *Organizational Behavior and Human Performance, 22*, 375–403.

Kerr, S., Schriesheim, C. A., Murphy, C. J., & Stogdill, R. M. (1974). Toward a contingency theory of leadership based upon the consideration and initiating structure literature. *Organizational Behavior and Human Performance, 12*, 62–82.

Ketrow, S. M. (1991). Communication role specializations and perceptions of leadership. *Small Group Research, 22*, 492–514.

Keyton, J. (1987). *An examination of the compatibility and effectiveness of self-selected small task groups.* Unpublished doctoral dissertation, Ohio State University, Columbus.

Keyton, J. (1991). Evaluating individual group member satisfaction as a situational variable. *Small Group Research, 22*, 200–219.

Keyton, J. (1993). Group termination: Completing the study of group development. *Small Group Research, 24*, 84–100.

Keyton, J. (1994). Going forward in group communication research may mean going back: Studying the groups of children. *Communication Studies, 45*, 40–51.

Keyton, J. (1995). Using SYMLOG as a self-analytical group facilitation technique. In L. R. Frey (Ed.), *Innovations in group facilitation: Applications in natural settings* (pp. 148–176). Creskill, NJ: Hampton.

Keyton, J. (1996). *Analyzing interaction patterns in dysfunctional teams.* Paper presented to the University of North Texas Symposium on Work Teams—Advanced Concepts Conference, Dallas.

Keyton, J., Harmon, N. A., & Frey, L. R. (1996, November). *Grouphate: Implications for teaching group communication.* Paper presented at the Speech Communication Association Convention, San Diego.

Keyton, J., & Hirokawa, R. Y. (1997). *Comaraderie: Revitalizing the cohesiveness construct.* Unpublished manuscript.

Kim, M., & Sharkey, W. F. (1995). Independent and interdependent construals of self: Explaining cultural patterns of interpersonal communication in multi-cultural organizational settings. *Communication Quarterly, 43*, 20–38.

Kinlaw, D. C. (1993). *Team-managed facilitation: Critical skills for developing self-sufficient teams.* San Diego: Pfeiffer.

Kirchmeyer, C. (1993). Multicultural task groups: An account of the low contribution level of minorities. *Small Group Research, 24*, 127–148.

Kirchmeyer, C., & Cohen, A. (1992). Multicultural groups: Their performance and reactions with constructive conflict. *Group & Organization Management, 17*, 153–170.

Knutson, T. J., & Holdridge, W. E. (1975). Orientation behavior, leadership and consensus: A possible functional relationship. *Speech Monographs, 42*, 107–114.

Knutson, T. J., & Kowitz, A. C. (1977). Effects of information type and level of orientation on consensus-achievement in substantive and affective small group conflict. *Central States Speech Journal, 28*, 54–63.

Kochman, T. (1981). *Black and white styles in conflict.* Chicago: University of Chicago Press.

Kolb, J. A. (1996). A comparison of leadership behaviors and competencies in high- and average-performance teams. *Communication Reports, 9*, 173–183.

Kolb, J. A. (1997). Are we still stereotyping leadership? A look at gender and other predictors of leader emergence. *Small Group Research, 28*, 370–393.

Kopelman, R. E. (1986). Objective feedback. In E. A. Locke (Ed.), *Generalizing from laboratory to field settings: Research findings from industrial-organizational psychology, organizational behavior, and human resource management* (pp. 119–145). Lexington, MA: Lexington Books.

Korten, D. C. (1962). Situational determinants of leadership structure. *Journal of Conflict Resolution, 6*, 222–235.

Kramer, M. W., Kuo, C. L., & Dailey, J. C. (1997). The

impact of brainstorming techniques on subsequent group processes: Beyond generating ideas. *Small Group Research, 28,* 218–242.

Lammers, J. C., & Krikorian, D. H. (1997). Theoretical extension and operationalization of the bona fide group construct with an application to surgical teams. *Journal of Applied Communication Research, 25,* 17–38.

Larkey, L. K. (1996). The development and validation of the workforce diversity questionnaire: An instrument to assess interactions in diverse workgroups. *Management Communication Quarterly, 9,* 296–337.

Larson, C. E., & LaFasto, F. M. J. (1989). *TeamWork: What must go right/what can go wrong.* Newbury Park, CA: Sage.

Larson, C. U. (1971). The verbal response of groups to the absence or presence of leadership. *Speech Monographs, 38,* 177–181.

Laughlin, P. R. (1996). Group decision making and collective induction. In E. H. Witte & J. H. Davis (Eds.), *Understanding group behavior: Consensual action by small groups* (pp. 61–80). Mahwah, NJ: Erlbaum.

Leathers, D. G. (1972). Quality of group communication as a determinant of group product. *Speech Monographs, 39,* 166–173.

Leathers, D. G. (1979). The impact of multichannel message inconsistency on verbal and nonverbal decoding behaviors. *Communication Monographs, 46,* 88–100.

Lee, J. (1997). Leader-member exchange, the "Pelz Effect," and cooperative communication between group members. *Management Communication Quarterly, 11,* 266–287.

Lewin, K., Lippitt, R., & White, R. K. (1939). Patterns of aggressive behavior in experimentally created "social climates." *Journal of Science Psychology, 10,* 271–299.

Liden, R. C., & Graen G. (1980). Generalizability of the vertical dyad linkage model of leadership. *Academy of Management Journal, 23,* 451–465.

Littlejohn, S. W., & Jabusch, D. M. (1982). Communication competence: Model and application. *Journal of Applied Communication Research, 10,* 29–37.

Littlepage, G. E., Cowart, L., & Kerr, B. (1989). Relationships between group environment scales and group performance and cohesion. *Small Group Behavior, 20,* 50–61.

Littlepage, G. E., & Silbiger, H. (1992). Recognition of expertise in decision-making groups: Effects of group size and participation patterns. *Small Group Research, 23,* 344–355.

Mabry, E. A. (1989a). Developmental aspects of nonverbal behavior in small group settings. *Small Group Behavior, 20,* 190–202.

Mabry, E. A. (1989b). Some theoretical implications of female and male interaction in unstructured small groups. *Small Group Behavior, 20,* 536–550.

Mackie, D. M. (1986). Social identification effects in group polarization. *Journal of Personality and Social Psychology, 50,* 720–728.

May, L. (1987). *The morality of groups: Collective responsibility, group-based harm, and corporate rights.* Notre Dame, IN: University of Notre Dame Press.

McCanne, L. P. F. (1977). Dimensions of participant goals, expectations, and perceptions in small group experiences. *The Journal of Applied Behavioral Science, 13,* 533–540.

McClane, W. E. (1991). The interaction of elder and member characteristics in the leader-member exchange (LMX) model of leadership. *Small Group Research, 22,* 283–300.

McCroskey, J. C. (1977). Oral communication apprehension: A summary of recent theory and research. *Human Communication Research, 4,* 78–96.

McCroskey, J. C., & Richmond, V. P. (1976). The effects of communication apprehension on the perceptions of peers. *Journal of the Western Speech Communication Association, 40,* 14–21.

McCroskey, J. C., & Richmond, V. P. (1987). Willingness to communicate. In J. C. McCroskey & J. A. Daly (Eds.), *Personality and interpersonal communication* (pp. 129–156). New Park, CA: Sage.

McCroskey, J. C., & Richmond, V. P. (1992). Communication apprehension and small group communication. In R. S. Cathcart & L. A. Samovar (Eds.), *Small group communication: A reader* (6th ed., pp. 361–374). Dubuque, IA: Brown.

McDonald, G. M., & Zepp, R. A. (1990). What should be done? A practical approach to business ethics. *Management Decision, 28*(1), 9–14.

McGrath, J. E. (1984). *Groups: Interaction and performance.* Englewood Cliffs, NJ: Prentice-Hall.

McGrath, J. E., Berdahl, J. L., & Arrow, H. (1995). Traits, expectations, culture, and clout: The dynamics of diversity in work groups. In S. E. Jackson & M. N. Ruderman (Eds.), *Diversity in work teams: Research paradigms for a changing workplace* (pp. 17–45). Washington, DC: American Psychological Association.

McIntyre, R. M., & Salas, E. (1995). Measuring and managing for team performance: Emerging principles from complex environments. In R. A. Guzzo & E. Salas (Eds.), *Team effectiveness and decision making in organizations* (pp. 9–45). San Francisco: Jossey-Bass.

McKinney, B. C. (1982). The effects of reticence on group interaction. *Communication Quarterly, 30,* 124–128.

McKinney, B. C., Kelly, L., & Duran, R. L. (1997). The relationship between conflict message styles and dimensions of communication competence. *Communication Reports, 10,* 185–196.

Mennecke, B. E., Hoffer, J. A., & Wynne, B. E. (1992). The implications of group development and history for group support system theory and practice. *Small Group Research, 23,* 524–572.

Meyer, C. (1994, May–June). How the right measures help teams excel. *Harvard Business Review,* pp. 95–103.

Meyers, R. A. (1989). Testing persuasive argument theory's predictor model: Alternative interactional accounts of group argument and influence. *Communication Monographs, 56,* 112–132.

Meyers, R. A., & Seibold, D. R. (1987). Interactional and noninteractional perspectives on interpersonal argument: Implications for the study of group decision-making. In F. H. van Eemeren & R. Grootendorst (Eds.), *Studies of argumentation in pragmatics and discourse analysis* (pp. 205–214). Cinnaminson, NJ: Foris.

Montgomery, B. M., & Norton, R. W. (1981). Sex differences and similarities in communicator style. *Communication Monographs, 48*, 121–132.

Moosbruker, J. (1988). Developing a productivity team: Making groups at work work. In W. B. Reddy & K. Jamison (Eds.), *Team building: Blueprints for productivity and satisfaction* (pp. 88–97). San Diego: NTL Institute for Applied Behavioral Science and University Associate.

Mudrack, P. E., & Farrell, G. M. (1995). An examination of functional role behavior and its consequences for individuals in group settings. *Small Group Research, 26*, 542–571.

Mullen, B., Anthony, T., Salas, E., & Driskell, J. E. (1994). Group cohesiveness and quality of decision making: An integration of tests of the groupthink hypothesis. *Small Group Research, 25*, 189–204.

Myers, D. G., & Bishop, G. D. (1971). Enhancement of dominant attitudes in group discussion. *Journal of Personality and Social Psychology, 20*, 386–391.

Nadler, D. A. (1979). The effects of feedback on task group behavior: A review of the experimental research. *Organizational Behavior and Human Performance, 23*, 309–338.

Neck, C. P., & Moorhead, G. (1995). Groupthink remodeled: The importance of leadership, time pressure, and methodical decision-making procedures. *Human Relations, 48*, 537–557.

Nelson, D. R., & Obremski, T. E. (1990). Promoting moral growth through intra-group participation. *Journal of Business Ethics, 9*, 731–739.

Nichols, M. L., & Day, V. E. (1982). A comparison of moral reasoning of groups and individuals on the "defining issues test." *Academy of Management Journal, 25*, 201–208.

Nicotera, A. M. (1994). The use of multiple approaches to conflict: A study of sequences. *Human Communication Research, 20*, 592–621.

Nord, W. R., & Tucker, S. (1987). *Implementing routine and radical innovations.* Lexington, MA: Heath.

Northcraft, G. B., Polzer, J. T., Neale, M. A., & Kramer, R. M. (1995). In S. E. Jackson & M. N. Ruderman (Eds.), *Diversity in work teams: Research paradigms for a changing workplace* (pp. 69–96). Washington, DC: American Psychological Association.

Norton, R. (1983). *Communicator style: Theory, applications, and measures.* Beverly Hills: Sage.

Norton, R., & Brenders, D. (1996). *Communication and consequences: Laws of interaction.* Mahwah, NJ: Erlbaum.

Norton, R. W. (1978). Foundation of a communicator style construct. *Human Communication Research, 4*, 99–112.

Nye, J. L., & Forsyth, D. R. (1991). The effects of prototype-based biases on leadership appraisals: A test of leadership categorization theory. *Small Group Research, 22*, 360–379.

Oetzel, J. G. (1995). Intercultural small groups: An effective decision-making theory. In R. L. Wiseman (Ed.), *Intercultural communication theories* (pp. 247–270). Newbury Park, CA: Sage.

Oetzel, J. G., & Bolton-Oetzel, K. (1997). Exploring the relationship between self-construal and dimensions of group effectiveness. *Management Communication Quarterly, 10*, 289–315.

Offner, A. K. Kramer, T. J., & Winter, J. P. (1996). The effects of facilitation, recording, and pauses on group brainstorming. *Small Group Research, 27*, 283–298.

Ogilvie, J. R., & Haslett, B. (1985). Communicating peer feedback in a task group. *Human Communication Research, 12*, 79–98.

Osborn, A. F. (1963). *Applied imagination* (3rd ed.). New York: Scribner's.

Pace, R. C. (1990). Personalized and depersonalized conflict in small group discussions: An examination of differentiation. *Small Group Research, 21*, 79–96.

Pavitt, C. (1993). What (little) we know about formal group discussion procedures: A review of relevant research. *Small Group Research, 24*, 217–235.

Pavitt, C., & Sackaroff, P. (1990). Implicit theories of leadership and judgments of leadership among group members. *Small Group Research, 21*, 374–392.

Peek, L. E., Peek, G. S., & Horras, M. (1994). Enhancing Arthur Andersen business ethics vignettes: Group discussions using cooperative/collaborative learning techniques. *Journal of Business Ethics, 13*, 189–196.

Pelz, D. (1952). Influence: A key to effective leadership in the first line supervisor. *Personnel, 29*, 209–217.

Phillips, G. M. (1965). "PERT" as a logical adjunct to the discussion process. *Journal of Communication, 15*, 89–99.

Pondy, L. R. (1967). Organizational conflict: Concepts and models. *Administrative Science Quarterly, 12*, 296–320.

Pood, E. A. (1980). Functions of communication: An experimental study in group conflict situations. *Small Group Behavior, 11*, 76–87.

Poole, M. S. (1983). Decision development in small groups: III. A multiple sequence model of group decision making. *Communication Monographs, 50*, 321–344.

Poole, M. S. (1991). Procedures for managing meetings: Social and technological innovation. In R. A. Swanson & B. O. Knapp (Eds.), *Innovative meeting management* (pp. 53–110). Austin: 3M Meeting Management Institute.

Poole, M. S. (1994). Breaking the isolation of small group communication studies. *Communication Studies, 45*, 20–28.

Prapavessis, H., & Carron, A. V. (1997). Cohesion and work output. *Small Group Research, 28*, 294–301.

Propp, K. M. (1995). An experimental examination of biological sex as a status cue in decision-making groups and its influence on information use. *Small Group Research, 26*, 451–474.

Propp, K. M. (1997). Information utilization in small group decision making: A study of the evaluative interaction model. *Small Group Research, 28*, 424–453.

Putnam, L. L. (1979). Preference for procedural order in

task-oriented small groups. *Communication Monographs, 46,* 193–218.

Putnam, L. L. (1982). Procedural messages and small group work climates: A lag sequential analysis. In M. Burgoon (Ed.), *Communication Yearbook 5* (pp. 331–350). New Brunswick, NJ: Transaction.

Putnam, L. L., & Poole, M. S. (1987). Conflict and negotiation. In F. M. Jablin, L. L. Putnam, K. H. Roberts, & L. W. Porter (Eds.), *Handbook of organizational communication* (pp. 549–599). Newbury Park, CA: Sage.

Putnam, L. L., & Stohl, C. (1990). Bona fide groups: A reconceptualization of groups in context. *Communication Studies, 41,* 248–265.

Putnam, L. L., & Wilson, C. E. (1988). Communicative strategies in organizational conflicts: Reliability and validity of a measurement scale. In M. Burgoon (Ed.), *Communication Yearbook 6* (pp. 629–652). Beverly Hills: Sage.

Riggs, C. J. (1983). Dimensions of organizational conflict: A functional analysis of communication tactics. In R. N. Bostrom (Ed.), *Communication Yearbook 7* (pp. 517–531). Beverly Hills: Sage.

Rose, S. R. (1989). Members leaving groups: Theoretical and practical considerations. *Small Group Behavior, 20,* 524–535.

Rosenthal, S. B., & Buchholz, R. A. (1995). Leadership: Toward new philosophical foundations. *Business & Professional Ethics Journal, 14,* 25–41.

Ruback, R. B., Dabbs, J. M., & Hopper, C. H. (1984). The process of brainstorming: An analysis with individual and group vocal parameters. *Journal of Personality and Social Psychology, 47,* 558–567.

Rubin, R. B., Rubin, A. M., & Jordan, F. F. (1997). Effects of instruction on communication apprehension and communication competence. *Communication Education, 46,* 104–114.

Salazar, A. J. (1995). Understanding the synergistic effects of communication in small groups: Making the most out of group member abilities. *Small Group Research, 26,* 169–199.

Salazar, A. J. (1996). An analysis of the development and evolution of roles in the small group. *Small Group Research, 27,* 475–503.

Salazar, A. J., Hirokawa, R. Y., Propp, K. M., Julian, K. M., & Leatham, G. B. (1994). In search of true causes: Examination of the effect of group potential and group interaction on decision performance. *Human Communication Research, 20,* 529–559.

Sargent, J. F., & Miller, G. R. (1971). Some differences in certain communication behaviors of autocratic and democratic group leaders. *Journal of Communication, 21,* 233–252.

Scheerhorn, D., Geist, P., & Teboul, JC B. (1994). Beyond decision making in decision-making groups: Implications for the study of group communication. In L. R. Frey (Ed.), *Group communication in context: Studies of natural groups* (pp. 247–262). Hillsdale, NJ: Erlbaum.

Schittekatte, M., & Van Hiel, A. (1996). Effects of partially shared information and awareness of unshared information on information sampling. *Small Group Research, 27,* 431–449.

Schultz, B. (1974). Characteristics of emergent leaders of continuing problem-solving groups. *Journal of Psychology, 88,* 167–173.

Schultz, B. (1986). Communicative correlates of perceived leaders in the small group. *Small Group Behavior, 17,* 51–65.

Schultz, B., Ketrow, S. M., & Urban, D. M. (1995). Improving decision quality in the small group: The role of the reminder. *Small Group Research, 26,* 521–541.

Schutz, W. C. (1966). *The interpersonal underworld.* Palo Alto, CA: Science & Behavior Books.

Schwarz, R. M. (1994). *The skilled facilitator: Practical wisdom for developing effective groups.* San Francisco: Jossey-Bass.

Schweiger, D. M., & Leana, C. R. (1986). Participation in decision making. In E. A. Locke (Ed.), *Generalizing from laboratory to field settings: Research findings from industrial-organizational psychology, organizational behavior, and human resource management* (pp. 147–166). Lexington, MA: Lexington Books.

Schweiger, D. M., & Sandberg, W. R. (1989). The utilization of individual capabilities in group approaches to strategic decision-making. *Strategic Management Journal, 10,* 31–43.

Schweiger, D. M., Sandberg, W. R., & Ragan, J. W. (1986). Group approaches for improving strategic decision making: A comparative analysis of dialectical inquiry, devil's advocacy, and consensus. *Academy of Management Journal, 29,* 51–71.

Seibert, S., & Gruenfeld, L. (1992). Masculinity, femininity, and behavior in groups. *Small Group Research, 23,* 95–112.

Seibold, D. R. (1995). Developing the "team" in a team-managed organization: Group facilitation in a new-design plant. In. L. R. Frey (Ed.), *Innovations in group facilitation: Applications in natural settings* (pp. 282–298). Creskill, NJ: Hampton.

Seibold, D. R., Meyers, R. A., & Sunwolf. (1996). Communication and influence in group decision making. In R. Y. Hirokawa & M. S. Poole (Eds.), *Communication and group decision making* (pp. 242–268). Thousand Oaks, CA: Sage.

Senge, P. M. (1990). *The fifth discipline: The art and practice of the learning organization.* New York: Currency Doubleday.

Sessa, V. I., & Jackson, S. E. (1995). Diversity in decision-making teams: All differences are not created equal. In M. M. Chemers, S. Oskamp, & M. A. Costanzo (Eds.), *Diversity in organizations: New Perspectives for a changing workplace* (pp. 133–156). Thousand Oaks, CA: Sage.

Sharf, B. F. (1978). A rhetorical analysis of leadership emergence in small groups. *Communication Monographs, 45,* 156–172.

Shaw, M. E. (1973). Scaling group tasks: A method for dimensional analysis. *JSAS Catalog of Selected Documents in Psychology, 3,* 8.

Shaw, M. E. (1981). *Group dynamics: The psychology of small group behavior.* New York: McGraw-Hill.

Shea, G. P., & Guzzo, R. A. (1987). Groups as human resources. In K. M. Rowland & G. R. Ferris (Eds.), *Research in personnel and human resources management* (pp. 323–356). Greenwich, CT: JAI.

Shonk, J. H. (1992). *Team-based organizations: Developing a successful team environment.* Homewood, IL: Business One Irwin.

Sias, P. M. (1996). Constructing perceptions of differential treatment: An analysis of coworker discourse. *Communication Monographs, 63,* 171–187.

Sias, P. M., & Jablin, F. M. (1995). Differential superior-subordinate relations, perceptions of fairness, and coworker communication. *Human Communication Research, 22,* 5–38.

Sibbet, D. (1981). *Workbook/guide to group graphics.* San Francisco: Sibbet & Associates.

Sillars, A. L., & Wilmot, W. W. (1994). Communication strategies in conflict and mediation. In J. A. Daly & J. M. Wiemann (Eds.), *Strategic interpersonal communication* (pp. 163–190). Hillsdale, NJ: Erlbaum.

Silver, W. S., & Bufanio, K. M. (1996). The impact of group efficacy and group goals on group task performance. *Small Group Research, 27,* 347–359.

Smith, K. K., & Berg, D. N. (1987). *Paradoxes of group life.* San Francisco: Jossey-Bass.

Sniezek, J. A. (1992). Groups under uncertainty: An examination of confidence in group decision making. *Organizational Behavior and Human Decision Processes, 52,* 124–155.

Socha, T. J., & Socha, D. M. (1994). Children's task-group communication: Did we learn it all in kindergarten? In L. R. Frey (Ed.), *Group communication in context: Studies of natural groups* (pp. 227–246). Hillsdale, NJ: Erlbaum.

Sorenson, P. S., Hawkins, K., & Sorenson, R. (1995). Gender, psychological type and conflict style preferences. *Management Communication Quarterly, 9,* 115–126.

Spink, K. S. (1990). Group cohesion and collective efficacy of volleyball teams. *Journal of Sport and Exercise Psychology, 12,* 301–311.

Spink, K. S., & Carron, A. V. (1994). Group cohesion effects in exercise classes. *Small Group Research, 25,* 26–42.

Spitzberg, B. H. (1983). Communication competence as knowledge, skill, and impression. *Communication Education, 32,* 323–328.

Spitzberg, B. H., & Cupach, W. R. (1984). *Interpersonal communication competence.* Beverly Hills: Sage.

Spitzberg, B. H., & Cupach, W. R. (1989). *Handbook of interpersonal competence research.* New York: Springer-Verlag.

Steiner, I. D. (1972). *Group process and productivity.* New York: Academic Press.

Stogdill, R. M. (1948). Personal factors associated with leadership: A survey of the literature. *Journal of Psychology, 25,* 35–36.

Stogdill, R. M. (1974). *Handbook of leadership.* New York: Free Press.

Stohl, C., & Putnam, L. L. (1994). Group communication in context: Implications for the study of bona fide groups. In L. R. Frey (Ed.), *Group communication in context: Studies of natural groups* (pp. 284–292). Hillsdale, NJ: Erlbaum.

Stohl, C., & Schell, S. E. (1991). A communication-based model of small-group dysfunction. *Management Communication Quarterly, 5,* 90–110.

Stoner, J. A. F. (1968). Risky and cautious shifts in group decisions: The influence of widely held values. *Journal of Experimental Social Psychology, 4,* 442–459.

Street, M. C. (1997). Groupthink: An examination of theoretical issues, implications, and future research suggestions. *Small Group Research, 28,* 72–93.

Street, M. C., Robertson, C., & Geiger, S. W. (1997). Ethical decision making: The effects of escalating commitment. *Journal of Business Ethics, 16,* 1153–1161.

SYMLOG Consulting Group. (1986). *The Bales report to your group.* San Diego: Author.

Taps, J., & Martin, P. Y. (1990). Gender composition, attributional accounts and women's influence and likability in task groups. *Small Group Research, 21,* 471–491.

Thibaut, J. W., & Kelley, H. H. (1959). *The social psychology of groups.* New York: Wiley.

Thomas, E. J., & Fink, C. F. (1961). Models of group problem solving. *Journal of Abnormal and Social Psychology, 63,* 53–63.

Thomas, K. W. (1977). Toward multi-dimensional values in teaching: The examples of conflict behaviors. *Academy of Management Review, 2,* 484–490.

Thomas, K. W. (1988). The conflict-handling modes: Toward more precise theory. *Management Communication Quarterly, 1,* 430–436.

Thomas, K. W. (1992). Conflict and negotiation processes in organizations. In M. D. Dunnette & L. M. Hough (Eds.), *Handbook of industrial and organizational psychology* (pp. 651–717). Palo Alto, CA: Consulting Psychologists Press.

Thomas, K. W., & Pondy, L. R. (1977). Toward an "intent" model of conflict management among principal parties. *Human Relations, 30,* 1089–1102.

Thomas, R. R., Jr. (1995). A diversity framework. In M. M. Chemers, S. Oskamp, & M. A. Costanzo (Eds.), *Diversity in organizations: New perspectives for a changing workplace* (pp. 245–263). Thousand Oaks, CA: Sage.

Tjosvold, D. (1995). Cooperation theory, constructive controversy, and effectiveness: Learning from crisis. In R. A. Guzzo & E. Salas (Eds.), *Team effectiveness and decision making in organizations* (pp. 79–112). San Francisco: Jossey-Bass.

Triandis, H. C. (1995a). A theoretical framework for the study of diversity. In M. M. Chemers, S. Oskamp, & M. A. Costanzo (Eds.), *Diversity in organizations: New perspectives for a changing workplace* (pp. 11–36). Thousand Oaks, CA: Sage.

Triandis, H. C. (1995b). The importance of contexts in studies of diversity. In S. E. Jackson & M. N. Ruderman (Eds.), *Diversity in work teams: Research paradigms for a changing workplace* (pp. 225–233). Washington, DC: American Psychological Association.

Tuckman, B. (1965). Developmental sequence in small groups. *Psychological Bulletin, 63,* 384–389.

Tuckman, B. W., & Jensen, M. A. C. (1977). Stages of small-group development revisited. *Group & Organization Studies, 2,* 419–427.

Van de Ven, A. H., & Delbecq, A. L. (1971). Nominal versus interacting group processes for committee decision-making effectiveness. *Academy of Management Journal, 14,* 203–212.

Van de Ven, A. H., & Delbecq, A. L. (1974). The effectiveness of nominal, delphi, and interacting group decision-making processes. *Academy of Management Journal, 17,* 605–621.

Verdi, A. F., & Wheelan, S. A. (1992). Developmental patterns in same-sex and mixed-sex groups. *Small Group Research, 23,* 356–378.

von Bertalanffy, L. (1968). *General systems theory.* New York: Braziller.

von Cranach, M. (1996). Toward a theory of the acting group. In E. H. Witte & J. H. Davis (Eds.), *Understanding group behavior: Small group processes and interpersonal relations* (pp. 147–187). Mahwah, NJ: Erlbaum.

Waldman, D. A., Bass, B. M., & Yammarino, F. J. (1990). Adding to contingent-reward behavior. *Group & Organization Studies, 15,* 381–394.

Wall, V. D., Jr., & Galanes, G. J. (1986). The SYMLOG dimensions and small group conflict. *Central States Speech Journal, 37,* 61–78.

Wall, V. D., Jr., Galanes, G. J., & Love, S. B. (1987). Small, task-oriented groups: Conflict, conflict management, satisfaction, and decision quality. *Small Group Behavior, 18,* 31–55.

Wall, V. D., & Nolan, L. L. (1986). Perceptions of inequity, satisfaction, and conflict in task-oriented groups. *Human Relations, 39,* 1033–1052.

Walter, G. A. (1975). Effects of videotape feedback and modeling on the behaviors of task group members. *Human Relations, 28,* 121–138.

Warfield, J. N. (1993). Complexity and cognitive equilibrium: Experimental results and their implications. In D. J. D. Sandole & H. van der Merwe (Eds.), *Conflict resolution theory and practice: Integration and application* (pp. 65–77). New York: Manchester University Press.

Watanabe, S. (1993). Cultural differences in framing: American and Japanese group discussions. In D. Tannen (Ed.), *Framing in discourse* (pp. 176–209). New York: Oxford University Press.

Watkins, C. E. (1974). An analytic model of conflict. *Speech Monographs, 41,* 1–5.

Watson, E. W., Kumar, K., & Michaelsen, L. K. (1993). Cultural diversity's impact on interaction process and performance: Comparing homogeneous and diverse task groups. *Academy of Management Journal, 36,* 590–602.

Watson, K. W. (1996). Listener preferences: The paradox of small-group interactions. In R. S. Cathcart, L. A. Samovar, & L. D. Henman (Eds.), *Small group communication: Theory & practice* (7th ed., pp. 268–282). Madison: Brown & Benchmark.

Weinberg, S. B., Smotroff, L. J., & Pecka, J. C. (1978). Communication factors of group leadership. *Journal of Applied Communication Research, 6,* 85–91.

Weisbord, M. R. (1988). Team work: Building productive relationships. In W. B. Reddy & K. Jamison (Eds.), *Team building: Blueprints for productivity and satisfaction* (pp. 35–44). San Diego: NTL Institute for Applied Behavioral Science and University Associates.

Wellins, R. S., Byham, W. C., & Wilson, J. M. (1991). *Empowered teams: Creating self-directed work groups that improve quality, productivity, and participation.* San Francisco: Jossey-Bass.

Wetlaufer, S. (1994, November–December). The team that wasn't. *Harvard Business Review,* pp. 22–26, 28, 30, 32, 34, 36, 38.

Wheelan, S. A., & Hochberger, J. M. (1996). Validation studies of the group development questionnaire. *Small Group Research, 27,* 143–170.

Wheelan, S. A., & Kaeser, R. M. (1997). The influence of task type and designated leaders on developmental patterns in groups. *Small Group Research, 28,* 94–121.

Wheelan, S. A., & McKeage, R. L. (1993). Developmental patterns in small and large groups. *Small Group Research, 24,* 60–83.

White, R. K., & Lippitt, R. (1960). *Autocracy and democracy: An experimental inquiry.* Westport, CT: Greenwood.

Witteman, H. (1991). Group member satisfaction: A conflict-related account. *Small Group Research, 22,* 24–58.

Wong, C. L., Tjosvold, D., & Lee, F. (1992). Managing conflict in a diverse work force: A Chinese perspective in North America. *Small Group Research, 23,* 302–321.

Wood, C. J. (1989). Challenging the assumptions underlying the use of participatory decision-making strategies: A longitudinal case study. *Small Group Behavior, 20,* 428–448.

Wood, J. T., & Phillips, G. M. (1990). Teaching groups alternative patterns of decision making. In G. M. Phillips (Ed.), *Teaching how to work in groups* (pp. 50–65). Norwood, NJ: Ablex.

Zander, A. (1982). *Making groups effective.* San Francisco: Jossey-Bass.

Zimmermann, S. (1994). Social cognition and evaluations of health care team communication effectiveness. *Western Journal of Communication, 58,* 116–141.

Credits

Text and Illustrations
Chapter 2 p. 40, Reprinted with permission of The Free Press, a Division of Simon & Schuster from *SYMLOG: A System for the Multiple Level Observation of Groups*, by Robert F. Bales, Stephen P. Cohen, with Stephen A. Williamson. Copyright © 1979 The Free Press. **Chapter 3** p. 69, Adapted from Benne, K. and Sheats, P., 1948, "Functional roles of group members," *Journal of Social Issues*, 4(2), 41–49. Used with permission from Blackwell Publishers. p. 78, Adapted from Keyton, J., Harmon, N.A. & Frey, L. R., November 1996, "Group hate: Implications for teaching group communication." Paper presented at the Speech Communication Association Convention, San Diego. Used with permission from the authors. **Chapter 4** p. 116, Adapted from Eldred, J. P., 1996 "A procedure for teaching criteria generation," *Speech Communication Teacher*, 10(2), 9–10. Used by permission of the National Communication Association. **Chapter 5** p. 136, From J. E. McGrath, 1991, *Groups: Interaction & Performance*. Copyright © 1991 Prentice-Hall, Inc. Reprinted by permission of Prentice-Hall, Inc., Upper Saddle River, NJ. **Chapter 6** Adapted from Wellins, R. S., Byham, W.C. & Wilson, J. M., 1991, *Empowered Teams: Creating Self-Directed Work Groups That Improve Quality, Productivity, and Participation*, Jossey-Bass. p. 165, Copyright © 1987 Jossey-Bass, Inc. Publishers. Reprinted with permission of the publisher. p. 162, Adapted from Norton, R.W., 1978, "Foundation of a communicator style construct," *Human Communication Research*, 4, 99–112. Copyright © 1978 Sage Publications, Inc. Reprinted by permission of Sage Publications, Inc. **Chapter 8** p. 228, Adapted from R. S. DeStephen and R. Y. Hirokawa, 1988, "Small group consensus: Stability of group support of the decision, task prrocess, and group relationships," *Small Group Behavior*, 19, 227–239. Copyright © 1988 Sage Publications, Inc. Reprinted by permission of Sage Publications, Inc. p. 240, From Putnam, L. L., 1979, "Preference for procedural order in task-oriented small groups," *Communication Monographs*, 46, 193–218. Used by permission of the National Communication Association. p. 242, From Gouran, D. S., Brown, C. & Henry, D. R., 1978, "Behavioral correlates of perceptions of quality in decision-making discussions," *Communication Monographs*, 45, 51–63. Used by permission of the National Communication Association. **Chapter 10** Table 10.1, A. G. Jago, "Leadership: Perspectives in theory and research," *Management Science*, Vol. 28, No. 3, March 1982. Copyright © 1982 The Institute of Management Sciences (currently INFORMS), 901 Elkridge Landing Road, Suite 400, Linthicum, MD 21090-2909. Reprinted by permission. Fig. 10.2, From Hersey, P., Blanchard, K. H., Johnson, D. E., 1996, *Management of Organizational Behavior: Utilizing Human Resources*, 7th edition, Prentice-Hall. The Situational Leadership ® Model is the registered trademark of the Center for Leadership Studies, Escondido, CA. Used with permission. All rights reserved. p. 304, Adapted with the permission of The Free Press, a Division of Simon & Schuster from, *Leadership and Performance Beyond Expectations*, by Bernard M. Bass. Copyright © 1985 by The Free Press. **Chapter 11** p. 323, Reproduced with permission of authors and publisher from Kilmann, R. H. & Thomas, K. W., "Interpersonal conflict-handling behavior as reflections of Jungian personality dimensions," *Psychological Reports*, 1975, 37, 971–980. Copyright © 1975 Psychological Reports. p. 328, Adapted from Jarboe, S. C. & Witteman, H. R., 1996, "Intragroup conflict management in task-oriented groups: The influence of problem sources and problem analyses. *Small Group Research*, 27, 316–338. Copyright © 1996 Sage Publications, Inc. Reprinted by permission of Sage Publications, Inc. p. 330, Modified and Reproduced by special permission of the publisher, Consulting Psychologists Press, Inc., Palo Alto, CA 94303 from, *Handbook of Industrial and Organizational Psychology*, Vol. 3, Second Edition, by Marvin D. Dunnette and Leaetta M. Hough, editors. Copyright © 1992 by Davies-Black Publishing. All rights reserved. Further reproduction is prohibited without the publisher's written consent. p. 334, Adapted from Riggs, C. J., 1983, "Dimensions of organizational conflict: A functional analysis of communication tactics," in R. N. Bostrom, ed., *Communication Yearbook* 7, 517–531. Copyright © 1983 Sage Publications, Inc. **Chapter 12** p. 366 and **Chapter 13** p. 399, From Gardenswartz, L. & Rowe, A., 1994, *Diverse Teams at Work: Capitalizing on the Power of Diversity*. Reproduced with permission of The McGraw-Hill Companies.

Photos
p. 1, © Rudi Von Briel/PhotoEdit. **Chapter 1** p. 8, © Loren Santow/Tony Stone Images; p. 9T, © Cindy Charles/PhotoEdit; p. 9B, © Rudi Von Briel/PhotoEdit. **Chapter 2** p. 33, © Nita Winter/The Image Works; p. 39, © Billy Hustace/Tony Stone Images. **Chapter 4** p. 104, © Kaluzny/Thatcher/Tony Stone Images. **Chapter 5** p. 133T, © Cindy Charles/PhotoEdit; p. 133BL, © Sean Arbabi/Tony Stone Images; p. 133BR, © David Young-Wolff/PhotoEdit. **Chapter 6** p. 165TL, © Michael Newman/PhotoEdit; p. 165TR, © Eric Millette/The Picture Cube, Inc.; p. 165B, © Charles Gupton/Tony Stone Images. **Chapter 7** p. 177, © David Young-Wolff/PhotoEdit; p. 199TL, © Michael Newman/PhotoEdit; p. 199TR, © HMS Images/The Image Bank; p. 199B, © Rudi Von Briel/PhotoEdit; p. 203, © James Smalley/The Picture Cube, Inc. p. 215, © Bruce Ayres/Tony Stone Images. **Chapter 8** p. 233, © Michael Newman/PhotoEdit. **Chapter 10** p. 285, © Nathan Nourok/PhotoEdit; p. 303L, © Mike Smith/FPG International; p. 303R, © Bob Daemmrich/The Image Works. **Chapter 11** p. 316L, © Bruce Ayres/Tony Stone Images; p. 316R, © Bruce Ayres/Tony Stone Images; p. 326, © Donna Binder/Impact Visuals; p. 341, © Paul Conklin/PhotoEdit. **Part Three** p. 349, © Stephen McBrady/PhotoEdit. **Chapter 12** p. 353, © A. Ramey/PhotoEdit. **Chapter 13** p. 382, © Michael Newman/PhotoEdit; p. 391, © Mark Richards/PhotoEdit. **Chapter 14** p. 417, © Stephen McBrady/PhotoEdit.

Author Index

Adamson, R. S., 286
Adato, A., 364
Adelman, M. A., 27
Adler, N., 210
Allen, M., 341, 342
Allen, V. L., 98
Ammons, R. B., 415
Anatol, K., 271
Ancona, D. G., 93–94, 108–109
Andersen, P. A., 34
Anderson, C. M., 167
Anderson, L. R., 300
Anderson, S. D., 285
Andrews, P. H., 197
Anthony, T., 180
Applbaum, R. L., 271
Archer-Kath, J., 412, 414
Argyle, M., 35
Armed forces, 228
Arrow, H., 210, 369, 370
Atkinson, M. L., 98
Avolio, B., J., 302
Avruch, K., 337, 339

Back, K., 72
Baird, J. E., Jr., 197, 285
Baker, D. C., 285
Bales, R. F., 27, 40–41, 317
Bandura, A., 411
Bantz, C. R., 203, 204, 208, 209
Barge, J. K., 189, 257, 260, 291, 301, 302, 306
Barker, J. R., 411
Bass, B. M., 286, 301, 302, 304–305, 306
Bauer, T. N., 299
Baxter, L. A., 316
Beatty, M. J., 226
Bechler, C., 47
Bednar, D. A., 160
Bell, M. A., 317, 339
Benne, K., 64, 65, 69–71, 292
Benson, S., 376
Berdahl, J. L., 210, 369, 370
Berg, D. N., 317, 318, 325, 431
Berteotti, C. R., 27
Bettenhausen, K. L., 13, 72, 73, 77
Biddle, B. J., 64
Bishop, G. D., 254, 255
Black, P. W., 337, 339
Blake, R. R., 293

Blanchard, K. H., 295, 296
Bocialetti, G., 396, 397
Bolton-Oetzel, K., 202, 209
Bormann, E. G., 27, 64, 286
Bormann, N. C., 64
Bradbury, T. N., 331
Bradley, P. H., 186
Brenders, D., 160
Brewer, M. B., 9
Broome, B. J., 102, 340
Brown, C., 242–243
Buchholz, R. A., 302
Bufanio, K. M., 411
Burgoon, J. K., 34, 35, 158
Burke, W. W., 393
Burrell, N. A., 341, 342
Byham, W. C., 152, 357, 359, 360, 361, 362, 365

Caldwell, D. F., 93
Canary, D. J., 327, 331
Carley, K., 370
Carron, A. V., 178
Cartwright, D., 80, 179, 351
Cathcart, D., 37
Cathcart, R., 37
Cawsey, T. F., 286
Chemers, M. M., 197, 282
Cissna, K. N., 364
Clark, R. D. III., 254
Cline, R. J. W., 268
Cohen, A., 329
Cohen, S. G., 371
Cohen, S. P., 27, 40–41, 317
Comer, D. R., 411
Conrad, C., 327
Cook., J., 238
Courtright, J. A., 268
Cowart, L., 179
Cox, T., Jr., 210
Cox, T. H., 202
Cronshaw, S. F., 286
Cupach, W. R., 165

Dabbs, J. M., Jr., 32, 33, 231
Dailey, J.C., 232, 234
Daly, J. A., 32
Dansereau, F., 299
Davis-Sacks, M. L., 274
Day, V. E., 404
DeLamater, J., 9

Delbecq, A. L., 218, 232, 234
de Reuck, A., 327
De Souza, G., 287
DeStephen, R. S., 224, 228–229
Deszca, G., 286
Deutsch, M., 12, 314, 316, 329, 330
Devine, D. J., 179
Diehl, B. J., 161
Dion, K. L., 178
Di Salvo, V. S., 153, 411
Donohue, W. A., 341, 342
Downs, C. W., 300
Driskell, J. E., 180
Duran, R. L., 332
Dyce, J., 178

Eagly, A. H., 197
Einstein, W. O., 302
Eldred, J. P., 116–117
Elias, F. G., 178
Ellis, D. G., 31
Ellis, R. J., 286
Erbert, L., 85, 236, 243, 267
Evans, C. R., 178
Evans, M. S., 32, 33

Farrell, G. M., 64, 68
Feldman, D. C., 68, 74
Ferrari, A., 191
Festinger, L., 72
Fiedler, F. E., 294, 295
Fincham, F. D., 331
Fink, C. F., 131
Firestien, R. L., 101, 232
Fisher, B. A., 22, 28, 282
Forsyth, D., 194
Forsyth, D. R., 199, 300, 410
Fortman, J. B., 178
Fourre, J. P., 271
Freeman, K. A., 198
French, J. R. P., 183
Frey, L. R., 27, 78–79, 115, 198
Frost, P. J., 189, 258
Fuehrer, A., 178
Fulbright, L., 102

Galanes, G. J., 318, 325, 327, 329
Gardenswartz, L., 206, 366, 399
Gastil, J., 44, 153, 290, 292, 389
Gayle, B. M., 198
Geier, J. G., 288

Geiger, S. W., 404
Geist, P., 138, 376
Gemmill, G., 194
Gersick, C. J. G., 76, 77, 274, 367, 370
Gibb, J. R., 49–50
Ginnett, R. C., 354
Gist, M. E., 411
Gladstein, D. L., 103
Glaser, H. F., 187
Glaser, S. R., 396
Golembiewski, R. T., 178
Goodman, P. S., 128
Goodstein, L. D., 398
Gouran, D. S., 92, 103, 105, 219, 242–243, 249, 251, 261, 263, 265, 266, 267, 276, 292, 300
Graen, G. B., 299
Graham, E. E., 249
Green, S. G., 231, 299
Green, T. B., 232, 234
Greene, C. N., 178
Gruenfeld, L., 200
Gudykunst, W. B., 338
Guetzkow, H., 64, 320
Gully, S. M., 179
Gurman, E. B., 198
Gustafson, D. H., 232
Guzzo, R. A., 398, 411
Gyr, J., 320

Hackman, J. R., 22, 76, 77, 87, 101, 105, 146, 176, 273, 275, 354, 367, 370
Haga, W. J., 299
Hall, B. J., 338
Hamblin, R. L., 282
Hansford, B. C., 161
Hanson, P. G., 396
Hare, A. P., 13, 14, 59, 225, 226, 230
Harmon, N, A., 78–79, 115, 198
Haslett, B., 419, 420
Hawes, L. C., 28, 315, 327
Hawkins, K. W., 160, 197, 199
Henry, D. R., 242–243
Herold, D. M., 141, 143
Hersey, P., 295, 296
Heston, J. K., 158
Hill, T. A., 308
Hirokawa, R. Y., 27, 85, 92, 102, 181, 218, 219, 224, 228–229, 236, 238, 243, 247, 249, 251, 261, 263, 265, 266, 267, 302, 307
Hochberger, J. M., 357
Hoffer, J. A., 356
Hoffman, L. R., 225
Hofstede, G., 201, 203
Holdridge, W. E., 292
Hollander, E. P., 282, 283, 284, 285, 286
Homans, G. C., 64

Hopper, C. H., 231
Horras, M., 404
Hunt, J. G., 300
Hurst, A., 85, 236, 243, 267

Ice, R., 238
Infante, D. A., 34

Jablin, F. M., 300
Jabusch, D. M., 165, 166, 401
Jackson, J., 72
Jackson, S. E., 205
Jacobs, T. O., 283
Jago, A. G., 282, 289, 292
Janis, I. L., 61, 109, 263, 268
Jarboe, S. C., 146, 222, 234, 236, 327, 328, 329, 339
Jensen, M. A. C., 357
Jermier, J. M., 309
Johannesen, R. L., 402
Johansen, R., 376
Johnson, B. M., 325, 326
Johnson, B. T., 197
Johnson, D. E., 295, 296
Johnson, D. W., 319, 325, 326, 412, 414
Johnson, M. E., 178
Johnson, R. T., 412, 414
Johnson, S C., 47
Johnson, V., 219
Johnston, D. D., 247
Jones, T. S., 344
Jordan, F. F., 160
Julian, K. M., 218, 251
Jurma, W. E., 298

Kaeser, R. M., 357
Kameda, T., 218
Karau, S. J., 197
Katzenbach, J. R, 107, 128, 371
Kelley, H. H., 176
Kelley, K. N., 199, 410
Kelly, L., 332
Keltner, J. W., 342, 343, 408, 412, 416
Kendon, A., 35
Kerr, B., 179
Kerr, S., 300, 309
Ketrow, S. M., 63, 252, 253, 282, 283
Keys, C., 178
Keyton, J., 27, 78–79, 102, 115, 180, 181, 189, 190, 192, 198, 257, 260, 307, 363, 364
Kim, M., 202
Kinlaw, D. C., 394–395
Kirchmeyer, C., 207, 329
Klein, H. J., 287
Kleinman, G. B., 225
Knutson, T. J., 292, 321, 339
Kochman, T., 338
Kolb, J. A., 286, 307

Kopelman, R. E., 412, 414
Korten, D. C., 292
Kowitz, A. C., 321, 339
Kramer, M. W., 232, 234
Kramer, R. M., 207, 209, 210
Kramer, T. J., 231
Krikorian, D. H., 97
Kumar, K., 209
Kuo, C. L., 232, 234

LaFasto, F. M. J., 11, 152, 153, 196, 307, 352, 411, 422, 423
Lammers, J. C., 97
Larkey, L. K., 205
Larson, C. E., 11, 152, 153, 196, 307, 352, 411, 422, 423
Larson, C. U., 287
Laughlin, P. R., 218
Leana, C. R., 219
Leatham, G. B., 218, 251
Leathers, D. G., 32, 37
Lee, F., 208
Lee, J., 299, 300
Lewin, K., 289, 290
Liden, R. C., 299
Liebscher, V. K., 300
Lippitt, R., 289, 290, 291
Littlejohn, S. W., 165, 166, 401
Littlepage, G. E., 138, 179
Lobel, S. A., 202
Long, K., 198
Love, S. B., 325, 327, 329
Lubin, B., 396

Mabry, E. A., 36, 198
Mackie, D, M., 256, 257
Makhijani, M.G., 197
Mann, L., 61, 268
Martin, A., 376
Martin, M. M., 167
Martz, A. E., 92, 261
May, L., 402
McCanne, L. P. F., 14
McCanse, A. A., 293
McClane, W. E., 299
McCroskey, J. C., 32, 158
McDonald, G. M., 404
McGrath, J. E., 126, 136, 181, 210, 254, 369, 370
McIntyre, R. M., 408, 416, 419, 423
McKeage, R. L., 13
McKinney, B. C., 158, 332
McLeod, P. L., 202
McPherson, M. B., 249
Mennecke, B. E., 356
Meyer, C., 430
Meyers, R. A., 253, 254, 255, 256, 257
Michaelsen, L. K., 209
Miller, G. R., 290
Mittman, R., 376

Monroe, C., 153, 411
Montgomery, B. M., 160
Moorhead, G., 268, 269
Moosbruker, J., 357, 361
Mouton, J. S., 293
Mudrack, P. E., 64, 68
Mullen, B., 180
Murnighan, J. K., 72, 73
Murphy, C. J., 300
Murphy, S. E., 197
Myers, D. G., 254, 255

Nadler, D. A., 408, 409, 410, 414, 421, 422, 423
Neale, M. A., 207, 209, 210
Neck, C. P., 268, 269
Nelson, D. R., 404
Nichols, M. L., 404
Nicotera, A. M., 327, 331
Nikkel, E., 153, 411
Nolan, L. L., 325
Nolan, T. M., 398
Nord, W. R., 269, 270
Northcraft, G. B., 207, 209, 210
Norton, R. W., 160, 162–164
Nye, J. L., 300

Obremski, T. E., 404
O'Connor, B. P., 178
Oetzel, J. G., 201, 202, 209
Offner, A. K., 231
Ogilvie, J. R., 419
Osborn, A. F., 231

Pace, R. C., 219, 320, 322
Papa, M. J., 249
Pavitt, C., 222, 231, 234, 282, 288
Pecka, J. C., 288
Peek, G. S., 404
Peek, L. E., 404
Pelz, D., 300
Pfeiffer, J. W., 398
Phillips, G. M., 144, 146, 271
Pickett, T., 300
Polzer, J. T., 207, 209, 210
Pondy, L. R., 324
Pood, E. A., 319, 377
Poole, M. S., 27, 234, 235, 239, 327, 365, 375
Prapavessis, H., 178
Pratt, J., 286
Propp, K. M., 198, 218, 253
Putnam, L. L., 96, 97, 236, 240–241, 286, 327, 331

Ragan, J. W., 223
Rancer, A. S., 34
Raven, B., 183
Richmond, V. P., 32, 158

Riggs, C. J., 334–335
Robertson, C., 404
Rose, S. R., 363
Rosenthal, S. B., 303
Rowe, A., 206, 366, 399
Ruback, R. B., 32, 33, 231
Rubin, A. M., 160
Rubin, R. B., 160

Sackaroff, P., 282, 288
Saffo, P., 376
Salas, E., 180, 408, 416, 419, 423
Salazar, A. J., 23, 68, 115, 218
Sandberg, W. R., 23, 223
Sargent, J. F., 290
Scandura, T., 299
Schachter, S., 72
Scheerhorn, D. R., 138, 219, 269, 376
Schell, S. E., 190, 192
Schittekatte, M., 110, 269
Schriesheim, C. A., 300
Schultz, B., 63, 252, 253, 286, 292
Schutz, W. C., 154
Schwarz, R. M., 380, 383, 433
Schweiger, D. M., 23, 219, 223
Seesa, V. I. 205
Seibert, S., 200
Seibold, D. R., 27, 253, 254, 255, 256, 257
Senge, P. M., 22, 243
Sharf, B. F., 286
Sharkey, W. F., 202
Shaw, M. E., 141, 142, 178
Shea, G. P., 398, 411
Sheats, P., 64, 65, 69–71, 292
Shonk, J. H., 400
Sias, P. M., 300
Sibbet, D., 376, 383
Silbiger, H., 138
Sillars, A. L., 327, 330, 333, 343
Silver, W. S., 411
Smith, D. H., 315, 327
Smith, D. K., 107, 128, 371
Smith, K. K., 317, 318, 325, 431
Smotroff, L. J., 288
Sniezek, J. A., 218
Socha, D. M., 27
Socha, T. J., 27
Sorenson, P. S., 198
Sorenson, R., 198
Spink, K. S., 178, 411
Spitzberg, B. H., 165, 307, 327, 331
Steiner, I. D., 129, 267
Stewart, R. A., 160
Stogdill, R. M., 281, 288, 300
Stohl, C., 96, 97, 190, 912
Stoner, J. A. F., 255
Street, M. C., 110, 269, 404
Sunwolf, 253, 254, 255, 256
SYMLOG Consulting Group, 433

Taber, T. D., 231
Taps, J., 198
Teboul, JC B., 138, 376
Thibaut, J. W., 176
Thomas, E. J., 131
Thomas, K. W., 314, 315, 322, 323, 324, 327, 329, 330, 331, 332
Thomas, R. R., Jr., 205, 209
Tolson, J., 300
Tompkins, P. K., 411
Tjosvold, D., 208, 412
Triandis, H. C., 204, 208
Tropman, J. E., 376
Tucker, S., 269, 270
Tuckman, B. W., 357

Urban, D. M., 63, 252, 253

Van de Ven, A. H., 218, 232, 234
Van Hiel, A., 110, 269
Verdi, A. F., 200
Von Bertelanffy, L., 28
von Cranach, M., 118–121

Waldman, D. A., 302
Wall, V. D., Jr., 318, 325, 327, 329
Walter, G. A., 428
Wanberg, K, W., 285
Warfield, J. N., 319
Watanabe, S., 204
Watkins, C. E., 315
Watson, E. W., 209
Watson, K. W., 38, 40, 42, 43
Weinberg, S. B., 285, 288
Weisbord, M. R., 392
Wellins, R. S., 152, 357, 359, 360, 361, 362, 365
Wetlaufer, S., 193
Wheelan, S. A., 13, 200, 357
White, R. K., 289, 290, 291
Whitney, D. J., 179
Wilder, D. A., 98
Wilmot, W. W., 327, 330, 333, 343
Wilson, C. E., 331
Wilson, J. M., 152, 357, 359, 360, 361, 362, 365
Winter, J. P., 231
Witteman, H. R., 180, 320, 327, 328, 329, 339
Womack, D. F., 34
Wong, C. L., 208
Wood, C. J., 62
Wood, J. T., 144, 146
Wynne, B. E., 356

Yammarino, F. J., 302

Zander, A., 11, 80, 351
Zepp, R. A., 404
Zimmermann, S., 152

Subject Index

acceptance level, 143
accommodating, 330
action-oriented listening style, 42, 43
active listening, 45
activity. *See* task
additive task, 132
affection, 154
affective conflict, 320
affiliative constraints, 264–265
agenda, 377
appointed leader, 283
appropriateness, 166, 167
area of freedom, 143
artifacts, 34
autocratic leadership, 289–290, 292
avoiding, 330–331

battles, 139
behavior feedback, 416
bona fide group, 96
boundary management, 93–94
boundary spanning, 91–92
brainstorming, 231–232
breakpoint, 366–367

camaraderie, 182, 184–185
cautious-shift, 255
centralized networks, 82–84
Challenger, 92–93
changing communication climate, 53
chronemics, 34, 36
cliques. *See* subgroups
closed-loop communication, 416–419
coalition formation, 7
code of conduct, 398, 400, 401
coercive power, 183
cognitive conflict, 321
cognitive conflict task, 138
cognitive constraints, 263–264
cognitive task, 131, 133
cohesiveness, 177–180, 181
collaboration, 327–328, 333–336
collectivistic cultures, 201
communication
    apprehension, 158, 160
    climate, 48–55
    competence, 165–167

listening, 38–48
    models, 14–19
    networks, 80–87
    nonverbal, 33–37
    overload, 81
    underload, 82
    verbal, 29–32
    verbal and nonverbal, 37–38
communication competency approach to leadership, 302–306
communication perspective for studying groups, 27–28
communicator style, 160–164, 392
competing, 329–330
competitive conflict, 320
competitive task, 139
compromising, 331
conducting meetings, 380–388
conflict
    aftermath, 324–325
    cultural differences, 336–339
    defined, 314–315
    gender differences, 198–199
    intergroup, 325–326
    management strategies, 326–333
    mediation, 341–344
    minimizing ineffective, 339–344
    orientation toward, 315–316
    personal, 392
    process model, 322–325
    reasons for, 317–319
    role of communication, 319–320
    sources of, 320
    strategy selection, 331–333
    types of, 320–322
conjunctive task, 131, 133
connectivity, 96–98
consensus, 224–228
constraints on decision making
    affiliative, 264–265, 266
    cognitive, 263–264, 265, 266
    egocentric, 265, 266–267
    recognizing, 265–266
    responding to, 266–267
content-oriented listening style, 42, 43
contests, 139

contextual influences, 257–260
contingency model of group development, 365–367
control, 154
cooperative conflict, 320
creativity task, 137
critical advisor, 63, 222–224
cultural bias, 201
cultural differences, and conflict, 336–339
cultural differences, dysfunctional reactions to, 205, 207–208
cultural distance, 204
cultural diversity, 200–210

decentralized networks, 81–82
decision implementation. *See* implementing decisions
decision logic, 243–244
decision making
    assumptions about, 247–249
    constraints on, 263–267
    faulty, 261–269
    groups vs. individuals, 217–218
    influences on, 253–260
decision-making effectiveness, 242–244
decision-making procedures
    brainstorming, 231–232
    comparing procedures, 234–236, 237, 238–239
    consensus, 224–228
    critical advisor, 222–224
    nominal group technique, 232–234
    problems in using, 238
    ranking, 230–231
    reasons to use, 218–220, 239
    standard agenda, 220–222
    tips for using, 239
    voting, 228–230
decision-making task, 138
decision outcomes
    monitoring, 276
    evaluating, 276
decision quality, 146–147
decision rule orientation, 226–228

I-4

defensive communication climate
  defined, 49
  certainty, 52
  control, 50–51
  evaluation, 50
  neutrality, 51–52
  strategy, 51
  superiority, 52
democratic leadership, 289–292
denial of external threat, 109–110
dependence, 174–175
dependencies, 100–103
descriptive feedback, 420
devil's advocate. *See* critical advisor
disagreement of verbal and nonverbal communication, 37–38
discretionary task, 132
disjunctive task, 130–131
distributive conflict management strategy, 329–330
diversity problems, overcoming, 208–210
dyadic interaction, 7

effectiveness, 165–166, 167
egocentric constraints, 265
elected leader, 283–284
embeddedness, 96–98
emergent leader, 284–287
emotions, 396, 397
equity, 194
ethics, 401–405
ethnocentric, 201
evaluating decision outcomes, 276
evaluative feedback, 420–421
expectations, 100–103
expert power, 185
expressed needs, 154–157

false consensus, 144–145
faulty decision making, 261–269
feedback
  audiotape, 428–430
  defined, 408
  interaction diagrams, 425–429
  levels, 421–425
  negative, 430–431
  questionnaires, 425
  receiver, 15
  types, 420–421
  surveys, 424
  system, 28, 31–32
  videotape, 429
feedback bias, 409–411
feedback levels
  group, 423–424
  individual, 422–423

organizational, 424–425
  procedural, 421–422
  relational, 422
  task, 421–422
feedback style, 419–420
feedback systems
  advantages, 411
  designing, 430–432
  limitations, 414–416
  types, 409
feedback types
  descriptive, 420
  evaluative, 420–421
  prescriptive, 421
FIRO-B, 154
follower readiness, 296–298
formal roles, 59, 60–64
forming, 357–359
functional leadership, 292
functional theory, 249–252

gender composition, 199, 200
gender influences, 196–200
goals, affiliation, 114–115
group, defined, 7, 13
group charge, 110–111
  See also group goal
group charge, developing, 114
group charter, 398, 400
group climate, changing, 53
group continuity, 148
group development
  defined, 356
  multiple-sequence perspective, 365–368
  punctuated equilibrium, 367–368
  stages, 357–365
group efficacy, 100–101, 411
group environment, 103–110
group facilitation, 375–405
group feedback, 423–424
group goal, 11–12
  See also group charge
grouphate, 115
group identity, 11
group influence
  on environment, 92–93
  on individuals, 98–99
groupings, 11
group maintenance roles, 64, 66
group member assimilation, 355–356
group member ethics, 401–405
group member fit, 353–354
group member selection, 352–355
group origination, 351–355
group process, 147, 356–357
group response strategies, 108–109

group roles, 12, 59–68
group size, 7–8, 13–14
group size, effects, 181
group structure, 12–13, 59
groupthink, 109–110, 267–269
group types, 125–126, 128
groups vs. individuals, 22–23

haptics, 34
impact of communication, 21
implementing decisions
  criteria for success, 270
  PERT, 271–273
  time pressures, 273–275
inclusion, 154
individual feedback, 422–423
individual roles, 64, 66–67
individualistic cultures, 201
inequity. *See* equity
informal interaction, 167–169
informal roles, 59–60, 64
in-group, 257
input, 28
integrative conflict management strategy, 327–329
intellective task, 137–138
intentionality, 20
interaction diagrams, 84–85, 425–429
interactional model of communication, 15–16, 18
interdependence, of members, 8–11, 175–177
interpersonal conflict, 321
interpersonal needs, 154–158
intrinsic interest, 142

judgment conflict, 321

kinesics, 34

language patterns, 30–32
law of inherent conflict, 319
leader
  appointed, 283
  elected, 283–284
  emergent, 284–287
  multiple, 308
leader-member exchange model, 299–300
leadership
  autocratic, 289–290, 292
  communication competency universal approach, 303–306
  contingency approach, 294–301
  contingency model, 294–295
  defined, 281–282
  democratic, 289–290

I-5

evaluation, 307
functional, 292
gender differences, 197
leader-member exchange model, 299–300
managerial grid, 293–294
relational competencies, 306
situational, 295–298, 309
styles, 292–294
substitutes for, 309–310
task competencies, 305
technical competencies, 306
traits, 288–289
transactional, 301
transformational, 301–303, 304–305
approach, 288–294, 300–301
leadership role, 61–62
leadership styles, 292–294
learning dimension, 22
legitimate power, 183
listening
adapting listening style, 43–44
complexity in groups, 38
effectiveness, 39, 45–48
pitfalls, 44–45
styles, 39–44

macro-system perspective, 90–91
making group assignments, 386
managerial grid, 293–294
material resources, 104–105
maximax decision rule, 226–227
maximin decision rule, 226–227
maximizing task, 129, 130
maximum expected utility decision rule, 226–227
meanings, of words, 30
mediation, 341–344
meeting planning, 376–380
meeting closure, 388
meeting management, 376–392
meeting visuals, 383–386
membership changes, 369–371
message, defined, 14
message feedback, 342–344, 412–414, 416
micro system, 28
minutes, 388
mixed-motive task, 138–139
models of communication, 14–19
monitoring decision outcomes, 276
multichannel communication, 18
multiple leaders, 308

need compatibility, 157–158
negative feedback, 430–431

negotiating latitude, 299
network, selection of, 85–86
noise
physical, 14–15
psychological, 14–15
nominal group technique, 232–234
nonverbal communication
artifacts, 34
chronemics, 34, 36
defined, 33
functions of, 34–36
haptics, 34
kinesics, 34
meanings of, 36–37
proxemics, 34, 36
vocalics, 33, 36
with verbal communication, 37–38
norms
as social control, 72
change in, 79–80
consequences of, 77–78
defined, 68
development of, 72–74
explicit, 75
implicit, 75
influence on groups, 77–78
initiating, 74–75
uniqueness, 77
norming, 360–362
normative conflict, 322
number of group members, *See* group size

opinions, 113–114
optimizing task, 129–130
organizational feedback, 424–425
output, 28, 115, 118
out-group, 257
overcoming meeting obstacles, 389–392

people-oriented listening style, 41–42, 43
performance task, 139
performing, 362
personalized conflict, 320
persuasive arguments theory, 255
PERT, 271–273, 381,385
physical environment, 103–105
planning task, 137
political decision logic, 244
population familiarity, 142
power
as control over resources, 188–189
bases for, 183, 186
coercive, 183, 186
dynamics, 186–188

expert, 183, 186
imbalances, 190–194
in relationships, 182, 190–194
legitimate, 183, 186
referent, 183, 186
reward, 183, 186
situationally enhanced, 189–194
power distance, 203
prediscussion influence, 253–254
premeeting planning
leader, 376–379
member, 379–380
preference for procedural order, 236–238, 240–241
prescriptive feedback, 421
primary provoker, 190–193
problem solving
in conflict management, 333–336
See also decision making
procedural conflict, 321
procedural feedback, 421
procedural roles, 67
process, 19
process advisor, 46
process loss, 267
postmeeting follow-up, 388–389
proxemics, 34, 36
pseudo-listening, 46
psychological environment, 105–107
psycho-motor task, 139
punctuated equilibrium model of group development, 367–368

questions of fact, 111–112
questions of policy, 112–113
questions of value, 112

ranking, 230–231
rational decision logic, 243–244
recorder, 62–63
referent power, 183
reflective feedback, 416
relational dimension, 21–22
relational feedback, 422
reminder role, 252–253
responsiveness, 167
reward power, 183
risky-shift, 254
role conflict, 98–99
roles
critical advisor, 63, 222–224
formal, 59, 60–61
individual, 64, 66–67
informal, 59–60, 64
leadership, 61–62
maintenance, 64, 66
procedural, 67

roles *(continued)*
   reminder, 252–253
   secretary, 62–63
   task, 64, 65–66

satisfaction, 180–181
satisficing, 61
scapegoat, 194
secondary provoker, 190–193
secretary, 62–63
selective listening, 47
self-construal, 202–203
sender, 14
shared meaning, 21
situational leadership model, 295–298, 309
social comparison theory, 254–255
social complexity, 143–144
social exchange theory, 176
social identify theory, 256–257
social influences, 257–260
social interaction perspective, 257
social loafer, 411
social loafing, 14
solution multiplicity, 141
stages of group development
   forming, 357–359
   norming, 360–362
   performing, 362
   storming, 359–360
   termination, 362–364
standard agenda, 220–222
storming, 359–360
substantive conflict, 320
substitutes for leadership, 309–310
superordinate goal, 10
supportive communication climate
   defined, 49
   description, 50
   empathy, 51–52
   quality, 52
   problem orientation, 50–51
   provisionalism, 52–53
   spontaneity, 51
synergy, 23
system, defined, 28
systemic complexity, 95–98
systemic interdependence, 95

system influence on groups, 100, 101, 102–103, 107
system perspective, 6, 28
system theory, 118–121

task/activity constraints, 144–146
task/activity outcomes, 146–148
task characteristics
   acceptance level, 143
   area of freedom, 143
   intrinsic interest, 142
   population familiarity, 142–143
   social complexity, 143–144
   solution multiplicity, 141–142
   task difficulty, 141
task difficulty, 141
task dimension, 21
task outcome ambiguity, 146
task roles, 64, 65–66
task/procedural feedback, 421–422
tasks
   additive, 133
   battles, 139
   cognitive, 131, 133
   cognitive conflict, 138
   competitive, 139
   conjunctive, 131, 133
   contests, 139
   creativity, 137
   decision-making, 138
   discretionary, 133
   disjunctive, 130–131
   divisible, 129, 130
   intellective, 137–138
   mixed-motive, 138–139
   optimizing, 129–130
   performance, 139
   planning, 137
   psycho-motor, 139
   unitary, 129–130
   See also group charge
   See also group goal
teambuilding 392–393, 396–398
team effectiveness, 396–398
termination, 362–364
throughput, 28
time-oriented listening style, 42–43
trait leadership, 288
transactional leadership, 301
transactional model of communication, 18
transformational leadership, 301–303, 304–305
trust, 195–196
types of groups, 125–126, 128

uncertainty avoidance, 203–204

verbal communication, 29–32, 37
vocal activity, 32
vocalics, 33, 36
voting, 228–230
wanted needs, 154–158
words
   abstract, 30
   concrete, 30
   meanings of, 30